DATE DUE

DEMCO 38-296

CONTEMPORARY MUSICIANS

ISSN 1044-2197

CONTEMPORARY MUSICIANS

PROFILES OF THE PEOPLE IN MUSIC

JULIA M. RUBINER,
Editor

VOLUME 9
Includes Cumulative Indexes

Gale Research Inc. • *DETROIT* • *WASHINGTON, D.C.* • *LONDON*

STAFF

Julia M. Rubiner, *Editor*

Sonia Benson, Nicolet V. Elert, L. Mpho Mabunda, Mary K. Ruby, *Associate Editors*

Marilyn Allen, *Editorial Associate*

Robin Armstrong, David Bianco, Barbara Carlisle Bigelow, Jenny Bleier, Suzanne M. Bourgoin, Susan Windisch Brown, Marjorie Burgess, John Cohassey, Tim Connor, John Cortez, Amy Culverwell, Mary Scott Dye, Stewart Francke, Alan Glenn, Simon Glickman, Nina Goldstein, Joan Goldsworthy, Joyce Harrison, Lloyd Hemingway, Barry Henssler, Kevin Hillstrom, Anne Janette Johnson, Janice Jorgensen, Michael L. LaBlanc, Ondine E. Le Blanc, Jeanne M. Lesinski, James M. Manheim, Matthew Martin, Marcia Militello, Louise Mooney, Diane Moroff, John Morrow, Rob Nagel, Nancy Pear, Debra Power, Nancy Rampson, Glenn Rechler, Joseph M. Reiner, Marta Robertson, Megan Rubiner, Michele Schachere, Jeffrey Taylor, Jordan Wankoff, Elizabeth Wenning, Christian Whitaker, *Contributing Editors*

Peter M. Gareffa, *Senior Editor, Contemporary Biographies*

Jeanne Gough, *Permissions Manager*
Margaret A. Chamberlain, *Permissions Supervisor (Pictures)*
Pamela A. Hayes, Keith Reed, *Permissions Associates*
Arlene Johnson, Barbara Wallace, *Permissions Assistants*

Mary Beth Trimper, *Production Director*
Shanna Philpott Heilveil, *Production Assistant*
Cynthia Baldwin, *Art Director*
C. J. Jonik, *Desktop Publisher/Typesetter*

Special thanks to the Biography Division Research staff

Cover Illustration by John Kleber

 This book is printed on acid-free paper that meets the minimum requirements of American National Standard for Information Sciences— Permanence Paper for Printed Library Materials, ANSI Z39.48-1984.

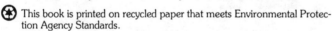 This book is printed on recycled paper that meets Environmental Protection Agency Standards.

ISBN 0-8103-2217-X
ISSN 1044-2197

10 9 8 7 6 5 4 3 2 1

The trademark **ITP** is used under license.

Contents

Introduction   ix

Photo Credits   xi

Cumulative Subject Index   293

Cumulative Musicians Index   305

Introduction

Fills the Information Gap on Today's Musicians

Contemporary Musicians profiles the colorful personalities in the music industry who create or influence the music we hear today. Prior to Contemporary Musicians, no quality reference series provided comprehensive information on such a wide range of artists despite keen and ongoing public interest. To find biographical and critical coverage, an information seeker had little choice but to wade through the offerings of the popular press, scan television "infotainment" programs, and search for the occasional published biography or expose. Contemporary Musicians is designed to serve that information seeker, providing in one ongoing source in-depth coverage of the important figures on the modern music scene in a format that is both informative and entertaining. Students, researchers, and casual browsers alike can use Contemporary Musicians to fill their needs for personal information about the artists, find a selected discography of the musician's recordings, and read an insightful essay offering biographical and critical information.

Provides Broad Coverage

Single-volume biographical sources on musicians are limited in scope, focusing on a handful of performers from a specific musical genre or era. In contrast, Contemporary Musicians offers researchers and music devotees a comprehensive, informative, and entertaining alternative. Contemporary Musicians is published twice yearly, with each volume providing information on 80 to 100 musical artists from all the genres that form the broad spectrum of contemporary music—pop, rock, jazz, blues, country, new wave, New Age, folk, rhythm and blues, gospel, bluegrass, rap, and reggae, to name a few, as well as selected classical artists who have achieved "crossover" success with the general public. Contemporary Musicians will occasionally include profiles of influential nonperforming members of the music industry, including producers, promoters, and record company executives.

Includes Popular Features

In Contemporary Musicians you'll find popular features that users value:

- **Easy-to-locate data sections**—Vital personal statistics, chronological career summaries, listings of major awards, and mailing addresses, when available, are prominently displayed in a clearly marked box on the second page of each entry.

- **Biographical/critical essays**—Colorful and informative essays trace each personality's personal and professional life, offer representative examples of critical response to each artist's work, and provide entertaining personal sidelights.

- **Selected discographies**—Each entry provides a comprehensive listing of the artist's major recorded works.

- **Photographs**—Most entries include portraits of the artists.

- **Sources for additional information**—This invaluable feature directs the user to selected books, magazines, and newspapers where more information on listees can be obtained.

Helpful Indexes Make It Easy to Find the Information You Need

Contemporary Musicians features a Musicians Index, listing names of individual performers and musical groups, and a Subject Index that provides the user with a breakdown by primary musical instruments played and by musical genre.

We Welcome Your Suggestions

The editors welcome your comments and suggestions for enhancing and improving *Contemporary Musicians*. If you would like to suggest musicians or composers to be covered in the future, please submit these names to the editors. Mail comments or suggestions to:

The Editor
Contemporary Musicians
Gale Research Inc.
835 Penobscot Bldg.
Detroit MI 48226-4094
Phone : (800) 347-4253
Fax: (313) 961-6241

Photo Credits

PHOTOGRAPHS APPEARING IN *CONTEMPORARY MUSICIANS,* VOLUME 9, WERE RECEIVED FROM THE FOLLOWING SOURCES:

Courtesy of Bugle Boy Productions: p. 1; Photograph by Buckmaster, courtesy of Elektra Entertainment: p. 5; Archive Photos: pp. 9, 117, 230; AP/Wide World Photos: pp. 13, 21, 34, 64, 67, 74, 141, 144, 151, 183, 187, 197, 207, 211, 238, 251; Photograph by John Harrell, © 1992 Reprise Records: p. 16; Photograph by Todd Gray: p. 24; Courtesy of International Record Syndicate, Inc.: p. 26; Photograph by Dennis Keeley, © 1990 Warner Bros. Records, courtesy of Opal Records: p. 30; Photograph by Deborah Feingold, courtesy of Concord Records: p. 38; Courtesy of Capitol Records: p. 42; MICHAEL OCHS ARCHIVES/Venice, CA: pp. 45, 155, 159; Courtesy of Hervey & Company Incorporated: p. 49; Photograph by Josh Jordan, courtesy of Elektra Entertainment: p. 53; Courtesy of Tommy Boy Records: p. 57; Courtesy of Great Northern Arts, Ltd.: p. 61; Photograph by Dennis Keeley, © 1990 MCA Records, Inc.: p. 70; Photograph by Cesar Vera, courtesy of MCA Records: p. 77; Courtesy of RCA Records: pp. 80, 215; Photograph by The Douglas Brothers, courtesy of Caroline Records: p. 83; Reuters/Bettmann: p. 88; UPI/Bettmann: pp. 92, 106, 173, 201; © 1992 Sony Music Entertainment Inc., courtesy of Epic Records: p. 96; Photograph by Chris Carroll, courtesy of A&M Records: p. 100; Photograph by Robert Cahen, courtesy of London Records: p. 103; Archive Photos/Imapress: p. 109; Photograph by Steve Paige, © 1992 Warner Bros. Records: p. 112; Archive Photos/Central Press: p. 121; Courtesy of Jive Records: p. 124; © 1981 Waring Abbott/MICHAEL OCHS ARCHIVES/Venice, CA: p. 128; Photograph by John F. Cooper, courtesy of High Street Records™: p. 131; Archive Photos/Camera Press: p. 135; Photograph by Carol Friedman, courtesy of Verve Records: p. 147; Courtesy of Abby Hoffer Enterprises: p. 162; Photograph by Gene Kirkland, 1992, courtesy of Capitol Records: p. 165; Photograph by Bradford Branson, © 1990 CBS Records Inc., courtesy of Columbia Records: p. 169; Photograph by Jules Allen, courtesy of Antilles Records: p. 177; Photograph by Mary Murphey, © 1992 Warner Bros. Records: p. 180; Courtesy of Gallin · Morey · Associates: p. 191; Photograph by Irene Young, courtesy of GNP Crescendo Records: p. 194; Photograph by Michael Miller, courtesy of A&M Records: p. 204; Courtesy of Five Corners Music: p. 220; Photograph by Peter Anderson, © 1990 Def American Recordings, Inc. Distributed by Geffen Records: p. 223; © 1992 Warner Bros. Records: p. 227; Photograph by Enrique Badulescu, © 1992 The David Geffen Company: p. 234; Courtesy of Arista Records: p. 241; Photograph by Randee St. Nicholas, courtesy of Gurley & Co.: p. 244; Photograph by Michael Lavine, © 1992 Zoo Entertainment: p. 248; Photograph by Jules Allen, © PolyGram 1992, courtesy of Axiom Records: p. 255; Photograph by Bettina Rheims, © 1992 Reprise Records: p. 258; Photograph by Aaron Rapoport, © 1992 Warner Bros. Records: p. 261; Photograph by Irene Young, courtesy of Windham Hill Records: p. 265; Courtesy of Agnes Bruneau and Associates: p. 268; Photograph by Victoria Pearson, courtesy of Kahane Entertainment: p. 271; Archive Photos/Strick: p. 274; MCA/Chess Files: p. 278; UPI/Bettmann Newsphotos: p. 281; © David Provost, courtesy of Eastwest Records America: p. 284; Photograph by Diego Uchitel, © 1991 Reprise Records: p. 287.

CONTEMPORARY MUSICIANS

The Andrews Sisters

Vocal trio

To evoke the happy, patriotic feeling of the 1940s, simply mention the Andrews Sisters—or for that matter, just the names Patty, Maxene, and LaVerne. The "girl" trio of Patty, Maxene, and LaVerne Andrews sang for the troops in Europe during World War II, starred in films, collaborated on several tremendous hits with superstar Bing Crosby, and continued to sing for decades. During their career the trio recorded some 1,800 songs and sold over 90 million records, earning 19 gold disks along the way. Although they added numbers to their repertoire through the years, they are most remembered for their earliest hits, among them "Beer Barrel Polka," "Beat Me Daddy, Eight to the Bar," "Boogie Woogie Bugle Boy," and "Don't Sit Under the Apple Tree." When co-producers Kenneth Waissman and Maxine Fox wanted to recreate the 1940s in their 1974 musical review *Over Here!*, they hired the Andrews Sisters. When choreographer Paul Taylor wanted to dramatize his memories of the war years, he created choreography with the Andrews Sisters as his muses. Into the early 1990s Maxene Andrews was still

M embers included **LaVerne Andrews,** born July 6, 1911, in Minneapolis, MN; died of cancer, 1967; married Louis A. Rodgers, 1948. **Maxene Andrews,** born January 3, 1916, in Minneapolis; married Lou Levy (the trio's manager), 1941 (divorced, 1949). **Patty Andrews,** born February 16, 1918, in Minneapolis. **Joyce de Young,** replaced LaVerne c. 1967-68.

Toured Midwest with Larry Rich, 1932-37; performed with Leon Belasco, New York City, 1937; signed with Decca Records, released "Bei Mir Bist du Schoen," 1938; featured on radio shows *Just Entertainment* with Jack Fulton, 1938, and *Honolulu Bound* with Phil Baker, 1939; broke up, 1954; regrouped 1956; retired, 1968.

Film appearances include *In the Navy* and *Buck Privates,* 1941; *Private Buckaroo,* 1942; *How's About It?* and *Always a Bridesmaid,* 1943; *Follow the Boys, Hollywood Canteen,* and *Swing-Time Johnny,* 1944; and *Road to Rio,* 1947.

Maxene Andrews became instructor of drama and speech and dean of women, 1968, and vice president in charge of planning and development, 1969, Tahoe Paradise College; appeared, with Patty Andrews, in stage production *Over Here!,* 1974; resumed singing career, c. 1974; appeared in dance production *Company B,* 1992. Author of memoir *Over Here, Over There,* Zebra Books, 1993.

Awards: 19 gold records; Medal of Distinguished Public Service, Department of Defense, 1987.

Addresses: DRG Records Inc., 130 West 57th St., New York, NY 10019.

singing the old songs with gusto, and fans still loved her.

The Andrews Sisters began performing as teens, in the early 1930s. They listened to the Boswell Sisters and tried on their style. "LaVerne had a wonderful musical memory," Maxene told the *New Yorker.* "She figured things out. She would listen to a Boswell Sisters record and then teach me and Patty the parts." Patty sang soprano and any solos, Maxene second soprano, and LaVerne alto. For several years they toured the Midwest on the vaudeville circuit. In 1937 they relocated to New York City. At first they had no luck, but when they were almost to the point of giving up, Lou Levy, who would become their manager—and Maxene's husband— brought them to the attention of Jack Kapp, who signed the sisters to a recording contract with Decca Records.

Their first release, "Why Talk About Love," sold poorly; their second attempt, 1938's "Bei Mir Bist du Schoen," however, became a million-seller.

Mobbed by Servicemen Overseas

"We only really became aware of how popular we were when we went overseas during the war and all the servicemen just mobbed us," Maxene told the *New Yorker.* The sisters were very popular, indeed, singing regularly on radio in the late 1930s and 1940s. They also performed with other popular musicians of the day, including crooner Bing Crosby and premiere swing outfit the Glenn Miller Orchestra. Between 1940 and 1948 Patty, Maxene, and LaVerne made 16 films, often portraying themselves. Their popularity was nearly matched by their financial reward; in 1949 Levy reported in *Billboard* magazine that the trio planned over one million dollars in bookings—and this figure did not even account for record royalties.

In the early 1950s musical styles began to change, and although the Andrews Sisters tried to keep up, they encountered some rough times. In 1954 Patty left the act to try a solo career. The following year Maxene performed on her own as well. In 1956, however, the siblings regrouped, vowing to remain together. A *Variety* reviewer wrote of their act, "They place an emphasis on their avowed pledge that [their] war is over when they take time out to kid the woes that befall an act that splits." For the next decade the Andrews Sisters continued to perform on the nightclub circuit. They mixed some new tunes into their repertoire but primarily relied on the old favorites. *Variety* opined in 1963 that their sound was attractively nostalgic: "In fact, the girls weave a nostalgic spell with a reprise of their disc licks." While the trio's vocal gifts were the main focus of their performances, they also enlivened their act with comedy routines and dance—from the Charleston to what *Variety* called a "bump and grind routine by Patty that's good for plenty of laughs."

Loss of LaVerne

The Andrews Sisters remained strong and popular well into the 1960s, but in 1966 the eldest, LaVerne, was forced to retire due to ill health. The following year she died of cancer. For a while, Patty and Maxene kept the trio alive, performing with Joyce de Young. But the act broke up for good in 1968 when Patty returned to solo work and Maxene traded in show business for an academic career. That year, the latter became an instructor of drama and speech and the dean of women at Tahoe Paradise College, a small liberal arts school. In 1969 she was made vice president in charge of planning and development. Maxene told *Billboard,* "It's a whole new world. Working and living and studying with young people is the biggest kick I've ever had. It beats a million-seller."

Interest in the trio was revived in 1973 when singer Bette Midler scored a hit with a cover version of the Andrews Sisters classic "Boogie Woogie Bugle Boy." Then, stage producers Kenneth Waissman and Maxine Fox decided to mount a Broadway show depicting the World War II years and big-band era and asked the sisters to star in it. *Over Here!* opened at the Shubert Theatre in 1974 to rave reviews. Actress Janie Sell, playing a comic spy, completed the singing trio. After the run of the show Maxene decided to resume her singing career. *Variety* reviewed her new act, reporting that she pleased her older fans and then some: "Andrews' style and catalog have relevancy to today. She recalls moments from the sisters' vast catalog of hits, but there are also moments from contemporary writing. In all, she does more than try to live up to a memory. It's another bag for her and apparently she has applied herself assiduously in meeting today's conditions." Maxene continued performing—and wowing audiences—into the next decade. In 1983 *Variety* again reviewed one of her performances, concluding, "Andrews looks in fine fettle, is obviously in fine voice and her 65-minute show is a lot of fun 'nostalgia' without cloying schmaltz, thanks in great part to Andrews' lively, infectious will."

Company B

In the early 1990s the Andrews Sisters received fresh attention when the Paul Taylor Dance Company choreographed a new work to nine of the Andrews Sisters' original recordings. The dance, *Company B,* contrasted the sisters' exuberance and good cheer with depictions of some of the harsher realities of World War II. Maxene attended the Kennedy Center opening of *Company B* in June of 1991 and loved the portrayal of both the joy and tragedy of the era. "I was entranced with having it explained in dance," she told the *New York Times.* "There was a dark side to the period, even though the whole country banded together and pitched in like a wonderful love-in. And [choreographer] Paul [Taylor] did it so clearly, so seamlessly. You knew the darkness was there, but no one thing stood out." In 1992 Maxene even shared the bill with the dancers; at age 76, she was still singing. And in later years she

became active in a host of charities, including the American Heart Foundation, the Save a Heart Foundation, and several AIDS organizations.

The music of the Andrews Sisters has captured the spirit of and cheered America for much of the twentieth century. Even when the trio finally disbanded, their music kept going strong. As Maxene put it in the *New York Times,* "Bette [Midler] brought the Andrews Sisters into the '70s. Now I think Paul [Taylor] will bring us into the '90s." As a cherished gem of Americana, the music of Patty, LaVerne, and Maxene will undoubtedly be heard into the next century as well.

Selected discography

Boogie Woogie Bugle Girls, MCA, 1973.
16 Great Performances, MCA, 1975.
In Blossom, Columbia Special Products, 1978.
Rarities, MCA, 1984.
50th Anniversary Collection, MCA, Volume 1, 1987, Volume 2, 1990.
Greatest Hits, CURB/Cema, 1990.
At Their Best, Pair, 1991.
The Andrews Sisters: Capitol Collectors Series, Capitol, 1991.
The Andrews Sisters, Pearl, 1991.
Over Here! (soundtrack), Sony Broadway, 1992.
(Contributors) *Capitol Sings Cole Porter,* Capitol, 1992.
The Best of the Andrews Sisters (two volumes), MCA.
(With Bing Crosby and Bob Hope) *Boogie Woogie Bugle Boy,* ProArte.

By Maxene Andrews

Andrews Sisters, Bain, 1985.
(With Dick Hyman, Mundell Lowe, Bucky Pizzarelli, and Chuck Mangione) *Maxene: An Andrews Sister,* DRG, 1992.

Sources

Books

Oxford Companion to Popular Music, Oxford University Press, 1991.

Periodicals

Billboard, September 24, 1949; August 19, 1950; April 9, 1955; May 20, 1967; September 20, 1969.
Christian Science Monitor, April 11, 1974.
New York Times, November 1, 1991; July 30, 1992.
New Yorker, November 11, 1991.
Newsweek, November 11, 1991.

Variety, December 8, 1954; June 30, 1954; April 25, 1956; December 14, 1960; August 21, 1963; May 25, 1966; August 30, 1966; May 10, 1967; July 17, 1968; August 14, 1968; October 1, 1975; October 3, 1979; November 21, 1979; February 11, 1981; October 12, 1983.

Village Voice, June 25, 1980.

—*Robin Armstrong*

Anita Baker

Singer, songwriter, producer

"Fear doesn't overcome me," singer Anita Baker told *Ms.* "I say if it's going to be done, let's do it. Let's not put it in the hands of fate. Let's not put it in the hands of someone who doesn't know me. I know me best." This determination has not only allowed Baker to weather early struggles with recording industry exploitation and later media battles, it has also made her an accomplished artist of enormous popularity, with almost complete control over her creative projects.

Known for her three-octave vocal range and exceptional evocative power in the recording studio and onstage, Baker described her voice in *Ebony* as "a tool that was given to me that would allow me to take care of myself and to rise above my beginnings." Baker grew up in inner-city Detroit, where she became aware of her vocal powers while singing in small church choirs. As a child she idolized gospel great Mahalia Jackson and as a teenager became enamored of the sounds of jazz singers Sarah Vaughan and Nancy Wilson. While these women continue to inspire Baker, she identifies her aunt, Lois Landry, a beauty salon owner with whom Baker lived from infancy to adulthood, as the individual whose love and encouragement most allowed her to develop her talent. Baker dedicated her landmark recording, 1986's *Rapture,* to Landry.

Although Landry gave consistent emotional support to Baker, she and other family members worried about the practicality of Baker's quest to become a singer. They encouraged her to attend community college and get a nine-to-five job when she graduated from high school in 1976. Baker enrolled briefly in community college, then quit to begin singing with bands in Detroit nightclubs. At the Cabaret Lounge, on the city's east side, David Washington, bassist for Detroit funk group Chapter 8, heard Baker and asked her to join the group. Baker agreed and spent the next several years touring with Chapter 8 and recording for Ariola Records. Although the album yielded one hit, "I Just Want to Be Your Girl," in 1980 Ariola chose not to renew the band's contract. At the time, Ariola executives said they were dropping Chapter 8 because Baker's singing was substandard. Baker later concluded that this assessment was most likely Ariola's attempt to mask its imminent demise; hindsight aside, she was devastated by the company's judgment. She decided to take her family's advice and gave up singing altogether in favor of traditional employment. Waiting tables in a bar for a short time, she soon found a job as a receptionist at a Detroit law firm, Quin and Budajh.

For the Record. . .

Born January 26, 1958, in Toledo, OH. Raised in Detroit, MI, by an aunt, Lois Landry (owner of a beauty salon), and uncle, Walter Landry (an auto worker); married Walter Bridgforth, Jr. (a marketing specialist), 1988; children: Walter Baker Bridgforth. *Education:* Attended community college in Detroit.

Singer, songwriter, producer. Performed with various bands in Detroit nightclubs, c. 1976; with group Chapter 8, toured and recorded for Ariola Records, late 1970s; waited tables and worked as a receptionist for Detroit law firm Quin and Budajh, c. 1980; released first solo album, *The Songstress,* Beverly Glen Records, 1983; signed with Elektra Records, served as executive producer for first Elektra release, *Rapture,* 1986; toured with Luther Vandross, 1988; performed at inauguration of president George Bush, 1989, and at Montreaux Jazz Festival. Created Bridgforth Foundation.

Selected awards: Grammy Awards for best female vocalist, rhythm and blues, for *Rapture,* and song of the year, rhythm and blues, for "Sweet Love," and American Music Awards for favorite female vocalist, soul/rhythm and blues, and favorite album, soul/rhythm and blues, all 1987; Grammy Awards for best rhythm and blues song and best female vocal, rhythm and blues, 1989, for "Giving You the Best That I Got"; Grammy Award for best female vocalist, rhythm and blues, for *Compositions,* and American Music Award for favorite female vocalist, soul/rhythm and blues, both 1990.

Addresses: *Home*—Grosse Pointe, MI. *Record company*—Elektra Records, 75 Rockefeller Plaza, New York, NY 10019.

Enticed Back to Music After Stint at Law Firm

Baker had not performed in a year and a half when she received an offer from Otis Smith, a former Ariola executive who had formed Beverly Glen Records. After Smith promised her an apartment and a salary matching what Baker was earing at Quin and Budajh, she agreed to move to Los Angeles and record a solo album for Beverly Glen. *The Songstress* was released in 1983, sold more than 300,000 copies, and was on Billboard's black music charts for more than a year. The record included the hit singles "No More Tears" and "Angels."

The treatment Beverly Glen dished out was no better than Ariola's, however: Baker did not receive royalties from *The Songstress.* The label claimed the album hadn't made enough money to cover recording costs and continually delayed release of a new Baker album. When Baker informed the company that she was leaving, executives threatened to sue any company that signed her. Ignoring these threats, Baker hired Sherwin Bash as her manager, a man she told *Ms.* was "as old as God" and had managed "everyone from the Carpenters to Neil Diamond." Bash arranged a deal with Elektra Entertainment, the president of which, Bob Krasnow, was willing to go to court with Beverly Glen. Baker signed with Elektra after a long court battle, with permission to work as executive producer on her first Elektra release, *Rapture.*

Finished *Rapture* With Own Funds

Enlisting the production assistance of Michael Powell, guitarist for Chapter 8, Baker threw herself into the project. Resolving not to squander what she saw as her chance to finally prove she could succeed, Baker personally paid for recording costs greatly in excess of Elektra's budget; *Rapture* was released in 1986. The record won two Grammy awards in 1987, and by 1988 it had sold 5 million copies. Spinning off two hit singles, "Sweet Love" and "You Bring Me Joy," *Rapture* earned Baker an invitation to perform at George Bush's inaugural festivities. She also appeared at the prestigious Montreaux Jazz Festival, accompanied by jazz luminaries including David Sanborn on sax, Freddie Washington on bass, and Al Jarreau's rhythm section, all under the musical direction of the esteemed George Duke.

In 1988 Elektra released Baker's *Giving You the Best That I Got.* Like *Rapture* a collection of soul and R & B love songs, the record revealed Baker's strategy of sticking with a winning formula. Although several reviewers commented that the songs Baker chose for *Giving You the Best That I Got* were inadequate vehicles for her richly varied voice, the album was a respectable success, selling over three million copies, winning a Grammy, and eliciting a three-month tour with R & B superstar Luther Vandross.

With the triumph of Baker's first two Elektra albums came trouble with the media, which had begun to exploit Baker's personal life. Widespread coverage of Baker's 1988 miscarriage made healing from the traumatic event more difficult and forced Baker and her husband, IBM marketing specialist Walter Bridgforth, Jr., to retreat to Maui, Hawaii, for several weeks. Baker tried to remain positive about the unwanted publicity, stating in *Ms.,* "Since [the miscarriage] happened, hundreds of women have shared their experiences with me and let me know I wasn't alone. That was good.

The bad thing was having the whole world know. Families can suffer their problems and difficulties with each other and it's not easy, but it's multiplied a million times when everyone knows about it."

To avoid media intrusion into her personal life, Baker had not notified the press of her pregnancy. She has also consistently resisted media efforts to place her in opposition to other popular black female vocalists. In *Ebony,* Baker said she feels a "sisterhood" with these artists, referring to Oleta Adams as "a complete artist," calling Vesta a "bottomless pit of vocal dynamics," describing Regina Belle as "awesome," and naming Whitney Houston as a "super talent [who gets a] bum rap because she's at the top." Of phenomenon Mariah Carey, Baker said, "I ain't gonna lie, I'm jealous!"

Felt the Sting of Criticism

Despite this graciousness, Baker did not escape the label "bitch"—commonly assigned to women who assert their professional autonomy in the music industry. She initially earned this dubious moniker when she reportedly chastised sound crews onstage when they made mistakes during her first tours. Baker has since acknowledged that she engaged in some unprofessional behavior. Luther Vandross's comments on the Oprah Winfrey Show implying that he and Baker were in conflict during their 1988 tour perhaps added to Baker's reputation as a "difficult" performer. Baker, however, did not make any negative statements about Vandross, telling *Ebony,* "I just wish that Luther and I had talked face-to-face, just once. We didn't. . . . We should have talked instead of our managers and promoters talking."

With *Compositions,* her 1990 Elektra release, Baker demonstrated that she had developed considerably as a songwriter while at the same time becoming adept at unraveling publicity snarls. She did not write most of the songs on *Rapture* or *Giving You the Best That I Got,* although this clearly was not because she lacked ability—she received Grammys for co-writing "Sweet Love" and "Giving You the Best That I Got." While working on *Compositions* Baker built on both the confidence of those two successes and the skills she had been gaining in music theory classes. "I did a lot more writing on [*Compositions*] than I ever thought I would," she told *Jet.* "After my first Grammy for songwriting I had a little more confidence. . . . I leaned into it a little bit more." Her efforts were well rewarded: In addition to selling 1.5 million copies and winning a 1991 Grammy, *Compositions* gave Baker a credibility in the jazz world that she had not previously enjoyed. "[*Compositions*]

got me the respect of people whose respect I wanted. . . . Betty Carter will talk to me now," Baker joked in *Ebony.* The album also gained recognition from other artists and the public for its warmth and immediacy—as executive producer, Baker chose to record half the songs in live studio sessions with a rhythm section. *Compositions* included the hits "Talk to Me," "Whatever It Takes," and "Fairy Tales."

Established Bridgforth Foundation

The aftermath of *Compositions* found Baker taking time off from recording and touring. In 1991 she enjoyed herself at home with her husband, in Grosse Pointe, Michigan, a short distance from her family in Detroit. Never idle, however, Baker continued to work on various projects. One that holds her attention is the Bridgforth Foundation, which Baker created and through which she has established a college endowment for a class of 25 children at Berry Elementary School, in Detroit. The Foundation also funds a program to educate young musicians in recording industry negotiation, teaching them how to promote their work in a commercially viable manner, retain competent attorneys, and control their finances. In establishing the program, Baker hoped to help other musicians learn from the missteps she had made during the early stages of her career.

Although Baker has enjoyed great success writing and singing varied and sophisticated love songs, she suggested in *Ebony* that new songs may broach topics other than love. "There are things that go on in my life besides the battle of the sexes," said Baker. "That is a part of life, but there are other things that are equally important." On January 19, 1993, Baker gave birth to an 8-lb., 5-oz. son whom she and her husband named Walter Baker Bridgforth.

Selected discography

(With Chapter 8) *Chapter 8* (includes "I Just Want to Be Your Girl"), Ariola, 1980.
The Songstress (includes "No More Tears" and "Angels"), Beverly Glen, 1983.
Rapture (includes "Sweet Love," "Same Ol' Love," "You Bring Me Joy," "Been So Long," "Watch Your Step," "Mystery," and "No One in the World"), Elektra, 1986.
Giving You the Best That I Got (includes "Priceless," "Lead Me Into Love," and "Giving You the Best That I Got"), Elektra, 1988.
Compositions (includes "Talk to Me," "Perfect Love Affair," and "Fairy Tales"), Elektra, 1990.

Sources

Chicago Tribune, January 6, 1991.
Down Beat, October 1990.
Ebony, July 1989; July 1991.
High Fidelity, March 1989.
Jet, February 1988; February 1989; July 1989; October 1990.
Ms., June 1989.
New Yorker, March 20, 1989.
People, July 30, 1990.
Rolling Stone, October 23, 1986; December 15, 1988; August 9, 1990.
Stereo Review, March 1989; December 1990.
Variety, September 23, 1987; June 6, 1990.

—Jenny Bleier

The Band

Rock band

The five musicians who would become known collectively as the Band—Robbie Robertson, Rick Danko, Garth Hudson, Richard Manuel, and Levon Helm—first joined forces as a backup band for rockabilly singer Ronnie Hawkins in the early 1960s. In 1965 and 1966 they toured with Bob Dylan for a memorable series of concerts, Dylan literally electrifying the world with his new sound. After the tour, the Band settled near Woodstock, New York, and began recording their influential first album, *Music From Big Pink*. They also continued to record songs with Dylan. Throughout their career together—which ended on Thanksgiving Day, 1976, with a concert filmed by director Martin Scorsese—the Band released a variety of important original material, much of which is today considered classic rock and roll.

The Band's roots originated in the early form of rock and roll known as rockabilly. As the craze for this rhythm and blues/country hybrid began to decline in the U.S. in the late 1950s, Arkansas-based Ronnie Hawkins decided to take his band of musicians, which

For the Record. . .

Group included **Rick Danko** (born December 9, 1943, in Simcoe, Ontario, Canada), bass and vocals; **Levon Helm** (born May 26, 1942, in Marvell, Arkansas), drums, mandolin, and vocals; **Garth Hudson** (born August 2, c. 1943, in London, Ontario), organ and saxophone; **Richard Manuel** (born April 3, 1945, in Stratford, Ontario; died of apparent suicide by hanging, March 6, 1986, in Winter Park, FL), piano and vocals; and **Jaime** (some sources say James) **Robbie Robertson** (born July 5, 1944, in Toronto, Ontario) guitar and vocals.

Group formed as backing ensemble for singer Ronnie Hawkins; by 1963, had left Hawkins and become known as Levon and the Hawks, performing variously as the Crackers and the Canadian Squiers; recorded with folk/blues singer John Hammond, Jr., New York City, 1964; supported Bob Dylan on tour, 1965-66, 1974; signed with Capitol Records, and released first album, *Music From Big Pink,* 1968; ended career with five-hour performance at the Winterland, San Francisco, Thanksgiving Day, 1976, excerpts of which, titled *The Last Waltz,* were later released as an album and film; regrouped to perform with Dylan at Absolutely Unofficial Bluejeans Bash honoring the inauguration of President Bill Clinton, 1993.

included drummer Levon Helm, to Canada. Touring the Great White North, he picked up Canadian musicians along the way. Guitarist Robbie Robertson was only 15 when he joined the Hawkins aggregation in Toronto, and the other members of what would later become the Band signed up one by one.

Eventually, Hawkins fell out of style with Canadian audiences, too, so his backup group continued without him as Levon and the Hawks. When asked by *Melody Maker* in 1971 to explain how a primarily Canadian band had absorbed so much of the American South, Robertson replied, "When we first got rolling, we spent five years together playing almost totally in the South . . . with Ronnie [Hawkins] and without Ronnie."

Arrived as Things Got Electric

After half a decade as a road band, the Hawks moved to New York City at the invitation of folk and blues singer John Hammond, son and namesake of the renowned talent recruiter and record producer. They arrived just as Hammond, Bob Dylan, and other New York-based folk singers were experimenting with electric amplification. Dylan and Robertson occasionally jammed to-

gether, and both Robertson and Helm were part of the band that backed Dylan for the electrified second half of his August 28, 1965, Forest Hills, New York, concert. Helm told *Rolling Stone* in 1968, "We had never heard of Bob Dylan, but he had heard of us. He said, 'You wanna play Hollywood Bowl?' So we asked him who else was gonna be on the show. 'Just us,' he said."

Dylan played the Hollywood Bowl on September 3, 1965, beginning a world tour that would take him through the U.S., Canada, Europe, and Australia. The tour showcased Dylan's newly electrified sound, which was also featured on his just-released *Highway 61 Revisited.* Winding up at London's Royal Albert Hall in May of 1966, the tour concluded with two legendry concerts. Dylan's backup band—Robertson on guitar, Richard Manuel on piano, Garth Hudson on organ, Rick Danko on bass, and Levon Helm on drums—remained unnamed. Although Helm played a few concert dates in September and October of 1965, he was replaced—after a falling out with Dylan—for the rest of the tour by Sandy Konikoff and then by Mickey Jones. Of the Band's stature as a result of their road time with Dylan, the *Rolling Stone Illustrated History of Rock & Roll* related, "People came to see Dylan and went away marveling at his band; by the end of the tour, their place in rock and roll history was secure."

After the tour the Band decided to get off the road for a while and settled down in West Saugerties, New York. Not coincidentally, Dylan lived nearby, in Woodstock. Together, they jammed in a home recording studio in the basement of a house they dubbed "Big Pink." As *Rolling Stone* described it, "Big Pink is one of those middle-class ranch houses of the type you would expect to find in development row in the heart of suburbia rather than on an isolated mountaintop high above the barn architecture of New York State's rustic Woodstock."

Friends Just Called Them "the Band"

"The band began to grow mustaches and beards and wear hats. It was in Woodstock that people started referring to them as The Band," *Rolling Stone* reported. Robertson explained their nameless status to the magazine, stating, "You know, for one thing, there aren't many bands around Woodstock and our friends and neighbors just call us the band and that's the way we think of ourselves. And then, we just don't think a name means anything."

The Band's first album was appropriately titled *Music From Big Pink.* It included cover versions of three previously unreleased Dylan compositions, "I Shall Be

Released," "This Wheel's on Fire," co-written with Danko, and "Tears of Rage" co-written with Manuel. Most of the other songs on the album were penned by Robertson or Manuel. According to the *Rolling Stone Illustrated History of Rock and Roll*, "[*Music From Big Pink*] was a revolutionary album in many ways: The emphasis was on ensemble work rather than on the soloing that had previously dominated rock; the melodies, few of them blues based, were delivered by an ensemble that was almost orchestral in scope, yet comprised of only five musicians; the lyrics were elusive, like Dylan's, but with a distinctive and compelling cast. Enigmatic? You bet." In addition to recording songs for their first album, the Band had also backed Dylan in the studio on some of his compositions, which were released in 1975 on the two-album set *The Basement Tapes*.

The Band's second album, simply titled *The Band*, was their breakthrough LP; though the group had by then relocated to Hollywood, this tribute to rural living and times gone by earned them sizeable financial reward and enabled them to tour as a headlining act. Soon other artists, including Joan Baez, began recording their songs. *Billboard* described the group's sound in a 1969 concert review, explaining, "The Band is essentially a folk group with a souped-up sound, and yet, though highly amplified, their tones do not jar. They are, instead, listenable, even soothing." By this time Robertson had emerged as a gifted songwriter and producer.

Piano *and* Organ Created Unique Sound

One of the unique aspects of the Band's sound was their use of both piano and organ. When asked by *Melody Maker* how they happened upon this innovative combination, Robertson said, "We were into gospel music . . . not particularly spiritual gospel music, black gospel music, but white gospel music. It was easier to play, and it came more natural to us. We were trying to get a bigger sound going on—we had like piano, guitar, bass and drums for a long time, and we tried horns and all kinds of things but there were too many people. So we realized that the only instrument that could make that fullness, and take the place of horns or anything like that, was an organ. We met Garth [Hudson] at that time, who was a hundred times superior to any of us. . . . I mean he was, to us, just a phenomenon. He could play rings around all of us put together." Robertson concluded by saying he liked the sound because "it's full, it feels much more secure."

The Band's next releases, *Stage Fright* and *Cahoots*, disappointed many of their fans and received mixed reviews. At the end of 1971 they mounted a New Year's

Eve concert at New York's Academy of Music; recordings from the show were released as the two-record *Rock of Ages*. It was a strong effort, but it contained little new material. The group's next album—the title of which, *Moondog Matinee*, was a reference to pioneering rock disc jockey Alan Freed's radio show—contained rock and roll oldies.

Toward the end of 1973 members of the Band appeared as backing musicians on Dylan's *Planet Waves* LP. Shortly after the recording sessions, Dylan and the Band announced a joint tour. It was Dylan's first scheduled tour in eight years; fittingly, it had been the Band who had accompanied him on his last tour, the landmark mid-1960s world expedition. The 1974 cross-country tour began in Chicago and ended in Los Angeles. Most of the tour dates were at large venues, including stadiums and coliseums like New York City's Madison Square Garden and Los Angeles's Forum.

Dylan Remained Catalyst to Greatness

The tour was a major event. The concerts featured alternating sets—the Band backing Dylan, Dylan accompanying himself on acoustic guitar, and the Band doing its own songs. On a good night, some 30 songs might be performed. But, as noted by *Billboard*'s Sam Sutherland in his generally enthusiastic review of a concert in Philadelphia, "One of the few disappointments of the afternoon was the lack of new material from The Band. Robbie Robertson's own writing has revealed a richness of style, and a unique sense for distinctly American problems and experiences. . . . But their sets here . . . focused on their older material."

Sutherland went on, however, to compliment the Band on its role as backup for Dylan. "As it stood, their contributions to Dylan's tunes were extraordinary. Had they simply recaptured the drive of those tunes performed during their tours in the mid '60s, the music would have been strong enough. But their evolution since, while subtle, became palpable in the new force behind those tunes, a force equally generated by Dylan." The superb two-album set *Before the Flood* captures the excitement of that 1974 tour and includes many of Robertson's most popular and highly regarded compositions. Among these are the best-selling "Up on Cripple Creek" and "The Weight" and "The Night They Drove Old Dixie Down," which gained much recognition as a Joan Baez cover.

In 1975 the Band released *Northern Lights-Southern Cross*, their first album of original material since 1971. The following year they played live for the first time since 1974, at Stanford University, where they were received with great enthusiasm. Later in 1976 they announced that they would no longer appear live. Their final national performance was on NBC-TV's *Saturday Night Live.*

Legendary concert promoter Bill Graham staged a farewell concert for the Band on Thanksgiving Day, 1976, at San Francisco's Winterland—where, according to the *The Rolling Stone Encyclopedia of Rock & Roll,* they had first performed as the Band in 1969. The Band was onstage throughout the concert, which featured guest appearances by luminaries including Dylan, Joni Mitchell, Neil Young, Van Morrison, Eric Clapton, Neil Diamond, Muddy Waters, Dr. John, Stephen Stills, Ringo Starr, and the man who had given them their break and whom by then they had eclipsed, Ronnie Hawkins. The five-hour concert was recorded and released as an album; an acclaimed film of the extravaganza, by director Martin Scorsese, was released in 1978. Both the album and film were titled *The Last Waltz.*

Early in 1977 the Band released *Islands,* the last fruit of their contract with Capitol Records. Although the group had curtailed concert performances, there were expectations that they would continue to record together. But this was not to be. Individual members went on to solo projects or became involved in record production; Helm, for one, dabbled in acting—his role as country singer Loretta Lynn's father in 1980's *Coal Miner's Daughter* was widely praised. Robertson, who also did some acting, has perhaps been the most visible and successful in his solo career. In the end, though, the group that Sam Sutherland had called "our most mature and authentic rock 'n' rollers" simply disappeared after reigning at the forefront of popular music for more than a decade.

Selected discography

On Capitol Records, except where noted

Singles

"The Weight," 1968.
"Up on Cripple Creek," 1969.
"Rag Mama Rag," 1970.
"Time to Kill," 1970.
"Life Is a Carnival," 1971.

"Don't Do It," 1972.
"Ain't Got No Home," 1973.
"Ophelia," 1976.

Albums

Music From Big Pink, 1968.
The Band (includes "The Night They Drove Old Dixie Down"), 1969.
Stage Fright, 1970.
Cahoots, 1971.
Rock of Ages, 1972.
Moondog Matinee, 1973.
(With Bob Dylan) *Before the Flood,* Asylum, 1974.
(With Dylan) *The Basement Tapes,* Columbia, 1975.
Northern Lights-Southern Cross, 1975.
The Best of the Band, 1976.
Islands, 1977.
The Last Waltz, Warner Bros., 1978.
Anthology, 1978.

Sources

Books

The Rolling Stone Encyclopedia of Rock & Roll, edited by Jon Pareles and Patricia Romanowski, Rolling Stone Press/Summit Books, 1983.
The Rolling Stone Illustrated History of Rock & Roll, edited by Jim Miller, Rolling Stone/Random House, 1980.
Stambler, Irwin, *The Encyclopedia of Pop, Rock and Soul,* St. Martin's, 1989.

Periodicals

Billboard, October 25, 1969; November 24, 1973; January 19, 1974; July 10, 1976; November 20, 1976; December 11, 1976.
Guitar Player, December 1976; January 1988.
Look, August 25, 1970.
Melody Maker, May 29, 1971.
Musician, September 1987.
Rolling Stone, August 24, 1968; January 29, 1976; December 16, 1976; December 30, 1976; May 19, 1977; June 26, 1980; November 4, 1991.
Time, January 12, 1970; March 17, 1986.

—David Bianco

George Benson

Guitarist, singer, composer

George Benson straddles the pop and jazz worlds, managing to garner fans in both. Although he is well known for his warm singing voice, which is featured on many commercially successful albums, he initially drew notice in the music industry as a young and innovative jazz guitarist. After many years of recording and performing primarily pop music, he resumed playing traditional jazz in the late 1980s.

Benson's singing career apparently began soon after he could talk: in 1947, when he was just four years old, he won a singing contest and performed on the radio as "Little Georgie Benson." Benson sang in nightclubs and on the street, where at age ten he was heard by a talent scout. This discovery led to his first recording, the R&B song "She Makes Me Mad," on the RCA label. Benson cites jazz great Eddie Jefferson as an early influence on his singing. He told *Down Beat* reporter Lois Gilbert, "I felt he was one of the greatest jazz singers the world had known—he was to me the Bebop King." Listening to recordings of groundbreaking saxophonist Charlie Parker and guitarist Grant Green increased his interest in jazz, and at seventeen, he led a five piece R&B group, in which he played rhythm guitar and sang.

Benson's big break came in 1961 when he joined Jack McDuff's organ trio as an electric guitarist. He toured and recorded with McDuff until 1965, when he left to lead his own quartets. In addition to singing and playing electric guitar with his own group, he played as a sideman for such jazz masters as Ron Carter, Billy Cobham, Miles Davis, Herbie Hancock, Freddie Hubbard, and Lee Morgan. Benson's first album as a leader, *Benson Burner,* was released in 1967. Although his singing was considered unremarkable, his brilliantly searing guitar solos were hailed as the work of a promising new jazz guitarist.

From Jazz to Pop

Benson's guitar style—especially his octave playing and soft tone—reflects the influence of Wes Montgomery, the legendary guitarist who set the pattern for the younger musician's career. Both worked under producer Creed Taylor, who first steered Montgomery from jazz playing to pop success, and then did the same for Benson. Benson initially worked with Taylor at A&M Records, joining Taylor's newly established CTI label in 1970. Although Benson still played guitar, Taylor worked to showcase his singing, backing his vocals with orchestras. Benson continued to record some highly praised jazz, particularly on his 1971 album *Beyond the Blue Horizon.*

For the Record. . .

Born March 22, 1943, in Pittsburgh, PA; wife's name, Johnnie; children: Keith Givens (deceased), Robert, Marcus, Christopher, Stephen, George, Jr.

Guitarist, singer, composer. Played electric guitar in Brother Jack McDuff's quartet, 1962-65; worked as sideman and led own quartets as guitarist and singer, beginning in 1965; recording artist with Columbia Records, 1965-68; worked with producer Creed Taylor, first at A&M Records, then at Taylor's CTI label, 1968-72; recording artist with Warner Bros. Records, beginning in 1976.

Awards: Numerous Grammy awards, including record of the year, 1977, best instrumental performance, 1977, best R&B male vocal performance, 1980, best jazz vocal performance, 1980, and best pop instrumental, 1983; multiplatinum award for *Breezin';* several other platinum and gold records; honorary degrees in music.

Addresses: *Record company*—Warner Bros., 3300 Warner Blvd., Burbank, CA 91505-4694.

Benson disliked his lack of autonomy under Taylor, so he moved to Warner Bros. and producer Tommy LiPuma. Benson and his group recorded with LiPuma, who overdubbed the strings section to sweeten their sound. At this time Benson developed his style of scat singing the identical line he was playing on the guitar. His 1976 Warner Bros. album *Breezin',* which includes the hit "This Masquerade," sold four million copies and broke the instrumental sales record for that year.

Benson started the 1980s by attempting to break into the dance market with *Give Me the Night.* Produced by Quincy Jones, who also produced Michael Jackson's phenomenally popular dance album *Off the Wall,* Benson's album achieved moderate success. Benson told Gilbert that he was striving to appeal to a variety of listeners: "I don't ever want to be pigeon-holed, and I don't want to make records that just sit on a shelf," he said in *Down Beat.* "I want them to be spinning on somebody's turntable."

Return to Jazz

Benson's commercial success in the 1970s and early 1980s was coupled with criticism for his virtual abandonment of traditional jazz. Jazz purists were disappointed that Benson's early promise as a jazz guitarist had not been fulfilled. Although Benson had dabbled in playing jazz guitar—as in his performance with Benny

Goodman on public television's *Soundstage Tribute to John Hammond*—he did not dedicate an entire album to his jazz playing until 1989, when he collaborated with jazz masters McCoy Tyner, Lenny Castro, and Ron Carter on the hit *Tenderly.* Benson also toured with the McCoy Tyner Trio throughout the summer of 1989. Commenting in *Down Beat* on his decision to shift back to jazz guitar, Benson noted, "With *Tenderly,* I very much felt I was reestablishing my jazz credentials and, although it took audiences a little while to get used to it, the response was eventually overwhelming."

Benson took this favorable response to his jazz playing as encouragement to pursue a jazz recording with the Count Basie Orchestra (CBO). Their collaboration, the 1990 album *Big Boss Band,* was well received. Benson joined the CBO for several songs at the NorthSea Jazz Festival that same year, standing in for Ella Fitzgerald at the last minute. Benson reported to *Down Beat* writer Michael Bourne, "We had no rehearsal except for what we'd done in the studio, but the great vibe was still there."

Scatting Benson-Style

Benson's trademark—scat singing a line identical to the melody he plays on the guitar—has earned him the admiration of fans and music critics alike. Although he generally sings in unison with the guitar, he occasionally sings an octave higher or lower than he plays. Even more rarely, he sings in harmony with his guitar. He told *Down Beat's* Michael Bourne, "My guitar can do things my voice can't do. It can soar and makes my voice try to follow, and I end up singing in octaves my voice can't do when I'm just doing the vocal. When I'm doing it with the guitar, my voice doesn't stop. It follows the guitar all the way up the scale and down. I don't know how I'm able to get that much range, but I can."

Benson's attempts to juggle the roles of guitarist and vocalist, jazz innovator and pop success, have occasionally led to criticism of his lack of dedication to pure jazz. However, his efforts in the late 1980s to fulfill his early promise as a jazz performer have resulted in the expansion of his pop audience with jazz enthusiasts. Throughout the early 1990s that expansion gave signs of continuing as Benson worked on an album with Jon Hendricks, Al Jarreau, and Bobby McFerrin and considered a world tour with the Count Basie Orchestra.

Selected discography

Benson Burner, Columbia, 1967.
Giblet Gravy, Verve, 1968.

Shape of Things, A&M, 1968.
(With Miles Davis) *Miles in the Sky,* Columbia, 1968.
Beyond the Blue Horizon, CTI, 1971, reissued, 1987.
White Rabbit, CTI, 1971.
The Electrifying George Benson, Affinity, 1973.
Breezin', Warner Bros., 1976.
Weekend in L.A., Warner Bros., 1977.
Give Me the Night, Warner Bros., 1980.
While the City Sleeps, Warner Bros., 1986.
Twice the Love, Warner Bros., 1988.
Bad Benson (recorded in 1974), CTI, 1988.
George Benson in Concert at Carnegie Hall (recorded in 1975), CTI, 1988.
(With McCoy Tyner, Ron Carter, and Lenny Castro) *Tenderly,* Warner Bros., 1989.
Big Boss Band Featuring the Count Basie Orchestra, Warner Bros., 1990.
(With Jack McDuff) *George Benson and Jack McDuff,* Prestige.
The Other Side of Abbey Road, A&M.
20/20, Warner Bros.
Livin' Inside Your Love, Warner Bros.

Sources

Books

Feather, Leonard, and Ira Gitler, *The Encyclopedia of Jazz in the Seventies,* Horizon, 1976.

Lyons, Len, and Don Perlo, *Jazz Portraits: The Lives and Music of the Jazz Masters,* William Morrow, 1989.
The New Grove Dictionary of Jazz, volume 1, edited by Barry Kernfeld, Macmillan, 1988.

Periodicals

Audio, February 1987; December 1989.
Chicago Tribune, August 3, 1992.
Down Beat, November 1980; November 1987; March 1988; July 1988; November 1988; November 1989; December 1990; January 1991; October 1991.
Guitar Player, October 1987; January 1992.
High Fidelity, September 1988.
Los Angeles Magazine, January 1990.
New York Times, October 10, 1991.
People, October 24, 1988.
Rolling Stone, October 5, 1989.
Stereo Review, September 1988; November 1989; March 1991.
Variety, July 4, 1990.
World Monitor, November 1991.

Additional information for this profile was obtained from Warner Bros. Records press material, 1991.

—Susan Windisch Brown

Black Sabbath

Rock band

Much of the credit—or blame, depending on your outlook—for both the sound and sensibility of contemporary heavy metal and "grunge" rock may be laid at the feet of the English group Black Sabbath. The sonic barrage they pioneered, consisting of Tony Iommi's riff-driven, bluesy guitar and a pounding rhythm best exemplified by bassist "Geezer" Butler and drummer Bill Ward, would form the model for a generation of hard rock bands. Meanwhile, the anguish and rage expressed in Sabbath classics like "Paranoid" and "War Pigs" gave voice to the confused aftermath of the 1960s counter-culture clash and has been a clear influence on the songwriting of later metal bands. By the release of its 1992 album *Dehumanizer*, Black Sabbath had marked nearly a quarter century of recording, touring, and personnel changes.

The quartet—Iommi, Butler, Ward, and singer John "Ozzy" Osbourne—originated in Birmingham, England, in 1967; at first they called themselves Earth and played fairly conventional music in various nightspots. "People were boozing and talking and drowning us

out," Iommi told *Melody Maker* in a 1976 interview. "We were playing our nice little jazzy/blues numbers and no one was taking a blind bit of notice. So we turned up the volume and blasted them with it." The group soon discovered they weren't the only group called Earth, so in 1969 the foursome chose the moniker Black Sabbath after a song they'd written.

Black Sabbath was signed to Vertigo Records in England and to Warner Bros. in the U.S. They released their self-titled debut LP on Friday the 13th of February, 1970. The title track, with its rain-and-thunder sound effects and punishing guitar riff, became an instant standard. Legendary rock critic Lester Bangs, however, was singularly unimpressed with the debut; his response in *Rolling Stone* set the tone for the group's early critical reception: "stiff recitations of [blues-rock supergroup] Cream cliches that sound like the musicians learned them out of a book, grinding on and on with dogged persistence." Despite such reviews, the album sold phenomenally well, as would many subsequent Sabbath outings.

Black-Magic Mystique

Not surprisingly, given their name, Black Sabbath found it necessary to defend themselves from charges of Satanism. By 1971 they were loudly protesting to *Melody Maker* that they were, in fact, "anti-black magic." Osbourne took it upon himself in 1973 to defend the group against the charge that they played "downer" music. "We just play music," he insisted to *Melody Maker.* Yet drummer Ward had told *Rolling Stone* two years earlier, "Most people live on a permanent down, but just aren't aware of it. We're trying to express it for people." In any case, the band's appeal to a disaffected, young, mostly male audience was undeniably due in part to the mystique and danger of its name and perhaps undeserved reputation. "The black magic thing did help us in the beginning," Iommi told *Rolling Stone* in 1971. Nonetheless, *Melody Maker's* Chris Charlesworth insisted that "Black Sabbath are pretty ordinary Midlands boys who love their mums, dads and wives, drink only moderately, and carry out their lives as members of a successful rock group with almost humdrum attitudes."

The group's second LP, *Paranoid,* was originally slated to be titled *War Pigs.* The single "Paranoid," however, was such a huge success—it went to Number Four on the rock charts and was by far the group's biggest single—that the album was named after it. The single appeared in late 1970, the album in 1971. It remains one of the group's most influential records, featuring the songs "War Pigs" and "Iron Man," which stand beside "Paranoid" as Sabbath anthems. Late in 1971 the group released *Master of Reality,* which included the hit "Sweet Leaf." Even Bangs changed his tune, writing with guarded approval in *Rolling Stone,* "Rock & roll has always been noise, and Black Sabbath have boiled that noise to its resinous essence."

Soon thereafter the band's relentless international touring schedule began to take its toll; but even as the members of the group announced their intention to tour less, their popularity continued to increase. 1972 saw the release of *Volume 4,* an ambitious excursion that brought more converts into the Sabbath fold. The LP included the gospel-tinged ballad "Changes," in which Osbourne's melancholy vocals were accompanied by strings and piano, and the kinetic rocker "Supernaut." Next came 1973's *Sabbath, Bloody Sabbath.* By that time, *Rolling Stone's* response had become downright respectful. Reviewer Gordon Fletcher called the record "an extraordinarily gripping affair" and dubbed the group "a true Seventies band"—a compliment at the time. More sonically varied than most of the band's previous efforts, the LP included such embellishment as orchestral arrangements. Years later, in a retrospective of musical "guilty pleasures," Ken Richardson of *High Fidelity* called the record "a fierce, multidimensional revival that holds up well." For Richardson, however, *Sabbath, Bloody Sabbath* was the group's last important recording.

In the early 1970s Black Sabbath became involved in a squabble with their management and found themselves on a couple of different British labels—World Wide Artists and NEMS—though they would return to Vertigo

> "Rock & roll has always been noise, and Black Sabbath have boiled that noise to its resinous essence."
> —Lester Bangs

in 1976. The group had resumed its intensive touring schedule after a hiatus and released a new album, *Sabotage,* in 1975. Sabbath touted the record in a *Rolling Stone* interview as a return "to basic roots." Even so, the group recorded a choir for part of the album and took keyboardist Jezz Woodruff on tour; Iommi, too, played some keyboards on the record. "*Sabotage* is not only Black Sabbath's best record since *Paranoid,*" opined Billy Altman in his *Rolling Stone* review, "it might be their best ever." *Melody Maker* found that with their 1976 follow-up, *Technical Ecstasy,* the group could "break the mould and still provide fresh exciting music." That year also saw the release of the two-record retrospective *We Sold Our Soul for Rock 'N' Roll,* which featured many of Sabbath's most popular songs.

Exit Ozzy

Ozzy Osbourne gradually became set on a solo career, and in 1978 he recorded his last studio album with Black Sabbath, *Never Say Die.* "It would be churlish not to wish Sabbath good health and congratulations on their tenth anniversary of splattering brains upon living room walls," acknowledged *Melody Maker's* Colin Ir-

win in his review of the record, though he had difficulty with the group's "one-dimensional music" and "pretensions." In any event, Osbourne departed and the group eventually settled on American vocalist Ronnie James Dio, late of the groups Rainbow and his own Dio. "We met up with Ronnie at a party in L.A. and invited him down for a blow [audition]," Iommi told *Melody Maker.* "We hadn't really looked at other vocalists and when we heard his voice we all liked the way he put things across. We got along almost immediately, so it was logical to work with him." Ward also left the band, but in 1980 the re-tooled Sabbath, with new drummer Vinnie Appice, put out the successful album *Heaven and Hell.* That year also saw the release of *Live at Last,* a live album featuring Osbourne; *Melody Maker* condemned it as a "totally inept retrospective."

In 1981 the group released *Mob Rules. Rolling Stone's* J. D. Considine opined: "After 1980's harder and faster *Heaven and Hell,* there was reason to believe that singer Ronnie James Dio might pull Black Sabbath off the heavy-metal scrapheap. Didn't happen. *Mob Rules* finds the band as dull-witted and flatulent as ever." As if that comment weren't enough, trouble erupted between Dio and his bandmates in 1982, during the mixing of the album *Live Evil.* In January of 1983 Iommi told *Melody Maker* that he and Butler had split with Dio and Appice, and that the two—without a band—had signed a new deal with old management associate Don Arden. *Live Evil* was released that year to reasonably positive reviews; it fared superbly with heavy metal fans, containing a mixture of Ozzy-era Sabbath classics and some of the strongest material recorded by Dio. In April Ian Gillan, former lead singer for Deep Purple, joined the group, and Ward once again took up his drumsticks. The re-formed Sabbath released the album *Born Again* that year, but soon Gillan, too, departed. Even Butler left to do solo work in 1985.

1980s Drift

The band, as Iommi admitted in a 1992 *Guitar School* interview, "went off on a tangent" after Gillan left, with a dizzying series of personnel shuffles and some very poorly received records. The 1986 album *Seventh Star* was intended as an Iommi solo record—the cover read "Black Sabbath Featuring Tony Iommi"—and vanished quickly. *Melody Maker* called it "a revolting, incestuous amalgam of everything Iommi has picked up along the way and a stark, grating reminder of all he has lost." 1987's *The Eternal Idol* featured a variety of new players, including singer Tony Martin, bassists Dave Spitz and Bob Daisley, percussionist Bev Bevan—Ward's temporary replacement after his first departure—and drummer Eric Singer. Also in 1987, Sabbath and fellow hard rock veterans Status Quo were criticized by the anti-Apartheid movement for appearing at South Africa's racially exclusive Sun City. The group's downward spiral continued with the 1989 I.R.S. Records release *Headless Cross.* "It's sad to report," wrote Simon Price of *Melody Maker,* "but Black Sabbath have switched their guitars to *unleaded."* His ultimate conclusion: "This is paganism in a condom. Don't waste your money."

In 1990 Black Sabbath put out the concept album *Tyr.* The *Wilson Library Bulletin* described the release as "a thematic saga about the son of [Norse god] Odin. It's all very grandiose, with lyrics singing the glories of 'Valhalla' [the great hall in Norse mythology where the souls of heroes slain in battle are received] or establishing the fearful presence of the title character, 'The Law Maker.' Guitarist and band founder Tony Iommi's martial music is well echoed by lyricist Tony Martin's strident vocals. *Tyr* is a suitable accompaniment to catching the latest news from the war front."

Revival With "Grunge" Recognition

Despite this lapse into what many critics would call self-parody, Black Sabbath found the 1990s a kinder, more appreciative decade, thanks in part to the ascendancy of new, alternative and grunge metal bands. As bassist Ben Shepherd of the well-regarded Seattle band Soundgarden told *Spin,* "We've taken everything we know from Black Sabbath." Supergroups like Metallica expressed similar indebtedness. Sabbath was finally acknowledged for their influence on a generation of rockers, and this acknowledgment may have fueled Iommi's decision to reunite with Butler, Appice, and Dio for a new album and tour. "Geezer met Ronnie in the States at one of his shows and got up and played with him," Iommi told the *Detroit Free Press.* "They spoke after the show, had a few drinks and a few more drinks, and they started talking about putting this lineup of the band back together." At first, Iommi wanted to recruit drummer Cozy Powell, who'd played on several Sabbath albums in the 1980s, but Powell and Dio didn't hit it off and when an injury sidelined the drummer, the group hired Appice.

In 1992 the foursome released *Dehumanizer* on Warner's Reprise label. *Pulse!* called it "the best thing the band's done in years," while Seattle's *Rocket* admitted,

"Dio has once again taught the old farts how to rock." A Reprise press kit quoted Butler on the songwriting process: "All the songs have come from rehearsals or jams. There are more tempo changes and intricate things than we have ever done before. It goes from riff to riff on this album." *Dehumanizer* focused on some serious issues, as Dio noted in an interview with *Circus:* "We didn't want to be dinosaurs that did an album about witches and devils. There's plenty to be angry about out there—the fact that we have what might be the worst government America's ever had, the education problem, the lack of attention to the AIDS crisis. We had plenty to be angry about and that is reflected throughout *Dehumanizer."* The group wrote the song "Time Machine" for the soundtrack of the megahit film *Wayne's World,* which amply reflected the continuing relevance of Sabbath to the teen rock sensibility. Of one of the group's live performances, Paul Gallotta of *Circus* noted, "The band handled the set with an air of professionalism sorely lacking in a lot of younger bands."

With its 1992 tour Sabbath celebrated twenty-five years in the music business. "It's nice, I suppose," Iommi told the *Detroit Free Press.* "But I've just kind of gone along with it all these years. I don't really think, 'Oh, it's been 25 years. How wonderful!'" When asked by *Guitar School's* Jeff Kitts if he had ever considered retirement, the guitarist replied, "Oh, no—I could never do that. I'll be fighting it out until the end. The problems we had over the last few years were very frustrating—but not enough to make me give up."

Far from throwing in the towel, in November of 1992 Iommi and company reunited with erstwhile vocalist Ozzy Osbourne for the last date of Osbourne's so-called farewell tour. Although Sabbath had performed with Osbourne at 1985's Live Aid extravaganza, this evening's show featured original drummer Bill Ward. Dio was conspicuously absent, reportedly not wanting to be involved in the reunion rigmarole. As a warm-up to Osbourne's appearance the band played a few numbers with headbanger idol Rob Halford, who had recently split with his bandmates in Judas Priest. Osbourne's arrival at first seemed anticlimactic. Quoted *Daily Variety's* Troy J. Augusto: "When Osbourne finally trudged out at 8 p.m., he looked like he needed, very badly, to retire. But the man is a living legend and deserves to be treated as such. So what if he used a teleprompter, or that his stage conversation was limited to his usual soundbites of 'I love you all!' and 'go (expletive) crazy!' Or that his stage presence is made up of incessant pacing and leap-frog jumps? He's Ozzy!" Apparently Osbourne's romp with his former cohorts hit the spot; in March of 1993 it was announced that he would rejoin Black Sabbath for a new record and tour.

Selected discography

On Warner Bros. Records, except where noted

Black Sabbath (includes "Black Sabbath"), 1970.
Paranoid (includes "Paranoid," "War Pigs," and "Iron Man"), 1971.
Master of Reality (includes "Sweet Leaf"), 1971.
Volume 4 (includes "Changes" and "Supernaut"), 1972.
Sabbath, Bloody Sabbath, 1973.
Sabotage, 1975.
We Sold Our Soul for Rock 'N' Roll, 1976.
Technical Ecstasy, 1976.
Never Say Die, 1978.
Heaven and Hell, 1980.
Live at Last, 1980.
Mob Rules, 1981.
Live Evil, 1983.
Born Again, 1983.
Seventh Star, 1986.
The Eternal Idol, 1987.
Headless Cross, I.R.S., 1989.
Tyr, I.R.S., 1990.
Dehumanizer (includes "Time Machine"), Reprise, 1992.
(Contributor) "Time Machine," *Wayne's World,* 1992.

Sources

Circus, October 31, 1992.
Daily Variety, November 17, 1992.
Detroit Free Press, July 31, 1992.
Guitar School, September 1992.
High Fidelity, July 1989.
Melody Maker, March 14, 1970; July 11, 1970; September 19, 1970; October 31, 1970; January 16, 1971; September 11, 1971; February 12, 1972; October 7, 1972; October 14, 1972; August 11, 1973; February 23, 1974; July 6, 1974; March 27, 1976; October 16, 1976; November 12, 1977; October 14, 1978; March 22, 1980; July 26, 1980; January 31, 1981; January 8, 1983; January 15, 1983; January 22, 1983; March 5, 1983; April 16, 1983; September 24, 1983; March 24, 1984; March 1, 1986; November 28, 1987; April 29, 1989; November 18, 1989.
Pulse!, August 1992.
Reflex, Issue 29.
Rocket (Seattle), August 1992.
Rolling Stone, September 17, 1970; May 13, 1971; November 25, 1971; December 7, 1972; February 14, 1974; September 25, 1975; October 9, 1975; October 19, 1978; February 18, 1982.
Spin, September 1992.
Wilson Library Bulletin, December 1990.

Additional information for this profile was obtained from Reprise Records media information, 1992.

—Simon Glickman

Julian Bream

Classical guitarist, lutenist

"It would be untrue to attribute the explosion of contemporary interest in the classical guitar solely to Julian Bream," Tony Palmer clarified in *A Life on the Road,* which he coauthored with Bream, "but there can be little doubt that his example as a performer, his choice of repertoire, his willingness to spend much of his life on the road proselytizing, has had a profound influence on the development and future of the guitar." Indeed it is Bream's playing of Elizabethan and Baroque lute pieces and his commissioning of guitar works from twentieth-century composers—a repertoire literally spanning centuries—that has showcased the versatility and vitality of the guitar and its family of instruments. This expansive approach, however, has piqued purists of the authentic music movement who disapprove of Bream's modern stylings on the lute; he quickly dismisses them. For Bream, playing music is not a show of technique but a passionate attempt to reveal to an audience a piece's spiritual and mystical qualities. "Ideally the performer has a special function," he theorized in *A Life on the Road,* "which is to bring the listener to the edge of that experience and to open the doors of this perception in such a way that those who wish to enter can."

Bream was born in Battersea, England, on July 15, 1933. Bream's first exposure to musical performance came from his father, Henry Bream, a commercial artist and amateur guitarist who taught his young son the basics of the instrument. But inspiration for Bream's future course came from recordings by the great Spanish classical guitarist Andrés Segovia. Segovia was considered an aberration, as solo guitar was not commonly a choice for classical performance at the time, but Bream was determined to follow a similar musical life. Though his father urged jazz studies, Bream chose to enroll in the Royal College of Music in London with an emphasis on piano, composition, and cello, while doggedly focusing on the classical guitar. Unable to reconcile the conservative faculty to his pursuit, Bream left the college in 1952. He was subsequently drafted by the British Army where he played electric jazz guitar in the Royal Artillery's dance band for three years.

Entranced by Elizabethan Music

Bream earned money in college by playing incidental music for dramas—usually sixteenth- and seventeenth-century historical plays—broadcast by the British Broadcasting Corporation (BBC). He had always been interested in the Elizabethan period of English history; in researching music for the plays, he was further drawn to the era's music and its popular instrument, the lute. "I felt instinctively that this was a

For the Record. . .

B orn July 15, 1933, in Battersea, England; son of Henry
G. Bream (a commercial artist); married Margaret
Williamson (divorced); married second wife (divorced). *Education:* Attended Royal College of Music, London.

Made professional debut, 1947; recorded incidental music
for BBC radio plays, late 1940s-early 1950s; served in
British Army, playing in dance band, 1952-55; began
recording and touring career, 1955; made U.S. debut,
1958; formed Julian Bream Consort, 1960. Subject of
television biography *A Life in the Country,* 1976. Author,
with Tony Palmer, of *A Life on the Road,* Macdonald,
1982.

Awards: Named commander of the Order of the British
Empire; received Villa-Lobos Gold Medal, 1976; six Grammy
awards; two Edison awards.

Addresses: *Office*—c/o Harold Holt, Ltd., 31 Sinclair
Rd., London W14 0NS, England.

musical period in these islands rich in beauty, inventiveness, and vitality," he recounted in his book. "And it seemed to me I had a possibility to help revitalize some of this music. I had a mission almost: to present this music in a way that was not of the museum, but of *now,* although still retaining the music's essential spirit."

In the early 1950s very few lute players or instructors existed. In lieu of training, Bream improvised by adapting his guitar technique to the lute. Traditionally the lute was played or plucked with the fingertips near the bridge, yielding the soft, intimate tone characteristic of a courtly instrument. Bream, however, played with his fingernails, plucking the strings between the fingerboard and the bridge, producing considerable differences in tone and dynamics—important aspects of any solo concert instrument.

Lute Technique Reproached

Bream's first efforts in the mid-1950s captured both the public's ear and imagination. But his growing recognition, along with that of the lute, also brought out traditional lute devotees who were exceedingly critical of his guitar-based style. Bream was unmoved, confirming that his approach to music has always been to champion expression over technique. "It's the sincerity and the heart behind the friggery that is for me the vital clue," he has written. "I like to play the lute full-bloodedly, with passion, as well as with delicacy and, I hope, refine-

ment." Almost 30 years later, William Ellis agreed. Reviewing a reissue of Bream's early works, Ellis opined in *American Record Guide* that the recordings still had "much to teach younger players of the instrument. Inherent in his occasional vibrato and wide dynamics (for a lute, that is) is an abundant musicality that more historically (or should I say 'politically') correct players would do well to study."

Part of a Continuing Tradition

In 1960 Bream formed the Julian Bream Consort, an instrumental group based on Elizabethan models, largely because he wanted to experience the repertoire available to this setting of instruments. But he was not content to explore only the lute and its ancient music. "One thing you learn very rapidly in this business is that you are part of a continuing tradition," Bream noted, adding "that the future of the guitar, for instance, is every bit as important as its past." This insight prompted Bream to commission guitar pieces from such eminent modern classical composers as Benjamin Britten, Malcolm Arnold, and William Walton. All the works have greatly impacted the classical guitar community and one, Britten's *Nocturnal,* has since become a standard piece in the repertoire for modern guitar.

"I'm all for change and variety," Bream told Allan Kozinn in *Guitar Review.* "Your experience of life is to a large part distilled into your performing. As you grow older, you concentrate on aspects of music that you perhaps only touched on earlier." This vital propensity for change was no more evident than in the late 1970s and 1980s when Bream set his lute aside to once more concentrate on the guitar. He again commissioned new works, sought out standard pieces in the Spanish guitar literature he had overlooked, and filmed a video series, *¡Guitarra!,* which explored the development of the Spanish guitar and the repertoire.

Bream returned to the lute in the early 1990s, playing a slightly different, more historically correct form. But his approach to music hasn't changed; he still "believes that interpretive values are more important than authentic timbres," acknowledged Kozinn. Perhaps more than anything, it is Bream's lack of zealous devotion to the technical aspects of the guitar repertoire that truly allows him to express its intangible qualities. "There is no piece of guitar music that has the formal beauty of a piano sonata by Mozart, or the richly worked out ideas and passion of a late Beethoven string quartet, or for that matter the beautiful mellifluous poetry of a Chopin Ballade," he opined. "[But] I know that I can invest unsophisticated, naïve, even corny guitar music with a poetry which can entice the ear, and with it create an experience that is perfectly valid for present-day musical circumstances. I only need a handful of notes, nothing special, and I'm away."

Selected discography

An Anthology of English Song, Decca, 1955.
A Bach Recital for the Guitar, Westminster, 1957.
The Art of Julian Bream, RCA, 1959.
(With the Julian Bream Consort) *An Evening of Elizabethan Music,* RCA, 1962.
Baroque Guitar, RCA, 1965.
Lute Music From the Royal Courts of Europe, RCA, 1966.
20th Century Guitar, RCA, 1966.
Classic Guitar, RCA, 1968.
Elizabethan Lute Songs, RCA, 1970.
Romantic Guitar, RCA, 1970.
Julian Bream Plays Villa-Lobos, RCA, 1971.
(With John Williams) *Together,* RCA, 1971.
The Woods So Wild, RCA, 1972.
Julian Bream '70s, RCA, 1973.
The Lute Music of John Dowland, RCA, 1976.
The Music of Spain, Vol. 1, RCA, 1979.
Dedication, RCA, 1981.
The Music of Spain, Vol. 5: The Poetic Nationalists, RCA, 1982.
Guitarra: The Guitar in Spain, RCA, 1985.
Bach: Suites for Lute, RCA, 1986.
(With the Julian Bream Consort) *Fantasies, Ayres, and Dances,* RCA, 1988.
Two Loves, RCA, 1989.
La Guitarra Romantica, RCA, 1991.

Also released *¡Guitarra!: The Guitar in Spain With Julian Bream, Vols. 1-4* (video series), Home Vision, 1984.

Sources

Books

Bream, Julian, and Tony Palmer, *A Life on the Road,* Macdonald, 1982.

Periodicals

American Record Guide, January 1985; September/October 1991.
Chicago Tribune, February 19, 1987.
Economist, January 11, 1992.
Guitar Player, June 1990; January 1992.
Guitar Review, Spring 1990.
New York Times, March 25, 1990; April 3, 1990.
Stereo Review, December 1986.

—*Rob Nagel*

Jheryl Busby

"Times have changed," Jheryl Busby, president and chief executive officer of Motown Records, announced to Pamela Shariff in *Black Enterprise,* "and Motown can't be what it was in the 1960s. Today, I want to position this company as a beacon to black executives and to black talent." While Busby acknowledged in the *New York Times* that Motown's past was stellar when Marvin Gaye, the Four Tops, the Jackson Five, Stevie Wonder, Smokey Robinson, and Diana Ross and the Supremes were regularly contributing classic songs to the Top 40, he proposed a different course for "the second chapter of Motown." When Busby took office, however, he did not foresee legal battles with his promotional distributor, MCA Records, that in the early 1990s threatened to destroy his visionary aims. Nonetheless optimistic, he disclosed to Jeffrey Ressner in *Entertainment Weekly,* "If you're a Christian like me, you realize there is a God. And the last time I checked, He was on Motown's side."

Born in Los Angeles, California, Busby attended Long Beach State College. He began his career as an inventory clerk at Mattel Toys, working his way up to new-toy coordinator. Later Busby joined Stax Records—the legendary Memphis-based 1960s soul alternative to Motown's crossover pop that, with its subsidiary, Volt, introduced Carla Thomas, Otis Redding, Sam and Dave, Booker T. and the MGs, and the Staples Singers. Eventually, Busby became head of West Coast promotion and marketing for the label. During the early 1980s, he did promotional work for several record companies, including Casablanca, CBS, A&M, and Atlantic. Employed by MCA Records as vice-president of the black music division in 1984, Busby enjoyed phenomenal success. His promotion of such established singers as Patti LaBelle and up-and-coming acts like New Edition catapulted record sales to $50 million in the mid-1980s. When he ended his career at MCA in the late 1980s—as president of the black music division—his sector was number one in the industry in black album sales.

Offered the opportunity to head Motown in 1988, Busby told Michael Lev in the *New York Times,* "I thought it couldn't get any better: president and CEO of probably the most important record label in America in terms of black music." But revitalizing Motown, he would find, involved a mass of legal red tape and required learning "a more aggressive marketing-oriented approach to developing new talent," he revealed to *Black Enterprise's* Shariff.

In September of 1989 Busby united Los Angeles-based Motown with its cultural counterpart on the East Coast, New York City's mecca for black talent, the historic Apollo Theatre, to form Apollo Theatre Records, a new

For the Record. . .

Born c. 1949, in Los Angeles, CA; children: three. *Education:* Attended Long Beach State College.

Record company executive. Inventory clerk, purchasing agent (in production supplies), and new-toy coordinator for Mattel Toys; regional promotional representative and head of West Coast promotion and marketing for Stax Records; independent album promoter; performed promotional duties for Casablanca, Atlantic Records, CBS Records, and A&M Records, 1980-83; began as vice-president, became president of black music department for MCA Records, 1984-88; president and chief executive officer of Motown Records, 1988—; developed, with New York City's Apollo Theatre, Apollo Theatre Records, 1989.

Addresses: *Office*—Chief Executive Officer, Motown Records, 6255 Sunset Blvd., 17th Floor, Los Angeles, CA 90026.

label that Motown would promote and distribute. Filmmaker Spike Lee and recording artists and producers Kool Moe Dee, Heavy D, and Teddy Riley, among others, were invited by Apollo Theatre Records to form an advisory committee. Performers who appeared at the celebrated "Amateur Night at the Apollo" and area clubs were selected by Motown and the Inner City Broadcasting Corporation, owner of the Apollo, to record for the new label. When Busby announced the Apollo venture at a press conference, he asserted, as was reported in *Black Enterprise,* "Motown's objective is to make these talented young adults into full-fledged performing artists."

Forming a training program for would-be record executives was another part of Busby's agenda at Motown as the 1980s drew to a close. He also persuaded superstar Diana Ross to come back to the Motown label, for which she had recorded some of her greatest hits, including "Ain't No Mountain High Enough." Busby told Richard W. Stevenson in the *New York Times,* "It's like the queen returning home."

In 1990 Motown outscored all other record labels in the rhythm and blues category, producing five Number One hits. Busby's leadership took Motown from tenth to fourth place on the black album charts with releases like Stevie Wonder's soundtrack from the motion picture *Jungle Fever.* And Busby registered platinum records with multimillion dollar sales after launching the careers of kiddie rappers Another Bad Creation, rhythm-and-blues crooner Johnny Gill, and the harmony-heavy Boyz II Men—whose "End of the Road" became the longest-running Number One single of the rock era in October of 1992.

In his effort to make Motown more profitable, Busby entered into a dispute with the label's distributor and part owner, MCA Records, a unit of Matsushita Electric Company of Japan. According to the original agreement, MCA was to manufacture, market, and promote Motown records for a relatively high fee, but by 1991 Busby had become disillusioned by the distributor's performance. *Black Enterprise* reported that he charged the company with "ineptitude and deliberate misconduct" and "egregious distribution failures" in a lawsuit seeking to terminate Motown's contract with MCA. MCA countersued, its representatives claiming in the *New York Times* that Motown was "unprofitable and many in the industry think of it as uninspired." Busby's next move was to establish a distribution relationship with PolyGram—while still under contract with MCA—because, he argued in *Entertainment Weekly,* MCA treated Motown "like a third world company."

Embroiled in legal problems and plagued by the defection of some of the label's top talent, Busby faced litigation in the early 1990s that threatened to unsettle Motown indefinitely. With plans to merchandise the Motown label to generate income throughout the 1990s, Busby expressed regret over Motown's difficulties with MCA, telling *New York Times* contributor Lev, "I never thought I wouldn't be able to sit down with people I spent five years with and talk about where we go in the future."

Sources

Black Enterprise, November 1989; December 1991.
Entertainment Weekly, October 25, 1991.
New York Times, February 19, 1989; May 19, 1991.
Washington Post, June 2, 1991.

—*Marjorie Burgess*

The Buzzcocks

Rock band

Other than the London-based Sex Pistols, the Buzzcocks are considered the most successful and influential of the late-seventies British punk/pop bands. With their rapid, rudimentary songs of romantic boredom and frustration, the Buzzcocks represented the punk ideal in both form—scratchy guitars, strident realism, manic rhythms, joyful minimalism—and practice: by releasing their debut EP, *Spiral Scratch,* on their own label, they demonstrated that the independent method was a viable, if not preferable, alternative to the major labels that dominated the recording industry's economics in 1976.

The Buzzcocks originated in Manchester, England, through the friendship of Howard Trafford and Peter McNeish, both students at the Bolton Institute. McNeish had begun playing guitar in 1970; by late 1975 he was playing in a group called Jets of Air. Both Trafford and McNeish loved the seminal albums of Iggy and the Stooges and the Velvet Underground; they "knew all of them back to front," McNeish later said. While sitting in a pub they noticed a *New Musical Express* review of a

Sex Pistols show and were particularly drawn to a statement made by the Sex Pistols' Johnny Rotten. Upon completion of a Stooges' song, Rotten had bellowed, "We're not into music, we're into chaos."

McNeish and Trafford went immediately to High Wycombe, just north of London, and saw the Sex Pistols twice in February of 1976. With an increased sense of urgency, yet minus the Pistols' negative political agenda, McNeish and Trafford returned to Manchester to start a band similar in intent and style. They changed identities—McNeish became Pete Shelley (Shelley being his name had he been born a girl) while Trafford took the name Howard Devoto. "Buzzcocks" came from the closing line of a review of the classic pop serial "Rock Follies" in the London entertainment guide *Time Out.* The review ended simply, ". . . get a buzz, cock." As the critic Jon Savage later wrote in *England's Dreaming,* Manchester was not initially receptive to Shelley and Devoto's "dream of a music that was not about, in Richard Hell's phrase, 'this idea of rock star as idol,' but about sharp minded kids talking to each other about what they saw."

In the spring of 1976 the English punk movement was still so contained that Shelley and Devoto were able to lure the Sex Pistols to Manchester for a performance. In April, Shelley and Devoto booked the Lesser Free

Trade Hall in Manchester for only 32 pounds; the Sex Pistols' performance that night would influence an entire generation of Mancunian (the descriptive phrase for all things native to Manchester) musicians.

After meeting bassist Steve Diggle at the Trade Hall that night, Shelley and Devoto—the Buzzcocks in name only, having yet to play in public—hired a 16-year-old drummer named John Maher, who was responding to an advertisement in *Melody Maker.* On July 20, 1976, the Buzzcocks again brought the Sex Pistols to Lesser Free Trade Hall. Yet this time they opened the show—their first public concert—and found themselves standing in the center of what would soon be called punk.

Punk Ethos: Do It Yourself

Before Christmas of 1976 the Buzzcocks had played ten full shows, including their London debut as part of the Sex Pistols' Screen on the Green event. They were then managed by Richard Boon, a friend and Reading University student. Their influence was immediately felt. By the end of 1976, Manchester was, next to London, England's premier punk city. Yet the city's scene was more friendly than London's, largely due to the Buzzcocks' romantic, alienated ideal. "People were throwing in all these ideas," Shelley was quoted by Savage as saying of the time. "It wasn't only the freedom to make the music you wanted to, it was also that other people with other ideas were coming in. It was like going to college in a way."

In December of 1976 the Buzzcocks, with producer Martin Hannett, recorded the four-song *Spiral Scratch* EP. Unable to interest major record labels, they released it on their own New Hormones label with 500 pounds borrowed from Shelley's father. "There were no labels up there then," Devoto was quoted by Savage as saying. "Again it's the question of ambition. I don't think we had much of an idea of the way things were swelling. But we had some sort of wherewithal, which made us borrow money, book a recording studio, and have records made."

To Shelley, *Spiral Scratch* was an end in itself. "We only pressed 1000," he said. "It was a memento." Yet the Buzzcocks' vision spawned an international movement. "Indies"—the name eventually given to the entire network of independent labels—went on to make up an estimable portion of record sales, while their aesthetic influence on all of youth culture has been immense. *Spiral Scratch,* along with releases on labels such as Chiswick and Stiff, literally ushered in the alternative era. Despite the band's initial success, in March of

1977, after only 11 gigs, Devoto quit the group he had founded; his departure was ostensibly due to academic demands—yet he reportedly also felt that the punk movement was quickly becoming co-opted by the media and other commercial forces. The following summer he established the group Magazine.

From Singles to Albums

Shelley quickly reformed the Buzzcocks, moving Diggle to guitar and adding ex-Jets of Air bassist Garth Smith. The Buzzcocks' reputation grew as they toured extensively on the Clash's White Riot Tour, which also included the Slits and Subway Sect. On August 16, 1977—ironically the day of Elvis Presley's death—the Buzzcocks signed with United Artists for 75,000 pounds. Two months later they released their first major label single, the controversial "Orgasm Addict," backed with "Whatever Happened To?" "Orgasm Addict" was something of a stylistic matrix for the Buzzcocks—playful lyrics fueled by nervous, guitar-driven punk rhythms. Shelley by then had developed a camp stage persona to match the gender ambiguity of his songs.

In November of 1977 Smith was fired for drunkenness and replaced by Steve Garvey. After issuing another single, "What Do I Get?," the Buzzcocks released their first album, *Another Music in a Different Kitchen,* in

---

"Shelley and Devoto had a dream of a music that was not about . . . 'this idea of rock star as idol,' but about sharp minded kids talking to each other about what they saw."
—*Jon Savage*

March of 1978. Produced by Martin Rushent, the album included such songs as "Fast Cars" and "Moving Away From the Pulsebeat," which illuminated a more personal side to punk's anarchy. The jacket design was also important to the burgeoning independent scene. Designer Malcolm Garrett's collages carried fine art references (Marcel Duchamp, Paul Klee) as well as common mass culture iconography. After *Another Music in*

a Different Kitchen reached number 15 on the UK album chart, the Buzzcocks began the "Entertaining Friends" tour with the Slits. Another full album, *Love Bites,* was released in September, only seven months after *Another Music in a Different Kitchen. Love Bites* contained "Ever Fallen in Love," a song that became the group's greatest success, reaching number 12 on the charts. The Buzzcocks followed *Love Bites* with a tour titled "Beating Hearts Tour."

In January of 1979 Shelley took time out to produce "Alberto y Los Trios Paranoias." "Everybody's Happy Nowadays," a Buzzcocks single full of witty irony, was released in March, followed by a drunken, bizarre performance on the British television program *Top of the Pops.* The strain of watching the punk movement—initially an honest reaction to sociopolitical elements in Britain—become a tawdry fashion show was beginning to show in the Buzzcocks' performance. They were falling into the trap they sought to destroy: they now had a *career.*

In mid-September *Spiral Scratch* was reissued by United Artists along with a compilation of singles titled *Going Steady. A Different Kind of Tension,* their third and final album, was released in late 1979. The Buzzcocks toured Britain with Joy Division, a young Mancunian band that seemed to be beating the Buzzcocks at their own game: Joy Division was peaking in popularity with a stoic punk rock that commented on inner feelings with stark clarity.

Cracks in the Finish

By 1980, drugs had become a part of Buzzcock life; a tour called "Tour of Installments" was begun and canceled. Financial problems also began to plague the band. In 1980 United Artists was purchased by the huge conglomerate EMI. "It had been a completely different atmosphere," Savage quoted Shelley as saying of the change. "EMI wanted hits and we got sat on." Shelley began working on what was to be the fourth Buzzcocks album with producer Rushent. He wrote and recorded the gay-disco song "Homosapiens" yet ultimately released it as a solo project. "I found that I work best if I'm just left alone to do what I want," Shelley told Savage. "I wasn't into being an entertainer; I was always into the more intellectual, artistic side."

In February of 1981 the band split up; Shelley had sent each member a letter stating that he wished to sever all his commitments to the Buzzcocks. Bassist Garvey moved to New York; Diggle and Maher established the group Flag of Convenience; and Shelley continued with

Homosapiens and XL.1, two synth-pop records. A series of reissues and live albums throughout the eighties kept the band's name somewhat alive. By the late eighties, Diggle was still touring with Flag of Convenience, Maher had left that band to start a Volkswagen repair shop in Manchester, and Garvey remained in New York. Other than brief tours in 1982 and 1986, Shelley was inactive. Devoto closed down Magazine in 1983.

Yet as Diggle toured, he discovered that posters promoting Flag of Convenience gigs would often use the Buzzcocks name and logo. This activity led to Diggle and Shelley's decision to reform the band. Another factor was the 1990 release of Product, a well-received three-CD compilation of the Buzzcocks' entire career. The Buzzcocks toured Europe and the United States briefly, to tremendous critical praise. In 1990 Maher returned to his auto repair business, replaced by ex-Smith Mike Joyce.

The Buzzcocks have since reportedly recorded new material with producer Bill Laswell, but as of late 1992 they were still without a recording contract. A live album, Entertaining Friends, was released on IRS in November of 1992, along with a long-form video titled Playback. Playback was shot at the Hammersmith Odeum in 1979. A tribute album titled Something's Gone Wrong Again: The Buzzcocks Cover Compilation was issued by C/Z Records in the fall of 1992; it featured young alternative bands such as Naked Raygun, Dose, and the Lunachicks performing much of the Buzzcocks' rich late-seventies catalogue. Another greatest hits package, Operator's Manual: Buzzcocks Best, was also released in 1992. The Buzzcocks, as New Musical Express's Richard Cook wrote, brought to rock "a view of love as a source of boredom, resentment, very occasional relief: no great revelation, maybe."

Selected discography

Spiral Scratch (EP), New Hormones, 1977.

Another Music in a Different Kitchen, United Artists, 1978.
Love Bites, United Artists, 1978.
A Different Kind of Tension, United Artists, 1979.
Singles Going Steady, IRS, 1979.
The Peel Sessions, Strange Fruit, 1988.
Lest We Forget, ROIR, 1988.
The Fab Four (EP), EMI, 1989.
Product, Restless Retro, 1990.
Entertaining Friends, IRS, 1992.
Something's Gone Wrong Again: The Buzzcocks Cover Compilation, C/Z, 1992.
Operator's Manual: Buzzcocks Best, 1992.

Sources

Books

Rees, Dafydd and Luke Crampton, Rock Movers and Shakers, Billboard Books, 1991.
The Rolling Stone Encyclopedia of Rock and Roll, edited by Jon Pareles and Patricia Romanowski, Summit, 1983.
Savage, Jon, England's Dreaming, St. Martin's Press, 1991.
The Trouser Press Record Guide, fourth edition, edited by Ira Robbins, Collier, 1991.

Periodicals

CD Review, October 1992.
Cover, February 1990.
New Musical Express, June 26, 1982.
Select, October 1991.
Spin, January 1992.

Additional information for this profile was obtained from the video compilation Playback, EMI Records Ltd., 1992, courtesy of IRS Records.

—Stewart Francke

John Cale

Singer, songwriter, producer

In 1968, having become increasingly dissatisfied with his marginal role in the Velvet Underground, John Cale left the enormously influential avant-garde rock group to embark on a strange and prolific solo career. Cale's talents as a classically trained arranger and his interests in experimentalism had lent the Velvet Underground much of their mystique and musical sophistication. In addition to utilizing these elements, Cale's solo career proved that he was also a great songwriter and a mesmerizing performer—capable of both a dream-like frailty and a phobic fury that earned him the reputation of progenitor of the late 1970s punk rock movement.

Born in Wales in 1942, Cale trained to be a concert violinist and violist at an early age. Although he had heard rock and roll, he became primarily involved in electronic music and performance art after entering London's Goldsmith College. He received a scholarship in 1963 to study at the prestigious Tanglewood music center in Massachusetts with famed American composer Aaron Copland and Franco-Greek composer Iannis Xenakis. At Tanglewood Cale was not allowed to play his own pieces because they were considered too violent—one involved smashing a table with an axe. After Tanglewood, he gravitated to New York City, where he worked with leading avant-gardist La Mont Young and his performing group Theatre of Eternal Music. Cale then fell sway to the underground arts scene; in 1966, with singer/songwriter Lou Reed, he formed the Velvet Underground, which soon became associated with pop artist Andy Warhol.

Felt Velvets Contribution Was Minimal

Although his viola, bass, and musical approach was a significant influence on the band, Cale did not contribute to the writing of the group's material and was occasionally intimidated by Reed's compositional authority. "I did very little with the Velvets," he explained in *Beyond the Velvet Underground.* "It was very educational in its own way, but my contribution was, I felt, quite minimal."

Cale's first solo release, 1969's *Vintage Violence,* was a collection of pop songs sharing straightforward arrangements and a markedly detached surrealism. A promising debut, it featured a masked Cale on the cover. But in *Interview,* Cale said of the album, "You don't see the personality. I didn't realize it until I put the thing out, but the cover was really more about the album than I had thought."

Cale then recorded three albums that explored his classical background. *Church of Anthrax* was a collaboration with avant-garde composer Terry Riley.

Born December 5, 1942 (some sources say 1940), in Garnant (some sources say Crynant), Wales; married briefly to a woman named Cyndrella, c. 1970. *Education:* Attended Goldsmith College, London; attended Guildhall School of Music, London; studied with composer Humphrey Searle; studied with Iannis Xenakis and Aaron Copland at Tanglewood Music Center, c. 1963.

Recording and performing artist, producer. Participated in Boston Symphony summer festival and performed with La Mont Young's Theatre of Eternal Music, mid-1960s; co-founder, and member of the Velvet Underground, 1966-1968; released first solo album, *Vintage Violence,* on Columbia Records, 1969; staff producer and A&R representative for Warner Bros. and Elektra Records, consultant for Columbia Records, early 1970s; signed with Island Records; signed with Opal Records, 1989. Producer of the Stooges' *The Stooges,* Elektra, 1969; Jennifer Warnes's *Jennifer,* Reprise, 1972; Patti Smith's *Horses,* Arista, 1975; Jonathan Richman and the Modern Lovers' *The Modern Lovers,* Beserkley, 1976; Squeeze's *U.K. Squeeze,* A&M, 1977; and the Happy Mondays' *Squirrel and G-Man . . . .,* Factory, 1987. Contributed soundtracks to films *Heat,* 1972, and *Caged Heat,* 1974.

Awards: Leonard Bernstein Fellowship, 1963.

Addresses: *Record company*—Opal/Warner Bros., 330 Harrow Rd., London W9 2HP, England; 3300 Warner Blvd., Burbank, CA 91510.

John Rockwell of the *New York Times* remarked of the effort, "The results didn't always work, but they were never less than interesting." In 1972 Cale set out to record his first purely classical album. However, after deciding that the three symphonic pieces he had composed to this end did not work well on their own, he added other music to the album. The final product was titled *The Academy in Peril,* which Rockwell called, "an absolutely fascinating amalgam of quasi-movie music orchestral pieces, fragments of rock, dream-like sustained chordal textures with disembodied voice-overs and bizarre . . . arrangements."

Paris 1919 "A Pop Masterpiece"

Paris 1919, released in 1973, is regarded by many as Cale's best work. In it Cale makes the most of both his classical and pop sensibilities to create a natural blend of sheer pop elegance as his dark baritone delivers an eerie, post-World War I geo-political dream diary. Stephen Holden of *Rolling Stone* called *Paris 1919* "a pop masterpiece . . . closer to being a finished work of art than any previous attempt to effect a rock-classical synthesis" and "the most ambitious album ever released under the name 'pop.'" The *New York Times* observed, "What really binds the album together is a pervasive sense of dream-like distance, a sort of sadly schizophrenic nostalgia for something that has more to do with one's own memories than a particular place in time. Cale's arrangements and Chris [Thomas's] production emphasize lower-register strings, filtering techniques and overdubbing that transforms Cale's none-too-striking voice into a gentle chorus, and continually idiosyncratic instrumental and rhythmic effects."

Despite the critical raves, *Paris 1919* sold poorly. During this time Cale worked as a staff producer at Warner Bros. He then signed a six-record deal with Island and moved back to England, where he began another phase of his career. In 1974 he told *Creem* magazine, "There were glimmers of light on *Paris 1919*—I was beginning to come through the cracks. But these songs I'm doing now, make me feel like I'm a songwriter for the first time."

Collaborated With Eno

Soon after, Cale began to work with enigmatic art-rock high priest Brian Eno; the relationship remained an important one throughout both artists' careers. Cale made a rare live appearance on the album *June 1, 1974,* recorded in Paris with Kevin Ayers, Eno, and Cale's Velvet Underground colleague Nico. Cale's contribution included a blood-curdling rendition of the Elvis Presley classic "Heartbreak Hotel." Aided by Eno and Roxy Music guitarist Phil Manzanera, Cale released *Fear* in 1975. Though he stripped down the dreamy string effects that had become his trademark, the album, nonetheless, remained tuneful. *Fear* found Cale's paranoid delusions driving him to lyrical fury and Eno's eccentricities inspiring him to create the abrasive sound demonstrated on the songs "Gun" and "Fear Is a Man's Best Friend."

Cale's next four albums, *Slow Dazzle, Helen of Troy, Animal Justice,* and *Sabotage/Live* continued to explore a morbid recklessness and an assortment of threatening, claustrophobic nightmares commanded by the singer's tense, brooding vocals. Richard Mortifoglio of the *Village Voice* called *Sabotage/Live* "Cale's best songwriting to date. *Sabotage* makes up for its beery looseness by rocking hard, fast . . . [coming] close to matching *Helen of Troy* and *Paris 1919.* The whole of side one is a relentlessly spirited tour de force." These records played an influential role in the punk rock movement that flowered in the late 1970s, and Cale's outrageous performances during this period were highly acclaimed and often controversial. Cale's output through the early 1980s sought to widen his audience; although the music remained dark, it became less dangerous and more diffuse. Again, his work receives favorable reviews, but he did not see the commercial success he had hoped to achieve.

In 1986 Cale teamed with Eno again, on *Words for the Dying,* a work comprised of two lengthy orchestral pieces and one shorter section. Of his next project, Cale told *Melody Maker,* "While the Argentine flag was being raised on South Georgia [during the Falklands Islands War between Britain and Argentina in 1982], I was feverishly embarking on a comprehensive setting of the collective poems of Dylan Thomas. Each night I would sit thrashing about from one poem to another with the tape running. By the end of the war I had arrived at 'Lie Still, Sleep Becalmed'. . . . Of the nine poems done there were four that felt all of a piece." This eventually became 1989's "Falklands Suite," which, along with "Songs Without Words," comprises an ambitious, elegiac orchestral work that was recorded by the Orchestra of Symphonic and Popular Music of Gosteleradio, in Moscow.

1990's *Wrong Way Up* was the first project wherein Cale and Eno collaborated fully to produce a completely joint album. It was also Eno's first pop vocal performance in years. *Rolling Stone* contributor David Fricke called the release "a gem, if an oddly anachronistic one. [Cale and Eno's] trademarks—launching synth patterns, carefully plucked guitar strings, self-consciously simple lyrics, chant-like choruses and echoey production—have been so plundered by their proteges over the years that they have lost some of their initial mystique."

Reuinted With Reed for Warhol Tribute

In 1989 Cale and Lou Reed wrote and performed a stunning collection of songs titled *Songs for 'Drella,* a 50-minute portrait of former manager and mentor Andy Warhol. *'Drella* revealed the paradoxical nature of Warhol's personality and art—in its simplicity *and* complexity—while at the same time uncovering for the listener the similar contradictions at the center of both Cale and Reed's work. Fricke called *'Drella* "a dream come true, a brilliant landmark collaboration by two headstrong avant-rock pioneers . . . a testament to the continuing strength of Warhol's catalytic powers and the enduring force of the Velvet's deviant genius." Jon Pareles in the *New York Times* opined, "As tunes,

nearly every one of the song cycle's segments is memorable. Cale and Reed are past masters of making simplicity eloquent."

In 1992 Cale released *Fragments of a Rainy Season,* a live offering recorded in Europe earlier that year. Though not as celebrated as *Magic and Loss,* Reed's offering of 1992, *Fragments* did remind some critics of Cale's haunting musical legacy. A stripped-down affair of piano and voice, *Rolling Stone* concluded of the work, "*Fragments of a Rainy Season* covers the erratic sweep of John Cale's career. . . . [It] makes an informative primer for initiates, but veterans who (understandably) wrote Cale off in the Eighties may want to use it as a refresher course."

Equally significant as his own solo recordings is the work Cale has produced for other artists. His first landmark work outside the Velvet Underground was his production of the Stooges' *With the Stooges,* a collection of three-chord Detroit-style punk that was many years ahead of its time. Cale also produced Patti Smith's highly acclaimed debut album, *Horses,* and Jonathan Richman and the Modern Lovers' first two records, in 1976. In 1977 he worked with Squeeze on their debut. Although Cale's style as a producer has varied from album to album, he has consistently demonstrated a willingness to present artists as honestly as he can; as would be expected from a creative force so uncompromising in his own artistry, Cale has made it his mission to produce powerful statements that are as much about the raw personality of the artist as they are about the artist's music.

Selected discography

With the Velvet Underground

The Velvet Underground and Nico, Verve, 1967.
White Light/White Heat, Verve, 1967.

Solo releases

Vintage Violence, Columbia, 1970, reissued, Columbia/Legacy, 1991.
(With Terry Riley) *Church of Anthrax,* Columbia, 1971.
The Academy in Peril, Reprise, 1972.
Paris 1919, Reprise, 1973.
Fear, Island, 1974.
(With Kevin Ayers, Brian Eno, and Nico) *June 1, 1974,* Island, 1974.
Slow Dazzle, Island, 1975.
Helen of Troy, Island UK, 1975.
Guts (compilation of *Fear, Slow Dazzle,* and *Helen of Troy*), Island, 1977.
Animal Justice (EP), Illegal, 1977.

Sabotage/Live, IRS, 1979.

Honi Soit, A&M, 1981.

Music for a New Society, Ze/Island, 1982.

Caribbean Sunset, Ze/Island, 1984.

John Cale Comes Alive, Ze/Island, 1984.

Artificial Intelligence, PVC/Jem, 1985.

Even Cowgirls Get the Blues (live recordings, 1978-79), Special Stock, 1986.

Words for the Dying, Opal/Warner Bros., 1989.

(With Lou Reed) *Songs for 'Drella,* Sire/Warner Bros., 1990.

(With Eno) *Wrong Way Up,* Opal/Warner Bros., 1990.

Paris S'Eveille—Suivi D'Autres Compositions, Crepuscule (Belgium), 1992.

Fragments of a Rainy Season, Hannibal/Rykodisc, 1992.

Sources

Books

The Rolling Stone Encyclopedia of Rock & Roll, edited by Jon Pareles and Patricia Romanowski, Rolling Stone Press/Summit Books, 1983.

Stambler, Irwin, *The Encyclopedia of Pop, Rock, and Soul,* St. Martin's, 1989.

Thompson, Dave, *Beyond the Velvet Underground,* Omnibus, 1989.

Periodicals

Atlantic, April 1990.

Creem, October 1974.

Interview, August 1972.

Melody Maker, February 11, 1989; December 9, 1989.

Metro Times (Detroit), November 4, 1992.

New York Times, December 21, 1974; December 24, 1976; April 22, 1981; December 1, 1989.

Rolling Stone, May 10, 1973; January 11, 1990; December 10, 1992.

Spin, December 1992.

Village Voice, August 2, 1976.

Additional information for this profile was obtained from Opal Records media information, 1989.

—*Glenn Rechler*

Pablo Casals

Cellist, conductor, composer

From the age of ten, Pablo Casals began each day with a walk, taking inspiration from nature. These outings were always followed by playing two Johann Sebastian Bach preludes and fugues on the piano when he returned home. It was, Casals expressed in *Joys and Sorrows: Reflections by Pablo Casals as Told to Albert E. Kahn,* "a rediscovery of the world of which I have the joy of being a part. It fills me with an awareness of the wonder of life, with a feeling of the incredible marvel of being a human being." A deeply reflective man, Casals imbued his life with his own spiritual triumvirate: the wonder of nature, the music of Bach, and God. This in turn informed his art. Technically masterful, revolutionary even, his cello playing was elevated by his belief, as he defined it for Kahn, that "music [was] an affirmation of the beauty man was capable of producing."

Casals always felt it his obligation to share with others this access to beauty that transcended languages and borders. When political and egotistical pursuits caused conflicts between his fellow men, however, Casals fought for peace by silencing that beauty. At the height of his artistic prowess he remained in exile, his cello quiet. Nobel Prize-winning writer Thomas Mann, quoted by Bernard Taper in *Cellist in Exile: A Portrait of Pablo Casals,* believed Casals's art was "allied to a rigid refusal to compromise with wrong, with anything that is morally squalid or offensive to justice."

Casals was born on December 29, 1876, in the seaside town of Vendrell, located in the Catalonian region of Spain. As a child he was surrounded by music. According to H. L. Kirk, author of *Pablo Casals: A Biography,* "The atmosphere of music cradled Casals's earliest fantasies; much later he spoke of being bathed in it all the time." Casals's father, the local church organist and choirmaster, would play the piano while the infant Casals, barely old enough to walk, would rest his head against the instrument and sing along to the music he felt. By the age of four, Casals was playing the piano. The following year he joined the church choir. A year later he was composing songs with his father, and by the age of nine he had learned how to play the violin and organ.

Unusual Techniques Evoked More From Cello

When he was 11, Casals decided to study the cello after having seen the instrument in a chamber music recital. Though his father wanted him to apprentice to a carpenter, his mother insisted he follow his inclination toward music, enrolling him in the Municipal School of Music in Barcelona, Spain. The young Casals disa-

For the Record. . .

Born Pau Carlos Salvador Casals y Defilló, December 29, 1876, in Vendrell, Catalonia, Spain; died October 22, 1973, in San Juan, Puerto Rico; son of Carlos (a church organist and choirmaster) and Pilar Ursula (Defilló) Casals; married Susan Metcalfe, 1914 (separated, 1928; divorced, 1957); married Marta Montañez, 1957. *Education:* Graduated with honors from Municipal School of Music, Barcelona, 1893; studied with Tomás Bretón and Jesús de Monasterio, 1894-96.

First solo recital, Barcelona, 1891; played in cafe trio, Barcelona, 1891-93; performed for Queen Regent of Spain, 1894; appeared with orchestras in Paris and Madrid, 1895-97; debut as soloist with Lamoureux Orchestra, Paris, 1899; began worldwide concert tours, often playing solo, 1900—; performed with trio including pianist Alfred Cortot and violinist Jacques Thibaud, 1904-37; organized and led Orquesta Pau Casals, Barcelona, 1920-36; in exile from Spain, 1936—; sporadic appearances in France and Switzerland, 1939-42; participated in Prades Festival, Prades, France, 1950-66; organized and led Casals Festival, San Juan, Puerto Rico, 1957-72; conducted special concert for United Nations General Assembly inaugurating his composition "Hymn of the United Nations," October 24, 1971. Led master classes in cello performance in Switzerland, Italy, and the U.S.

Selected awards: Order of Carlos III; Grand Officer of the French Legion of Honor; United Nations Peace Medal; inducted into the Academia de Bellas Artes de San Fernando of the Spanish Academy.

greed with the technical constraints advocated by his instructors, preferring to bow and finger the cello in his own manner. His progress was extraordinary, however, and soon Casals's revolutionary techniques had exposed "a range of phrasing, intonation, and expressiveness that had not previously been thought possible, and [made] the cello an instrument of high purpose," Taper noted in *Cellist in Exile.*

Among those impressed by the ability of the young virtuoso was the Spanish composer and pianist Isaac Albéniz. Upon hearing Casals play in a cafe trio, Albéniz gave him a letter of introduction to Count Guillermo de Morphy, secretary to the Queen Regent of Spain, Maria Cristine. In 1894 Casals traveled to Madrid and gave informal concerts for the queen and her court. Over the next few years, his reputation spread as he played with various orchestras in Paris and Madrid. With his formal debut as a concert soloist in Paris in 1899—where he

appeared with the prestigious orchestra of French conductor Charles Lamoureux—Casals's career was assured.

What audiences heard in Casals's playing was a suffused reverence for everything around him. "I have the idea of God constantly," he declared in *McCall's.* "I find Him in music. What is that world, what is music but God?" Those feelings were heightened for Casals in nature and in the music of Bach, as he indicated when he continued, explaining his morning ritual: "I go immediately to the sea, and everywhere I see God, in the smallest and largest things. I see Him in colors and designs and forms. . . . [And] I see God in Bach. Every morning of my life I see nature first, then I see Bach."

Casals's devotion to the music of Bach was no more fully realized than in the Six Suites for solo cello. Sometime in 1890 while browsing through a Barcelona bookstore with his father, Casals found a volume of the suites. The discovery was enlightening. Previously the suites were considered merely musical exercises, but, even at that young age, Casals saw in them something deeper, richer. "How could anyone think of them as being cold, when a whole radiance of space and poetry pours forth from them," he marveled in *Joys and Sorrows.* "They are the very essence of Bach, and Bach is the very essence of music." Casals studied and practiced the suites every day for a dozen years before he exposed them to the public, and he continued to play at least one suite every day for the rest of his life.

Garnered New Respect for Bach's Music

His performance of the suites both shocked and astounded listeners. During the nineteenth-century revival of Bach's music, only the cantatas and the religious works were played in public. It was believed that the solo music for strings had no warmth, no artistic value. With these "exercises," however, "Casals displayed the [German] master as a fully human creator whose art had poetry and passion, accessible to all people," author Kirk stated in *Pablo Casals: A Biography.* "[Bach], who knows everything and feels everything, cannot write one note, however unimportant it may appear, which is anything but transcendent," Casals stressed to José Maria Corredor in *Conversations With Casals.* "He has reached the heart of every noble thought, and he has done it in the most perfect way."

Casals's interpretation of the suites, his true testament, came into disfavor after the 1940s when a more historically correct reading of lightness and spontaneity was advanced, in marked contrast to his dramatic renderings. "Almost every movement of the suites, in Casals's hands," William H. Youngren maintained in the *Atlantic,* "vividly projects the image of a powerful Romantic sensibility engaged in an unceasing, heroic struggle with itself and with the universe." However, in a *Strad* review of a recent remastering of Casals's performances for compact disc, Tully Potter justified his passionate, ennobling vision: "He builds up great waves of sound and tension, achieving an enormous physical and emotional release towards the end of each one—a Romantic approach, perhaps, but valid here because the player's heart, soul, and sinew are so completely behind every note. . . . [It is] a spiritual exaltation rare in any performance and still more so on record."

As he approached Bach and music, so did Casals approach life and other people. "The pursuit of music and the love for my neighbors have been inseparable with me, and if the first has brought me the purest and most exalted joys, the second has brought me peace of mind, even in the saddest moments," Casals affirmed to *Conversations With Casals* author Corredor. "I am everyday more convinced that the mainspring of any human enterprise must be moral strength and generosity." In 1891, while still in school, Casals came to understand the suffering and inequality of man as he walked among the poor on the streets of Barcelona. He vowed to use his gift from God—his music—for the welfare of his fellow people.

Silenced Cello in Protest of Oppression

Throughout his career, Casals championed the oppressed and neglected by writing letters and organizing concerts. He refused to perform in countries practicing political tyranny and repression: the Soviet Union in 1917, Germany in 1933, and Italy in 1935. In 1920, for the benefit of the Catalonian people, Casals organized and led the Orquesta Pau Casals, using the Catalonian version of his name. He supported the Republican cause during the Spanish Civil War in the 1930s, and when Nationalist General Francisco Franco rose to power in 1939, Casals announced he would never return to Spain while Franco was in power. He settled in Prades, France, giving sporadic concerts until 1946 when he renounced the stage altogether. In order to take a stand against dictatorships, Casals vowed never to perform again. As author Kirk put it in *Pablo Casals: A Biography,* "His withdrawal into silence was the strongest action he felt he could make."

However, in 1950, urged on by friends, Casals resumed conducting and playing, taking part in the Prades Festival organized to celebrate the bicentennial of Bach's death. Though he picked up his cello again, he did not forget his cause—at the end of the festival and every concert he gave after that, Casals played his arrangement of the Catalonian folk ballad "Song of the Birds" as a protest to the continued oppression he saw in Spain.

Casals never returned to Spain. In 1956 he settled in Puerto Rico, his mother's homeland, where he inaugurated the world-famous Casals Festival that spurred artistic and cultural activities on the island, including the founding of a symphony orchestra and a conservatory of music. During the rest of his life, Casals balanced his stand on the issues with his creative impulses. In 1958 he joined his friend, Nobel Prize-winning French philosopher and musicologist Albert Schweitzer, in calling for peace and nuclear disarmament. Casals also spoke and played before the United Nations General Assembly. He appeared before the General Assembly again in 1971, at the age of 95, when he conducted the first performance of his "Hymn of the United Nations."

Though Casals had resumed performing, he refused to play in any country that officially recognized the totalitarian Franco government—as did the United States. Until he died in 1973, Casals did not waver from this position, but for one important exception—in 1961 he performed at the White House at the request of U.S. President John F. Kennedy, a man Casals greatly admired. In *Cellist in Exile,* Taper quoted Kennedy's introduction of Casals on that day: "The work of all artists—musicians, painters, designers, and architects—stands as a symbol of human freedom, and no one has enriched that freedom more signally than Pablo Casals."

Throughout his life, Casals exalted in the divine presence he found in music and in nature. He also sought to inspire and promote harmony among people, both with his cello and his silence. At his funeral, a recording of "The Song of the Birds" was played. "At that moment," Kirk recounted in *Pablo Casals: A Biography,* "the noble voice of Pablo Casals's cello commanded pause in the ceremony of the day, a last salutation, eloquent, profound, overwhelming."

Selected writings

(With Albert E. Kahn) *Joys and Sorrows: Reflections by Pablo Casals as Told to Albert E. Kahn,* Simon and Schuster, 1970.

Song of the Birds: Sayings, Stories, and Impressions of Pablo Casals, compiled, edited, and with a foreword by Julian Lloyd Webber, Robsons Books, 1985.

Selected compositions

"Cançó a la Verge," "El Pessebre," "Eucaristica," "Hymn of the United Nations," "O Vos Omnes," "Recordare Virgo Mater," "Rosari," "Salve Regina," and "Sardana."

Selected discography

As performer

Bach: The Six Cello Suites, EMI, 1988.
Beethoven: Cello Sonatas, CBS Masterworks, 1990.
Casals Festivals at Prades, Vols. 1 & 2, Music & Arts, 1991.
Encores: Boccherini and Haydn, Pearl, 1989.
Hommage à Pablo Casals: Dvorak and Bach, AS Disc, 1991.
Pablo Casals Plays Works for Cello and Orchestra, Pearl, 1989.
Schubert: String Quintet, Supraphon, 1991.
The Victor Recordings (1926-1928), Biddulph, 1991.

As conductor; on Sony Classical, 1990

Bach: Brandenburg Concertos 1-3.
Bach: Brandenburg Concertoes 4-6.
Bach: Orchestral Suites 2 & 3.
Beethoven: Symphonies 1 & 6.
Mendelssohn: Symphony 4.
Mozart: Serenades 11, 12; Eine Kleine Nachtmusik.
Schubert: Symphony 8; Schumann: Symphony 2.

As composer

Casals: Sacred Choral Music, Koch-Schwann, 1991.

Sources

Books

Blum, David, *Casals and the Art of Interpretation,* Holmes & Meier, 1977.
Casals, Pablo, *Song of the Birds: Sayings, Stories, and Impressions of Pablo Casals,* Robsons Books, 1985.
Casals, Pablo, and Albert E. Kahn, *Joys and Sorrows: Reflections by Pablo Casals as Told to Albert E. Kahn,* Simon & Schuster, 1970.
Corredor, José Maria, *Conversations With Casals,* Hutchinson, 1956.
Kirk, H. L., *Pablo Casals: A Biography,* Holt, Rinehart, & Winston, 1974.
Littlehales, Lillian, *Pablo Casals,* Greenwood, 1970.
Quintana, Arturo O., *Pablo Casals in Puerto Rico,* Gordon Press, 1979.
Taper, Bernard, *Cellist in Exile: A Portrait of Pablo Casals,* McGraw-Hill, 1962.

Periodicals

American Record Guide, July/August 1991; November/December 1991; January/February 1992; March/April 1992.
Américas, July/August 1985.
Atlantic, November 1981.
McCall's, May 1966.
Musical America, July 1991.
New Yorker, April 19, 1969.
Strad, February 1989; September 1990.

—Rob Nagel

Rosemary Clooney

Singer

The distinctively unpretentious, deep, rich, and smooth voice of Rosemary Clooney has earned her recognition as one of America's premiere pop and jazz singers. According to Clooney's record company press biography, *Life* magazine, in a tribute to America's "girl singers" named her one of "six preeminent singers . . . whose performances are living displays of a precious national treasure . . . their recordings a preservation of jewels." First-class crooner Frank Sinatra stated, as was also reprinted in Clooney's press biography, "Rosemary Clooney has that great talent which exudes warmth and feeling in every song she sings. She's a symbol of good modern American music."

The singer noted for her decades-long mastery of American popular song started life amid the poverty of small-town Maysville, Kentucky. Her childhood was a difficult one; Clooney and younger siblings Betty and Nick were shuttled among their alcoholic father, Andy, their mother, Frances—who traveled constantly for her work with a chain of dress shops—and relatives, who would take turns raising the children. When Clooney was 13 her mother moved to California to marry a sailor, taking Nick with her but leaving the girls behind. Her father tried to care for Rosemary and Betty, working steadily at a defense plant, but he left one night to celebrate the end of World War II—taking the household money with him—and never returned.

A Difficult Childhood

As Clooney described in her autobiography, *This for Remembrance,* she and Betty were left to fend for themselves. They collected soda bottles and bought meals at school with the refund money. The phone had been disconnected, the utilities were about to be turned off, and the rent was overdue when Rosemary and Betty won an open singing audition at a Cincinnati radio station. The girls were so impressive, in fact, that they were hired for a regular late-night spot at $20 a week each. "The Clooney Sisters," as they became known, began their singing career in 1945 on WLW in Cincinnati.

This work brought them to the attention of bandleader Tony Pastor, who happened to be passing through Ohio. In 1945 The Clooney Sisters joined Pastor's orchestra. They toured with Pastor as featured singers until 1948, at which point Betty decided to return to Cincinnati and her radio career. Rosemary continued as a solo vocalist with Tony Pastor for another year. Then, in 1949, deciding she needed to expand her

For the Record. . .

Born May 23, 1928, in Maysville, KY; daughter of Andrew (a defense plant worker and house painter) and Frances (an employee of a dress-shop chain; maiden name, Guilfoyle) Clooney; married Jose Ferrer (an actor), 1953 (divorced, 1961), remarried Ferrer (divorced, 1967); children: Miguel Jose, Maria Providencia, Gabriel Vincente, Monsita, Rafael.

Formed duet with sister Betty and performed on radio station WLW, Cincinnati; as "The Clooney Sisters," duet toured the U.S. with the Tony Pastor orchestra, 1945-48; performed with Pastor as solo artist, 1948-49; signed with Columbia Records, 1950, and recorded "Come On-a My House," 1951; performed with Bing Crosby on CBS Radio songfest show, early 1950s; under contract to Paramount Pictures, 1953-54; film roles include *The Stars Are Singing* and *Here Come the Girls,* both 1953, and *White Christmas, Red Garters,* and *Deep in My Heart,* all 1954; appeared in television programs the *Rosemary Clooney Show,* KKTV, WRCA-TV, WPIX, 1956-57, and *Lux Music Hall,* NBC-TV, 1957; appeared with Bing Crosby on his 50th anniversary tour, 1976; signed with Concord Jazz, 1977. Author of autobiography *This for Remembrance,* Playboy Press, 1977.

Awards: Gold records for "Come On-a My House, 1951," "Tenderly," 1952, "Botcha Me," 1953, "Half as Much," 1953, and "Hey There," 1954; special award from *Look* magazine, 1954; James Smithson Bicentennial Medal, 1992, for contribution to American arts.

Addresses: *Record company*—Concord Jazz, Inc., P.O. Box 845, Concord, CA 94522.

professional career, she left the band; at age 21 Clooney struck out on her own and headed for New York City.

Enlistment in World War II and the draft drastically depleted the personnel of most bands, creating the need for orchestras to highlight a charismatic singer. After the war, singers who had stolen the limelight from bands became even more indispensable as audiences increasingly came to demand them. Leaders of popular bands discovered and nurtured singers like Bing Crosby, Doris Day, Frank Sinatra, Peggy Lee, Ella Fitzgerald, and Dinah Washington and became associated in the public eye with their finds. Clooney's arrival in New York was perfectly timed with the rage for orchestra-backed singers; she was immediately signed to a recording contract with Columbia Records. By then

"girl singers," as they came to be known—Kay Starr, Day, and Lee—were emerging as recording stars.

"Come On-a My House"

It was at Columbia that Clooney began an important association with Mitch Miller, one of the company's A&R [Artists and Repertoire] representatives and top entertainers. In 1951 Miller convinced Clooney to record an oddball song, "Come On-a My House," written by Ross Bagdasarian with lyrics by William Saroyan. When Miller first suggested the song, Clooney was highly skeptical, insisting the song was not her kind of material. She felt it was silly and demeaning; she believed the double-entendres were a cheap lyrical device and felt uncomfortable putting on an Italian accent. But Miller was persistent and finally persuaded Clooney to record "Come On-a My House." He conceived a novel instrumental effect utilizing a harpsichord to accompany Clooney. Much to her surprise, the song was an immediate and enormous success, topping the charts to become a gold record. "Come On-a My House" made Rosemary Clooney a star. A household name, she became known simply as "Rosie."

In the early 1950s radio made a strong bid to issue a challenge to the growing magnetism of television. Star-studded variety programs were created, and week after week Hollywood studios offered musical programs by big names. Clooney was signed to co-host, with beloved vocalist Bing Crosby, a songfest radio show, which aired every weekday morning on CBS radio. Film roles abounded; Clooney's appearance in *White Christmas* was generally credited with the film's enormous success, which made it the top grosser of 1954. Co-starring with hot properties Bob Hope and Crosby and accompanied by the music of Irving Berlin, Clooney was lauded for her performance, in which she sang the ballad "Love, You Didn't Do Right by Me."

The Hollywood Life

As her popularity swelled, Clooney began a romance with dancer Dante Di Paolo, her co-star in the films *Here Come the Girls* and *Red Garters.* Nonetheless, to her friends' and the public's amazement, Clooney eloped in the summer of 1953 with Oscar-winning actor Jose Ferrer, 16 years her senior. "Rosie" and her whirlwind marriage became a favorite topic of the tabloid journals. Clooney and Ferrer moved into a glamorous

Clooney • 39

Beverly Hills home once owned by composer George Gershwin and entertained with lavish pool-side parties attended by the toast of Hollywood. Their first child was born in 1955 and by 1960, the family had grown to seven.

Clooney became the star of her own television series in 1956. The *Rosemary Clooney Show,* which ran through 1957, was syndicated to more than one hundred television stations. But by that time, Clooney had begun to feel the strain of stardom and her relentlessly hectic schedule. The pressure of raising five children while pursuing careers as a television, movie, radio, and recording star, coupled with the deteriorating state of her marriage, soon took its toll. Clooney developed an addiction to tranquilizers and sleeping pills. Although her life appeared idyllic to the public, the singer's addiction to drugs worsened. Clooney and Ferrer divorced in 1961, reconciled for a few years, then divorced again in 1967. Recalling in her autobiography how she fell prey to "the '50s myth of family and career," the singer confessed, "I just did it all because I thought that I could, it certainly wasn't easy."

Collapse

For Clooney, the world came crashing down in 1968. She was standing only yards away when her close friend Bobby Kennedy, then campaigning for the Democratic presidential nomination, was assassinated in Los Angeles at the Ambassador Hotel. The tragedy, compounded with her drug addiction, triggered a public mental collapse: At a Reno engagement she cursed at her audience and stalked off the stage. She later called a press conference to announce her retirement at which she sobbed incoherently. When a doctor was summoned, Clooney fled and was eventually found driving on the wrong side of a dangerous mountain road. Soon thereafter she admitted herself to the psychiatric ward of Mount Sinai Hospital in Los Angeles. Clooney remained in therapy for many years. She worked when she could—at Holiday Inns and small hotels like the Ventura and the Hawthorne and selling paper towels in television commercials.

In 1976 Clooney's old friend Bing Crosby asked her to join him on his 50th anniversary tour. It would be Crosby's final tour and Clooney's comeback event. The highlight of the show came when Clooney joined Crosby in a duet of "On a Slow Boat to China." The next year, Clooney signed a recording contract with Concord Jazz, taking the next step on her comeback trail—one that would produce a string of more than a dozen successful recordings, inaugurated with *Everything's Coming Up Rosie.*

Salvation Through Singing

"I'll keep working as long as I live," Clooney vowed in an interview with *Lear's* magazine, "because singing has taken on the feeling of joy that I had when I started, when my only responsibility was to sing well. It's even better now . . . I can even pick the songs. The arranger says to me, 'How do you want it? How do you see it?' Nobody ever asked me that before."

Along with her renewed recording efforts, Clooney created a living memorial to her sister Betty, who died in 1976 from a brain aneurysm: the Betty Clooney Center in Long Beach, California, a facility for brain-injured young adults. The first of its kind in the U.S., the center is supported by grants and donations as well as the annual star-splashed benefit concert that Clooney hosts. After receiving the James Smithson Bicentennial Medal in 1992 in recognition of her contribution to American music, Clooney told the *Washington Post,* "It's for showing up day after day, for small increments of time and achievement." Claiming that singing has become her salvation, Clooney added, "I'm the only instrument that's got the words, so I've got to be able to get that across." As her top-selling jazz albums indicated, Clooney was still able to mesmerize audiences with her warmth, depth of feeling, honesty, and unsurpassed craft.

Selected discography

Children's Favorites, 1956.
Everything's Coming Up Rosie, Concord, 1977.
Rosie Sings Bing, Concord, 1978.
Here's to My Lady, Concord, 1979.
Rosemary Clooney Sings Ira Gershwin Lyrics, Concord, 1980.
With Love, Concord, 1981.
Rosemary Clooney Sings the Music of Cole Porter, Concord, 1982.
Rosemary Clooney Sings the Music of Harold Arlen, Concord, 1983.
(With Woody Herman) *My Buddy,* Concord, 1983.
Rosemary Clooney Sings the Music of Irving Berlin, Concord, 1984.
Rosemary Clooney Sings Ballads, Concord, 1985.
Rosemary Clooney Sings the Music of Jimmy VanHeusen, Concord, 1986.
Rosemary Clooney Sings the Lyrics of Johnny Mercer, Concord, 1987.
Show Tunes, Concord, 1989.

Rosemary Clooney Sings Rodgers, Hart & Hammerstein, Concord, 1990.
For the Duration, Concord, 1991.
Girl Singer, Concord, 1992.
Rosemary Clooney Sings the Music of Harold Allen, Concord, 1992.
Do You Miss New York?, Concord, 1993.

Sources

Books

Clooney, Rosemary, *This for Remembrance,* Playboy Press, 1977.
Ewen, David, *All the Years of American Popular Music,* Prentice-Hall, 1977.

Periodicals

Lear's, February 1990.
Newsweek, March 9, 1992.
New York Times, February 9, 1992.
Stereo Review, June 1991.
Variety, October 28, 1991.
Village Voice, October 16, 1991.
Washington Post, March 28, 1992.

Additional information for this profile was obtained from Concord Jazz, Inc., press materials, 1992.

—*Michele Schachere*

Lloyd Cole

In 1984, soon after the release of his group's first album, Lloyd Cole told *Melody Maker's* Helen Fitz-Gerald, "I've always liked people who've been artistically unpredictable. . . . People like that are much more *interesting* than the others, don't you think?" Cole could well have been speaking of himself. From the invigorating sound and striking literacy of his early work with the Commotions, through his sudden dissolution of the group and move to New York in 1988, to the inclusion of lush string arrangements on 1991's *Don't Get Weird on Me, Babe,* Cole has always followed an unconventional path. The press has called him pretentious, derivative, and brilliant, but has rarely described him as predictable.

Cole belongs to a generation of British pop stars that includes Boy George and Morrissey, with whom he is frequently compared. Yet his work lacks the outrageous showmanship of George or the quintessentially British wit of Morrissey. More than many of his compatriots, Cole has turned to the culture of the United States as a source of inspiration for his music—which echoes such diverse U.S. artists as singer/songwriters Lou Reed and Bob Dylan, country star Glen Campbell, and early blues singer Robert Johnson. His image, described by Stewart Francke of the *Metro Times* as that of "a haunted, glamorously grubby, urban cowboy," also has an American flair. In fact, Cole's move to the United States in 1988 and immersion in the cultural life of New York City's Greenwich Village can be seen as a "homecoming" of sorts.

Lloyd Cole was born on January 31, 1961, in Buxton, Derbyshire, in south central England. In the early 1980s Cole's parents moved to Glasgow, Scotland, to manage a golf course, and Lloyd accompanied them, entering the University of Glasgow in 1981. While in college Cole studied English and philosophy, an experience that would be mined for numerous literary references later in his songwriting career. He also developed a talent for observing other people's lives; as he recalled in *Melody Maker,* "I went to all these wild parties . . . and I'd sit in a corner taking notes. That's the kind of person I am. I like making observations and speculations about other people." This skill at capturing the details of human nature and the unfolding narrative of people's lives is reflected in the vivid characters that dwell in Cole's songs—characters like Louise in 1984's "Perfect Skin": "She's got cheeks like geometry and eyes like sin/And she's sexually enlightened by *Cosmopolitan.*"

For the Record. . .

Born January 31, 1961, in Buxton, Derbyshire, England; son of Brenda and Brian Cole; married, c. 1990, wife's name, Elizabeth. *Education:* Attended University of Glasgow, 1981-83.

Singer and songwriter. Formed Lloyd Cole and the Commotions, 1983; signed with Polydor Records and released debut album, *Rattlesnakes,* 1984; toured North America and Europe, 1985-86; band dissolved, 1988; released first solo album, *Lloyd Cole,* 1990; toured internationally, 1991.

Addresses: Booking agent—Triad Artists, Inc., 10100 Santa Monica Blvd., Ste. 1600, Los Angeles, CA 90067. *Record company*—Capitol Records, Inc., 810 Seventh Ave., New York, NY 10019.

Formed the Commotions

While Cole was studying at the University of Glasgow he met guitarist Neil Clark and keyboardist Blair Cowan; the three musicians formed the nucleus of Lloyd Cole and the Commotions, later adding to the group bassist Lawrence Donegan and drummer Stephen Irvine. In February of 1984 the band signed a contract with Polydor Records, and in September of that year the Commotions' first album, *Rattlesnakes,* was released. The fresh, guitar-oriented sound of the band, appearing at a time when synthesizers and drum machines were the rage, was widely praised in the press, as was the literary prowess Cole showed in some of his lyrics, including those of the title track: "She looks like [actress] Eve-Marie Saint in *On the Waterfront*/She reads [twentieth-century French author] Simone de Beauvoir in her American circumstance."

Lloyd Cole and the Commotions recorded two more albums, *Easy Pieces* in 1985 and *Mainstream* in 1987, and toured extensively in 1984 and 1987. Then in 1988 Cole disbanded the group and moved to New York City; as he told the *San Francisco Chronicle,* "I left London, because I was only there for two reasons: it was where the band recorded and it was where my girlfriend lived. I left to escape the shadow of these things after they had gone wrong. It was a chance to start over."

Began Solo Career in New York

After settling in his new home, Cole began work on his first solo effort, titled simply *Lloyd Cole,* which was released in February of 1990. The album features the singer's trademark sultry voice, though with a newfound depth and dynamic range, and evokes what *Melody Maker's* Simon Reynolds called "a certain kind of autumnal melancholy: the wilting of youthful idealism, love losing its bloom, romance stagnating into habitude." The lyrics show a subtlety not found in Cole's earlier work with the Commotions, reflecting the singer's own reassessment of his early work; as he told Reynolds, "I do think I over-estimated what the possibilities of the pop song were. I over-reached at times, wrote more to say less." The album was a critical and popular success, reaching Number Ten on the British charts, providing Cole with his first French gold disc, and earning a spot on charts throughout the rest of Europe.

Cole titled his second solo album *Don't Get Weird on Me, Babe;* the phrase, typically, is an obscure reference to a poem by Raymond Carver. The record was released in September of 1991 and was really two albums in one. The first side—which was actually the *second* side in all markets except that of the United States—contained the kind of straight-ahead, country-influenced rock tunes for which Cole had become known. The second side featured full orchestral arrangements by Paul Buckmaster. As Cole explained to Dev Sherlock of *Boston Rock,* "Obviously half [of the songs] were totally suitable for just guitar, bass and drums—but the other ones just wouldn't have taken that sort of arrangement, so I needed to find a different way of doing them." This section of the album was made in Capitol Records' legendary Tower Studio in Hollywood, where Frank Sinatra recorded with Nelson Riddle's orchestra in the 1950s.

Continued Musical Explorations

In 1992 Steve Simels of *Stereo Review* gave *Don't Get Weird on Me, Babe* a best recording of the month citation, calling it "one of the most genuinely nervy and idiosyncratic major-label rock albums of the year." It is fitting praise for the work of an artist who has developed a loyal following without compromising his artistic integrity. Cole told Randi Gollin of *In Fashion,* "What I'm doing is incredibly glamorous to me. I'm actually living what was my dream as a child, and I'm doing it in my own way. I don't have bellbottoms on and I'm not throwing my guitar off the stage."

In the fall of 1991 Cole began work on his third solo album, tentatively titled *Can't Get Arrested.* In this next effort, Cole planned to extend some of the ideas from his previous album, this time combining orchestra and electric guitar. For inspiration he has turned to the work of soul singer Al Green. "I have an idea that the rhythm section on the next album should sound basically like an Al Green-type rhythm section," he commented in *Boston Rock.* "They've all got Hammond organ, they've all got electric guitar, and yet most of them have brass and strings on them. A lot of his records sound really sparse, but when you add up all of the different elements, there's a lot going on."

Selected discography

With Lloyd Cole and the Commotions

Rattlesnakes, Polydor, 1984, reissued, Capitol, 1988.
Easy Pieces, Geffen, 1985, reissued, Capitol, 1988.
Mainstream, Polydor, 1987, reissued, Capitol, 1988.
1984-1989, Capitol, 1989.

Solo releases; on Capitol Records

Lloyd Cole, 1990.

Don't Get Weird on Me, Babe, 1991.

Sources

Boston Rock, November 1991.
Cover, October 1991.
In Fashion, Winter 1991.
Melody Maker, May 19, 1984; November 3, 1984; November 28, 1987; February 17, 1990.
Metro Times, June 27-July 3, 1990.
Musician, July 1988.
New Musical Express, August 31, 1991; September 14, 1991.
San Francisco Chronicle, December 1, 1991.
Stereo Review, January 1992.

—Jeffrey Taylor

Cream

Rock band

Cream, for better or worse, brought instrumental virtuosity to rock and roll. *Rolling Stone* once referred to them as "rock's first true supergroup." The first real power trio, Cream reestablished the link between rock and the blues, and their freewheeling improvisations took them into territory that was once the province of jazz musicians. By breaking the strictures of pop song forms and making instrumental solos the heart of their sound, they paved the way for Led Zeppelin and heavy metal bands that followed.

Though Cream found its greatest popularity in the United States, all three members had strong individual reputations in England before they decided to join forces. Jack Bruce was a classically trained cellist who took up jazz bass in his teens. He eventually earned a scholarship to the Royal Scottish Academy of Music and began playing in a dance band to support himself. The academy, however, disapproved of its students playing jazz. "They found out," Bruce told *Musician* correspondent Jim Macnie, "and said 'you either stop, or leave college.' So I left college."

For the Record. . .

Members included **Ginger Baker** (drums; born Peter Baker, August 19, 1939, in Lewisham, England), **Jack Bruce** (bass, vocals; born May 14, 1943, in Lanarkshire, Scotland), and **Eric Clapton** (guitar; born March 30, 1945, in Ripley, England; son of Patricia Clapp; married Patti Boyd Harrison, March 27, 1979 [divorced, 1988]; children: [with Lori Del Santo] Conor [deceased]; attended Kingston College of Art).

Band formed by Baker in 1966; toured Europe and U.S., 1967-68; released debut album, *Fresh Cream*, Atco, 1967; disbanded, 1968.

Selected awards: Inducted into the Rock and Roll Hall of Fame, 1993.

In the early 1960s Bruce played in a series of traditional jazz, rhythm and blues, and jump blues groups. In 1965, while playing a recording session, he borrowed an electric bass. He recalled to Dan Hedges of *Guitar Player*, "[I] found that I . . . could get a completely different kind of thing out of it."

By that time Bruce was working with Ginger Baker in the Graham Bond Organisation, a group that also included fusion guitarist John McLaughlin. Baker also came from a jazz background and was particularly influenced by the avant-garde work of Ornette Coleman and John Coltrane. He had played in the house band at Ronnie Scott's, London's premier jazz club, and in Alexis Korner's Blues, Inc., the band that gave birth to the British blues revival, before leaving to pursue a more progressive direction with Bond.

Guitarist Eric Clapton became a star with the Yardbirds, a band that won a following in England for their extended blues jams on stage and their exotic Eastern-tinged pop experimentation in the studio. Feeling that they had sold out by abandoning the blues for pop music, Clapton quit the band immediately after they recorded their first hit single. He then played in John Mayall's Bluesbreakers but left the group shortly after Bruce joined it.

Formation of a Supergroup

In 1966 Baker, Bruce, and Clapton were all at loose ends in their careers. Baker and Bruce had been playing throughout London as a jazz rhythm section, but, as Bruce recalled it to Macnie, "We'd had a kind of falling out. [Baker] thought my bass playing was getting too busy. . . . I was trying to make the bass stand up there with the other instruments. Ginger didn't agree with that. But when he went to Eric and said, 'Let's form a band,' Eric said, 'Yeah, but you've got to have Jack in it; he's the singer.' So we went by Ginger's little suburban pad and set up in his living room. And it was obvious from the start that there was a magical thing happening."

The trio may have had magic, but they lacked material; rehearsals consisted mainly of blues jams. Bruce, the most experienced songwriter in the band, wrote a light pop tune for their first single, "Wrapping Paper." It was the opposite of what everyone expected from three jazz/blues virtuosos, and it flopped. Cream's next record, however, another Bruce composition, "I Feel Free," made the British charts and set the band on their way to acclaim.

Cream didn't really hit their stride until they toured the United States in 1967. Though their first album, *Fresh Cream,* had only moderate sales in America, they had a considerable word-of-mouth reputation among music fans in the growing "underground" scene. American fans seemed more receptive to experimental music, and it was during Cream's stint at San Francisco's Fillmore West in 1967, Bruce told MacNie, that the band "got into the more improvised thing. . . . The audience began shouting 'Just play!' We were getting a bit bored just doing the tunes, actually, and were quite happy to open up."

Cream Rose to the Top

The new improvisational direction thrilled audiences, and Cream quickly became one of the hottest bands in rock. *Time* praised their "exultant technical mastery that surpasses anything yet heard in rock;" *Newsweek* noted "a new freedom of self-expression that, if not a step toward jazz, is running on a parallel course." The first American tour was followed in short order by a new album, *Disraeli Gears,* and a hit single, "Sunshine of Your Love."

Cream's success as a recording band, however, only underscored the disparity between their live work and their efforts in the studio. They seemed almost to be two bands, and the critical response fell roughly into two camps: those who considered Cream's live shows a harbinger of a new freedom in rock, but found their recorded output to suffer from mediocre songwriting, undistinguished vocals, and poor production; and those who judged the studio recordings interesting, if inconsistent, and felt the extended onstage jamming was merely self-indulgent. Clapton himself was ambivalent, commenting in *Rolling Stone* in 1967, "That's where I want to be at: where I just don't ever have to play anything but improvisation." But in 1988 he told David Fricke in the same magazine, "Maybe we should not have been allowed that much luxury. We probably started burning out at that point. We were just going for the moon every time we played, instead of confining it and economizing."

On their third album, *Wheels of Fire,* Cream tried to have the best of both worlds, recording one disc in the studio and one live at the Fillmore. *Rolling Stone* correspondent Jann Wenner dismissed the studio half of the project: "Cream is good at a number of things; unfortunately songwriting and recording are not among them." Wenner went on to praise the live portion of *Wheels of Fire,* observing, "This is the kind of thing that people who have seen Cream perform walk away raving about and it's good to at last have it on a record." Even so, the studio disc featured "White Room," one of Cream's biggest hits, and the live sides included what Phil Hardy described in *The Faber Companion to 20th Century Popular Music* as "the excesses of 'Train Time' and 'Toad''s seventeen minutes of drumming."

Disbanded at Their Peak

By the time *Wheels of Fire* began to climb the charts, relationships among the members of Cream had soured. Musical disagreements, personality clashes, and egos—Bruce and Baker resented the fact that the public saw Cream as Clapton's band, even though Bruce was the chief singer and songwriter and Baker's drumming was a vital component of the sound—had created such tension that the three often stayed in separate hotels when on tour. In August of 1968 Clapton announced that Cream had lost its musical direction and were disbanding. They played their last concert on November 26 at the Royal Albert Hall in London, where a more enthusiastic audience then they had ever before found in their homeland shouted "God save the Cream!" as the trio left the stage.

Clapton and Baker stayed together for a year in the short-lived band Blind Faith, while Bruce went on to a successful, though lower profile, solo career, playing jazz with the Tony Williams Lifetime and Mose Allison and more blues-rock with West, Bruce, and Laing and BLT, as well as making a series of innovative solo albums. Baker eventually built a recording studio in Nigeria and recorded with Fela Kuti and other African musicians. He also formed the jazz-rock bands Ginger Baker's Air Force and the Baker-Gurvitz Army. In 1989 Baker rejoined Bruce for an album, *A Question of Time,* and a brief tour. Clapton went on to form Derek and the

Dominos and to build a career as one of rock's senior superstars.

Short as its ascendancy was, Cream permanently changed the nature of rock and roll. Clapton defined the role of the guitar hero; Bruce brought the bass out of the shadows of the rhythm section, revealing its possibilities as a melodic instrument; and Baker introduced new levels of rhythmic complexity to rock percussion. Nineteen years after Cream's farewell, *Rolling Stone* characterized the group as "essentially a jazz trio playing blues changes with rock muscle. Clapton, Bruce and Baker were liberating rock bands once and for all from the constraints of the Top Forty pop song."

Selected discography

Fresh Cream, Atco, 1967, reissued, DCC Classics, 1992.
Disraeli Gears, Atco, 1967, reissued, MFSL, 1992.
Wheels of Fire, Atco, 1968, reissued, DCC Classics, 1992.
Goodbye, Atco, 1969.
The Best of Cream, Atco, 1969.
Live Cream, Atco, 1970.
Live Cream, Volume II, Atco, 1972.
Heavy Cream, Polydor, 1973.
The Best of Cream Live, Polydor, 1975.
Early Cream, Springboard, 1978.
Strange Brew: The Very Best of Cream, Polydor, 1983.

Solo releases by Jack Bruce; on Polydor Records, except where noted

Songs for a Tailor, 1969.
Things We Like, 1970.
Harmony Row, 1971.
Out of the Storm, 1974.
How's Tricks, 1977.
I've Always Wanted to Do This, Epic, 1980.
A Question of Time, Epic, 1989.
Will Power, 1989.

Solo releases by Ginger Baker

Ginger Baker's Air Force, Polydor, 1970.
Horses and Trees, Celluloid, 1986.
Middle Passage, Axiom, 1990.

Solo releases by Eric Clapton; on Polydor Records, except where noted

Backless, reissued, 1986.
No Reason to Cry, reissued, 1987.
E. C. Was Here, reissued, 1987.
Rainbow Concert, reissued, 1987.
There's One in Every Crowd, reissued, 1987.
August, Warner Bros., 1987.
Time Pieces/Best of E. C., 1988.

Time Pieces II/Live in the Seventies, 1988.
24 Nights, Reprise, 1991.
Unplugged, Duck, 1992.
Behind the Sun, Warner Bros.
Journeyman, Reprise.
Money & Cigarettes, Warner Bros.
Crossroads.
Slowhand.
Eric Clapton.
461 Ocean Boulevard.
Just One Night.
Another Ticket.

Sources

Books

Hardy, Phil, *The Faber Companion to Twentieth-Century Popular Music,* Faber and Faber, 1990.

The Rolling Stone Interviews, edited by Jann Wenner, Straight Arrow, 1971.

Periodicals

Down Beat, March 1990; November 1990.
Guitar Player, June 1968; August 1975.
Musician, January 1988.
Newsweek, March 18, 1968.
Rolling Stone, November 9, 1967; January 12, 1968; July 20, 1968; April 5, 1969; June 4, 1987; August 23, 1988; October 17, 1991; February 4, 1993.
Time, October 27, 1967.

—*Tim Connor*

Andraé Crouch

Singer, composer, pianist, producer

"Long before Amy Grant, Chris Christian, and B. J. Thomas were thinking about it, Andraé Crouch was doing it," wrote Bob Darden in *Billboard* magazine. "Along with Larry Norman, Crouch is one of religious music's original groundbreakers." Indeed, as contemporary gospel's perennial frontrunner, Crouch is most widely recognized as the first black gospel artist to appeal to both religious and secular audiences across multiracial lines. A prolific songwriter with some 300 titles to his credit—many of which have become industry standards—Crouch has been a driving force since he appeared on the music scene in the late 1960s. Darden elaborated by noting that the six-time Grammy winner was the first to receive significant airplay and sales in the mainstream marketplace, the first contemporary gospel act (as Andraé Crouch and the Disciples) to appear on national television, and the first to accumulate more than a million in sales. According to Walter Rico Burrell in *Ebony* magazine, Crouch has "cleverly combined elements of disco, progressive jazz, rhythm and blues, pop and even rock, while at the same time walking a fine line between his traditional grass roots gospel background and outright top-40 funk. . . . He has carved a niche for himself in the music world usually reserved for non-religious artists."

Perhaps because of his enormous success, Crouch has had his share of detractors who, according to Ed Ochs in *Billboard,* "say that [he] is not a gospel artist anymore, but a pop artist singing gospel lyrics." His use of electronic and acoustic instruments as well as his nontraditional lyrics have garnered a significant amount of criticism from those who think he has strayed too far from his roots. In particular, Crouch's 1981 venture with Warner Bros.—resulting in the release of the heavily commercial album *Don't Give Up*—elicited accusations that Crouch had "sold out." Yet Crouch remains faithful to his interpretation of gospel music and his mission as a singer: "God gave me my talent to use for Him and I'll use it for Him all my life," he was quoted as saying in a publicity release from his agent. "My reward is my music. Love is the main message of the Bible, and that's what I want to portray in my music."

Crouch was born and raised in Los Angeles, California. As children, he and his twin sister, Sandra, and their older brother, Benjamin, formed a group called "The Crouch Trio." Their father was a street preacher who eventually wound up with a church of his own in Val Verde, California. At the age of nine Crouch became a Christian, and at age eleven he "received the gift of music," as he put it in his autobiography, *Through It All,* which enabled him to become the pianist at his father's small church. Though he had no formal training, Crouch

For the Record. . .

B orn Andraé Edward Crouch, July 1, 1942, in Los Angeles, CA; son of Benjamin Jerome (a preacher and owner of a dry-cleaning business) and Catherine Dorothea (maiden name, Hodnett; a homemaker and dry cleaner) Crouch. *Education:* Studied elementary education, Valley Junior College, San Fernando, CA; studied personal evangelism and scripture, LIFE Bible College, Los Angeles. *Religion:* Pentecostal Church of God in Christ.

Gospel singer, songwriter, pianist, and record producer. Debuted as gospel singer with the COGICS (Church of God in Christ Singers) while in high school; organized group the Disciples, 1965, and toured with them as lead singer and pianist until 1980; first album, *Take the Message Everywhere,* released by Light Records, 1971; recorded 12 additional albums for Light featuring contemporary gospel music, including *No Time to Lose,* produced by Crouch Music Corporation, 1984; recorded nontraditional gospel album for Warner Bros., *Don't Give Up,* 1981. Formed Andraé Crouch Choir; performed and collaborated with other artists, 1981—. Author of autobiography, *Through It All,* Word Books, 1974.

Selected awards: Grammy awards with the Disciples, 1975, for *Take Me Back,* 1978, for *Live in London,* 1979, for *I'll Be Thinking of You,* 1980, for "The Lord's Prayer," and 1981, for *Don't Give Up;* Grammy Award for solo work, 1984, for *No Time to Lose;* Dove awards, 1976, for *This Is Another Day,* 1978, for *Live in London,* and 1984, for *No Time to Lose;* Daviticus Award, 1979, for *I'll Be Thinking of You;* Gospel Music Excellence Award for best male vocalist, 1982, for *More of the Best;* ASCAP Special Songwriter Award; two NAACP Image awards; Golden Halo Award; Oscar nomination.

Addresses: *Agent*—Triad Artists, Inc., 10100 Santa Monica Blvd., 16th floor, Los Angeles, CA 90067. *Management*—The Hervey Company, 9034 Sunset Blvd., Beverly Hills, CA 90069.

played at all services and later started a choir. By the time he was 14, Crouch had written his first song, "The Blood Will Never Lose Its Power." When he was in junior high school, the family moved to Pacoima near the San Fernando Valley, where Crouch's father became the pastor of the fledgling Christ Memorial Church.

While in high school Crouch formed his first group, the COGICS (Church of God in Christ Singers), featuring his twin sister, Sandra, and future Grammy winner Billy Preston. The group recorded an album and received

several awards but eventually split up when Preston left to pursue a career in secular music. Following graduation Crouch attended Valley Junior College for two years and later took courses at the LIFE Bible College in Los Angeles. During this time he worked as a counselor and choir director for recovering drug addicts at the local Teen Challenge Center. In the mid-1960s Crouch organized his second group, the Disciples, with whom he would perform as lead singer and pianist for eleven years.

The Disciples Discovered

The Disciples, which included Crouch's sister and Danniebelle Hall as vocalists, were discovered in 1968 by Ralph Carmichael, founder of gospel-oriented Light Records. Their first album, *Take the Message Everywhere,* was released in 1971 to critical acclaim; Crouch debuted as a soloist on the Light label in 1972 with *Just Andraé.* The Disciples recorded more than half a dozen additional albums for Light before they disbanded in 1980. Their tours throughout the United States, Europe, Africa, and the Far East helped establish a strong foothold in both the traditional gospel and secular soul markets. "Andraé Crouch insists he isn't an entertainer," wrote Burrell in *Ebony.* "If you ask him, he'll tell you he's 'a minister spreading God's word through song.'. . . The simple truth of the matter is that Crouch has concocted a winning formula of highly energized rhythm and blues production values and techniques of song construction with explosively charged religious messages, and has emerged as one of the hottest, most commercially successful practitioners of gospel music in the country, if not the entire world."

In 1975 Andraé Crouch and the Disciples became the first gospel group to perform for sold-out crowds at New York City's Carnegie Hall, to which they returned in 1979 with similar fanfare. The group was also the first of its kind to perform at the Sydney Opera House in Australia and the Royal Albert Hall in London. Later, Crouch became the first gospel artist to perform in New York's Radio City Music Hall. In 1980 Crouch and the Disciples broke ground again as the first gospel group to perform on NBC-TV's *Saturday Night Live;* a second solo performance by Crouch followed four years later when then-presidential candidate Jesse Jackson hosted the show. During their decade-long roll Crouch and the Disciples were honored with multiple awards including four consecutive Grammies for each original work produced between 1978 and 1981, and several Dove awards, gospel music's equivalent of the Grammy.

Broadened Scope

In 1981 Crouch's first album without the Disciples, *Don't Give Up,* was released by Warner Brothers amid much controversy. It was the first of a planned four-record deal negotiated in an attempt to broaden Crouch's foothold in the secular market. The album included songs about abortion and prostitution and was the product of more sophisticated sound engineering. At the same time, Crouch signed with Light Records for another four albums so as not to lose his main audience. "Every album I've done has been controversial," Crouch told *Billboard's* Cary Darling. "I feel this album [*Don't Give Up*] has the potential to reach a different kind of person than the Light Records audience. . . . It's not anything new for me. It's just time for me to say it."

Reviews were generally positive: "With a vocal style and arrangements reminiscent of [Motown legend] Stevie Wonder, Crouch lets his message flow naturally on upbeat numbers like 'I Can't Keep It to Myself,' 'Don't Give Up,' and 'Start All Over Again,'" *People* magazine noted. "His convictions are unmistakable, but this is also a classy R&B work." In 1984 Crouch released *No Time to Lose,* the first record distributed by Light on the Crouch Music Corporation label. Peter Gross of the *Christian Herald* deemed it a hit, noting that the album had a "refined, polished sound that dances off the grooves."

Sometimes Crouch's music translated better on vinyl than in person, however. "Gospel-goes-disco and ends up a wallflower best describes Andraé Crouch's 60-minute turn of pop/secular music," a *Variety* reviewer commented about a 1982 concert. "The band rocked, in the rock 'n' roll sense rather than in the gospel tradition, much to the chagrin of the audience, who were as quiet as the proverbial church mouse throughout several tunes." Several years later another concert was reviewed in *Variety* that deemed Crouch "straightforward and big-voiced—but there was an element of calculation about his performance."

Explored Other Media

In 1986 Crouch became the first contemporary religious artist to receive an Oscar nomination for his work as gospel historian on the film adaptation of Alice Walker's novel *The Color Purple.* Working under the direction of famed record producer Quincy Jones, the film's executive producer and music supervisor, Crouch wrote 15 songs and directed and sang with all gospel choirs on the soundtrack. The "rousing Gospel sound" was praised by Chris Albertson in *Stereo Review.* This collaboration led to future work on Jones's *Back on the Block* album, as well as to work with pop artists Michael Jackson (on his *Bad* and *Dangerous* albums) and Madonna (on *Like a Prayer*). Crouch ventured into the television market when he wrote and produced the theme song "Shine on Me" for NBC's long-running sitcom *Amen.*

In addition to orchestrating his own successful career, Crouch helped launch the careers of other gospel artists. He and his sister Sandra co-produced her Grammy-winning debut album, *We Sing Praises,* as well as her follow-up album, *We're Waiting.* He also produced *Introducing the Winans,* the debut album of the three-time Grammy-winning group. Other musicians Crouch has assisted include Walter and Tremaine Hawkins, Gloria Jones, and Tata Vega, who is most recognized for her vocals in the film *The Color Purple.* Mainstream chart-topping artists who have recorded Crouch's songs include Elvis Presley, Barbara Mandrell, and Paul Simon.

Crouch has been sporadically working on material for a new album since 1984. In his autobiography, Crouch wrote of his music: "God just happens to use me. I'm not His first choice, not His second, maybe not even His hundredth; but so be it, He chose me. He gave me some songs and you just happen to hear those songs. I trust that through it all, something I write or sing will be a blessing to you."

Selected discography

With the Disciples; on Light Records/Lexicon Music, Inc.

Take the Message Everywhere, 1971.
Keep On Singing, 1971.
Soulfully, 1972.
Live at Carnegie Hall, 1973.
Take Me Back, 1974.
This Is Another Day, 1976.
Live in London, 1978.
I'll Be Thinking of You, 1979.

Solo releases

Just Andraé, Light Records/Lexicon Music, Inc., 1973.
Don't Give Up, Warner Bros., 1981.
Andraé Crouch—More of the Best, Light Records/Lexicon Music, Inc., 1982.
Finally, Light Records/Lexicon Music, Inc., 1982.
No Time to Lose, Crouch Music Corporation/Light Records, 1984.

Composer of *Amen* theme song, "Shine on Me," NBC-TV.

Sources

Books

Crouch, Andraé, and Nina Ball, *Through It All,* Word Books, 1974.
Jenkins, Keith Bernard, *The Rhetoric of Gospel Song: A Content Analysis of the Lyrics of Andraé Crouch* (dissertation), Florida State University, Fall 1990.

Periodicals

Billboard, September 27, 1980; November 7, 1981; March 22, 1986.
Christian Herald, May 1983.
Christianity Today, March 4, 1983.
Ebony, September 1982.
Jet, August 23, 1982; September 13, 1982.
People, January 29, 1982.
Stereo Review, June 1986.
Variety, September 1, 1982; July 2, 1986.

Additional information for this profile was obtained from Light Records, 1992, courtesy of Triad Artists, Inc.

—Mary Scott Dye

Deee-Lite

Deee-Lite struck the dance-music scene in 1990 like a lightening bolt. The group's extravagantly campy look and irresistibly funky, upbeat songs were a marked contrast to the generally introverted cool of most hip-hop, and the distinctive vocals of lead singer Lady Miss Kier—whose 1970s-inspired wardrobe made her an instant fashion icon—helped set the group apart from the droves of diva-meets-dance-machine records dominating the club scene. Part of the appeal of Deee-Lite's music has been its inclusiveness—Christian Logan Wright wrote in *Mademoiselle* that "as a group, they're a festival of individuality; as a band, they're a party anyone can attend." With their first hit single, "Groove Is in the Heart," from their gold debut album, *World Clique,* they injected the feel-good bounce of 1970s "P-Funk" into house music and created a sensation. Then 1992's *Infinity Within* made the group's political agenda a more literal part of the music.

The seeds of the group were sown in 1982 when Miss Kier—born Kier Kirby—met a Russian emigré musician

named Dmitry Brill in New York City's Washington Square Park. Brill, who was raised in the Ukraine, had played in a rock cover band in the Soviet Union and arrived in New York City expecting an atmosphere of lavish excitement. The city and its prospects initially disappointed him, but he discovered the joys of funk music, particularly the P-Funk, or pure funk sound of George Clinton's groups, Parliament and Funkadelic. Meanwhile Brill deejayed in some large dance clubs where he soon found a soulmate in Kier. A native of Pittsburgh, Kier grew up attending political rallies with her activist mother. Later she worked a variety of jobs, including textile designer, waitress, and coat check attendant. In 1986 Kier and Brill decided to form a group; after writing songs together for a while, the twosome made their first appearance at Siberia, a local club.

Eclectic Origins

Shortly afterward Brill and Kier received a demo tape from a Japanese computer whiz named Towa Tei, who had just arrived in the United States. He became the band's "DJ," mostly producing sounds via computer. Like Brill, Towa had escaped a cultural climate he considered stultifying: "When I was in high school, everyone listened to [commercial hard rockers] Whitesnake, or Japanese versions of Whitesnake," he related in *Rolling Stone.* The group continued playing gigs and soon began presenting a homemade demo tape to record labels. An article in *Details* noted that

apart from vague rejections, the group received only one formal reply: "Sorry, we can't use your stuff. It's completely unoriginal." Nonetheless the group began gathering crowds as a live act, drawing a cross section of the various dance scenes of New York City. As Jeff Giles described in *Rolling Stone,* "They were drawing vivid, multiracial, pan-sexual crowds that were often a thousand strong, and Kier was throwing daisies from the stage."

Soon several record companies were courting Deee-Lite. "We turned down a lot of offers waiting for someone who understood our art," Kier told Giles. "At a lot of the labels, the only people in power were white men. There were no minorities working in high positions. And you could see what was coming. You could *smell* it. They'd say: 'You're a Top Forty band. You could be the next. . . .' And we'd say, 'Sorry, but you miss what we're about.'" If nothing else, the band was about the sense of freedom and diversity their audience embodied: politically progressive as well as stylish, convinced that the groove of Deee-Lite was the sound of liberation on several levels.

Hit Big With Debut

In 1989 Brill, who by then was becoming better known as Dmitry, and Towa did production work with a number of up-and-coming artists, including Sinead O'Connor, the Jungle Brothers, and A Tribe Called Quest. These projects were, for the members of Deee-Lite, part of the process of defining the "Sampledelic" sound—a fusion of P-Funk groove and the eclectic sampling instincts of rap's bohemian fringe.

After signing a deal with Elektra Records in 1990, Deee-Lite released their debut album, *World Clique.* The single "Groove Is in the Heart" was a huge hit, dominating dance-oriented radio and the clubs. Several subsequent singles also fared well. *People's* Craig Tomashoff, admittedly not usually a fan of dance music, suggested that "Deee-Lite is the aspirin of dance music. Maybe because this trio of New York City-based hipsters has a sense of humor. Maybe it's because they actually use some real instruments and real musicians, instead of just sampling them. Whatever the reason, *World Clique* bubbles with energy." *Entertainment Weekly* referred to the album as "one of the major musical happenings of 1990." In Kier's own words, as cited by Wright in *Mademoiselle,* "It's funk, soul, curly, wiggly music." As proof the group enlisted bassist-guitarist-vocalist Bootsy Collins along with several other Parliament-Funkadelic alumni to play on some tracks, cementing Deee-Lite's connection with the legacy of 1970s funk.

During 1990, as Dmitry and Towa continued producing for various artists—including post-production work and remixing on a track by labelmates They Might Be Giants—Kier became a familiar face on the international fashion scene, sharing the spotlight with designers like Thierry Mugler. She used the spotlight for a number of causes, from helping to raise money for AIDS relief, to filming a pro-choice public service announcement with other women musicians, to protesting the war in the Persian Gulf between the United States and Iraq. Deee-Lite wrote an anti-war song, "Riding on Through," but it ended up backing a single rather than appearing on *World Clique*. Kier continually spoke out during the war, but was frustrated to find her comments excised from published profiles. "We were censored by the media cowards," she assessed in *Details*. Indeed, many journalists appeared baffled by Deee-Lite's mixture of fashion consciousness and political awareness. Kier appraised the situation in her interview with Giles of *Rolling Stone:* "People think that to make a political statement you have to wear a poncho and Birkenstocks [German-made sandals] and, like, love beads. And that's an anachronism. It's twenty, twenty-five years old, and it's really ridiculous."

Taking their politics out on the road, Deee-Lite toured to support *World Clique* with a nine-piece band that included Collins; Towa had chosen to co-produce an album by Japanese artist Hajime Tachibana instead. The tour highlight was an appearance at the prestigious Montreux Jazz Festival where Deee-Lite was invited to share the stage with P-Funk pioneer George Clinton for a rendition of the Funkadelic hit "(Not Just) Knee Deep." The band's press biography later quoted Kier as commenting, "Playing live is in the true spirit of techno soul."

New Political Package: *Infinity Within*

Deee-Lite released "Good Beat," the last single from *World Clique,* in 1991. Kier and Dmitry got married, and by the following year Deee-Lite had a new album to promote. For its 1992 effort, *Infinity Within,* Deee-Lite developed a number of its political concerns, giving some of their ideas practical form. For starters, the CD was released in a format called "Eco-Pak" rather than the traditional—and, according to most environmentalists, very wasteful—longbox. "The Eco-Pak's overall package has no disposable parts, uses 33% less plastic than conventional [plastic CD] jewel boxes and 15% less paper than current longboxes," an Elektra press release stated. Deee-Lite had finally created the appropriate context for its environmental ode "I Had a Dream I Was Falling Through a Hole in the Ozone Layer." *Infinity* also contained "Rubber Lover," a track

featuring vocals by Collins that advised the use of condoms, and a brief ditty called "Vote, Baby, Vote" in support of Kier's sentiments towards voting privileges. She maintained in an interview with *Reflex,* "[I'd] like to see a law: as soon as you get a social security number, as soon as you turn 18, you're automatically registered to vote." Lastly, Deee-Lite pledged a portion of the profits from the album to the environmentalist group Greenpeace.

At first this heightened political emphasis alienated some critics. Yet for the most part, reviewers found the dance beat of the second album—augmented by the inclusion of P. Funk's legendary "Horny Horns" duo, Maceo Parker and Fred Wesley, who joined several of their former bandmates on the album—just as irresist-

---

> *"People think that to make a political statement you have to wear a poncho, Birkenstocks, and like, love beads. And that's an anachronism. It's really ridiculous."*
> —Lady Miss Kier

---

ible as that of the first. *Infinity Within* yielded a house-influenced single called "Runaway," and offered songs with guest raps by celebrated newcomers Arrested Development and Michael Franti of The Disposable Heroes of Hiphoprisy.

"Deee-Lite, those neo-disco darlings, have succumbed to the fashion for politically correct dance music," observed Jeremy Hellingar of *People.* "The irony is that this bandwagon-esque approach provides some of the album's best musical moments." *Time's* reviewer concluded, "The deee-lightful result: good message, great dance beat." *Entertainment Weekly's* Greg Sandow objected, however, to the "mundane specificity" of the political sentiment. "Your [Deee-Lite's] politics worked better two years ago when you made the words vague, and let your music tell the story." Despite issuing that mild rebuke, Sandow gave the album a "B."

But Kier insisted in *Reflex* that the emphasis of the album was a progression, not a departure. "The reason why we titled this new album *Infinity Within*—to balance out [*World Clique's*] idea of looking outward and thinking about unity—is if you look outward, you should look inward to see what you're doing as an individual. Because people seem to be so passive—I'd like to see people turn their TV sets off and start protesting."

Deee-Lite's mixture of funk, soul, disco, house, and rap brought together a huge, varied listenership; their mixture of style and political substance helped make them one of the most influential forces in dance music in the early 1990s. Lady Miss Kier, Dmitry, and Towa have all expressed the hope that their music will contribute to positive global change and Kier has remained philosophical about her group's impact. "Deee-Lite is not guiding anything," she insisted in *Details*. "We're reflecting it. But I can feel something happening right now. It's like when animals know that there's an earthquake coming and they all start running out of the forest."

Selected discography

On Elektra Records

World Clique (includes "Groove Is in the Heart"), 1990.

"Good Beat"/"E.S.P." and "Riding on Through," (singles), 1991.
Infinity Within (includes "I Had a Dream I Was Falling Through a Hole in the Ozone Layer," "Rubber Lover," "Runaway," and "Vote, Baby, Vote"), 1992.

Sources

Details, July 1992.
Entertainment Weekly, June 26, 1992.
Mademoiselle, December 1990.
Musician, August 1992.
Newsweek, March 18, 1991.
People, July 29, 1991; July 13, 1992.
Reflex, June 23, 1992.
Rolling Stone, July 9, 1992; September 17, 1992.
Time, June 29, 1992.

Additional information for this profile was obtained from Elektra Records press releases, 1992.

—*Simon Glickman*

Digital Underground

Rap group

Digital Underground helped usher in a new style of rap music during the late eighties, a style heavily influenced by the sound and attitude of seventies funk bands like George Clinton's groups, Parliament and Funkadelic. Sampling from recordings by Clinton's various "P-Funk" bands, the Underground also emulated the wild stage shows featuring bizarre and funny characters that were the other side of the P-Funk legacy. From its independent debut single, through hits like "The Humpty Dance" and "Doowutchyalike," Digital Underground has broadened its appeal, continuing to live up to its self-description as an "all-Atlantic, all-Pacific, all-city, grand-imperial dance music and hip hop dynasty." As *Newsday* commented in 1990, "Digital Underground looks like the new face of hip hop, as the music tries to make sense of its expanded range of possibilities."

Before becoming a "dynasty," Digital Underground was the brainchild of musician and rapper Shock G, whom Eric Weisbard of the *San Francisco Weekly* described as "a hip hop jack-of-all-trades: He plays drums, piano and other instruments; is a capable MC and disc jockey; produces his records; makes his own videos; [and] designs and choreographs his stage show." Born Greg Jacobs in Far Rockaway, Queens, New York, c. 1963, Shock G played drums in a band that only knew one song—the Commodores' funk hit "Brick House." Hip hop was a fledgling form, but the excitement of early rappers like Grandmaster Flash left an indelible impression on the young musician. Soon, Shock was asking his parents for turntables and a mixer, the main instruments of a rap DJ. In an interview with Weisbard, Shock G recounted, "We'd constantly spend time at 42nd Street Records, Downstairs Records, getting all the break beats."

Founded by Shock G and Chopmaster J

Shock G's family moved to Tampa, Florida, in 1980. He landed a job there disc jockeying on radio station WTMP and participated in a rap group known alternately as Spice or Chill Factor. He also picked up work recording demos for other rappers. His outlook changed, however, when his parents divorced; Shock dropped out of high school and became involved in various illegal activities, including pimping and selling drugs. He served a number of jail terms but after a few years went straight, got his high school diploma, and began pursuing music. While monitoring rap's development, he took music theory classes at a neighborhood college.

Shock moved to Oakland, California, in the mid-1980s and began working in the keyboard and drum machine

---

For the Record. . .

Original members include **Chopmaster J** (born Jimmy Dright), DJ, and **Shock G** (born Greg Jacobs, c. 1963, in Queens, NY), rapper, keyboardist, composer. Other members have included **Big Money Odis,** rapper; **DJ Fuse** (born David Elliot); **MC Clever,** rapper; **Money B** (born Ronald Brooks), rapper; **Ramone PeeWee Gooden,** keyboardist, percussionist, vocalist; **Schmoovy Schmoove,** vocalist; and **2Pac,** rapper.

Group formed in Oakland, CA, c. 1987; recorded first single, "Underwater Rimes"/"Your Life's a Cartoon," 1987; signed with Tommy Boy Records and released *Sex Packets,* 1989.

Awards: Platinum record for *Sex Packets* and for single "The Humpty Dance."

Addresses: *Record company*—Tommy Boy Records, 1747 First Ave., New York, NY 10128. *Fan club*—Digital Underground Fan Club, 13624 Sherman Way, #450, Van Nuys, CA 91405.

department of a music store in neighboring San Leandro. One day a customer named Jimmy Dright—an experienced drummer trained in jazz but determined to jump on the hip hop bandwagon—spent several thousand dollars on equipment. Sensing an opportunity, Shock struck a deal with Dright: he would teach him to use the new equipment if Dright would let him make a demo with it. That night, according to Weisbard's article, the Dright and Shock recorded four-track versions of the two songs that would grace Digital Underground's first single: "Underwater Rimes" and "Your Life's a Cartoon." Dright sent the tape to a producer friend in Los Angeles, who offered to oversee the re-recording of the tracks. A partnership had been created. Though Shock was leery of allying himself with an acoustic drummer who considered himself a hippie, he knew his new friend had business savvy. Shock was right; soon Dright became "Chopmaster J" and Digital Underground had a 12-inch single.

Unfortunately the song's release was held up by a number of complications. Consequently the duo spent a couple of lean years without a record contract. At one point they were even living off of a $10,000 loan they received from a bail bondsman, but the money ran out before anything spectacular happened. Meanwhile hip hop was maturing into a multifaceted art form, and emerging artists like De La Soul were reaping praise and profit from a style that Shock G and Chopmaster J felt they had helped invent. Turnabout came in the fall of 1988 when Digital Underground's new manager, Atron Gregory, finally got the record released on TNT/Macola Records. Daria Kelly of Leopold's Records—described by Weisbard as "one of the guardian angels of Bay Area rap"—sent the 12-inch to the hip hop label Tommy Boy. Interested, the company signed Digital Underground in 1989.

By this time Shock G and Chopmaster J had recruited two new members—DJ Fuse, also known as David Elliot, and his friend and roommate Money B., also known as Ronald Brooks. Shock G particularly admired the new recruits because, as he told Weisbard, "Money B and DJ Fuse eat, sleep, and drink hip hop." The revamped Digital Underground fell halfway between the hardcore Oakland rapping style that was Money B's preferred mode and the extravagant strangeness of Shock's P-Funk model. Trouble hadn't strayed far, though; the ensuing album, *Sex Packets,* was not released until early in 1990 due to legal problems related to samples the group had selected.

Tall Tales and *Sex Packets*

Thematically *Sex Packets* juxtaposes sex, fun, and silliness with a few more serious subjects, most notably street life as in "The Danger Zone." The album also spawned the infectious hit "Doowutchyalike," a tune *Billboard* branded "a hilarious party record espousing personal freedom," in addition to "The Humpty Dance" and "Underwater Rimes." The latter songs showcased the rapping talents of two mysterious figures, Humpty Hump and MC Blowfish. Though Shock G never admitted to providing the voices for these two characters, his talent for different voices is legendary in the rap community. Stories circulated in press releases and interviews about Humpty's former career as a soul singer and the tragic accident that deformed his face and ruined his voice—hence the necessity of his wearing a rubber nose in videos and other appearances. MC Blowfish, according to the band, pursued the group by swimming back and forth between the two coasts.

The yarns escalated; Shock even claimed in his interview with *Musicmakers* that the group formed when "we were all out eating pizza. The ground rumbled and opened up and this voice said 'You are the chosen ones.' We were sucked down into this underground recording lab and the equipment in that place was so fabulous that we didn't even worry about what was happening." The story continued: "This light blinded us, we lost consciousness, and two days later we had these master tapes in our hands and our name was Digital Underground."

Perhaps the most controversial element of *Sex Packets* was the legendary—and, many claim, fictional—substance that gave the album its name. Shock told interviewers around the world that sex packets were a special drug originally designed for astronauts; "All they have to do is put a capsule on their tongue in order to have an orgasm," he explained to *Musicmakers.* Given Shock's flair for tall tales, the sex packets story was taken with a grain of salt by most reviewers. Though critics were skeptical about the existence of the drug, they were believers when it came to the record. *Detour* proclaimed, "This is one hyped up album." *Rolling Stone* called it an "inventive debut," and *Sounds* declared that "*Sex Packets* is consistently engaging in a way that many rap albums aren't. It also shows there are no rules in hip-hop." Billy Kiernan of the *San Francisco Independent* dubbed the effort "a concept album that will be considered a landmark in rap music for years to come." Kiernan's praise was modified only by his distaste for some of the album's "sexist imagery."

"The Humpty Dance" made its way into *Billboard's* Top 100 with a bullet, dominating both radio and dance clubs, and helping propel the album to gold status. Another sales-pushing factor was the innovative sampling featured on *Sex Packets.* For example, "Underwater Rimes," the self-described "Underwater Hip Hop Extravaganza" and sequel to Parliament's deep-sea funk epic "Aqua Boogie," sampled that Parliament tune as well as "Chameleon" by jazz-rock pioneer Herbie Hancock; the latter was a sly choice, given Shock's chameleonlike character changes. "The Humpty Dance" nicked its large-nosed character's groove from Parliament's nasally fixated LP *Trombipulation;* "The Way We Swing" lifted a riff from "Who Knows" by guitar legend Jimi Hendrix, looping it to emphasize the swing in its rhythm. "Doowutchyalike" and two other tracks sampled different parts of Parliament's hit "Flash Light."

Digital Underground toured the planet, discovering a worldwide audience that was mad for P-Funk-inspired hip hop. In Vienna, when a computer program lost all the group's samples, a DJ loaned them all the records they needed to redo the program.

A World Tour, an EP, and New Personnel

1990 saw the advent of *This Is An EP Release.* The seven-track recording featured the single "Same Song" and marked the debut of rapper 2Pac, who would later release a hit solo album entitled *2Pacalypse Now.* The Underground had also recruited rapper-drummer Big Money Odis and singer-musician-producer Ramone

PeeWee Gooden. Digital Underground continued touring and reaching ever-larger audiences in the United States, Europe, and Japan. By 1991, as noted in *The Source,* the band had "sold more product, domestically, than any other Tommy Boy artist, including De La Soul." That year Chopmaster J left the group to start his own project, Force One Network.

In 1992 Digital Underground released *Sons of the P.* The new album sported a more ambitious batch of Funkadelic samples than either of its predecessors, and none other than George Clinton himself appeared on the record to hand the mantle of P-Funk over to the

> *"Funk can be rock, funk can be jazz, and funk can be soul. We say, 'Do what feels good.'"*
> —Shock G

Underground. "Digital Underground is where Parliament left off," Shock insisted to James Bernard in the *New York Times.* "Funk can be rock, funk can be jazz, and funk can be soul. Most people have a checklist of what makes a good pop song: it has to be three minutes long, it must have a repeatable chorus, and it must have a catchy hook. That's what makes music stale. We say, 'Do what feels good.' If you like it for three minutes, then you'll love it for thirty." The joy-in-repetition argument certainly applies to the record's first single, "Kiss You Back," which Bernard described as "an irresistible, playful ode to cuddling and snuggling." He further observed that the album "focuses attention on the ground-shaking bass, which seems injected with adrenaline."

Yet *Sons of the P* also takes up more sober topics. Even the relatively comical "No Nose Job"—narrated by Humpty, of course—makes some tough arguments about cosmetic surgery as a retreat from ethnicity. "Heartbeat Props" insists that too many people don't get "proper respect" until they die; to remedy this, the song lists dozens of prominent African Americans, from Muslim minister Louis Farrakhan to rapper Queen Latifah.

Most of all, though, *Sons of the P* takes the legacy of P-Funk as its major focus; the recurring theme here is the legendary "DFLO Shuttle"—the mythical train that transports Clinton's successors from the underground to the outside world. This concept, like the cover photo of the group members sleeping in glass pods, makes reference to Parliament's 1976 album *The Clones of Dr. Funkenstein.* And yet Digital Underground didn't merely pay homage to those funkmasters in efforts like "Tales of the Funky," a song detailing the highlights of P-Funk tours over a sample of Funkadelic's "One Nation Under a Groove." "We've come out and declared that this isn't a tribute to P-Funk, it is P-Funk," Shock told *The Source.* "Instead of harping on how live everything that George [Clinton] did was, he's on the album, doing it. It's like the next step in funk." New personnel included singer Schmoovy Schmoove and young rapper MC Clever. Shock emphasized that Digital Underground "is a liquid band," and that the rotating personnel—and multiple MCs—reflect a desire "to bring fresh new perspectives into Black music. If we just sealed ourselves off and said 'these are the members,' where would the opportunity be for other brothers? Plus, it keeps it fun."

Fun, of course, has been the name of the game all along for Digital Underground—a band that, in *New York Times* contributor Bernard's words, "make the kind of music that would make Scrooge laugh, if he were not too busy dancing." As Shock G was quoted as saying in *Spin,* "We're trying to break out of the normal modes of music. There's no one out there like us." Like Clinton, Shock expanded a band into a small musical industry, and the fluctuating musical talents of Digital Underground serve to get more solo projects onto the market while infusing Underground records and tours with fresh blood. Of course, into every hip hop dynasty a little rain must fall; "Humpty's been on an attitude trip and doesn't show up unless he has to," Shock reported to Bernard. "He doesn't do any interviews until 'No Nose Job' comes out."

Selected discography

"Underwater Rimes"/"Your Life's a Cartoon" (single), TNT/Macola, 1988.

Sex Packets (includes "Doowutchyalike," "The Humpty Dance," "Underwater Rimes," "The Way We Swing," and "The Danger Zone"), Tommy Boy, 1989.

This Is an EP Release (includes "Same Song"), Tommy Boy, 1990.

Digital Underground, Tommy Boy, 1991.

Sons of the P (includes "Kiss You Back," "No Nose Job," "Heartbeat Props," "Good Thing We're Rappin'," "The DFLO Shuttle," and "Tales of the Funky"), Tommy Boy, 1992.

Sources

BAM, November 4, 1988.
Billboard, September 23, 1989.
Detour, October 1990.
Echoes, December 2, 1989.
Face, September 1989.
Hip Hop Connection, October 1989.
Mixmag, April 1990.
Musicmakers, March 1990.
Music Week, December 16, 1989.
New Musical Express, April 14, 1990.
Newsday, January 7, 1990.
New York Times, November 3, 1991.
Reflex, Number 20.
Rockpool, July 15, 1990.
Rolling Stone, April 19, 1990.
San Francisco Independent, March 27, 1990.
San Francisco Weekly, March 21, 1990.
Soul Underground, April 1990.
Sounds, March 31, 1990.
Source, December 1991.
Spin, October 1989.
Village Voice, April 10, 1990.

—*Simon Glickman*

Donovan

Singer, songwriter

A pale, diminutive Scottish lad, Donovan launched his career imitating American folk-rock hero Bob Dylan. While that brought him some notoriety, he didn't fully come into his own until he shed the protest singer image. Blossoming into a mystical, flower-power singer—idol to hippies the world over—Donovan soon found a broad following for his folksy, psychedelic music. The second half of the 1960s found him at the height of his popularity, evidenced by international tours and sell-out crowds. He went into semi-seclusion during the following decade, lending his talents to film scores. The 1980s saw him involved primarily in political causes and protest marches. Although his star burned brightly only for a few years, Donovan's songs have become classics and remain classic-radio staples.

Born Donovan Leitch in Glasgow, Scotland, the singer grew up in the working-class Gorbals section of Glasgow. "We left Glasgow when I was ten," Donovan recalled in *Look* magazine, elaborating, "We were in the slums there. My father was afraid for his children. We moved to England where it was green and grassy." The family relocated to Hertfordshire, in the country outside of London. In school Donovan discovered a talent for painting and writing. "My son always had that little pencil in his hand and that little paper," his mother commented in *Look*.

Donovan continued writing throughout his adolescence, running the gamut from ghost stories to poems hinting at sexual frustrations. He became fascinated with the American beat movement and tried to imitate the free-form writing he found there. When faced with the possibility of taking a job as a tailor, he rebelled, quitting school and opting for a career as a singer. He made a living at odd jobs: working in a toothpaste factory, making cardboard boxes, manufacturing plastic soldiers. These spotty occupations afforded him the time to hitch-hike around England, where he found solace on the lonely, haunting Cornwall coast. During his travels he composed fragments of songs on his acoustic guitar and played in any pub or cafe that would let him. He was also active in the "Ban the Bomb" movement flowering in England at the time.

First Television Appearance

At 18 Donovan was discovered in a club in southeast England, after which he was enlisted to perform on the popular British television program *Ready Steady Go*. By then he had adopted a Dylan-inspired protest singer persona—complete with harmonica harness and a guitar bearing the slogan "This Machine Kills," an expression Dylan had taken from Woody Guthrie, whose

For the Record. . .

Born Donovan Leitch, May 10, 1946, in Glasgow, Scotland; married a woman named Linda, c. 1970; children: three, including daughter Ione Skye.

Worked at odd jobs, including in a toothpaste factory, making cardboard boxes, and manufacturing plastic soldiers, and performed in bars and clubs throughout England, c. 1963-65; discovered in British Club, c. 1965; performed on British television program *Ready Steady Go*, 1965; made U.S. debut at Newport Folk Festival, 1965; recording artist, 1966—; composer of film scores, 1969-79, including *If It's Tuesday, This Must Be Belgium, Brother Sun, Sister Moon*, and *The Pied Piper*; appeared in films *If It's Tuesday, This Must Be Belgium* and *The Pied Piper*; continued to write songs and perform at peace rallies in Europe, 1980—.

Addresses: *Management*—Great Northern Arts, Ltd., 114 Lexington Ave., New York, NY 10016.

slogan had actually been "This machine kills fascists." Television gained him widespread exposure in 1965 and despite his obvious influences, he had hits with two original songs: "Catch the Wind" and "Colours." Also in 1965, Donovan made his U.S. performing debut at the famed Newport Folk Festival.

By 1966 Donovan's image began to change; the activist folksinger role gave way to that of peace-loving "flower power" hippie. Denims fell by the wayside—replaced by love beads and the flowing white robes of a guru. Musically too, critics noted, Donovan had come into his own. Though his songs retained a folksy, soft-rock element, they were now laced with the ubiquitous psychedelia of the era, evinced on the Number Two hit "Mellow Yellow"—a ditty that engendered a brief fad of smoking banana peels. Perhaps his biggest hit, however, was the jaunty "Sunshine Superman," which reached Number One in 1966.

The following year Donovan traveled to India to receive the teachings of Maharishi Mahesh Yogi. There he continued to write songs, immersing himself in philosophies that would change his life. "I was in India," Donovan related in press material from Great Northern Arts, Ltd., "with four Beatles, one Beach Boy and [actress] Mia Farrow. We were gathered together on the roofs of our bungalows, under the tropical Indian stars. We broke out the guitars and I started to write this song. George Harrison turned to me and said: 'I could write a verse for that song, Don.' And he did—but I didn't record it." The song turned out to be the hit

"Hurdy Gurdy Man"; the verse Harrison wrote was tucked away and recorded by Donovan over 20 years later on the album *Donovan: The Classics Live.*

Espoused Natural High

Donovan returned to the West with a new agenda—to preach of the wonders of life without drugs. "I've done all drugs," the singer told Allan Parachini of the *Detroit News*, "and what it's led me to believe is that there's no high like a natural high. . . . Meditation is the only way to find what you're looking for when you get stoned." The newly sober singer reached the peak of his popularity in 1968 and 1969, the period during which he released the albums *Hurdy Gurdy Man* and *A Gift From a Flower to a Garden*. The singles "Wear Your Love Like Heaven" and "Jennifer Juniper" became huge hits and Donovan was lauded for the melodic, upbeat direction of his songcraft. *Christian Science Monitor* contributor David Sterritt wrote that Donovan's "current music returns to the time of the troubadour, the wandering musician whose songs were poetically influenced by the trees and green fields on his way from town to town." He added that the artist's approach to his work was "unique . . . in its total lack of pessimism and its childlike delight in subject matter as basic and unpretentious as the composer's own singing style."

During the 1970s Donovan briefly retired to Ireland. When he returned, he found that he had faded somewhat from the public eye. He released a few records and toured sporadically but never again reached the popularity he had enjoyed during the late 1960s. He wrote musical scores for several films, including *If It's Tuesday, This Must Be Belgium, Brother Sun, Sister Moon*, and *The Pied Piper*, in which he also took the lead role. He also wrote a much-loved children's double album entitled *H.M.S. Donovan*. 1974's *7-Tease*, a concept album, was accompanied by a theatrical tour that made its way to the U.S. featuring Donovan and a company of dancers.

Inspired New Generation

Donovan's career became even more low-key during the 1980s; not ready to retire, however, he spent the decade recording and marching in support of Europe's peace movement, singing at rallies in Britain, Holland, and Germany. In the 1990s three alternative rock bands—No Man, Happy Mondays, and the Butthole Surfers—each released cover versions of popular Donovan compositions. In 1991 the singer even launched a tour of the U.K. with Happy Mondays. That year he also released the album *Donovan: The Classics Live.*

Although his heyday was relatively short-lived, Donovan's impact on popular music has been significant. Many of his songs have stood the test of time, sounding fresh decades later—testimony to their irresistible hooks, unusual orchestration, and lyrical creativity. Furthermore, as a spokesperson for various concerns the singer has done much to promote world peace over the many years since the 1960s golden era of activism. Despite the uncertainty of renewed commercial success, Donovan's voice has remained in the mix of popular music, influencing a new generation of songwriters and performers.

Selected discography

Catch the Wind, Hickory, 1965.
Sunshine Superman, Epic, 1966.
In Concert, Epic, 1968.
Hurdy Gurdy Man, Epic, 1968.
A Gift From a Flower to a Garden, Epic, 1968.
(With Jeff Beck) *Barabajagal,* Epic, 1968.
Greatest Hits, Epic, 1969.
Open Road, Epic, 1970.
Colours, Hallmark, 1972.
Cosmic Wheels, Epic, 1973.
7-Tease, Epic, 1974.
Donovan, Rak, 1977.
The Donovan File, Pye, 1977.
Greatest Hits, Embassy, 1979.
Donovan: The Classics Live, Great Northern Arts, 1991.
Troubadour: The Definitive Collection/1964-76, Epic/Legacy, 1992.

Island of Circles (tribute album), Nettwerk, 1992.

Also released albums *H.M.S. Donovan, Love Is Only Feeling, Lady of the Stars,* and *Neutronica.*

Sources

Books

Hardy, Phil and Dave Laing, *Encyclopedia of Rock,* Schirmer Books, 1987.
Rolling Stone Encyclopedia of Rock, edited by Jon Pareles and Patricia Romanowski, Rolling Stone Press/Summit Books, 1983.

Periodicals

Christian Science Monitor, April 9, 1968.
Detroit Free Press, November 23, 1974.
Detroit News, November 30, 1969; November 15, 1971.
Look, April 2, 1968.
New York Times, November 7, 1971.
Playboy, May 1967.
Rolling Stone, December 10, 1992.

Additional information for this profile was obtained from Great Northern Arts, Ltd., press material, 1992.

—*Nancy Rampson*

Duane Eddy

Guitarist

Duane Eddy was known as one of the most famous guitarists in the years from 1958 to 1963. He hit a wave of popularity when instrumental songs were making it big, and rode it until the musical tides began to change. Eddy was known specifically for his "twangy" guitar style that fused country, rhythm and blues, and rock and roll. His popularity in the music field led him to earn several screen roles, and he composed scores for movies. After a short time in the limelight and 15 Top 40 hits, Eddy faded from view, but his influence was to live on. The distinctive Duane Eddy "twang" was often imitated by others in the business. Eddy continued to tour the United States after 1963, but never reached his previous level of fame. In England, however, he enjoyed a greater amount of popularity and has spent time touring there.

Eddy was born in 1938 in Corning, New York, and his family packed up and moved to Phoenix, Arizona, when he was a teenager. Eddy began playing the guitar at a very early age. "When I was five or six years old, I started picking at the strings, and the first thing I knew I was playing," Eddy told Louella O. Parsons in the *Detroit News.* "I have always liked the guitar, in fact, I like music period." When he was 16, he quit school and started working as a regular in local clubs. It was then that he got a custom-made Chet Atkins-model Gretsch guitar that he was to play for many years. He teamed up with guitarist Al Casey, taking lessons from Casey's jazz guitarist, Jim Wybele. In 1957 a local disc jockey, Lee Hazlewood, signed up the young Eddy for a recording contract.

Hazlewood pushed right ahead to produce Eddy's first hit. They formed a band made up of Al Casey, Larry Knechtel, and Steve Douglas called the Rebels. Hazlewood produced "Movin' 'n' Groovin'," an instrumental single featuring Eddy's soon-to-be-famous "twangy" guitar. He achieved this specialized sound by tuning his six string down an octave, performing the melody line on the top strings and feeding the sound through a combination of echoes. This sound became Eddy's trademark and was a creative fusion of rock, country, and rhythm and blues.

The record caught on and was a hit almost immediately. In a *Musician* article John Fogerty commented that the record sounded "big" both in a sense of it being new and in the actual sound quality itself. Eddy told Fogerty, "I knew we had to have something that counted, something that was big. . . . We did go for a big sound. I have to give a lot of credit to Lee Hazlewood. He mixed things for AM radio in those days so that they would come rockin' out of the radio."

One Hit After Another

The band's second release was the single "Rebel Rouser" in 1958. The record went gold in a relatively short amount of time, and Eddy's group soon earned the chance to perform on Dick Clark's *American Bandstand.* It was on this show that Eddy had an opportunity to launch another hit. Clark had asked the group if they would perform a song to close the show. Eddy reported in *Musician* that he said to Clark, "'Well, we could do "Ramrod," a thing I cut last year and never did anything with.' So we ran it down and Dick said, 'That's perfect, great.' So we did it to close the show, the credits. And Monday morning there was orders for 150,000 copies at the record company." And the orders kept coming in—up to 250,000 by Tuesday of that same week. "Fortunately," related Eddy to Mike Gormley in the *Detroit Free Press,* "we had the basic tracks recorded for the song so we finished them up and had the record out by Friday."

More hits followed for the hard-working Eddy, including "Cannonball," "Peter Gunn," and "40 Miles of Bad Road." The name for the latter hit came from a conversation Eddy overheard while attending a movie. He related in *Musician,* "We were standing in line to see a movie one day and just sort of monitoring the conversations around us, and we heard these old Texans talking about their evening before, how much fun it was. They were kidding each other and laughing and suddenly this guy says, 'Well, that girl you were with, boy, she wasn't so hot either.' And the other guy says, 'Well she was better 'n yours! Yours had a face like 40 miles of bad road.'" Eddy picked up on that last phrase immedi-

ately, realizing it would make a great title for a hit single, which it did in 1959.

Aimed for Movie Career

In 1960 Eddy was so popular that he was voted Number One Pop Personality by the *New Musical Express.* Change was in the air for him as he decided to split with Hazlewood and produce himself. He also launched an acting career, starring in the movie *Thunder of Drums* and the television series *Have Gun, Will Travel.* "All my life I've dreamed of being in motion pictures," he told the *Detroit News.* He also acted in and wrote the theme for *Because They're Young,* and wrote the theme for the 1961 release *Ring of Fire.*

While Eddy was earning fame on the screen, his self-produced efforts were going nowhere in the United States, although several of the singles he released in 1961 and 1962 scored steadily on the British Top 40. In 1962 he once again reunited with Hazlewood for "Dance With the Guitar Man," featuring backup by the all-female Rebellettes. Reaching number 12 on U.S. charts, the single was one of the last records to achieve success in the United States.

Eddy turned to touring and session work in the late 1960s, occasionally recording albums. None of the albums met with great success. He found, though, that he still had a popular base in England and Europe, and he ended up living in England for several years. Interviewed by the *Detroit Free Press* in 1970, Eddy commented: "I'm interested in commercial stuff and would like to have a hit. . . . I'm not trying to get rich now."

Repeatedly Attempted Comebacks

In 1975 he found success with the recording "Play Me Like You Play Your Guitar," which ended up in the Top Ten in England. He reemerged with "You Are My Sunshine" in 1978, with vocals by Willie Nelson and Waylon Jennings. And in 1986 he redid his famous "Peter Gunn" theme with Trevor Horn's Art of Noise.

Despite the relatively few years of his stardom, Eddy has had an inestimable impact on the rock music scene. Fogerty commented in *Musician* that "it's certainly my opinion that [Eddy] stood at the crossroads of rock 'n' roll and transformed things by putting the musician out front. . . . Duane came along and was a real musician and was in front." His guitar technique was so legendary that producers everywhere instructed musicians to "do Duane Eddy." Asked how he felt about influencing generations of musicians, Eddy commented in *Musician* that it "is an unexpected bonus. It makes me feel more important than I otherwise would. It's a confirmation, many years later, that it was the right thing. And we had no way of knowing at the time. We got confirmation in the fact that the records were hits. That's the first big joy. But after that it dies down. . . . Then suddenly somebody comes along and says, 'You started me in this business.'"

Selected discography

Have Twangy Guitar Will Travel, Jamie, 1959.
Especially for You, Jamie, 1959.
The Twang's the Thang, Jamie, 1960.
Songs of Our Heritage, Jamie, 1960.
A Million Dollars' Worth of Twang, Jamie, 1961.
Girls, Girls, Girls, Jamie, 1961.
A Million Dollars' Worth of Twang: Volume 2, Jamie, 1962.
In Person, Jamie, 1962.
16 Greatest Hits, Jamie, 1962.
Twistin' and Twangin', RCA, 1962.
Dance With the Guitar Man, RCA, 1962.
Best of Duane Eddy, RCA, 1965.
Pure Gold, RCA, 1965.
Twangy Guitar, London, 1970.
Movin' 'n' Groovin', London, 1970.
Duane Eddy Guitar Man, GTO, 1975.
Legend of Rock, Deram, 1975.

Duane Eddy Collection, Pickwick, 1978.
Greatest Hits of Duane Eddy, Ronco, 1979.
20 Terrific Twangies, RCA, 1980.
Duane Eddy, Capitol, 1987.

Also performed on singles "You Are My Sunshine," with Willie Nelson and Waylon Jennings, 1978, and "Peter Gunn," with The Art of Noise, 1986.

Sources

Books

Hardy, Phil and Dave Laing, *Encyclopedia of Rock*, Schirmer Books, 1987.
Rees, Dafydd, and Luke Crampton, *Rock Movers & Shakers*, ABC-CLIO, 1991.
The Rolling Stone Encyclopedia of Rock & Roll, edited by Jon Pareles and Patricia Romanowski, Rolling Stone Press/Summit Books, 1983.
Stambler, Irwin, *The Encyclopedia of Pop, Rock and Soul*, St. Martin's, 1989.

Periodicals

Detroit Free Press, August 28, 1970.
Detroit News, June 4, 1961.
Musician, November 1991.

—*Nancy Rampson*

Roy Eldridge

Jazz trumpeter, vocalist

When Otto Hardwick, a reed player with Duke Ellington's orchestra, gave Roy Eldridge the lasting nickname "Little Jazz," he was referring to Eldridge's physical stature, not his standing as a jazz performer. Although Eldridge's name may not be as familiar to the general public as those of fellow trumpeters Louis Armstrong and Dizzy Gillespie, his immense talent had a profound effect on the history of jazz. In addition to playing an important role in jazz's transition from the swing styles of the 1930s to the bebop styles of the 1940s and 1950s, Eldridge was an exceptional soloist in his own right. He combined a somewhat abrasive personality with a deep sensitivity and created a musical style that, as drummer Phil Brown told *Musician*'s Burt Korall, "went directly to the heart."

Korall described Eldridge as "a crucial link on trumpet between Armstrong's New Orleans-inflected 'hot jazz' and the bebop innovations Gillespie helped pioneer." The musical succession from Armstrong to Eldridge to Gillespie is audible on recordings; yet, seeing Eldridge as merely a transitional figure does him a great disservice, for he was one of the most gripping performers jazz has produced. Gary Giddins maintained in *Rhythm-a-ning: Jazz Tradition and Innovation in the 80s* that, of the trumpeters of his generation, "Eldridge was the most emotionally compelling, versatile, rugged, and far-reaching." He had a tone like no other, which Giddins described as holding "an urgent, human roughness that gave his music an immediacy of its own. You felt you could hear the sound start in the viscera and work its way through his small body, carving a path in his throat, and bursting forth in breathtaking release."

Eldridge first heard Armstrong in 1932, and he learned much from the trumpeter's sense of logic and climax. Unlike Armstrong, however, he played uptempo numbers with a passion and relentless energy that sometimes verged on the demonic; as Whitney Balliett described in *American Musicians: Fifty-Six Portraits in Jazz,* "He would work so hard and grow so excited that he would end up caroming around his highest register and sounding almost mad." However, though Eldridge was undoubtedly Gillespie's most important early influence—indeed, the younger musician's first recordings sound almost like a carbon copy of Eldridge's playing—he never completely assimilated the bebop techniques that Gillespie later used to such advantage, remaining at heart a swing-era player.

Deeply Influenced by Saxophone

Eldridge began playing drums at the age of six; he later learned to play the bugle, and then the trumpet, receiving some early training on that instrument from his brother Joe, a fine musician in his own right. As he became proficient on the trumpet, Eldridge turned for inspiration not just to brass players such as Rex Stewart and Red Nichols, but also to saxophonists, whose work he admired for its speed and fluidity. In fact he was given one of his first jobs—in a carnival—because he could play note-for-note saxophonist Coleman Hawkins's solo on Fletcher Henderson's recording of "The Stampede." Eldridge's fascination with sax playing would continue to be an important influence on his style; later he would come under the spell of such players as Lester Young and Chu Berry.

Eldridge formed his first band in Pittsburgh while he was still a teenager, using the pseudonym Roy Elliott. During the 1920s he played with several important groups, including Horace Henderson's Dixie Stompers and Zach White's band. In 1930 he moved to New York City, and soon carved out a niche for himself with many of Harlem's finest ensembles, including those led by Cecil Scott, Charlie Johnson, Teddy Hill, and Elmer Snowden. The trumpeter came to national prominence

in the mid-1930s, when he was a featured soloist with Fletcher Henderson's orchestra. In 1936 Eldridge began a two-year residency at Chicago's Three Deuces club, with an ensemble that included his brother Joe on alto sax. According to Stanley Dance in *The World of Swing,* Eldridge called this group, which was featured on a radio broadcast seven nights a week, "the best little band I ever had."

Wounded by Prejudice

During the 1940s Eldridge played with the ensembles of two important white band leaders, Gene Krupa and Artie Shaw. At a time when integration of musicians on the bandstand was still a subject of great controversy, Eldridge's presence in the brass section of these groups represented an important step forward. Yet, Eldridge himself had to face frequent humiliation from club owners and the managers of restaurants and hotels. A sensitive and proud man, this wounded Eldridge deeply, and the scars never entirely healed.

As an example, Eldridge once recalled an episode that took place at a club in San Francisco while he was on tour with Artie Shaw's orchestra. Having just played a successful job at a ballroom in Oakland, across the bay, he was excited about the upcoming performance, and showed up early. However, he found that, because he was black, he was not allowed in the front door, even though his name was on the marquee. Although he was eventually allowed to enter, he was so upset he couldn't perform. As he told *Musician*'s Korall, "I threw my mutes and things around; I began to cry. I knew it wasn't my fault. Finally I was told to take the evening off. And all I wanted to do was play my horn!"

In 1950 Eldridge went to Europe with a sextet that featured clarinetist Benny Goodman, tenor saxophonist Zoot Sims, and pianist Dick Hyman. Because of the relative lack of racial tensions in Europe and the immense appreciation that audiences there showed him, Eldridge decided to settle in Paris. He lived there for almost two years, during which he played, recorded, and wrote a music column for the *Paris Post.*

Returned to United States

After returning to New York in 1951, Eldridge made a highly acclaimed appearance at Old Stuyvesant Casino, and then spent much of the 1950s playing with Norman Granz's Jazz at the Philharmonic, an ensemble founded to present jazz performances in a concert setting. For two years he was a member of the group that accompanied singer Ella Fitzgerald; he also played briefly with Count Basie's orchestra in 1966.

In 1970 Eldridge began what was to become a ten-year run at Jimmy Ryan's, a club that featured Dixieland—a style of jazz playing that revived the instrumentation, repertory, and playing styles popular in jazz of the teens and the 1920s. Although many jazz fans viewed this type of music as archaic, Eldridge approached each evening's performance with typical enthusiasm and inventiveness.

A heart attack in 1980 brought Eldridge's run at Ryan's, as well as his trumpet playing career, to a close. Thereafter he performed only occasionally, usually as a singer, drummer and even pianist. Tired of the demanding life of a full-time musician, he began to spend more time at home with his wife, Vi, and focus on his hobbies of carpentry, radio engineering and electronics. Eldridge died in 1989, just three weeks after his wife.

Selected discography

After You've Gone (recorded in 1936, 1943-46), Decca Jazz, 1991.

Roy Eldridge at the Three Deuces, Chicago—1937, reissued, Jazz Archives, 1975.

Roy Eldridge at the Arcadia Ballroom—1939, reissued, Jazz Archives, 1973.

At Jerry Newman's (recorded in 1940), Xanadu.

Roy Eldridge and the Swing Trumpets (recorded in 1944), Mercury, 1987.

Roy and Diz, Clef, 1954.

The Urbane Jazz of Roy Eldridge and Benny Carter, Verve, 1955.

At the Opera House, Verve, 1957.

Tour de force, Verve, 1957.

The Nifty Cat (recorded in 1970), reissued, New World, 1986.

(With Paul Gonsalves) Mexican Bandit Meets Pittsburgh Pirate (recorded in 1973), Fantasy, 1986.

Happy Time (recorded in 1975), Fantasy/OJC, 1991.

The Art Tatum Group Masterpieces: Tatum/Eldridge, reissued, Pablo, 1975.

Roy Eldridge Four: Montreux '77, reissued, Fantasy/OJC, 1989.

All the Cats Join In, reissued, MCA, 1982.

Louis Armstrong—Roy Eldridge/Jazz Masterpieces, reissued, Franklin Mint Record Society, 1982.

Roy Eldridge: The Early Years, reissued, Columbia, 1982.

Little Jazz, Columbia Jazz Masterpieces, 1989.

Uptown, reissued, Columbia, 1990.

Hawkins! Eldridge! Hodges! Alive! At the Village Gate!, reissued, Verve, 1992.

The Best of Roy Eldridge, Pablo.

Loose Walk, Pablo.

Oscar Petersen and Roy Eldridge, Pablo.

Roy Eldridge, GNP Crescendo.

Sources

Books

Balliett, Whitney, American Musicians: Fifty-Six Portraits in Jazz, Oxford University Press, 1986.

Collier, James Lincoln, The Making of Jazz: A Comprehensive History, Dell, 1978.

Dance, Stanley, The World of Swing, Scribner's, 1974.

Giddins, Gary, Rhythm-a-ning: Jazz Tradition and Innovation in the 80s, Oxford University Press, 1985.

Gillespie, Dizzy, with Al Fraser, To Be or Not . . . To Bop: Memoirs, Doubleday, 1979.

Shapiro, Nat, and Nat Hentoff, The Jazz Makers: Essays on the Greats of Jazz, Rinehart, 1957.

Periodicals

Down Beat, February 4, 1971; May 1989.

Jazz Journal International, April 1989.

Musician, November 1987.

—Jeffrey Taylor

Danny Elfman

Composer

Danny Elfman's exotic collection of folk objects—ranging from Ecuadoran shrunken heads to Mexican Day of the Dead figures—has often inspired him in his musical creation of a dark, humorous, and fantastic world. Elfman has scored over 15 films, concocted numerous television themes, and until 1990 was writing songs and performing with the rock band Oingo Boingo. Despite his successes with film music, however, he is largely considered an amateur composer. He explained in *American Film,* "It is a generally accepted feeling within the music industry, of composers and would-be composers and wanna-be composers, that I don't write my own music, that I hire ghosts." But Elfman has successfully exorcised his ghosts with the orchestral works *Batman* and *Edward Scissorhands,* thus firmly establishing himself in the realm of contemporary film composers that includes giants like John Williams and Jerry Goldsmith.

In 1971 Elfman returned home to Los Angeles after a yearlong trip through Africa, where he had unearthed the musical roots for both his film work and the sound that would define his band, Oingo Boingo. Upon his return, Elfman's brother Richard asked him to join a theater ensemble called the Mystic Knights of the Oingo Boingo. The Mystic Knights performed a multimedia theatrical revue, initially in the streets, then moving on to more elaborate indoor shows. After eight years with the troupe, Richard redirected his efforts toward independent filmmaking, leaving Danny to form Oingo Boingo from the remaining Mystic Knights. The group had its first Top 40 hit in 1985 with the theme song from the film *Weird Science.* Despite his eventual triumph in Hollywood, Elfman continued to write songs for the group as well as perform guitar and percussion duties. All of Elfman's scores are orchestrated by Steve Bartek, Oingo Boingo's lead guitarist, who also assists Elfman in producing his soundtrack albums. Dividing his time between scoring and songwriting, Elfman nonetheless allowed in *American Film* that songs reach "people on a much more personal, direct level" than does orchestral music for film.

Piqued Pee-wee's Interest

Elfman composed his first score in 1980 for his brother's cult film *Forbidden Zone;* it included several songs by the Mystic Knights. Actor Paul Reubens—more popularly known as Pee-wee Herman—saw the film; it piqued his interest in acquiring a non-traditional composer for his project *Pee-wee's Big Adventure,* which was released in 1985. This became Elfman's first full orchestral score. He told *Keyboard* in 1987 that he

Born May 29, 1953 (some sources say 1955), near Amarillo, TX; married, two daughters.

Singer, songwriter, guitarist, and percussionist for group Oingo Boingo, 1979—. Composer of film scores, including *Pee-wee's Big Adventure*, Warner Bros., 1985; *Batman,* Warner Bros., 1989; and *Dick Tracy,* Buena Vista, 1990; and television themes, including *The Simpsons,* Fox-TV, and *Batman: The Animated Series,* Fox-TV. Contributor to soundtrack of film *Buffy the Vampire Slayer,* Twentieth Century Fox, 1992.

Awards: Grammy Award for best instrumental and Grammy Award nomination for best score, 1990, for *Batman;* Grammy Award nomination for best score, 1991, for *Dick Tracy.*

Addresses: *Home*—Santa Monica, CA. *Agent*—The Kraft Agency, Inc., 6525 Sunset Blvd., Ste. 407, Hollywood, CA 90028. *Management*—LA Personal Development, 1201 Larrabee, Penthouse 302, West Hollywood, CA 90069.

"really learned to write [music] on *Pee-wee's [Big] Adventure.* My scores aren't what you would call legit, but they communicate my ideas effectively, and ultimately that's what composition is all about."

Elfman learned how to communicate with an audience from some of the great soundtrack masters. He revealed to *Egg,* "As a kid I would see movies five, six, seven times if I liked them, and I learned early on that a lot of my favorite '50s and '60s fantasy films had wonderful music by Bernard Herrmann." As a teenager he "would go out at least three nights a week, see every Truffaut, every Fellini—Nino Rota's music became like second nature to me." His awareness at such a young age of the intimate relationship between a film's soundtrack and elements of mood and character made writing soundtracks a very personal endeavor. Composers like Rota, whose work includes the venerable *8 1/2* and *The Godfather,* and Bernard Herrmann, the genius behind the scores of both *Psycho* and *Citizen Kane,* are still his inspiration, and their styles are echoed in many of his works. In *Fanfare,* Elfman wrote of *Pee-wee's Big Adventure* that he "was looking for a type of music that was very innocent and light. Bringing in the Nino Rota element felt right for me. . . . I wanted to find something that immediately put [Pee-wee] over as something from another world living here." Herrmann's influence, too, is evident, particularly in the film's dream sequences.

Fruitful Collaborations With Burton

Pee-wee's Big Adventure marked Elfman's first collaboration with director Tim Burton, with whom he has enjoyed a strong partnership. His relationship with Burton began early on to resemble those of other filmmakers and their composers—Fellini and Rota, Hitchcock and Herrmann. Elfman told *Fanfare,* "Tim puts me into areas that are very challenging and fun to work with, and yet he allows me the creativity of figuring out how to make it come alive musically." Their second film together was 1988's *Beetlejuice.* Often cited as Elfman's finest work, the *Beetlejuice* score combines circus, calypso, and horror motifs to create a discordant musical montage that skillfully complements the comic film. "A funnier, more boldly innovative or more manic score would be virtually impossible to imagine. . . . Elfman's work is as joyous and rollicking as the film itself," wrote Frederic Silber in *Fanfare.*

Then, in 1989, Elfman and Burton collaborated on *Batman,* one of the most commercially successful movies of all time. Burton's tale of the Dark Knight was tailor-made for Elfman's dark, visionary style. The score earned the composer a Grammy nomination for best score and the prized statuette, for best instrumental, in 1990. In an interview with *Keyboard,* Elfman remarked that the visual imagery of the film helped him create the score, which is filled with driving percussion, energetic horns, and haunting organs. "As soon as I saw Gotham [the setting of the film], I heard the music," Elfman professed. "Tim and I had talked about doing a kind of darkly operatic and Romantic score. . . . I got my major thematic ideas right there, sitting in the theater and singing into this tape recorder the very first time I was seeing the movie." Once again, Elfman's musical sensibilities were easily wed to Burton's highly developed visual perceptions. *Keyboard* contributor Robert L. Doerschuk noted in 1989 that *Batman* could change the face of the movie soundtrack forever. "By writing a soundtrack that stands on its own as an album release *and* could challenge the *Star Wars* theme in pops concert programs, Elfman demonstrates that with sufficient talent and dedication . . . [he] can transcend the idiom formerly defined by the technology of his studio and write effectively for orchestra."

The composer's next film with Burton, 1990's *Edward Scissorhands,* produced a score that deftly evoked Burton's fairy-tale imagery. Elfman used a choral backdrop to develop a melancholic vision of the world, producing a work that many feel stands on its own while simultaneously enhancing the title character's feelings and expressions.

Approached for "Contemporary Score"

Between his ventures with Burton, Elfman composed for a wide range of directors and genres. In 1988 he scored *Wisdom,* a box-office bomb written, directed by, and starring Emilio Estevez. *Fanfare's* Silber wrote of Elfman's contribution, "Suspenseful, hypnotic, pulsating, dream-like, the score succeeds so admirably in every thematic aspect where the film failed so miserably." Also in 1988, Elfman composed scores for two comedies: *Hot to Trot* and *Big Top Pee-wee,* the follow-up to *Pee-wee's Big Adventure.* But the film Elfman considers a turning point is yet another 1988 offering, the box-office hit comedy *Midnight Run.* The composer noted in *Fanfare,* "Finally, after all those years, I was asked to do a 'contemporary' score." His next film, however, 1988's horror-comedy *Scrooged,* was a composer's nightmare: Most of his music was either buried in the film or not used at all.

The following year, two film projects, *Nightbreed* and *Darkman,* brought Elfman back to the genre he loves best—horror. Both scores featured shadowy themes combined with tribal chanting and dramatic overtures. Instead of taking the usual route—reviewing scripts to decide which film to score—Elfman sought out director/writers Clive Barker, the mastermind of *Nightbreed,* and Sam Raimi, father of *Darkman.* "I wanted very much to work with them, since I love horror," Elfman wrote in *American Film.* "So I've returned to the genre that inspired me in the first place."

Elfman's soundtrack for another 1990 film, *Dick Tracy,* directed by and starring Warren Beatty, used Gershwin-esque themes to conjure the 1930s-era setting of the Dick Tracy comic strip. The film earned Elfman a second Grammy nomination for best score. But by 1992, he had again changed directions, this time with the soundtrack for *Article 99,* the story of a Vietnam veteran's hospital. That score took a more traditional approach to film music but still featured Elfman's signature style. 1992 also found Elfman following up his *Batman* efforts with the score to Burton's *Batman Returns. Entertainment Weekly's* Ty Burr, for one, was unimpressed with the results. Asserting that Elfman had run out of ideas, Burr groused: "Here are the same windswept demon choirs, tinkling music boxes, Fellini carny music, and chic Wagnerian pooting that sounded so great in *Edward Scissorhands,* Elfman's peak. But like *Batman Returns* itself, this new score is neurotically hyperactive. It's as if Elfman, stumped for new material, simply opted to throw the old stuff at us faster and louder. That's fine if you're a punching bag. If not, not."

In addition to soundtracks, Elfman has composed several television themes for successful shows like Fox-TV's extremely popular animated *The Simpsons* and HBO's highly acclaimed *Tales From the Crypt.* These and other television and soundtrack themes were released in 1990 on a compilation album called *Music for a Darkened Theatre: Film and Television Music Volume One.*

Throughout his composition adventures, whether with Oingo Boingo, in film, or in television, the prolific Elfman has remained close to the origins of his fascination with the theatrical power of music. "Even now, the way I get around my lack of training and technique is by drawing on my having grown up in a world of movies," he told *Fanfare.* "Very often, when I'm not sure how to approach something, I say, 'How would I approach this if I were thirteen years old, sitting in a theater, and watching the movie?' In other words, what would make me come alive?" These instincts have, indeed, served him well, which has perhaps given him the confidence to branch out yet again, this time into screenwriting and directing. In January of 1992 *Entertainment Weekly* reported that Elfman was "developing several oddball projects, including an 'over-the-top' musical titled *The World of Jimmy Callicut* at Fox and 'a strange and stylized ghost story' he'll also direct called *Julian,* which Tim Burton is executive producing for Warner Bros."

Selected discography

With Oingo Boingo

Oingo Boingo (EP), IRS, 1980.
Only a Lad, A&M, 1981.
Nothing to Fear, A&M, 1982.
Good for Your Soul, A&M, 1984.
Dead Man's Party, MCA, 1986.
BOI-NGO, MCA, 1987.
Boingo Alive, MCA, 1988.
Skeletons in the Closet, A&M, 1988.
Dark at the End of the Tunnel, MCA, 1990.
Best O'Boingo, MCA, 1991.

Film scores

Pee-wee's Big Adventure/Back to School, Varese Sarabande, 1985.
Beetlejuice, Geffen, 1988.
Big Top Pee-wee, Arista, 1988.

Midnight Run, MCA, 1988.
Wisdom, Varese Sarabande, 1988.
Hot to Trot, 1988.
Scrooged, 1988.
Batman, Warner Bros., 1989.
Forbidden Zone, Varese Sarabande, 1990.
Darkman, MCA, 1990.
Dick Tracy, Sire, 1990.
Edward Scissorhands, MCA, 1990.
Nightbreed, MCA, 1990.
Article 99, Varese Sarabande, 1992.
Batman Returns, Warner Bros., 1992.
Sommersby, Warner Bros., 1993.
"March of the Dead Theme," *Army of Darkness,* Varese Sarabande, 1993.

Other

So-lo, MCA, 1985.
Music for a Darkened Theatre: Film and Television Music Volume One, MCA, 1990.

Sources

Books

Stambler, Irwin, *The Encyclopedia of Pop, Rock, and Soul,* St. Martin's, 1989.

Periodicals

American Film, February 1991.
Egg, December/January 1991.
Entertainment Weekly, January 24, 1992; July 24, 1992.
Fanfare, September/October 1988; May/June 1989; November/December 1989.
Keyboard, September 1987; October 1989.
New York Times, December 9, 1990.
Seventeen, August 1987.

—Debra Power

The English Beat

Rock band

The Beat, known as the English Beat in the United States to avoid confusion with the California pop group of the same name, was a prominent band in the ska revival movement in England in the early 1980s. Perhaps the most widely known and certainly the longest lived band associated with that movement, the Beat did not confine themselves to ska rhythms, but experimented with a variety of Latin and African beats and eventually incorporated more mainstream pop forms, such as the love ballad, into their repertoire.

Vocalist David Wakeling, guitarist Andy Cox, and classically trained bassist David Steele began playing a punk/rock mix in 1978. They were soon joined by Everett Morton, a West Indian who had drummed for Joan Armatrading. His addition of reggae and other Jamaican rhythms to the group's style, as well as the band's now biracial makeup, led to their identification as part of the ska revival.

As with other musical trends, such as the British Invasion in the mid-1960s, the ska revival borrowed heavily from black music, in this case, blue beat and reggae. Opposing the English skinhead movement, which endorsed racial intolerance, ska advocated racial unity. In the *Village Voice* Robert Christgau defined ska, sometimes referred to as 2-tone, as "left-liberal: an alternative to anarchistic punk rage and apocalyptic reggae mysticism that politicized power pop's nostalgia for limits in a context at once biracial and specifically English."

In March of 1979 the quartet played its first gig, opening for a punk group at a Birmingham club. Ranking Roger, the drummer for the headliner, began "toasting," or chanting over the songs, during the Beat's performance. The combination proved irresistible, and Ranking Roger joined as the group's second vocalist.

Debut Single a Hit

The Jamaican saxophonist Saxa joined the Beat to record their first single, a remake of Smokey Robinson's "Tears of a Clown." Saxa's experience, gained while playing with such renowned ska musicians as Prince Buster, Laurel Aitken, and Desmond Dekker, contributed to the instant success of the group's debut record. In Britain the single rose to Number Six on the pop charts, which perhaps influenced Saxa's decision to join the group permanently.

The group's next two releases, "Hands Off . . . She's Mine" and "Mirror in the Bathroom," hit the Top Ten in the U.K. The Beat released them on their own newly formed label, Go Feet, which they used for all of their subsequent singles and albums. Their first album, *I Just Can't Stop It,* came out in 1980 and quickly rose to Number Three in Britain.

I Just Can't Stop It firmly entrenched the group's identity as a ska band. Although the Beat relied on Jamaican rhythms and other island rhythm and blues techniques, they differed from other ska revivalists by raising the intensity of their music with punk. In *Rolling Stone* Milo Miles described their first album as "a rambunctious cluster of singles held together by tenor saxophonist Saxa's winning, authoritative blowing and a rhythm section . . . that cared more about adventure than duplicating antique reggae." The frenzied guitar in "Twist and Crawl" and the manic pace in "Click Click" set the tone for the album, where even the leisurely horns in "Tears of a Clown" were presented in a context of strain and tension. James Hunter in the *Village Voice* explained the appeal of this first album: "Two things made them winning beyond awesome technical accomplishment: their speed, which tended always to beat you across the room, and their heart—this great nervous band for the nervous world had feelings as insistent as its riffs."

Opened for Pretenders and Talking Heads

While the Beat's debut album was soaring up the charts, the group was touring Europe. David "Block-head" Wright accompanied them, eventually becoming a keyboardist for the group. In the fall of 1980 they began their first American tour, opening for the Pretenders and the Talking Heads. In 1981 the group released their second album, *Wha'ppen?,* to enthusiastic reviews. While popular reaction in the United States was lukewarm, the album went to Number Two in Britain. The group still employed some reggae, but they also experimented on this album with a variety of beats, from Motown to steel band rhythms.

Unlike *I Just Can't Stop It,* which was simply a collection of unrelated songs, *Wha'ppen?* was designed with each song as an integral part of the whole. Critics noted that the pacing of the album, with its building suspense, is less exuberant but more mature than that of *I Just Can't Stop It.* According to *Rolling Stone*'s Miles, "Except in sheer pep, *Wha'ppen?* marks an advance for the English Beat: truly complex love-and-jealousy tales, politics that are more keenly defined."

The group's third album, *Special Beat Service,* was not the chartbuster in England that the group's previous albums had been, although it was the group's most popular in the United States. The album moved into more mainstream pop territory, which perhaps explains its success in the United States. Love songs and pop ballads set the album's direction, although the Latin and African rhythms show the group's continued interest in experimenting with a variety of beats.

Shift in Musical Direction

Steele explained the group's shift in musical direction to *Musician:* "It has changed in that we all had similar musical interests when we first started, mainly punk and reggae, but now everyone's into totally different stuff. That's why you get different music from track to track on the new LP, and you'll probably get an even wider variety of differences on the next one. I still don't think we have the proper mix. We've always been searching for the right sound, and I don't think we've found it yet."

The Beat's search for a sound kept them alive longer than the other popular bands of the ska movement. Wakeling protested the group's label as a ska band to Bill Holdship of *Musician,* "Ska is a specific beat, and we've only had two or three songs out of something like forty that used the ska beat. . . . I think we mainly got labeled ska because people saw blacks and whites together." Wakeling, however, admits the group's affinity with the movement: "It did say something very strong about racial unity. . . . Although I sometimes get annoyed when people complain that the third Beat LP isn't a ska record, I still think it was an honor to have been involved with 2-tone."

In 1982 poor health forced Saxa to retire. His replacement, saxophonist Wesley Magoogan, previously a member of Helen O'Connor's band, earned Wakeling's approval because of his discipline as a musician. However, Wakeling's comment on Saxa's retirement to *Musician* writer Bill Holdship proved prophetic: "[Saxa] was one of the cornerstones [of the band], and the idea of losing someone that important had us worried that the whole thing might fall apart."

Special Beat Service was indeed the group's final album. Yet the group's exuberant mix of rhythms made them an important influence on the rock world in the 1980s. Early in the group's career, *Rolling Stone*'s Miles predicted, "The English Beat have an instant legend aura about them, weaving an eccentric path between black and white, calculation and craziness."

Selected discography

I Just Can't Stop It, Go Feet, 1980.

Wha'ppen?, Go Feet, 1981.
Special Beat Service, I.R.S., 1982.

Sources

Books

The Rolling Stone Encyclopedia of Rock & Roll, edited by Jon Pareles and Patricia Romanowski, Rolling Stone Press/Summit Books, 1983.
Stambler, Irwin, *The Encyclopedia of Pop, Rock and Soul,* St. Martin's, 1989.
Who's New Wave in Music: An Illustrated Encyclopedia, 1976-1982, edited by David Bianco, Pierian Press, 1985.

Periodicals

Musician, February 1983.
Rolling Stone, October 1, 1981; March 17, 1983.
Village Voice, October 21, 1981; December 7, 1982.

—Susan Windisch Brown

Eric B.
and Rakim

Rap duo

With their debut single "Eric B. Is President"/"My Melody," Eric B. and Rakim introduced themselves as a tough, frosty rap act devoid of gimmickry and hype. DJ Eric Barrier laid down funky, soulful, and occasionally spacey sounds to support the supple, powerful rhymes of rapper Rakim. Nelson George of the *Village Voice* declared Rakim the "master rapper of 1987 (damn near '86)." The duo followed these auspicious beginnings with a series of straightforward albums that largely ignored fashionable musical and cultural trends. *Reflex* magazine noted that such consistency "would translate into stylistic stagnation for anyone else. But hip-hop's supreme poet was always years ahead of his time." As Rakim himself told *Rolling Stone,* "We don't change. We make changes."

As the 1980s drew to a close and the 1990s brought an ever-widening mainstream audience to hip-hop music, rap began to separate into "schools": the "gangsta" sound of N.W.A., Ice-T and the Geto Boys; the "Native Tongues" psychedelic funk-rap of De La Soul and A Tribe Called Quest; the consciousness-raising of Public Enemy and Boogie Down Productions; and, of course, the highly staged pop rap of Hammer and Kriss Kross. Eric B. and Rakim, however, remained true to their own unique sound, described by *Rolling Stone's* Alan Light as "Rakim's cool, menacing delivery of intricate rhymes over Eric's subtly shifting beats." The *Voice's* George elaborated, revealing, "Rakim's intonation itself conjures wintry images of cold-blooded killers, chilly ghetto streets and steely-eyed hustlers. There's a knowing restraint in his voice that injects danger into even harmless phrases." A series of successful albums solidified Eric B. and Rakim's place at the top of their medium, despite a two-year hiatus between 1988 and 1990. With 1992's *Don't Sweat the Technique,* the pair showed no sign of slowing down. "The music Eric B. and Rakim make kicks because it sneaks into the ear like careless whispers before exploding on the brain like dynamite," wrote Havelock Nelson in his *Rolling Stone* review of *Sweat.* "Eric B.'s tracks are mellow and mean, while Rakim's lyrics are at once eloquent and threatening."

"Presidential" 1986 Debut

Eric Barrier grew up in Queens, New York, while William Griffin, alter ego of Rakim, was raised in Wyandach, Long Island, New York. Eric told *Melody Maker* that he grew up loving the music of versatile composer Quincy Jones and the Beatles. "I always wanted to play music and be up on the stage," he confessed. "I guess that's every little kid's fantasy, to be up on the stage with 20,000 people screaming. You see rock stars on televi-

For the Record. . .

Members include **Eric B.** (born Eric Barrier in New York City, c. 1965), DJ; and **Rakim** (born William Griffin in New York City, c. 1968), rapper.

Recording and performing duo, 1986—. Released debut single "Eric B. Is President"/"My Melody," 4th & B'Way Records, 1986; released album *Paid in Full,* 1987; signed with MCA Records, 1987, and released MCA debut *Follow the Leader,* 1988. Contributed to soundtracks of films *House Party II* and *Juice.* Eric B. founded Lynn Starr Productions and Mega Starr Management companies, 1990.

Awards: Gold records for *Paid in Full* and *Follow the Leader.*

Addresses: *Record company*—MCA Records, 70 Universal Plaza, Universal City, CA 91608; 1755 Broadway, 8th Floor, New York, NY 10019.

sion, like in the Beatles movies, and people screaming and ripping their clothes off and going crazy. That's always your dream. That person onstage, you always see it as being you." Griffin—who took the name Rakim when he became a Muslim—was only 18 when the duo hit the rap scene with "Eric B. Is President"/"My Melody." In 1987 the duo released their debut record, *Paid in Full,* on 4th & B'Way Records. *Melody Maker's* David Stubbs called it "an alienating, enticing album, a reminder of the endless possible permutations for hip hop." *Village Voice* contributor George reported, "Throughout *Paid in Full* there are moments when Rakim's voice and words, complemented by Eric B.'s dictionary of James Brown beats, make mesmerizing hip hop."

Indeed, Eric's "sampling" of Brown, the undisputed "King of Soul," helped begin one of rap's sturdiest trends. The single "I Know You Got Soul" was a case in point and one of the reasons the album went gold. In 1992 *Rolling Stone's* Nelson asserted that Rakim's claims in the song "defined the essence of great hip-hop." Fellow rappers Stetsasonic immortalized the duo and their contribution to the art form when they rhymed: "James Brown was old/ Till Eric and Rak came out with 'I Got Soul.'" As Rakim insisted in a *Rolling Stone* interview, "I don't think we were the first ones to use James Brown, but we were the first to use it right." Eric pointed out to *Melody Maker* that unlike other rap acts, "people see our group as a unity. I'm more than just a DJ, just somebody putting on records. Maybe in other groups people don't see the DJ as having any significance at all but, in our group, I'm more of a figure." By

way of illustration, he also revealed, "I always said to Rakim, the money should always be split 50-50. If we're partners we're partners and friends all the way through."

Moved to Major Label

Eric B. and Rakim scored again with their sophomore effort, *Follow the Leader.* Released in 1988 on MCA Records, this album went gold as well. *Melody Maker* dubbed it "seminal" and "superb." Vince Aletti of the *Village Voice* observed, "*Follow the Leader* is powerful not just because Rakim's boasting rocks so hard but because it's so convincing. Fueled by a mixture of arrogance, anger, wit, and brilliance, he raps like a man on fire." Aletti further noted that Eric provided "a sound that leads rap back into left field rather than further into the pop mainstream," capturing "hiphop's mood of apprehensive exhilaration, the excitement of peering over the edge of oblivion, the delusion of being totally in control." Earlier in the year, however, control of Eric B. and Rakim as an act was disputed in court. According to *Variety,* Zakia Records and Profile Records both sued MCA, claiming to have signed prior agreements with the act. Zakia and Profile alleged that MCA had urged Eric B. and Rakim to breach their previous agreements. Nonetheless, the duo remained with MCA, leaving the battle to the label's legal department.

The two years that elapsed before the release of their next album led many to believe that Eric B. and Rakim were history. Despite the recording lapse, the two were indeed busy; in 1989 they appeared on Jody Watley's Top Ten single "Friends," and January of 1990 saw Eric founding two companies dedicated to new talent, Lynn Starr Productions and Mega Starr Management. Still, the demand for innovation and constant need for visibility is particularly steep in hip hop, and many worried that the duo wouldn't recover from such a long hiatus. It was even rumored that Rakim was in prison for selling cocaine. "There were a lot of setbacks," the rapper told *Rolling Stone's* Light. "My father passed, one of the kids who was helping us make the music passed, then there were a lot of problems at the studio."

Rhythm Too Hard for Radio

Finally, in 1990, *Let the Rhythm Hit 'Em* hit the stores. James Bernard of the *Village Voice* noted that the pair's "vocal and instrumental nuances threaten to whiz past you, unless you drop everything to listen hard. Like [metal hitmakers] Metallica, the focus and fun are in the technical proficiency." Mark Coleman's *Rolling Stone* review insisted that the duo's traditional approach was no "gold-chain throwback" but a way of "upholding the Seventies funk canon and advancing rap's original verbal mandate." Even so, Coleman admired the group's versatility: "Masters of their appointed tasks, Rakim and DJ Eric B. are also formal innovators. They both can riff and improvise like jazzmen, spinning endless variations on basic themes and playing off each other's moves with chilly intuition. The resulting music is as stark, complex and edgy as Rakim's stone-cold stare on the album cover." *Let the Rhythm Hit 'Em* concluded with the track "Set 'Em Straight," on which Rakim explained that he was never imprisoned—but stated, "If I go to jail it won't be for selling keys/ It'll be for murdering MC's." Rakim told *Reflex* that *Rhythm* "was too motherf——ing hard" for radio stations, and that the record label "was like, 'Yo, your shit is slamming, but you don't get radio.'" The rapper admitted that he toned down his material somewhat on the pair's next album, though one listen put to rest any worry that he had streamlined his concerns.

When *Rolling Stone* contributor Nelson once called the group's sound "cinematic," he wasn't kidding. Eric B. and Rakim sent MCA a seven-song tape while working on their next album, and the label selected "What's On Your Mind" for the soundtrack of the film *House Party II*. Rakim was also approached by noted hip-hop producer Hank Shocklee and asked to contribute a song to the soundtrack of the film *Juice*. Shocklee told *Pulse!* he thought of Rakim as "one of those people who doesn't like anything," but in this instance the producer was pleasantly surprised. After viewing the film, Rakim wrote "Know the Ledge," a tense, jazzy song about the perils of gang warfare. The tune became the *Juice* theme, and a video of Rakim and Eric performing it was interspersed with clips from the movie.

"Know the Ledge" also appeared on Eric B. and Rakim's 1992 album *Don't Sweat the Technique*. "The title track, like almost all of the other cuts on the album," wrote Dimitri Ehrlich in *Pulse!*, "is steady, mid-tempo and extremely tasteful." The record included the relentless boasting of "The Punisher" and an unorthodox take on U.S. military involvement in the Persian Gulf called "Casualties of War." *Sweat* "activates the mind," Nelson proclaimed, calling it "erotic, playful, violent, dramatic, funky, jazzy and definitely dope."

Hip-hop may have changed since Eric B. and Rakim emerged in 1986, but the duo have stuck with their original vision. Even so, Eric's inventive repertoire of sounds and Rakim's thoughtful, ferociously versatile rhyming remain the standard against which most rap is measured. "We try to give people more than just rhymes, something they can take home and use for themselves in everyday life," Rakim told *Rolling Stone*. For his part, Eric—normally the silent one—couldn't help trumpeting the pair's achievements in a *Melody Maker* interview: "People say we got a strong style, strong bass, strong vocal, strong feeling. Nobody can do what we do best, nobody can take our place. People already say our albums are legendary, they say our albums are like rap archives."

Selected discography

"Eric. B. Is President"/"My Melody" (single), 4th & B'Way, 1986.
Paid in Full (includes "I Know You Got Soul"), 4th & B'Way, 1987.
Follow the Leader, MCA, 1988.
(Contributors) Jody Watley, "Friends," *Larger Than Life*, MCA, 1989.
Let the Rhythm Hit 'Em (includes "Set 'Em Straight"), MCA, 1990.
(Contributors) *House Party II* (soundtrack; "What's on Your Mind"), MCA, 1992.
(Contributors) *Juice* (soundtrack; "Know the Ledge"), MCA, 1992.
Don't Sweat the Technique (includes "What's On Your Mind," "Know the Ledge," "The Punisher" and "Casualties of War"), MCA, 1992.

Sources

Melody Maker, September 12, 1987; June 25, 1988; July 30, 1988; August 6, 1988; August 11, 1990.
Pulse!, July 1992.
Reflex, October 1992.
Rolling Stone, August 23, 1990; October 18, 1990; July 9, 1992.
Variety, February 17, 1988.
Village Voice, August 25, 1987; July 26, 1988; October 16, 1990.

Additional information for this profile was obtained from MCA Records publicity material, 1992.

—Simon Glickman

Lita Ford

Singer, guitarist

"**R**ock and roll is basically a man's world," guitarist and vocalist Lita Ford explained in *People.* "You have to play, sing and shake your ass onstage—and not be afraid to let your make-up run." Once a bandmate of Joan Jett in the 1970s all-female rock band the Runaways, Ford has led her own band—besides her, all men—since 1983. She was the first woman to appear on the cover of *Hit Parader* after the publication became a heavy metal magazine, and was the first woman in two decades to be inducted into *Circus* magazine's Hall of Fame. Winner of several Best Female Performer magazine polls, including *Metal Edge* and *Guitar,* she is considered the foremost female guitarist in the macho world of heavy metal. Karen Schoemer surmised in the *New York Times* that Hard Rock Queen Lita Ford survives "the male-dominated metal world by simultaneously fulfilling the stereotypes of both sexes."

Ford chose her profession, aware of its solitary nature. "I don't know why there are so few women metal acts," she divulged to Peter Watrous in the *New York Times.* "It's just something that women don't do. Not that they're encouraged, because, face it, it's not a feminine industry. Hard rock isn't a woman's type of music or job. But they love listening to it, and I play a lot of songs that reflect the fact that I think like a woman, not like a man."

Born in England, Ford grew up in Long Beach, California. Her mother, Lisa, a dietary supervisor at a local hospital, encouraged her to develop musical talent. When Ford was 11 years old, she began guitar lessons. Immediately upon playing the guitar, she wrote her first song. Her mother recalled in *People,* "It was a fancy Spanish piece. I loved it." The discovery of Jimi Hendrix records caused the adolescent Ford to alter her musical course. She listened to the music of similar performers, including the bands Deep Purple and Led Zeppelin.

As a teenager, Ford was invited to join the Runaways as a guitarist. The novelty of a rock band composed entirely of women, coupled with the talents of the band and lead singer Joan Jett, made the group successful in the era of bands that included the Clash, Blondie, and the Sex Pistols. Influenced by her idol Jimi Hendrix's solo act, Ford left the Runaways in the early 1980s. She told *Teen* that she "wanted to be able to sing and play as well as any man can sing and play."

Fought for Place in Male-Dominated Genre

While Ford studied voice, she struggled to support herself working at a gas station and selling perfume. "I like money," Ford revealed in *People.* "It sucks when you don't have a job." She shared an apartment with future Mötley Crüe bass player Nikki Sixx in Los Angeles, where the two dined mostly on macaroni and cheese. A fitness instructor at a gym before her career gained momentum, Ford endured snubs from male metal guitarists. Chris Holmes, who was one of her boyfriends and a guitarist for the band W.A.S.P., told *People,* "She doesn't like guys to say chicks shouldn't play guitar. She plays better than 90 percent of the guys I know."

The influence of the Runaways lingered in Ford's debut album *Out for Blood.* Ralph Novak stated in *People* during the early 1980s that Ford exhibited "the same brash, steel-edged approach to rock 'n' roll and the Jett black outlook on romance." Impressed with her first solo record, Jon Pareles wrote in *Mademoiselle* that Ford "backs up her commands with the crunch and thud of heavy metal. It's a familiar pose, but Ford knows how to make it convincing." Her second album, *Dancin' on the Edge,* made with drummer Randy Castillo, keyboardist Aldo Nova, and bassist Hugh McDonald, contains the scores "Dressed to Kill," "Lady Killer," and "Take the $ and Run." Novak wrote that the songs convey "the general idea that we're not talking syrupy, lovey-dovey stuff here." Although Novak called Ford "a first-class rock guitar player," he pegged her in 1984 as playing with a "thoughtful, light-metal sort of touch."

Became a Smash Success

In 1986 Ford's career soared upon the release of her third album, *Lita.* The LP, which went platinum, show-cased two Top Ten songs, including the gold single "Close My Eyes Forever" and the popular "Kiss Me Deadly." Sixx and Lemmy Kilmister of Motorhead worked with Ford on the soundtrack, and Ozzy Osbourne joined her on the duet "Close My Eyes Forever." Critical response was enthusiastic. Although *Stereo Review* stated her lyrics ranged "from the vapid to the incomprehensible," the magazine credited Ford for her "inspired solos." *Teen* postulated that Ford stood "alone in her field," while *Guitar Player* wrote that Ford "turns in the performance of her career." In *People* Novak called her "a little old for [the] dopey vulgarity" he saw in the album's lyrics, but praised Ford's "instinct for abandon" that "often produces a positively charged variety of runaway rock." Novak summarized: "Anyone in the market for hard rock modulated by a feminine sensibility might find this record a rewarding challenge."

Her next release, *Stiletto,* solidified Ford's image "with the kind of 'nasty girl' tunes her followers expect," wrote the *Wilson Library Bulletin* in 1990. The album, which includes the song "Lisa" that gives homage to Ford's mother, lacked the critical acceptance of *Lita. Guitar Player* asserted the album was drab and contrived. "Sure, Ford has an undeniable spark of what it takes to attain MTV guitarstardom, but her moments of guitar glory suffocate beneath a morass of misdirection." Although Kim Neely stated in *Rolling Stone* that the album struck "a safer balance between talent and titillation," the critic objected to Ford's persona. "If this guitar-slinging Goldilocks ever stops sabotaging her inventiveness with coy sexual innuendo," wrote Neely, "she will give her skeptical male counterparts a raucous run for their money."

Accused of Making "Formula Pop"

When Ford followed *Stiletto* with the album *Dangerous Curves,* music critic Watrous noted in 1991 that the "title may or may not refer to her figure, which is usually a prominent part of her marketing plan." *Entertainment Weekly* critic Janiss Garza regretted that Ford's albums since *Lita* appeared to "bow down to too-slick formula pop." Garza contended that *Dangerous Curves* revealed that "the struggle for Ford's musical soul continues. When she sticks to her fierce roots, as she does on 'Larger Than Life' and 'Hellbound Train,' the brazen fire of her singing and playing almost busts through the glossiness to recapture her long-dormant raw power. Almost, but not quite." *Billboard* panned the album's title as a misnomer, declaring that "Ford's ultrasafe MTV ready rock is anything but dangerous."

Critical rebuff will not dissuade heavy metal star Lita Ford from making more albums. She has already survived the test of hard rock audiences. Ford divulged to Watrous, "If you're good and can hold your own, they like you. If I was terrible, they'd throw things at me and I would throw them right back. . . . Not any more so much, but I've had situations where the audience will try and see if I'll crack. They'll yell obscenities at me. You just deal with it, it's no big deal. I'm not going to cry and run off stage or anything."

Selected discography

Out for Blood, Mercury.
Dancin' on the Edge (includes "Dressed to Kill," "Lady Killer," and "Take the $ and Run"), Polygram.
Lita (includes "Close My Eyes Forever" and "Kiss Me Deadly"), RCA, 1986.
Stiletto, RCA/Dreamland, 1990.
Dangerous Curves (includes "Larger Than Life" and "Hellbound Train"), RCA, 1991.

Best of Lita Ford, RCA, 1992.

Sources

Billboard, November 30, 1991.
Entertainment Weekly, November 8, 1991.
Guitar Player, May 1988; August 1990.
Mademoiselle, August 1983.
New York Times, November 20, 1991; November 26, 1991.
People, June 11, 1984; February 15, 1988; May 2, 1988.
Rolling Stone, August 9, 1990.
Stereo Review, June 1988.
Teen, September 1988.
Variety, March 23, 1992.
Wilson Library Bulletin, September 1990.

—*Marjorie Burgess*

Robert Fripp

Guitarist, producer, educator

"Find the new." This phrase characterizes Robert Fripp, guitarist extraordinaire whose career has been a strobe-light session of brilliant exposure and self-imposed retreats. Fripp leapt into public consciousness in 1969 as guitarist for King Crimson, the inventive assemblage that blended jazz and classical orchestration with rock rhythms on their first release, *In the Court of the Crimson King*. The record went gold, and Fripp's biographer, Eric Tamm, insists that the first generation of King Crimson continues to exert tremendous influence on rock and helped to launch "several musical movements, among them heavy metal, jazz-rock fusion, [and] progressive rock."

Fripp remains best known for his role as guiding spirit of the four incarnations of King Crimson that appeared intermittently from 1969 to 1984. Yet throughout the 1980s Fripp served as dazzling soloist, producer of Peter Gabriel, Talking Heads, and other talents, and sessions player for and/or colleague to rock innovators Brian Eno, former Police guitarist Andy Summers, and pop star David Bowie. He also found time to explore dance-club music with the League of Gentlemen and, between 1985 and 1991, found and lead the Guitar Craft school, which trained 700 students, some of whom appeared in the school's acoustic ensemble, the League of Crafty Guitarists.

Through these endeavors Fripp opened rock's frontiers to classical music, jazz, avant-garde electronics, and worldbeat influences while enhancing his reputation as rock intellectual. *Guitar World* writer Bill Milkowski dubbed Fripp "the Mr. Spock of rock," and *Rolling Stone* critic Mark Dery dryly remarked that "Robert Fripp . . . makes music for would-be Mensa members." Many Fripp projects, in fact, can be described as brainy, and his work has received consistently mixed reviews. In 1991 *Guitar Player* reviewer Andy Widders-Ellis praised Fripp's "intelligent lyrics, odd meters, highly-crafted guitar parts, and weird processed sounds [that] make for superb progressive rock." But a year earlier *Melody Maker's* Simon Reynolds had panned some of King Crimson's early work as "dated . . . a baroque'n'roll calamity . . . scrofulous, overwrought improvisation."

"Somewhat of an Enigma"

Some observers feel that Fripp has used his intellect as a defense; from his podium in *Musician, Player and Listener,* and *Guitar Player* magazines and in record liner notes, he has espoused his musical philosophies, attacked music industry "dinosaurs," and promoted his Guitar Craft school. While such efforts have kept Fripp

For the Record. . .

Born in 1946 in Wimborne Minster, Dorset, England; father owned a real-estate business; married Toyah Willcox (a singer and actress). *Education:* Attended real-estate management program at Bournemouth College.

Guitarist, producer, educator. With drummer Michael Giles and bassist Peter Giles, recorded *The Cheerful Insanity of Giles, Giles and Fripp,* Deram, 1968; member of rock band King Crimson, 1969-1984; toured with Peter Gabriel, 1977; performed and recorded with the League of Gentlemen, early 1980s, and the League of Crafty Guitarists and Sunday All Over the World, early 1990s. Session player on recordings by Blondie, David Bowie, Brian Eno, Flying Lizards, Gabriel, Andy Summers, David Sylvian, Talking Heads, and Toyah Willcox. Producer of recordings by Gabriel, Daryl Hall, the Roches, and Keith Tippet, among others. Student and innovator of plectrum (picking) guitar technique; founded, 1985, and led school Guitar Craft, Charles Town, WV, and Cranbourne, England, 1985-1991. Contributor to periodicals, including "Guitar Craft" column in *Guitar Player,* 1989-90.

Addresses: *Record distributor*—Caroline Records, 114 West 26th Street, New York, NY 10001.

in the public eye, he also has interrupted his musical career for concentrated periods of self-examination and spiritual development. It's little wonder that *Robert Fripp* author Tamm tagged him as "somewhat of an enigma."

Although Fripp began performing at 14, his first success was in 1967, with a little-known psychedelic rock novelty act that included drummer Michael Giles and bassist Peter Giles. After the flop of the band's 1968 album *The Cheerful Insanity of Giles, Giles, and Fripp,* the trio dissolved. Michael Giles and Fripp, however, decided to further explore their musical alliance. They formed King Crimson in November of 1968 with bassist Greg Lake (who would later form Emerson, Lake, and Palmer), composer and multi-instrumentalist Ian McDonald (who would go on to a career with Foreigner), and lyricist Peter Sinfield.

Tamm chronicled in Fripp's biography how the musicians allowed their songs to evolve, inviting inspiration through collaborative improvisation—a method Fripp has adopted as his guiding modus operandi. Although he consistently maintained that King Crimson was primarily a band for the stage and not the studio, performances led to the release in October of 1969 of *In the Court of the Crimson King,* which enjoyed more than

500,000 in sales. Almost half of the album's songs, including Fripp's compositions "Twentieth Century Schizoid Man" and "Epitaph," continued to appear on Crimson compilations released as much as two decades later.

First King Crimson Short-Lived

The first King Crimson was short-lived, disbanding the same year as their performing debut. Fripp later wrote that he was crushed but determined to carry on the Crimson project. The band reformed featuring a shifting roster of musicians from reed player Mel Collins and pianist Keith Tippet to bassists Lake, Gordon Haskell, or Boz Burrell and drummers Mike Giles, Andy McCulloch, or Ian Wallace. Fripp remained the group's guitarist and composed or co-wrote many of Crimson II's songs.

Between tours the second King Crimson released four albums: 1970's *In the Wake of Poseidon* and *Lizard,* 1971's *Islands,* and the live *Earthbound,* from 1972. *In the Court of the Crimson King* and *Poseidon* are Fripp's only recordings to hit the *Billboard* Top 40; the everwilder experiments of *Lizard* and *Islands* mystified many fans. When critics lauded or damned these recordings for their ambitious/pretentious, daring/jarring mixes of orchestral music, rock, and jazz, Fripp shrugged—he was exploring rock's frontiers. As he later told *Musician, Player and Listener's* Vic Garbarini, "Since rock music is for me the most mobile of the musical forms, one can, under the general banner of rock music, play in fact any kind of music whatsoever."

In light of Crimson II's mixed reception, it was no surprise that between 1973 and 1974 a new, third King Crimson appeared. It was comprised of Fripp, Yes drummer Bill Bruford—he takes second to Fripp in Crimson longevity—and bass player John Wetton, also known for his work with Uriah Heep and Asia. This trio was supplemented by string and Mellotron player David Cross and percussionist Jamie Muir. Sharply contrasting the increasingly mellow Crimson II, the new band offered a driving, almost heavy metal sound, kicked to overdrive by Fripp's power chords and Bruford's assertive rhythms. The rock press couldn't ignore the disparity between the old Crimsons and the new band's output on their 1973 recording *Larks' Tongues in Aspic,* as well as the 1974 releases *Starless and Bible Black* and *Red.* Asked by *Rolling Stone's* Cameron Crowe to clarify the band's intentions, Fripp replied, "I'm not interested in being pegged down with narrow definitions . . . as soon as one defines, one limits."

Collaborated With Eno

From 1972 to 1974 Fripp defied other rock boundaries in conspiracy with synthesizer player and sound-treatment wizard Brian Eno, of Roxy Music fame. Their records *No Pussyfooting* and *Evening Star,* released in 1973 and 1975, respectively, can be viewed as lab notes on the use of the signal loop and layering technologies that Fripp later refined with his improvised "Frippertronics." Crimson production work also engaged Fripp at the time; he edited the band's live recordings *Earthworks* and *USA,* as well as Fripp, Bruford, and Wetton's *Starless and Bible Black.* Fripp's production of *Starless* was so subtle that few critics noted that the "live recording" was enhanced with studio touches.

During the summer of 1974 Fripp took the first of his hiatuses from rock. "[An] accumulation of doubts and powerful personal experiences had led Fripp to a position when he felt compelled to disband King Crimson," Tamm wrote. Fripp wound up his affairs and relocated to Sherborne, England, where he installed himself at the Academy for the Harmonious Development of Man. There he studied for ten months under John G. Bennett, a disciple of mystic George Gurdjieff. Notoriously tight-lipped with interviewers, Fripp has issued few public statements about his stay at the Academy. Its monkish surroundings were most likely ideal, however, to the rock guitarist who told *Musician* in 1984, "Me and a book is a party. Me and a book and a cup of coffee is an orgy." After this spiritual sojourn, Fripp remained in retreat for two more years, enticed to perform only on Brian Eno's 1975 outing *Another Green World* and his *Before and After Science,* of 1977.

That year was one of a resurgent Fripp's most productive. He inched his way back into rock with session work on Peter Gabriel's first solo album after the singer's departure from Genesis. Fripp impressed Gabriel so much that he was invited to produce and perform on Gabriel's second solo recording and to share the stage during a 1977 tour. Fripp further shattered his self-imposed isolation by moving from England to New York City, where the punk and new wave musicians of the seminal club CBGB were assailing the corporate music industry. Here Fripp took up development of the tape-loop technology he'd begun exploring with Eno, formerly christening the system "Frippertronics." In 1977 Eno and David Bowie coaxed Fripp into a studio in Berlin, where his session work enlivened several songs on Bowie's *Heroes.*

Developed "Frippertronics"

From Berlin Fripp joined singer Daryl Hall, of Hall and Oates, in New York and produced an album so removed from Hall's popular blue-eyed soul that RCA Records and Hall's handlers refused to release it. Fripp nonetheless fought to get the disc into stores, and *Sacred Songs* finally reached the public in 1980. In defending *Sacred Songs* Fripp was actually defending Frippertronics, which made its recording debut on Hall's album. In a 1986 *Guitar Player* article, Tom Mulhern described Frippertronics as a system that allowed Fripp to improvise "with himself using a pair of tape recorders, his pedalboard, and a variety of guitars." Frippertronics inspired Fripp to begin a new era in his musical development and a period of great activity in the music industry.

Improvisation is one of Fripp's musical obsessions, and Frippertronics enabled him to probe its potential. Using tape recorders, Fripp could lay down a musical line, loop it through a tape replay, and improvise over his

> *"I'm not interested in being pegged down with narrow definitions. As soon as one defines, one limits."*

own playing. The method came to full bloom with *Exposure,* the guitarist's first solo recording, released in 1979. Predictably, critics greeted the LP with ambivalence. Even Tamm—usually sympathetic to Fripp—commented "*Exposure* gels as a whole but not in its parts." Tamm conceded, however, that perhaps Frippertronics was most exciting at Fripp's 1979 live dates.

These concerts and Frippertronics were actually part of a bigger project that Fripp tagged "The Drive to 1981," in which he mixed Frippertronics with another of his inventions, "Discotronics"—dance music with a cerebral edge; Fripp even coined the term "Barbertronics," to describe his guitar work at London's Virgin Records store, where he was accompanied by a beautician cutting hair. "Drive" it was; Fripp whirled like a dervish—granting interviews; recording and releasing the dual Frippertronics/Discotronics works *God Save the Queen/Under Heavy Manners* and *Let the Power Fall: An Album of Frippertronics*; pumping Frippertronics in a 72-date 1979 tour; and publishing articles in *Musician, Player and Listener.* Aside from all this, there was Fripp's session work with Talking Heads, David Bowie, Flying Lizards, the Screamers, and Janis Ian. Plus, Fripp produced the first two recordings of the folk-feminist trio of sisters called the Roches.

Frippertronics/Discotronics was further synthesized in 1980 when Fripp spawned the League of Gentlemen, a dance band featuring XTC organist Barry Andrews (later of Shriekback), bassist Sarah Lee (who would graduate to Gang of Four), and drummer Johnny Toobad. Their 77 performance dates in 1981 resulted in *Robert Fripp and the League of Gentlemen,* released the following year.

Fourth Incarnation of the Crimson King

The League's dance music spurred Fripp to regenerate King Crimson. Late in 1980 he sought out veteran Crimson drummer Bill Bruford, who had spent the 1970s hybridizing progressive rock with Genesis and on solo projects. Bruford and Fripp fleshed out their troupe with noted guitarist Adrian Belew and bassist/Chapman stick player Tony Levin. Their goal: to compose improvised dance-club music that pieced together cutting-edge influences from art-rock, mysticism, minimalism, and new wave.

Introduced on the 1981 King Crimson album *Discipline,* these ideas were embellished with worldbeat touches and Frippertronics on 1982's *Beat* and *Three of a Perfect Pair,* from 1984. Some critics greeted these efforts with superlatives. *Guitar Player* dubbed Fripp's work of this period "exciting adventurism"; *Rolling Stone* seconded that assessment with "a marvel of control and technique." Others reviewers, however, complained of a cerebral chill that undercut the music's passion—even at King Crimson IV live shows. One 1984 concert, in fact, was chastened by *New York Times* contributor John Rockwell as "cool, careful, and bit too calculated." *Billboard* critic Ethlie Ann Vare seemed to concur, tagging the concert "an IQ test" conducted by "four certified musical geniuses."

Tamm suggested that for Fripp, the collaboration of these great musical minds degenerated into a clash of "egotistical aspirations. . . . Clearly, by 1984, Fripp's heart was already elsewhere." He turned to Police guitarist Andy Summers, with whom Fripp released the collaborative recordings *I Advance Masked,* from 1982, and 1984's *Bewitched.* By the mid-1980s, though, Fripp had devoted himself to teaching.

Founded Guitar Craft School

With the disbanding of the fourth King Crimson, Fripp once again withdrew from the rock stage to renew his ties with his guru, John G. Bennett—only this time, he landed not in a monastic cell but in the seminar rooms of the American Society for Continued Education in Charles Town, West Virginia. There Fripp founded Guitar Craft. As Joao Botelho da Silva wrote in *The Christian Science Monitor,* Guitar Craft represented "a whole new way of approaching the guitar, including a new tuning, a precise study of how to play with a pick, and underneath the technical details, something of a way of life." Between 1985 and 1991 more than 700 students attended the guitar master's residential seminars in the U.S., UK, and Europe. Fripp proteges were treated to a regimen of daily individual and group guitar lessons, instruction in relaxation, meditation, and concentration techniques, discussions of musicology, and practice.

Like other Fripp endeavors, Guitar Craft evolved over time. Fripp nurtured its growth not only through teaching but by popularizing his pedagogies and philosophies through interviews or in his *Guitar Player* "Guitar Craft" columns published from 1989 to 1990. Eventually Guitar Craft became a complex enterprise engendering instructional monographs and an informal network of "Crafties" linked by newsletter, as well as the all-acoustic performing ensemble the League of Crafty Guitarists.

Five Crafty Guitarist recordings were issued between 1986 and 1991, 1988's *Get Crafty, I* and the following year's *Show of Hands* deemed the most important. As was expected, they garnered mixed reviews, as did Crafty Guitarist concerts. A *Variety* reporter perched firmly on the fence while describing a March, 1990, show as "viscerally and technically appealing . . . achieving a sort of terrible beauty . . . but one wonders what kind of career can be ahead for Robert Fripp clones." *Down Beat*'s Art Lange, for his part, condemned the ensemble's 1990 Victoriaville, Quebec, Musique Actuelle performance as "the fest's biggest flop."

Such notices perhaps prompted Fripp to entrust Guitar Craft to other hands in 1991. As of 1992, his income reportedly came not from music or teaching, but from real estate. Nonetheless, Fripp occasionally surfaced with new recordings, including collaborations with his wife, singer Toyah Willcox, and the ephemeral band Sunday All Over the World, whose single recording, *Kneeling at the Shrine,* was issued in 1991. Fripp also renewed his collaboration with Brian Eno, providing session work for Eno's 1992 release *Nerve Net.*

By 1993 Fripp's principal musical pursuit appeared to be management of the King Crimson properties. He remastered the studio recordings of all four generations of King Crimson; the work, marketed in single albums or sets, was widely available in 1992. A three-disc compilation of previously unreleased King Crimson concert recordings from 1973 and 1974 also made its way into record stores in 1993.

Although Fripp retained his low profile, the continued availability and sheer range of King Crimson and Fripp solo material perpetuates his reputation among rock audiences. His persistent record of innovation also keeps him in the back of critics' minds. As Garbarini noted in *Musician, Player and Listener*, "If there's any one thing that's predictable about Robert Fripp, it's that he'll consistently do the unexpected."

Selected discography

With King Crimson

In the Court of the Crimson King: An Observation by King Crimson, 1969, reissued, Editions EG, 1989.
In the Wake of Poseidon, 1970, reissued, Editions EG, 1989.
Lizard, 1970, reissued, Editions EG, 1989.
Islands, 1971, reissued, Editions EG, 1989.
Earthbound, Editions UK, 1972.
Larks' Tongues in Aspic, Editions EG, 1974.
Starless and Bible Black, Editions EG, 1974.
Red, Editions EG, 1974.
USA, Editions EG, 1975.
Discipline, Editions EG, 1981.
Beat, Editions EG, 1982.
Three of a Perfect Pair, Editions EG, 1984.
The Compact King Crimson, Editions EG, 1987.
The Essential King Crimson: Frame by Frame, Editions EG, 1991.
The Abbreviated King Crimson, Caroline, 1922.
The Great Deceiver Live 1973-74, Virgin, 1992.

With the League of Crafty Guitarists

Live!, Editions EG, 1986.
(With Toyah Willcox; featuring the League of Crafty Guitarists) *The Lady or the Tiger?,* Editions EG, 1986.
Get Crafty, I, Editions EG, 1988.
Show of Hands, Editions EG, 1989.

Solo releases

(With Brian Eno) *No Pussyfooting,* Antilles, 1973.
(With Eno) *Evening Star,* Antilles, 1975.
Exposure, 1979, reissued, Editions EG, 1985.
God Save the Queen/Under Heavy Manners, Polydor, 1980.

(With the League of Gentlemen) *Robert Fripp and the League of Gentlemen,* Editions EG, 1980.
Let the Powers Fall, Editions EG, 1981.
(With Andy Summers) *I Advance Masked,* A&M, 1982.
(With Summers) *Bewitched,* A&M, 1984.
Network, Editions EG, 1984.
(With Willcox) *Ophelia's Shadow,* 1991, Caroline.
(With Sunday All Over the World) *Kneeling at the Shrine,* Editions EG, 1991.

Other

(With Michael Giles and Peter Giles) *The Cheerful Insanity of Giles, Giles and Fripp,* Deram, 1968.

Also produced or contributed session work to Brian Eno's *Here Come the Warm Jets,* Island, 1973; *Another Green World,* Island, 1975; *Before and After Science,* Island, 1977; *Music for Films,* Polydor, 1978; and *Nerve Net,* Warner Bros., 1992; David Bowie's *Heroes,* RCA, 1977; Peter Gabriel's *Peter Gabriel,* Atco, 1977, and *Peter Gabriel,* Atlantic, 1988; Blondie's *Parallel Lines,* Chrysalis, 1978; Talking Heads' *Fear of Music,* Sire, 1979; Daryl Hall's *Sacred Songs,* RCA, 1980; The Roches' *The Roches,* RCA, 1980, and *Keep on Doing,* RCA, 1982; and David Sylvian's *Gone to Earth,* Virgin, 1986.

Sources

Books

The Rolling Stone Encyclopedia of Rock & Roll, edited by Jon Pareles and Patricia Romanowski, Rolling Stone Press/Summit Books, 1983.
Tamm, Eric A., *Robert Fripp: From King Crimson to Guitar Craft,* Faber & Faber, 1990.

Periodicals

Billboard, June 23, 1984.
Christian Science Monitor, November 5, 1990.
Down Beat, February 1991.
Guitar Player, February 1982; January 1986; July 1991.
Guitar World, September 1984.
Melody Maker, February 3, 1990.
Musician, February 1989.
Musician, Player and Listener, August 1979.
New York Times, July 23, 1978; June 28, 1984.
Rolling Stone, December 6, 1973; May 10, 1984; August 8, 1991.
Variety, April 14, 1990.

—Amy Culverwell

Bob Geldof

Singer, songwriter, activist

Previous to the desiccation of Ethiopia, as witnessed by the Western world in 1984, Bob Geldof was almost better known in British and Irish rock circles for his brash and sometimes abrasive personality than for his incisive songwriting and passionate singing. *Life* magazine described him this way: "When you meet this man you wonder, 'Why?' Did God knock at the wrong door by mistake and when it was opened by this scruffy Irishman, think, 'Oh, what the hell—he'll do.'" Simply put, he was an unlikely candidate for the nickname "Saint Bob," and nothing in his childhood would have led one to guess that he'd earn rights to the name anyway.

The grandson of Belgian immigrants, Geldof was born in Dublin, Ireland, in 1954. His mother died when he was in elementary school, and he grew up rebellious, often in conflict with his father, his older sisters, and the priests at the prestigious private school he attended. Just your average kid next door, Geldof wrote in his autobiography *Is That It?,* "My main claim to fame was the fact that I knew the lyrics of every song Cliff Richard ever recorded." Richard was soon replaced by the Rolling Stones, who "looked and sounded like they were saying 'f--- you' to everything. They were my boys." Geldof recalled, "That racket was the first thing I'd ever heard that felt like someone knew what *it* felt like." By the time he was 14, the Kinks, the Who, and the Small Faces had appended his list of role models.

Though he did poorly in school, Geldof was a voracious reader, especially of philosophy, history, and politics. He also dabbled in political activism, joining antiapartheid demonstrations and forming a local chapter of the Campaign for Nuclear Disarmament, though he admitted in his book, "We were too lazy to actively campaign. . . . The things I was interested in were passive—reading, listening to music, talking politics—and yet I wanted to be active. I wanted to play music not listen to it, to be involved in politics not talk about it." The Simon Community, a group that aided the homeless and hungry in Dublin, served as an outlet for his frustrated activism; he paid less attention than ever to his studies.

Such a quixotic background left Geldof in limbo, as he disclosed in *Is That It?,* revealing, "When I left school, I ran out of the front gates, and didn't look back once. . . . I had no hopes when I left, no ambitions, no clue as to what I should do." His father had hoped he would get a university education, but he failed his exams for the Leaving Certificate, the Irish equivalent of a high school diploma. Running out of options, Geldof went to England and worked on a road construction crew for a while, then drifted to London, where he lived with a group of squatters in an abandoned building and worked occasionally at odd jobs, including photographing rock concerts and playing guitar in subway stations.

Began as Journalist

Exhaustion and a bout of drug-induced paranoia finally moved Geldof to escape from his dead-end London life. He found a teaching position in Spain where his lack of credentials would not be a liability. "The sole qualification for being able to teach [English] in the school was that you knew no Spanish," he recounted. Looking for a change of scenery after his short stint in education, Geldof decided to try Canada. There he achieved the first real success of his life, becoming a reporter, then music editor for Vancouver's underground newspaper *Georgia Strait.* He became a minor local celebrity and was sure he wanted to spend his life in Canada. However, he was also an illegal immigrant; to get a proper visa he would have to return to Ireland.

Back in Dublin, Geldof attempted to engage his newly found enterprising spirit in starting his own alternative paper, to be modeled on a Vancouver classified-ad weekly. But, he discovered, "What was a successful and prosperous idea in North America was . . . impossible in the unenterprising atmosphere of Ireland." While Geldof tried to negotiate the bureaucratic and financial roadblocks, he was also spending time with several old friends who were talking about creating a band, but having trouble getting organized. To take his mind off the woes of beginning a paper, he offered to help them

launch and manage the band; jack-of-all-trades, he was soon drafted as lead singer. A few months later the band got its first gig, under the name "Nightlife Thugs." Between sets, Geldof thought of the name of a children's gang in American folksinger Woody Guthrie's autobiography *Bound for Glory,* which he had been reading the night before. On the spot, the Nightlife Thugs became the Boomtown Rats.

The Rats scuttled along, due in large part to Geldof's flair for promotion and his philosophy that "you need to act like stars from the word go." Though other local bands considered the Rats musically inept, their performances were always exciting and they soon had a following, not only in Dublin but throughout Ireland. Unfortunately, however, no real music industry existed in Ireland. The Rats opted to go to England, where they were signed to Ensign Records in 1976.

Scurried Into Number One Hit

The Boomtown Rats hit England at the height of the punk movement and were immediately associated with it, though Geldof noted in his autobiography, "We did not feel ourselves to be primarily part of any new grouping. . . . All we had in common [with the punks] was the conviction that something new needed to happen in music." While the Rats considered themselves raw and their musicianship less than adequate, their 18 months of performing experience was nearly 18 months more than many English punk bands had had when they moved into the spotlight. The Rats sound, rooted in rhythm and blues, reggae, and pop, was less harsh than that of the Sex Pistols or the Damned, and unlike some of the very political punk bands, they made no bones about the fact that they wanted to sell records. Punk ideologues labelled them sellouts for appearing on the British TV show *Top of the Pops,* but they began to have hits almost immediately and finally had a Number One single with "Rat Trap" in late 1978.

For the next two years the Boomtown Rats stayed at the top of the British pop scene. They toured Asia and the United States, but never really broke through in America. This was in part because Geldof's outspokenness alienated U.S. recording executives and radio station program directors. It didn't help that their most successful single on the U.S. charts, 1979's "I Don't Like Mondays," was withdrawn by Columbia Records under the threat of lawsuits. The song was inspired by an incident in San Diego, in which a girl named Brenda Spencer shot several people from her bedroom window. The title came from the answer she gave a journalist who asked her why she did it. When Geldof explained in an interview what the song was about,

Spencer's parents threatened to sue. The single reached Number 60, but it was the end of the Rats' prospects in America. The Boomtown Rats also suffered commercial decline in Britain. By 1984 they were broke and fighting an uphill battle against indifference from both their record company and the public. They toured the university circuit to raise money for recording their sixth album, *In the Long Grass*, but the first three singles from that release stiffed in spite of a successful tour. A catalyst was needed.

The first flash of "Saint Bob" occurred in November of 1984. Geldof related in *Is That It?:* "All day I had been on the phone trying desperately to get something happening with the single. It was coming to the end of 1984 and I could see no prospect for the release of *In the Long Grass,* which we'd sweated over and were proud of. I went home in a state of blank resignation and switched on the television. I saw something that placed my worries in a ghastly new perspective. The news report was of famine in Ethiopia. . . . This was horror on a monumental scale."

Melded Activism and Popular Music

Geldof conceived the idea of making a record to raise money for famine relief, but he realized that a Boomtown Rats record wouldn't sell very well. Instead he asked friends who played in other bands to collaborate. They responded enthusiastically, and by the recording date of November 25, Band Aid's roster was a Who's Who of British rock. Geldof also persuaded Phonogram Records, the distributors, the retailers, and everyone else involved in the production to forego any profit on the record. He had expected to raise about 72,000 pounds, but by Christmas Eve of 1984, "Do They Know It's Christmas" had rung up sales of over five million pounds.

Geldof told *Rolling Stone* in 1990: "I did a thing that I thought would last three weeks. It didn't, and I'm glad it didn't." Band Aid spawned an American imitation, USA for Africa, and climaxed with the transatlantic benefit concert Live Aid, which raised over $120 million. Geldof spent most of the next two years overseeing the distribution of the enormous sums of money. He was knighted by Queen Elizabeth II, nominated for the Nobel Peace Prize, received by heads of state, and lionized by the press. Ironically though, the effect on his own life, he told *Rolling Stone,* was "disastrous . . . financially, professionally, personally." Of his moniker he said, "I don't want to be 'Saint Bob,' because halos are heavy and they rust very easily, and I know I have feet of clay because my socks stink."

Geldof went out of his way to avoid any appearance that he was using the publicity generated by Band Aid to boost his own career. Consequently whatever attention the Boomtown Rats' last album might have received was swept aside and *In The Long Grass* sank without a trace. The Rats played at Live Aid, but broke up in 1986, just as they were on the verge of signing a new recording contract. Geldof, who took no salary for his administrative work on Band Aid, wrote his autobiography to raise money to pay his own bills. *Is That It?,* which *Rolling Stone* called "a witty, open recounting of his first thirty-three years," was a best-seller in Britain and relieved his immediate financial problems, but it was not until late 1986 that he was able to return to music.

His first solo album, *Deep in the Heart of Nowhere,* was released in 1987 to mixed reviews and tepid sales. As Geldof later observed in *Rolling Stone,* "When I got back to pop . . . nobody wanted to accept it." 1990's *The Vegetarians of Love* met with a better critical reception. *Rolling Stone* described it as "loose and often lovely. . . . The songs themselves are the strongest Geldof has come up with since the Rats' third album." J. D. Considine of *Musician* praised the songs' "tuneful charm and garrulous wit."

Geldof still get requests to aid in fund-raising for various causes, all of which he declines. "The big concert is seriously devalued currency," he remarked to *Rolling Stone.* "John Lennon was quite right when he said 'You can be benefited to death.'" *Rolling Stone* interviewer Rob Tannenbaum asked him: "Was there ever a point . . . when you thought, 'I'm really good at this . . . maybe I should do this full time?'" Geldof replied, "No, I didn't, because I didn't enjoy it. The same logic applies to pop music: 'Gee, I know a lot about this, I'm as good as anybody else'—[smiles] that's *my* opinion of it—'maybe I should do it full time.' And I *do* like that."

Selected discography

Deep in the Heart of Nowhere, Atlantic, 1986.
The Vegetarians of Love, Atlantic, 1990.

With the Boomtown Rats

The Boomtown Rats, Mercury, 1977.
A Tonic for the Troops, Columbia, 1979.
The Fine Art of Surfacing, Columbia, 1979.
Mondo Bongo, Columbia, 1981.

Five Deep, Columbia, 1982.
In the Long Grass, Columbia, 1985.
The Best of the Boomtown Rats (1977-1982), Columbia, 1987.

Sources

Books

Geldof, Bob, *Is That It?,* Weidenfeld & Nicholson, 1986.
The Rolling Stone Encyclopedia of Rock & Roll, edited by Jon Pareles and Patricia Romanowski, Rolling Stone Press/Summit Books, 1983.
Rees, Dafydd, and Luke Crampton, *Rock Movers & Shakers,* ABC-CLIO, 1991.
Stambler, Irwin, *The Encyclopedia of Pop, Rock and Soul,* St. Martin's, 1989.

Periodicals

Down Beat, October 1986.
Life, January 6, 1986.
High Fidelity, May 1987.
Musician, November 1990.
New York Times Book Review, March 22, 1987.
People, October 22, 1990.
Playboy, August 1987.
Rolling Stone, December 5, 1985; December 4, 1986; February 12, 1987; November 15, 1990; September 6, 1990.
Time, January 6, 1986.
Variety, August 27, 1986

—Tim Connor

Glenn Gould

Pianist

When pianist Glenn Gould died in October of 1982, he left behind a legacy of recordings, television and radio programs, interviews, and articles in which he offered opinions and interpretations that continue to exert a profound influence on contemporary music. He was a complex figure and a mass of contradictions: a recluse who made himself, through the media, extraordinarily accessible; a man greatly sensitive to the cold who had a fascination with the Canadian Arctic; a romantic who dismissed most of the music of the romantic 19th century and whose playing displayed a notable lack of sentiment. Yet there was a consistency beneath the contradictions. In 1962, two years before he stopped performing in order to devote himself solely to recording, Gould contributed an article to *Musical America,* called "Let's Ban Applause!," in which he made a statement that came to represent his view of life for the next 20 years: "The purpose of art is not the release of a momentary ejection of adrenaline but is, rather, the gradual, lifelong construction of a state of wonder and serenity."

Glenn Herbert Gould was born on September 25, 1932, the only son of Russell Herbert Gould, a Toronto furrier, and Florence Greig Gould. His mother claimed to be a descendant of Norwegian composer Edvard Grieg. Both parents were amateur musicians, and the young Gould displayed his own musical abilities at an early age. His mother taught him piano until he was ten; he then enrolled at the Toronto Conservatory of Music (now the Royal Conservatory of Music), studying piano with Alberto Guerrero. He attended the Williamson Road Public School until 1945, later advancing to Malvern Collegiate Institute, a public high school.

Gould's formal debut was not as a pianist but as an organist, at Toronto's Eaton Auditorium on December 12, 1945. On May 8, 1946, he gave his premiere performance as a pianist, playing the first movement of Beethoven's fourth piano concerto with the Toronto Conservatory Symphony Orchestra at Toronto's Massey Hall. That year he also received an associate diploma from the Toronto Conservatory.

U.S. Debut

In 1951 Gould left Malvern Collegiate without receiving his diploma; he stopped studying with Guerrero in 1952. By this time he was performing throughout Canada, establishing a reputation as one of the country's most promising musicians. On January 2, 1955, Gould made his U.S. debut at the Phillips Gallery in Washington, D.C.; a week later he appeared at New York City's Town Hall. His programs at that time were character-

For the Record. . .

Born Glenn Herbert Gould, in Toronto, Ontario, Canada, September 25, 1932; died of a stroke October 4, 1982, in Toronto; son of Russell Herbert (a furrier) and Florence Greig (a piano teacher) Gould. *Education:* Studied piano with his mother, c. 1935-42; studied piano with Alberto Guerrero, organ with Frederick C. Silvester, and music theory with Leo Smith, Toronto (now Royal) Conservatory of Music, 1942-46.

Pianist. First public performance, on organ, 1945; debut as pianist, with Toronto Conservatory Orchestra, 1946; first solo piano recital, 1947. Performed throughout Canada, 1951-54; U.S. debut, Washington, D.C., 1955; signed with Columbia Records, 1955, and recorded Bach's Goldberg Variations; international solo and orchestral performances, 1957-64. Composer of chamber music and film scores.

Made over 80 recordings with Columbia, 1956-82; appeared in over 70 radio and 20 television broadcasts for the Canadian Broadcasting Corporation, 1964-82; hosted weekly radio program "The Art of Glenn Gould," 1966-68, 1969; wrote and produced *Solitude Trilogy* series of radio broadcasts, including "The Idea of North," 1967, "The Latecomers," 1969, and "Quiet in the Land," 1977; wrote and hosted four-part television series on twentieth-century music, "Music in Our Time," 1974-77; numerous television appearances. Author of liner notes and contributor to periodicals.

Awards: Lady Kemp Scholarship; honorary doctorate of law, University of Toronto, 1964; Grammy Award, 1973, for liner notes to his recording of Paul Hindemith's *Sonata No. 2 in G Major.*

ized by a taste for intellectually rigorous music and a conspicuous absence of the 19th-century staples that dominate the repertory of most pianists.

The day after the New York recital Gould was offered a recording contract with Columbia Records—unprecedented considering he had mounted only a single performance in New York City. His first recording, of Bach's *Goldberg Variations,* was released in 1956 and became a best-seller. Gould was on his way to becoming a celebrity, known not only for his piano playing but also for his eccentricities: He sang and conducted himself as he played, sat in a low chair that put him at about shoulder level with the keyboard, carried a suitcase of pills for various ailments, soaked his hands in hot water before concerts, kept bottled water at his

side, and wore wool sweaters under his tuxedo vest to ward off the cold of drafty concert halls.

Although his reputation continued to grow in the 1960s, Gould became increasingly uncomfortable as a concert performer. "At live concerts I feel demeaned, like a vaudevillian," he told *Holiday* magazine in 1964, as was recalled by Tim Page in his introduction to *The Glenn Gould Reader.* On April 10th of that year he gave his last public performance. His withdrawal from concert life shocked both critics and the public, who felt he was turning his back on them at the height of his fame. But Gould had been planning to leave for years and had been telling reporters as much since the 1950s. He had his reasons. The most notorious of these was a belief that the live concert would cease to exist by the year 1999 and would be replaced exclusively by recordings. He felt that a piece of music could neither be played nor appreciated as well in a concert hall as it could via recording in one's living room. Moreover, as he wrote in "The Prospects of Recording," a piece he penned for *High Fidelity,* "In the course of a lifetime spent in the recording studio [the performer] will necessarily encounter a wider range of repertoire than could possibly be his lot in the concert hall." And in establishing what was perhaps most significant to him, Gould concluded that recording "enables the performer to establish a contact with a work which is very much like that of the composer's own relation to it. It permits him to encounter a particular piece of music and to analyze and dissect it in a most thorough way, to make it a vital part of his life for a relatively brief period, and then to pass on to some other challenge and to the satisfaction of some other curiosity."

"Creative Cheating"

Gould put these ideas into practice for the next 18 years, making over 80 recordings in which he engaged in what he called "creative cheating," where multiple "takes"—different recorded versions of the same material—were recorded, the most appropriate of these spliced together to create the perfect whole. He compared this process to the making of films, where scenes are frequently shot out of sequence and then pieced together in the editing room. Gould even imagined a time in the future when the home listener could obtain an editing kit by which his or her own ideal performance could be produced by splicing together, say, one orchestra playing the first movement of a symphony, another playing the second movement, and so on.

In a 1982 interview, reprinted in *Piano Quarterly,* Gould told music critic Tim Page, "All the music that really interests me—not just some of it, all of it—is contrapuntal

Gould • 93

music"—music in which individual musical lines overlap. Gould's recordings displayed his facility for playing such music with remarkable clarity and accuracy. His interpretations were often controversial because he approached each piece of music from a fresh point of view, refusing to concern himself with how the piece "should" be played or with what other performers had done in the past. "If there's any excuse at all for making a record, it's to do it differently," he remarked in a 1968 interview captured on Volume 1 of *The Glenn Gould Legacy*, "to approach the work from a totally recreative point of view . . . to perform this particular work as it has never been heard before. And if one can't do that, I would say, abandon it, forget about it, move on to something else."

Solitude Trilogy

Gould participated in dozens of radio and television broadcasts, mostly for the Canadian Broadcasting Corporation (CBC). Perhaps his most important undertaking for these media was the *Solitude Trilogy*, a series of three docudramas he wrote and produced for CBC radio: "The Idea of North," "The Latecomers," and "Quiet in the Land." Each of these explored the concept of isolation in various forms, the participants' comments often overlapping to create a kind of counterpoint.

In addition to his roles as pianist and media figure, Gould was also a composer and writer. He wrote articles and essays throughout his life that developed his ideas about musical interpretation and analysis, the recording industry, and the electronic media, many of which were published in North American periodicals. Gould wrote a string quartet in his youth; his 1964 *So You Want to Write a Fugue?* is a humorous piece for voices and instruments. He was also involved in creating music for films, including *Slaughterhouse Five*, in 1972, and *The Wars*, in 1982. Toward the end of his life Gould became interested in conducting; three months before his death he conducted members of the Toronto Symphony Orchestra in a recording of Wagner's *Siegfried Idyll*.

Gould allowed observers to believe that his reclusive, highly controlled lifestyle was a reflection of his attempt to construct the "state of wonder and serenity" that was his ideal. In reality, his reclusive habits were most likely due more to Gould's high-strung and extremely sensitive temperament. Nonetheless, one can reason that by avoiding the distractions of the outside world, Gould was able to explore music and ideas in a way that would have been otherwise impossible. When listening to Gould's recordings, the listener can't help but feel that he or she is in the presence, so to speak, of a highly original and utterly intelligent musical mind. As Nicholas Spice wrote in the *London Review of Books* in 1992, "[Gould] delivers the music to us as someone might place in our hands a fragile and priceless object which he loved beyond anything else."

Selected compositions

String Quartet, Op. 1, 1956.
So You Want to Write a Fugue? (for four-part chorus of mixed voices with piano or string quartet accompaniment), 1964.

Also composed scores for films, including *Slaughterhouse Five*, 1972, and *The Wars*, 1982.

Selected discography

On CBS/Sony, except where noted

Bach, *Goldberg Variations*, 1956.
Beethoven, *Sonata No. 30 in E Major, Op. 109*, 1956.
Berg, *Sonata, Op. 1*, 1959.
Krenek, *Sonata No. 3, Op. 92, No. 4*, 1959.
Schoenberg, *Three Piano Pieces, Op. 11*, 1959.
String Quartet, Op. 1, 1960.
Brahms, *Intermezzi: Op. 76, Nos. 6 and 7; Op. 116, No. 4; Op. 117, Nos. 1-3; Op. 118, Nos. 1, 2, and 6; Op. 119, No. 1*, 1961.
Schoenberg, *Five Piano Pieces, Op. 23*, 1966.
Schoenberg, *Piano Pieces, Op. 33a and b*, 1966.
Scriabin, *Sonata No. 3 in F-sharp minor, Op. 23*, 1969.
Byrd, *A Voluntary; Sixth Pavan and Galliard; First Pavan and Galliard; Hughe Aston's Ground; Sellinger's Round; Gibbons, Orlando. Lord of Salisbury Pavan and Galliard; Allemand, or Italian Ground; Fantasy in C Major*, 1971.
The Idea of North, CBC Learning Systems, 1971.
The Latecomers, CBC Learning Systems, 1971.
Hindemith, *Sonata No. 3 in B-flat Major*, 1973.
A Glenn Gould Fantasy, 1980.
So You Want to Write a Fugue?, 1980.
Haydn, *Selected Sonatas*, 1982.
Bach, *Goldberg Variations*, 1982.
The Glenn Gould Legacy, Volume 1, 1984; Volume 2, 1985 Volume 3, 1986; Volume 4, 1986.
Glenn Gould the Composer, 1992.
The Art of Glenn Gould, 1992.
The Glenn Gould Edition, 1992.

Sources

Books

Cott, Jonathan, *Conversations With Glenn Gould*, Little, Brown, 1984.

Friedrich, Otto, *Glenn Gould: A Life and Variations,* Random House, 1989.

The Glenn Gould Reader, edited by Tim Page, Knopf, 1984.

Glenn Gould Variations: By Himself and His Friends, edited by John McGreevy, Quill, 1983.

Payzant, Geoffrey, *Glenn Gould: Music & Mind,* Van Nostrand Reinhold, 1978.

Periodicals

Canadian Music Journal, Fall 1956.

High Fidelity, April 1966; August 1975.

London Review of Books, March 26, 1992.

Musical America, February 1962.

New Republic, October 1, 1986; June 26, 1989.

Newsweek, October 18, 1982.

New York Times, October 5, 1982.

Piano Quarterly, Winter 1982/83; Summer 1974.

Pulse!, October 1991.

Saturday Review, December 1980.

Vanity Fair, May 1983.

Additional information for this profile was obtained from a recorded interview, "Glenn Gould: Concert Dropout," *The Glenn Gould Legacy,* Volume 1, CBS/Sony, 1984.

—Joyce Harrison

Al Green

Singer, songwriter

Al Green emerged from relative obscurity—he recorded one moderately successful single in the 1960s—to become one of the premiere soul vocalists of the early 1970s and an unrivaled hitmaker. His impassioned, sensual delivery and silky charisma made him a sex symbol as well, and he seemed prepared to dominate the world of rhythm and blues throughout the decade with hits like "Love and Happiness" and "Let's Stay Together." Something unexpected happened, however, that exerted a profound effect on the course of Green's career: he converted to Christianity, made his way back to the gospel music he had sung in childhood, and eventually became the minister of his own church in Memphis, Tennessee. Although this decision cost Green the chance to be the king of soul music, he has recorded a string of albums since then, some of them quite successful, and has introduced many secular listeners to the power of gospel. In his prime as a mainstream soul singer, though, according to Geoffrey Himes of *Musician.* "Green created a body of work that stands with the best black pop of the 70s."

Green was born in 1946 in Forrest City, Arkansas. His father played bass in a traveling gospel group, the Green Brothers, and by the age of nine, Al was singing alongside his brothers in the band. The family moved to Grand Rapids, Michigan, when Al was about sixteen, and there he discovered the joy of secular music: the nongospel work of Sam Cooke and, most especially, the sounds of rhythm and blues legend Jackie Wilson. "I had told my father and my brothers that I had this idea about me becoming a real popular singer and they didn't like it," Green told *Melody Maker* in a 1975 interview. "They didn't believe I could do it and they thought I was kidding them. . . . They thought I was nuts." They also thought pop music was sinful. Green further confessed in the interview that he would "sneak out" to a friend's house to listen to pop records.

"Back Up Train"

Having decided on a career in pop music, Green assembled a group known as Al Green and the Creations; when that group broke up he formed Al Green and the Soul Mates. In 1967 Green and the group recorded his first single, "Back Up Train." Released by Bell Records, the song was a Top Five hit, though Green never made a penny from it. He began singing his one hit on the "chitlin circuit," as the black music nightspots of the time were known. "I can remember doing the Apollo in New York as the opening act when I had just eight minutes to sing my record on stage," he recalled to *Melody Maker.* "Four of those minutes it takes to get from the tenth floor dressing room all the way down to the bottom and by the time you're into the song, they're calling you from the side, ready for the next act." Green added, "After one song they wouldn't let me do any more. I tried to do some Sam and Dave tunes, but they'd only let me sing 'Back Up Train.'" Green reportedly told a skeptical floor manager that he'd be back one day, "with a dressing room on the first floor instead of the tenth."

After a couple of directionless years, Green hooked up with trumpeter-producer Willie Mitchell in Midland, Texas. The two had been ripped off by the same club owner and vowed to escape the torpor of the circuit. Mitchell had a label in Memphis called Hi and was prepared to make killer soul records. Mitchell, together with brothers Tennie, Leroy and Charles Hodges (on guitar, bass, and keyboards) and drummers Howard Grimes and Al Jackson, Jr.—the latter formerly of the stellar Memphis band Booker T. and the MGs—needed only a singer whose voice would define the sound. "Green's was that voice," wrote Himes in *Musician*. "It seemed to defy gravity as it grew in intensity, as it rose in pitch. It had a soft-slurring sensuality that blended the urban sophistication of Northern soul with the holy roller roots of Southern soul." With its tough, funky rhythm section and buoyant, often string-laden melodic arrangements, the Hi house band could match Green's vocal flights. "It was a good package," said Green with characteristic understatement in a *Down Beat* interview; he told *Rolling Stone* in 1987 that "Willie would

write the music, I wrote the words, and then Al Jackson would come in and say, 'Let me hear that.' It was just a combination that clicked."

String of Soul Hits

After grappling with some inappropriate material—notably attempts to cover songs by the Beatles and soul hitmaker Isaac Hayes—they hit with a Green original, "Tired of Being Alone," in 1971. Green explained to *Melody Maker*, "Nobody was writing the kind of material that I heard in my head and wanted to sing. My only choice was to write my own." The single was a million seller; that same year saw the release of the album *Al Green Gets Next to You*, which also contained "I Can't Get Next to You" and "Are You Lonely for Me."

Green reached the number one position on the pop and rhythm and blues charts with his next big hit, "Let's Stay Together." The album that bore the single's title, released in 1972, went platinum, as did its successor of the same year, *I'm Still in Love With You*. Dean and Nancy Tudor wrote in their 1979 book *Black Music* that "Green's voice is very flexible: he can growl, scream, shout, croon, scat, and so forth with no apparent effort, including a rising falsetto." They maintain that *Let's Stay Together* and *I'm Still in Love With You* "contain his best work to date." *Rolling Stone*'s special 1988 list of "The Top 100 Singles of the Last 25 Years" put "Let's Stay Together" at number 45. It was, wrote the editors, the song that "established Green as one of the great soul singers." The *Rolling Stone* piece also cites a story Mitchell told in a 1984 documentary: "We were over here in the ghetto area, and there was a bunch of winos drinking with themselves out there. We said, 'Let's get four or five gallons of wine—bring these people into the studio!' So we brought about fifty people in here, all the winos drinking wine and lying on the floor while we were cutting the record. If you notice, on the *Let's Stay Together* album, there's a lot of noise in the background. Well, it's the winos."

Finding His Religion

In 1973 Green was riding high. He released three albums that year, two of which, *Livin' for You* and *Call Me*, went gold. "I think my best singing was done on *Call Me*," Green told *Rolling Stone* in 1987. The magazine referred to the record as "perhaps the epitome of [the Green-Mitchell] collaboration," featuring Green's versions of a couple of country songs, including the Hank Williams classic "I'm So Lonesome I Could Cry" and Willie Nelson's "Funny How Time Slips Away." The gospel song "Jesus Is Waiting" also appeared on *Call*

Me, reflecting the fact that in the midst of his pop success and recognition, the singer had found religion. "I was born again in 1973," Green told *Musician,* insisting that he underwent a lengthy "transformation" rather than being turned around by a single incident. Instead of switching to straight gospel music performances as a result of his experience, Green attempted a synthesis between popular soul and the intense religious ferment he felt.

The year 1974 saw the release of *Al Green Explores Your Mind,* which featured the single "Take Me to the River." That song—covered by many artists in the ensuing decades—is at once a riveting ode to sexual desire and a cry for spiritual redemption. The tension of secular and sacred in the song gives it a compelling

> "Nobody was writing the kind of material that I heard in my head and wanted to sing. My only choice was to write my own."

edge. The straightforwardly upbeat 1974 single "Sha-La-La (Make Me Happy)" was a huge hit as well. But the year may be more notable for an incident that pushed Green further toward his eventual ministerial destination. A woman he knew and had rejected scalded the singer while he bathed by pouring a pot of steaming grits down his back. She then locked herself in his bedroom and committed suicide. This traumatic experience moved Green—who was hospitalized for his burns—to reflect on his life and eventually to seek solace and illumination in the scriptures.

Hi released a *Greatest Hits* package in 1975, signalling, consciously or not, the end of Green's reign as a soul music hitmaker; it went gold. It was, however, the beginning of a new era. In 1976 he became a minister, though he had to open his own church—the Full Gospel Tabernacle—in Memphis to escape the scorn of the religious establishment. The next year, Green went into his own studio for Hi—but without Mitchell—to produce *The Belle Album.* Although Greil Marcus of *Rolling Stone* called it "idiosyncratic," he asserted that "we may someday look back on *The Belle Album* as Al Green's best." Of the song "All 'n All" Marcus remarked that "it carries a sense of liberation and purpose deep enough to make the sinner envy the saved." *Musician*'s

Himes called *Belle* "the crowning artistic achievement of Green's career." The record was not, however, a commercial success, at least measured against Green's previous efforts.

"God's Way of Saying Hurry Up"

Rolling Stone's Dave Marsh wrote of Green's 1979 follow-up *Truth n' Time* that it "lacks the monumental peaks" of *Belle* but "it has much more focus." Green was still struggling for balance, mixing gospel songs like "King of All" with such pop covers as "To Sir With Love" and a nod in the direction of disco. He lost his balance quite literally that year, falling from the stage during an appearance in Cincinnati, Ohio, and he was subsequently hospitalized for two weeks. "I was moving towards God, but I wasn't moving fast enough," Green was quoted as saying in a *Musician* profile. "It was God's way of saying hurry up." Green hurried up and recorded his first album of exclusively gospel songs, 1980's *The Lord Will Make a Way,* for the Texas religious music label Myrrh Records. Although he was no longer a contender for massive pop sales, Green was honored with a Grammy that year for best gospel performance. He continued in this vein with *Higher Plane* in 1981 and *Precious Lord* in 1982. Tom Carson wrote in *Rolling Stone* that *Higher Plane* "may be the most intimately seductive gospel album ever recorded." *Melody Maker* called *Precious Lord* "a lovely collection of songs." Also in 1982, Green appeared in the Broadway gospel musical *Your Arms Too Short to Box With God.* And he continued performing live, though his sexually dynamic stage presence alienated some gospel fans.

Green's 1986 record *He Is the Light* reunited him with Mitchell and saw him return to a major label, A&M. According to *Rolling Stone,* "Green and Mitchell have successfully recreated the sound of the classic soul albums they cut for Hi Records." 1988 saw Green re-emerge momentarily on the pop scene with "Put a Little Love in Your Heart," a duet with rock diva Annie Lennox on the *Scrooged* movie soundtrack. In 1989 he released *I Get Joy,* which *Cosmopolitan* called "smoldering." Hi/MCA released a collection of pre-gospel Green material called *Love Ritual* in 1990. Then Green moved to Word/Epic for the 1991 compilation *One in a Million,* which gathered songs from his eighties gospel albums, and 1992's *Love Is Reality.* On *Love* he was produced by former Motown recording artist Tim Miner, who surrounded Green with up-to-date production touches and arrangements, including new jack swing. Green also made some videos to promote *Love Is Reality.* "It's kind of like a boxer fighting his fight," Green stated in the Epic press release. "He just goes in and hits it at the level he's at. We cut the album very fast. I wrote it in the studio. I wrote it at home. I wrote it in the hotel. I wrote one tune in the elevator, on the back of a legal pad."

By the time of *Love Is Reality,* Green had been recording gospel records for over twelve years. Yet critics and many fans continued to treat his gospel career, for the most part, as a footnote to his brief blaze of glory as a soul singer. Green, however, managed to bring the various camps together in part because he never recognized the formal boundaries. "There are different degrees of love and different kinds of celebration," he told *Cosmopolitan.* "I sang gospel music as a child, then wrote and sang pop songs for ten years, before I was born again in nineteen seventy-three. I've never known what the dividing lines were and still don't."

Selected discography

"Back Up Train" (single), Bell Records, 1967.

On Hi Records

Al Green Gets Next to You (includes "Tired of Being Alone," "I Can't Get Next to You," and "Are You Lonely for Me"), 1971.
Let's Stay Together (includes "Let's Stay Together"), 1972.
I'm Still in Love With You, 1972.
Al Green, 1972.
Green Is Blues, 1973.
Call Me (includes "Call Me," "I'm So Lonesome I Could Cry," and "Funny How Time Slips Away"), 1973.
Livin' for You, 1973.
Al Green Explores Your Mind (includes "Take Me to the River" and "Sha-La-La [Make Me Happy]"), 1974.
Greatest Hits, 1975.
Al Green Is Love, 1975.
The Belle Album (includes "All 'n All"), 1977.
Greatest Hits, Volume II, 1977.
Truth n' Time (includes "King of All" and "To Sir With Love"), 1979.
Love Ritual, 1990.

On Myrrh Records

The Lord Will Make a Way, 1980.

Higher Plane, 1981.
Precious Lord, 1982.

On A&M Records

He Is the Light, 1986.
(Contributor; with Annie Lennox) *Scrooged* (soundtrack; "Put a Little Love in Your Heart"), 1988.
I Get Joy, 1989.

On Word/Epic Records

One in a Million, 1991.
Love Is Reality, 1992.
White Christmas.

Sources

Books

The Rolling Stone Illustrated History of Rock & Roll, edited by Jim Miller, Random House, 1976.
Tudor, Dean, and Nancy Tudor, *Black Music,* Libraries Unlimited, 1979.

Periodicals

Audio, January 1990.
Cosmopolitan, October 1989.
Down Beat, April 5, 1979.
Ebony, June 1991.
Melody Maker, August 18, 1973; December 27, 1973; January 12, 1974; March 29, 1975; April 19, 1975; January 14, 1978; August 25, 1979; December 18, 1982; July 15, 1989.
Musician, April 1983; March 1986.
Rolling Stone, February 23, 1978; March 9, 1978; March 22, 1979; March 18, 1982; September 13, 1984; January 30, 1986; March 27, 1986; August 27, 1987; September 8, 1988.

Additional information for this profile was obtained from an Epic Records press release, 1992.

—*Simon Glickman*

Robyn Hitchcock

Singer, songwriter

"I wished for the impossible when I was a kid," British rocker Robyn Hitchcock once told *Rolling Stone.* "When I couldn't realize it, I retreated into fantasy." Thirty-some years and 11 albums later, the eccentric Hitchcock has yet to fully emerge. With his witty lyrics and surrealist imagery, the singer and songwriter has created an elaborate fantasyscape populated by bizarre life forms—slimy amphibians, antennaed insects, and creepy crustaceans. And in the psychedelic ooze these inventions trail is a devoted cult following; Hitchcock's fans have developed quite a taste for his peculiar brand of primordial soup.

Born in London in 1953, Hitchcock developed an "intense contempt for normalcy in all its forms" at an early age, he told the *San Francisco Chronicle.* Inspired by Bob Dylan's "Like a Rolling Stone," he gravitated toward music as a means of expressing that contempt. At 16 Hitchcock discovered William Shakespeare and avant-garde rock figure Captain Beefheart, the two influences that would establish the foundation for his unique musical perspective. In the early 1970s his interest in Shakespeare led him to study English at Cambridge University, while the allure of Beefheart propelled Hitchcock to the coffeehouse folk scene, where he explored his burgeoning musical style as a solo guitarist.

On the coffeehouse circuit Hitchcock developed the distinctive right-hand picking style that *Guitar Player* called "a kind of finicky folk that's not sentimental enough for the coffeehouses, and too acerbic and sharply poetic for most rock audiences." Hitchcock explained: "There weren't chorus pedals in the early '70s, and it was hard to make a nice noise, so I innately started picking, which makes you sound like [folk-rocker] Roger McGuinn or something. Everybody else was trying to play like Eric Clapton, but when I did leads I tried to play like Barry Melton from Country Joe and the Fish."

"Avoid Cliche Whenever Possible"

Following the demise of his short-lived acoustic quartet, Maureen and the Meatpackers, Hitchcock formed his first recording group with bassist and keyboardist Andy Metcalf and drummer Morris Windsor in 1976. Dubbed the Soft Boys, the art-punk rock band derived its title from two William Burroughs novels, *The Soft Machine* and *The Wild Boys.* Its mission: to "avoid cliche whenever possible." That was "our manifesto," Hitchcock told the *Chronicle.*

It was with the Soft Boys that Hitchcock perfected his signature surrealist style. Although characterized by a psychedelic quality typical of the musicians of his generation, his was a method, he insisted, that was not drug-induced. "I was influenced by people who had taken LSD," he told the *Chicago Tribune,* but "I didn't take very much acid. I don't think I needed to, really, because I'd already thought myself into that state." The effect of that condition was captured on the single "Kingdom of Love," recorded in the late 1970s. Offering a classic Hitchcockian juxtaposition of the familiar and the bizarre, it laments: "You've been laying eggs under my skin/ Now they're hatching out under my chin/ Now there's tiny insects showing through/ All them tiny insects look like you." Although labeled a "classic paranoid delusion" by a psychologist, Hitchcock explained to *Rolling Stone,* the song was "intended to describe the way people have an effect on each other and sometimes have kids."

Soft Boys a Casualty of Punk

Although the Soft Boys developed a consistent following after the release of the band's first recordings in 1977 and '78, their irreverent pop sound was ultimately drowned out by angrier young men like the Sex Pistols; unable to withstand the punk-rock tide, the group disbanded in 1981.

Three years later the Soft Boys were reborn as the Egyptians; in addition to Hitchcock, Metcalf, and Windsor, the group counted two new members, Otis Horns Fletcher and Roger Jackson. The band fared well stateside in its new incarnation. The albums *Fegmania!, Gotta Let This Hen Out!,* and *Elements of Light,* on the alternative Slash and Relativity labels, rated high on college radio playlists. The band's reputation was enhanced by the enthusiastic endorsement of R.E.M. guitarist Peter Buck, with whom they began a lasting musical collaboration. In 1988 the Egyptians recorded *Globe of Frogs,* their first album on the major label A&M. *Queen Elvis* and *Perspex Island* followed in 1989 and '91, respectively.

Perspex Island, Hitchcock's first recording with an outside producer, Paul Fox, was "mixed on a car stereo in L.A. because it's designed to be listened to in traffic," reported the *Chicago Tribune.* Here the artist emerged for the first time from behind his well-fortified wall of crustaceans and alien vegetation. "There's a side of me I've been hesitant to reveal in the past," he told *Pitch* magazine. "I've always avoided being too vulnerable, too open, afraid of coming off maudlin."

Perspex Island Marked a Departure

The emotional openness reflected on *Perspex Island* could be credited to Hitchcock's new-found contentment. "I haven't had therapy or anything," he explained to the *Chicago Tribune,* "I just have a great girlfriend." Peter Buck and R.E.M. vocalist Michael Stipe also had something to do with the new confessional mode. Hitchcock told *Pitch,* "They're very into that sort of thing." Buck played guitar and mandolin on eight of the album's 11 tracks, and Stipe contributed vocals to the cut "She Doesn't Exist."

Despite its sincerity, *Perspex Island* did not sacrifice the surreal imagery so dear to Hitchcock's diehard fans. The album's title, in fact, was inspired by an acrylic material that's used to make souvenir paperweights; trinkets are suspended in the substance, creating a fossilized Jello effect. "Birds in Perspex," one of the singles off the album, "is basically about wanting something that's dead or frozen to suddenly reanimate," Hitchcock explained in an A&M Records press release. In fact, that "something" does come alive on the album's cover, a creature-filled composition of Hitchcock's own making.

Critics were overwhelmingly positive about *Perspex Island's* accessible love songs, assuring Hitchcock that his fear of "coming off maudlin" was unfounded. Quickly becoming a college favorite, the album was praised not only for its exacting rhythms and three-part harmonies but also for its disarming candor. The first single, "So You Think You're in Love," rose to the top of the CMJ Album Network, Gavin Report, and Radio and Records Alternative charts.

Fittingly, *Perspex Island's* popularity mirrors Hitchcock's feelings about his shift in musical style. "For a long time,

I would rather have been [1960s Pink Floyd guitarist] Syd Barrett or Bob Dylan than me," he told *Spin.* "It's taken about half my life to actually stagger into accepting being Robyn Hitchcock. My aim now is to write songs that have emotion."

Selected discography

With the Soft Boys

Underwater Moonlight (import), Armageddon, 1980.

With the Egyptians

Fegmania!, Slash, 1985.
Gotta Let This Hen Out!, Relativity, 1985.
Element of Light, Relativity, 1986.
Globe of Frogs, A&M, 1988.
Queen Elvis, A&M, 1989.
Perspex Island, A&M, 1991.
Respect, A&M, 1993.

Solo releases

I Often Dream of Trains, Relativity, 1984.

Eye, Twin/Tone, 1990.

Sources

Chicago Tribune, February 23, 1992.
Guitar Player, April 1992.
High Fidelity, May 1988.
Lincoln Journal (Lincoln, NE), September 1991.
Los Angeles Reader, September 13, 1991.
Musician, September 1991; April 1992.
Pitch (Kansas City, MO), August 21, 1991.
Pulse!, September 1991.
Rolling Stone, January 29, 1987; November 4, 1991.
San Antonio Light, August 18, 1991.
San Francisco Chronicle, September 22, 1991.
Spin, September 1991; October 1991.
Washington Post, January 31, 1992.

Additional information for this profile was obtained from an A&M Records press release, 1991.

—Marcia Militello

Marilyn Horne

Opera singer

Marilyn Horne has become one of the twentieth century's most celebrated opera singers, despite her decision to concentrate on the mostly supporting roles of a mezzo-soprano. Her vast range, technical precision, and confident stage presence have earned her great respect, lending force to her efforts to revive the florid singing of bel canto operas.

Horne, who was born in 1934 and as a child wished to become a famous diva, was already singing professionally by the time she was seven years old. Trained by her father, a semiprofessional tenor, Horne and her sister appeared together in churches and United Service Organizations (USO) centers during World War II. In 1951 she entered the University of Southern California on a voice scholarship and began studying with William Vennard. Horne later took masters classes with soprano Lotte Lehmann. She left the university in 1953 in order to concentrate on her career.

In 1954 Horne made her operatic debut with the Los Angeles Guild Opera in the mezzo-soprano role of Hata in Czech composer Bedrich Smetana's *The Bartered Bride.* The same year she dubbed the singing voice of actress Dorothy Dandridge in the film version of *Carmen Jones.* Conductor Robert Craft helped further her career by featuring her in his Los Angeles Monday Evening Concerts. He also introduced her to composer Igor Stravinsky for whom she sang in several concerts and recording sessions.

Horne left the United States for Europe in 1956 to gain more experience. Stravinsky and Craft helped arrange her appearance at that year's Venice Festival, her first major exposure in Europe. The following year she joined the Municipal Opera of Gelsenkirchen—a city in West Germany's Ruhr valley—where she sang such roles as Mimi in *La Boheme,* Tatiana in *Eugene Onegin,* and Fulvia in *Ezio.* She went on to perform in Italy, Vienna, Southern California, and Alaska in a variety of formats, including operas, concerts, radio broadcasts, and music festivals.

More significant than Horne's experience with various formats was her ability to sing a wide variety of roles. Her range extended from a low E to a high C—nearly two octaves—and she could alter her tone to sing soprano, mezzo-soprano, and mezzo-coloratura roles. Horne admitted to *Vogue* reporter David Daniel, "I could and would sing almost anything anyone asked me to. I was young, I figured, and I had nothing to lose. . . . I was going to make it no matter what."

For the Record. . .

Born Marilyn Berneice Horne, January 16, 1934; daughter of Bentz J. (a city assessor and semiprofessional tenor) and Berneice P. (Hokanson) Horne; married Henry Lewis (an orchestra conductor), 1960 (divorced, 1976); children: Angela. *Education:* Attended University of Southern California; studied with William Vennard and soprano Lotte Lehmann. *Religion:* Episcopalian.

Opera and concert singer, c. 1941—. Performed at churches and USO centers, 1940s; made operatic debut with the Los Angeles Guild Opera, 1954; appeared at Venice Festival, 1956; performed major soprano and mezzo-soprano roles with the Municipal Opera of Gelsenkirchen, West Germany, 1957-60; sang mezzo-soprano role in *Beatrice di Tenda,* 1961; first performance as Arsace in *Semiramide,* 1964; debuted at London's Covent Garden, 1964, Milan's La Scala, 1969, and New York City's Metropolitan Opera, 1970; sang the part of Semira in *The Ghost of Versailles,* 1991; performed at inauguration of U.S. President Bill Clinton, 1993. Author, with Jane Scovell, of *Marilyn Horne, My Life,* Atheneum, 1983.

*Addresses: Home—*New York, NY. *Record company—*London Records, 825 Eighth Ave., New York, NY 10019.

Especially Enjoyed Roles for Mezzo-Soprano

Horne returned to the United States in 1960, making her debut that summer as Marie in *Wozzeck* with the San Francisco Opera Company. Soon thereafter, she performed several important roles, including Carmen for the San Francisco Opera Company in 1961, Lora in the premiere of Vittorio Giannini's *The Harvest* at the Chicago Lyric Opera the same year, and Adalgisa in Bellini's *Norma* for the Vancouver Opera in 1962.

Though she was able to sing a wide range of roles, Horne had discovered that she enjoyed singing the more ornate passages of Handel oratorios and Bach cantatas. Coloratura roles, with their difficult combinations of trills, rapid scales, arpeggios, and roulades challenged her already superb technical mastery and interpretive skills. Just such a role presented itself in 1961 when the mezzo-soprano who was to sing with Joan Sutherland in *Beatrice di Tenda* canceled three weeks before the opening. Horne replaced her, singing the role of Agnese to great critical praise.

At that time, such bel canto operas as *Beatrice di Tenda* had been virtually forgotten. According to Philip

Kennicott of *Musical America,* these baroque operas were "considered dramatically flimsy and vocally strenuous," and "many of these works hadn't been staged for nearly a century." However, some singers, including Joan Sutherland, were renewing the operas' popularity, and Horne's speed, flexibility, and vast range made her voice a natural for this genre. Although Horne sang several soprano roles over the next few years—including her 1970 Metropolitan Opera (Met) debut as Adalgisa in *Norma*—she soon began to specialize in mezzo-soprano, bel canto music.

Often Sang Male Roles

In 1964 Horne first performed a bel canto role that she would sing many times during the next 30 years—Arsace, the commanding general of the Babylonian army in Gioacchino Rossini's *Semiramide.* This initial performance in Los Angeles, with Joan Sutherland in the title role, was such a success they performed it that same year at Carnegie Hall. Described as an opera of "fiendish difficulty" by *Vogue* correspondent David Daniel, it was an immense success in New York City. Winthrop Sargeant reported in the *New Yorker,* "Marilyn Horne, a mezzo-soprano of brilliant agility, backed [Joan Sutherland] to the hilt in the transvestite part of Arsace . . . and the duet between the two at the end of the third act was as spectacular a display of trilling and cascading pyrotechnics as I have ever come across."

With her choice of a soprano or mezzo career, some think it unusual that Horne chose the mostly supporting roles of a mezzo-soprano. However, as she explained to Kennicott in *Musical America,* "I think I get some pretty gutsy characters in these [bel canto] operas. Many of them are male roles, of course, but that also gives them a lot of dramatic thrust, accent, and power." Kennicott attested to the success of her choice: "Through years of hearing her sing with different sopranos, audiences have marveled at Horne's ability to blend, shade and color her voice, making it a confident, yet never self-serving accompaniment to everyone on stage."

Horne began to eliminate certain roles from her repertoire as she entered her sixties, an age at which most opera singers have retired. She no longer performs in Verdi operas, except for *Falstaff* in which she plays Dame Quickly. However, she continues to sing the demanding bel canto roles of Rossini and to learn new roles. In 1991 Horne played Semira—a role written especially for her—in the premiere of John Corigliano's *The Ghost of Versailles.*

Played Major Part in Revival of Bel Canto Opera

Horne's appearance in *Semiramide* at the often conservative Met in 1990, surrounded by young American bel canto singers, indicated the enormous influence she has had in the revival of bel canto singing. Noted Rossini scholar Philip Gosset stressed to *Musical America* correspondent Philip Kennicott, "I don't think the Rossini revival could possibly have taken place without [Horne's] central position in it." In recognition of her contributions to the revival of such operas, Horne received an invitation to perform at Avery Fisher Hall in New York's Lincoln Center the day of Rossini's 200th birthday, February 29, 1992.

Horne, considered one of the greatest mezzo-sopranos of her time, not only led the revival of bel canto opera, but has entranced audiences in a myriad of roles. *Musical America's* Kennicott described the reasons for her vast success: "She not only had a distinctive and beautiful voice, but also an incomparably even technique that allowed her to fly through the tortuous roulades and runs of Rossini as if her voice were a dark wooden flute, played with superhuman dexterity."

Selected discography

(With Joan Sutherland and Richard Conrad) *The Age of Bel Canto,* London Records, 1964.
Presenting Marilyn Horne, London Records, 1965.
Souvenir of a Golden Era, London Records, 1966.
(With Sutherland and Luciano Pavarotti) *Requiem,* London Records, 1968.
(With Sutherland) *Semiramide,* London Records, 1969.
Bach and Handel Arias, London Records, 1969.
Marilyn Horne Sings Carmen, London Records, 1970.
(With Elena Souliotis, Nicolai Ghiaurov, and John Alexander) *Anna Bolena,* London Records, 1970.
Marilyn Horne's Greatest Hits, London Records, 1973.
Marilyn Horne, London Records, 1974.

(With the Chicago Symphony Orchestra and Chorus) *Mahler's Symphony No. 3,* RCA, 1976.
(With Sutherland and Pavarotti) *Il Trovatore,* London Records, 1977.
Sheherazade, CBS, 1978.
Diva!, CBS, 1981.
(With Samuel Ramey, Ernesto Palacio, and Kathleen Battle) *L'Italiana in Algeri,* RCA, 1981.
Giovanna D'Arco and Songs, CBS, 1982.
In Concert at the Met, RCA, 1983.
Airs D'Operas, Erato, 1984.
Rarities From Her Repertoire, Standing Room Only 800 Series, 1992.
(With Sir Colin Davis) *Falstaff,* RCA Victor Red Seal, 1992.
(With Chris Merritt and Rockwell Blake) *Ermione,* Legato Classics, 1992.
All Through the Night, RCA, 1992.
Beautiful Dreamer, London Records.

Sources

Books

Horne, Marilyn, with Jane Scovell, *Marilyn Horne, My Life,* Atheneum, 1983.
The Metropolitan Opera Encyclopedia: A Comprehensive Guide to the World of Opera, edited by David Hamilton, Simon and Schuster, 1987.

Periodicals

Modern Maturity, December 1991/January 1992.
Musical America, January/February 1992.
New Yorker, February 29, 1964.
Pulse!, November 1992.
Time, February 19, 1965.
Vanity Fair, February 1992.
Vogue, December 1990.

—*Susan Windisch Brown*

Elvin Jones

Jazz drummer

Many music critics regard Elvin Jones as the most influential drummer in the history of jazz. His revolutionary style transformed the drums as a traditional time-keeping instrument. Employing a multilayered, rhythmic approach, he created a dynamic interplay with soloists unprecedented by earlier drum stylists. Early in his career, Jones performed with such jazzmen as Charles Mingus, Bud Powell, Sonny Rollins, and Miles Davis. But it wasn't until he joined the John Coltrane Quartet in 1960 that Jones began to attract international recognition. During his six years with Coltrane's group, Jones contributed to some of the most celebrated recordings in the history of modern jazz. For over four decades, his innovative rhythmic technique has served as a catalyst for drummers who seek greater improvisational freedom.

Jones was born on September 9, 1927, in Pontiac, Michigan, not far from Detroit. The youngest of ten children, he belonged to a musical family. Aside from his two brilliantly talented brothers, Hank and Thad, he had two sisters who studied piano and violin. Jones's early interest in music preceded his later affinity for jazz.

Around the age of five or six, Jones visited a fairgrounds in Pontiac where the Ringling Brothers circus drummers performed. That experience—combined with local radio broadcasts of symphonic music that introduced him to the sound of the tympani drums—inspired him to become a percussionist. Whether at a parade or at a football game, Jones could be found observing a musical rhythm section with intent fascination. Much to the frustration of his mother, he began to practice rhythms on various objects around the family home. When he reached age fourteen, his older sister loaned him money to purchase his first set of drums.

While in junior high school, Elvin acquired a drum method book from which he quickly learned the rudiments of percussion. "Being able to read music," Jones explained to Herb Nolan in *Down Beat,* "opened up a whole world of possibilities," since it provided techniques that could be applied to other musical forms. Jones's high school band instructor Fred N. Weist contributed to the young drummer's knowledge and approach to percussion. But after a year, Jones—desiring a career as a professional drummer—left school. In 1946, he ventured to Boston in search of employment. On the East Coast, he enlisted in the U.S. Army. For the next three years, he performed in various military bands.

B orn September 9, 1927, in Pontiac, MI; son of a Baptist deacon and lumber inspector; married; wife's name, Keiko.

Jazz drummer and recording artist; performed with Charles Mingus, Bud Powell, Sonny Rollins, and Miles Davis; member of John Coltrane Quartet, 1960-66. Appeared in film *Zachariah*, 1970. *Military service*: U.S. Army, 1946-49.

Awards: Member of Percussive Arts Society Hall of Fame.

Addresses: *Record company*—Enja, c/o Koch International Corp., 177 Cantiague Rock Rd., Westbury, NY 11590.

From Detroit to New York

Returning to Pontiac in 1949, Jones played in groups with his brothers, Hank and Thad. In clubs around the Detroit area, Jones shared the stage with such local greats as guitarist Kenny Burrell, bassist Paul Chambers, and pianist Tommy Flannagan. As a member of Billy Mitchell's house band at the Blue Bird, Jones performed with the finest Detroit musicians as well as jazz legends like trumpeter Miles Davis and saxophonist John Coltrane. "They took me as one of their own, and I began to use my abilities," reminisced Jones in the *Detroit Free Press*. "It was a great camaraderie there."

In 1955 Jones left for New York to audition for Benny Goodman's band. He did not get the job, but within two weeks, he joined a group led by bassist Charles Mingus. "Elvin was a 'prophet,'" declared Mingus in *Mingus: A Critical Biography*. "I never swung so much or rather lived so much in my life." After touring with Mingus, Jones performed for over a year with pianist Bud Powell, a musician he considers one of the "masters" of modern jazz. In 1957 Jones toured Europe with trombonist J. J. Johnson. Throughout the late 1950s he recorded with such musicians as Sonny Rollins and Stan Getz and Detroiters like Chambers and Flannagan.

Became Drummer in John Coltrane Quartet

But one of Jones's crowning achievements came when he joined John Coltrane's Quartet in 1960. Replacing Billy Higgins on drums, Jones helped form one of the most formidable ensembles in modern jazz. Coltrane's group provided Jones with the opportunity to freely improvise within the arrangements. Along with bassist Jimmy Garrison and pianist McCoy Tyner, Jones and

Coltrane conducted a powerful exchange of musical ideas. "The most impressive thing about working with Trane was a feeling of steady, collective learning," recalled Jones in Arthur Taylor's *Notes and Tones: Musician to Musician Interviews*. "I admired Coltrane both as a person and as a musician," he added. "It was the best of both possible worlds." In 1966 Coltrane added a second drummer, Rashied Ali. Jones, who considered this arrangement incompatible with his musical direction, chose to leave the group.

Following a brief stint in Europe with Duke Ellington's band, Jones returned to the United States where he founded several trios under his own name. The first of these featured bassist Wilbur Ware and saxophonist-flutist Joe Farrel. Soon afterward, Ware was replaced by former Coltrane member Garrison. Because the trio did not have a guitar or piano to lay down harmonic foundations, making the group work proved a challenge for Jones. For as he explained in *Down Beat*, the drummer's role within this format "is like a root of tree. . . . You gotta be there, and firmly there." Among the trio's recordings was *Puttin' It Together*.

Toured Internationally

Beginning in the 1970s, Jones organized tours to Europe, Asia, and South America and performed at clubs, clinics, high schools, and free outdoor concerts. His appearance on recordings with Ron Carter on bass and Tyner on piano influenced a new generation of musicians to take up the study of acoustic jazz, and he gained a reputation as a nurturer of new jazz talent. "Giving someone a chance is the greatest gift that you can give to another person," he commented in an interview with Ken Franckling in *Down Beat*. Leading his own groups, Jones employed the talents of such saxophonists as Farrel, Frank Foster, Dave Liebman, and George Coleman. By the 1990s, the line-up of his group, known as the Elvin Jones Jazz Machine, featured saxophonists Sonny Fortune and John Coltrane's son, Ravi—musicians who seem to share his philosophy. "The whole point is to play jazz, not any of its hybrid forms," Jones continued in *Down Beat*. "You need to have a deep, spiritual feeling for the music."

Using only a standard drum kit—without the aid of any electronics—Jones changed the face of percussion in the jazz world. He is responsible for the innovation of a circular style of drumming, an approach that uses broad sweeping movements across the drums. Often beginning an arrangement by introducing a simple pattern or theme, he perpetually builds the rhythm into a near-kinetic state. By removing the traditional four-

four beat on the bass drum, Jones is able to create what he calls a more "constant flow of rhythm." On the snare drum and cymbals, he plays irregular accents that often accompany soloists in furious dialogue. Although many modernist drummers try to imitate Jones's techniques, they often lack his skillful execution. For as Jones stresses, no matter how abstract the arrangement, a drummer's main responsibility is to keep time.

Elvin Jones has had a profound impact on modern music. His improvisational approach helped lay the foundations for avant garde and fusion jazz movements. During the 1960s he was idolized by a number of rock musicians, including Jimi Hendrix's drummer, Mitch Mitchell. A unique and gifted individual, Jones has redefined the role of the drums in jazz music. His influence extends to a new school of jazz drummers who perform on concert stages throughout the world. As he stated in the film documentary *Different Drummer,* Jones believes his exceptional approach stems from the fact that he could never "comply to the standard form." Impelled by this rebellious spirit, he continues to devote his life to the pursuit of infinite rhythmic variations and creative expression.

Selected discography

Solo releases

Elvin!, 1962.
Puttin' It Together: The Elvin Jones Trio, Blue Note, 1967.
In Europe, Enja, 1992.
Youngblood, Enja, 1993.
Yesterdays, Precision.
That's the Way I Feel Now (Tribute to Thelonious Monk), A&M.
Live at the Lighthouse, Black Sun.
Poly-Currents, Black Sun.

With John Coltrane

My Favorite Things, Atlantic, 1960.
Ballads, Impulse, 1961.
Live at Birdland, Impulse, 1961.

Impressions, Impulse, 1961.
A Love Supreme, Impulse, 1963.
New Thing at Newport, Impulse, 1965.

With others

(With McCoy Tyner) *Elvin Jones and McCoy Tyner Quintet Reunion,* Black Hawk, 1982.
(With Pharoah Sanders) *Ask the Ages,* Axiom, 1992.
(With Tyner) *Today and Tomorrow,* Impulse.
(With Tyner) *Trident,* Milestone.

Sources

Books

Balliet, Whitney, *Ecstacy at the Onion: Thirty-one Pieces on Jazz,* Bobbs-Merrill, 1971.
The New Grove Dictionary of Jazz, edited by Barry Kernfield, MacMillan, 1988.
Priestly, Brian, *Mingus: A Critical Biography,* Quartet Books, 1982.
Taylor, Arthur, *Notes and Tones: Musician to Musician Interviews,* Perigee, 1982.
Thomas, J. D., *Chasin' the Trane: The Mystique of John Coltrane,* Doubleday, 1975.

Periodicals

Detroit Free Press, November 5, 1991.
Down Beat, October 2, 1969; March 2, 1972; November 8, 1973; March 1992; July 1992; September 1992; November 1992.
Jazz Journal, April, 1975.
Rolling Stone, February 4, 1993.

Additional information for this profile was obtained from liner notes by Billy Taylor to *Puttin' It Together: The Elvin Jones Trio,* Blue Note, 1967; the documentary *Different Drummer: Elvin Jones,* directed by Ed Gray, 1979; and a recording of a Wayne State University drum clinic, Detroit, MI, November 15, 1991.

—John Cohassey

Grace Jones

Singer

"**G**race Jones slinks on stage wearing a floor-length wedding veil, a black corset, and fishnet stockings held up by fancy garters. Flicking a long red leather whip, she struts from one end of the small stage to the other, singing her hit song, *I Need a Man,* and inspecting two half-naked male dancers as though they are tigers in her cage. The whip snaps and off come the dancers' baggy pants to reveal their black jock straps. Grace steps back and inspects the wares, occasionally slapping the dancers' bare buttocks with her red whip. She's not satisfied. She dismisses the bejocked dancers, and from the audience that jams three sides of the stage grabs a man by the collar ('Come on! I know you're a hot number!'), pulls him onto the stage and demands that he remove his shirt. Before long, there are dozens of half-dressed men on stage, and Grace is almost lost in a sea of sweaty, gyrating bodies. One fellow takes off *all* his clothes." It is precisely this kind of performance, described in *Ebony* in 1979, that made Grace Jones famous.

After her first album, *Portfolio,* in 1977 and a series of hit dance singles, Jones became a virtual legend with nightclub audiences. Although her music always stayed right in step with the latest trends, it was more accurately Jones's appearance and performances that catapulted her to fame. A strikingly handsome Afro-Caribbean woman, Jones deliberately accented her sculptured features with a shaved head, dramatic make-up, and outlandish clothing. She cultivated an image so unusual to mainstream American audiences that it led to a variety of rumors and questions about her identity, as the *Ebony* writer demonstrated: "So is she European? African? South American? Isn't she really a man? Did she have a sex change?"

She also cultivated the behavior that made her an icon for the late 1970s nightclub audiences that anticipated the rise of New Wave and punk music and fashion. The games that Jones played in particular with gender roles and sexuality brought her solid success with gay male audiences, as well as the title "Queen of the Gay Discos." She inspired such adoration that, after a performance, she would receive lines of admirers backstage, many bearing gifts. One man even handcuffed himself to her ankle during a performance.

Childhood in Jamaica, Success in Paris

Jones's image began in a large, religious, middle-class family in Spanish Town, Jamaica. She and a twin brother, Christian, were born on May 19, 1952, to the Reverend Robert Jones and Marjorie Jones—both the offspring of powerful Afro-Caribbean families. Jones described the environment in *Rolling Stone:* "My fa-

For the Record. . .

Born May 19, 1952, in Spanish Town, Jamaica; immigrated to U.S., c. 1965; daughter of Robert (a minister) and Marjorie Jones; married Jean-Paul Goode, c. 1979 (divorced, 1982); married Chris Stanley, c. 1989 (divorced, 1990); children: (first marriage) Poalo. *Education:* Studied theater at State University of New York at Syracuse, c. 1968.

Worked variously in theaters and nightclubs in Philadelphia, late 1960s to early 1970s; became employed by Wilhelmina Modeling Agency, New York City; moved to Paris to pursue modeling career, mid-1970s; recorded first album, in France, c. 1975; signed with Island Records and released *Portfolio,* 1977; signed with Capitol and Manhattan Records, late 1980s; re-signed with Island, 1991. Worked with ACT UP and other AIDS relief organizations, late 1980s. Appeared in films *Gordon's Wars,* 1977; *Conan the Destroyer,* 1984; *A View to a Kill,* 1985; *Vamp,* 1987; *Siesta,* 1987; and *Boomerang,* 1992.

Addresses: *Record company*—Island Records, 14 East 4th St., New York, NY 10012.

ther's side of the family was heavy into politics. The bank and the library—real government stuff. We were kept away from them because my mother's side was very religious." The religion—Pentecostal—was so strict that Jones was required always to wear dresses with high necks and long sleeves. Not surprisingly, she sees this upbringing as the beginning of her later rebelliousness. The discipline increased when Jones's parents moved from Jamaica to Syracuse, New York, and she was left to the care of her grandparents. She described those years in a 1985 *Los Angeles Times* interview with Robert Hilburn: "As a little child I wasn't allowed to do anything. . . . No television, no radio, no movies, nothing. I wasn't even allowed to straighten my hair or wear open-toed shoes. . . . Even when I moved to Syracuse to live with my parents when I was 13, I had to go by strict rules."

By the time she was 17, she was studying theater at Syracuse University. Before the first semester was over, Jones decided to pursue her interest in performance through different channels. First she moved to Philadelphia where, for a few months, she held odd jobs at theaters and nightclubs. In the early 1970s she moved again, this time to New York City, where—according to *Mademoiselle*—she "began to be seen nightly in the city's shadier discos." *Newsweek* reported that "she shaved her head, became a nudist, tried go-go dancing." New York also provided her with her

first break: a modeling job with the Wilhelmina Modeling Agency. When one last move took her to Paris to join her brother who was already a model there, Jones succeeded as a top international model. The career that began with a cover for *Essence* in the early 1970s soon led to covers for *Elle, Vogue,* and *Der Stern.*

For Jones, however, the modeling career was only a stepping stone to the stage and film work that she had always wanted. Her "discovery" came in 1974, according to *Ebony:* "While dining with friends, Grace got so carried away when she heard 'Dirty Old Man' by the Three Degrees that she jumped on the restaurant table and sang to the record. Her captivated audience applauded. . . . One of the models with her was so impressed by the impromptu performance that she told her boyfriend, who just happened to be a record producer." The first record was produced by a small French label that couldn't market the work well. In 1977 Jones signed instead with Island, an important British label, and cut the album *Portfolio,* which launched her career as a disco performer. By 1980 she had released three more albums, *Fame, Muse,* and *Warm Leatherette,* as well as a string of singles that were successful on the dance charts: "I Need a Man," "Do or Die," "La Vie en rose," and "Love Is a Drug."

A Change in Image

In the late 1970s, when Jones met and eventually married French artist Jean-Paul Goode, she moved away from the provocative performances that had made her a favorite at New York nightclubs like Studio 54. Under Goode's management, the "Queen of the Gay Discos" began giving concerts intended to broaden her audience. The 1981 release of *Nightclubbing* and a 1982 tour, promoting both *Nightclubbing* and new material for *Living My Life,* the album she would release later that year, introduced audiences to the new Grace Jones: less shocking, more "aesthetic." Goode carefully redesigned Jones's stage show, replacing the animals and whips with a series of "Tableaux Vivants"—living pictures.

Although her concerts received mixed reviews—some critics appreciated the new quality of the show, others clearly missed the exhibitionism—*Nightclubbing* kept Jones right in sync with the dance music trend, just as her earlier albums had. "Pull Up to the Bumper" reached number five on the charts—the biggest hit Jones had ever had; "Nipple to the Bottle," from *Living My Life,* became one of the dance hits of 1983. According to *Melody Maker,* "[Jones's] 'Nightclubbing' album changed the path of dance music."

Despite persistent ambivalence on the part of critics who wanted musical quality out of Jones, she had in fact moved into a realm of greater seriousness among her peers. Chris Blackwell, the president of Island, still handled the production of her albums; his co-producer for *Nightclubbing*, Alex Sadkin, had worked with such successful New Wave bands as the B-52s and the Plastics. Several songs were penned by respected New Wave musicians, including David Bowie and Iggy Pop's "Nightclubbing" and Sting's "Demolition Man." Robbie Shakespeare and Sly Dunbar, probably the most sought after rhythm section in reggae music, worked with Jones for the second time on *Nightclubbing*.

By the mid-1980s, Jones was enjoying the peak of her fame. *Newsweek* noted: "She seems to be turning up everywhere—astride a blood-red Honda in a TV commercial, curtsying to the Princess of Wales at the London premiere of 'A View to a Kill.' In the July issue of *Playboy*, Jones and her Swedish boyfriend, Dolph Lundgren . . . are splashed across the pages." Probably the most important consolidation of Jones's fame came with her two major film roles—*Conan the Destroyer* in 1984 and *A View to a Kill* in 1985. Both of these, unlike Jones's first film appearance in 1977 in *Gordon's Wars*, were high visibility roles: the first was the sequel to the immensely successful *Conan the Barbarian*; the second, one in the long series of James Bond films dating from the 1960s.

Myriad Troubles

It was soon after the release of *Slave to the Rhythm* in 1987 that Jones's career began to falter. Although the album did well enough, other problems beset the singer. *Vamp*, a 1987 horror movie in which Jones plays a vampire/stripper, had no success with movie audiences. Consequently, from 1987 to 1990, Jones was scarce on the public scene, except in news stories that focused on distress in her personal life. She had declared bankruptcy in 1986 and was still working against a debt that some sources estimated at $750,000; her largest creditor, American Express, eventually sued for $80,000. In 1989 a series of news reports focused on Jones's appearance at a drug trial after she was charged with cocaine possession; she was eventually acquitted. She was married to and then divorced from Chris Stanley. Her attempt at a comeback in the late 1980s—including a move to Capitol Records and then Manhattan, the release of *Bulletproof Heart* in 1989, and a limited concert tour—failed to fan the waning flames.

In a 1991 interview for *The Advocate*, Jones added a different perspective to the stories about what had happened to her career in the late 1980s. The performer who had first found her fame, her most adoring audience, and many of her good friends among gay men, found herself losing many of those people to AIDS (Acquired Immune Deficiency Syndrome): "It was a strange period. . . . I got very depressed for about two years. . . . So many of my close friends were sick and passing away. As I said at the benefit I did last year for [artist and activist] Keith [Haring] and ACT UP [AIDS Coalition To Unleash Power], 'I felt like dying along for a while.'"

In response to her sense of loss, Jones became involved with AIDS benefits and relief work in general. She described the kind of support that she gained from these activities: "I always perform at gay clubs, even if I have an international movie or whatever big success. I still go back. That's where I have the most fun! Gays appreciate me more than anybody." In a similar gesture of homecoming, Jones re-signed with Island Records in 1991, intending to once again produce an album with Chris Blackwell.

Selected discography

Portfolio (includes "I Need a Man" and "La Vie en rose"), Island, 1977.
Fame, Island, 1978.
Muse, Island, 1979.
Warm Leatherette (includes "Love Is a Drug"), Island, 1980.
Nightclubbing (includes "Pull Up to the Bumper," "Nightclubbing," and "Demolition Man"), Island, 1981.
Living My Life (includes "Nipple to the Bottle"), Island, 1982.
Island Life, Island, 1985.
Slave to the Rhythm, Island, 1987.
Bulletproof Heart, Capitol, 1989.
Inside Story, Manhattan, 1990.

Sources

Advocate, September 10, 1991.
Ebony, July 1979.
Essence, June 1985.
Jet, May 1, 1989; September 25, 1989; February 5, 1990.
Los Angeles Times, May 18, 1985.
Mademoiselle, November 1982.
Melody Maker, January 24, 1987; April 7, 1990.
Newsweek, July 1, 1985.
People, June 8, 1992.
Rolling Stone, August 20, 1981.
Stereo Review, May 1986.

—Ondine E. Le Blanc

Chaka Khan

Singer, songwriter, producer

In his notes to one volume of Rhino Records' CD series *Soul Hits of the 70's: Didn't It Blow Your Mind!,* Paul Grein called Chaka Khan "the most influential female vocalist in R&B since Aretha Franklin." This was not the first time that Khan had been compared to the "Queen of Soul." As a teeny-bopper singing with a group of friends, she became known as "Little Aretha." But the comparison would have a double edge: many critics accused her of lacking a distinctive style. As Curtis Bagley of *Essence* remarked, Khan was at the time of her early stardom in the mid-seventies "a new breed of singer: one who was self-taught, not manufactured; one who ignored tradition and recorded exactly as—and what—she wanted to."

Scoring early hits with the funk-rock group Rufus, she established herself as a solo artist in the late seventies, moving through the following decade with several huge hits, a slew of Grammy awards, and a growing roster of distinguished musical collaborators. Though several reviewers found her solo career spotty and often lamented her choice of material and use of multiple producers on her records, she moved with the times. Her 1992 album *The Woman I Am* yielded a smash single and further demonstrated her staying power.

Chaka Khan was born Yvette Marie Stevens in 1953 in Great Lakes, Illinois. Her mother worked at the National Opinion Research Center at the University of Chicago, and her father was a free-lance photographer. Khan described her family as "upper middle class" to *Melody Maker*'s Ian Pye. She confided in a *Rolling Stone* interview that when she was ten years old, her grandmother read her palm and told her, "One day, many, many people are going to know your name." Soon she was showing signs of fulfilling this prediction, singing with her vocal group the Crystalettes at talent shows.

Began Singing in Clubs at 15

At the age of 15, Khan made her professional debut, singing in a Chicago club. She would soon enter what *Rolling Stone*'s Debby Bull called her "African Awareness Phase," singing with a group called Shades of Black and another Afrocentric ensemble known as The Pharaohs. An African priest gave her the name Chaka Adunne Adufle Yemoja Hodarhu Karifi. She found strength and a degree of rebellion in the doctrine of the politically radical Black Panter Party and helped organize her school's Black Student Union. This was no mere phase. Years later she told *Melody Maker* that she

For the Record. . .

Born Yvette Marie Stevens, March 23, 1953, in Great Lakes, IL; given the name Chaka Adunne Adufle Yemoja Hodarhu Karifi by an African priest, c. 1970; daughter of a researcher and a free-lance photographer; involved in long-term relationship with Assan Khan (a musician), beginning 1970; married Richard Holland (a songwriter and producer), 1978 (divorced, 1980); children: Milini (daughter); (with Holland) Damien (son).

Began singing as a teenager with vocal group the Crystalettes; worked as a file clerk, 1968; singer and songwriter, 1968—; recording artist, 1972—; joined group Rufus and recorded debut album, 1972; signed with Warner Bros. Records; released first solo album, *Chaka,* 1978.

Awards: Numerous Grammy awards, including two with Rufus for best R&B performance by a duo or group, for "Tell Me Something Good" and "Ain't Nobody"; for solo work, including best female vocalist and best vocal arrangement, 1983, for "Bebop Medley," best R&B single by a female vocalist, 1984, for "I Feel For You," and best R&B vocal performance, female, 1993, for "The Woman I Am"; honored by International Association of African-American Music for career excellence, 1992.

Addresses: Record company—Warner Bros., 75 Rockefeller Plaza, 20th floor, New York, NY 10019.

retained her radical views: "The Panthers were telling the truth—America is the most fascist country; capitalism does suck."

Soon she dropped out of high school; at sixteen she ran away from home. "When I left I was very broke but very happy," she told *Rolling Stone*'s Fred Schruers, "and I wanted to prove to my parents and my peers that I could do it." At seventeen she entered a quasi-marriage—"All we went through were some Indian rites" for the ceremony, she told *Rolling Stone* in 1974—with Assan Khan, bassist for the Babysitters, for whom she was singing at the time. During this time she worked in an office for $2.60 an hour and sang in the clubs at night with various bands. She was also smoking a lot of marijuana and living a life that—despite her ostensible marriage—was far from domestic. In 1972 she joined up with Chicago's Ask Rufus, a versatile group made up of former members of the successful pop act American Breed. Ask Rufus was fronted at the time by singer Paulette McWilliams, with whom Khan became close. By the time McWilliams left the band, Khan knew all their songs and was a natural choice for her replacement.

Stole Spotlight With Rufus

The group paid more dues on the club scene, shortened its name to Rufus, and got new management; after many ups and downs they forged a deal with ABC Records. Even with the group's solid credentials, however, it became clear that the new lead singer would monopolize the limelight. A *Down Beat* review of a Rufus appearance in Los Angeles in 1973 demonstrates this. After lauding the group's material and musicianship, reviewer Eric Gaer wrote, "Chaka Khan, black, beautiful female vocalist, hides her true ability until about halfway into the set. But the minute she opens her mouth we know she can put us away—and does."

The band's self-titled debut LP made a few ripples—the single "Whoever Is Thrilling You Is Killing Me" did fairly well on black radio—but was by no means a smash. Then superstar singer-performer Stevie Wonder, an admirer of Khan's who had contributed the song "Maybe Your Baby" to the group's first record, appeared at a session for their next album. He offered a song called "Tell Me Something Good." Khan recalled to *Rolling Stone* that she didn't like a previous song that Wonder had offered for the session. "So he said, 'What's your birth sign?' I said, 'Aries-Pisces,' and he said, 'Oh, well here's a song for you.' And he wrote 'Tell Me Something Good.'" The two collaborated on the lyrics. Released as a single in 1974, the song helped the LP on which it appeared, *Rags to Rufus,* go gold. "Tell Me Something Good" garnered a Grammy Award for best R&B performance by a group or duo. The album also yielded the dance hit "Once You Get Started" and Ray Parker Jr.'s "You Got the Love"; both songs made it into the Top 20. Also in 1974 Khan had her first child, her daughter Milini. Assan was not the father.

The next year saw the release of *Rufusized,* which also went gold. The group was by now calling itself Rufus Featuring Chaka Khan; as *Rolling Stone* critic Jim Miller asked, "Is Rufus a group or is it Chaka Khan with a backup band?" Miller answered his own question by declaring that "Rufus has become a vehicle for showcasing Khan and her idiosyncratic voice," a voice he praised while noting its owner's tendency toward "histrionic displays." Miller found the material on the album lacking "the kind of creative spark that animated 'Tell Me Something Good.'"

Subsequent albums fared well commercially, if not always critically. *Rufus Featuring Chaka Khan,* released in 1976, went gold, as did its Top Five single "Sweet Thing." Even so, *Rolling Stone*'s Tom Vickers, while admitting that Khan's vocals had "calmed down recently," insisted that she lacked "emotion." The 1977 release *Ask Rufus* went platinum and finally earned the approval of *Rolling Stone:* "With time and experience Chaka Khan has broken away from her screeching Aretha Franklin imitations and found her own voice in both the musical and poetic senses of the term," wrote Russell Gersten, who dubbed *Ask Rufus* "one of the year's best pop albums." Of 1978's *Street Player,* the magazine's Joe McEwen noted that Khan's departure from the group was expected and suggested that the group had little to offer without her. "Chaka Khan has been one of the most iconoclastic pop singers of the Seventies, but she has yet to make a substantial album," McEwen concluded. "It's about time."

Solo Career

Khan did in fact embark on a solo career and began recording for Warner Bros. in 1978, though she still periodically recorded with Rufus on ABC and later on MCA, the label that acquired it. Her first solo album, *Chaka,* received mixed reviews. *Melody Maker* called it a "clinker," while *Rolling Stone* declared: "Here she achieves an emotional depth only hinted at on other albums." The record went gold and contained the hit "I'm Every Woman." Produced by R&B wizard Arif Mardin and enlisting members of Rufus and the Average White Band, *Chaka* was recorded quickly and relatively inexpensively. By 1979 Khan was pregnant again and gave birth to a son, Damien, by her husband, songwriter/producer Richard Holland.

Khan next recorded *Masterjam* with Rufus; it was produced by Quincy Jones and released in 1980. *Rolling Stone,* while asserting that Khan was "the group's most attractive feature," judged that "the songs aren't so good. Chaka Khan's not in top form and neither is

---

"It was a little scary at first, making all the decisions, but I learned a lot, and having done it, I know I could never go back to the way it was."

Rufus." *Masterjam* contained three hit singles, including "Do You Love What You Feel." The same year Khan put out another solo album, *Naughty;* it featured the hits "Clouds" and "Papillon (Hot Butterfly)." Her 1981 solo LP *What Cha' Gonna Do for Me* was a smash, despite

another pan from *Rolling Stone.* "Chaka Khan has grown up into an overly facile stylist," wrote Laura Fissinger of the album, which includes Khan's rendition of the jazz classic "A Night in Tunisia." The album went gold. In 1981 Khan also appeared on the Rufus album *Camouflage* and provided the soundtrack for the public television production of the play *For Colored Girls Who Have Considered Suicide / When the Rainbow is Enuf.*

Khan's marriage to Holland ended in 1980, and she took Milini and Damien and moved to New York to live with her boyfriend, Harlem schoolteacher Albert Sarasohn. She appeared with Chick Corea and his group of stellar musicians for the jazz standards album *Echoes of an Era* in 1982 and released her next solo album, *Chaka Khan,* that same year; for the latter project she enlisted the help of producer Mardin and experimented with a wide variety of styles. Perhaps the most ambitious track on the album is "Bebop Medley," which touches on a handful of jazz classics. *Stereo Review,* while acknowledging that with Khan "you either like her or you don't," called the album "a sizzling summary of the state of her art" that demonstrated her evolution into "a solo artist whose performance is as classy as it is brassy." Khan won two 1983 Grammies for "Bebop Medley." She also shared a trophy with Rufus for their single "Ain't Nobody" from that year's *Live Stompin' at the Savoy.*

The 1984 solo release *I Feel for You* went platinum, thanks in large part to the smash title track. The song was written by Prince and featured pioneering rapper Grandmaster Melle Mel and a harmonica part by Stevie Wonder. Khan walked off with another Grammy, this time for best R&B vocal performance. "Khan has always been a singer of great range and eclectic tastes," opined Don Shewey in his *Rolling Stone* review, "but they've never been shown to greater advantage than on *I Feel for You.*"

Khan didn't please the critics as much with her 1986 album *Destiny,* however. "Her attempt to be every singer for every taste falls into the gaps between the formats," read the *Rolling Stone* review of *Destiny.* "I'm a big gambler with life," Khan told *Essence* in 1986, adding that she felt daunted by the prospect of singing jazz: "There is a conscious part of me that doesn't think Chaka is a very good jazz singer." That same year, she drew attention for her backing vocals on Steve Winwood's hit single (and video) "Higher Love."

In 1988 Khan released *C.K.,* which sports collaborations with Prince and jazz legend Miles Davis. Prince contributed two songs, "Eternity" and "Sticky Wicked"; Khan also recorded Wonder's "Signed, Sealed, Delivered." For *New Yorker* critic Mark Moses, "Once you've relinquished the hope that Khan will ever make a consistent solo album—this is a career that is crying out for a 'best of' compilation to make sense of it—the record reveals charms (and, even more surprising, an unshowy depth) that you wouldn't have dared to let yourself expect." *Melody Maker* called the album "just dandy." To the latter periodical Khan admitted disgust at the cobbled-together release *Life Is a Dance.* "I didn't do this LP," she said. "Warner Brothers did it totally themselves without my knowledge and without my consent and it pisses me off a lot." The record contains a number of collaborations between Khan and other artists over a ten-year period.

Oversaw Next Project

Khan took a sabbatical after *C.K.,* relocating to Europe—she has homes in London and Germany—and envisioning her next project. It would take a few years to germinate, with Khan (now going only by the name Chaka) co-writing several songs and undertaking the task of overseeing the project herself. "Usually I'd hire a producer and let him do the work of pulling the sessions and songs together," she was quoted as saying in a Warner Bros. press release. "But this time, I wanted to take that responsibility myself. It was a little scary at first, making all the decisions, but I learned a lot, and having done it, I know I could never go back to the way it was." The result was the 1992 album *The Woman I Am.* The album's single "Love You All My Lifetime" was a Number One single on the *Billboard* Dance chart and the *R&R* Urban chart. "Her fiery contralto is in total command" on all of the album's tracks, read a *Time* review, "swooping effortlessly from a raunchy growl to a soulful wail. The result is frisky, hip-shaking music. Go ahead," concluded the review, citing a line from "Once You Get Started" by Rufus, "party hearty." *Pulse!* called *The Woman I Am* "a superb album," though *Entertainment Weekly* gave it a "C-" grade, labeling the multi-producer approach unfocused and closing its review with the question: "Where is Rufus when we need them?"

Chaka, as usual, cared little for reviews. "I think this is the best representation of me, the person, that I've ever done," she said of *The Woman I Am* in the Warner Bros. press release. "There came a point in my life where I really wanted to get serious and this is the result. I've always been my own biggest competition so I guess if I feel good about it, I must be doing something right."

Chaka joined a number of singing stars—Wonder included—for the Hallelujah Chorus section of Quincy Jones's 1992 endeavor *A Soulful Celebration,* which puts a rhythm and blues spin on Handel's classic *Messiah.* She was honored the same year by the International Association of African-American Music for her career work as a recording artist. Having come a long way from the funky siren of "Tell Me Something Good," she further demonstrated her staying power in the music world.

Selected discography

With Rufus

Rufus (includes "Whoever Is Thrilling You Is Killing Me" and "Maybe Your Baby"), ABC, 1974.
Rags to Rufus (includes "Tell Me Something Good," "Once You Get Started," and "You Got the Love"), ABC, 1974.
Rufusized, ABC, 1975.
Rufus Featuring Chaka Khan (includes "Sweet Thing"), ABC, 1976.
Ask Rufus, ABC, 1977.
Street Player, ABC, 1978.
Masterjam (includes "Do You Love What You Feel"), MCA, 1980.
Camouflage, MCA, 1981.
Live Stompin' at the Savoy (includes "Ain't Nobody"), MCA, 1983.

Solo releases; on Warner Bros. Records

Chaka (includes "I'm Every Woman"), 1978.
Naughty (includes "Clouds" and "Papillon [Hot Butterfly]"), 1980.
What Cha' Gonna Do for Me (includes "A Night in Tunisia"), 1981.
Chaka Khan (includes "Bebop Medley"), 1982.
I Feel for You (includes "I Feel for You"), 1984.
Destiny, 1986.
C.K. (includes "Eternity," "Sticky Wicked," and "Signed, Sealed, Delivered"), 1988.
Life Is a Dance, 1989.
The Woman I Am (includes "Love You All My Lifetime"), 1992.

With others

Ry Cooder, "Down in Hollywood," *Bop 'Til You Drop,* Warner Bros., 1979.
Chick Corea, Joe Henderson, Freddie Hubbard, and others, *Echoes of an Era,* Elektra, 1982.
Steve Winwood, "Higher Love," *Back in the High Life,* Island, 1986.
Quincy Jones, "I'll Be Good to You," *Back on the Block,* Qwest, 1989.
Jones, "Hallelujah Chorus," *A Soulful Celebration,* Warner Bros., 1992.
Whitney Houston, "I'm Every Woman," *The Bodyguard* (soundtrack), Arista, 1992.

Sources

Books

Stambler, Irwin, *Encyclopedia of Pop, Rock and Soul,* revised edition, St. Martin's, 1989.

Periodicals

Down Beat, October 11, 1973.
Entertainment Weekly, May 1, 1992; May 15, 1992.
Essence, January 1986.
Jet, June 10, 1985.
Melody Maker, July 12, 1975; December 9, 1978; April 14, 1984; February 9, 1985; January 7, 1989; June 3, 1989.
New Yorker, March 20, 1989.
Pulse!, July 1992.

Rolling Stone, October 24, 1974; March 27, 1975; January 29, 1976; April 8, 1976; May 19, 1977; April 6, 1978; January 25, 1979; April 5, 1979; March 20, 1980; August 6, 1981; November 8, 1984; February 14, 1985; October 9, 1986.
Stereo Review, April 1983.
Time, May 11, 1992.
Upscale, August/September 1992; October/November 1992.

Additional information for this profile was obtained from liner notes by Paul Grein to *Soul Hits of the 70s: Didn't It Blow Your Mind!,* Volume 13, Rhino Records, 1991; and from a Warner Bros. publicity biography, 1992.

—*Simon Glickman*

The Kingston Trio

Folk group

Folk music's first appearance on the pop charts was rather short lived. During the early 1950s the Weavers and other folksingers had a number of hits, but the anticommunism sentiment prevalent in the United States at the time—which associated folk music with left wing organizations—put an end to that. Before the decade was over, however, the Kingston Trio and their distinctive harmonies brought folk music back to the mainstream, beginning the so-called "folk boom." With their clean-cut, collegiate image, they were able to circumvent the political stigma that haunted so many other folksingers.

The trio's critics have called them "opportunistic," according to Irwin Stambler in *The Encyclopedia of Folk, Country, and Western Music*—"essentially a pop group that happened to sing folk or folk-flavored material rather than an authentic folk group." Authenticity notwithstanding, the Kingston Trio was instrumental in bringing folk music to a mass audience, and in doing so, they set the stage for such singers as Bob Dylan, Joan Baez, and Peter, Paul and Mary. "Using only

acoustic guitars and banjos," wrote Tom Ray in the *Bermuda Sun*, "they revolutionized the popular music of the day with simple, catchy melodies, imbued with the ageless, timeless quality of American traditional and folk."

The Kingston Trio's roots were not in Jamaica, as their name would suggest, but in Hawaii where Dave Guard and Bob Shane grew up. They met at the Punahou School in Honolulu, where they often sang together. After high school both went to Northern California for college—Shane to Menlo Park School of Business Administration, and Guard to Stanford University to study economics. At Menlo Park, Shane met Nick Reynolds, another business student with a musical bent,

and the three began performing at college functions. At this time, according to Stambler and Landon, the trio wasn't considering a musical career, and after graduation, Shane returned to Hawaii to pursue a career in business.

Before long the trio re-formed, inspired, Stambler and Landon noted, by a revival in the public's interest in folk music. They began playing in a Stanford hangout called the Cracked Pot, where they were paid in beer and food. Frank Werber, a San Francisco publicist, heard the trio and was so impressed he had them sign a contract he wrote on a table napkin.

The group chose the name Kingston because of its reference to Jamaica's capital, where Calypso music—popular in the United States at the time—originated. The trio debuted with a well-received but unspectacular week-long engagement at a San Francisco club, the hungry i, and then moved to the Purple Onion across the street. Here audience response picked up—especially when the group sent postcards to everyone they knew inviting them to come—and their gig was extended, eventually to seven months. They began playing around the San Francisco area and before long had gigs in New York City and Chicago. In 1958 the Kingston Trio signed with Capitol Records, presumably on something more sturdy than a napkin.

First Single Skyrocketed

The trio's self-titled debut album released in June of 1958 was a mild success, but "Tom Dooley," a track from the LP released as a single, became a huge hit—the first folk song to gain popularity since the Weavers had been blacklisted several years earlier. The song rose to Number One on the charts and earned the Kingston Trio a gold record and a Grammy Award for best country western record (the folk category had not yet been established).

The trio had gambled well on the musical mood of the country. Rock icon Elvis Presley had been drafted into the army and wholesome singer Pat Boone was not to everyone's taste. Roy Harris Jr. wrote in the *Wall Street Journal*, "Kingston Trio songs were the perfect accompaniment for the times: [the Soviet satellite] Sputnik and the space race created the need for a traditional, but still good-humored style of music to rally the maturing [post-World War II] baby boom Americans, without alienating their parents."

While many critics have disparaged the Kingston Trio for their "commercial" or "pseudo" folk music, the mainstream press seemed thrilled to find popular music that wasn't the rock and roll for which they had so much disdain. Magazine articles touted the trio's wholesome image and devoted more space to descriptions of their picture perfect marriages than to their music. "The brightest new sounds heard through all the racket of rock 'n' roll comes from the voices and the instruments of three college grad cutups," wrote a *Life* correspondent in 1959. "Despite the surprising facts that every chord is in tune and every lyric is in good taste, *The Kingston Trio at Large* is now the best selling LP in the country."

Began Rediscovery of Folk Music

The Kingston Trio often performed traditional songs, updating them with new lyrics and arrangements. They also collected compositions from a number of different musicians, including Bob Dylan, Pete Seeger, and Woody Guthrie, and penned many themselves. As the decade of the 1960s began, they became one of the most popular vocal groups in the world, earning eight gold records and two Grammy awards. "People in all parts of the country started playing the guitar and banjo in imitation of the Kingston Trio, and new groups sprang up everywhere as the country 'rediscovered' folk music," wrote Kristin Baggelaar in *Dave Guard and the Whiskey Hill Singers.*

In 1961, after a world tour, Guard decided to leave the group. His departure came over a "whole gang of differences," as reported in *Life* in 1961. Part of the trio's differences, according to *Life,* was Shane's insistence that the band begin playing more "authentic" folk music as well as learn to read music. *Life* commented on the loss of Guard: "He is the group's personality kid, and personality is really their stock in trade, not music. An old friend of the Kingstons observed, 'To say Dave Guard is the best musician is to say that a school kid who can spell c-a-t is the most literate boy in class.'"

Despite Guard's departure, the Kingston Trio survived. Guard went on to form the Whisky Hill Singers and continued to write music and pursue an interest in folklore until he died of cancer in 1991. Shane and Reynolds replaced Guard with John Stewart. Stewart, who had been performing with another folk trio, the Cumberland Three, had already worked with the Kingston Trio, writing and arranging songs. Although the change was smooth, in retrospect Stewart did not feel it worked. According to Baggelaar, he said, "At first it was an exciting idea to take the place of Dave Guard, but then, when I got into it, I realized that the reason I had liked the Trio was because Dave Guard was in it!. . . The sound was different, and I thought it was much better with Dave."

Rock Revival Overshadowed Folk

By the mid-1960s, with the invasion of British groups and the revival of rock, listeners' tastes moved away from the Kingston Trio's folk-flavored music. As the 1960s wore on, ticket and record sales dropped off, and in 1967, the trio's members decided to bow out gracefully, as Reynolds later told Thomas Arnold in the *Los Angeles Times.* Reynolds retired to a ranch in Oregon, and Stewart pursued a solo career, finding moderate success in the late 1970s. Shane, however, found it difficult to stay away from the Kingston Trio for long. He bought the rights to the name and in the early 1970s formed a new version of the trio with Roger Gambill and George Grove.

In 1981 the original Kingston Trio met at California's Magic Mountain Amusement Park for a reunion concert that was taped by PBS. At the time Harris wrote that the reunion was good musically, but the relationship among the three—especially between Shane and Guard—was quite strained. Future reunions seemed unlikely.

> *With its clean-cut, collegiate image, the Kingston Trio was able to circumvent the political stigma that haunted so many other folksingers.*

Meanwhile, Shane's revival group toured with modest success and recorded on the Nautilus and Xeres labels. Gambill died in 1985, and by 1989 Shane had coaxed Reynolds back into the trio.

Reynolds's return came at a time when Americans were once again rediscovering folk music, and many returned to hear their old favorites. Younger fans also joined the audiences, and Capitol Records jumped on the bandwagon, reissuing many of the trio's early albums. While some critics complained of the nostalgia or that their songs and shtick were outdated, most found their voices and music in fine form and their enthusiasm and rapport with the audience impressive. In his review of a 1989 concert, David Silverman of the *Chicago Tribune* wrote that although it had been quite a few years since they started out, "there is not a bit of tarnish on the Kingston Trio. They have achieved a fine musical patina that never grows old, only finer, sweeter and more pleasing."

Some critics noted that in the turmoil of the late 1980s and early 1990s, it was nice to return to the apparent idealism of the pre-Vietnam era and such groups as the Kingston Trio. "They're just having such a *damn* good time up there, and it's just a tonic for the generically jaded audience of the late '80s," Barbara Shulgasser noted in a *San Francisco Examiner* concert review. "The middle-age crowd was whooping and clapping for the trio as if time hadn't passed, as if we hadn't waged tragic wars, suffered assassinations, sold arms to Iran, broken into Democratic Party headquarters. Tom Dooley hung down his head and all was right with the world."

Selected discography

Singles; on Capitol Records

"Tom Dooley," 1958.
"Raspberries, Strawberries," 1959.
"The Tijuana Jail," 1959.
"M.T.A.," 1959.
"A Worried Man," 1959.
"Everglades," 1960.
"Where Have All the Flowers Gone," 1962.
"Scotch and Soda," 1962.
"Greenback Dollar," 1963.
"Reverend Mr. Black," 1963.

Albums; on Capitol Records, except where noted

The Kingston Trio (includes "Tom Dooley"), 1958, reissued with *From the hungry i,* 1992.
From the hungry i, 1959.
Stereo Concert, 1959.
At Large, 1959, reissued with *Here We Go Again!,* 1991.
Here We Go Again!, 1959.
Sold Out, 1960, reissued with *String Along,* 1992.
String Along, 1960.
The Last Month of the Year, 1960.
Make Way!, 1961.
Goin' Places, 1961.
Encore, 1961.
Close-Up, 1961.
College Concert, 1962.
The Best of the Kingston Trio, 1962.
Something Special, 1962.
New Frontier, 1962.
#16, 1963.
Sunny Side!, 1963.
Sing a Song With the Kingston Trio, 1963.
Time to Think, 1964.
Back in Town, 1964.
Folk Era, 1964.

Nick-Bob-John, Decca, 1965.
The Best of the Kingston Trio, Volume 2, 1965.
Stay Awhile, Decca, 1965.
Somethin' Else, Decca, 1965.
Children of the Morning, Decca, 1966.
The Best of the Kingston Trio, Volume 3, 1966.
Tom Dooley/Scarlet Ribbons, 1970.
Once Upon a Time, Tetragrammaton, 1969.
Tom Dooley, Pickwick, 1971.
The Kingston Trio, Pickwick, 1972.
Where Have All the Flowers Gone, Pickwick, 1973.
The Kingston Trio—25 Years Non-Stop, Xeres, 1982.
Kingston Trio's Greatest Hits, Curb Records, 1990.
The Kingston Trio Collectors' Series, 1990.

Other

(Dave Guard and the Whiskey Hill Singers) *Dave Guard and the Whiskey Hill Singers,* Capitol, 1962.
(John Stewart) *Dream Away Dream Babies,* RSO, 1979.
(Stewart) *Dream Babies Go Hollywood,* RSO, 1980.

Sources

Books

Baggelaar, Kristin, and Donald Milton, *Folk Music: More Than a Song,* Thomas Y. Crowell Co., 1976.
Helander, Brook, *The Rock Who's Who,* Schirmer Books, 1982.
The New Rolling Stone Record Guide, edited by Dave Marsh and John Swenson, Random House, 1983.
Nite, Norm N., *Rock On, Vol. 1,* Harper & Row, 1982.
The Penguin Encyclopedia of Popular Music, edited by Donald Clarke, Viking, 1989.
Stambler, Irwin, and Grelun Landon, *The Encyclopedia of Folk, Country, and Western Music,* second edition, St. Martin's Press, 1983.

Periodicals

Bermuda Sun, February 21, 1992.
Chicago Tribune, February 22, 1989.
Journal of American Folklore, October 1990.
Life, August 3, 1959; June 9, 1961.
Look, January 3, 1961.
Los Angeles Times, March 18, 1989; January 29, 1992.
San Francisco Examiner, June 8, 1989.
Wall Street Journal, March 12, 1982.

Additional information for this profile was obtained from a Fugi Productions press release, c. 1989.

—*Megan Rubiner*

Eartha Kitt

Singer, actress, dancer

Entertainer Eartha Kitt's five decades in show business approximate a roller coaster ride with peaks and valleys more considerable than most. The cabaret singer with the saucy delivery and sultry purr escaped a childhood so daunting that, according to *People* magazine's John Stark, it made Charles Dickens's fictitious urchin Oliver Twist's look good; yet by the time the song stylist had reached her mid-twenties she was headlining at top clubs in the United States and Europe and rubbing elbows with such twentieth-century heavyweights as physicist Albert Einstein and Indian prime minister Jawaharlal Nehru.

Early in her career, director Orson Welles pronounced Kitt "the most exciting woman alive" and cast her in her first dramatic role as Helen of Troy in his award-winning interpretation of *Faust;* later, the entertainer appeared in less distinguished cinematic vehicles—a downward trend she relates to her highly publicized confrontation with Lady Bird Johnson, former first lady of the United States, over the Vietnam War in 1968. The conflict blacklisted Kitt from performing at home during her prime years and left a seemingly permanent stain on her singing and acting career. Nevertheless, the philosophical performer told Judy Gerstel in the *Detroit Free Press:* "I'm still very much here, and I feel strongly that the stars are rising for me again. . . . As long as you are working, that gives you dignity and respect."

Endured Traumatic Childhood

Kitt was born in rural South Carolina to a 14-year-old black mother and a white father, whose identity she never knew. Her black stepfather was a sharecropper who soon abandoned the family; when Eartha was six, her mother also disappeared, and she and a half-sister survived on berries in the woods or picked cotton in exchange for food and shelter. Kitt's light skin made her a particular target for taunts and beatings in her hometown. At the age of eight, she was taken in by an aunt, who brought her to Harlem to live. But the aunt mistreated her. "She was a child abuser," Kitt told Veronica Webb in *Interview.* "I never knew when she was going to pick up a stool and hit me over the head with it. Not because I was doing anything wrong. . . . I went to school with black eyes and welts on my bottom, and I figured, Well, I guess that's the way it was meant to be."

While her aunt worked, Kitt practiced singing and dancing, talents that won her recognition in school. By age fourteen, she was earning a living as a sewer in a

---

For the Record. . .

Born Eartha Mae Kitt, January 26, 1928, in North, SC; daughter of William (a sharecropper) and Anna Mae (Riley) Kitt; married William McDonald (in real estate), 1960 (divorced, 1965); children: Kitt McDonald Shapiro. *Education:* Studied dance at New York High School for the Performing Arts and piano privately; received Katherine Dunham dance scholarship, c. 1944.

Worked in factory sewing military uniforms, Brooklyn, NY, c. 1942-44; dancer and singer with Katherine Dunham Dance Troupe, touring U.S. and abroad, 1944-49; solo nightclub performer, 1949—, debuting in Paris and headlining at clubs in Europe and U.S.; international stage performer, 1950—, recording artist, 1953—, and actress, 1954—. Performed cabaret act in New York City, Germany, and Australia, 1992. Television performer and film narrator.

Stage performances include *Time Runs,* 1950, *New Faces of 1952,* 1952, *Mrs. Patterson,* 1954, *Shinbone Alley,* 1957, *Jolly's Progress,* 1959, and *Timbuktu,* 1978; film appearances include *New Faces,* 1954, *Accused,* 1957, *The Mark of the Hawks,* 1958, *Anna Lucasta,* 1959, *Synanon,* 1965, *Erik the Viking,* 1989, *Ernest Scared Stupid,* 1991, and *Boomerang,* 1992; television appearances include the role of Catwoman on the series *Batman.*

Awards: Montreaux Film Festival Golden Rose Award, 1962, for *This Is Eartha;* named Woman of the Year, National Association of Black Musicians, 1968.

Addresses: *Agent*—Gurtman & Murtha Assoc., 162 West 56th St., New York, NY 10019.

factory, using her savings for piano lessons; two years later she got her big break when she landed a dance scholarship with the all-black Katherine Dunham Company in New York.

Kitt toured South America and Europe with the company and emerged as one of its solo stars when it was discovered that she could sing as well as dance. She was taught African, Haitian, and Cuban songs, capitalizing on her exotic beauty and facility with languages (born of her youth in New York's ethnically rich neighborhoods). The entertainer's blend of sensuality and sophistication made her an instant hit with international audiences; her individual stardom also brought clashes with troupe leader Dunham, however, and the two ended their association in Paris in 1949. Kitt remained and became the toast of that city, performing at major clubs and cabarets there and in other continental capitals.

Kitt's 1950 dramatic debut in Welles's *Time Runs* in Paris drew critical acclaim and established her as a serious actress; she starred in two French films before returning to New York in 1952. After a fitful start, the performer reestablished her nightclub act there, and after appearing in the Broadway revue *New Faces of 1952* and its cinematic counterpart, she rose to new heights in popularity: she broke attendance records at New York's Blue Angel nightclub and the Mocambo in Hollywood. By the mid-fifties Kitt was recording her international repertoire for RCA Victor, and songs like "C'est Si Bon," "Angelitos Negros," the Turkish "Uska Dara," and calypso "Somebody Bad Stole de Wedding Bell" became hits, as did "An Old-Fashioned Girl," "I Want to Be Evil," and "Santa Baby." The entertainer also made frequent television appearances and engaged in additional stage and film work.

Faced Color Barrier

While Kitt prevailed as a variety artist, it was apparent by the 1960s that she was not destined for superstardom. The performer suspected that her color and cosmopolitan persona limited her; interviewer Gerstel suggested that "[Kitt] was always considered 'too high class' to play black women in dramas about the black experience." Kitt told Webb, "I didn't fit in. 'She thinks she's white. She doesn't sing blues. She doesn't sing jazz.' I was ostracized by . . . black people for twenty-five years because they were conditioned by the media into thinking that all black people should be singing the same kind of music."

Yet, writing about her long, failed relationships with Hollywood scion Arthur Loew, Jr., and cosmetics mogul Charles Revson in her 1989 autobiography *I'm Still Here,* Kitt determined that she was also "too black" to be accepted into white upper-crust society. Regardless, the performer had a comfortable club following, as well as a number of social and charitable interests that consumed much of her time. That was why she took her 1968 invitation to the White House so seriously, researching the topic for discussion—juvenile delinquency in America—beforehand, concluding that the Vietnam War was much to blame (due to the high proportion of minorities drafted and the deferment of those with criminal records). When Kitt discovered that the luncheon was merely a public relations event with a staged visit by President Lyndon B. Johnson, she confronted Mrs. Johnson with her findings, and news of the clash spread.

Blacklisted in the U.S.

In her 1976 autobiography, *Alone With Me,* Kitt recalled how her career in the United States—worth about a million and a half dollars annually—was strangled for nearly seven years by the incident: "Club contracts were cancelled or 'lost,' with the contractors refusing to draw up new ones. The television quiz show on which I was a semi-regular never invited me back, and the phones stopped ringing." Fortunately, the international entertainer was still able to perform and record abroad.

In the mid-1970s, Washington, D.C., columnist Jack Anderson disclosed that the Secret Service and other government intelligence agencies had compiled extensive dossiers on Kitt's professional and personal activities both before and after the 1968 luncheon. With that revelation the variety performer's bookings in the United States resumed, but the passage of time, or tastes, narrowed her appeal. When reviewing her 1984 album *I Love Men* for *People,* for instance, Michael Small found Kitt's purrs and snarls "high camp" and "sometimes catchy"; still, he admitted that with lyrics like "'I just need someone to spank me/ I just need someone to bank me/ Sugar Daddy/ Sugar Daddy,' she won't make a pal out of [noted feminist] Gloria Steinem." Nonetheless, the entertainer still tours widely and appears in such venerable settings as New York's Hotel Carlyle. She frequently performs a favorite—and appropriately titled—number, the Stephen Sondheim song "I'm Still Here."

Selected writings

Thursday's Child (autobiography), Duell, Sloan & Pearce, 1956.
Alone With Me (autobiography), Regnery, 1976.
I'm Still Here (autobiography), [New York], 1989, published as *Confessions of a Sex Kitten,* Barricade Books, 1991.

Selected discography

Eartha Kitt With the Doc Cheatham Trio (recorded 1950), Swing, 1986.

In Person at the Plaza (recorded 1965), GNP Crescendo, 1987.
C'est Si Bon (recorded 1983), Polydor.
I Love Men, Sunnyview, 1984.
My Way: A Musical Tribute to Reverend Martin Luther King, Jr., Caravan of Dreams, 1987.
Miss Kitt to You, RCA, 1992.
Thinking Jazz, ITM (German import), 1992.
Love for Sale, Capitol.
That Bad Eartha, RCA.
The Best of Eartha Kitt, MCA.
The Romantic Eartha Kitt, Capitol.

Has also recorded dramatic readings, including *Black Pioneers in American History: Nineteenth Century,* with Moses Gunn, Caedmon, 1968; *Folk Tales of the Tribes of Africa,* Caedmon, 1968; and *Young Brer Rabbit,* 1987.

Sources

Books

Contemporary Authors, Volumes 77-80, Gale, 1979.
Kitt, Eartha, *Alone With Me,* Regnery, 1976.
Kitt, *I'm Still Here,* 1989, published as *Confessions of a Sex Kitten,* Barricade Books, 1991.
The New Grove Dictionary of American Music, Volume 2, Macmillan, 1986.

Periodicals

Detroit Free Press, October 16, 1991.
Ebony, September 1991.
Interview, January 1992.
Jet, January 18, 1988; July 23, 1990.
Newsweek, January 29, 1968.
People, February 4, 1985; February 12, 1990.
Pulse!, December 1992.
Time, February 13, 1978.
Washington Post, January 19, 1978.

—*Nancy Pear*

Kool Moe Dee

Rap singer

In a review of Kool Moe Dee's 1991 album *Funke, Funke Wisdom, Rolling Stone*'s Alan Light referred to the artist as "one of rap's founding fathers." From the rapper's pioneering work with the Treacherous Three in the early 1980s to his highly successful solo work, Kool Moe Dee has honed his distinctively hard-edged but stylish delivery and pursued his cherished theme of black independence. Poised between the mass market giants of pop-rap and the hardcore underground, he has for many years forged a middle path; he mixes political and social commentary with playful rhyming and dancefloor beats. "Funk is definitely necessary" to convey serious messages, he told *Billboard*. "The idea is to entertain first."

Moe was born Mohandas Dewese in Harlem, New York, in the early 1960s. He attended Norman Thomas High School in New York City and was an avid rapper as a teen; he started out, according to his Jive Records biography, "by grabbing the mike at house parties." His interest in rap grew out of a long-standing fascination with wordplay. "My group of friends growing up were considered, like, the outcasts of the neighborhood because we weren't caught up in doing drugs and crime and things like that," he told Stephen Fried of *GQ*. "We were, like, the next step from a nerd. We weren't bookworms, but we considered ourselves the intellectual street kids. We had fun with words. We used to like to show how much we knew. Our competition was over vocabulary. Throw a word in there, and see if anybody can respond. And if the person doesn't respond correctly, it means he didn't understand the word—or sometimes we'd overlook it and then run home and look it up." He added that he "was fascinated with words. [Illustrator and rhyme-obsessed author] Dr. Suess, *The Cat in the Hat*, was *phenomenal* to me at 5 or 6. [Former heavyweight boxing champion] Muhammad Ali [was, too], not just because of the way he boxed but his poetic style. Loved that stuff."

Began Recording as a Teenager

Moe formed the rap group Treacherous Three with his friends L.A. Sunshine and Special K. The trio debuted on Spoonie Gee's 1980 Enjoy Records single "The New Rap Language." Harry Allen, introducing Moe's testimonial in the *Village Voice,* called the single "a futuristic record that showed the lyrical and percussive possibilities of hip-hop right up your auditory canal." Treacherous Three soon began to generate excitement with singles like 1981's "Bodyrock" and "Heartbeat." Soon they were signed to Sugarhill Records, the home of some of the guiding lights of early rap. They released a number of singles, including "Action" and "Yes We Can," showcasing their skill as complex rhymesters. Soon, though, their style was eclipsed by the emergence of hardcore rap; groups like Run-DMC and Whodini captivated audiences with a tougher, simpler style. Moe left the Three—and the music world, for a time—and attended the State University of New York at Old Westbury, Long Island, earning a B.A. in communications.

He couldn't stay away from rap for long, however. His solo single "Go See the Doctor," a wry cautionary rhyme about sexual promiscuity, appeared on Rooftop Records and caught the attention of Jive/RCA. The company bought Kool Moe Dee's self-titled debut album and released it in 1986. "Moe Dee's style is slack-jawed and straight-faced, laced with menace," observed Lloyd Richards of *Melody Maker.* "There's something disturbing in his voice," Richards remarked, suggesting that "Go See the Doctor" might have misled listeners into expecting more "goofy" rap. He chided Moe for the apparent misogyny of certain tracks; the album, he concluded, is "psycho rap for stranglers in the night."

Second Album Went Platinum

Moe's first effort after signing with Jive, *How Ya Like Me Now?,* was his big breakthrough. It went platinum and marked the beginning of Moe's feud with fellow rapper L.L. Cool J. The two have exchanged lyrical blows intermittently ever since. Fried noted that on the inner sleeve of the record, "he arrogantly offered his own report card on the industry. Grading on the Kool Moe Dee curve, the rapper rated himself and twenty-four of his competitors in ten categories (including vocabulary, articulation and 'sticking to themes'), assigning final scores that—what a surprise—mathematically proved him to be first in his class."

How Ya Like Me Now? was a hard act to follow, but Kool Moe Dee reemerged in 1989 with *Knowledge Is King,* a solid success in its own right though not as big a smash as its predecessor. *Knowledge* includes the single "I Go to Work," produced by hip-hop wizard Teddy Riley; Alan Light of *Rolling Stone* called the song "stunning." While much of the album devotes itself to issues of black autonomy and political power, "I Go to Work" is a straightforward boast—albeit one that gives Moe the chance to stretch out lyrically: "Every rhyme's a dissertation/You wanna know my occupation?/I get paid to rock the nation." Nelson George of the *Village Voice* noted that calling *Knowledge* Moe's best album "isn't saying much," but added, "Everything on the first half of *Knowledge* hits hard, along with one solid uppercut in the second," even if the album overall "sounds too clean."

"Socially Conscious Rapper"

Fried remarked in *GQ* that *Knowledge* "may not have been the most politically important rap record in the year of Public Enemy's 'Fight the Power,' but it was arguably the most accomplished in terms of balancing lyrics, music and performance.' He added that the record sold 625,000 copies—still impressive though markedly less so than the 950,000 copies of *How Ya Like Me Now?* The year of *Knowledge Is King,* Kool Moe Dee became—according to his press biography—the first rap artist ever to perform at the Grammy awards. *Billboard's* Janine McAdams observed that Kool Moe Dee "has aligned himself with the new breed of socially conscious rappers. The title track of the new album is the clearest evidence of that commitment." Moe's other activities included voiceovers for TV commercials and an appearance on *The Arsenio Hall Show.*

In 1990 Moe released an unsuccessful EP called *God Made Me Funke;* he also shared rapping duties with Ice-T and rap trailblazer Melle Mel on the title track of composer-producer Quincy Jones's album *Back on the Block*. As part of his commitment to improving conditions in the black community, Moe rapped on the gold charity single "Self-Destruction" for the Stop the Violence project organized by rapper-activist KRS-One of Boogie Down Productions and contributed a short prose piece to the project's book *Stop the Violence: Overcoming Self-Destruction*. In his essay he addresses the issue of black-on-black violence, particularly at rap concerts. "The violence is not caused by rap fans," he insists. "It's caused by bandits who come to prey on young kids who are there to enjoy the show." He also asserts that "rap artists are into something besides making money. It's at the point where we're trying to show that we really care about the fans, and not just the fans but the black community, because that's where rap music is generated from, and for. We think that because we have this spotlight and the attention of youth we can utilize this to become young black leaders, so to speak, since they don't have any real positive images to identify with." His rap on the *STV* record was even more to the point: "I never had to run from the Ku Klux Klan/And I shouldn't have to run from a black man."

Re-emerged with *Funke, Funke Wisdom*

According to Havelock Nelson of *Billboard*, Moe "went back to the streets for inspiration" after *God Made Me Funke* faltered. "I'm a perfectionist," he admitted to McAdams. "I think speaking is an art form in itself. [My style is] a way to ride and accent certain parts of a sentence to make it stick. I think a lot of rappers just rap to go through it, while I'm thinking: What message am I trying to get across? What's the most important part of this sentence? I'm always trying to take myself to another level lyrically."

He found his next level with 1991's *Funke, Funke Wisdom*. Relying on samples from funk standbys like James Brown, Parliament, and Sly and the Family Stone, *Funke, Funke Wisdom* places the emphasis on dance rhythms even as it broaches social issues. Moe is joined by KRS-One and Public Enemy rapper Chuck D. for the track "Rise 'n' Shine," while he has another go at L.L. Cool J with "Deathblow." Jive executive Barry Weiss told Nelson that "Rise 'n' Shine" was first released as a video, then as a single, before the album's release. It went to number one on the Hot Rap Singles chart. "People at street level and at retail were screaming for the record" by that time, he said. "At its best," Light opined, *Funke, Funke Wisdom* "marks a return to the joyous words-for-words'-sake looseness that powered hip-hop's early classics." Light found "Deathblow" the only real flaw on the album, continuing as it

does "a rivalry which grew tired long ago." According to Fried, *Funke, Funke Wisdom* "will neither incite inner-city youth to riot nor further suburbanize rap music. Nor will it likely be compared to the hardest-cutting edge of rap—Public Enemy, Ice Cube, N.W.A.—which has been embraced by critics as the new punk rock. But it will, once again, walk the fine line between political and musical correctness—balancing message and music, function and fun."

Kool Moe Dee found his niche with this balancing act. A quote in his biography offers a key to his longevity: "The only reason I can say that I'm still around today, is because unlike other old school rappers, I pay attention to what people like. I make music for them. You can't get caught up in yourself." That may be, but he has also survived because—as both Light and George have observed—he has *focused* on himself; his playful raps have often been a celebration of his own prowess. After all, the second single on *Funke, Funke Wisdom* asks the musical question "How Kool Can One Black Man Be?"

Selected discography

Singles; with the Treacherous Three

"The New Rap Language," Enjoy, 1980.
"Bodyrock," Enjoy, 1981.
"Heartbeat," Enjoy, 1981.
"Action," Sugarhill.
"Yes We Can," Sugarhill.

Solo releases

"Go See the Doctor" (single), Rooftop, 1985.
Kool Moe Dee, Jive/RCA, 1986.
How Ya Like Me Now?, Jive/RCA, 1987.
Knowledge Is King (includes "I Go to Work"), Jive/RCA, 1989.
"God Made Me Funke" (single), Jive/RCA, 1990.
Funke, Funke Wisdom (includes "Rise 'n' Shine" and "How Kool Can One Black Man Be?"), Jive/RCA, 1991.

Contributor to Stop the Violence project single "Self-Destruction," Jive/RCA, 1989; Quincy Jones's *Back on the Block*, Qwest/Warner Bros., 1990; and *Zebrahead* soundtrack, Ruffhouse, 1992.

Sources

Books

Stop the Violence: Overcoming Self-Destruction, edited by Nelson George, Pantheon, 1990.

Periodicals

Billboard, July 22, 1989; July 27, 1991.
GQ, June 1991.
Melody Maker, January 24, 1987.
Rolling Stone, July 11, 1991.
Village Voice, August 1, 1989; January 2, 1990.

Additional information for this profile was obtained from a Jive/RCA press biography, May 1991.

—Simon Glickman

Kraftwerk

Pop group

Out of the historical and spiritual vacuum created in Germany after World War II and set against the gray spires of factory smokestacks filling the landscape a generation later, a new musical approach and sound appeared. Inspired by the German Bauhaus movement—a 1920s artistic crusade that attempted to seal the rift between the artist's vision and the craftsman's technical expertise—the group Kraftwerk melded man and machine into a singular unit, creating music that reflected man's existential freedom in the modern, mechanized world. Despite major commercial successes—ironic given the group's numerous recording hiatuses and lack of significant tours in support of its work—Kraftwerk's musical legacy has been its great and varied influence, from such esteemed and established artists as David Bowie and Neil Young, to disco artists of the late 1970s, to such electronic pop groups of the 1980s as the Human League and Ultravox.

The two founding members of Kraftwerk, Ralf Hütter and Florian Schneider, met in the late 1960s while both

were studying classical music at the Düsseldorf Conservatory. They found the traditional medium bereft of the means to express their personal musical vision and sought not only artistic definitions but ontological ones as well. "After the war," Hütter explained to Lester Bangs in *Creem,* "German entertainment was destroyed. The German people were robbed of their culture, putting an American head on it. I think we are the first generation born after the war to shake this off, and know where . . . to feel ourselves."

Mechanized World Provided Basic Sound

Hütter and Schneider found a musical identity in what surrounded them: the mechanized sounds of the German factories and language. They acquired electronic keyboards and amplifiers and in 1970 set up their own recording studio, Kling Klang, which means Ringing Tone in English, in an oil refinery. "There's smoke and fire around it," Schneider described to Ray Townley in *Rolling Stone,* "and when you emerge from the studio you hear this hissing sound all around you." That same year they joined a five-piece band, Organisation, and released an album, *Tone Float,* but quickly left the group to form their own, Kraftwerk, which means power plant in English.

"Kraftwerk is not a band," Schneider told Townley. "It's a concept. We call it 'Die Menschmaschine,' which means 'the human machine.' We are not the band. I am

me. Ralf is Ralf. And Kraftwerk is a vehicle for our ideas." The group's ideas are conceived not in standard linear notation but visually, completely. With machines, Hütter and Schneider are able to transmit their visions to an audience like an aural film. But the machines are not merely conduits, nor even prosthetic extensions. As Bangs noted, the relationship between Hütter and Schneider and their machines is an organic, symbiotic one: "The machines not merely overpower and play the human beings but *absorb* them, until the scientist and his technology, having developed a higher consciousness of its own, are one and the same."

After a few limited releases in their native Germany, Hütter and Schneider added Wolfgang Flür and Klaus Roeder to Kraftwerk in 1974 and released *Autobahn,* the group's seminal work. Side one of the LP contains the title track, a twenty-two-and-a-half-minute paean to driving on Germany's super highway, delivered not as a human response to the experience but as a machine-like statement about it—clean, precise, hypnotic, endless. "What have both we and these poor krauts been seeking desperately ever since the Second World War if not the penultimate nonrush provoked by the *absence of feeling?*" Bangs wrote in a review of the album, which reached Number Five on the *Billboard* charts. An edited version of the title cut, "Wir farh'n farh'n farh'n auf der Autobahn" ("We're driving, driving, driving on the Autobahn"), was also a popular success, peaking on the singles charts at Number 25.

Influenced Other Musicians

Although not quite equaling the commercial acclaim of *Autobahn,* subsequent works solidified Kraftwerk's standing through their impact on other artists and musical mediums. Musician David Bowie credited Kraftwerk's 1976 *Radio-Activity* with influencing some of the arrangements on his album *Low,* while the mercurial Neil Young significantly patterned his *Trans* release on 1981's *Computer World.*

The disco craze of the late 1970s also latched onto the Kraftwerk beat. Extended versions of "Trans-Europe Express" and "Showroom Dummies"—both from the 1977 album *Trans-Europe Express*—were heard in discos worldwide. And hip-hop deejay Afrika Bambaataa reworked "Trans-Europe Express" into the 1982 hit "Planet Rock," which, as Mark Dery pointed out in the *New York Times,* "helped spawn 'electro-boogie,' a rap subgenre characterized by video arcade bleeps, cartoon sound effects, and locomotive rhythms. Electro-boogie is a forerunner of the Detroit 'techno' school of house music, and house deejays continue to incorporate Kraftwerk records in their live mixes."

Dismissing its danceable rhythms, some critics found the music of Kraftwerk to be severely devoid of human emotional involvement. "With its efficient modern-world toys—synthesizers, speech synthesizers, synthesized percussion—Kraftwerk strikingly creates a sound so antiseptic that germs would die there," Mitchell Schneider wrote in a review of 1978's *The Man Machine* for *Rolling Stone*. And Mark Peel, reviewing the 1986 release *Electric Café* for *Stereo Review*, went as far as to suggest that there is no human input even in the act of creation: "Maybe it's some kind of neo-Expressionist statement about the domination of technology, or maybe the group's machines really did take over the recording session—maybe the guys are tied up in the studio and the synthesizers are out spending their royalty checks on one-night stands with cheap cable-ready TV's."

Approach Changed Shape of Musical World

According to others, however, it is exactly this predilection toward technology in the face of human emotions that has given Kraftwerk its lasting value. "Society has come to take the sort of technological advances celebrated by Kraftwerk for granted, become largely computer-literate without human beings having been reduced to mere automatons, as once feared," David Stubbs assessed in *Melody Maker*. "And musically, Kraftwerk have created a new orthodoxy."

In the end, perhaps, what Kraftwerk can be credited with developing is not a new musical doctrine, or religion. Through their intermingling of man and machine, they have helped create a new species, a jump in the evolution of music. It is not their own music but the sound and approach they have spawned that marks Kraftwerk as a significant event on the developmental line of popular music. "Certainly they're capable of moments of exceptional, accessible beauty," Paul Lester of *Melody Maker* noted, "and yet, in this area, the godlike Electronic are light-years ahead. Kraftwerk have long been content to let people—from the [Human] League to the hip hoppers—run away with their inventions. Maybe that's their greatness."

Selected discography

Var, Vertigo, 1971.
Kraftwerk, Vertigo, 1972.
Ralf and Florian, Vertigo, 1973.
Autobahn, Vertigo/Mercury, 1974, reissued, Elektra, 1988.
Radioactivity, Capitol, 1976, reissued, Elektra, 1986.
Exceller 8, Vertigo, 1976.
Trans-Europe Express, Capitol, 1977.
The Man Machine, Capitol, 1978.
Computer World, Warner Bros., 1981, reissued, Elektra, 1988.
Techno Pop, EMI (British import), 1983.
Electric Café, EMI, 1986, reissued, Elektra, 1988.
The Mix, Elektra, 1991.
Showroom Dummie, 1992.
The Model (The Best of), Cleopatra, 1992.

Sources

Art in America, March 1988.
Billboard, October 22, 1977; August 22, 1981.
Creem, June 1975; September 1975.
Down Beat, June 3, 1976.
Melody Maker, September 13, 1975; June 20, 1981; November 8, 1986; June 15, 1991; July 20, 1991.
New York Times, June 16, 1991.
People, September 28, 1981.
Rolling Stone, July 3, 1975; May 18, 1978.
Stereo Review, September 1981; March 1987.
Wilson Library Bulletin, October 1991.

—Rob Nagel

Patty Larkin

Singer, songwriter, guitarist

Although Patty Larkin does not twirl batons in her concerts—like folk music compatriot Christine Lavin—she seems to do everything else. Larkin is critically acclaimed for her singing, songwriting, guitar playing, and live performances. She writes, according to Steve Holden of the *New York Times,* "self-critical songs that balance passion against bitter observation," and what Scott Alarik of the *Boston Globe* described as "vivid, image-rich songs." For much of her career she has been relatively unknown in the mainstream music world, but she is a favorite in folk circles and in her home territory of New England. She has won seven Boston Music awards, including outstanding folk act, outstanding folk album, and outstanding song/songwriter, and was named best folk act in a Boston Phoenix-WFNX music poll. Though perhaps an underestimation, the *Washington Post* characterized her as a "triple threat," saying, "She dwarfs most of the folkie competition when it comes to playing acoustic guitar, writes first-rate ballads, broadsides and lampoons, and possesses a voice that can be quietly affecting one moment and hilariously on target the next."

Born in Iowa, Larkin grew up outside Milwaukee in the midst of a creative family. Her mother was an artist and both grandmothers taught piano. Larkin and her sisters began as pianists, but as she told Lis Kestier in a *Minneapolis Star Tribune* article, her sisters were much better players. After four years of studying classical piano, one of her uncles brought home a guitar, and that was the end of keyboards. "I was just enthralled by it," she told Kestier. "It was a very personal instrument. I could waddle into my room with it, close my door, and be by myself." By the time she was in high school she had begun making up chords and lyrics because, as she explained in a High Street Records biography, "I hit the wall at the number of folk songs I could learn."

Found Rock Limiting

After attending the University of Oregon, and according to one source, Notre Dame, Larkin studied at the Berklee College of Music in Boston, where she remained for a summer and then left to concentrate on performance. Larkin supported herself by working in a toy factory and playing music around Harvard Square in Cambridge, Massachusetts. She also played electric guitar in various ensembles. Though particularly drawn to jazz, she drifted away from it for a number of years. "I realized that if I was serious about becoming a jazz player, it would take me years to get where I wanted to be on the instrument, and that I'd have to get more contemporary—explore the whole rock thing and get

For the Record. . .

Born c. 1951 in Iowa; raised outside of Milwaukee, WI. *Education:* Attended University of Oregon, University of Notre Dame (according to one source), and Berklee College of Music.

Singer, songwriter, and guitarist. Played electric guitar with various jazz, rhythm and blues, and rock bands in Boston, late 1970s; switched to acoustic guitar, 1981—; toured with Richard Gates and Catherine David, opening for various folk performers; released *Step Into the Light,* Philo, 1986; toured solo and with other folk musicians, playing at numerous folk festivals; signed to High Street Records, 1991; helped establish audio narrative record label Gang of Seven, 1992.

Awards: Seven Boston Music awards, including outstanding folk act, outstanding folk album, 1987, for *I'm Fine,* and outstanding song/songwriter.

Addresses: *Home*—Wellfleet, MA. *Management*—Lamartine Productions, P.O. Box 662, Wellfleet, MA, 02667.

all the pedals," she recalled in *Guitar Player.* "It was a little too awesome, so I decided to concentrate on my songwriting instead." She played electric guitar with a rock/R&B band for some time but, as she told Kestier, found rock music too limiting. She preferred the freedom of styles she had when playing acoustic gigs, and in 1981, began playing acoustic guitar full time.

Larkin hooked up with bass player Richard Gates and vocalist Catherine David; they toured, performing opening sets for folk acts. By the mid-eighties she had carved out a place in the folk circuit and had developed a following, especially in New England. Her reputation for very entertaining and funny live shows grew as well. As she told Seth Rogovoy in the *Berkshire Eagle,* humor has always been an important part of relaxing and connecting with her audience. People did not get the joke on her first attempt at age 16—playing George and Ira Gershwin's "I Got Rhythm" out of rhythm. Audiences did catch on eventually, though, and as Joe Brown noted in the *Washington Post,* Larkin is now "notorious for such wickedly wry satirical songs as 'Not Bad for a Broad,' and 'I'm White'"—the latter including a lyric gem skewering singer Rickie Lee Jones: "There ain't no way that I can hide it / Rickie Lee Jones already tried it / She's still white." In another concert staple, "At the Mall," Larkin impersonates Marlene Dietrich, Carmen Miranda, and Ethel Merman. "As a songwriter, one would hope that your most requested song is some-

thing moving, and powerful, and almost spiritual," she conceded to Kevin Ransom of the *Ann Arbor News.* "But no. My most requested song is about shopping."

As her career moved along, Larkin released two albums—*Step Into the Light* in 1986 and *I'm Fine* in 1987—both on Philo Records. *I'm Fine* won a Boston Music Award for outstanding folk album of 1987, and in a review for *People,* critic Ralph Novak praised Larkin's "clean, unembellished approach," as well as her "warm, melodically pure vocal style."

Renewed Focus on Guitar

By 1987 Larkin found herself at a musical crossroads again. She explained to *Guitar Player*'s Kevin Ransom that she was "feeling stuck." Elaborating, she said, "I felt like I needed to put more tension in my chords, move around the neck more, and add more colors." Larkin's dissatisfaction led her back to the guitar study she had abandoned a decade earlier. She began devoting more attention to her instrument, combining elements of jazz, rock, and blues. She embarked on a three-year self-designed study to broaden her range and skills and in the process rediscovered much of the jazz styles she had developed in the late seventies. She used books and tapes to study, including folksinger and guitarist Richard Thompson's Homespun Tapes series. In the process, Thompson and his Celtic/British Isles music influenced her music, as did the guitar styles of Bruce Cockburn and Michael Hedges.

Meanwhile, Larkin continued rounding up fans and awards. In 1990 she released a live recording entitled *In the Square.* Larkin also joined a number of folk musicians in collaborative recordings and tours. She contributed to the folk music compilations *When October Goes (Autumn Love Songs)* and *On a Winter's Night,* and toured with other artists. She and Christine Lavin also toured with Sally Fingerette and Megon McDonough as the Four Bitchin' Babes, and released a live record called *"Buy Me, Bring Me, Take Me: Don't Mess My Hair. . .": Life According to Four Bitchin' Babes.*

Larkin's exploration of new styles led her to a new record company as well. Very impressed with her guitar playing, Will Ackerman of Windham Hill Records contacted her. Thrilled that the head of a major company had taken such an interest, she left the more folk-oriented Philo for High Street Records, a division of Windham Hill. The move made great sense; Larkin's music was growing beyond the albeit very fuzzy boundaries of traditional folk music, and as Ransom expressed in the *Ann Arbor News,* "The complex harmonic structure and rhythmic pulse of her music have more in common with modern acoustic players like [Windham Hill's] Michael Hedges than the Woody Guthrie school of traditional folk picking."

Tango **Exhibited Musical Growth**

The success of Larkin's *Tango* proved that the record company switch came at the right time. The album, which she and Ackerman coproduced, exhibited the attention she had paid to her musical style, as well as changes she had made in her singing. "I'm letting more air into my voice now, and a little more personality as well," she emphaszied to Ransom in the *Ann Arbor News*. The album also captured the quality of her live performances by recording her voice and guitar at the same time, as well as by featuring what Ransom proclaimed to be "a pristine, pared-down sound that puts her percussive strumming and breathy, airy vocals right up front." The critics took notice. In his feature in *Guitar Player*, Ransom wrote that Tango "reveals a growth in harmonic complexity and rhythmic pulse over her three previous releases on Philo/Rounder." *The New England Folk Almanac* called her voice "silky and lovely throughout," and praised her "brilliant, often stunning guitar work."

While concentrating on her music, Larkin did not forgo songwriting. The lyrics on *Tango* were marked by a concentration on Larkin's serious side—more self-exploratory and reflective and less dependent on humor. The album included songs focusing on relationships and human interaction as well as socially conscious songs like "Metal Drums," about a chemical plant toxic waste disaster in Hollbrook, Massachusetts. "I believe in looking beyond myself, and there's a lot going on beyond my personal world," Larkin reflected in a High Street press release. "To avoid these issues would be a sin of omission." *Tango* does however find room for Larkin's characteristic wit, especially in "Dave's Holiday," which the *New England Folk Almanac* called "excruciatingly sarcastic."

Armed with her favorite guitar, a 1946 Martin D-18, Larkin returned to her touring schedule, again drawing the attention of music critics. In the *San Francisco Chronicle*, Barr Nobles effused, "For my money, Patty Larkin could have sung the title track from *Tango* four or five times during her set. . . . Larkin is an exciting guitarist, relying on rich open tunings and blurry-fast arpeggios. She's obviously spent hours playing those scales, honing those chops." Having broadened her interests, she also included a bit of storytelling in her efforts. Teaming up with Ackerman, she helped establish Gang of Seven—a record label created to record narrative performers such as monologuist Spalding Gray and cartoonist Lynda Berry.

As her work is extoled and her relative obscurity bemoaned, it has become apparent that the success of *Tango* is only the beginning for Larkin. Critics agree that Larkin's voice is unique. "Like the best of today's singer-songwriters, Larkin is not willing to tie up tough truths in pretty hooks or easy platitudes," the *New England Folk Almanac* asserted. "There is a lilting musicality throughout, even when angry, fearful or sassy. Even at her most challenging, Larkin finds comfort in life's blurred edges, and makes it clear she likes much of what she sees when her sharp eyes turn our way." In the *Boston Globe* Scott Alarik agreed; "Anyone who can tell us such important things, offer insight into our lonely hearts and too-busy lives—and make such pretty music along the way—deserves our attention."

Selected discography

Step Into the Light, Philo, 1986.
I'm Fine, Philo, 1987.
In the Square (includes "At the Mall" and "I'm White"), Philo, 1990.
(With Sally Fingerette, Christine Lavin, and Megon McDonough) *"Buy Me, Bring Me, Take Me: Don't Mess My Hair": Life According to Four Bitchin' Babes* (includes "Not Bad for a Broad"), Philo, 1991.
Tango (includes "Dave's Holiday," "Metal Drums," and "Tango"), High Street, 1991.

Contributor to *On a Winter's Night,* North Star Records, 1990; *When October Goes (Autumn Love Songs),* Philo/Rounder, 1991; and *Legacy II,* High Street Records, 1992.

Sources

Books

Harris, Craig, *The New Folk Music,* White Cliffs Media Company, 1991.

Periodicals

Ann Arbor News (MI), October 18, 1991.
Berkshire Eagle (Pittsfield, MA), July 13, 1989.
Billboard, December 7, 1991.
Boston Globe, September 12, 1991.
Chicago Tribune, July 18, 1991.
Guitar Player, February 1992.
Minneapolis Star Tribune, October 17, 1991.
New England Folk Almanac, September 1991.
New York Times, March 1, 1992.

People, August 10, 1987.

Pulse!, July 1992.

San Francisco Chronicle, October 15, 1991.

San Francisco Examiner, March 14, 1989.

Washington Post, November 8, 1991; November 18, 1991.

Additional information for this profile was obtained from liner notes to *Tango,* High Street Records, 1991, and *Legacy II,* High Street Records, 1992, and a High Street press biography.

—*Megan Rubiner*

John Lennon

Singer, songwriter, guitarist

John Lennon was born as German bombs fell on Liverpool during the Battle of Britain—a time many considered Britain's "finest hour" until Lennon and the Beatles provided a finer one twenty-odd years later. He grew up in austere, depressed, postwar England. His father abandoned the family when John was a baby, and his mother never could bring herself to settle down to parenthood, leaving her son to be raised by his aunt, Mimi Smith, in a respectable, lower-middle class milieu in which he never really fit.

Lennon was a mediocre student, but his obvious intelligence and artistic talent enabled him to move through the rigidly stratified British school system in spite of poor grades. He went to high school and on to Liverpool Art College, but from the mid-fifties on, his attention was increasingly focused on music. In 1955, inspired by the popularity of skiffle—a sort of speeded up jug-band blues sound—Lennon persuaded his aunt to buy him a guitar. In the spring of 1957 he and some other students at Quarry Bank High School formed the Quarry Men; at one of their first performances, on July 6, he met Paul McCartney and invited him to join the group. George Harrison joined in February of 1958.

The Quarry Men's style began to move from skiffle to rock and roll; they graduated from playing youth club dances and church halls to pubs, nightclubs, and dance halls. Along the way they acquired amplifiers, a bass player, and a series of drummers. By the time they were booked into the Kaiserkeller Club in Hamburg, Germany, they were experienced, if not quite seasoned, musicians. Their two stints in Hamburg, in 1960 and 1962, made them professionals, though the crude recordings made at the Star Club in 1962 give little hint of the impact they were to have in only a few months.

Beatlemania

In 1964 Lennon and the Beatles "came out of the f---in' sticks to take over the world," as Lennon told *Rolling Stone* publisher Jann Wenner seven years later. They had taken over England the year before, exploding out of provincial, industrial Liverpool into a British pop music scene dominated by American rock and roll and jazz, and by feeble home-grown imitations. Almost overnight the Beatles' energy and originality made them the biggest stars in the history of British popular music. Skeptical Americans who doubted that foreigners could play such a distinctly American music as rock were won over almost as quickly.

The Beatles went on to revolutionize rock music several times over. "The Beatles are a pivotal part of rock's

For the Record. . .

Born John Winston Lennon, October 9, 1940, in Liverpool, England; died of gunshot wounds December 8, 1980, in New York City; son of Alfred (a merchant seaman) and Julia (Stanley) Lennon; married Cynthia Powell, August 23, 1962 (divorced, 1968); married Yoko Ono (an artist and singer), March 20, 1969; children: (first marriage) John Charles Julian, (second marriage) Sean Ono Taro. *Education:* Attended Liverpool College of Art, 1957-60.

Learned to play guitar, 1955; formed group the Quarry Men, 1957; group performed as Johnny and the Moondogs, the Moonshiners, the Rainbows, the Nurk Twins, and Long John and the Silver Beetles; group's name changed to the Beatles, 1960; performed in Liverpool area, northern England, Scotland, and Hamburg, Germany, 1960-62; group signed with EMI/Parlophone records and recorded first single, "Love Me Do," 1962; recorded more than a dozen albums and numerous singles and EPs, 1962-70; toured Europe, America, and Asia, 1963-66; appeared in films *A Hard Day's Night,* 1964, *Help,* 1965, *Yellow Submarine,* 1968, and *Let It Be,* 1970; group disbanded, 1970.

With Yoko Ono, released *Two Virgins,* Apple, 1968; with Ono and others, recorded several albums, 1968-80, and made occasional concert appearances. Author of books including *In His Own Write,* 1964, and *A Spaniard in the Works,* 1965. Graphic artist, works exhibited in Great Britain and the U.S.

Selected awards: With the Beatles, numerous Grammy awards and platinum albums; gold album for *Imagine,* 1971.

story," wrote Tim Riley in *Tell Me Why,* "not just because their music can still dazzle but because their arrival as rock 'n' rollers with an endless stream of original material challenged what anyone had imagined pop could become. . . . They may not be responsible for everything, but nearly everything that comes after would be impossible without them." As Griel Marcus wrote in *The Rolling Stone Illustrated History of Rock and Roll,* "What you heard was a rock and roll group that combined elements of the music that you were used to hearing only in pieces. . . . The Beatles combined the harmonic range and implicit equality of the Fifties vocal group, . . . the flash of a rockabilly band, . . . the aggressive and unique personalities of the classic rock stars, . . . the homey this-could-be-you manner of later rock stars, [and] endlessly inventive songwriting. . . . The result was that elusive rock treasure, *a new sound*—and a new sound that could

not be exhausted in the course of one brief flurry on the charts."

Perhaps more significant than the Beatles' sound was the way in which they made the recording studio their instrument and the long-playing record their medium. Though some producers, notably Phil Spector, had expanded the concept of recording beyond merely the capturing of a live performance, the Beatles were the first artists to make records the focus of their work. "The Beatles are our first recording artists, and they remain our best," Riley wrote. "The Beatles' work came to be conceived with the studio in mind—all the production values a mixing board had to offer were used to serve the ideas conveyed in their music. A Beatles record is more than just a collection of songs: it's a performance for tape. . . . As time went on, the Beatles weren't so much songwriters as they were *record* writers; the studio became a lab where musical ideas were exchanged, reworked, and restructured for tape."

The core of the Beatles' brilliance was the musical relationship between Lennon and McCartney, a relationship that was as complex as the music it spawned. McCartney had begun writing songs before he met Lennon, and inspired Lennon to try his hand at it. They sometimes wrote songs together (Hunter Davies, in his biography of the Beatles, describes them sitting down at a piano to write "With a Little Help From My Friends") but seem at least as often to have served as each other's editors, helping to fix or finish a song that the other was having a problem with. McCartney wrote the verses of "We Can Work It Out," and Lennon contributed the bridge; Lennon wrote most of "Ticket to Ride," but McCartney came up with the off-center drum pattern that anchors the rhythm. After the Beatles broke up, Lennon played down the importance of their teamwork, but in his final interview with *Playboy* he acknowledged, "I said that, but I was lying. . . . We wrote a *lot* of stuff together, one on one, eyeball to eyeball. . . . In those days we absolutely used to write like that—both playing into each other's noses."

That was particularly true in the early days, from the time they first went into Abbey Road studios in London in 1962—insisting to skeptical producer George Martin that they wanted to record their own songs—until the Beatles stopped touring in 1966. By that time, Lennon told *Playboy,* "the creativity of songwriting had left Paul and me . . . well, by the mid-Sixties it had become a *craft.*" Their personal relationship had become strained as well. According to Ray Coleman in *Lennon,* the tension began to build with the death of their manager, Brian Epstein, in 1967. Lennon was deeply into drugs, unhappy in his marriage, and bored with being a Beatle. McCartney took over the direction of the band, leading them into the ill-conceived and chaotically executed film project *Magical Mystery Tour* and taking the dominant role in most of their recordings.

Lennon reacted by withdrawing further from the Beatles and focusing on his relationship with artist Yoko Ono. He brought her to the 1968 sessions for *The Beatles,* the so-called White Album, breaking what Coleman called "a rigid, unwritten rule of the group: that their women would never be allowed in the studios." The other band members resented her presence and treated her coolly, alienating Lennon further. The resulting album, with its fragmented sound, heralded the disintegration of the Beatles into four individualistic musicians rather than a band.

The release of *The Beatles* was followed a week later by the release of *Two Virgins,* an album of avant-garde music Lennon and Ono had recorded in his home studio. The cover photo, which showed the couple nude, was banned in some countries and sold in brown paper wrappers in the United States. The music, an aural collage of electronic sounds, attracted much less attention. The Lennon-Ono relationship had become public. Lennon's divorce was in progress, and Ono suffered a miscarriage in November of 1968. They had also been arrested for possession of drugs, a hazard from which the Beatles had been considered exempt in spite of their public admission that they had used marijuana and LSD.

End of the Beatles

The Beatles' musical estrangement deepened and was documented in the movie *Let It Be,* filmed in 1969 as they worked on what was to be their last album. Their financial affairs were also in disarray: their company, Apple Corps, Ltd., was losing money rapidly, and Lennon said in an interview with Coleman in January of 1969 that "if it carries on like this all of us will be broke in the next six months." It was the business crisis that brought things to a head: Lennon invited Allen Klein, an American promoter, to take over as the Beatles' manager, but McCartney refused to sign a contract with Klein. Late in 1969 Lennon informed the others that he no longer considered himself a Beatle, but was persuaded not to make a public announcement until the group's financial position was stabilized. The breakup became public when McCartney released his first solo album in the spring of 1970.

Lennon had already moved on, forming the Plastic Ono Band with Yoko in 1969, releasing three singles, "Give Peace a Chance," "Cold Turkey," and "Instant Karma," and performing at the Toronto Peace Festival in Sep-

tember of 1969. He released his first real solo album, *Plastic Ono Band,* in 1970. The record, made in the wake of his primal scream therapy with psychiatrist Arthur Janov, was as much a therapeutic as a musical exercise. Riley, in *Tell Me Why,* wrote: "These confessional songs seek out the idealized state of childhood, the pain of individuation, the fragility of fantasies and the very real power of illusions. . . . The soul-baring leanness of the sound embodies the crux of what rock 'n' roll is all about: a restlessness with the status quo, a hopeful dissatisfaction, and a gnawing sense of encumbrance that finds release as it expresses itself."

Lennon's next album, *Imagine,* was much more successful commercially, and the title song became the most popular song of Lennon's solo career. Ben Gerson of *Rolling Stone,* who considered *Plastic Ono Band* "a masterpiece," found *Imagine* a disappointing follow-up, faulting it for it's "sloppiness and self-absorption." He wrote that *Plastic Ono Band,* "in its singing and instrumental work, was as much a triumph of artifice as of art. It managed to sound both spontaneous and careful, while *Imagine* is less of each. Even though it contains a substantial portion of good music, on the heels of [*Plastic Ono Band*] it only serves to reinforce the questioning of what John's relationship to rock really is."

Politics and Conceptual Art

Lennon was questioning that relationship, too. Freed from the confines of the Beatles' wholesome image—something he had resented and struggled against ever since Brian Epstein took the band out of black leather and put them in suits—he began branching out into other activities. Inspired by Ono's conceptual art, he made several avant-garde films and exhibited a series of erotic lithographs entitled "Bag One." He also began to speak out about politics, which had been another Beatle taboo. He had started to cross that line earlier with the song "Give Peace a Chance" and by returning the medal he had received when the Beatles were made members of the Order of the British Empire, partly as a protest against British support of America's war in Vietnam. He became especially outspoken after moving to New York City in 1971 and falling in with a group of prominent American radicals.

The radicals wanted Lennon to join the protests at the 1972 Republican Convention in San Diego. Lennon, who suspected they were trying to provoke a riot similar to the one at the Democratic Convention in Chicago in 1968, never intended to go. Nevertheless, rumors began to spread, and they were believed by some officials of the Nixon administration, who began a campaign to have Lennon deported as a convicted drug user. The FBI shadowed him, tapped his phone, and filled thousands of pages of files with notes on his musical and other activities. The case was finally settled in 1975 when a court declared that Lennon's British marijuana conviction was not grounds for deportation under U.S. law.

While Lennon was still under the influence of, as he wrote in *Skywriting by Word of Mouth*, "male-macho 'serious revolutionaries' and their insane ideas about killing people to save them from capitalism," he recorded a politically didactic single, "Power to the People"—which he recalled as "rather embarrassing"—and another album with Ono, *Some Time in New York City*.

> "Lennon's death was a crucial event in rock culture. . . . [It] was the ultimate example of the era's fragmentation. All the media pundits repeated the same phrase—'the dream is over'—and it was."
> —Ken Tucker

Rolling Stone's Stephen Holden called the record "incipient artistic suicide," while acknowledging that "John sings better than ever." Holden observed: "*Some Time in New York City* is . . . entirely devoted to propaganda. But as propaganda it is so embarrassingly puerile as to constitute an advertisement against itself. . . . The tunes are shallow and derivative and the words little more than sloppy nursery rhymes that patronize the issues and individuals they seek to exalt."

In 1973 Lennon and Ono separated, she staying in New York and he going to Los Angeles on what he later described to *Playboy* as a "lost weekend that lasted eighteen months." Drinking heavily, Lennon was thrown out of nightclubs and was a staple of gossip columns for much of that time. He also released three albums. The first two, *Mind Games* and *Walls and Bridges*, turned away from politics, back toward the musical territory of *Imagine*. While neither was particularly well received by critics, *Walls and Bridges* did bring Lennon his first American Number One hit, the single "Whatever Gets You Through the Night."

For his next record—which was to be his last for five years—he turned to legendary producer Phil Spector to make an album of old rock and roll songs. This was in part a legal obligation, part of an out-of-court settlement with Chuck Berry's publisher who claimed that Lennon had lifted the line "Here come old flattop" in "Come Together" from Berry's "You Can't Catch Me." To avoid a lawsuit, Lennon had agreed to record several Berry tunes, and he decided to fill out the album with other fifties classics. The sessions did not go well: Spector's eccentric, paranoid behavior, combined with Lennon's drinking, made the sessions prolonged, expensive, and unproductive. Finally Spector took the tapes and withdrew to his walled house with its armed guards and attack dogs and refused to give the recordings to Lennon. It took months to recover the tapes, and when Spector finally did relinquish them they turned out to be all but unusable. Eventually Lennon went into a New York studio to record ten songs in a week to complete the album. *Rock 'n' Roll* was released early in 1975 to lukewarm reviews and unimpressive sales, though a few critics, including Steve Simels of *Stereo Review*, considered it among his best work.

Five-Year Musical Hiatus

At about the same time Lennon and Ono were reconciled, and the Beatles were finally dissolved as a legal entity. Chet Flippo recalled in *The Ballad of John and Yoko* that Lennon later remarked to him that it was "the first time in thirteen years that he had not been under written contract to at least *someone*. . . . It was his desire now to exert that freedom by quitting rock & roll." Quit he did, resisting calls for a Beatles reunion from fans and promoters; he always insisted that he had no regrets about the breakup of the band and no desire to look back, and he believed that his solo work was as good as, if not better than, anything the Beatles had done. He retired to his apartment in the Dakota building on Central Park West to raise his new son, Sean, and dabble in house-husbandry. "I'm a housewife who also has a nanny and an assistant and a cook and a cleaner," he told *Playboy*. "I wasn't a poor strugglin' housewife who *had* to cook three meals a day. . . . [But] it wasn't a lark. The serious intent was to orchestrate what went into the baby's mind and body for at least five years."

Lennon's sabbatical came to an end in 1980 when, on a trip to Bermuda, he heard the music of the B-52s. "It sounds just like Yoko's music," he told Jonathan Cott of *Rolling Stone*, "so I said to meself, 'It's time to get out the old axe and wake the wife up!'" Lennon and Ono wrote 25 songs in the next few weeks, and were soon in the studio recording. The resulting album, *Double Fan-*

tasy, was different from their previous collaborations: it was their first album of pop songs on which they received equal billing, alternating writing credits and lead vocals throughout. Subtitled "A Heart Play," it presented, as *Rolling Stone*'s Holden wrote, "the Lennon's marriage as an exemplary pop fairy tale."

Double Fantasy received mixed reviews, with some critics expressing disappointment that the pop music trends of the late seventies seemed to have passed Lennon by. As Steve Simels of *Stereo Review* noted, much of the music on Lennon's comeback album was nearer to "what the industry calls Adult Contemporary" than to the cutting edge of rock. Nevertheless, the single "Starting Over" went quickly to number one, and Lennon and Ono continued to spend many hours in the studio working on their next record.

Upon returning home from a recording session on December 8, 1980, Lennon was shot five times by a self-described fan, Mark Chapman, for whom he had signed an autograph earlier that day. He was dead on arrival at Roosevelt Hospital. Crowds gathered outside the Dakota as soon as the news broke, and many remained there for days, singing "Give Peace a Chance," "Imagine," and other Lennon songs.

Ken Tucker wrote in *Rock of Ages:* "Lennon's death was a crucial event in rock culture. . . . [It] was the ultimate example of the era's fragmentation. All the media pundits repeated the same phrase—'the dream is over'—and it was: Rock fans were forever separated from the myth of the Beatles. There was nothing left but to face the future." Lester Bangs, writing in the *Los Angeles Times,* noted that much of the grief was at odds with Lennon's own attitude toward the past: "John Lennon at his best despised cheap sentiment and had to learn the hard way that once you've made your mark on history those who can't will be so grateful they'll turn it into a cage for you. . . . The Beatles were most of all a moment. . . . It is for that moment—not for John Lennon the man—that you are mourning."

Stereo Review's Simels summed up that moment: "John Lennon was the coolest guy in the universe. Cooler than Elvis (dumb greaser!), cooler than Brando or James Dean or Lord Byron or Willie Sutton or Muhammad Ali or Cary Grant or Robert de Niro or Bruce Springsteen. Cooler than Elvis Costello even. . . . He had wit, style, and songwriting genius. He invented the world's most exclusive men's club and made millions of dollars thumbing his nose at the Establishment. He gave countless people joy and in the process changed the world a couple of times. . . . His finest work . . . constitutes an achievement as personal and innovative and moving as can be found in the history of the music he helped shape."

Selected writings

In His Own Write, Simon & Schuster, 1964.
A Spaniard in the Works, Simon & Schuster, 1965.
John Lennon's Erotic Lithographs, edited by Ralph Ginzburg, Avant-Garde Media, 1970.
The Writings of John Lennon, Simon & Schuster, 1981.
Skywriting by Word of Mouth, Harper & Row, 1986.

Selected discography

With the Beatles

Please Please Me, Parlophone, 1963.
With the Beatles, Parlophone, 1963.
A Hard Day's Night, Parlophone, 1964.
Beatles for Sale, Parlophone, 1964.
Help!, Parlophone, 1965.
Rubber Soul, Parlophone, 1965.
Yesterday . . . and Today, Capitol, 1966.
Revolver, Parlophone, 1966.
Sgt. Pepper's Lonely Hearts Club Band, Parlophone, 1967.
Magical Mystery Tour, Capitol, 1967.
The Beatles, Apple, 1968.
Yellow Submarine, Apple, 1969.
Abbey Road, Apple, 1969.
Let It Be, Apple, 1970.
Hey Jude, Apple, 1970.
The Beatles—Circa 1960—In the Beginning, Polydor, 1970.
The Beatles 1962-1966, Apple, 1973.
The Beatles 1967-1970, Apple, 1973.
Rock 'n' Roll Music, Capitol, 1976.
The Beatles at the Hollywood Bowl, Capitol, 1977.
The Beatles Live! At the Star Club in Hamburg, Germany: 1962, Lingasong, 1977.
Love Songs, Capitol, 1977.
Rarities, Capitol, 1979.
Dawn of the Silver Beatles, PAC, 1981.
Reel Music, Capitol, 1982.
Twenty Greatest Hits, Capitol, 1982.
Past Masters Volume One, Parlophone, 1988.
Past Masters Volume Two, Parlophone, 1988.

With Yoko Ono

Unfinished Music No. 1: Two Virgins, Apple, 1968.
Unfinished Music No. 2: Life With the Lions, Apple, 1969.
Wedding Album, Apple, 1969.
Some Time in New York City, Apple, 1972.
Double Fantasy, Geffen, 1980.
Milk and Honey, Polydor, 1984.

With the Plastic Ono Band

The Plastic Ono Band—Live Peace in Toronto, Apple, 1969.
Plastic Ono Band, Apple, 1970.

Solo releases

Imagine, Apple, 1971.
Mind Games, Apple, 1973.
Walls and Bridges, Apple, 1974.
Rock 'n' Roll, Apple, 1975.
Shaved Fish, Apple, 1975.
The John Lennon Collection, Geffen, 1982.
Reflections and Poetry, Silhouette, 1984.
Menlove Avenue, Capitol, 1986.
John Lennon: Live in New York City, Capitol, 1986.
Imagine John Lennon: Music From the Original Motion Picture, Capitol, 1988.
Lennon, Capitol, 1990.

Sources

Books

The Ballad of John and Yoko, edited by Jonathan Cott and Christine Doudna, Rolling Stone Press, 1982.
Bangs, Lester, *Psychotic Reactions and Carburetor Dung,* Vintage Books, 1988.
Castleman, Harry, and Walter J. Podrazik, *All Together Now: The First Complete Beatles Discography,* Ballantine, 1975.
Coleman, Ray, *Lennon: The Definitive Biography,* McGraw-Hill, 1984, revised, Harperperennial, 1993.
Davies, Hunter, *The Beatles: The Authorized Biography,* McGraw-Hill, 1968.
Goldman, Albert, *The Lives of John Lennon,* Morrow, 1988.
Lennon, John, *Skywriting by Word of Mouth,* Harper & Row, 1986.
Lewisohn, Mark, *The Beatles: Recording Sessions,* Harmony Books, 1988.
Martin, George, *All You Need Is Ears,* St. Martin's, 1979.
Reinhart, Charles, *You Can't Do That: Beatles Bootlegs and Novelty Records,* Contemporary Books, 1981.
Riley, Tim, *Tell Me Why,* Knopf, 1989.
The Rolling Stone Illustrated History of Rock 'n' Roll, edited by Jim Miller, Rolling Stone Press, 1986.
Sheff, David, and G. Barry Golson, *The Playboy Interviews With John Lennon and Yoko Ono,* Berkley Books, 1981.
Wenner, Jann, *Lennon Remembers,* Popular Library, 1982.
Wiener, Allen J., *The Beatles: A Recording History,* McFarland, 1986.
Wiener, Jon, *Come Together: John Lennon and His Time,* Random House, 1984.
Ward, Ed, Geoffrey Stokes, and Ken Tucker, *Rock of Ages: The Rolling Stone History of Rock & Roll,* Rolling Stone Press, 1986.

Periodicals

Los Angeles Times, December 11, 1980.
Rolling Stone, October 28, 1971; July 20, 1972.
Stereo Review, March 1981.

—*Tim Connor*

Huey Lewis

Huey Lewis and his band the News are perhaps best described as the working man's Top 40 group. With their hard-driving rock and roll, catchy songs, and brisk *a capella* harmony, the band members have placed 16 songs in the Top Ten on the pop charts since 1982. Some of their most memorable hits include "I Want a New Drug," "Heart of Rock and Roll," "If This Is It," and "The Power of Love." Success came slowly for the California-based group, but since selling more than eight million copies of their 1983 album *Sports,* they have enjoyed superstar status in the United States and abroad.

People magazine contributor Roger Wolmuth wrote about Huey Lewis and the News, "No matter that the band's message has all the depth of Huey's chin dimple, or that its bouncy good-time sound seems straight out of rock 'n' roll's archives. Echoes of street corner doo-wop singing and urban gospel, of '50s rockabilly and '80s rock blend together like primary colors." The critic added that Lewis and his companions hardly fit the hard rocker mold with their short haircuts and shirt-and-jeans attire. "With Lewis," concluded Wolmuth, "there are only the chiseled good-guy looks and slap-on-the-back chumminess that make him seem as comfy as a cardigan to his fans. Think of him as an aging high school jock, a favorite drinking buddy or that lovable lug of an older brother."

Singer, songwriter, harmonica player

Bohemian Parents, Bohemian Son

Huey Lewis was given the unlikely name of Hugh Anthony Cregg III. Only the name was conservative, however. Lewis was born in 1951 to a set of parents who were a generation ahead of the bohemian revolution. A graduate of Duke University, his father gave up medical studies to play drums in a jazz band. His mother was a Polish refugee who was drawn to both jazz music and beatnik poetry.

After Lewis was born in New York City, the family moved west to Mill Valley, California, where the elder Lewis completed his medical studies and worked as a radiologist. Young Huey grew up in a racially mixed community where drug experimentation and a love of rock music went hand-in-hand. Lewis's own musical tastes leaned to the early hillbilly rock of Elvis Presley and Carl Perkins. He also loved rhythm and blues and taught himself how to play the harmonica.

When Lewis was 12 his parents divorced. Partly in order to remove him from the heady atmosphere of Mill Valley, Huey's father sent him to Lawrenceville Academy, a conservative boarding school in southern New Jersey. Lewis earned honor roll grades there, especial-

ly in math, but refused to conform to the school's strict codes of behavior. "I really hated prep school when I first got there," he recalled in *Rolling Stone.* "I couldn't believe there were people from everywhere in the world and they had the same tie on. I never was very cool. I didn't really distinguish myself at all, really."

Post-Prep Rebellion

Lewis's math grades were so high that he was accepted into a prestigious program at Cornell University. He graduated from high school at the age of 16—he had skipped a grade—and wanted to play baseball for the summer. Instead, his father persuaded him to fly to Europe. For three months in 1968 he used a rail pass and the youth hostel system to see much of Spain, Portugal, and Italy. When money ran low, he would earn pocket change "busking" his harmonica on street corners. "Europe taught me I could live on my own," he remarked in *Rolling Stone.* "From that day on, I decided I was never gonna work for anybody."

Lewis lasted only one semester at Cornell, and by late 1968 he found himself back in the San Francisco Bay area, jamming with old Mill Valley friends and trying to make good in a rock band. He called himself Huey Louie and in 1972 joined the soft-rock band Clover. The

band also boasted future News member Sean Hopper and future Doobie Brothers member John McFee.

Lewis told *Rolling Stone* that Clover had the talent but perhaps pressed too hard for success. "We kept trying to sound like a big-time rock band," he said. Nevertheless, the manager of the British group Dr. Feelgood caught a Clover show at the Palomino Club and offered the group a recording contract in England. Clover cut several albums in Great Britain, but none sold well. Disappointed, the members came back to San Francisco and went their separate ways.

In Lewis's case, the breakup of Clover meant a shift back to the minor leagues. He organized a Monday night jam session at a Marin County club called Uncle Charlie's. Lewis recruited more old friends, all of whom had been working with semisuccessful rock bands, and soon the personnel for a new group began to take shape. The musicians were lifted out of obscurity when Nick Lowe turned a Lewis line—"what looks best on you is me"—into a song. Lewis declined royalty payments and accepted a flight to London instead. There he and his companions cut a parody tune, "Exodisco," based on the theme from the motion picture *Exodus.*

By that time Lewis and his friends were calling themselves American Express. The U.K.-based Chrysalis Records offered them a recording contract but insisted upon a name change. The group became Huey Lewis and the News, and their first album was released in 1980. That work, *Huey Lewis and the News,* was recorded in three weeks. It briefly held a spot on the charts but soon faltered. The executives at Chrysalis were confident, however, and they gave the go-ahead for another album. *Picture This* hit the stores in 1982 and yielded the group's first Top 40 hits, "Workin' for a Livin'," "Do You Believe in Love," and "Hope You Love Me Like You Say You Do."

Scored Big With News and *Sports*

Huey Lewis and the News broke through as headliners with the 1983 album *Sports.* Most of the tracks were written by Lewis or other band members, and the work produced an astonishing number of hits. The News made the Top Ten with "Heart and Soul," "I Want a New Drug," "Heart of Rock and Roll," and "If This Is It." The long-form video of "Heart of Rock and Roll" won a Grammy Award, and Lewis was invited to join other talented artists for the "We Are the World" project, which yielded a single and video to aid famine relief in Ethiopia.

The group's next album, *Fore!,* was greeted with high expectations. It too produced such Top 40 hits as

"Stuck with You" and "Hip to Be Square." The News also contributed two songs to the popular film *Back to the Future,* including the chart-topping "Power of Love," which earned an Oscar nomination for best song of 1986.

This period of dizzying success was followed by a fallow time. The News' 1988 album, *Small World,* their most experimental work to date, featured Bruce Hornsby, the Tower of Power Horns, and the late jazz saxophonist Stan Getz. It failed to sell well, however, and Lewis and his band changed record labels and took a three-year hiatus to work on their next release.

Hard at Play, the News's first Capitol-EMI recording, was issued in 1991. The group went back to work on tour to help promote the album, appearing in the United States and Europe. *Hard at Play* went platinum in sales, but the venues that Huey Lewis and the News were playing in the early 1990s were not as vast as they once were. The group can be heard at Houston rodeos and at the New Orleans Jazz Festival rather than in arenas that seat many thousands. Lewis commented in the *Akron Beacon Journal,* "I enjoy our new profile. It's a little lower than it was in 1984, '85 and '86. Now it's just about the music and the show, you know? It's nice not being the bee's knees. It's fabulous. We have our fans. They come to see us play—and that's it. I love it. It's all I ever really wanted." The musician concluded, "I didn't want to be the talk of the town. I wanted to have a nice, successful band—and that's what we've got going."

Lewis has cautioned would-be musicians to make music for the love of it, and not for any fame that might come. "I never did this to make it," he declared in *Rolling Stone.* "Period. Neither fame nor fortune. And I didn't do this to get girls either. The real reason I did this was because when I was growing up, being in a great band looked like the coolest thing in the world. And you know what? It is the coolest thing in the world."

Selected discography

With Clover; released in Great Britain

Clover, 1977.

Unavailable, 1977.
Love on the Wire, 1977.

With the News

Huey Lewis and the News, Chrysalis, 1980.
Picture This, Chrysalis, 1982.
Sports (includes "I Want a New Drug," "Heart of Rock and Roll," "Heart and Soul," and "If This Is It"), Chrysalis, 1983.
(With others) *Back to the Future* (soundtrack; includes "Power of Love"), 1985.
Fore! (includes "Stuck With You" and "Hip to Be Square"), Chrysalis, 1986.
Small World, Chrysalis, 1988.
Hard at Play, Capitol-EMI, 1991.
Best of, Chrysalis, 1992.

Contributor to the single and video "We Are the World," 1984.

Sources

Books

Rees, Dafydd, and Luke Crampton, *Rock Movers & Shakers,* ABC-CLIO, 1991.
Stambler, Irwin, *The Encyclopedia of Pop, Rock and Soul,* St. Martin's, 1989.

Periodicals

Akron Beacon Journal (OH), July 19, 1991; July 20, 1991.
Desert News (Salt Lake City, UT), January 3, 1992.
Houston Post, February 20, 1992.
Newsweek, November 3, 1986.
People, January 19, 1987.
Rolling Stone, September 13, 1984; November 20, 1986; July 14, 1988.

—*Anne Janette Johnson*

Liberace

Pianist

A flamboyant musical showman, Liberace is remembered for his extravagant costumes and campy stage presence as much as for his talent as a pianist. The country's highest paid piano soloist for nearly 30 years, Liberace combined florid renditions of popular songs with abbreviated versions of the classics in a show that became a Las Vegas mainstay. His decision to reach for every excess and embrace it with just a hint of self-mockery paved the way for such androgynous superstar musicians as Michael Jackson, Boy George, and Elton John.

Newsweek correspondent Bill Barol described a Liberace concert at Radio City Music Hall: "Liberace flew in from the wings suspended on a wire; introduced his valet/chauffeur, put on a purple sequined-and-feathered robe; took it off; played Chopin on a Lucite piano with lacework trim; did a soft shoe; bestowed a selection of gifts on an audience member; shamelessly plugged his new book and Las Vegas restaurant; drove onstage in a red, white and blue Rolls-Royce; peeled away a red, white and blue sequined-and-feathered robe to reveal red, white and blue satin hotpants, and grabbed a red, white and blue sequined baton to lead the Rockettes in 'The Stars and Stripes Forever.' This was all before intermission."

Liberace constantly strove to outdo himself, and his audience never grew tired of seeing his extravagant and warmly amusing displays. *New Republic* correspondent Edward Rothstein wrote that Liberace's was "a material version of dazzling splendor, found in minks and jewels and capes and glitter. . . . But it is an image of the 'classics' refracted through rhinestones and diamonds—puffs of smoke rising from the floor."

Displayed Talent at Young Age

Throughout his life, Liberace was coy about his personal relationships. Biographers who sought to discuss his homosexuality were summarily dismissed, and only an official coroner's report revealed that he died of complications of acquired immune deficiency syndrome (AIDS). In a *People* magazine obituary, Michelle Green noted that at his death "the world lost an exotic original—a sweet-natured self-promoter who, for all of his extrovert showiness onstage, had been something of a lost soul." The reporter continued: "Liberace's was a life of exquisite paradox; for flamboyance and repression, kitsch and concealment."

Liberace was born Wladziu Valentino Liberace in 1919 in West Allis, Wisconsin. One of four children, he was the son of a french horn player who eventually earned a spot with the Milwaukee Philharmonic Orchestra. Liberace showed his musical talent early, learning to play the piano by ear when he was only four. At first his father tried to discourage his interest in piano, but timely praise from Poland's most noted pianist, Ignace Jan Paderewski, made the way clear for a musical career.

Tensions remained high in the Liberace household, however. Calling himself Walter Busterkeys, the young pianist made the rounds of speakeasies and movie theaters, earning wages for playing the popular melodies of the time. This infuriated his father, who was devoted to the classics. "Liberace's emotional difficulties surely sprang from his unsatisfactory relationship with his harsh father," wrote Green. "While proud of his son's musical abilities (the boy won a piano scholarship and later played with the Chicago Symphony), Salvatore was bitterly opposed to the popular music that his son loved. But songs like 'Sweet Jennie Lee' were the budding musician's preference, and to help keep the family afloat, young Liberace gladly played piano in silent-movie houses." Relations between father and son were further strained when Liberace discovered that his father had a mistress—his parents eventually divorced.

Developed Unique Style

At the age of 17, Liberace was offered a place with the federally funded Works Progress Administration Symphony Orchestra. This in turn led to a scholarship to the Wisconsin College of Music and to concert appearances in many major cities. He developed his trademark style quite by chance in 1939, when, after a classical recital, his audience requested a rendition of

the popular tune "Three Little Fishes." Liberace launched into the number, giving it impromptu, quasi-classical flourishes, and brought the house down. His sudden idea on "how to make piano playing pay" won him bookings at the Persian Room of the Hotel Plaza in New York City and other large nightclubs. By 1947 he was traveling with his own custom-made piano, an oversized Bluthner grand, insured for $150,000. He also decked his instrument with a candelabra, borrowing the idea from a Hollywood motion picture about composer Frederic Chopin.

Liberace was the star of the very first syndicated television program, *The Liberace Show,* filmed in Los Angeles. The show began in 1952 and quickly established Liberace as television's first matinee idol. Within two years it was being carried by more stations than either *Dragnet* or *I Love Lucy.* The performer added to his popularity by making frequent live appearances, in one instance drawing a sellout crowd—13,000 women and 3,000 men—to Madison Square Garden on May 26, 1954.

The star suffered a setback in 1956, though, during a tour of England. One of the newspapers there hinted at his homosexuality, prompting a quick lawsuit from the entertainer for defamation of character. Liberace won the case, but his popularity in the United States plummeted. He sought to remedy the matter by appearing in more conservative dress and offering more conservative concerts, but by the early 1960s he realized that he could draw more customers by capitalizing on his kitsch. He amassed a wardrobe worth millions, including lavish fur coats that could weigh as much as 150 pounds, and he joked, sang, and even danced during his concerts.

Master of Showmanship

"Critics were—and are—dismissive about [Liberace's] recordings," Green claimed. "Few dispute the fact that he possessed talent; but the consensus is that it was showmanship, rather than technique, that was his forte." Liberace could play Chopin's famed "Minute Waltz" in 37 seconds and a truncated version of Beethoven's "Moonlight Sonata" in approximately four minutes. His classical repertoire was often performed in abbreviated form because he felt he would lose the audience's attention otherwise. Rothstein called the entertainer a "representative of our time" who was simply "an exaggeration of the character of our musical life, which itself is a distorted, peculiar transformation of nineteenth-century musical culture, thriving on invoked images, ritualistic signs, and commercial energies."

Nevertheless, Liberace did indeed exert an influence on modern popular music. As Barol put it, "his apparent homosexuality—not acknowledged but not exactly hidden—must have given hope to millions of closeted gays in . . . less open years." Liberace's legacy lives on in the exuberant piano work of Elton John and Billy Joel as well as in the eye-catching costumes of Michael Jackson, Prince, and Little Richard.

Afflicted with heart disease and emphysema, Liberace nevertheless performed regularly until the autumn of 1986. It is estimated that he earned $5 million each year during the 1970s and 1980s. He spent lavishly on himself, his costumes, and his friends. However, he also became a serious patron of the fine arts by creating a Liberace Museum; profits from the museum's admission fees provide college scholarships to needy classical musicians.

Early in 1987 Liberace's condition deteriorated, and he died at his home in Palm Springs, California. To the time of his death he denied rumors that he was homosexual—even after a former chauffeur brought a "palimony" suit against him. An official autopsy ruled that the pianist died as a result of AIDS. His many fabulous artifacts, costumes, and furniture were disbursed at a much-publicized auction.

Liberace was never considered a serious concert musician. The critical barbs did little to deflate his spirit, though. For years his theme song was "I Don't Care," as he joked about his vast earning power. Behind the surface glitter of Liberace's image lay a solid grounding in classical music and the ability to transmit that music to a public that just wanted to hear popular songs. As Barol concluded, the ebullient Liberace "never disappointed an audience. . . . It is a measure of his talent that he made the two biggest celebrity cliches ring

quite true: there was no one else like him, and he will never be replaced."

Selected discography

Here's Liberace, MCA, 1968.
Greatest Hits, Columbia, 1969.
Concert Favorites, 3 volumes, Columbia, 1986.
16 Most Requested Songs, Columbia/Legacy, 1989.
The Golden Age of Television, Curb/CEMA, 1991.
Liberace Remembered, USA, 1992.
The Artistry of Liberace, MCA.
The Best of Liberace, MCA, reissued, RCA-Camden.
Liberace Christmas, MCA.
Liberace Plays Moon River and Other Great Songs, Richmond.
'Twas the Night Before Christmas.

Sources

Books

Thorson, Scott, and Alex Thorleifson, *Behind the Candelabra: My Life With Liberace,* Dutton, 1988.

Periodicals

American Weekly, July 18, 1954.
Life, December 7, 1953.
New Republic, July 2, 1984.
Newsweek, February 22, 1954; May 7, 1984; February 16, 1987.
New Yorker, June 5, 1954.
People, February 16, 1987; April 25, 1988.
Time, February 16, 1987.
Washington Post, February 5, 1987.

—*Anne Janette Johnson*

Abbey Lincoln

Singer, composer

Abbey Lincoln "is a culture bearer," jazz singer Cassandra Wilson told *Newsweek*'s John Leland. "There are certain people inside the African-American experience that act as *griots,* bearers of the culture, and they help to carry on the traditions and transmit knowledge and understanding of our heritage. [Singer] Paul Robeson was something like that. And so is she." For four decades Lincoln's life has been a constant transformation of experience, of awakenings into growth, of the communication of what she has witnessed. She has grown through many stages: a naive young lounge singer; a movie and jazz-club sex kitten; a vocal African American with a deepened cultural awareness; a sensitive actress contradicting cultural perceptions; an artistic and cultural exile; a poetic jazz sage. She has gone by many names, finding and then defining herself individually, culturally, and humanistically. Lincoln's music, which at first served as an attention-getting device, eventually grew into a means of expression, understanding, and communication.

Lincoln was born Anna Marie Wooldridge in Chicago in 1930. Soon after her birth, the family moved to Calvin Center, Michigan, her mother believing a rural environment was the best in which to raise a family. Since they were poor, the children often had to entertain themselves with singing, but as the tenth of twelve children, Lincoln had a difficult time distinguishing herself. "I preferred to sing alone—to be the centerpiece," she recounted to Francis Davis in *High Fidelity.* "The living room piano was my private space once I discovered that singing could win me attention and admiration." She also sang in school and church choirs, often as a soloist. Her musical approach was mainly influenced by the recordings of singers that her father borrowed from neighbors: Billie Holiday, Ella Fitzgerald, Sarah Vaughan, Lena Horne. "I was particularly impressed with Lena Horne; for a while I totally emulated her style and voice," Lincoln explained to Gary G. Vercelli in *Down Beat.* "Then I had the opportunity to see Lena perform. It was then that I knew I no longer wanted to be like Lena, 'cause her message was so loud and clear to be yourself."

Walked the Bar

Lincoln proved her singing capabilities at an amateur contest when she was 19 and then began her musical career in Los Angeles, singing in nightclubs. By 1952 she had moved to Honolulu to perform as a resident club singer under the stage name Anna Marie, but she still hadn't quite developed her own identity as a singer. "I sang songs I heard Rosemary Clooney sing, songs that were popular on the radio," Lincoln told Lisa Jones

For the Record. . .

Born Anna Marie Wooldridge, August 6, 1930, in Chicago, IL; performed variously under names Anna Marie, Gaby Lee, and Aminata Moseka; changed name to Abbey Lincoln, 1956; married Max Roach, 1962 (divorced, 1970). *Education:* studied music with prominent vocal and dramatic coaches, Hollywood, CA, early 1950s.

Worked as a maid, 1949-50; won amateur singing contest, 1950; moved to California to perform in nightclubs, 1951; resident club singer, Honolulu, HI, 1952-54; singer at various clubs, Hollywood, 1954-57; began recording career, 1956; soloist with group led by Max Roach, late 1950s-1960s; as a soloist, recorded and toured, including tours of Africa, Asia, Europe, and the Far East, 1970—. Assistant professor of African-American Theatre and Pan-African Studies, California State University, 1974.

Film appearances include *The Girl Can't Help It,* 1956, *Nothing But a Man,* 1964, *For the Love of Ivy,* 1968, *A Short Walk to Daylight,* 1972, and *Mo' Better Blues,* 1990; performed in music, dance, and legitimate theater productions; wrote, directed, and produced play *A Pig in a Poke,* 1975.

Awards: Best actress awards from the Federation of Italian Filmmakers, 1965, and First World Festival of Negro Arts, 1966, both for *Nothing But a Man;* most prominent screen person award, 1969, All American Press Association, for *For the Love of Ivy;* inducted into Black Filmmakers Hall of Fame, 1975.

Addresses: *Home*—New York, NY. *Record company*—Verve, 825 Eighth Ave., New York, NY 10019.

of the *New York Times.* "Singers would walk the bar back then, hollering and screaming like instruments, really entertaining the people."

Lincoln returned to Hollywood in 1954 to sing at the Moulin Rouge, a nightclub featuring a French-style revue replete with elephants and pink poodles. Wearing feathered hats and dresses with daring slits, she became Gaby Lee, a name the owners of the club thought sounded French. In 1956, at the advice of her manager, lyricist Bob Russell, she changed her name to Abbey Lincoln—a combination of London's Westminster Abbey and Abraham Lincoln. Also at that time, she recorded her first album, *Affair: A Story of a Girl in Love,* appearing on the cover in a centerfold pose. "I went along with [the cover pose] because I didn't know any better," she related to *High Fidelity's* Davis years later. "I didn't think of myself as a serious artist—or as a

serious person either. All I wanted was to be thought of as beautiful and desirable." Later that year, Lincoln solidified her sexy image by playing a bit part in the film *The Girl Can't Help It,* which starred Jayne Mansfield. In the film, Lincoln appeared in a dress that Marilyn Monroe had worn in *Gentlemen Prefer Blondes;* she subsequently landed on the cover of *Ebony,* in June of 1957, as "The Girl in Marilyn Monroe's Dress."

Down Beat's Dom Cerulli encapsulated the public and media impression of Lincoln in a review of a 1957 nightclub performance: "Definitely a visual as well as an aural performer. Miss Lincoln [is] a handsome women of striking proportions. . . . She must be seen as well as heard for full appreciation." But her increasing popularity was at odds with her burgeoning social and artistic sensibilities. "It was a contradiction in my life," Lincoln told Michael Bourne in *Down Beat.* "I was always a nice girl and now I was this *siren!* It was about to drive me crazy. I was scared."

Feeling she really wasn't as good a singer as she appeared to be, that she was faking it, Lincoln decided to drop the affectations that had put her in the limelight. Further enlightenment came from the great jazz drummer Max Roach, whom Lincoln met in the late 1950s and married in 1962. He convinced Lincoln that she didn't need Marilyn Monroe-type dresses in order to succeed in music and in life. "Max taught me to invest all my creative effort into everything I approach in life, not only the music," she told *Downbeat's* Vercelli. "Many of the things I learned from him continue to serve me today, especially the technique of always practicing, even when you are away from your instrument." In a symbolic gesture, she reportedly burned the Monroe dress soon afterward.

Pupil of Roach, Rollins, Coltrane, and Monk

Through Roach, Lincoln began singing with and learning from such jazz giants as Sonny Rollins, John Coltrane, and Thelonious Monk. She also began composing her own music and came in contact with black artists in other fields, intellectuals concerned with the plight of African Americans in American society. "It was the early days of the civil rights movement, and we were all asking the same questions," Lincoln explained to Davis. "But they were asking questions that glamour girls weren't supposed to ask. As I toured the country, I noticed that black people everywhere were living in slums, in abject poverty. I wanted to know why."

Lincoln's interest was heartfelt, her questions searching and insightful. She became more aware of her cultural heritage; she began wearing her hair natural.

Newsweek's Leland quoted Roach on Lincoln's social awareness: "She became a symbol for young black women because she was politically astute. [Writers] Amiri Baraka and Maya Angelou and other people would all come up and we'd have these debate sessions. Because she had the kind of visibility and beauty that you appreciated, it was unsettling to a lot of us men, including me. Because her position would be, not harder, but more pointed than ours. She'd get right down to it."

Lincoln lent her newly driven voice to Roach's 1960 recording *We Insist!: Freedom Now Suite,* which became the jazz anthem of the civil rights movement. One track on the album, "Prayer/Protest/Peace," a wordless duet that progressed from hopefulness to screams to peace, brought divided critical reaction. Because it was her voice that assailed the listener, Lincoln was labeled a radical. That view notwithstanding, her change and growth had indeed had an impact, as *New York Times* contributor Jones noted: "Her passage from a bouffant-coiffed starlet to a socially conscious jazz artist with an Afro presaged the course that black identity would take in the '60s."

Lincoln left music in the mid-1960s to focus on acting, but she continued to speak out against the oppression and stereotyping of African Americans, choosing to portray only fully realized characters. She starred opposite Ivan Dixon in the 1964 film *Nothing But a Man* and in 1968 played the title role opposite Sidney Poitier in the romantic comedy *For the Love of Ivy.* "Though very different, both films were landmarks because of their sensitive, nonpathological portrayals of love, sexuality, and intimacy between a Black woman and man," Jill Nelson wrote in *Essence.*

"An Image the Media Is Not Interested In"

Despite winning critical accolades for these film roles, Lincoln was relegated to minor television spots, never allowed to fulfill her potential as an actress. Film historian Donald Bogle, as quoted by Leland, believed Lincoln was an important transitional figure in the portrayal of African Americans on screen and that the only reason she did not progress as an actress was because of the social climate: "She was able to project intelligence and poise and sensitivity. She had color. She wasn't a nurturing mammy figure or oversexed. . . . It's an image the media is not interested in or not comfortable with from an African-American woman."

In 1970, frustrated by a stifled acting career and despondent over her recent divorce from Roach, Lincoln sought emotional relief, signing herself into a psychiat-

ric hospital in upstate New York for five weeks. Over the next decade, she rarely performed in the United States, touring and traveling occasionally abroad. In 1972, while on vacation in Africa, Lincoln was given her African names. President Sekou Toure of Guinea presented her the name "Aminata" in recognition of her inner strength and determination. "Moseka," a gift from Zaire's Minister of Information, is the god of love in female form.

In 1979, almost 15 years after her last U.S. recording had appeared, Lincoln released *People in Me.* She had spent the previous decade writing songs, training her

> "I come from a long line of great singers who were social and specific and sang about their lives and the lives of their people."

voice, and finding inner peace. The results were evident. "She shows an uncommon felicity with words," John S. Wilson wrote in *High Fidelity.* "Her settings and moods range from the expansive glow of 'Africa' to a satirical view of female vanity, from an imaginative duet with an inner voice to a listing—almost in Cole Porter fashion—of the mixtures of blood strains that flow through all of us." After almost ten years of self-exile, Lincoln had emerged as a "strong black wind, blowing gently on and on," poet Nikki Giovanni was quoted as saying by Vercelli.

Throughout most of the 1980s Lincoln labored "in the shadows, looking inward, taking the stuff of her own life—the loneliness, pain, and joy—and turning it into music," wrote *Essence* contributor Nelson. Her approach to songwriting is autobiographical; she records the world as she encounters it and offers it back in telling observations. "A singer has the power of the word," she explained to Peter Watrous in the *New York Times.* "What we say is direct. . . . I come from a long line of great singers who were social and specific and sang about their lives and the lives of their people."

Renewed Acclaim

Lincoln's voice has ascended to that of her predecessors not only in content but also in timbre. It is an instrument now often compared to one of her childhood idols, Billie Holiday, a "deep, rich voice . . . probably truer to the emotional content of her songs than to absolute pitch," Leland noted. "It can be off-putting or powerfully engaging, but—never prettified—it doesn't allow listeners much room for neutrality." The persuasive conviction behind the delivery of Lincoln's songs, mirroring her charged attention to life, "can leave an audience breathless with the tension of real drama," *New York Times* contributor Watrous revealed. "A slight, curling phrase is laden with significance, and the tone of her voice can signify hidden welts of emotion."

With two releases in the early 1990s—*The World Is Falling Down* and *You Gotta Pay the Band*—Lincoln earned both commercial and artistic success. The works were a testament to her life, artistic vision, and overall empathy for humanity. Calling *The World Is Falling Down* a "discourse on life and love from a well-traveled, still passionate soul," *People's* Eric Levin explained, "When she sings in the title cut (one of her own), 'The world is falling down/ Hold my hand, hold my hand,' the sound is of comfort offered rather than sought."

On 1991's *You Gotta Pay the Band,* Lincoln was joined by legendary jazz saxophonist Stan Getz, who died shortly after its release. The music they created and communicated together transcended not only the simple joys of life but the pain at its very end. *Down Beat's* Owen Cordle called it "an album with bittersweetness and poignancy in the air. Lincoln's voice is the black earth, Getz's saxophone soft summer clouds. Knowing he was dying, how could they get through Lincoln's 'When I'm Called Home' without pity? Such is the triumph of great art, of which this album is an example."

Selected compositions

"You and Me, My Lover," "Throw It Away," "Caged Bird," "Painted Lady," "Talking to the Sun," "The River," "People on the Street," "The World Is Falling Down," "I Got Thunder (and It Rings)," "First Song," "Bird Alone," "When I'm Called Home."

Selected discography

Affair: A Story of a Girl in Love, Liberty, 1956.
That's Him!, Riverside, 1957, reissued, Fantasy/OJC, 1983.
It's Magic, Riverside, 1958, reissued Fantasy/OJC, 1985.
Abbey Is Blue, Riverside, 1959, reissued Fantasy/OJC, 1983.
(With Max Roach) *We Insist!: Freedom Now Suite,* Candid, 1960.
Straight Ahead, Candid, 1961.
(With Roach) *It's Time,* Impulse, 1962.
People in Me, Inner City, 1979.
Golden Lady, Inner City, 1981.
Talking to the Sun, Enja, 1984.
Abbey Sings Billie, Enja, 1987.
The World Is Falling Down, Verve, 1990.
You Gotta Pay the Band, Verve, 1991.
Abbey Sings Billie, Volume 2, Enja, 1992.
Devil's Got Your Tongue, Verve, 1993.

Sources

Down Beat, February 20, 1957; September 6, 1979; December 1980; March 1982; January 1987; December 1991; February 1992.
Ebony, June 1957.
High Fidelity, June 1979; May 1986.
Jazz Journal International, May 1981.
Musician, February 1993.
Newsweek, January 6, 1992.
New York Times, March 3, 1989; August 4, 1991; August 11, 1991.
People, December 17, 1990.
Stereo Review, January 1985.

Additional information for this profile was obtained from the documentary *You Gotta Pay the Band: The Words, the Music, and the Life of Abbey Lincoln,* PBS-TV, 1992.

—*Rob Nagel*

John Lydon

Singer

Viewed by many as an icon of punk rock, John Lydon, known as Johnny Rotten when he fronted the legendary Sex Pistols—some say because of his fragrance, others because of his oft-repeated expression "You're rotten, you are"—has become nearly synonymous with that musical movement. He mocked, snarled, and raged with a fury that had not been seen in rock and roll before and rarely since. Nonetheless, as early as 1976, a year after the formation of the Pistols, Lydon felt trapped, sickened and confused by his audiences' expectations, his own deterioration, and his manager's exploitive antics.

"Before the Pistols began, English music was very bad, we tried to change all that but . . . before I realized what was happening, it had run away from us," Lydon told Jeff Hays of *Creem* in 1980. "As soon as they'd see anything with our name on it, they'd buy it—that's stupidity. I was accused of selling out when I became famous—now, who made me famous? The audience."

In 1978, slightly damaged but fundamentally undaunted by his misadventures with the Sex Pistols, Lydon dropped "Rotten" and formed the aptly named Public Image Ltd. with ex-Clash guitarist Keith Levene. Experimenting with throbbing dance rhythms, Asian and Arabic modalities, dense guitar layering, and angry, obtuse lyrics, Public Image Ltd., or PiL, succeeded in heralding and defining the post-punk era. To those who believed Johnny Rotten would engender cataclysmic changes in the social fabric, Lydon was an art-rock sell-out. But to those who merely sought redemption through art, Lydon delivered passionate, challenging music—that you could dance to.

Collaborative Beginnings With PiL

Early incarnations of PiL were collaborative efforts. Lydon and Levene were joined by the dub reggae-influenced Jah Wobble on bass and Jim Walker on drums. The band attempted to work as a cooperative in which each member would share equally in the responsibilities of band business. (In reality, a later member, Jeannette Lee, seems to have handled much of PiL's business).

The group's first single, 1978's "Public Image," attacked people's perceptions of Johnny Rotten: "You never listened to a word I said/ You only see me for the clothes I wear/ Or did the interest go so much deeper/ It must've been the color of my hair." The song and LP that followed backed Lydon's lyrical assault with an equally vicious sonic attack of loosely structured guitar patterns and pounding minimalist rhythms, Wobble's bass lines acting as backbone. Most pointed amid the din were Lydon's vocals—vehement ranting and terrifying chanting. Roundly panned, *Rolling Stone* called the record "post-nasal drip monotony." Perhaps to bolster its claim, *Rolling Stone* also recalled the *New Musical Express* appraisal of PiL's first album: "a zen lesson in idolatry." Worst of all, the band's American record company, Warner Bros., refused to release it. "It was self-indulgent, non-simplistic, and non-rock and roll; and those are the good points," Lydon told *Rolling Stone*. "But that's the kind of music we intend to make."

By the time PiL unleashed their second album, *Metal Box*—originally packaged in a round 12-inch metal container—the critical climate had shifted favorably toward the burgeoning trend of British bands experimenting with noise and dance rhythms. The enormously influential *Metal Box,* released as *Second Edition* in the U.S., found PiL more confident in their trance-like dirges and dub-reggae disco, aided by the work of new drummer Martin Atkins. *Downbeat* contributor Michael Goldberg reported, "PiL incorporates a bass sound that rattles teeth; melodies, when there are any, are strictly of the down-by-the-power-plant genre. Levene's lead guitar repeats slightly varying patterns that bore right into the brain. This is a rough, raw rock album and there is little instrumental expertise evident. Yet PiL have managed to create an emotionally and intellectually powerful record."

Murky Danceability

There was a formlessness to the music that Lydon attributed to improvisation. "We just do it. We don't talk

about it. We don't think about it. There's no intellectual reason," the singer told *Creem*. "Maybe Wobble will come up with a bass line, then the drums, singing, and Keith's guitar, and then we go to the mixing board. That's where all the fun is." That process gave way to the pulsating bog that intrigued audiences and critics and eventually became PiL's trademark. *Rolling Stone* elucidated the sound and its power to enthrall: "It begins by driving the listener away, offering murk, dopey horror sound effects, unexamined images of bad news. Yet the murk is artful—even arty—the self-pity merely the first face, the unexamined images often an entry into trance music. Obsessively danceable, once glimpsed [it] has to be pursued."

PiL had managed to achieve the unique status of pioneering artists, but it wasn't enough for Lydon to fully escape the shadow of Johnny Rotten. Audiences continued to cry out for Sex Pistols songs at PiL's critically acclaimed live shows. John Rockwell of the *New York Times* commented of such a performance, "Public Image's music is already so different from early punk that any kind of growth is possible. In its own strange, vanguardish way, this concert was as brilliant a moment as rock has seen in years."

PiL's follow-up LPs, *Paris au Printemps* and *The Flowers of Romance,* were no less challenging for listeners, even as the band's sound became more formalized. Both albums, however, reflect the gradual disintegration of the group: *Flowers of Romance* was recorded without Wobble, and Atkins appeared as a session player rather than a full-fledged bandmember. On the live album *Paris au Printemps,* Lydon, his stage presence unapologetically contemptuous, vociferously taunts the audience, who jeer and spit back at him. That Lydon released an album graphically depicting his confrontational relationship with his audience is testimony to how far he will go to present raw honesty and how willing he is to accept his uneasy public image. In keeping with his brazenly bad behavior, Lydon was arrested in October of 1980 for assault after a pub melee in Dublin; he was sentenced to three months in jail for disorderly conduct but was eventually acquitted on appeal.

On *Flowers of Romance,* PiL introduced Eastern influences and relied on a thunderous minimalism of vocals and percussion to transcend the murk, while Levene, according to Robert Palmer of the *New York Times,* went "to great lengths to avoid playing anything that sounds like a melody or chords on his guitar." In *Rolling Stone* Mikal Gilmore described the record as "the most brutal, frightening music Lydon has ever lent his voice to." Despite PiL's devoted following, Virgin balked at releasing *Flowers* because of its intrinsically uncommercial nature; Warner Bros., which had also declined to release *Paris au Printemps,* agreed to only a small pressing.

Ironic Accessibility

In 1983 Lydon and cohorts relocated to New York City, started their own short-lived label, and recorded the single "This Is Not a Love Song." With this release, PiL entered a new phase—one of unabashed accessibility and an ironic, spiteful commerciality. *Downbeat's* Jim Brinsfield called the single "the closest thing to straight rock PiL has recorded. The band is in top form, at ease in turning the simplest format into a series of searing climaxes that grow into aching intensity." The crude commercialization of PiL, however, was puzzling to many critics. *New York Times* contributor Palmer observed, "Lydon talked about wanting to destroy rock-and-roll, but he really seems to belong in front of a rock band. He seems to have decided that fronting a rock band as persuasive as Public Image isn't such a bad thing after all." And Jon Pareles, reviewing a PiL concert for the *Times,* revealed that "[Lydon] demanded more applause and urged fans to buy more souvenir T-shirts, making overt what some performers keep to themselves."

Then suddenly, Lydon and Levene ended their six-year collaboration; Lydon went on a ten-stop tour of Japan with Atkins and some New Jersey session musicians, covering the gamut of the band's history and even some Sex Pistols songs. The recorded result was the poorly received *Live in Tokyo.* *Melody Maker's* Michael Senate opined that the release "was in the best tradition of flogging a dead horse." *Downbeat's* Brinsfield relayed, "Lydon goes through his set in the most perfunctory manner, Atkins plays as though he's unfamiliar with his own tempos and cues, and the band—they aren't bad, but they aren't convincing."

Shortly thereafter, PiL released *This Is What You Want . . . This Is What You Get,* which had been recorded before Levene's departure. Lydon, however, had the guitarist's tracks erased and rerecorded. For those who accepted PiL's perpetual evolution, this album stood "in comparison with the best of the Public Image canon," according to *Melody Maker's* Lynden Barber. "And it is certainly the most consistent. This is what you get: bangs, balls, brass that'll tear the roses off the wallpaper and, in tune with the times, an appealing populism." But for some, Lydon's new support unit was a betrayal of the old PiL, much in the way some viewed the original PiL as a betrayal of the Sex Pistols. *Musician's* Scott Isler concluded, "Unlike earlier editions of PiL, this band is technically competent and not too

inspired. Then again, Lydon would probably sack musicians who tried to assert themselves."

All-Star Lineup

And sack them he did. For his next album, titled *Album*—the cassette version was titled *Cassette*—Lydon assembled some of the most innovative musicians of his time including Ginger Baker of Cream and jazz legend Tony Williams on drums, Ryuichi Sakamoto on keyboards, and Steve Vai on metal-guitar acrobatics. The contributions of these players were convincingly blended into one of the most powerful versions of PiL by producer Bill Laswell, who also played bass. In *Downbeat,* Roy Trakin called *Album* "the strongest selection of pop tunes Mr. Lydon has turned out." The record also featured the hit single "Rise," with its chant "Anger is an energy." A myriad of international stylistic influences, dense, guitar-heavy rhythms, and Lydon's enraged caterwauling merged to create PiL's first heavy metal record and certainly one of Lydon's most successful efforts.

The singer returned to a highly collaborative format for his next three records, teaming with former Siouxsie and the Banshees and Magazine guitarist John McGeoch and bassist Allan Dias. On *Happy?, 9,* and *That What Is Not,* Lydon solidified his reputation as the granddaddy

> *"It was self-indulgent, non-simplistic, and non-rock and roll; and those are the good points. But that's the kind of music we intend to make."*

of "alternative" rock. Critics found each album accessible but consistently edgy, containing many good songs and some great ones. McGeoch's guitar was noted for its ability to both shimmer ethereally and assail brutally. Although many critics remained stunned by the commercial nature of these releases, they were frequently equally stunned by the quality of the material and intensity of the production.

In 1992, after the release of *That What Is Not,* PiL appeared on MTV's 120 Minutes Tour with former Clash member Mick Jones's band Big Audio Dynamite II. True to form, Lydon and company disappointed those who longed for the difficult experimentalism of early PiL or the iconoclastic anarchy of the Sex Pistols.

In the increasingly predictable and formulaic world of pop music, John Lydon's constant betrayal of expectations can be viewed as an achievement in itself. As punk anarchist, primal artist, willing self-parody, or as career musician, he has continued to deliver his unique expressions of rage. If he maintains this committed betrayal of expectations, his best work may still be ahead of him.

Selected discography

With Public Image Ltd.

Public Image Ltd. (includes "Public Image Ltd."), Virgin, 1978.
Metal Box, Virgin, 1979, reissued as *Second Edition*, Virgin/Island, 1980.
Paris au Primtemps, Virgin, 1980.
Flowers of Romance, Virgin/Warner Bros., 1981.
"This Is Not a Love Song"/"Blue Water" (single), Virgin, 1983.
Live in Tokyo, Virgin, 1983.
This Is What You Want . . . This Is What You Get, Virgin/Elektra, 1984.
(With Afrika Bambaataa) *Time Zone* (includes "World Destruction"), Celluloid, 1984.
Album (includes "Rise"), Elektra, 1986.

Happy?, Virgin, 1988.
9, Virgin, 1990.
Greatest Hits So Far, Virgin, 1990.
That What Is Not, Virgin, 1992.

Sources

Books

Rees, Dafydd, and Luke Crampton, *Rock Movers & Shakers*, ABC-CLIO, 1991.
Stambler, Irwin, *The Encyclopedia of Pop, Rock and Soul*, St. Martin's, 1989.

Periodicals

Creem, August 1980.
Down Beat, July 1980; May 1984; July 1986.
Entertainment Weekly, May 29, 1992.
Melody Maker, September 24, 1963; July 28, 1984.
Musician, December 1984; July 1992.
New York Times, April 22, 1980; September 30, 1982; November 5, 1984.
Rolling Stone, May 29, 1980; May 28, 1981; May 14, 1992.

—Glenn Rechler

Lynyrd Skynyrd

Rock band

In the mid-1960s the nucleus of what would become one of the most popular southern boogie bands of the 1970s, Lynyrd Skynyrd, were students at Robert E. Lee High School in Jacksonville, Florida. Impressed by the sounds of the Yardbirds and Blues Magoos, buddies Ronnie Van Zant, Gary Rossington, and Allen Collins formed a band and played dances under a variety of names, including My Backyard and later, One Per Cent. By the early 1970s the group had begun attracting regional attention and settled on the name Lynyrd Skynyrd, immortalizing a high school gym teacher named Leonard Skinner who had persecuted Van Zant and others for their long hair. This gentle revenge must have satisfied the band, for in later years they invited Mr. Skinner to introduce them in concert.

Lynyrd Skynyrd reached national prominence in 1973 opening for the Who's *Quadrophenia* tour and issuing their debut album, *Pronounced Leh-Nerd Skin-Nerd.* The release featured Van Zant's grainy-voiced rendering of the band's trademark and somewhat mournful "Freebird." Performer/producer Al Kooper, best known

For the Record. . .

Early members included **Allen Collins** (born in Jacksonville, FL, c. 1949), guitar; **Steve Gaines** (born in Seneca, MO [one source says Florida], early 1950s; replaced **Ed King,** 1974; died in a plane crash, October 20, 1977, in Gillsburg, MS), guitar; **Billy Powell** (born in Florida, early 1950s), keyboards; **Artimus Pyle** (born in Spartanburg, SC; replaced **Bob Burns,** 1975), drums; **Gary Rossington** (born in Jacksonville, c. 1949), guitar; **Ronnie Van Zant** (born in Jacksonville in 1949; died in a plane crash, October 20, 1977, in Gillsburg), vocals; and **Leon Wilkeson** (born in Florida, early 1950s), bass.

Later members include **Randall Hall** (guitar), King, Powell, Pyle, Rossington, **Johnny Van Zant** (vocals), and Wilkeson.

Group formed in Jacksonville, FL, 1966; initially called My Backyard and later, One Per Cent; signed with MCA, and released debut LP, *Pronounced Leh-Nerd Skin-Nerd,* 1973; disbanded after 1977 plane crash; reformed, 1987.

Awards: Gold record for *Pronounced Leh-Nerd Skin-Nerd,* 1973.

Addresses: *Record company*—Atlantic Records, 75 Rockefeller Plaza, New York, NY 10019.

for his work with Blood, Sweat and Tears, produced the album on his Sounds of the South label for MCA, and it went gold. Later Skynyrd hits included 1974's "Sweet Home Alabama" and 1977's "That Smell." The former, a retort to Neil Young's southerner-bashing in his hit "Southern Man," appeared on the band's second album, *Second Helping,* and reached the Top Ten. In recognition of the song, Alabama governor George Wallace sent the group plaques conferring on them the status of honorary lieutenants in the state militia, a conscription the band regarded with marked ambivalence.

Three-Guitar Attack

During most of its tenure, Lynyrd Skynyrd boasted three lead guitars—bettering the two guitars of their fellow southerners, the more-popular Allman Brothers Band. Piling the third guitar atop those of Rossington and Collins, beginning in 1973, was Ed King, formerly of the Strawberry Alarm Clock and co-writer of that band's Number One hit "Incense and Peppermints." Billy Powell played keyboards, Bob Burns drums, and Leon Wilkeson bass. King left in late 1974 amid the band's inveterate use of drugs and alcohol and be-

cause of interpersonal tensions—at the end of the infamous "Torture Tour," some 64 dates in 83 days, Van Zant had knocked out the keyboardist's two front teeth. King was replaced by Steve Gaines. Artimus Pyle replaced Burns on drums in 1975 and fired away on the band's 1976 album *Gimme Back My Bullets.* This offering featured three female backup singers, among them Steve Gaines's sister, Cassie. By the time *Bullets* was released Lynyrd Skynyrd was one of the largest concert draws in the U.S.

Critics persistently characterized the group as the voice of the southland's working class. *Rolling Stone's* John Swenson asserted in December of 1977 that the Skynyrd tune "Things Goin' On," from the album *Skynyrd's First and . . . Last,* which begins "They're gonna ruin the air that we breath/ They're gonna ruin us all by and by," represented "the characteristic cry of the broken post-Reconstructionist South against the technological imperialism of the industrial North." Lynyrd Skynyrd certainly tried to play the southern rebel, routinely unfurling the confederate flag as a stage backdrop. How deep musical southernness actually ran is open to question. Dave Marsh, in his book of criticism *Fortunate Son,* noted the group's redneck bent but found in their music's "brash vulgarity" and lack of discipline the very definition of "male belligerence"—certainly not a quality limited to the South.

In fact, the band's belligerence was no stage act. Van Zant was arrested five times for drunkenness-related offenses in 1975 alone. In this he was in tune with his followers. As the singer noted in a 1976 *Time* profile, the band attracted "mostly drunk people and rowdy kids who come to shake." The *Time* piece went on to chronicle various Skynyrd exploits, among them the band's destruction of half the exercise machines in a Nashville hotel and Van Zant's heaving of an oak table out a fifth floor window in a British hostelry. If explaining to hotel management that the boys' behavior was merely "the characteristic cry of the broken post-Reconstructionist South" failed to appease, reparations were made by the band's road manager, who found himself paying damage bills averaging $1,000 a month. Eventually, hotels in many cities refused to accommodate Lynyrd Skynyrd.

Plane Crash

The hard partying and hitmaking came to a horrifying end on October 20, 1977, when the Convair 240 propeller plane carrying the band to a performance in Baton Rouge, Louisiana, crashed in swampy ground in

Gillsburg, Mississippi. Killed were Ronnie Van Zant, Steve and Cassie Gaines, and road manager Dean Kilpatrick. The pilot and co-pilot were also killed, and the rest of the band sustained serious injuries. Apparently the plane, which had exhibited mechanical problems and was due for retirement, ran out of fuel. The aircraft was a Dallas-based charter similar to the one that had crashed four years earlier, killing singer Jim Croce in Louisiana.

Southern man Ronnie Van Zant was buried in Florida with his favorite fishing pole. A memorial service was attended by, among others, Dickey Betts of the Allman Brothers Band, country-rock bandleader Charley Daniels, Al Kooper, and members of the Atlanta Rhythm Section. Shortly before the crash, MCA had released the Skynyrd album *Street Survivors,* which featured cover art depicting the band standing amid flames. This sleeve was replaced promptly after the accident. The album contained the song "That Smell," co-written by Van Zant and Collins, a reference to the "smell of death" and essentially a plea for less self-destructive behavior. The song was written partly in reaction to the events of the 1976 Labor Day weekend during which both Rossington and Collins injured themselves in separate car accidents.

In the emotional devastation following the plane crash, the surviving members of the band swore a "blood oath" not to capitalize on the death of Van Zant and the others by continued use of the name Lynyrd Skynyrd. After a year of grieving, the remaining bandmembers, except for drummer Artimus Pyle, formed a new entity called "The Rossington-Collins Band," taking a female vocalist, Dale Krantz, from the band .38 Special, an outfit fronted by Van Zant brother Donnie. Rossington-Collins concerts featured the by now anthemic "Freebird," performed without vocals as a tribute to Ronnie Van Zant. This was the second such duty for the song, which was originally written in tribute to Duane Allman of the Allman Brothers Band after the 24-year-old guitar hero was killed in a 1971 motorcycle accident. The Rossington-Collins Band produced an album entitled *Anytime, Anyplace, Anywhere,* which reached Number Thirteen on the charts in 1980. But the band broke up within a couple of years. Artimus Pyle went his own way, emerging with the Artimus Pyle Band in 1982.

The Phoenix Rises

In 1986 keyboardist Billy Powell, following his release from a 30-day jail stint, joined a Christian rock group called Vision. Powell quickly realized that the band's covers of Lynyrd Skynyrd tunes consistently proved more popular than Vision's born-again fare and quit to join Rossington, Pyle, Wilkeson, King, and Ronnie's brother Johnny Van Zant in forming a new Lynyrd Skynyrd. Collins did not join, owing to an auto accident the previous year that had left him paralyzed from the waist down and had killed his girlfriend. Ronnie Van Zant's widow sued the new bandmembers for violation of the blood oath proscribing the use of the name Lynyrd Skynyrd. In settlement of the case, the new band appended to their name the distinguishing phrase "Tribute Tour." The Lynyrd Skynyrd Tribute Tour hit the road in 1987.

The group attracted renewed attention in 1991 when they embarked on a world tour, kicking off the expedition at the venue to which the band had been flying 14 years earlier. Anyone still holding a ticket to the unperformed October, 1977, Baton Rouge concert was admitted free, along with a guest, and presented with the tour record *Lynyrd Skynyrd 1991.* A hundred people produced such tickets and attended along with some nine thousand others to hear an incarnation of Lynyrd Skynyrd that consisted of Johnny Van Zant, Gary Rossington, Ed King, Randall Hall on guitar, Billy Powell, and Artimus Pyle, who split percussion duties with a co-drummer known simply as "Custer." A *Rolling Stone* reviewer attending a concert that year reported that the performance seemed largely an oldies show for southern rockers, an impression duly reinforced by the superiority of the old songs to the new. Nonetheless, a quarter-century after its inception and 14 years since the band's seeming demise, the guitar-heavy bombast of Lynyrd Skynyrd was making the 1990s safe for southern rock.

Selected discography

Pronounced Leh-Nerd Skin-Nerd (includes "Freebird"), MCA, 1973.

Second Helping (includes "Sweet Home Alabama"), MCA, 1974.

Nuthin' Fancy, MCA, 1975.

Gimme Back My Bullets, MCA, 1976.

One More for the Road, MCA, 1976.

Street Survivors (includes "That Smell"), MCA, 1977.

Skynyrd's First . . . and Last (includes "Things Goin' On"), MCA, 1978.

Gold and Platinum, MCA, 1979.

The Best of the Rest, MCA, 1985.

Legends, MCA, 1987.

Southern by the Grace of God: The Lynyrd Skynyrd Tribute Tour, 1987, MCA, 1987.

Lynyrd Skynyrd 1991, Atlantic, 1991.

Last Rebel, Atlantic, 1993.

Sources

Books

Marsh, Dave, *Fortunate Son,* Random House, 1985.

Pareles, Jon and Patricia Romanowski, *The Rolling Stone Encyclopedia of Rock & Roll,* Rolling Stone Press/Summit Books, 1983.

Rees, Dafydd and Luke Crampton, *Rock Movers & Shakers,* Billboard Books, 1991.

Stambler, Irwin, *The Encyclopedia of Pop, Rock & Soul,* St. Martin's, 1989.

Walker, Dave, *American Rock & Roll Tour,* Thunder's Mouth, 1992.

Periodicals

Amusement Business, July 29, 1991.

Creem, August 1975; March 1976.

Rolling Stone, October 9, 1975; April 22, 1976; December 1, 1977.

Time, October 18, 1976.

—Joseph M. Reiner

The MC5

Rock band

The mid-1960s was a turbulent time for Detroit, and the music of the Motor City Five—or MC5, as they would become known—stood as an aural reflection of events like the Cass Corridor race riots and area youth protests. Although rock music has become synonymous with censorship issues and the confrontation of authority, the MC5, vocalist Rob Tyner, guitarists Wayne Kramer and Fred "Sonic" Smith, bassist Michael Davis, and drummer Dennis Thompson, were one of the first bands to stand up for freedom of speech and expression in performance. In explaining the band's enormous influence, *Village Voice* contributor Mike Rubin asserted in 1991 that the MC5's aggressive approach "lives on in any heavy metal band from Motley Crue to Metallica, and their antiestablishment posture was at a least as big an influence on punk rock."

The MC5 did not start out as the innovative bad boys they would later become. The band formed in the winter of 1964 from the ashes of Smith and Kramer's junior high rhythm and blues band, the Bountyhunters. Initially, the Five were a pedestrian rock and roll outfit whose

concert repertoire relied primarily on the material of other, more-famous performers. The band quickly earned a reputation with concert promoters, however, for showing up late—if at all—playing too loudly, and often not playing long enough to satisfy concertgoers. Not yet quite "bad," the MC5 were at this point merely irresponsible.

As if their unreliable reputation was not enough to hamper their progress, the MC5 soon found themselves in competition with the Motown sound. While Motown Records and its rhythm and blues acts were putting the Detroit music scene on the map, they were also creating a formidable shadow from which young rock and roll acts found it difficult to escape. Vocalist Tyner commented on this predicament in *Motorbooty* magazine, stating, "To be a white singer in Detroit at that time, you simply were the wrong man for the job; I did not feel comfortable as a performer until I could pull off James Brown material without flaw."

Met John Sinclair

As luck would have it, the MC5 found a patron of sorts in John Sinclair. Sinclair was a poet and musician, known around Detroit's Wayne State University as the "king of the beatniks." He was a fan of the Five and after witnessing their state of affairs—the band's equipment was being repossessed due to nonpayment—offered his services as manager. Along with his managerial approach, Sinclair instilled in the band his political beliefs, which leaned toward socialism. He viewed the group as a tool for the promotion of an ideology that he and the band developed in emulation of 1960s political agitators the Black Panthers. They dubbed their dogma

the White Panther Ten-Point Plan; its most infamous tenets were "dope, guns, and f---ing in the streets." Essentially, the plan called for freedom from everything and the abolition of money. In *Guitar Army,* Sinclair's book chronicling his life with the MC5, the poet-provocateur summed up the spirit of the time: "We were totally committed to carrying out our program. We *breathed* revolution. We were LSD-driven total maniacs in the universe. We would do anything we could to drive people out of their heads and into their bodies. Rock and roll was the spearhead of our attack because it was so effective and so much fun."

While Sinclair's guidance put the MC5 on a more professional path, difficulties with club owners continued; at one concert at Detroit's Grande Ballroom the Five burned an American flag onstage and raised in its place a banner with the word "Freak" emblazoned across it. At the end of the show, a nude fan climbed onstage and began to meditate. Club owner Gabe Glantz was none too amused. In *Guitar Army* Sinclair elaborated on the incident, recalling, "Glantz started ranting at Tyner and me about 'committing crimes' and 'obscenity' and 'Is that what you think of your country?,' threatening us with eternal expulsion from the Grande." The group was, in fact, temporarily banned from the venue. The exile did not last because the group attracted significantly large crowds to their concerts.

Played Democratic National Convention

In August of 1968 the MC5 were invited to perform at the Youth International Party's "Festival of Life" in Chicago's Lincoln Park. Although not officially labeled a protest of the Democratic National Convention, the "Yippie" festival was mounted simultaneously with the convention to show, as Sinclair put it in *Guitar Army,* "a sharp contrast to the way of death epitomized by the Democratic Death Convention." Securing their place in history, the MC5's appearance at the festival helped spark the 1968 Chicago riot. In *Motorbooty,* bassist Michael Davis recounted the event: "We were doing the show and everything was going okay when all of a sudden from over a hill came a huge line of policemen in riot gear charging toward the crowd. We packed up our gear as fast as we could and barely made it out before complete chaos ensued."

Events like the Chicago riot and the political reservations of concert promoters began to wear on the nerves of the band and created a rift between them and Sinclair. The division of the band's income became a major concern. Tyner commented in *Zig Zag* magazine, "I invested a lot of trust in John Sinclair, and he just kept bleeding us for money, we never knew where the money was going." Tyner elaborated in *Motorbooty*, stating, "[Sinclair's] politics were so out to lunch, [but] we were the ones getting our heads busted open onstage every night and he was the one getting the money."

The band's first LP, *Kick Out the Jams,* released by Elektra Records, was recorded live at the Grande Ballroom in October of 1968. *Zig Zag* called it "a quasi-political holocaust of white noise and skin-deep [jazz saxophonist John] Coltrane." While that comment was meant as a compliment, *Rolling Stone* compared the release unfavorably to the San Francisco band Blue Cheer and criticized the album's raw production values. Still, though the recording's quality perhaps failed to showcase the musical abilities of the MC5, it amply succeeded in capturing the energy, power, innovation, and political sloganeering of the Detroit group. Songs like "Come Together" called for the unification of youth, while "Starship" was a free acid-jazz odyssey featuring the band at their most experimental. Obscene lyrics in the title track caused such an uproar that Elektra was forced to terminate the MC5's recording contract.

Matured on *Back in the U.S.A.*

Back in the U.S.A., the group's second LP, was released by Atlantic Records in 1970. While not as overtly political as the band's previous effort, it did showcase the developing songwriting and musicianship of the performers. Owing largely to production values brought to the project by rock critic Jon Landau, the second LP was much more of a pop record than *Kick Out the Jams,* as was intimated by the selection of rock and roll pioneer Chuck Berry's song as the release's title track. *Cowabunga* magazine concluded that the Five were "rediscovering their roots" and that *Back in the U.S.A.* was primarily a work about "life as a teenager." The mood of the record was light, evidenced by the inclusion of 1950s shouter Little Richard's "Tutti-Frutti." Also featured on the record was the soulful ballad "Let Me Try." The Detroit publication *Big Fat* criticized the band's new direction, commenting, "Superficially it was fair rock and roll, best in its tightness and [conciseness] worst in its shallowness and lack of invention."

The MC5's third and last LP, *High Time,* attempted to combine the energy and inventiveness of *Kick Out the Jams* with the studio technology, control, and coherence of *Back in the U.S.A.* Unlike the first two LPs, *High Time* contained all original compositions, from the *Kick Out the Jams*-styled "Skunk" to the *Back in the U.S.A.*-reminiscent "Sister Anne." Though critically acclaimed

in some circles, *High Time* suffered the most dismal sales figures of the band's three releases.

Interest in the MC5 has remained constant since their demise in 1972. Indeed, their spirit lives on in the many "alternative" and mainstream bands who emulate their style and rebelliousness. The Seattle "grunge" revolution of the early 1990s owed much to Detroit's pioneering noisemakers, and the purveyors of that sound were not shy about disclosing this influence. In a retrospective of the MC5, *Big Fat* remembered, "Not since the summer of 1967 had a band possessed the power to illicit such a broad and strong response from an audience. If the Five's revolutionary ambitions were grand, so was their ability to win over and activate."

Selected discography

Singles

"I Can Only Give You Everything"/"One of the Guys," AMG Records, 1966.
"Looking at You"/"Borderline," A-Squared Records, 1967.

Albums

Kick Out the Jams, Elektra, 1969, reissued, 1992.
Back in the U.S.A., Atlantic, 1970, reissued, Rhino, 1992.
High Time, Atlantic, 1971, reissued, Rhino, 1992.

Sources

Books

Marsh, Dave, *Fortunate Son,* Random House, 1985.
Pareles, Jon and Patricia Romanowski, *The Rolling Stone Encyclopedia of Rock & Roll,* Rolling Stone Press/Summit Books, 1983.
Sinclair, John, *Guitar Army,* Douglas, 1972.

Periodicals

Big Fat, March 1970.
Cowabunga, November 1977.
Metro Times (Detroit), November 18, 1992.
Motorbooty, October 1990.
Rolling Stone, February 14, 1969; December 12, 1991; June 11, 1992; December 10, 1992.
Village Voice, October 1, 1991.
Zig Zag, September 1976; July 1977; August 1977; November 1977.

—*Barry Henssler*

Carmen McRae

Jazz singer, pianist

Carmen McRae sang and scatted in jazz clubs throughout the United States—and across the world—for over forty years. Schooled in the traditions of big bands, blues, and bebop, her style reflects an artful blend of traditional jazz with all three genres. She has strong opinions on her profession and her music; jazz, she told *Down Beat* magazine, "is all about improvising."

McRae's life was filled with music from the beginning. She began studying piano when she was eight, and the music of jazz greats like Louis Armstrong and Duke Ellington filled her home. She met singer Billie Holiday when she was just 17 years old. "We became friends the moment that I met her. We used to hang around together," she told *Jazz Forum.* McRae still considers Holiday to be her primary influence.

Growing up in the culturally rich environment of Harlem in New York City gave McRae a strong background in the blues. "The blues is like the national anthem of jazz," she theorized in *Jazz Forum.* But she is not a blues singer herself. "I have sung the blues . . . but more jazzy blues. . . . I think you have to have a special talent for [singing blues], which I don't have."

In her late teens and early twenties, McRae played piano at a New York club called Minton's, sang as a chorus girl, and worked as a secretary. She was admittedly too young and inexperienced to really make her living as a musician. However, she found herself in the right place at the right time to jam with the great pioneers of the blossoming bebop scene. McRae related in *Jazz Forum:* "I met [saxophonist] Charlie Parker when . . . I was 18. And I met [trumpeter] Dizzy Gillespie and [bassist] Oscar Pettiford [and drummer Kenny Clarke]. There was a place under Minton's where we used to go. Teddy Hill, who ran Minton's, used to have the guys come in. . . . They would work and after the club closed, which was [at] 4 o'clock, we'd go downstairs and other guys, other musicians, would come and we'd jam awhile." She also played short stints with bandleaders such as Count Basie, Benny Carter, and Mercer Ellington.

Early Days in Chicago

While McRae learned to play music in New York, she learned to survive in Chicago. In 1948 she moved there with comedian George Kirby. Later, their relationship soured. As she told *Down Beat* magazine, a friend suggested she sing for her supper. "I was having all of those problems waiting for George to send me the check to pay the rent, and she said, 'C'mon with me.' She took me someplace to play piano and sing. I said,

For the Record. . .

Born April 8, 1922, in Brooklyn, NY; married Teddy Wilson (divorced); married Kenny Clark, 1946. *Education:* Private training in piano.

Pianist with Benny Carter and Count Basie, 1944; made first recording as pianist with Mercer Ellington Band, 1946-47; regular on jazz-club circuit, beginning in 1948; made first solo record, 1953. Film appearances include *Hotel,* 1967, and *Jo Jo Dancer, Your Life Is Calling,* 1986. Television appearances include *Soul,* 1976, *Sammy and Company,* 1976, *Carmen McRae in Concert,* 1979, *From Jumpstreet,* 1980, *At the Palace,* 1981, *Billie Holiday: A Tribute,* 1981, and *L. A. Jazz,* 1982.

Addresses: *Agent*—Abby Hoffer Enterprises, 223 East 48th St., New York, NY 10017.

'Girl, I know about seven songs,' but she just thought I was great. I thought she was crazy.''

Chicago audiences thought she was great, too. She played piano steadily for almost four years before returning to New York. Those years in Chicago, McRae told *Jazz Forum,* "gave me whatever it is that I have now. That's the most prominent schooling I ever had."

Back in New York in the early 1950s, McRae got the record contract that launched her career. In 1954, she was voted best new female vocalist by *Down Beat* magazine. She had also reached the top spot as a jazz singer in the Metronome poll. For nearly four decades, she enjoyed a rich musical career, performing and recording in the United States, Europe, and Japan.

Kudos for *Carmen Sings Monk*

McRae's 1990 album *Carmen Sings Monk* was years in the making and epitomizes the uncompromising work ethic that earned her success and respect in the jazz arena. "I considered it one of the hardest projects I've ever worked on," she told *Down Beat.* She sorted through the music of jazz great Thelonious Monk to pick his finest tunes, had lyrics written for them, and then set out to record them. "His melodies are not easy to remember because they don't go where you think they're going to go." The reviews of the album hailed it as one of her absolute best.

This type of figurative collaboration, as well as literal collaboration, is a constant theme in McRae's work.

Early in her career, she recorded an entire album of Billie Holiday songs. More recently, she recorded *Sarah—Dedicated To You,* an album of favorites of singer Sarah Vaughan. She has also made albums in collaboration with other jazz musicians, including singer Betty Carter, pianist Shirley Horn, and pianist Harry Connick, Jr., and she recorded Latin American sounds with musician Cal Tjader.

McRae has strong opinions about the musicians with whom she works, about her profession, and what makes a good jazz singer: "You should know an instrument to be a good jazz singer," she said in *Down Beat.* "Ella [Fitzgerald] plays a little piano. Sarah [Vaughan] played piano; I play piano; Shirley Horn plays. All these ladies can sing Jazz." But not everyone who professes to be a jazz singer is one. Even the best singers, according to McRae, aren't really singing jazz if they don't improvise. "You have to improvise," she continued in *Down Beat,* "you have to have something of your own that has to do with that song. And you have to know where you're going when you improvise." Good singing alone does not make good jazz singing, "and I'll go to court on that one."

Candid About Downside of Performing

Although McRae loves the music, she has always been less enthusiastic about other aspects of the profession, namely the traveling, and performing in the typical jazz venue, the club. "It's not easy, traveling to appear in club after club," she told *Coda* magazine. And jazz musicians apparently do not receive the same respect that other musicians have. "I [got] sick of having to get dressed in offices because they [didn't] have proper dressing rooms—or even full-length mirrors—in some of these clubs. . . . All of this really detracts. Club owners don't seem to realize that the conditions in a lot of clubs aren't conducive to getting the best performances out of an artist."

McRae became ill in 1992 and is no longer able to perform. Throughout her long and distinguished musical career, she consistently gave her best, and she remains one of the finest jazz vocalists of her era. But McRae never enjoyed the general popularity of her contemporaries like Fitzgerald and Vaughan. Because her repertoire and style adhered so firmly to a pure jazz idiom, her following remained more limited to pure jazz enthusiasts. While lack of recognition sometimes irritated her, she never compromised her own unique style. Jazz, she told *Down Beat* is "something in your heart, and something that is you."

Selected discography

By Special Request, Decca, 1955.
After Glow, Decca, 1957.
Something to Swing About, Kapp, 1959.
The Great American Songbook, Atlantic, 1972.
Live at Birdland West, Concord Jazz, 1980.
Live at Bubba's, Kingdom Jazz, 1981.
You're Lookin' at Me, Concord Jazz, 1983.
(With Red Holloway, John Clayton, Paul Humphrey, Jack McDuff, and Phil Upchurch) *Fine and Mellow* (recorded in 1987), Concord Jazz, 1988.
Carmen Sings Monk, Novus, 1990.
Sarah—Dedicated to You, Novus, 1991.
Live at Century Plaza, Atlantic, 1991.
The Ultimate Carmen McRae, Mainstream Records, 1991.
Woman Talk, Mainstream Records, 1991.
(With others) *Here to Stay,* Decca Jazz, 1991.
Any Old Time, Denon.
(With George Shearing) *Two for the Road,* Concord Jazz.

Sources

Books

Crowther, Bruce, *The Jazz Singers,* Blanford Press, 1986.
Dahl, Linda, *Stormy Weather,* Limelight, 1989.

Periodicals

Coda, October/November 1987.
Down Beat, August 1990; November 1990; June 1991.
Ebony, July 1991.
Essence, October 1986.
Jazz Forum, No. 2, 1990.
Jazz Journal International, July 1988.
People, July 2, 1990; September 2, 1991.

—Robin Armstrong

Megadeth

Rock band

When Megadeth appeared on the scene in the mid-1980s, their combination of furious, high-speed sonic barrage and apocalyptic lyrics signaled the advent of a new and more serious brand of metal. Variously described as speedmetal, thrash-metal, or death-metal, Megadeth and a wave of other bands offered an alternative to the glam-pop stylings of the decade's successful "lite metal" acts. When the group arrived, wrote *Melody Maker*'s Caren Myers, "They were so lean, so mean, so rock that they made [arena-rockers] Guns N' Roses sound like a quaker picnic in Harmony, Arkansas." After battling with drugs and alcohol for years, the band's leader, Dave Mustaine—a former member of the metal supergroup Metallica—got sober. His recovery motivated a flurry of artistic production; in 1992 the band produced its most commercially accessible record, *Countdown to Extinction*. While some admirers of Megadeth's earliest, most uncompromising work found *Countdown* less intoxicating, the record advanced the group's popularity and visibility. As Mustaine told *Rolling Stone*, his goal was to create

"a jazz-oriented progressive music that's going to alter heavy metal as we understand it."

Mustaine experienced rootlessness and abuse during his childhood in southern California; after his parents divorced, he lived with his sisters and their husbands. A conflict with his brother-in-law over a record by metal pioneers Judas Priest helped steer Mustaine toward his career path. He explained in *Rolling Stone,* "I decided then that I was going to play this music. That would be my revenge." Indeed he played in various rock bands before meeting James Hetfield and Lars Ulrich while living in Nowalk, California; the three formed the core of Metallica's original lineup. Mustaine cowrote much of the material on the group's first three records, but he was fired in 1983. He claimed in a *Melody Maker* interview that he was ejected after a fight with Hetfield—"He kicked my puppy so I bashed his teeth in"—but in a 1991 issue of *Rolling Stone* he said that after various disagreements "One day, they woke me up and said, 'You're out of the band.'"

His bandmates in Metallica had been irked in part by Mustaine's drug use, and the disgruntled musician sank further into the dregs after being ejected from the group. In 1984, however, he met bassist Dave Ellefson. Again, as he told *Rolling Stone,* "revenge" provided the impetus to form a new, groundbreaking metal group. With Ellefson and the additions of guitarist Chris Poland

and drummer Gar Samuelson, Megadeth was born. The group released its first album, *Killing Is My Business . . . And Business is Good,* on the independent label Combat Records. The record's cover version of the 1960s song "These Boots Are Made for Walking" was selected for the film *Dudes* soundtrack.

Major Label, New Members

In 1986 Megadeth was signed to Capitol Records; their major-label debut, *Peace Sells . . . But Who's Buying?,* went gold, and the group's cover of "I Ain't Superstitious" earned the approval of the song's author, blues great Willie Dixon. In the interim before the group's gold 1988 follow-up, *So Far, So Good . . . So What!,* Poland and Samuelson departed and were replaced by guitarist Jeff Young and drummer Chuck Behler. That album featured "Hook In Mouth," a searing response to anti-metal censorship groups like activist Tipper Gore's Parents' Music Resource Center (PMRC), and a cover of "Anarchy in the U.K." by punk heavyweights the Sex Pistols. Jim Earber, reviewing *So Far. . .* for *Rolling Stone,* opined that "Megadeth belongs at the top of the thrash-rock heap." *Melody Maker's* inimitable critics The Stud Brothers concluded their review by declaring, "Megadeth are one of the finest bands we've ever heard." According to Mikal Gilmore in *Rolling Stone,* the group's best songs from this period "demonstrate a melodic and textural versatility that no other band in metal has matched."

Despite Megadeth's phenomenal success—they culminated their 1988 world tour with an appearance at metal's mecca, "Monsters of Rock" site Castle Donington in the United Kingdom—Mustaine's personal situation was deteriorating. "I became like a dope-seeking missile," he confessed to Gilmore, "and after a while I was losing my mind. I got to the point where I just *could not play* anymore. I knew that I was going to die if I didn't get sober, and even that didn't make me stop. I would have done anything for coke or heroin." It was only after Mustaine was stopped by police while driving under the influence that the decision to change was made for him. Forced to choose between permanent sobriety and a jail sentence, he opted for a recovery program and kicked drugs. As he reflected on his wasted years of substance abuse, Mustaine wavered between anger and thoughtfulness. "I've got the potential to be one of the biggest rock legends in the world and I wasted so much of my time," he fumed in a 1990 *Melody Maker* interview. "I'm an asshole for wasting so much time. I'm 28 years old right now. I'll be retired by the time I'm 35."

New Mustaine, New Members

Behler and Young left the band, and in 1990 a newly purposeful Mustaine announced that he, Ellefson, guitarist Marty Friedman, and drummer Nick Menza would be recording a new album in Los Angeles under the guidance of veteran rock producer Mike Clink. The result was *Rust in Peace,* an album that marked the end of Megadeth's great work for some hardcore early fans and critics. Even so, Robert Palmer of *Rolling Stone* felt the release "[carried] Megadeth's individuality into a broader, more open musical arena where nobody can touch them." For Palmer, *Rust's* instrumental landscape showed a real advance: "The arrangements, using multiple meters, multipart song structures, lightning-quick shifts in density, tempo and accenting, a variety of guitar overtones and sonics and occasional respites from the slamming, full-speed-ahead fervor, are consistently riveting." He praised all the players, and was particularly impressed with Menza's ability to make "the entire band swing like mad." Andrew Mueller of *Melody Maker* was less impressed, stating, "*Rust in Peace* is the sound of auto pilot running on empty." The album includes the corrosive rockers "Holy Wars," "Tornado of Souls," and "Hangar 18." With *Rust,* the band embarked on a new tour and released a home videocassette, *Rusted Pieces,* in 1991.

1992 brought forth *Countdown to Extinction,* a work that sharply divided critics and listeners. Though Jim Greer of *Spin* magazine argued that "it may be the finest thrash-metal album ever made," he worried that "the band members don't seem excited about anything they've accomplished musically; they're stoked because they've got a *great product* that will likely *move a lot of units.*" Many critics seemed to agree on the release's likely commercial appeal. *Pulse!* described the record's sound as "crunch with catchiness." *Entertainment Weekly* ventured, "The music has lost its former hurricane verve but keeps its crunch, and (a big mainstream plus) feels more rooted, even more melodic." *Spin* noted that "Megadeth tones down the pyrotechnics and pumps up the songcraft, resulting in perhaps its most accessible work yet."

Countdown Too Commercial for Some

For *Musician,* however, the band's "slicker" sound could not compensate for Mustaine's "conservative" arrangements and lyrical "poses." The singer's voice, the review mentioned, "seems to have two settings—cartoony-scary and cartoony-cartoony." Karen Csengeri of *Rolling Stone* was more blunt: "It's stylistically disappointing: the music, which is considerably more subdued than anything Megadeth has ever done, sounds formulaic; the musicianship is pedestrian; and the album as a whole seems to have been written for marketability rather than merit."

For good or ill, compared to Megadeth's earlier work—even *Rust in Peace*—the album is very accessible, even radio-friendly. Ellefson told *Spin's* Greer that "If anything was too high on the self-indulgent meter we'd just shorten it or pull it out completely." The video for the single "Symphony of Destruction" began appearing regularly on MTV, though Mustaine admitted to Greer that the music television network cut a potentially controversial "assassination scene" before agreeing to air "Symphony."

In its journey from the thrash underground to mainstream success, Megadeth has survived numerous personnel changes, Dave Mustaine's drug abuse and struggle for sobriety, attacks from censorship groups, and finally the charge that the band has sold out, an assessment that was furthered by some when Mustaine covered the Democratic National Convention for MTV News in 1992. Yet Megadeth's dark, skeptical political message has reached a larger audience than ever, and the influence of their pummelling, complicated musical arrangements continues to be seen across the hard rock spectrum. "In this year of rage," speculated *Entertainment Weekly,* "Megadeth might just follow Metallica to the top of the charts." As Mustaine boasted to *Rolling Stone,* "Bands like us are writing a new book in rock & roll history."

Selected discography

Killing Is My Business . . . And Business Is Good (includes "These Boots Are Made for Walking"), Relativity, 1985.

Peace Sells . . . But Who's Buying? (includes "I Ain't Superstitious"), Capitol Records, 1986.

(Contributors) *Dudes* (soundtrack; "These Boots Are Made for Walking") MCA, 1987.

(Contributors) *The Decline of Western Civilization: The Metal Years* (soundtrack; "In My Darkest Hour"), Slash/Warner Bros., 1988.

So Far, So Good . . . So What! (includes "Hook in Mouth" and "Anarchy in the U.K."), Capitol, 1988.

Rust in Peace (includes "Holy Wars," "Tornado of Souls," and "Hangar 18"), Capitol, 1990.

Countdown to Extinction (includes "Symphony of Destruction"), Capitol, 1992.

Sources

Circus, October 30, 1992.
Detroit Free Press, November 20, 1992.
Entertainment Weekly, July 24, 1992.

Guitar Player, November 1992.

Melody Maker, March 21, 1987; February 20, 1988; March 5, 1988; May 7, 1988; March 4, 1989; February 10, 1990; September 29, 1990.

Musician, September 1992; November 1992.

Pulse!, September 1992.

Reflex, Issue 29.

Rolling Stone, July 24, 1988; November 15, 1990; July 11, 1991; October 1, 1992.

Spin, September 1992; October 1992.

Additional information for this profile was obtained from Capitol Records media information, 1992.

—*Simon Glickman*

George Michael

Singer, songwriter

Although he began his musical career in 1980 as half of what some consider the lightweight pop outfit of Wham!, as a solo artist George Michael has been hailed as a leading creative force in popular songwriting and even mentioned as an heir to songwriting giants Paul McCartney and Elton John. *Faith,* his 1988 album, rose to Number One on the *Billboard* pop chart and sold 15 million copies. Though 1990's *Listen Without Prejudice, Vol. I* was not as lucrative for Michael as *Faith* had been, it was nonetheless applauded by critics as an important and accomplished work.

Michael was born Georgios Kyriakou Panayiotou in London in 1963. The son of a Greek Cypriot restauranteur, Michael was the youngest of three siblings. As a boy he dreamed of becoming a pilot; he was disappointed to find, however, that his myopia and color blindness would make that pursuit impossible. After receiving a tape recorder as a gift on his seventh birthday and unearthing some old Motown records and a phonograph, Michael hatched a new dream: He would become a recording artist. "I literally never entertained any other thought in my entire childhood and adolescence after that," Michael told *Rolling Stone's* Steve Pond.

In his early adolescence the restaurant that Michael's father owned became successful enough for the family to move to the affluent suburb of Bushey. While in school there Michael met Andrew Ridgeley, who would later become his partner in Wham! Ridgeley was popular, attractive, and stylish. At the time, Michael was shy and overweight. Though it seemed unlikely, the two became friends as they discovered a shared interest in pop music. The duo began recording songs together on Michael's tape recorder.

Quit School to Form Band

Although Michael's parents wanted him to enter a "respectable" profession like law or medicine, at the age of 16 he and Ridgeley quit school to form a band called The Executive. Tension among band members, however, led to a split before the ensemble had played a half-dozen gigs. Despite this turbulent beginning, Michael was not swayed from his dream. He continued to write songs while earning a living from a variety of odd jobs. In 1981 he and Ridgeley completed their first demo tape and sent it to a variety of record producers. By early 1982 the talented pair had won a contract with Innervision records.

With fame approaching, Michael decided to change his name from the intimidating Georgios Panayiotou to the more accessible George Michael. Taking their

For the Record. . .

Born Georgios Kyriakou Panayiotou, June 25, 1963, in London, England; son of Jack (a restauranteur) and Lesley Panayiotou.

With Andrew Ridgeley, formed group The Executive, 1979; worked at odd jobs while composing songs and working on demo tapes, 1980-82; signed with Innervision records, 1982, and released first Wham! album, *Fantastic;* performed with Wham!, 1982-86; toured China with Wham!, 1985; solo artist, 1986—. Producer and writer, *Trojan Souls* (featuring Anita Baker, Bryan Ferry, Aretha Franklin, and Elton John, among others), Hardback Records/Warner Bros.

Awards: Grammy Award nomination (with Ridgeley) for best pop performance by a duo, 1985, for "Wake Me Up Before You Go-Go"; American Video Award (with Ridgeley) for best new video artist, 1985; Igor Novello Award for best songwriter, British Academy of Songwriters, Composers, and Authors, 1985; Grammy Award (with Aretha Franklin) for best rhythm and blues performance by a duo, 1987, for "I Knew You Were Waiting (For Me)"; MTV Video Award for best direction, 1988, for video "Faith"; Grammy Award for album of the year, 1988, for *Faith;* American Music Awards for best pop male vocalist, best soul/rhythm and blues vocalist, and best soul/rhythm and blues album, all 1989, for *Faith.*

Addresses: *Home*—London, England. *Record company*—Columbia Records, 1801 Century Park W., Los Angeles, CA 90067.

group's moniker from a song Michael had written—"Wham! Rap (Enjoy What You Do)"—the duo released an album in the summer of 1982, *Fantastic,* that reached Number Four on the British charts.

The next Wham! album, *Make It Big,* made the pair teen idols in Britain and became popular in the States as well. Their style had changed from the previous record; on their first album, rap-style songs and a leather-clad bad-boy image prevailed. For *Make It Big,* Michael reached back to his early years to compose songs with a Motown feel. The single "Wake Me Up Before You Go-Go" became a Number One hit in England, the U.S., Australia, and a handful of other countries. It also garnered a Grammy nomination. Michael and Ridgeley won popular acclaim, but there was a price to pay; critics categorized Wham! as pretty-boy pop. "I totally threw away my personal credibility for a year and a half in order to make sure my music got into so many

people's homes," Michael told David Fricke in *Rolling Stone.* "It was a calculated risk, and I knew I would have to fight my way back from it."

Wham! completed another album in 1985 and took a tour of China, the first Western group to do so. But Michael was growing restless within the creative confines of the group. In 1986, still shaken by the dissolution of a long-term romantic relationship, Michael made the decision to dissolve Wham! The group was at the peak of its popularity. After a disagreement with his management, Michael chose to manage his career by himself.

Faith

To erase his teenybopper image, Michael recorded a duet with soul high priestess Aretha Franklin. The single, titled "I Knew You Were Waiting (For Me)," won a Grammy Award in 1987. Also that year, Michael released his first solo album, *Faith.* The album quickly soared to the Number One position and earned remarkable sales. One single in particular, "I Want Your Sex," caused quite a stir among radio programmers. Many stations banned it, and others restricted it only to late-hour play. The commotion was caused primarily by the song's lyrics—though the accompanying video was none too tame—which seemed to encourage people to have sex. Michael, however, contended that the message was a positive one that promoted monogamy in the age of AIDS, not promiscuity. Despite the hubbub, or perhaps because of it, "I Want Your Sex" became a Number Two hit.

Faith spun four more hit singles: the infectious title track, "Father Figure," "One More Try," and "Monkey." The album also topped the black album chart—the first time a white artist had achieved this honor. This was a moment of personal triumph for the Motown-inspired artist. He revealed to Gary Graff of the *Detroit Free Press,* "I was much happier with [*Faith*] being the No. 1 black album than I was when it became the No. 1 pop album. There was much more of a sense of achievement."

Faith was hailed as a crowning achievement by many reviewers. Stephen Holden wrote in the *New York Times* that the album "demonstrates that Mr. Michael's stylistic range and skill at integrating inventive new sounds into strong, well-shaped tunes is unequaled by any young pop craftsman with the possible exception of Prince." *Rolling Stone's* Mark Coleman opined, "George finally proves once and for all that he's no mere genius chart hack." Holden's rave concluded, "Mr. Michael's metamorphosis from journeyman to innovator has been so swift and dramatic that one can't begin to imagine where he'll go from *Faith.*"

In 1990 Michael followed up his enormous solo debut with *Listen Without Prejudice. Vol. I.* Despite the album's weightier themes, the singer's sex-symbol image continued to haunt him, partly because of a popular *Saturday Night Live* skit that parodied the unmistakable focus on Michael's rhythmically shaking rear end featured in the video for "Faith." In fact, *Listen Without Prejudice* was largely an attempt to once and for all dispel the superficial image of the Wham! days. One song, "Freedom," spawned a video of lip-synching models that featured several shots of the leather jacket Michael had worn in the "Faith" video bursting into flame—clear evidence of the artist's repudiation of the earlier video's relentless image selling. Further proof of this direction could be found in Michael's pointed absence from the video. "This time around," James Hunter wrote of the record in *Rolling Stone,* "George Michael has begun to think that he should provide something to his fans beyond fun and games." Hunter went on to point out that Michael "fashions just the kind of bold pop with rock and soul overtones that *Listen Without Prejudice* aims for." Though *Listen* did not rack up the sales that *Faith* had, it was viewed as definitive testimony of Michael's artistic legitimacy.

AIDS Activism and Record Company Battle

In 1992 Michael appeared at the star-studded Concert for Life, an AIDS awareness benefit and tribute to recently deceased Queen vocalist Freddie Mercury. Backed by a full gospel choir, Michael performed the demanding Queen classic "Somebody to Love" for a thousands-strong audience of diehard Queen fans massed at London's Wembley Stadium. His stunning rendition, in which, it seemed, he effortlessly approximated Mercury's soaring tenor, was a much commented upon highlight of the event. Later that year, Michael cut his teeth at directing, getting behind the camera to oversee the making of the "Too Funky" video. The song was one of three Michael contributed to the album *Red, Hot & Dance,* another project organized to raise funds for AIDS charities. Said project coordinator Leigh Blake of Michael's work, according to David Wild's *Rolling Stone* piece on *Red, Hot & Dance,* "We had already pretty much made the record when the possibility [of Michael's addition] came up. His involvement has made all the difference."

The singer made news in late 1992 with a lawsuit against Sony Music UK, his record label, charging in a London court that the agreement constituted a restraint of trade. Alleging in a prepared statement that was

reprinted in *People,* among other sources, that Sony regards "artists as little more than software," Michael sought to break his recording contract—due to expire in 2003—which requires that he produce six more albums for the label. Particularly revealing were the artist's remarks, reprinted in *Rolling Stone,* lamenting that "the great American music company that I proudly signed to as a teenager (has) become a small part of the production line for a giant electronics corporation, who, quite frankly, have no understanding of the creative process." Sony had purchased Michael's previous label, CBS, in 1988. Distilling the importance of the move, *Entertainment Weekly* postulated, "If Michael wins, the precedent could allow other bands to break from acquiring companies, doing to the music industry what free agency did for baseball."

The pending litigation overshadowed Michael's musical efforts of that time, including his production for Warner Bros. of *Trojan Souls,* an album of new Michael compositions performed by such artists as Anita Baker, Bryan Ferry, Aretha Franklin, and Elton John, with whom Michael had developed a close personal and working relationship, amply symbolized by their duet of John's "Don't Let the Sun Go Down on Me," recorded on the Elton John-Bernie Taupin tribute album, *Two Rooms. Listen Without Prejudice Vol. II,* the singer's apparently incomplete but much ballyhooed third album, was sentenced to limbo as a result of the Sony suit.

George Michael unabashedly championed pop music at a time when many had abandoned the form as so much glossy drivel. His dedication to the genre, however, did not insulate him from the insecurities of an artist torn between people-pleasing and critical success. He articulated his fears that his audience could not appreciate the duality of his creative output to the *Detroit Free Press's* Graff, suggesting, "If people can try to understand as opposed to being suspicious of it, maybe they can appreciate the music a bit more."

Selected discography

With Wham!

Fantastic, Innervision, 1982.
Make It Big, Columbia, 1984.
Music From the Edge of Heaven, Columbia, 1985.

Solo releases

Faith, Columbia, 1987.
Listen Without Prejudice. Vol. I, Columbia, 1990.

Contributor to *Two Rooms: Celebrating the Songs of Elton John & Bernie Taupin,* Polydor, 1991; *Red, Hot & Dance,* Columbia,

1992; and *A Very Special Christmas II,* A&M, 1992. Also recorded duet with Aretha Franklin, "I Knew You Were Waiting (For Me)," released as single, 1987.

Sources

Books

Crocker, Chris, *Wham!,* Simon & Schuster, 1985.

Periodicals

Chicago Tribune, September 4, 1988.

Detroit Free Press, August 21, 1988.
Entertainment Weekly, February 14, 1992; November 27, 1992; December 11, 1992.
Musician, February 1993.
New York Times, May 29, 1988.
New York Times Magazine, June 22, 1986.
People, September 23, 1985; March 10, 1986; November 30, 1992.
Rolling Stone, November 20, 1986; January 14, 1988; January 28, 1988; November 16, 1989; October 4, 1990; August 6, 1992; January 7, 1993.

—*Nancy Rampson*

Charles Mingus

Jazz bassist, composer

Charles Mingus is universally acknowledged as one of the most influential figures in the world of jazz, and many musicians consider even that expansive description too limited, believing that the great bassist should be ranked among the most important men in all of twentieth-century music. Mingus's accomplishments are certainly remarkable and wide-ranging. As an instrumentalist, he lifted the bass from its traditional role as a timekeeper and harmonic regulator to that of a full participant. His playing was technically brilliant, individualistic, and always deeply expressive. As a composer, he produced outstanding works of all types, from earthy, blues-oriented tunes to sophisticated orchestral numbers to free-form pieces. In performance and in composition, he demonstrated a deep understanding of virtually every style of jazz that existed during his lifetime. His talent for assembling groups and bringing out the best in both green and experienced players was legendary, and his influence continues to be profoundly felt years after his death.

Music was always considered important in the Mingus family. Growing up in the Watts section of Los Angeles, Mingus was exposed to classical music through the piano and violin lessons of his two older sisters. Another early influence—one that remained with him throughout his life—was the call-and-response singing practiced in the Holiness Church devoutly attended by his stepmother. Mingus's parents bought him a trombone when he was eight years old, but he felt uncomfortable with the instrument and soon took up the cello, which he loved. He switched to the double bass—the instrument on which he would build his reputation—in high school, where his fellow orchestra members included future jazz stars Dexter Gordon and Chico Hamilton. During his late teens Mingus augmented his classroom studies with private lessons; his tutors included jazzmen Joe Comfort and Red Callender, as well as a former bassist with the New York Philharmonic Orchestra, Herman Rheinschagen. He also studied composition with Lloyd Reese, and at least two of the songs he wrote at this time—"What Love," from 1939, and "Half-Mast Inhibitions," from 1940—would be recorded some twenty years later.

Mingus's activity in the jazz scenes of Los Angeles and San Francisco began even before he graduated from high school. In 1940 he replaced his former teacher, Red Callender, in Lee Young's band; the following year he joined Louis Armstrong's organization, where he remained until 1943. As "Baron Mingus" he led various ensembles of his own, but it was as a member of Lionel Hampton's band that he began to revolutionize jazz bass playing with his highly charged, lightning-fast solos. Economic pressures prompted Mingus to briefly

Born Charles Mingus, Jr., April 22, 1922, in Nogales, AZ; died of amyotrophic lateral sclerosis (Lou Gehrig's disease) January 5, 1979, in Cuernavaca, Mexico; son of Charles Mingus (a postal worker); married first wife, Barbara Jane Parks (divorced); married last wife, Susan Graham Ungaro; children: (first marriage) Charles III. *Education:* Studied privately with Joe Comfort, Red Callender, Herman Rheinschagen, and Lloyd Reese.

Jazz bassist, composer, and pianist, 1940-77. Bassist with Lee Young, 1940-41, Louis Armstrong, 1941-43, and Lionel Hampton, late 1940s; member of Red Norvo trio, 1950-51; played in and led various ensembles with Duke Ellington, Art Tatum, Dizzy Gillespie, Charlie Parker, and others. Established and performed with Jazz Workshop; founder of Jazz Artists Guild, Debut Records, and Charles Mingus Records. Instructor at State University of New York in Buffalo. Author of *Beneath the Underdog* (autobiography), Knopf, 1971.

drop music for a job with the U.S. Postal Service until 1950, when vibraphonist Red Norvo invited him to be part of a trio that would also include guitarist Tal Farlow. The Red Norvo trio attracted national attention for introducing the West Coast's "cool jazz" to a wide audience.

Became Involved in New York Jazz Scene

In 1951 Mingus relocated to New York City, a hothouse of jazz creativity where he worked regularly with such musicians as Art Tatum, Bud Powell, Dizzy Gillespie, and Charlie Parker. In 1953 he joined the band of his idol, Duke Ellington, but when a personality clash between Mingus and another bandmember led to a violent altercation, Mingus became one of the few musicians ever fired by Ellington. During the mid-1950s Mingus began to mature as a composer, modifying conventional forms by adding the startling rhythmic contrasts that would become his trademark. His aim was always to expand the horizons of jazz, and, to this end, he frequently experimented with atonality and dissonance. Some listeners found his music disturbing, but to others it was challenging and stimulating. As swing gave way to bop, and bop eventually gave way to avant-garde jazz, Mingus was able to keep pace with every new development, though he always maintained his individuality and avoided identification with any one school.

Mingus's energy led him to engage in many activities during the late 1950s, in addition to composing and upholding his reputation as one of the greatest soloists of all time. Angered by the unfair treatment meted out to musicians by major recording labels, Mingus established Debut Records in 1952. From 1953 to 1955, Mingus gave written contributions to the Jazz Composers Workshop, but in 1955 he founded his own workshop, based on his belief that written notation was not equal to his composing style. In his Jazz Workshop, Mingus carefully dictated each line of a composition to the appropriate player, thereby ensuring that all of his intended nuances were fully understood. His unique talent for putting together combos and bringing out the best in each player came to the fore during that era. J. J. Johnson, Kai Winding, and Thad Jones were but a few of the musicians who flourished under his direction. By the end of the decade, his continuing frustrations with the business side of the music industry spurred him to found the short-lived Jazz Artists Guild and act as a concert organizer.

Suffered Psychological Problems

During the early 1960s Mingus experimented with free-form jazz and also wrote some of his most richly textured, rhythmically complex music, including such pieces as "The Black Saint and the Sinner Lady" and the album *Mingus Mingus Mingus Mingus Mingus.* His influence on the young bass players of the day was incalculable, but, ironically, he gave up playing bass at this time. Instead he played piano, "on which he resembled a watery Thelonious Monk," according to jazz critic Whitney Balliet in his book *Such Sweet Thunder.* Mingus's behavior became increasingly erratic; frequently he ignored contracts, walked offstage early, or spent more time haranguing audiences about their ignorance and inattention than he did playing. Band members were routinely upbraided—even physically attacked—onstage for making mistakes or failing to show the proper attitude. Grappling with deep-seated psychological problems, Mingus dropped out of the music scene in the mid-1960s to concentrate on writing an autobiography. In 1968 he was evicted from his New York City apartment, and much of his written music was lost in that episode.

When Mingus finally returned to music—and the bass—in June, 1969, he was motivated mainly by economic pressures. To his surprise he found himself accorded the status of an elder statesman. His stream-of-consciousness autobiography, *Beneath the Underdog,* was published in 1971, the same year he received a Guggenheim fellowship for composition. He became a part-time instructor at the State University of New York in Buffalo; wrote music for films; collaborated with singer Joni Mitchell on her tribute recording *Mingus;* and traveled extensively with his workshop. In 1974 Mingus organized what Leroy Ostransky, author of *Understanding Jazz,* deemed "the greatest jam session since the expression was coined," which was recorded and released as *Mingus at Carnegie Hall.* In 1977 he became seriously ill, and in 1979 Charles Mingus died at the age of 56.

Legacy Lived on in *Epitaph*

Still, Mingus's music lived on. Shortly after his death, his widow formed the Mingus Dynasty group—with an ever-changing roster that often included former Mingus sidemen—in order to keep his works alive. In 1989, ten years after his death, a world premier was held at Lincoln Center in New York City for his composition "Epitaph," a masterwork that was discovered after his death. "It is the longest and most richly textured of jazz compositions," assessed *Time* contributor John Elson, adding that the piece was "a suite of 18 sections comprising nearly 4,000 bars of music, with a performance time of more than two hours." Composer Gunther Schuller, who conducted the 31-member ensemble that played "Epitaph," described the work to Elson as "a musical summary of one of the great jazz composers of the century, from the sweet and gentle Mingus to the angry Mingus."

Mingus fans will likely continue the debate over which of his many accomplishments was the greatest. Martin Williams, author of *The Jazz Tradition,* stated unequivocally that "Mingus the bassist . . . made the most important and durable contribution to jazz because he made people think of the instrument in a new way and because he was a virtuoso . . . outstanding enough to be numbered among the great soloists regardless of instrument." Yet few would argue with *Understanding Jazz* author Ostransky, who concluded that when Mingus's playing, his compositions, his leadership, and his continuing influence are all taken into account, "the classification for Charlie Mingus is catalyst."

Selected discography

Mingus at the Bohemia (recorded in 1955), Fantasy OJC, 1991.
Charles Mingus Quintet (recorded in 1955), Debut.
Charles Mingus Plus Max Roach (recorded in 1955), Fantasy/ OJC, 1990.
Pithecanthropus Erectus (recorded in 1956), Atlantic.
The Clown (recorded in 1957), Atlantic.
New Tijuana Moods (recorded in 1957), Bluebird, 1986.

Blues and Roots (recorded in 1959), Atlantic.
Mingus Ah Um (recorded in 1959), reissued, Columbia Jazz Masterpieces, 1987.
Mingus Dynasty (recorded in 1959), Columbia.
Shoes of the Fisherman's Wife (recorded in 1959 and 1971), Columbia Jazz Masterpieces, 1988.
Charles Mingus Presents Charles Mingus (recorded in 1960), Candid.
Pre-Bird (recorded in 1960), Mercury.
Mingus at Antibes (recorded in 1960), Atlantic.
Mingus Revisited (recorded in 1960), reissued, EmArcy, 1986.
Mysterious Blues (recorded in 1960), Candid, 1990.
Oh Yeah (recorded in 1961), reissued, Atlantic, 1988.
Tonight at Noon (recorded in 1961), Atlantic.
Town Hall Concert (recorded in 1962), United Artists.
The Black Saint and the Sinner Lady (recorded in 1963), reissued, MCA/Impulse, 1986.
Mingus Plays Piano (recorded in 1963), Impulse.
Mingus, Mingus, Mingus, Mingus, Mingus (recorded in 1963), MCA/Impulse.
Town Hall Concert 1964, Volume 1 (recorded in 1964), reissued, Fantasy/OJC, 1991.
Right Now: Live at the Jazz Workshop (recorded in 1964), reissued, Fantasy/OJC, 1991.
Mingus at Monterey (recorded in 1964), Charles Mingus Records.
Portrait (recorded in 1964 and 1965), Prestige.
Charles Mingus (recorded in 1965), Prestige.
Let My Children Hear Music (recorded in 1971), reissued, Legacy, 1992.
Mingus Moves (recorded in 1973), Atlantic.
Mingus at Carnegie Hall (recorded in 1974), Atlantic.
Cumbia and Jazz Fusion (recorded in 1976), Atlantic.
3 or 4 Shades of Blues (recorded in 1977), Atlantic Jazz.
Epitaph (recorded in 1989), Columbia, 1990.
The Complete Debut Recordings, Debut, 1990.
Mingus in Europe, reissued, Enja, 1990.
Live in Oslo, 1964, Volume II, Landscape, 1992.
Astral Weeks, Moon.
Jazzical Moods, Fresh Sound.
Jazz Workshop, Savoy Jazz.
Live at TBB-Paris, Volume 1, Soul Note.
Meditations on Integration, Bandstand/Sphere.
Mingus, Candid.
Reincarnation of a Lovebird, Prestige.

Sources

Books

Balliet, Whitney, *Such Sweet Thunder,* Bobbs-Merrill, 1966.
Mingus, Charles, *Beneath the Underdog* (autobiography), Knopf, 1971.
Ostransky, Leroy, *Understanding Jazz,* Prentice-Hall, 1977.
Priestly, Brian, *Mingus: A Critical Biography,* Salem House, 1983.

Williams, Martin, *The Jazz Tradition,* Oxford University Press, 1983.

Periodicals

Down Beat, February 1989; March 1989; September 1989; July 1990; October 1990; March 1991; September 1991.
High Fidelity, October 1988.
New Yorker, August 21, 1989.
Radio Free Jazz, February 14, 1979.
Reflex, Number 21.
Stereo Review, January 1988; August 1990; March 1991.
Time, September 10, 1990.
Village Voice, July 3, 1978.

—Joan Goldsworthy

Frank
Morgan

Saxophonist

"**S**eduction," suggested *Down Beat* correspondent Larry Birnbaum, is the expertise of jazz saxophonist Frank Morgan. "Lyrical, refined, unblushingly romantic, his alto sings a siren song, animating wordless tunes with the aching poetry of triumph and loss, fruition and desire. His poised, spare, sculpted lines mark him as an old master." "He's a virtuoso who makes deep feeling accessible," commented Eric Pooley in *New York*. "Through his horn, he sings shockingly intimate songs about loves lost and won, years irretrievably gone, death cheated but heading back to settle the score." Considered one of the greatest jazz saxophonists of all time, Morgan is a 1950s-generation bebop artist who regained popularity in the 1990s bebop revival.

Until Morgan opted to play straight in 1985, thievery and con games to support his drug habit designated him the recurrent star of prison bands. For several decades his alto reverberated on and off in numerous penitentiaries, including San Quentin, San Luis, Chino, and Obisbo. A media darling as a new jazz discovery since his 1980s revival, Morgan has appeared on the television news show *CBS Sunday Morning,* in such magazines as *Newsweek* and *Time,* and in an inspirational book *One Person Can Make A Difference.*

With the encouragement of his wife, Rosalinda, he cut nine albums amid personal turmoil and a media blitz. "It's my wife who saved my life," Morgan told Birnbaum. "She propped me up and said, 'If you love me and want to be with me, then you'll play your saxophone and stop going to prison.'"

Impelled by Jazz as Youth

Born in 1933, Morgan is the son of bebop guitarist Stanley Morgan, who played with jazz master Charlie Parker and later led the Ink Spots. Morgan's mother, Geraldine, gave birth to Morgan when she was a 14-year-old Minneapolis schoolgirl. "My father told me he used to play his guitar next to my mother's womb," Morgan related to Zan Stewart in *Down Beat.* "Then he would practice by my crib. I took my first guitar lesson when I was three."

Morgan was raised by his maternal grandmother and great-grandmother until he was six years old. He was sent to live with his paternal grandmother, "Mama Coot," in Milwaukee, Wisconsin. Since his parents were anchored in Detroit between engagements, Morgan was taken on short trips to Michigan. One memorable weekend with his father, the seven-year-old Frank became enthralled with alto saxophonist Charlie Parker's performance at the Paradise Theater. Backstage, he asked Parker's advice about playing an alto saxophone.

The next day Morgan put away his guitar and purchased the clarinet Parker recommended for childhood fingering. Three years went by before he got his first saxophone. By the age of 14, he had mastered the alto sax enough to mimic Parker. When his grandmother found the adolescent with marijuana, though, she shipped Frank off to Los Angeles to live with his divorced father.

Jeopardized Career at Onset

In 1948 Stanley Morgan was opening at the Casablanca, but he took Frank, who had recently joined him, to the nonalcoholic Crystal Tearoom to jam on Sunday afternoons. Morgan kept up his Parker-like play with Dexter Gordon, Wardell Gray, and others who frequented those sessions. At the age of 15, he was offered Johnny Hodges's former chair in Duke Ellington's band, but his father felt Frank was too young for road trips. Instead, Morgan backed famed jazz singers Billie Holiday and Josephine Baker in the house band at the Club Alabam.

While working at the club at night and attending Jefferson High School, where he played in the Jefferson Big Band by day, Morgan starting using heroin. When his idol Charlie Parker came to Los Angeles in 1952, Morgan assumed Parker—who also used the drug—would be pleased to know Frank had taken up the

habit. At first, Parker lectured, swore, and cried, begging the boy not to follow his example. But when Morgan offered him a half-ounce of the drug, Parker gleefully took it. "I'll always wonder," Morgan confessed to Pooley, "what would have happened if he had flushed it down the toilet instead."

By 1955—the year Parker died—Morgan was a serious junkie with his first drug arrest. His debut album, *Introducing Frank Morgan,* appeared the same year, but he had already embarked on the course of thievery and scams that would eventually land him in San Quentin in 1962. Though he left the prison in 1967, he would be a habitual offender for the next 20 years.

In 1978 Morgan's one-year marriage to a forensic pathologist was already failing when he met Rosalinda Kolb on a brief time-out from jail. An artist and model, Kolb lived with Parker after his divorce until the day in 1980 when he took money set aside for brake repairs to buy drugs. When the couple's car—driven by Morgan—nearly went off a cliff that night, Kolb left Morgan. Though she returned to Morgan periodically, by 1985 the relationship was over.

That same year, one of Fantasy Records' executives called Kolb, asking her to locate Morgan so he could sign a recording contract. Just out of prison in April, Morgan released *Easy Living*—plugged on the television show *Simon and Simon* when a character held up the album on camera—but turned himself in after using drugs in violation of his parole. He and Kolb were reunited prior to his release from his last incarceration on December 7, 1986; the couple married in 1988.

Triumphed After Prison

After his record company staff required he move to New York City so they could keep an eye on him, Morgan debuted to resounding success at the Village Vanguard in 1987. In New York, the saxophonist's career flourished. He appeared in several magazines, including *People,* and in the Off-Broadway production *Prison-Made Tuxedos*—a semi-autobiographical musical based on his days as a prison superstar. Also during the 1980s, he released the well-received albums *Lament, Bebop Lives!, Double Image, Major Changes,* and *Yardbird Suite.*

Reflections followed in 1989, but 1990's *Mood Indigo,* released on Morgan's new record label, Antilles, reached Number Four on *Billboard's* jazz charts. When *A Lovesome Thing* was released in 1991, Morgan had kept his life straight for many years. His methadone treatments and sometimes nightly Narcotics Anonymous meetings proved to be successful.

Morgan's immense talent has kept him in the favor of music critics. "Alto saxophonist Frank Morgan is a rarity among jazz musicians: a virtuoso who is not ashamed to tug at the heartstrings of his listeners . . . Morgan is capable of dazzling displays of musical finesse," wrote David Grogan in *People*. "But he is at his best when he launches into a familiar melody and caresses the notes with a tenderness that will make even the most jaded soul consider a surreptitious swoon or two." "He also plays an alto sax better than any man alive," penned Daniel Okrent in *Esquire*. And David Gates appraised in *Newsweek*, "His playing, of course, sounds like [Charlie Parker's]. But he pauses more often to caress a single note and to revel in the sheer texture of sound—from a frail piping, to a croon, to a lowdown honk. Parker was an innovator who played saxophone; Morgan is a *saxophonist*."

Morgan revealed to Birnbaum the resolve that motivates this reborn, master musician, "I have an assignment, a job to do. It's apparent to me that a force greater than me saved me from myself, so I could do what I'm doing now. . . . The more nice things they write about [me], the harder I'll practice and the harder I'll try to be a better human being. Just to be the best Frank Morgan I can be."

Selected discography

Introducing Frank Morgan, GNP Crescendo, 1955.

Easy Living, Contemporary, 1985.
Lament, Contemporary, 1986.
Bebop Lives!, Contemporary, 1987.
Reflections, Contemporary, 1989.
Mood Indigo, Antilles, 1990.
A Lovesome Thing, Antilles, 1991.
(With Bud Shank) *Quiet Fire*, Contemporary, 1992.
You Must Believe in Spring, Antilles, 1992.
Double Image, Contemporary.
Major Changes, Contemporary.
Yardbird Suite, Contemporary.

Sources

American Visions, April 1991.
Atlantic, October 1987.
Down Beat, June 1986; December 1988; April 1991.
Esquire, July 1988.
High Fidelity, August 1988.
Newsweek, April 6, 1987.
New York, February 12, 1990.
People, July 18, 1988; February 12, 1990; January 18, 1993.
Pulse!, December 1992.
Rolling Stone, March 8, 1990.
Time, March 26, 1990.

—*Marjorie Burgess*

Michael Martin Murphey

Singer, songwriter

Michael Martin Murphey has not only blazed a trail through pop music and into country as a performer, he has reaped considerable success by writing songs as well. His youthful good looks notwithstanding, Murphey is a seasoned veteran of the music business—he wrote hit songs for the pop group the Monkees and singer Kenny Rogers in the 1960s and made the pop charts himself in the 1970s. He was well into his thirties when his western-influenced country songs made him a star in Nashville. Today he is one of the most highly regarded recording artists in all of country music.

In *Who's Who in New Country Music,* Andrew Vaughan noted that Murphey's "longevity and determination have certainly paid off." The critic added that Murphey's career "proves that country music will embrace those artists more concerned with their art and integrity than big bucks." The singer has had major country hits with such singles as "A Long Line of Love," "Don't Count the Rainy Days," "Talkin' to the Wrong Man," and "What She Wants." More recently, a long-standing interest in the culture and history of the cowboy led to the release of *Cowboy Songs,* the first high-profile album of cowboy music to come from Nashville in more than twenty years.

Murphey was born in Texas and spent his youth on family farms and ranches where his relatives ran cattle. He was comfortable in a saddle from an early age and was fascinated by the songs he heard on the range. "There was a lot of music sung while they were working," Murphey remembered of his family in the *Chicago Tribune.* "I learned a lot of it from being around people who were working cattle, and my uncle, who was and is a real fan of music, had tons of 78 [r.p.m.] records by people like [western singers] Carl T. Sprague, Jules Verne Allen and other guys that go back way before [singing cowboy and actor] Roy Rogers." At the age of 17, Murphey took his first job in the music industry—he played western songs around the campfire at a Texas ranch.

As a youth Murphey also enjoyed other musical genres, including the country and folk music of such performers as Hank Williams, Bob Wills, and Woody Guthrie. After high school he moved to California where he played guitar with the pop group The Lewis and Clark Expedition and attended the University of California, Los Angeles, majoring in medieval history. Murphey was anxious to work his way into the music business as a singer and songwriter, however, seeing little disparity between his education and the career he wanted to follow. Murphey illustrated this for *Country Music*'s Michael Bane: "I was fascinated with the troubadour, the old oral tradition. . . . You go back and read classic history, most of it comes from recited history . . . [and] the traveling minstrels. The closest thing we have in modern life is the wandering musician, the songwriter." For a time he lived hand-to-mouth in the Mojave Desert, writing songs for Kenny Rogers and country duo Flatt & Scruggs. His big break came through Mike Nesmith, an old friend from Texas.

Big Break From a Monkee

Nesmith, himself a folk-rock singer, had landed a job with The Monkees, an enormously popular television pop group. At Nesmith's request, Murphey wrote a song for a Monkees album—"What Am I Doing Hangin' Round"—and the album sold some five million copies. The success of that song earned Murphey a song publishing contract with Screen Gems. He penned a few more numbers for The Monkees but soon became disenchanted with the Los Angeles scene.

In 1971 Murphey returned to Texas and became an active member of the so-called "outlaw" movement there. He played and sang, mixing such genres as country, rock, and folk, and was often on the bill with other maverick performers such as Willie Nelson and Jerry Jeff Walker. One of his best-known songs from this period is "Geronimo's Cadillac," a forceful plea for Indian rights that became an unofficial anthem for the Indian movement in the early 1970s.

As a very young man, Murphey had written a sentimental song about a woman and her wild pony. He was not particularly fond of the song, and he put off recording it. Seven years later, after the constant urging of a sister-in-law, he finally released the piece. "Wildfire" became a Number One pop hit in 1975, Murphey's first. The singer had another charted pop release the following year with "Carolina in the Pines."

Preferred Country Music

Murphey's success in the pop format was fleeting, mainly because he preferred to sing and write country music. By 1979 he was living in New Mexico and creating songs based on country, rock, Spanish, Indian, and western styles. He also decided to add his middle name "Martin" to his professional name, and this added to the confusion about exactly who and where he was. He did not languish in obscurity for long, however. By the mid-1980s he was a regular on the country charts, with hits such as "What's Forever For," "What She Wants," and "Don't Count the Rainy Days."

In 1984 Murphey was named "best new artist" by both the Country Music Association and the Academy of Country Music. The irony was not lost on the performer, who, at that point, had been a professional musician for more than 15 years. Murphey was glad for the recognition, however, and he has lived up to his potential by producing still more hit singles, including "A Long Line of Love" and a Grammy Award-nominated duet with singer Holly Dunn, "A Face in the Crowd." Murphey also scored a hit with a song he sings with his son Ryan. Based on a real incident, in which Ryan sought his father's advice about women, "Talkin' to the Wrong Man" affords a poignant view of father-son relations and concerns that leap from generation to generation.

Late in 1990 Murphey released an album on which he had labored for several years. The work, *Cowboy Songs,* was not expected to be a commercial success, since there hadn't been a recording of authentic cowboy music in more than two decades. Even Murphey was reluctant to release singles or make music videos based on the project. He reconsidered this decision, however, and the first single, "Cowboy Logic," became a hit. The song helped to sell the album, which performed far better than expected.

Quite apart from its commercial success, *Cowboy Songs* earned the praises of country and folk music critics nationwide. *Chicago Tribune* correspondent Jack Hurst, for instance, called the work "not only one of the finest albums of [the] year but also one of the finest of the last decade. Its 22 riveting cuts represent a labor of not only love but also scholarship; it raises a cult musical genre to the level of mainstream art." Hurst concluded that *Cowboy Songs* "is a hands-down masterpiece capable of wringing laughter, sadness, and sometimes even terror from its hearers."

Champion of the West

Cowboy Songs certainly reflects an ongoing interest in Murphey's case—the artist has long been a champion of the western wilderness and its creatures. In 1986 he founded an annual festival, WestFest, celebrating western art and culture, and he has been almost single-handedly responsible for resurrecting the cowboy's image in Nashville. *Richmond Times-Dispatch* contributor Molly Carpenter noted: "Murphey's love for the American West clearly comes through in his songs, painted with vivid images of the rugged mountains and vast deserts of southwest landscapes, all evidence of his travels from his native Texas to California's Mojave Desert, Colorado's Rockies and the wild diversity of New Mexico, his home for the past 10 years." In a further effort to preserve the traditions of the West, Murphey has led a group of performers in a combination poetry reading and songfest called "Cowboy Logic." Murphey—along with poet and cowboy Waddie Mitchell and Don Edwards, a western music historian and troubadour—has taken the improvisational show to such unlikely places as New York and Las Vegas because, as he maintained in the *New York Times,* he wants "to make people take a second look at the agrarian tradition of [the] country and the culture it has produced. The basis of all economy is growing things and producing food. Without an agricultural tradition that is respected, a country dies,"

Murphey is also concerned with issues other than the survival of western culture, including Indian rights and finding a middle ground between ranchers and activists on opposite sides of environmental problems. Murphey feels he has more opportunity than most to be "a real citizen involved in the community instead of being a guy who lives over the hill and plays the guitar or sits around town being a personality," as he explained in a Warner Bros. press release.

Not all of Murphey's songs are about the land out West. Many of his best-known country hits are more personal—glimpses of family life, love, and heartbreak. Murphey told the *Richmond Times-Dispatch,* "Periodically I like to write music about people because I've written so many songs about landscapes and other things." He concluded with a laugh, "I mean, my biggest hit was about a horse."

Selected discography

The Heart Never Lies, EMI America, 1986.
Tonight We Ride, Warner Bros., 1986.
Americana, Warner Bros., 1987.
Best of Michael Martin Murphey, EMI America, 1987.
River of Time, Warner Bros., 1988.
Land of Enchantment, Warner Bros., 1989.
The Best of Country, Curb/CEMA, 1990.
Cowboy Songs, Warner Bros., 1990.
Cowboy Christmas: Cowboy Songs II, Warner Bros., 1991.
Wide-Open Country, Warner Bros., 1993.
Cowboy Songs III, Warner Bros., 1993.
Blue Sky Night Thunder (includes "Wildfire" and "Carolina in the Pines"), Epic.
Cosmic Cowboy Souvenir, A&M.
Geronimo's Cadillac, A&M.
Michael Martin Murphey (includes "What's Forever For"), Liberty.

Also recorded albums *Swans Against the Sun* and *Flowing Free Forever.*

Sources

Books

Vaughan, Andrew, *Who's Who in New Country Music,* St. Martin's, 1989.

Periodicals

Atlanta Constitution, April 8, 1988.
Atlanta Journal/Atlanta Constitution, May 10, 1986.
Chicago Sun-Times, August 1, 1990.
Chicago Tribune, January 27, 1985; May 22, 1988; September 23, 1990; December 2, 1990.
Country Music, July/August 1991; November/December 1992.
Houston Post, June 3, 1991.
New York Times, May 22, 1992.
People, February 24, 1986; March 23, 1987; August 1, 1988.
Richmond Times-Dispatch, April 14, 1989.
Stereo Review, June 1986; December 1987; January 1991.

Additional information for this profile was obtained from Warner Bros. press material, 1990.

—Anne Janette Johnson

Carl
Perkins

Singer, songwriter, guitarist

Rock and roll pioneer Carl Perkins and his two brothers, Jay and Clayton, were raised on a west Tennessee cotton plantation called the Wilbur Walker Farm. Theirs was the only white family working the fields, and Perkins grew up hearing the sounds of black gospel music as the sharecroppers worked together during the day. In an April, 1990, interview with *Rolling Stone,* Perkins described how this gospel tradition, along with a heap of Mississippi-Delta blues, bled into the country music he was listening to on the evening radio. As a young man he also soaked up the new wave of bluegrass coming over the radio waves, particularly the sounds of Bill Monroe as he performed at the Grand Ole Opry. Perkins fell in love with bluegrass because "it was uptempo from the other country dudes." He explained to *Rolling Stone*'s Dave McGee, "There's a lot of kinship to bluegrass and early rockabilly—I mean a lot."

John Westbrook, an elderly fixture on the Walker plantation, sold a guitar to Perkins's father when Carl was just seven or eight. Soon thereafter the boy could frequently be found on Westbrook's porch when the day's work was over, learning every blues guitar lick the old man could teach him. At night, he learned country hits from various radio programs, speeding them up as he played them on Westbrook's old guitar—accelerating them to the point that his father would interrupt, saying, "That's not the way [Opry great] Roy Acuff does it!" Perkins recalled in *Rolling Stone* that he would keep playing away, saying only, "I know it, Daddy."

Sun Records and "Blue Suede Shoes"

The first song Perkins wrote was also the first he recorded; it was called "Movie Magg." The song described an adolescent's life in Lake County, Tennessee, where "you took your girl to the picture show on the back of a mule." With songs of that ilk and a developing, distinctive musical style, Perkins began playing around west Tennessee accompanied by his brothers. By the early 1950s, the Perkins Brothers were sending off demo tapes to Nashville and New York, all of which were politely rejected. "It's not bad," the record company people would say, "but we don't know what it is."

Perkins knew those days of incomprehension and rejection were numbered when he heard a recording of a young Elvis Presley, cut at the Sun studios up in Memphis. Some say the song Carl heard in his kitchen that night was the bluegrass classic "Blue Moon of Kentucky," to which Presley gave his own rocking twist. Others insist it was Presley's version of the Arthur Crudup composition "That's All Right (Mama)." That detail notwithstanding, Perkins immediately realized

For the Record. . .

Born April 9, 1932, in Lake City (one source says Tiptonville), TN; married wife Valda, 1954; children: Stan, Steve, Greg, Debbie.

Performed with brothers Jay and Clayton as the Perkins Brothers, early 1950s; signed with Sun Records, 1955; wrote and recorded "Blue Suede Shoes," 1956; toured with Johnny Cash, 1960s; appeared regularly on Cash's television show, 1969-71; signed with Columbia Records, 1969; signed with Jet Records, 1978; wrote and recorded with various artists, including Paul McCartney, Jeff Lynne, and NRBQ, 1970s and '80s; with George Harrison, Ringo Starr, Dave Edmunds, and the Stray Cats, among others, appeared in own television special, c. 1986; continued to record and tour, 1990s.

Awards: Gold record for "Blue Suede Shoes," 1956; inducted into the Rock and Roll Hall of Fame, 1987.

Addresses: *Home*—Jackson, TN. *Management*—Carl Perkins Enterprises, 27 Sunnymeade Dr., Jackson, TN 38305.

that he had found a kindred spirit—another musician who understood what the newly emerging rockabilly sound was all about.

After more dues-paying on a local radio show, Perkins and his brothers went to Memphis and pleaded with legendary Sun Records founder Sam Phillips for an audition. By 1955 Perkins had been signed by Sun, and by 1956 was on the top of the country, rhythm and blues, and pop charts simultaneously with his first hit, "Blue Suede Shoes"—the first song ever to achieve this triple play. In his *Encyclopedia of Pop, Rock, and Soul,* Irwin Stambler related the origins of this celebrated "early [anthem] of teenaged identity": "The song was inspired by a boy at a dance where Carl was playing. Poor but proud of his blue suede shoes, the youth wouldn't let anyone step too near them. At 3 in the morning after the dance, Carl got out of bed in his subsidized housing project and dashed off the song on a potato sack since there was no writing paper in the house."

Perkins wasn't on the charts for long before he participated in an event which has, in retrospect, taken on unusual prominence in the history of rockabilly and, indeed, rock and roll itself. On December 4, 1956, while still enjoying chart-topping fame, Perkins and his trio of backing musicians were working at Sun studios, rehearsing new material with another up-and-coming

rockabilly artist, Jerry Lee Lewis. Elvis Presley, who was at the time unsuccessfully trying to break into the Vegas lounge circuit, stopped by "to say howdy." Country giant Johnny Cash, another prominent Sun artist, was also in the studio that day, and soon all four were gathered around the piano singing everything from hymns to country ballads. Phillips kept the tape recorders rolling, and a local newspaper photographer managed to put a picture of the four onto the following day's front page, dubbing them "The Million Dollar Quartet." The name stuck, and it underscored the idea that here was a distinctive, new, and potentially lucrative brand of popular American music. The tapes resulting from that session, containing ragged arrangements that begin and end in fits and starts, were finally released in 1988, prompting some critics to suggest that the event may have been more culturally than musically significant. As it turned out, Johnny Cash went home that day before the recording got underway—hence the Million Dollar Quartet remains more the stuff of legend than of pop music history.

Disastrous Crash

Perkins was at the height of his career at the time of the "Quartet" sessions. In 1956, after producing other hits for Sun and some for Columbia Records, he was, in his words, going "toe-to-toe with that good-lookin' Elvis." That same year, however, just outside of Wilmington, Delaware, Carl was in an automobile accident on the way to a taping for Perry Como's television show, at which he was to be presented with a gold record for "Blue Suede Shoes." The crash fractured his neck in three places, broke the neck of his brother Jay, and killed their manager, David Stewart. Jay died six months later of injuries sustained in the crash, and Carl was forced to recuperate while Presley took "Blue Suede Shoes" on its second trip to the top of the pop charts, where it would sell even more than Perkins's version had. These events marked a turning point for Perkins's career; no longer would he remain "toe-to-toe" with Elvis and no longer would the Perkins brothers perform together. Some have speculated over the years, including Presley, that if not for the accident, Perkins may have emerged the bigger star. During a year of convalesce, Perkins began a long battle with drug and alcohol abuse.

The 1960s found Perkins the performer more often than not sidelined by younger or more successful acts, although Perkins the songwriter continued to be revered by bands like the Beatles. For much of the decade—during which fashion forced Perkins to leave rockabilly behind in favor of country music—he toured with Johnny Cash, serving as both opening act and lead guitar player. From 1969 to 1971 Perkins would be a regular on Cash's network TV show. In 1963, however, while touring England with early rocker Chuck Berry, he met up with the Beatles, who threw a party for him, afterward bringing him to Abbey Road studios, where they recorded his songs "Honey Don't," "Matchbox," and "Everybody's Trying to Be My Baby." These recordings, and their subsequent renown, went nearly as far as the artist's own work had in the 1950s to insure that there would always be a spot for Perkins in the Rock and Roll Hall of Fame, into which he was officially inducted in 1987.

Perkins's alcohol problem became most acute during the 1960s. Then, one night in 1971 at the Shrine Auditorium in Los Angeles, he walked onstage drunk and struggled through only three songs before giving up. He left the stage, threw his guitar against the wall, and sat for a while in the tour bus, sobbing. That night marked the end of his drinking days. By 1977 Perkins was touring again on his own, this time with his sons Stan and Greg serving as back-up.

Million Dollar Quartet Redux

The Million Dollar Quartet lived on in legend long enough to prompt an unlikely reunion—unlikely in that Presley died eight years and one month before the event. But on September 16, 1985, an illustrious rockabilly lineup returned to the cramped studios at 706 Union Avenue in Memphis to record some new originals. Hair-raising tenor Roy Orbison joined Perkins, Cash, and Jerry Lee Lewis in place of "the King." Other notables in attendance included Sun Records artist Charlie Rich; Scotty Moore, Presley's lead guitarist; Creedence Clearwater Revival's John Fogerty, whose tribute to the Sun legends, "Big Train From Memphis," was recorded during the session; and the mother-daughter country vocal duo the Judds, who sang back-up. Perkins hadn't been in the tiny studio since 1958 and was clearly touched by the gathering. "That little studio changed my life," he told Rolling Stone. "[It] gave my kids new bicycles and gave me some new sharkskin britches that I could never have gotten out of the cotton patch. I tried sending tapes everywhere. But it was Sun Records that gave me a chance."

In 1992 Perkins released Friends, Family and Legends. Though not pleased with what he felt was overly glossy production, Pulse!'s Ted Drozdowski nevertheless reported in his review of the album, "Carl Perkins still sings like a god—all goosed up on the religion of rock'n'roll, the gospel for which he helped write." Shortly after the record's debut, the singer was diagnosed

with throat cancer. But at 60, Perkins was every bit the survivor he was in his twenties. In an interview with Musician's Scott Isler in August of 1992, Perkins reported that the more than 30 radiation treatments he had undergone appeared to have been successful and that he was "feeling stronger everyday." When he got up in a club after regaining his voice that year, intending "to do a couple of songs," five "slipped by . . . real fast." The man, and the performer, it seemed, were incapable of quitting. By the fall of 1992 Perkins was on the road again, playing to enthusiastic houses in Europe, "fronting a series of star-studded anniversary parties for the Hard Rock Cafe, including one where longtime fan George Harrison dropped in," reported the Metro Times. Pulse! also tracked Perkins touring in Britain, where he had always been revered, with Presley band alumni Moore and drummer D. J. Fontana. Fans could almost have expected such a recovery from the guitar- and cotton-picker who, despite all the hardship and tragedy in his life, was able to tell one interviewer, "I have been and am to this day a very happy man."

Selected discography

Blue Suede Shoes, Sun, 1956, reissued, 1969.
Boppin' the Blues, Sun, 1956.
Your True Love, Sun, 1957.
Pink Pedal Pushers, Columbia, 1958.
Whole Lotta Shakin', Columbia, 1959, reissued, Sony Music Special Products "Collector's Series."
Greatest Hits, Columbia, 1969.
On Top, Columbia, 1969.
(With NRBQ) Boppin' the Blues, Columbia, 1970, reissued, 1990.
Ol' Blue Suede's Back, Jet, 1978.
(With Johnny Cash and Jerry Lee Lewis) The Survivors, Columbia, 1982.
Original Sun Greatest Hits (1955-1957), Rhino, 1986.
(With the Million Dollar Quartet) The Complete Million Dollar Session: December 4th, 1956, Sun/Charly, 1988.
Honky Tonk Gal: Rare and Unissued Sun Masters, Rounder, 1989.
Jive After Five: The Best of Carl Perkins, 1958-1978, Rhino, 1990.
Blue Suede Shoes and Other Big Hits, Such a Deal, 1990.
The Best of Carl Perkins, Sound, 1991.
Friends, Family and Legends, Platinum, 1992.
(With NRBQ) Restless: The Columbia Years, Columbia/Legacy, 1992.
Best of Carl Perkins, Curb, 1993.
Twenty Golden Pieces, Bulldog.
Introducing Carl Perkins, Boplicity.
Born to Rock, Liberty.
Class of '55.
(Contributor) Rockabilly Stars, Volume 1, Sony Music Special Products "Collector's Series."

Sources

Books

Rock Movers & Shakers, edited by Dafydd Rees and Luke Crampton, ABC-CLIO, 1991.

The Rolling Stone Encyclopedia of Rock & Roll, edited by Jon Pareles and Patricia Romanowski, Rolling Stone Press/Summit Books, 1983.

Stambler, Irwin, *The Encyclopedia of Pop, Rock and Soul,* St. Martin's, 1989.

Stambler, Irwin, and Grelun Landon, *The Encyclopedia of Folk, Country & Western Music,* St. Martin's, 1983.

Periodicals

Country Music, July/August 1992.

Metro Times (Detroit), September 9, 1992.

Musician, August 1992.

Pulse!, August 1992; October 1992.

Rolling Stone, October 24, 1985; November 21, 1985; February 25, 1988; April 19, 1990.

Stereo Review, November 1986.

—*Matthew Martin*

Tom Petty

Singer, songwriter, guitarist

Like many American boys growing up in the late 1950s and early 1960s, Tom Petty was first inspired to pick up a guitar after seeing rock and roll icon Elvis Presley perform. Unlike many other aspiring musicians, Petty's long rock and roll road has led to fame, wealth, millions of albums sold, a Grammy Award, and a hard-earned reputation as one of rock's most enduring stars and accessible songwriters. For nearly two decades, Petty, along with his band, the Heartbreakers, has won audiences with consistently insightful and exciting albums and energetic live shows. Though his rise to rock stardom was anything but easy, his late 1980s association with other rock music legends as part of the Traveling Wilburys, as well as his hugely successful 1989 solo release, *Full Moon Fever,* cemented his place in rock history.

Born the son of an insurance salesman on October 20, 1950, in Gainesville, Florida, Tom Petty seemed destined for a future in rock and roll from the age of 11. He met Elvis Presley when the King of Rock and Roll came to Gainesville in 1961 to shoot the film *Follow That Dream.* "[Presley] didn't have much to say to us," Petty recalled in *Rolling Stone,* "but to a kid at an impressionable age, he was an incredible sight." The next day young Petty traded his slingshot for a friend's collection of Presley and Little Richard records. "And that," related Petty, "was the end of doing anything other than music with my life. I didn't want anything to fall back on because I was *not* going to fall back."

Petty learned to play on a guitar purchased from a Sears, Roebuck & Co. catalogue, and by 14 he was playing with various Gainesville bands, including a bar band called the Epics and, ultimately, a country-rock band known as Mudcrutch. Part of the Mudcrutch line-up—guitarist Mike Campbell and keyboardist Benmont Tench—would later become members of the Heartbreakers.

Went West With Mudcrutch

At 17 Petty quit high school to go on the road with Mudcrutch, ending up in Los Angeles in the early 1970s in search of a record contract. After sending a demo tape around, Mudcrutch signed with an MCA label, Shelter Records. The band broke up in an L.A. recording studio while working on their first album. One afternoon in 1975, Petty reunited in a demo session with Campbell and Tench and two other musicians he knew from Gainesville—bassist Ron Blair and drummer Stan Lynch. The quintet sparked together and decided to form a band with Petty as the frontman, calling themselves Tom Petty and the Heartbreakers.

For the Record. . .

B orn October 20, 1950, in Gainesville, FL; son of an insurance salesman; married, c. 1973, wife's name, Jane; children: Adria, Kim.

Played in various Gainesville, FL, bands, including the Epics and Mudcrutch; guitarist and vocalist with the Heartbreakers, 1975—; group released self-titled debut LP on Shelter Records, 1976; performed at Live-Aid concert, 1985; recorded and performed with Traveling Wilburys, 1988—; solo recording artist, 1989—.

Selected awards: Grammy Award, 1989, for *Traveling Wilburys, Vol. One.*

Addresses: *Record company*—Warner Bros. Records, 3300 Warner Blvd., Burbank, CA 91505-4694.

The band's eponymously titled debut album was released in 1976 on Shelter—now owned by ABC—and featured such Petty staples as "American Girl" and "Breakdown," which became his first Top 40 single in the United States. "American Girl," a hit for the band in England in 1976, was also the first of Petty's songs to be covered by another artist, Petty idol and former Byrds leader Roger McGuinn.

By the time of the release of the band's second album, 1978's *You're Gonna Get It!,* Petty and the Heartbreakers were the hottest band on the L.A. club circuit, regularly drawing wall-to-wall crowds at such venues as the famed Whiskey A Go Go. In the disco-infested American music scene of 1978, the driving, jangling guitars of Tom Petty and the Heartbreakers were hard to classify. Many young, guitar-oriented rock bands drawing media attention were mislabeled as part of the punk movement filtering across the Atlantic from England, and the Heartbreakers were no exception. Lack of a clear media identity, though, quickly took a backseat to the string of contract and legal hassles that began to plague Petty after the second album's release.

Damned the Torpedoes and Contract Problems

ABC sold Shelter Records back to MCA, and Petty declared himself a free agent, prompting a lawsuit against him by MCA and Shelter that prevented him from signing with another label. Finding himself $500,000 in debt, Petty declared bankruptcy in mid-1979 to prevent further prosecution then signed a $3 million contract with a small, MCA-affiliated label called Backstreet Records. An out-of-court settlement was

reached later with Shelter, and Petty and the Heartbreakers went into the studio to record the album that propelled them to superstar status.

With such hard-driving cuts as "Refugee" and "Even the Losers" and moodier yet radio-friendly tunes like "Here Comes My Girl" and "Don't Do Me Like That," *Damn the Torpedoes* hit Number Two on the album charts and sold two-and-a-half million copies. *Newsweek* characterized the record as "melodic mainstream at its best." While the sounds of the band's third album filled rock airwaves, arena audiences across the country realized what L.A. club crowds had known for years—that Petty and the Heartbreakers brought good-time music to the stage with all the fire and spontaneity that great live rock demands.

Waited Out Another Impasse With MCA

MCA executives planned to capitalize on the popularity of Tom Petty and the Heartbreakers by raising the price on the band's fourth album, *Hard Promises,* from $8.98 to $9.98. An angry Petty refused to allow it and even threatened to rename the album *$8.98.* After a month-long standoff, MCA finally agreed to release the album at the lower price. The 1981 album, which sold 1.5 million copies, was less of a straightforward rock album than its predecessor, and included "Insider," a duet with California pop diva Stevie Nicks of Fleetwood Mac. Petty and the Heartbreakers later returned the favor by writing and playing on Nicks's hit single "Stop Draggin' My Heart Around." Among the radio staples from *Hard Promises* was "The Waiting" and "A Woman in Love (But It's Not Me)," a pair of tunes exploring the rocky world of romantic relationships, each featuring the characteristic Heartbreaker hook connecting Petty's soulful lyrics.

Long After Dark, the 1982 follow-up to *Hard Promises,* included the hit single "You Got Lucky." The futuristic video for the song received heavy play on MTV, which helped boost album sales. Though it had more of a pop feel than anything Petty had done to date, "You Got Lucky" became one of his biggest hits. The album also featured such rock radio hits as "Change of Heart" and "Straight Into Darkness." The initial wave of mass popularity of Petty and the Heartbreakers peaked with the release and subsequent supporting tour of *Long After Dark.* The record also marked the first and only personnel change in the band: bassist Ron Blair left the Heartbreakers and was replaced by Howie Epstein.

Though Petty and the Heartbreakers continued to record through the rest of the 1980s, they sold gradually fewer albums, and empty seats began to appear in the top rows of the arenas they had been selling out. "To the people buying the albums," wrote David Wild in *Rolling Stone,* "or, increasingly, *not* buying the albums, Tom Petty and the Heartbreakers were in danger of becoming just another bunch of not-so-new kids on the block. Frustratingly for Petty . . . he found himself making more news when he broke his hand during the recording of 1985's *Southern Accents,* or when his home burned down in 1987, than when he made a new record."

Recovered From Hand Injury

Indeed, after an extended break from touring, not much was heard from Petty until the infamous wall-punching incident during the *Southern Accents* sessions in 1984. His right hand was severely damaged, and it was thought that his guitar-playing days were over. The other Heartbreakers took to referring to him as L.V., which stood for "lead vocalist." Petty's hand was repaired with steel inserts, and he recovered in time not only to play guitar for a tour supporting *Southern Accents* but also to perform in the landmark Live-Aid concert on July 13, 1985.

Southern Accents, a collection of songs influenced by growing up in the South, particularly the title track and the infectious "Rebels," marked a return to the band's Gainesville roots. Despite the hit single "Don't Come Around Here No More," which spawned a unique video spoofing *Alice in Wonderland, Southern Accents* failed to outsell its predecessors. A 1986 live album, *Pack Up the Plantation,* documented the band's subsequent tour and included some older live numbers. The two-record set excluded some of Petty's major hits but featured a blistering version of the Byrds' "So You Want To Be a Rock 'n' Roll Star," two duets with Stevie Nicks, and a raucous version of the Isley Brothers' crowd-pleasing "Shout."

In 1986 Petty and the Heartbreakers embarked on a momentous world tour backing Bob Dylan, taking their place among such renowned acts as the Band and the Grateful Dead, who have backed rock's legendary poet laureate. The chemistry onstage between Dylan and the Heartbreakers and a strong opening set of Heartbreaker material won the band legions of new fans. In a hotel room one night in the midst of the tour, Petty, Dylan and Mike Campbell wrote the rocking "Jammin' Me," which appeared on the Heartbreakers' 1987 album, *Let Me Up (I've Had Enough).* The band's eighth release, *Let Me Up* was laced with the same fiery guitar-driven rock that had made them famous.

Traveled With Wilburys

Following a 1987 arson-induced fire that destroyed the Petty family home in California's San Fernando Valley—a case that was never solved—Petty's fortunes began to turn around when he became part of the Traveling Wilburys. A chance meeting with former Electric Light Orchestra leader Jeff Lynne in Los Angeles led to Petty's involvement in a gathering of rock legends that led to the creation of the Wilburys, which included Petty, Lynne, Dylan, former Beatle George Harrison, and the late Roy Orbison. The group got together to record strictly for fun under fictitious names and produced *Traveling Wilburys, Vol. One,* complete with wacky liner notes penned by Monty Python alum Michael Palin. The collection of acoustically based, good-time music won widespread critical acclaim and earned Petty a Grammy Award. The Wilburys reunited in 1990 to record their whimsically titled second album, *Traveling Wilburys, Vol. Three.*

In between the two Wilburys releases, Petty recorded his first solo effort, *Full Moon Fever,* which became the most popular of his career, selling three million copies in the United States alone and staying in the Top Ten—

> *Petty's long rock and roll road has led to fame, wealth, millions of albums sold, a Grammy Award, and a hard-earned reputation as one of rock's most enduring stars.*

where it peaked at Number Three—for 34 weeks. The album spawned hit after hit, including "Free Fallin'," "I Won't Back Down," and "Runnin' Down a Dream." Hailing the album as an "infectious fever," *Rolling Stone* ranked it as one of the Top 100 albums of the 1980s.

In 1991 Petty reunited with the Heartbreakers for the band's ninth record, *Into the Great Wide Open.* Despite mixed reviews, the album sold one million copies within a month of its release and produced the radio hits "Learning to Fly" and the title track. The work also included the spirited "Makin' Some Noise," which revealed that Petty, despite the trials and tribulations of his traumatic rise to superstardom, has retained the inner urge to rock that moved him after his boyhood Elvis encounter.

In 1992 Petty signed a $20 million, six-album deal with a new label, Warner Bros. "The deal was made [in 1989] at a time when Petty's MCA albums weren't selling well," according to *Rolling Stone*. "Ironically, on the heels of the secret agreement [between Petty and Warner Bros.], his next album for MCA, *Full Moon Fever*, went triple platinum, and [*Into the Great Wide Open*] has sold more than a million copies." The magazine also reported that Petty's first album for Warner Bros. was not due to be released before 1995. Plans were underway in the meantime for a compact disc box set of the musician's work.

Selected discography

With the Heartbreakers

Tom Petty and the Heartbreakers (includes "American Girl" and "Breakdown"), Shelter, 1976.
You're Gonna Get It! (includes "Listen to Her Heart"), Shelter, 1978.
Damn the Torpedoes (includes "Refugee," "Even the Losers," and "Don't Do Me Like That"), MCA, 1979.
Hard Promises (includes "The Waiting" and "A Woman in Love"), MCA, 1981, reissued, 1992.
Long After Dark (includes "You Got Lucky" and "Change of Heart"), MCA, 1982.
Southern Accents (includes "Don't Come Around Here No More"), MCA, 1985.
Pack Up the Plantation—Live!, MCA, 1985.
Let Me Up (I've Had Enough) (includes "Jammin' Me"), MCA, 1987.
Into the Great Wide Open (includes "Learning to Fly"), MCA, 1991.

"We Need Peace in L.A." (single), 1992.

With the Traveling Wilburys

Traveling Wilburys, Vol. One, Warner Bros., 1988.
Traveling Wilburys, Vol. Three, Warner Bros., 1990.

Solo releases

Full Moon Fever (includes "Free Fallin'" and "I Won't Back Down"), MCA, 1989.
(Contributor) *A Very Special Christmas*, A&M, 1992.

Sources

Books

Rees, Dafydd, and Luke Crampton, *Rock Movers & Shakers*, ABC-CLIO, 1991.
The Rolling Stone Encyclopedia of Rock & Roll, edited by Jon Pareles and Patricia Romanowski, Rolling Stone Press/Summit Books, 1983.
Stambler, Irwin, *The Encyclopedia of Pop, Rock, and Soul*, St. Martin's, 1989.

Periodicals

Interview, June 1992.
Newsweek, January 17, 1980; July 8, 1991.
Orlando Sentinel, October 25, 1991.
Pulse!, July 1992.
Rolling Stone, January 16, 1986; April 20, 1989; October 5, 1989; August 8, 1991; April 30, 1992; May 14, 1992.

—*John Cortez*

The Pointer Sisters

Vocal group

The Pointer sisters were raised in a strict religious atmosphere by parents who were both ministers at the West Oakland Church of God in Oakland, California. As young girls, Anita, Bonnie, June, Ruth, and their two older brothers sang in the church choir. Irwin Stambler, in his *Encyclopedia of Pop, Rock, and Soul,* quoted Ruth as having said in 1978, "Our parents naturally, as ministers, wanted to protect us from the bad lives people had led in the blues and jazz worlds. We weren't allowed to go to the movies or hear music other than gospel and TV soundtracks. . . . In the beginning we had no one to imitate. We'd never heard of the Andrews Sisters or nostalgia," both of which would later become associated with the group.

According to *Jet,* the senior Pointers were apprehensive about their daughters' choice of careers until "after the turnaround, when [they] had health insurance and money in the bank; then [their parents] could come to the shows and enjoy themselves." Besides the gospel music with which they grew up, the sisters developed a passionate interest in other musical genres, from jazz to

rhythm and blues, scat, country, rock, and pop, all of which influenced their music.

Initially a duo featuring Bonnie and June, the Pointer Sisters later became a trio, with the addition of Anita. In the early 1970s the group sang backup for various artists, including Elvin Bishop, Taj Mahal, Tower of Power, Dave Mason, Sylvester, Boz Scaggs, and Esther Phillips. While backing Bishop at Los Angeles's celebrated Whisky-a-Go-Go, the four were spotted by Atlantic Records executive Jerry Wexler, who shortly thereafter signed them to his label. According to Stambler, two unsuccessful rhythm and blues singles for Atlantic Records were heard only in the Pointer living room. In 1972 Ruth joined the group, and as a quartet the Pointer Sisters sang backup on recordings of Bishop's "Don't Fight It, Feel It" and Chicago's "Skinny Boy." Their debut at Doug Weston's Troubadour, also in Los Angeles, established the Pointer Sisters as an independent act. The increasingly popular foursome, buoyed by their initial retro 1940s look, was soon seen on television's *Tonight Show* and *Midnight Special*.

Struck Gold With *The Pointer Sisters*

In 1972 the sisters were offered a recording deal with ABC/Blue Thumb through the connections of their friend, producer David Robinson. The Blue Thumb debut album, *The Pointer Sisters*, included the Allen Toussaint rhythm and blues single "Yes We Can Can," which went to number 11 on the *Billboard* pop chart in 1973. The album was the group's first to be certified gold by the Recording Industry Association of America, on February 7, 1974.

Despite their frequent categorization as a soul group, the Pointer Sisters were the first African-American female singers to perform on the stage of that bastion of country music, Nashville's Grand Ole Opry. In 1974 they won a Grammy Award for best country vocal performance by a duo or group for "Fairytale," written by Anita and Bonnie, which went to number 13 on the pop chart. With "Fairytale" the Pointer Sisters became the first African-American female group to score a Number One hit on the country chart. The quartet made their movie debut in 1976 as the Wilson Sisters in *Car Wash*.

Even with their chart-topping and Grammy triumphs, however, the Pointer Sisters lacked consistent success. Because of their wide range of styles, which defied musical categorization, the sisters became typecast as a nostalgia group by their label. In *The Encyclopedia of Pop, Rock, and Soul* June recalled, "We didn't read contracts in those days and we lived on the road and came home broke. But we enjoyed singing so much we just kept on." Compounding their difficulties, June was plagued in the mid-1970s by a much publicized nervous disorder.

Quartet Became a Trio

Finally, after a short breakup in 1977, Bonnie left the group to pursue a solo career. Anita, June, and Ruth resurrected the Pointer Sisters in 1978 and began working with producer Richard Perry, who is credited by *New Grove Dictionary of American Music* author Barry Kernfield as having "emphasized their affinities with soul music." *Energy*, the debut album on Perry's Planet Records, became the Pointer Sisters' third gold record. The group's first gold single, "Fire," a cover of Bruce Springsteen's smoldering lust song, reached Number Two on the pop chart in 1978. As Kernfield noted, the recipe for commercial success was found in "an appealing blend of pop and soul music."

The Pointer Sisters continued to make musical history with the 1981 album *Black and White*, which earned them the *Billboard* title of Rhythm and Blues Group of the Year. The gold single "Slow Hand" was heard that year in the film *Taps* and in 1982's *Partners*. Their succession of hits in the mid-1980s established the sisters as the female rhythm and blues group of the decade. 1984's *Break Out* included the hit single "Neutron Dance," which helped give the enormously popular film *Beverly Hills Cop* some of its characteristic energy. *Break Out* also produced the singles "Jump (for My Love)," a smash hit that earned a Grammy Award for best pop performance by a duo or group with vocal, and "Automatic," Grammy winner for best vocal arrangement for two or more voices.

More Label Jumping

In 1985 the Pointer Sisters switched to RCA Records, where they produced 1988's *Serious Slammin'*, their 16th album. *People's* Ralph Novak described the release as "full of fun, funk, romance and just about everything else on earth that's admirable except glazed doughnuts." Jumping labels again, this time to Motown, the trio released 1991's *Right Rhythm*. Motown press information pointed out that in much of their material, particularly "Slow Hand," "He's So Shy," "Fire," and "The Man With the Right Rhythm," the Pointer Sisters have consistently "[projected] strong images of women who know what they want—emotionally and physically—out of life" and that singles like "Real Life" carried a clear message that "superficial, material things ain't where they're at." While the Pointer Sisters have drawn stylistically from their diverse musical heritage, their lyrics show the influence of their strong moral background. *Right Rhythm's* "Billy Said Yes," for example, which featured a rap break—in both English and French—addressed the pressure on young people to use drugs.

In the spring of 1992, the trio again changed labels, moving to SBK Records. The sisters continued to maintain a wide and varied touring schedule, performing for audiences at New York City's Carnegie Hall; soldiers in the Persian Gulf; on television in tributes to comedian Richard Pryor and former heavyweight champ Muhammad Ali; and at the opening of the Disney-MGM Studios Theme Park in Orlando, Florida.

The Pointer Sisters have influenced both music and fashion throughout their many years of popular suc-

cess. Motown's press information remembered how "they [had gone] back in time to resurrect the '40s look and caused thousands of young women across the nation to copy their fashion sense and hundreds of hopeful female trios to try to scat." With an uncanny sixth sense, the group is "always pointed in the right direction whatever the road traveled or musical direction."

Selected discography

The Pointer Sisters (includes "Yes We Can Can"), Blue Thumb, 1973.
"Fairytale" (single), Blue Thumb, 1974.
Energy (includes "Fire" and "Happiness"), Planet, 1978.
Special Things (includes "He's So Shy"), Planet, 1980.
Black and White (includes "Slow Hand" and "What a Surprise"), Planet, 1981.
So Excited, Planet, 1982.
Break Out (includes "Jump [for My Love]" and "Automatic"), Planet, 1983.
Contact, RCA, 1985.
Serious Slammin', RCA, 1988.
Right Rhythm (includes "Real Life" and "Billy Said Yes"), Motown, 1991.

Sources

Books

Kernfield, Barry, *The New Grove Dictionary of American Music*, Macmillan, 1986.
The Rolling Stone Encyclopedia of Rock & Roll, edited by Jon Pareles and Patricia Romanowski, Rolling Stone Press/Summit Books, 1983.
Stambler, Irwin, *The Encyclopedia of Pop, Rock, and Soul*, St. Martin's, 1989.

Periodicals

Jet, April 24, 1989.
People, May 2, 1988; May 25, 1992.
Variety, May 10, 1989.
Stereo Review, October 1991; March 1991.

Additional information for this profile was obtained from a Motown Records publicity release, 1991.

—*Marta Robertson*

Queen Ida

Singer, accordionist

Queen Ida related in her book of recipes and stories, *Cookin' With Queen Ida: "Bon Temps" Creole Recipes (& Stories) From the Queen of Zydeco Music,* the way in which she acquired her stage name. At the end of a masquerade dance on Mardi Gras night in California's Bay Area in 1975, Ida Lewis Guillory was brought onstage with the introduction "Tonight we're going to crown you Ida—Queen of the Zydeco Accordion and Queen of Zydeco Music." A reporter in the crowd, Peter Levine, did a story on the dance that appeared a few weeks later in the Sunday magazine of the *San Francisco Chronicle,* and soon calls were coming in from Bay Area clubs to book "Queen Ida" for appearances. At that point, however, she didn't even have a band. She'd just been sitting in that night with her brother, Al Lewis—better known as Al Rapone—and his Latin/soft rock group, the Barbary Coast Band.

Since the early 1970s she'd been playing the accordion and singing with the Barbary Coast Band, or with another group called the Playboys, at private dances held by the African-American community that had relocated from Louisiana to California. In *Cookin' With Queen Ida,* she wrote that "one of the reasons they wanted me to sit in was that a woman accordion player was such a novelty. Every time I played one or two songs with the Playboys at those dances, the area in front of the stage would fill up with men." But Queen Ida was always taking on jobs sometimes thought to be more suitable for men. As a young girl she had learned to drive a tractor and hired out to help neighboring rice farmers, experience that proved helpful later when she began driving a school bus.

Initially Queen Ida hesitated to accept the invitations that followed her press exposure, but her brother told her he had already agreed to many of them, and they appeared as "The Barbary Coast Band, featuring Queen Ida." To reflect her importance as she expanded her repertoire and did more songs with the band, they became "Queen Ida and the Barbary Coast Band." Still later the group's name changed to "Queen Ida and the Bon Temps Zydeco Band."

Though she moved with her family from Lake Charles, Louisiana, to Beaumont, Texas, when she was ten, and then on to San Francisco when she was eighteen, Queen Ida never really left Louisiana behind. Her first language was French, and her father, a rice farmer until he moved to California, even brought his own rice with them when they moved so the family would be sure to have plenty to eat. There were a growing number of friends and relations in the Bay Area who were from Louisiana, and Queen Ida's young adult years were filled with the music and food of her former home.

Learned to Play Her Mother's Accordion

Queen Ida came from a musical family—her father played the harmonica, and her uncles played the accordion and fiddle. Her mother also played the accordion, and it was her instrument that Queen Ida first learned to play, after taking piano lessons for a time. For years, however, music was only a part of her social life. After she married, she attended nursing school, but quit to have her first child. When her three children grew older, she took a part-time job driving a school bus. It was only gradually, with the encouragement of her family and friends, that she began to perform occasionally in public.

The word zydeco—a corruption of the French term "les haricots," meaning beans—attests to the music's humble beginnings with the French-speaking people of color in southwest Louisiana and southeast Texas. Having little money to buy instruments or pay for entertainment, washboards and spoons became the means for making music in these areas. Eventually the accordion became the instrument most closely associated with zydeco. Queen Ida differs from the great zydeco player Clifton Chenier and Cajun accordion players in that she plays neither the piano accordion nor the button accordion with only 11 keys. Queen Ida's accordion has 31, allowing her to play more melodically because she can play notes from more than one key. She also tends to use the treble side of the accordion, as many Mexican accordionists do, to better blend with the other instruments in the band. The Bon Temps Zydeco Band also incorporated a fiddle player, which

is unusual for a zydeco band though common in Cajun music. Traditional tunes were part of the group's repertoire in addition to Queen Ida's own songs, including "Rosa Majeure," or Rosa of Legal Age.

Cooked Up a "Musical Gumbo"

Queen Ida's music is an eclectic mix of rhythm and blues, Caribbean, and Cajun, though the presence of her accordion always keeps it traditional. She explained in *Keyboard:* "It was Zydeco music I started with. It was Zydeco music my parents—my mother especially—asked my brothers to keep alive. And now we have a following for Zydeco music. There are songs that I play that are not totally Zydeco. But Zydeco has always been a musical gumbo because it's got all the elements. It's not rock, it's not country, it's not blues, but it has all those elements. Also, the nature of the accordion carries a lot of its weight into making whatever we play sound like Zydeco." Queen Ida has become an ambassador for the accordion, which is now often used in pop music by such artists and groups as Paul Simon, John Mellencamp, and They Might Be Giants.

By 1976 Queen Ida had appeared at the Monterey Jazz and Blues Festival and landed her first record contract, with GNP/Crescendo Records, a Los Angeles record company that specializes in jazz and with whom she has recorded all her albums. Still, as she noted in *Cookin' With Queen Ida,* "I didn't feel that music would be a full-time career for me." She kept her job as a school bus driver until her youngest daughter, Ledra, went to college and she started to tour more widely.

In 1978 Queen Ida met her agent, John Ullman, and things began to change. The following year she was nominated for a Bammy, or Bay Area Music Award. She lost out to Taj Mahal, though it was he who suggested she tour Europe and had his agent arrange for Queen Ida's first two-week European tour. Her brother Willie joined the band as washboard player for the tour, and, though her brother Al eventually left the band to resume his own career, it has remained a family business. Her husband Ray left his job as a truck dispatcher in 1986 to become the group's manager, while her son Myrick replaced Willie on washboard, in addition to providing help on the accordion and vocals. The group was soon touring Europe several times a year, performing for appreciative audiences.

Gained Popularity in United States

Queen Ida's career was progressing in the United States, as well. In 1980 she was nominated for a

Grammy Award for her album *Queen Ida and the Bon Temps Zydeco Band in New Orleans.* A Grammy Award for the best ethnic/folk album came her way in 1982 for *Queen Ida on Tour,* recorded in Denmark. She felt the band always sounded best live and most of her albums have been recorded while she was on tour.

Since then Queen Ida has appeared in Francis Ford Coppola's movie *Rumblefish* and a documentary about Louisiana music by Les Blank called *J'ai Ete au Bal.* She has also performed on the television shows *Saturday Night Live* and *Austin City Limits.* In 1988 Queen Ida became the first zydeco musician to tour Japan, and a year later she went on a tour of Africa sponsored by the State Department. She added Australia and New Zealand to the list in 1990.

Though she began her career later in life, Queen Ida has yet to slow down and serves as an inspiration to many of her fans. In her 1992 GNP/Crescendo Records biography she maintained: "When I was a little girl, women in Louisiana were expected to raise their children, tend chickens, go to church, and bake bread. I tell older women that they are just now mature, and that they just now know what direction they want to go in, something they didn't know at an earlier age. Sometimes I feel like a teacher or a missionary, but I believe it's never too late to expand your human potential."

Selected discography

On GNP/Crescendo Records

Queen Ida on Tour, 1982.
Caught in the Act, 1986.
Cookin' With Queen Ida and Her Zydeco Band, featuring Myrick "Freeze" Guillory, 1989.

Also recorded the albums *On a Saturday Night, Queen Ida and the Bon Temps Zydeco Band in New Orleans, Queen Ida in San Francisco, Zydeco,* and *Zydeco a la Mode.*

Sources

Books

Broven, John, *South to Louisiana: The Music of the Cajun Bayous,* Pelican, 1987.
Guillory, Ida, and Naomi Wise, *Cookin' With Queen Ida: "Bon Temps" Creole Recipes (and Stories) From the Queen of Zydeco Music,* Prima, 1990.
Harris, Craig, *The New Folk Music,* White Cliffs, 1991.

Periodicals

Billboard, July 9, 1983; November 30, 1985.
Down Beat, August 1986; April 1991.
Keyboard, August 1990.
Living Blues, Number 64, 1985.
Melody Maker, August 9, 1980; March 21, 1981.
Ms., Volume 6, Number 6, 1977.
Sing Out!, Volume 27, Number 6, 1979; Volume 29, Number 2, 1983; Volume 32, Number 1, 1986.
Stereo Review, March 1991.
Variety, April 27, 1983; June 22, 1983.

Additional information for this profile was obtained from a GNP/Crescendo Records press biography, 1992, and the documentary *J'ai Ete au Bal,* 1991, by Les Blank.

—John Morrow

The Ramones

Rock band

In the often harsh, sometimes unjust world of popular music, the true innovator is often overlooked; trends come and go—their origins unknown and originators unrecognized. The punk rock phenomenon of the late 1970s was no exception. In just two years, four glue-sniffing high school dropouts calling themselves the Ramones almost single-handedly changed the course of rock music when, as David Fricke wrote in *Rolling Stone,* they "torched the sluggish Seventies with their debut album, *Ramones,* the punk-rock blast that shook the world." In one of the more rancorous episodes of music history, however, the Ramones were forced to watch as other bands became symbolic of the movement they had so tirelessly promoted—a situation that endured for more than 15 years.

The original Ramones—Dee Dee, Johnny, Joey, and Tommy—came together as a band in 1974 in Forest Hills, a community within the New York City borough of Queens. Juvenile delinquents in the narrowest sense of the term, the pre-Ramones Ramones were a mixture of big-city desperation and adolescent hostility directed

at a system they felt had nothing to offer them. None had finished high school, none could hold a job, their drug use was on the rise, and Dee Dee, at least, was drifting into a life of crime. "John and I used to sit on rooftops and sniff glue and drop television sets on people," Dee Dee told *Musician.* "Actually, John used to drop the television sets. I only threw firecrackers. We didn't receive proper guidance from our parents." He added, "I had my last rites three times before I figured out maybe I should straighten up. It gets pretty expensive: seventeen-, eighteen-hundred-dollar bills for emergency room stuff."

Rock Stardom the Only Escape

As they saw it, their only chance of escape from this quagmire was rock stardom. This seemed unlikely, however, since none of the Ramones were at that time accomplished musicians. Moreover, they found the overwhelming tepidity of most mid-1970s rock and roll profoundly uninspiring. A turning point came when they began attending the growing number of area low-budget, reactionary "garage" concerts, especially those by the New York Dolls, a locally popular hard rock

group both Johnny and Dee Dee have listed prominently among their influences. "I couldn't believe you could just be in a band and be so rebellious without spending $10,000 on amplifiers," Dee Dee said in *Musician.* "I learned you could be what you wanted to be, and after the Dolls, I wouldn't settle for anything less. That's something you didn't get after seeing [British rock guitar virtuoso] Jeff Beck."

Thus inspired, Dee Dee and Johnny bought an inexpensive bass and guitar, respectively, and began practicing two or three times a week. Despite the fact that they could hardly play a note between them, they had some very definite ideas about how they wanted to make music. "It had to sound loud and fast and heavy rock with no guitar solos or anything like that," Dee Dee told *Guitar Player.* "Just heavy power chords and exciting songs." Johnny had similar notions: "I always wanted the guitar to sound like energy coming out of the amplifier. Not even like music or chords; I just wanted that energy coming out." Unfortunately—or perhaps fortunately, depending on one's outlook—their first rehearsals didn't go quite as expected. "We didn't know what to do when we started trying to play," Dee Dee recalled in *Spin.* "We'd try some Bay City Rollers songs, and we absolutely couldn't do that. We didn't know how, so we just immediately started writing our own stuff."

Nostalgic for the simple vitality of 1960s pop, the Ramones quickly amassed a repertoire consisting wholly of two-minute bursts of what Johnny called in *Rolling Stone* "pure rock and roll with no blues or folk or any of that stuff in it," but with a definite twist. Using stark and often darkly humorous lyrics—"We decided to sing about something that we found amusing . . . and *daring*"—hammered into bubble gum melodies that were then pasted over sparse, high-energy, buzz-saw guitar, the Ramones managed to "reinvent rock 'n' roll," as Jim Greer testified in *Spin.* Their anger and frustration with the state of mainstream rock, and with life in general, found vent in such (barely) musical onslaughts as "Beat on the Brat," "Blitzkrieg Bop," "Now I Wanna Sniff Some Glue," "I Don't Wanna Walk Around With You," and "I Don't Wanna Go Down to the Basement."

Became a Sensation at CBGB

With Joey as lead vocalist and Tommy on drums, the Ramones—their name was coined when Dee Dee read that Paul McCartney had called himself "Paul Ramon" during early Beatles tours—played their landmark gig in August of 1974 at CBGB, a dilapidated nightclub on lower Manhattan's seedy Bowery. There they quickly became an underground sensation, attracting the attention of music fans and critics bored with increasingly bloated mainstream rock. In November of 1975 the Ramones signed with then-fledgling Sire Records and immediately recorded their first album, *Ramones,* for the incredibly small sum of $6,400. Largely derided at the time of its release, *Ramones* has since become a classic: *Rolling Stone* voted it Number 69 of the Top 100 rock albums of the years 1967-1987, calling it "perhaps the purest expression of head-first rock velocity in the music's history . . ., *Ramones* recalled the glory days of the rock & roll single: every song was short, fast and—to those so disposed—unforgettable."

The next step was to tour, and tour massively. The Ramones always spent the major portion of their time on the road, but with record company backing, they made it all the way to England for a series of concerts that many now regard as the spark that ignited the punk rock phenomenon. "When we played the Roundhouse in London for the first time on July 4, 1976, it was just incredible," remembered Dee Dee in *Musician.* "All the gobs of spit—that's how you could tell if they liked you." Among those contributing saliva were the core of Britain's soon-to-be punk scene. With safety pin in cheek, these angry young Anglicans wrathfully answered the (some say imagined) call and, in a sense, made it their own, supplementing the Ramones' minimalist approach with sociopolitical virulence. "Somehow after we went over there," Dee Dee continued, "the feeling expanded. All these bands started coming out of nowhere. Everyone was saying, 'I'm starting a band,' whether they knew how to play or not."

As more and more groups swelled its ranks, punk rock quickly became a powerful movement. Commercialism soon took hold, however, and punk became just another fad in an already fad-ridden decade, with people simply exchanging their pet rocks for punk rock. The Ramones, meanwhile, seemed to get lost in the shuffle. At the height of the punk era, they found themselves eclipsed by their imitators and those they had inspired; most of the media was directed at English bands with "weird pointy haircuts," as Johnny described them in *Rolling Stone,* and when punk's popularity began to wane with the start of a new decade, the Ramones became a band without a genre. They were justifiably bitter. "By 1979, all these soft new wave bands who came after us had made it: Elvis Costello, Blondie, [the] Cars, Graham Parker," Joey told *Musician* in 1983, the same year the video of the Ramones tune "Psycho Therapy" earned the dubious distinction of being among the first such clips banned from airplay on MTV. "We stuck by our guns through it all, played our own music. Now it's time for us to happen, and if we don't the hell with everybody."

Sold-Out but Hitless

It was with no small amount of audacity that the Ramones continued to churn out inflammatory, wickedly satirical songs dealing with such diverse and taboo topics as drug use, intolerance, and mental disorders—specifically as they occur in U.S. presidents. Unfortunately, titles like "Teenage Lobotomy," "Gimme Gimme Shock Treatment," "Pinhead," "I Wanna Be Sedated," "Psycho Therapy," "Cretin Hop," "The KKK Took My Baby Away," and "Bonzo Goes to Bitburg," among others, were not destined to receive maximum airplay—or, for that matter, any airplay at all—in the resurgently conservative 1980s. The Ramones were a music industry paradox: They were lucky if their records broke the Top 100, but at the same time they played to sold-out crowds around the world. And while many reviewers, especially *Rolling Stone*'s, gushed praise from seemingly every bodily orifice, detractors labeled the Ramones cartoonish ninnies—"D-U-M-B/ Everyone's accusing me," sang Joey rather pointedly on "Pinhead." Even critics who initially perceived the Ramones as a studied parody of a rock and roll band began to complain that the joke was wearing thin.

What followed was nearly a decade of producer-hopping—from Graham Gouldman, co-author of the hit single "Bus Stop," to Eurythmics' Dave Stewart. The low point of this approach came when the Ramones commissioned legendary producer Phil Spector to outfit them with his trademark "wall of sound" for *End of the Century.* But Spector, architect of countless 1960s mega-hits including "Be My Baby" and "You've Lost That Lovin' Feelin'," by the 1980s was becoming better known for his personal eccentricities than his production talents. As Dee Dee recalled in *Spin:* "It was getting so out of hand, people were trying to get hits out of Punk Rock. Some of it was getting big, but it wouldn't work with the Ramones. And someone thought we could have a hit record if Phil Spector produced us. But it was a nightmare. One night he pulled out his gun and wouldn't let us leave. We had to sit there in the living room and listen to him play 'Baby I Love You' over and over again."

The Ramones chafed under restrictions imposed by producers who tried to alter their sound in order to make it more palatable to mainstream radio programmers. Discord erupted among bandmembers about where they were going with their music, and, moreover, who would lead them there. Add to this their grueling tour schedule—at least nine months of every year— and the results were inevitable: the loss of two drummers, Tommy, in 1978, and Marky, in 1983, and, finally, one bassist. Disillusioned by their lack of recognition and tired of both the constant touring and the Ramones' intentional lack of musical growth, founding member Dee Dee left the band in 1989 to pursue a solo career. More as a declaration of independence than a musical statement, he quickly released the rap-rock *Standing in the Spotlight,* for Sire, under the name Dee Dee King.

'90s Renaissance

Despite these tribulations, the band continued to enjoy the worship of legions of dedicated fans the world over. By the early 1990s, Ramones lyrics managed to find their way into a growing number of hip magazine articles and newspaper headlines. In 1992 *Spin* hailed the Ramones as one of the Top Seven bands of *all time,* placing them in such illustrious company as the Beatles and the Rolling Stones: "No group in the last 18 years has been more important or influential," wrote Jim Greer. That year the band released *Loco Live* and *Mondo Bizarro.* In his enthusiastic review of the former, *Spin* contributor Jon Young reported, "Studies have shown that New York's beloved Ramones are the inspiration for 95 percent of the rock'n'roll you listen to these days." Describing the release as "30-something of the Ramones' best onstage in grungy low fidelity," Young allowed parenthetically, "By the way, anyone who wonders why the Ramones haven't changed much since 1976 must not realize they were nearly perfect to begin with."

Mondo Bizarro marked the Ramones' departure from Sire Records; their first studio album of new material in over three years, the disc was released on Radioactive Records. Ed Stasium, who oversaw production of 1977's *Rocket to Russia,* produced the record, bassist C.J.'s first with the band. Featuring Living Colour guitarist Vernon Reid on the cut "Cabbies on Crack," *Mondo Bizarro* also included a remake of the Doors' "Take It as It Comes" and Joey's "Censorshit," an ode to Tipper Gore, co-founder of the record-stickering Parents' Music Resource Center and wife of Vice President Al Gore. Assessed *Rolling Stone's* Dave Thompson, "The Ramones sound fiercer than they have in years."

Indeed, the Ramones' ferocity helped recruit new fans as an increasing number of popular bands cited them as an influence. "I know that we're a staple," Joey had told *Musician* in 1991. "But we're not just this and nothing more. I think we're the blood and guts of what rock 'n' roll always was." But it was Dee Dee who perhaps best summed up the band's prospects when he wrote in a 1990 issue of *Spin:* "I don't know what's gonna happen to them, but I think there [sic] gonna do just fine."

Selected discography

On Sire Records, except where noted

Ramones (includes "Beat on the Brat," "Blitzkrieg Bop," "I Don't Wanna Go Down to the Basement," "I Don't Wanna Walk Around With You," "Now I Wanna Sniff Some Glue"), 1976.
Leave Home (includes "Gimme Gimme Shock Treatment" and "Pinhead"), 1977.
Rocket to Russia (includes "Cretin Hop" and "Teenage Lobotomy"), 1977.
Road to Ruin (includes "I Wanna Be Sedated"), 1978.
It's Alive (U.K. import), 1978.
(Contributors) *Rock 'n' Roll High School* (soundtrack), 1979.
End of the Century (includes "Baby I Love You"), 1980.
Pleasant Dreams (includes "The KKK Took My Baby Away"), 1981.
Subterranean Jungle (includes "Psycho Therapy"), 1983.
Too Tough to Die, 1984.
Animal Boy (includes "My Brain Is Hanging Upside Down [Bonzo Goes to Bitburg]"), 1986.
Halfway to Sanity, 1987.
Ramones Mania, 1988.
Brain Drain, 1989.
Lifestyles of the Ramones (video), Reprise/Warner Bros., 1990.
All the Stuff (and More), Volume One, 1990.
All the Stuff (and More), Volume Two, 1991.
Loco Live, 1992.
Mondo Bizarro (includes "Cabbies on Crack"), Radioactive/MCA, 1992.

Sources

Books

Rees, Dafydd, and Luke Crampton, *Rock Movers & Shakers,* ABC-CLIO, 1991.
The Rolling Stone Encyclopedia of Rock & Roll, edited by Jon Pareles and Patricia Romanowski, Rolling Stone Press/Summit Books, 1983.
Stambler, Irwin, *The Encyclopedia of Pop, Rock and Soul,* St. Martin's, 1989.

Periodicals

Entertainment Weekly, September 18, 1992.
Esquire, April 1980.
Guitar Player, April 1985.
Musician, July 1983; November 1991; December 1991.
Pulse!, October 1992.
Rolling Stone, February 8, 1979; July 12, 1979; July 17, 1986; August 27, 1987; September 20, 1990; October 29, 1992.
Spin, April 1990; April 1992; June 1992.
Stereo Review, October 1978.
Time, March 10, 1980.

—*Alan Glenn*

Helen Reddy

Singer, songwriter, actress

In 1971 Australian-born entertainer Helen Reddy wrote and recorded the pop song "I Am Woman," a celebration of female strengths and consciousness that became the anthem of the burgeoning women's liberation movement in her adopted United States. While not necessarily a staunch feminist, Reddy became identified with the movement nonetheless, a perception that quickly propelled her to stardom and narrowed her appeal once the fervor of feminism had died. Still, the pop singer with the clear country voice and strong, clipped delivery had cultivated loyal fans along the way, enough to keep her performing and recording into the 1990s. In a 1991 interview with *Detroit Free Press* reporter Judy Gerstel, the straight-talking Reddy related, "I can't say that I follow trends. I couldn't even tell you what's on the charts. That aspect of the music business applies to teenagers." To *People* correspondent Jeff Jarvis she remarked, "I think I'll be around for another 100 years."

Reddy was born into a show business family, the second daughter of vaudevillian performers. At age four she joined the act, singing and dancing; for most of her childhood she toured with her family until she was sent to boarding school for her education. Restless with the desire to perform, Helen left school at 15 to join a traveling theatrical company, where she continued to polish her singing and acting skills. Later, a stint as a vocalist with a band in Melbourne led to regular appearances on the popular late-night variety show *Melbourne Tonight* and a guest role on the long-running television series *Sunnyside Up*. At the age of 18 the performer was given her own television program, a 15-minute spot that aired twice weekly, called *Helen Reddy Sings*. Still, despite her prodigious success in her native country, the young entertainer was eager to continue her career in the United States.

In 1966 it appeared that Reddy would get her chance when she won a national talent contest that awarded her a trip to New York City and an audition with Mercury Records. Once she was in the United States, however, Mercury balked at its offer, and the vocalist had to support herself with any singing job she could find, including performing at weddings, hospitals, and resorts. When she was down to just a few dollars, her friends in New York threw a fund-raising party to keep her going. It was there she met talent agent Jeff Wald, a man whose hunger for success matched her own. The two married a few weeks later, and Wald became her manager. He also represented such performers as Tiny Tim, comedian George Carlin, and the rock group Deep Purple, and he used his extensive connections to secure nightclub engagements and television guest appearances for his wife. For the next few years, though, real success eluded Reddy, until a 1970 performance

For the Record. . .

Born October 25, 1941 (some sources say 1942), in Melbourne, Australia; naturalized U.S. citizen, 1974; daughter of Max (a theatrical producer, writer, and actor) and Stella (an actress; maiden name, Lamond) Reddy; first marriage ended in divorce; married Jeff Wald (a talent agent), 1966 (divorced, 1982); children: (first marriage) Traci, (second marriage) Jordan. *Education:* Attended University of California, Los Angeles.

Singer, songwriter, and actress, c. 1945—. Made stage debut in family vaudeville act at Tivoli Theatre in Perth, Australia, c. 1945; performed with family in Australian theaters and on radio; singer and actress with Australian traveling theater company, c. 1957; fronted band at Chevron Hotel, Melbourne; regular performer on late-night television variety show *Melbourne Tonight,* late 1950s; star of television program *Helen Reddy Sings,* beginning in 1960; signed first U.S. recording contract, 1970; club and concert performer, mid-1970s; hosted television programs the *Helen Reddy Show,* 1973, and the *Midnight Special,* beginning in 1975; appeared in films *Airport '75,* 1974, and *Pete's Dragon,* 1977; has appeared in musical theater.

Awards: NAACP IMAGE Award for best female pop vocalist, 1973; Artist of the Year Award, Music Operators of America, 1973; Grammy Award for best female pop vocal, 1973, for "I Am Woman"; American Music Award for top pop/rock female artist, 1974.

Addresses: *Office*—Helen Reddy, Inc., 820 Stanford St., Santa Monica, CA 90403.

on *The Tonight Show* caught the attention of Capitol Records.

Reddy's first recording for Capitol was a favorite song, "I Believe in Music," with "I Don't Know How to Love Him" from the rock musical *Jesus Christ Superstar* on the flip side. Leaving nothing to chance, she and Wald drove from radio station to radio station handing out records that winter. The couple's perseverance paid off—"I Don't Know How to Love Him" charted for 22 weeks, prompting a follow-up album of the same title in 1971.

Reddy's "I Am Woman," co-written with Ray Burton, also appeared on the LP, but drew little attention until it was included on the soundtrack of Mike Frankovich's 1972 film about women's liberation, *Stand Up and Be Counted.* Pressed by Wald, Capitol reluctantly re-re-leased the piece as a single—including an additional verse—while executives worried that the strident song would quash Reddy's fledgling career. Wald again distributed the record to radio stations around the country, and it reached Number One on the pop charts in late 1972.

"I Am Woman" sold more than one million copies, with 80 percent of those purchased by women. When Reddy won a Grammy Award for the song in 1973—edging out industry heavyweights Barbra Streisand, Aretha Franklin, and Roberta Flack—she accepted the award, thanking Wald and God "because She makes everything possible." With that declaration the singer became a willing spokesperson for the feminist movement and made her work ripe for interpretation. *New York Sunday News* critic Lillian Roxon, for example, wrote that Reddy can restate "a man's song . . . so that it gives you the most amazing insight into the way a woman thinks and feels." Over the next five years, the vocalist recorded a dozen more Top Forty hits, including "Delta Dawn," "Leave Me Alone," "You and Me Against the World," "Angie Baby," and "Ain't No Way to Treat a Lady." She frequently performed at top clubs, on television, and in concert, her earnings approaching $30 million.

By the late 1970s, however, Reddy's popularity had waned considerably. Critics often cited the singer's lack of musical versatility; as one *People* writer put it, "The strident, acerbic edge that served her well on *I Am Woman* is not always useful." Discussing Reddy's 1979 album, *Take What You Find,* in *Stereo Review,* Peter Reilly concurred; while acknowledging the singer's technically accomplished voice, he regretted her "inability to transmit the tenderer emotions of pop music," adding that "she's fine on fire and ice, but hearts and flowers seem alternately to baffle and annoy her." Following poor-selling albums in 1981 and 1983, Reddy lost major-label representation. Still, she seemed unperturbed by the development, having explained to one reporter, according to Irwin Stambler in the *Encyclopedia of Pop, Rock and Soul,* "I'll always sing, but I would like that to become a smaller part of my life." Focusing more on writing, women's issues, and environmental concerns, the vocalist still performs regularly at clubs and corporate conventions around the country.

Selected discography

I Don't Know How to Love Him, Capitol, 1971.
Helen Reddy, Capitol, 1971.
I Am Woman, Capitol, 1972.
Long Hard Climb, Capitol, 1973.

Love Song for Jeffrey, Capitol, 1974.
Free and Easy, Capitol, 1974.
No Way to Treat a Lady, Capitol, 1975.
Helen Reddy's Greatest Hits, Capitol, 1975.
Music, Music, Capitol, 1976.
Ear Candy, Capitol, 1977.
Pete's Dragon (soundtrack), Capitol, 1977.
We'll Sing in the Sunshine, Capitol, 1978.
Live in London, Capitol, 1978.
Take What You Find, Capitol, 1979.
Reddy, Capitol, 1980.
Play Me Out, MCA, 1981.
Imagination, MCA, 1983.
Lust for Life, Pair, 1986.
Feel So Young, Helen Reddy, Inc.

Sources

Books

Simon, George T., and others, *The Best of the Music Makers,* Doubleday, 1979.
Stambler, Irwin, *The Encyclopedia of Pop, Rock and Soul,* St. Martin's, 1989.

Periodicals

Detroit Free Press, May 23, 1991.
New York Sunday News, January 16, 1972.
People, June 29, 1981; March 21, 1983; May 16, 1983.
Stereo Review, October 1980; September 1981; June 1983.

—*Nancy Pear*

Zachary Richard

Accordionist, singer

Cajun accordionist and singer Zachary Richard commented in a 1990 A&M press biography that it is important for him "to express a depth of feeling that transcends the typical Cajun rave-up, bon temps, boogie-woogie, wanna dance?" And though he is proud of his family's 200 years in Louisiana and the 200 years his ancestors spent in Canada before they were exiled by the British in 1763, he considers himself a creator rather than an archivist. Louisiana and—since 1974—Canada and France serve more as the meeting places for the gumbo of musical styles that go into what Richard calls Cajun, or Swamp Rock.

Steeped in rock and roll and rhythm and blues, Richard played the harmonica while he was in college in New Orleans. He moved to New York City after graduating and was signed by Elektra Records to produce an album of his own country-rock tunes. Elektra soon merged with Warner Bros., though, and the record was never released. Richard used the money he received in the deal with the record company to buy a Gibson 335 guitar and a French accordion.

Returning to Louisiana, Richard resumed his intense practicing schedule: four hours on piano, two hours on guitar, and two hours on accordion every day. He learned to play the accordion by listening to recordings of Cajun greats Aldus Roger and Ira LeJeune as well as by his acquaintance with his one-time neighbor Clifton Chenier. It soon replaced the guitar as his primary instrument.

Gained Popularity in Canada

In 1974 Richard got together with Kenneth Richard and Michael Doucet, who would later go on to form the band Beausoleil. Calling themselves the Bayou Drifter Band, the three musicians combined the sounds of traditional Cajun instruments like the accordion and fiddle with rock and roll. Their music failed to win popularity with local audiences, but in Canada the band was an enormous success. As Barry Ancelet pointed out in *The Makers of Cajun Music,* Richard's choice to sing in french created "a viable market in Quebec, which, in the early 1970s, was gearing for a drive for independence."

Richard's earnest militancy in promoting awareness of the plight of the Cajun people, who were forced out of Canada by Great Britain, further alienated him from Louisiana audiences. At the Tribute to Cajun Music Festival in 1975, the band performed before a flag with a "green live oak on a field of bayou blue upon which was written 'Solidarité et Fierté' [Solidarity and Pride]. There was even a drop of blood somewhere on there,

For the Record. . .

Born September 8, 1950, in Lafayette, LA. *Education:* Tulane University, B.A., 1972.

Cajun singer and accordionist. Sang in Bishop's Boys Choir, c. 1957-63; played in Louisiana blues bands; signed by Elektra Records, 1972; with Michael Doucet and Kenneth Richard, formed Bayou Drifter Band; toured Canada and France, 1974; left band and released debut album, *Bayou des Mystères,* Kebec Disc, 1976; performed primarily in Canada until 1980; performed in U.S. clubs, early 1980s—.

Selected awards: Prix de la Jeune Chanson, France, 1980.

Addresses: *Record company*—A&M, 1416 North La Brea Ave., Hollywood, CA 90028.

for one reason or another," Richard recalled in *The Makers of Cajun Music.* "Everyone sitting in the bleachers looked at us and wondered why I was so angry."

Richard has traced his anger back to his experience as a rebellious student in 1968 and 1969 in New Orleans, but there may be a more personal reason for his feelings. According to Tom Moon in the *Philadelphia Inquirer,* Richard, who was raised by parents who no longer spoke French, was unaware of what it meant to be Cajun. "It was considered ignorant. The Cajun music had no credibility. It wasn't anything anybody was proud of."

Between Tradition and Innovation

Richard was part of the vanguard of young people in Louisiana in the late 1970s who sought to rediscover the heritage of Cajun music. In that light, the lyrics to his early song "Réveille!," set in the eighteenth century, served as a wake up call to his generation: "Awaken! The English are coming to burn the fields/ Awaken, men of Acadia, to save the village." But, in trying to bring Cajun music to the young, Richard added contemporary elements that alienated him from older Cajun traditionalists. Not yet completely accepted by newer Cajun music fans and not quite conservative enough for Cajun old-timers, Richard found his musical opportunities in the United States severely limited. He set out on his own in 1976 and played before Canadian audiences until 1980.

By the time he returned to Louisiana, it was not only hip to be Cajun, but the rest of the country was catching on

to Louisiana culture as well, from the dinner table to the dance floor. Musicians of all kinds were in demand. Richard was thus afforded the freedom to keep his eclectic mix of styles—not quite Cajun, not quite Zydeco, with a dash of New Orleans blues.

That mix has been reflected and influenced by the varied musicians that have backed Richard over the years, from his earlier work with traditional musicians to his work in the mid-1980s with trumpeter Warren Caesar, keyboardist Craig Lege, and drummer Dudley Fruge. He later added bassist Leon Medica and guitarist Marcus Elizondo. According to the *San Francisco Examiner,* Richard called his 1987 tour a "Mardi gras carnival," and "in keeping with the carnival mood, he and his four colleagues arrived on stage bedecked as birds, with headpieces, colorful satin 'body feather' strips, and so forth." The rest of the group's costume, reported the *San Francisco Chronicle,* "consisted of black tights, a gold, green and purple skirt and a lavish mask complete with veil."

Signed by Major Label

Richard's move from Rounder to A&M in 1991 signaled that he was once again on the verge of major recognition. But unlike his experience in New York City in 1972, this time he was assured that his records would be widely promoted and distributed. His 1991 album, *Women in the Room,* brought together well-known musicians: Brian Stoltz of the Neville Brothers band on guitar, Sonny Landreth from John Hiatt's Goners on slide, Joe Hammer on drums, and numerous other musicians, including Jimmy Buffet doing background vocals on "Who Stole My Monkey." Richard's powerful voice was characterized by Tom Moon in the *Miami Herald* as "a mixture of Van Morrison sass, Honky Cat-era Elton John and Sting that becomes more eloquent—even romantic—when he sings in Creole."

The make-up of Richard's band may keep changing, but throughout his career he has maintained the rhythmic elements at the heart of his music, never straying too far from traditional Cajun and Zydeco accordion riffs. He continued in this vein on his 1992 release, *Snake Bite Love.* Calling the album "pure country magic," Stewart Francke declared in the Detroit *Metro Times,* "*Snake Bite Love* evokes the Acadian pathos of Louisiana more precisely than any recording since Dr. John's *Gumbo.*" The reviewer also noted Richard's unique musical style on the album and concluded, "Naming the genre that Richard works in is ultimately unimportant; emotive transference this true should never be ignored."

Selected discography

Bayou des Mystères, Kebec Disc, 1976.
Migration, CBS Canada, 1977.
(Contributor) *The Big Easy* (soundtrack), Mango, 1987.
Zack's Bon Ton, Rounder, 1988.
Mardi Gras Mambo, Rounder, 1989.
Women in the Room, A&M, 1990.
Snake Bite Love, A&M, 1992.
Mardi Gras, Arzed Records.
Allons Danser, Arzed Records.
Live in Montreal, Arzed Records.
Vent D'Été, Kebec Disc.
Zack Attack, Arzed Records.
Looking Back, Arzed Records.
Zydeco Party.

Sources

Books

Ancelet, Barry Jean, *Cajun Music: Its Origins and Development,* Center for Louisiana Studies, 1989.

Ancelet, Barry Jean, *The Makers of Cajun Music,* University of Texas Press, 1984.
Broven, John, *South to Louisiana: The Music of the Cajun Bayous,* Pelican, 1987.

Periodicals

Billboard, August 18, 1990.
Metro Times (Detroit), December 1, 1992.
Miami Herald, May 10, 1987.
Philadelphia Inquirer, November 2, 1988.
Rolling Stone, December 13, 1990.
San Francisco Chronicle, January 29, 1988.
San Francisco Examiner, January 29, 1988.

Additional information for this profile was obtained from an A&M Records press biography, 1990.

—*John Morrow*

Marty Robbins

Singer, songwriter

V ersatile singer and songwriter Marty Robbins was one of the artists most successful at adding western flavor to his country hits. Over a recording career that lasted roughly thirty years, he scored smashes with such songs as "Singing the Blues," "El Paso," "Devil Woman," and "My Woman, My Woman, My Wife." Robbins also had hits in the rock and pop genres— including the classic "White Sport Coat"—in addition to recording Hawaiian, Caribbean, and gospel music. He won Grammys and several songwriting awards for his efforts and was a frequent performer at the Grand Ole Opry until his death in 1982.

Marty Robbins was born September 26, 1925, in Glendale, Arizona. His childhood was spent in a desert area where he received little exposure to music. Thus Robbins was particularly influenced by his father, who played the harmonica for Marty and his siblings, and his grandfather, Texas Bob Heckle, a traveling medicine man who told stories and sang songs about cowboys. Irwin Stambler and Grelun Landon quoted Robbins on the subject of his grandfather in their book *The Encyclopedia of Folk, Country, and Western Music:* "A lot of the songs I've written . . . were brought about because of stories he told me. Like 'Big Iron' I wrote because he was a Texas Ranger. At least he told me he was." Robbins also enjoyed going to see western movies as a child, and he idolized singing cowboy star Gene Autry.

Learned Guitar During Navy Off-Hours

It wasn't until he enlisted in the Navy at the age of 19 that Robbins began to actively pursue his ambition to follow in Autry's footsteps. While off duty, he learned to play the guitar and quickly began writing songs for the instrument. At the end of his three-year hitch, Robbins returned to Phoenix, Arizona, where his family had moved when he was twelve. A friend asked Robbins to play with his group, and, though he gratefully accepted, he soon realized he was able to sing and decided to form his own band. Robbins and the K-Bar Cowboys performed in Phoenix-area clubs, eventually landing a job on a local radio show. It wasn't long before the station's television affiliate recruited Robbins to host his own musical variety show, *Western Caravan.*

Though *Western Caravan* was a local television program, it was important enough to attract guests like country star Little Jimmy Dickens, who noticed Robbins's talent. Dickens suggested that Columbia, his own rec-

Born Martin David Robinson, September 26, 1925, in Glendale, AZ; died of a heart attack, December 8, 1982, in Nashville, TN; son of Jack Joe and Emma (Heckler) Robinson; married Marizona Baldwin, 1945; children: Ronnie (son), Janet.

Singer, songwriter, and guitarist. With K-Bar Cowboys, played in small clubs and on radio shows, AZ, late 1940s; host of local television show *Western Caravan,* c. 1950; solo recording artist and concert performer, 1952-82. Film appearances include *Buffalo Gun,* 1962; *Ballad of a Gunfighter,* 1963; *Honkytonk Man,* 1982; *The Gun and the Gavel; The Badge of Marshal Brennan;* and *Guns of a Stranger;* star of syndicated television show *Marty Robbins's Spotlight,* 1977. Raced stock cars on the National Association for Stock Car Auto Racing (NASCAR) circuit, 1960s and 1970s. Author of *Small Man* (novel), 1966. *Military service:* U.S. Navy, 1944-48.

Selected awards: Grammy awards for best country and western recording, 1960, for "El Paso," and for best country song, 1970, for "My Woman, My Woman, My Wife"; voted Man of the Decade, 1970, Academy of Country Music; NASCAR Rookie of the Southern 500, 1972; inducted into Nashville Songwriters Association Hall of Fame, 1975; Gold Trustees Award, National Country Hall of Fame, 1979; inducted into Country Music Hall of Fame, 1982.

ord label, audition the young musician. The company sent one of its executives to hear Robbins perform, and he was signed as a Columbia act in 1951. Robbins didn't create much of a stir with his first two singles, but Columbia had faith in their new discovery and continued to release his efforts. Finally Robbins began climbing the country charts with "I'll Go It Alone" and "I Couldn't Keep From Crying." Because these hits were Robbins's own compositions, he attracted the attention of Acuff-Rose Music Publishing, who signed him to a songwriting contract. Promoters for the Grand Ole Opry had also noticed Robbins, and by 1953 he had become a regular performer on its stage.

Island music was a favorite of Robbins's, and in 1953 he recorded the first of what would prove to be many Hawaiian and Caribbean songs. *Country Music's* Rich Kienzle described him as "a peerless Hawaiian-style vocalist, able to handle even falsetto singing." Robbins went on to record two complete albums of Hawaiian music—*Song of the Islands,* released in 1957, and the 1963 release *Hawaii's Calling Me.*

Hit Number One on the Country Charts

Robbins scored his first Number One country hit in 1956 with "Singing the Blues." The following year, however, he became famous with pop fans nationwide when he released the smash "White Sport Coat." Another of his own compositions, Robbins recorded the hit in New York with producer Mitch Miller and arranger Ray Conniff during the first of several sessions he had with the pair over the course of two years. He followed up this success with the singles "She Was Only Seventeen" and "Stairway of Love," but it was not until 1959 that Robbins gave audiences his best-remembered, trademark hit, "El Paso." One of Robbins's many story songs, "El Paso" concerns a young man who shoots another man over a Mexican dancing girl. He flees, but is unable to stay away from the dancer and returns, only to be shot by a posse and die in the woman's arms. "El Paso" not only garnered Robbins his first Grammy Award, but received the first Grammy ever awarded in the country and western category.

The western storytelling tunes and bluesy country love songs continued to do well for Robbins during the 1960s. He had hits with "Big Iron" in 1960, "Don't Worry" in 1961, the melodious "Devil Woman" in 1962, and "The Cowboy in the Continental Suit" in 1964. In a testament to Robbins's ability to write, sing, and play, Fred Dellar and Roy Thompson, in their book *The Illustrated Encyclopedia of Country Music,* deemed Robbins "a first-rate songwriter," allowing, "his musical versatility is astonishing." Robbins also had smashes with other writers' efforts, including "Ruby Ann," "Ribbon of Darkness," and "Tonight, Carmen."

In addition to music, the multitalented Robbins also extended his versatility into the acting realm. He proved a competent performer in that arena as well, appearing in several westerns, including *Buffalo Gun*—his first film, released in 1962—*Ballad of a Gunfighter,* and *The Gun and the Gavel.* His last film appearance was a cameo role in the 1982 film *Honkytonk Man,* starring Clint Eastwood.

Kept up Pace, Despite Heart Trouble

In the late 1960s Robbins suffered a massive heart attack, and underwent bypass surgery in 1970—according to some reports he was only the fifteenth patient ever to have the operation. He recovered quickly, though, and later that year came back with his second Grammy-winning single, the love ballad "My Woman, My Woman, My Wife." He even managed to tour extensively during the 1970s, performing in England, Australia, and Japan.

Robbins had many interests, including cattle ranching and, as owner of several record labels and a movie production company, the business side of the music and film industries. His favorite, however, was stock car racing, which he took up in the 1960s. Robbins refused to let his heart trouble keep him from pursuing his hobby, and by 1972 he was competing professionally in National Association for Stock Car Auto Racing (NASCAR) races against well-known race drivers. He did so well, in fact, that he was named Rookie of the Southern 500 by NASCAR that same year. In 1974, however, Robbins was involved in three bad racing accidents—reportedly in one of them, he deliberately drove into a wall in order to avoid broadsiding another driver—and he decided to rededicate himself to the music business.

Robbins released another successful single in 1976 with "El Paso City," a kind of sequel to "El Paso." Although "El Paso City" was Robbins's last real hit, he continued to be an active recording artist and performed at the Grand Ole Opry almost until his death from another massive heart attack on December 8, 1982.

Selected discography

Singles; on Columbia Records

"That's All Right," 1955.
"Singing the Blues," 1956.
"White Sport Coat," 1957.
"She Was Only Seventeen," 1958.
"Stairway of Love," 1958.
"El Paso," 1959.
"Big Iron," 1960.
"Don't Worry," 1961.
"Devil Woman," 1962.
"Ruby Ann," 1962.
"Begging to You," 1963.
"Ribbon of Darkness," 1965.
"Tonight, Carmen," 1967.
"My Woman, My Woman, My Wife," 1970.
"El Paso City," 1976.

Albums; on Columbia Records, except where noted

Singing the Blues, 1956.
The Song of Robbins, 1957.
Song of the Islands, 1958.
Marty's Greatest Hits, 1958.

Marty Robbins, 1958.
Gunfighter Ballads and Trail Songs, 1959.
More Gunfighter Ballads and Trail Songs, 1960.
More Greatest Hits, 1961.
Just a Little Sentimental, 1961.
Portrait of Marty, 1962.
Devil Woman, 1962.
Hawaii's Calling Me, 1963.
Return of the Gunfighter, 1963.
Island Woman, 1964.
R.F.D., 1964.
Turn the Lights Down Low, 1965.
What God Has Done, 1966.
The Drifter, 1966.
My Kind of Country, 1967.
Tonight, Carmen, 1967.
It's a Sin, 1969.
Marty's Country, 1969.
My Woman, My Woman, My Wife, 1970.
Greatest Hits, Volume 3, 1971.
Marty Robbins Today, 1971.
The World of Marty Robbins, 1971.
All Time Greatest Hits, 1972.
Bound for Old Mexico, 1972.
El Paso City, 1976.
American Originals (recorded 1976-1982), 1990.
Best of Marty Robbins, Curb/CEMA, 1991.
The Essential Marty Robbins 1951-1982, 1991.
Border Town Affair, Embassy.
Encore, CBS.
Good 'n' Country, MCA.
A Lifetime of Song (recorded 1951-1982).
The Marty Robbins Collection, Hallmark.
Marty Robbins/Johnny Horton, K-tel.
Two Gun Daddy, MCA.

Also recorded *Adios Amigo, Alamo, The Bend in the River, Biggest Hits, By the Time I Get to Phoenix, Christmas With Marty Robbins, Come Back to Me, El Paso, From the Heart, Greatest Hits, Volume 4, Gunfighter Ballads/My Woman, My Woman, My Wife, Have I Told You Lately That I Love You, Heart of Marty Robbins, I've Got a Woman's Love, I Walk Alone, Marty After Midnight, No Signs of Loneliness Here, Saddle Tramp, Some Memories Just Won't Die, The Story of My Life,* and *Streets of Laredo,* all on Columbia.

Sources

Books

The Annual Obituary 1982, St. Martin's, 1983.
Dellar, Fred, and Roy Thompson, *The Illustrated Encyclopedia of Country Music*, Harmony Books, 1977.
Stambler, Irwin, and Grelun Landon, *The Encyclopedia of Folk, Country, and Western Music*, St. Martin's, 1984.

Periodicals

Country Music, January/February 1986; September/October 1986; May/June 1990; July/August 1990; November/December 1991; January/February 1992.

Los Angeles Times, December 27, 1991.

Newsweek, December 20, 1982.

People, December 9, 1991.

Pulse!, February 1992.

Washington Post, May 29, 1992.

—Elizabeth Wenning

Richard Rodgers

Composer, songwriter

M any observers agree that Richard Rodgers did not merely write Broadway musicals—he created the Broadway musical. Working first with Lorenz Hart and then with Oscar Hammerstein, he left two legacies: Rodgers and Hart wrote clever, witty, and sometimes cynical musical comedies; Rodgers and Hammerstein wrote serious and heartwarming musical dramas. The two pairs transformed the American musical from a light, cliche-ridden play with songs to a tightly knit, completely integrated theatrical/musical work.

Rodgers's life was focused on music and theater from a very early age. His mother, an amateur pianist, and father, a doctor with a lovely baritone voice, would sing selections together from current musicals as evening entertainment. Rodgers began picking these tunes out on the piano by ear when he was four year old. He took piano lessons long enough to learn the basics of piano technique and reading music but eventually quit because he much preferred improvising tunes over scales and exercises. Rodgers also loved to go to the theater; he would see the same show many times just to study how it worked. He was particularly impressed with the efforts of Broadway composer Jerome Kern who, with his partners Guy Bolton and P. G. Wodehouse, was the first composer to reject the mythological and historical subjects of European operettas in favor of more intimate, realistic American settings.

Found Partner and Friend in Hart

As a teenager, Rodgers, with the encouragement of his family, began writing music in earnest. In 1916 he copyrighted his first song, "The Auto Show Girl." The following year he wrote his first musical score, *One Minute Please,* for an Akron Club fund-raiser at the Hotel Plaza. Throughout high school he wrote songs with many partners; friends and family contributed lyrics—often of poor quality—for his earliest songs. The composer needed a lyricist. While Rodgers was a freshman at New York City's Columbia University, a friend introduced him to Lorenz Hart, a poet in search of a composer. They talked for hours during their first meeting at Hart's home. The writer taught the composer much about the structure and purpose of lyrics. Rodgers, in turn, impressed Hart as a serious composer. They quickly became partners and friends. Their first collaboration was Columbia's varsity show that year; at age 17, Rodgers was the youngest person ever to write for the show.

Hart also grew up with a great interest in theater; he saw his first play at age seven and was especially devoted to the works of Shakespeare. He never doubted that he wanted to pursue language as a profession. At Colum-

211

For the Record. . .

Born Richard Charles Rodgers, June 28, 1902, in Hammels Station, NY; died December 30, 1972, in New York City; son of William (a physician) and Mamie Rodgers; married Dorothy Feiner, 1930; children: Mary, Linda. *Education:* Attended Columbia University, 1919-21; attended Institute of Musical Arts (now the Juilliard School), 1921-23.

Copyrighted first song, "The Auto Show Girl," 1916; composed first musical score, *One Minute Please,* 1917. With Lorenz Hart, composed score for first amateur show, *Fly With Me,* 1919; composed score for first professional show, *Garrick Gaieties,* 1925; Broadway shows include *Dearest Enemy,* 1925, *Peggy-Ann,* 1926, *A Connecticut Yankee in King Arthur's Court,* 1927, *Babes in Arms,* 1937, and *Pal Joey,* 1940. With Oscar Hammerstein, composed Broadway show *Oklahoma!,* 1943; other shows include *Carousel,* 1945, *South Pacific,* 1949, *The King and I,* 1951, *Flower Drum Song,* 1958, and *The Sound of Music,* 1959; shows for television include *Cinderella,* 1952. Author of autobiography *Musical Stages,* Random House, 1975.

Selected awards: Special Pulitzer Prize for Drama, 1944, for *Oklahoma!;* New York Drama Critics Circle Award for best musical, 1944, for *Carousel;* Academy Award for best song, 1945, for "It Might as Well Be Spring" (from *State Fair);* New York Drama Critics Circle Award for best musical, 1949, for *South Pacific;* Tony Awards for best musical, best book, and best score, 1949, for *South Pacific;* Pulitzer Prize in Drama, 1950, for *South Pacific;* New York Drama Critics Circle Award for best musical, 1951, for *Pal Joey;* Tony Awards for best musical and best score, 1951, for *The King and I;* Academy Award for best score, 1955, for *Oklahoma!;* Academy Award for best score, 1956, for *The King and I;* Tony Awards for best musical, best book, and best score, 1959, for *The Sound of Music.*

bia he amused himself and his classmates by writing witty verses and passing them around. During his second year there he entered the school of journalism but did not stay long. When Hart met Rodgers, he was supporting himself by translating German plays for the Schubert brothers, famous theatrical producers.

Their partnership did not catapult Rodgers and Hart to instant fame. They wrote songs for scores of amateur productions but had little luck in the professional world. Several of their songs were used in shows produced by comedian Lew Fields, but when they offered their songs

to publishers, they were rejected. In 1921 Hart returned to translating for the Schubert brothers, and Rodgers entered the Institute of Musical Arts—later renamed the Juilliard School—for classical musical training. For two years they continued their attempts to find professional work; they landed their first job the very day Rodgers was ready to give up.

Almost Took Sales Job

At age 23 Rodgers had yet to hold a full-time job. He decided it was time to get one and settle down. A children's clothing manufacturer offered him a sales and management-trainee position at fifty dollars a week; he told the man he would let him know the next day if he would take the position. By the next morning he had decided to take the job, but before he had a chance to let the manufacturer know, he received a phone call from his friend Ben Kaye, who wanted to hire him to write the music for a show. He agreed—on the condition that Hart be hired to write the lyrics. *Garrick Gaieties* opened in 1925, effectively launching the partnership of Rodgers and Hart.

Rodgers and Hart also collaborated with a third partner, Herbert Fields, who wrote the books for their early shows. Together, the trio wrote shows that not only thrilled their audiences but also began to change the shape of the Broadway musical. Instead of the trite boy-meets-girl story, they sometimes chose unusual subjects, such as the historical tale that formed the basis of 1925's *Dearest Enemy,* set during the Revolutionary War; Freudian dream-fantasies were the subject of the following year's *Peggy-Ann.* With that show, Rodgers and Hart began to diverge from the established structure of musical comedy, in this case abandoning the typical opening chorus number. In other shows, like 1928's *Chee-Chee* and *Present Arms,* they explored the integration of songs into the plot and added transitional music to strengthen the cohesion of the action.

In 1930 Rodgers and Hart moved to Hollywood to write songs for the film industry, but the pair did not take to Tinsel Town and returned to New York City in 1934. Their subsequent efforts further altered the musical comedy. The story of *On Your Toes* revolved around the world of classical ballet and was the first musical to incorporate ballet into dance sections; "Slaughter on Tenth Avenue," the big hit from that show, was Rodgers's first extensive orchestral piece. Frequently, songs in musicals were only loosely connected to the story, but Rodgers and Hart were determined that their songs center on plot situations and be completely integrated into the action. With 1937's *Babes in Arms* they produced a show in which every song advanced the story.

Several of their best-known songs, all remarkably distinct, were written for this show, including the lyrical ballad "My Funny Valentine," the sophisticated "The Lady Is a Tramp," and the funny and rhythmic "Johnny One Note." One of their last collaborations, *Pal Joey,* was also one of their best. Again, they picked an unusual subject, the seamy side of life; the main character was an unsavory fellow whose existence was filled with illicit love affairs, opportunism, and blackmail. *Pal Joey's* "Bewitched, Bothered, and Bewildered" is one of Rodgers and Hart's most famous songs.

After their final show, *By Jupiter,* Hart, an alcoholic, sought rest and recuperation in Mexico. On his return he worked for a while on the revival of the earlier Rodgers and Hart hit *A Connecticut Yankee in King Arthur's Court.* Hart died shortly thereafter. In the 25 years of their collaboration, Rodgers and Hart wrote 27 musicals, becoming one of the most productive and prolific creative teams in the history of musical theater. Many of their songs were hits in their day but have also endured over half a century later. In addition to the aforementioned classics, Rodgers and Hart brought the world such standards as "Where's the Rainbow," "Thou Swell," "My Heart Stood Still," "There's a Small Hotel," "I Wish I Were in Love Again," and "This Can't Be Love." In 1948 Hollywood immortalized their partnership with the biographical film *Words and Music.*

Enter Hammerstein

When Hart left for Mexico, Rodgers sought another lyricist. He chose Oscar Hammerstein II. Hammerstein grew up in a theatrical family. Although like Hart he had a desire to write for the theater, he was forbidden by his parents to consider a theatrical career. His grandfather and namesake, an opera impresario, so soured his father, a vaudeville theater manager, on opera and theater, that his parents forced young Oscar to study law instead of theater. Although he was fascinated by literature and plays all of his life, he did enter Columbia in pre-law and then attended Columbia University Law School. He also wrote for and acted in every varsity show Columbia produced while he studied there. Shortly after his father died, during his second year of law school, Hammerstein quit his studies to work for his uncle Arthur Hammerstein, a successful Broadway producer. He spent the next few years working his way up from office boy to stage manager, learning the business of the theater.

In 1918 Hammerstein wrote his first full-length stage work, a play called *The Light.* It flopped, but it did encourage him to concentrate on musicals. His first

such work, *Always You,* with music by Herbert Stothart, appeared on Broadway in 1920. Although the lyrics were good, the libretto was weak, so his uncle suggested he team up with a librettist. His next show, *Tickle Me,* a collaboration with Otto Harbach, Frank Mendel, and Stothart was a success. During the 1920s Hammerstein continued to collaborate with Harbach, and together they produced a string of hits, including 1923's *Wildflower,* with music by Vincent Youmans; 1924's *Rose-Marie,* with music by Rudolf Friml; and 1925's *Song of the Flame,* music by George Gershwin, and *The Desert Song,* music by Sigmund Romberg. All of these followed the European operetta formula: serious, often unrealistic stories set in far-away places—a marked contrast to the light comedies of Rodgers and Hart. With his next undertaking, 1927's *Show Boat,* Hammerstein and his partner Jerome Kern broke new ground in musical theater by producing what has since become recognized as the first modern American musical play: a serious story with an American locale, believable characters, and songs that fit the action of the plot. Hammerstein wrote both the lyrics and libretto for this show and many subsequent ones.

In the 1930s Hammerstein went to Hollywood. While audiences loved the film adaptations of his stage shows, the original musicals he wrote for the screen with composer Sigmund Romberg failed miserably, so he returned to New York. Offsetting Hammerstein's many disappointments of the decade was his successful 1932 collaboration with Kern, *Music in the Air.*

Oklahoma!

In 1942, with Hart out of the picture, Richard Rodgers chose Hammerstein to help him turn Lynn Riggs's play *Green Grow the Lilacs* into a musical. The two brought in renowned classical dancer and choreographer Agnes de Mille to join the project. All three agreed from the outset to produce a fully integrated musical play in which every song and dance would have a dramatic purpose. They practically had to beg to find backers for the project. The reviews of the pre-Broadway run of the show were good but not great, and advanced sales were small. Nonetheless, *Oklahoma!* became the biggest hit in the history of musical theater. The songs "Oh What a Beautiful Morning," "I'm Just a Girl Who Can't Say No," and "People Will Say We're in Love," among others from the show, quickly became favorites with the public and critics. *Oklahoma!'s* choreography stunned audiences; although ballet had been introduced to Broadway in earlier shows, de Mille's unique mastery of the art and Rodgers's musical foundation made it standard fare.

The partnership of Rodgers and Hammerstein became official after the death of Lorenz Hart, in 1943. They continued to develop the genre, incorporating music, songs, dance, and comedy into the action of the drama, producing classic after classic of the American theater, including *Carousel,* in 1945, *South Pacific,* in 1949, *The King and I,* in 1951, and *The Sound of Music,* in 1959.

Richard Rodgers could not have selected two more different partners if he had made a concerted effort to do so. Hart, a man of excessive habits who was often professionally unreliable, wrote clever, witty, and sometimes cynical lyrics; one of Rodgers and Hart's most celebrated love songs, "My Funny Valentine" actually extols the imperfections of the loved one. "Bewitched, Bothered, and Bewildered" is more about sex than love and is almost always watered down in modern performance. And perhaps Hart's most (blackly) humorous lyrics are those of "To Keep My Love Alive," a first-person "how-to" about a woman who maintains her ardor by killing her husbands. Oscar Hammerstein, on the other hand, kept regular habits and was a rock of professional dependability. With creative roots in the European operetta, his lyrics were romantic and heartwarming, his love songs sincere and straightforward, as in the charming waltz "Ten Minutes Ago," from *Cinderella.* Hammerstein's humor was without malice, as was evinced in "The Lonely Goatherd," from the *Sound of Music.* Though he could be bitter if the situation called for it, his intent was always instructive, as in "You Have to Be Taught to Hate," from *South Pacific.*

What Hart and Hammerstein had in common was a gift for capturing in rhythm and rhyme the spirit of the stories they helped create. Rodgers's brilliance was in his ability to adapt his music to the personalities of both lyricists; he not only provided the perfect foil for his partners' lyrics but composed beautiful melodies that stand easily on their own. Perhaps this is the true genius of Rodgers and Hart and Rodgers and Hammerstein: The lyrics alone are poetry, and the music is memorable without the words. But the two combined, along with the innovations pioneered by Rodgers and his partners, are what forged the essence of modern musical theater.

Selected discography

Pal Joey, Capitol, 1957.

Flower Drum Song, MCA, 1961.
Me and Juliet, RCA Victor, 1964.
Pipe Dream, RCA Victor, 1965.
Cinderella, Columbia, 1965.
The Rodgers and Hart Songbook, Verve, 1977.
The King and I, MCA, 1980.
The Musical World of Richard Rodgers, Columbia, 1980.
The Rodgers and Hart Album, RCA, 1981.
On Your Toes, Polydor, 1983.
More Rodgers and Hart, RCA Red Seal, 1983.
The Rodgers and Hart CD, RCA Red Seal, 1986.
The Sounds of Music, Telarc, 1988.
South Pacific, CBS, 1988.
Babes in Arms, New Word, 1990.
Carousel, MCA, 1990.
Oklahoma!, MCA Classics, 1990.

Sources

Books

Ewen, David, *Richard Rodgers,* Holt, 1957.
Green, Stanley, *The Rodgers and Hammerstein Story,* Da Capo, 1980.
Harriman, Margaret Case, *Take Them Up Tenderly,* Knopf, 1944.
Hart, Lorenz, *The Complete Lyrics of Lorenz Hart,* Knopf, 1986.
Marx, Samuel, *Rodgers & Hart: Bewitched, Bothered and Bedeviled,* Putnam, 1976.
Nolan, Frederick, *The Sound of Their Music: The Story of Rodgers and Hammerstein,* Walker, 1978.
The Rodgers and Hart Fact Book, edited by Stanley Green, Lynn Farnol Group, 1980.
Rodgers, Richard, *Musical Stages: An Autobiography,* Random House, 1975.
Taylor, Deems, *Some Enchanted Evenings: The Story of Rodgers and Hammerstein,* Harper, 1953.

Periodicals

American Heritage, September/October 1990.
Connoisseur, July 1989.
Life, Fall 1990.

—*Robin Armstrong*

Roy Rogers

Singer, film and television star

The great wellspring of American mythology suggested by the figure of the cowboy may have reached its high watermark with Roy Rogers. Singing cowboy films emanated rapidly from Hollywood between the mid-1930s and mid-1950s, and Roy Rogers was one of the most renowned of the performers that appeared in them. He inherited from Gene Autry the title of "King of the Cowboys" and kept it for what in Hollywood's terms qualifies as eons.

Rogers made 91 films in all, went on to a successful television career after that, and released dozens of 78 rpm and LP recordings. In late 1991, at the age of 79, he ascended the country sales charts with a new album pairing him in duets with leading contemporary singers in the country genre. He achieved worldwide fame— *Collier's* reported in 1948 that he had edged out Bing Crosby as England's biggest box-office draw—and inspired the creation of thousands of fan clubs, whose members took to the Rogers legend wholeheartedly and churned out an unprecedented volume of fan mail.

It was not simply good looks and Hollywood promotion that generated and sustained Rogers's popularity. His own musical activities helped to launch his film career: he founded the Sons of the Pioneers, the greatest of the Western musical acts that flourished along with the cowboy movie craze, and his energy kept the group together when its other members were ready to throw in the towel. Rogers's musical accomplishments marked the beginning of a spectacular success story. But they took shape in the midst of a serious Depression-era struggle of the kind faced by so many Americans.

Restless Family

Rogers was born Leonard Franklin Slye on November 5, 1911, in Cincinnati, Ohio. His father, Andrew, worked in a shoe factory, and the family lived in a tenement near where the Cincinnati Reds' Riverfront Stadium now stands. The Slye family, like many others in industrializing America, was restless, torn between farm life and steady but demoralizing urban wage-earning. They traveled up the Ohio River in a homemade houseboat when young Leonard was a year old, spent several years in the city of Portsmouth, and ended up on a farm in Duck Run, Ohio, 12 miles back in the hills. Andrew Slye continued to work in Portsmouth, and at times would go two weeks without returning home.

Both parents and all three of Leonard's sisters were musical—his father had entertained professionally on a river steamer for a time—and before his voice changed Leonard began to participate fully in the musical life of a

For the Record. . .

Born Leonard Franklin Slye, November 5, 1911, in Cincinnati, OH; married Arlene Wilkins, 1936 (died, 1946); married Dale Evans, 1947; children: Roy, Jr., Robin Elizabeth (deceased), John (deceased), Cheryl, Linda Lou, Marion, Scottish Ward, Mary, Little Doe, Deborah Lee (deceased).

Recording artist, television performer, and star of 91 films. Founded western musical group the Sons of the Pioneers, 1930s; hired as singing-cowboy replacement for Gene Autry, 1936; first starring role, *Under Western Stars*, 1938; other films included *Billy the Kid Returns*, 1938, *Red River Valley*, 1941, *Sons of the Pioneers*, 1942, *King of the Cowboys*, 1943, *The Cowboy and the Senorita*, 1944, *Hollywood Canteen*, 1944, and *Melody Time*, 1948; recorded for Decca Records, late 1930s and 1940s; became top-grossing western star in Hollywood, 1943; starred in various network television series, 1951-65; recorded for Capitol and RCA Records, 1960s and 1970s; recorded *Tribute* album of duets, RCA, 1991.

Selected awards: Inducted into the Country Music Hall of Fame, 1988; member of the Cowboy Hall of Fame; National Film Society's Humanitarian Award; Kiwanis Decency Award.

Addresses: *Record company*—RCA/BMG Music, One Music Circle N., Nashville, TN 37203-4310.

rural community where most music had to be self-made. He played the guitar and mandolin, sang in a church choir, and called square dances. On the farm he learned to handle a horse, but to ride one at full tilt was a skill he acquired only in Hollywood. Much of his time was spent on farm chores; in school he recalled being "pretty good at sports, not bad at the clarinet, okay with my studies, and a galloping failure with the girls." When Leonard was 17, the family moved back to Cincinnati. Leonard joined his father at the shoe factory and dropped out of high school shortly thereafter.

When the chance came to escape hard times and dead-end work by joining a relative in California, nobody in the family needed much persuading. In the spring of 1930 the Slyes embarked on the voyage made by many other American families. But at the end of the rainbow lay no pot of gold, only long months of driving a gravel truck for Leonard and migratory fruit picking for the whole clan. When the former gravel truck driver later read *The Grapes of Wrath*, John Steinbeck's classic tale of Dust Bowl migrants, his comment was this: "There are parts in that book that made me wonder

if maybe Mr. Steinbeck wasn't looking over the shoulders of the Slye family."

Breaking Into Western Music

Leonard Slye was known among the migrant families he encountered as a fine impromptu guitarist, singer, and square dance caller. Soon he teamed with a cousin; the pair billed themselves as the Slye Brothers and began to play for parties and dances, earning what they could by passing the hat. Probably they believed that at the height of the Depression, music offered as reasonable a chance at a decent living as any other work did. The duo was short-lived, but soon Leonard, goaded on by his sister Mary, entered a talent contest presented on a small radio station in Inglewood, California. He did not win, but he did attract the attention of the promoter of a western music group, the Rocky Mountaineers, and was invited to join the group. This act was not especially successful, either—the performer later recalled that in the rainy spring its members would tour the canyons above Los Angeles, hoping to come upon cars stuck in the mud and be generously tipped for helping to push them out. But the group attracted two prolific and original songwriters, Bob Nolan and Tim Spencer, and the nucleus of what would become the Sons of the Pioneers was formed.

Before that group's debut, though, Leonard embarked in 1933 on an ill-planned tour of the Southwest with the O-Bar-O Cowboys, a group that also included Tim Spencer. This group, subsisting at times on a diet of rabbit and hawk that they procured with a borrowed rifle, turned to a time-honored trick among destitute radio performers: mentioning food on the air in the hope that a musically impressed and kindhearted listener might take the hint. During an otherwise unprofitable radio appearance in Roswell, New Mexico, Leonard fulfilled a request for the "Swiss Yodel" in exchange for a lemon pie from a girl named Arlene Wilkins. The two were married in 1936; the singer has said it was "love at first sight."

The O-Bar-O Cowboys sputtered to their demise in Lubbock, Texas, "so broke," Rogers later said, "we couldn't pay attention." Back in Hollywood, he worked briefly with another radio western outfit, the Texas Outlaws. But he continued to dream of breaking through to stardom. Sensing the talents of Nolan and Spencer, he persuaded them to give up their day jobs and join him in serious rehearsals for an act to be called the Pioneer Trio. The name was changed to the Sons of the Pioneers after a radio announcer botched an introduction. Historian Douglas Green (leader of the present-day Sons of the Pioneers imitators Riders in the Sky) called Rogers the group's "sparkplug."

His part in creating the Sons of the Pioneers remains Rogers greatest purely musical accomplishment. With the addition to the group of two swing-playing Texas brothers, Hugh and Karl Farr, the Sons of the Pioneers offered a combination of beautifully wrought, poetic lyrics (Nolan was a serious student of the classics of English poetry), perfect trio and quartet harmonies, Rogers's yodeling, and crack instrumental playing that set the standard for western music for years to come. The group, with various changes in personnel (Rogers left when he achieved film stardom), endured for more than half a century, and such pieces as "Tumbling Tumbleweeds" remain country classics.

Into the Movies

By 1935 the group was working steadily and often provided background music for western films. This work led to a series of bit parts for Rogers, who billed himself as Dick Weston for a time. The following year, Gene Autry became embroiled in a contract dispute with Republic Pictures, and Rogers, through a chance encounter in a hat shop, learned that Republic was auditioning replacements. He rushed to the scene, sneaked into the building, and became the studio's new singing cowboy. His first starring role came in the 1938 film *Under Western Stars.* Studio executives gave Leonard Slye the name Roy Rogers, Rogers after the recently deceased humorist Will Rogers, and Roy for its alliterative quality. Rogers adopted his new name legally in 1942. The following year Rogers, by the luck of the lottery, escaped the military draft that claimed Autry and became the top-grossing cowboy star in Hollywood—the "King of the Cowboys."

Studio publicity executives changed more of Rogers's life than just his name. *Life* wrote of Rogers in 1943 that he "is playing a part not only during the hours he spends before the camera. He is under compulsion to play it almost 24 hours a day." Rogers took naturally to his good-guy role. *Collier's* reported that "there never are weeks in which some sobbing mother or pleading doctor doesn't call Roy to come and see a desperately ill or dying child." Rogers did his best to respond to such entreaties, and always set aside space for handicapped children at his personal appearances.

At the height of his career in the mid-1940s, Rogers was the object of unparalleled adulation among young people. Two thousand fan clubs were in operation in the United States, with more overseas. Western films have always attracted male audiences, but Rogers had

many female followers as well; one fan magazine caused a momentary sensation when it queried its readers as to whether Rogers should break with cowboy-movie tradition and kiss his leading lady in his next screen outing. Traditionalists prevailed.

Rogers never gave the girl an onscreen kiss, but would often kiss his horse, Trigger, who, like Rogers, received great volumes of fan mail. The horse, purchased by Rogers himself from a rental stable near Los Angeles, eventually acquired a repertoire of more than 50 tricks, including doing simple arithmetic and signing an "X"

Artificial as the singing-cowboy genre might have been, Rogers seemed believable as a cowboy and often took on an almost personal presence in the lives of his fans.

---

with a pencil. "The World's Smartest Horse" was featured prominently at Rogers's many stage shows and personal appearances, which included an annual visit to the giant World's Championship Rodeo at Madison Square Garden in New York.

Artificial as the singing-cowboy genre might have been, Rogers seemed believable as a cowboy and often took on an almost personal presence in the lives of his fans. One reason for this kind of identification was that Rogers usually appeared on film "as himself"—as a character named Roy Rogers. In a 1992 interview with *Country Music* magazine, Rogers pointed to this scriptwriting innovation as a contributor to his success: "Other actors played different characters, but I didn't. It put my name before the public with the whole picture, in the form of a story." In 1945 the *New York Times* reported that the volume of fan mail Rogers received had eclipsed all previous records. He has since traded on his good name and image by endorsing a large variety of commercial products and in recent years lending his name to a chain fast-food venture of which he is part-owner.

Rogers's films, like Autry's, were called B-Westerns—they were quickly turned out, relied on formulas, and were aimed at the vast audience that went to the movies weekly (or more often) and wanted simple new installments of its heroes' adventures on a regular basis, much as television audiences do today. Rogers made 87 films for Republic Pictures between 1938 and 1951. In most of them, his rescue of a ranch family or small town would conclude neatly at sunset, and Rogers and Trigger would ride away into that sunset.

At various plot junctures a song might be featured, with Rogers accompanying himself on the guitar while muted strings hummed in the background. Songs along the trail were addressed to Trigger or to longtime sidekick Gabby Hayes. Most of the songs were contributed by composers employed by the film studios, but Rogers wrote some songs himself and his films continued to employ the talents of the Sons of the Pioneers. Sometimes, Rogers told *Country Music,* the music generated the movie: "We'd take a song like 'Don't Fence Me In' and write a story around it. That way, we'd get a lot of good publicity from the song and from the people who recorded the song."

Remarriage and Personal Tragedy

The music always included a serenade directed at Rogers's leading lady. From 1944 on, Rogers was paired with Dale Evans, whom he married in 1947 after the sudden death of his first wife. (It was Evans who composed "Happy Trails," the tune with which Rogers is most closely associated. She wrote the song in 20 minutes as a theme song for a television program the pair inaugurated in 1951.) They have been professionally as well as personally teamed ever since. But tragedy continued to wind its dark counterpoint around Rogers's success story. The only child born to Rogers and Evans, named Robin Elizabeth, died a victim of mongolism in 1953, and two children they adopted later died in freak accidents. Rogers and Evans sought solace in their Christian faith, and have gained some prominence as inspirational writers and lecturers.

In Rogers's heyday, his recording career was always less important than his movie work. "Recording was my second or third priority," he told Deborah Fruin of *Country Fever.* "Back in those days I was making seven or eight pictures a year. When I got a day off I'd do a personal appearance somewhere, Madison Square Garden or a state fair." For a time, too, the best new musical material that Republic acquired was offered to Autry, a practice that caused some friction between the two men. Nevertheless, *Newsweek* reported in 1943 that Rogers's 78 rpm singles on Decca Records were

selling at the rate of 6,000 per week. His recordings alternated cowboy-movie fare with Texas-style vocal swing; he once offered a fine reading of Bob Wills's "Time Changes Everything." But Hollywood strings were heard more often in his music than Texas fiddles.

Rogers had carefully negotiated with Republic for the rights to his name, voice, and likeness, and when his second seven-year contract expired in 1951, he was able to make a lucrative move to television by preventing the studio (through a lengthy court battle) from distributing his previous films in edited versions for television presentation. Always in partnership with Evans, he was featured in a string of network western series and specials that were successful into the mid-1960s. Rogers also made a series of LP recordings for Capitol during the 1960s and early 1970s, but gradually his appearances in the spotlight dwindled to award presentations and occasional musical-program guest slots. He and Evans kept up a steady succession of evangelistic activities.

Rogers caught the public eye and ascended the country charts once more in late 1991, when RCA Records coaxed him out of retirement to record an album called *Tribute.* It featured Rogers singing duets with leading contemporary singers in the country field. Included were duets with such stars as Kathy Mattea, Randy Travis, K. T. Oslin, Alan Jackson, and Tanya Tucker. "I defy you to find any other 79-year-old man singing like that," his producer said; Rogers even yodeled on several selections. The most successful collaboration was a duet with Clint Black called "Hold On Partner," which was released as a single. Many people noticed the eerie physical resemblance between Rogers and the younger singer, and must have felt a sort of shock of recognition at how deeply Rogers's image is implanted in the minds of most Americans. Some have noted that he seemed able, like some Hindu deity, to reincarnate himself.

Selected discography

Tribute (contains "Hold On Partner"), RCA, 1991.
Roy Rogers, MCA, 1992.
The Country Side of Roy Rogers, Capitol.
A Man From Duck Run, Capitol.

With the Sons of the Pioneers

Sons of the Pioneers (includes "Tumbling Tumbleweeds"), Columbia, 1982.
Sons of the Pioneers, MCA, 1991.

Sources

Books

Rogers, Roy, with Carlton Stowers, *Happy Trails,* Word Books, 1979.

Rothel, David, *The Roy Rogers Book: A Reference-Trivia-Scrapbook,* Empire, 1987.

Periodicals

Antiques & Collecting Hobbies, August 1992.
Billboard, September 21, 1991.
Collier's, July 24, 1948.
Country Fever, August 1992.
Country Music, March/April 1992.
Journal of Country Music, May 1978.
Life, July 12, 1943.
Newsweek, March 8, 1943.
New York Times Magazine, November 4, 1945.
People, August 17, 1987.
Pulse!, November 1991.
Saturday Evening Post, June 9, 1945.

—James M. Manheim

Rosenshontz

Family entertainers

ogether Gary Rosen and Bill Shontz make up the popular family entertainment duo Rosenshontz, old timers in the growing crowd of children's performers taking to stages in the 1990s. Since Rosenshontz's formation in 1974, the team has entertained millions of people of all ages throughout the United States and Canada with its brand of whimsical, melodious music that invites the audience to join in.

Gary Rosen, who graduated from Oberlin College, is the composer of numerous songs for *Sesame Street* characters. He was later employed as a music group worker in New York City's Division of Senior Centers, for which he was awarded the Community Volunteer Award for his initiation of outreach programs. Furthering his education at the Greenwich House Music School in New York, he later studied privately with Juan de la Mata and Ralph Towner, an internationally known composer and performer. Rosen went on to pen more than sixty songs for Rosenshontz and other performers, including *Sesame Street*'s Big Bird and Oscar the Grouch, and opera singer Roberta Peters.

For the Record. . .

Members include **Gary Rosen** (born March 24, 1947, in New Haven, CT; son of Philip [a physics professor] and Jeanne Penn Rosen; married, wife's name, Mary Shea; children: Lela, Penn, Jaime [deceased]; received A.B. from Oberlin College, 1968; attended Greenwich House Music School, 1969-70; studied privately with Jean de la Mata and Ralph Towner), and **Bill Shontz** (son of Bill [an ice cream store owner and amateur musician] and Marie Shontz; married, wife's name, Barbara [a writer]; children: four; received M.A. in music from Ohio State University).

Duo formed in 1974. Performed in concert halls throughout North America; television appearances include *Kaleidoscope Concerts, Rosenshontz Family Concert,* and *Romper Room;* featured on National Public Radio; appeared at children's festivals in Vancouver, Edmonton, Toronto, Wolf Trap, Halifax, Pittsburgh, and Philadelphia. Authors of children's sing-along books and producers of videos.

Selected awards: Notable children's recording citations, American Library Association, 1982, for *Rosenshontz Tickles You,* 1983, for *Share It,* 1985, for *It's the Truth,* and 1987, for *Rock 'n' Roll Teddy Bear;* New England Emmy Award nomination for children's television, 1986, for *Rosenshontz Family Concert.*

Addresses: *Booking agent*—Judith Z. Miller, Five Corners Music, P.O. Box 838, Great Falls, VA 22066.

Bill Shontz was trained in classical clarinet and earned a masters degree in flute, clarinet, saxophone, and recorder from Ohio State University. He also played solo clarinet with the Ohio State University Orchestra and Concert Band and the University of Illinois Orchestra and Wind Ensemble. In addition to performing with the Lima (Ohio) Symphony and as guest soloist with the Simion String Quartet, Shontz has taught at the University of Illinois, Ohio State University, Bluffton College, and Muskingum College.

Fateful Ping-Pong Game

In 1974 Rosen and Shontz met over a Ping-Pong table in New York City, where they were both trying to make it on the cabaret circuit. Their first joint performances took place between the seal pond and the gorilla cage in the Central Park Zoo. There they would sing and play for passersby; children and parents alike stopped to listen and proved to be an appreciative audience. Rosen remarked in *Newsweek,* "When we realized that

the parents loved us too, we knew we must be on to something." That something turned out to be a popular and award-winning family entertainment duo.

Since their stints at the zoo, Rosen and Shontz have appeared nationwide at children's festivals, before general audiences, with symphony orchestras, and on public television and radio. With what a *Newsweek* critic called "acute wit and marvelous melody," Rosenshontz's songs touch on all facets of life: "Eat It Up" extols the values of eating vegetables; "Sleep, Sleep" lists various bedtime excuses; "A Good Friend" teaches consideration for others; and "Garbage" deals with the issue of pollution. While their musical styles range from rock and roll to swing to gentle sing-alongs, empathy with children and humor are constants. "Our style is a combination of MTV and rock 'n' roll with family messages. We write from imagination and personal experience," Rosen explained in *USA Weekend.*

The Vermont state arts council hired Rosen and Shontz to develop school music programs in 1977, and the duo moved to their present location in Brattleboro, Vermont. Like many children's performers who were ignored by large record companies, they were forced to establish their own record company—RS (Rosenshontz) Records. The duo's 1982 debut album, *Rosenshontz Tickles You,* features humorous songs that explore issues relevant to children.

Spotted Market for Family Entertainers

Several subsequent Rosenshontz albums have received awards from *Parents' Choice* magazine and have been listed as notable children's recordings by the American Library Association. They began appearing on television on such shows as *Rosenshontz Family Concert,* aired on WCVB-TV in Boston, and NBC's *Today Show.* In 1986 Rosenshontz was nominated for a New England Emmy for children's television.

Many wonder why music for children has become such a big business. Rosen believes that parents, often well-educated professionals who waited until after their careers were in full swing to have children, are interested in spending quality time and participating in quality activities with their children. Attending concerts and listening to records together are just two such activities. "A lot of the songs appeal to the adults as much as to kids," Rosen pointed out to David Browne of the *New York Daily News.* "It's uplifting and not as negative as a lot of rock 'n' roll is," he added. "The message is to feel good about yourself and take your place in the world."

It took several decades for children's musicians in general to attract the serious attention of major record labels. "The competition has increased in the past few years. There's been a proliferation of really good performers," Rosen told Martin F. Kohn of the *Detroit Free Press* in 1991. "It's a double-edged sword. When people come and join in, you know there's a market for it. We've known there's a market for top-notch family entertainment for years; it's just that the media didn't know."

Signed by Major Label

In 1991 Rosen and Shontz caught the eye of recording giant BMG and signed a record contract for duo performances. All of Rosenshontz's previous recordings will appear on the record giant's Lightyear label. "It means more time to write songs, to play with my kids, to tour and do concerts," Rosen told Kohn, "and less time to be concerned about the business of a record company."

Though they aim to continue to work as a duo, Shontz and Rosen also plan to record solo albums that will reflect their varied interests. Shontz wishes to express his concerns about the environment. Rosen, on the other hand, inspired by his pre-school children, plans to record for the toddler set.

At a time when many parents are particularly looking for quality children's music, Rosenshontz is as refreshing as it is timely. "At one time, people would come up to us and say, 'Very nice, but what do you really do for a living?,'" Rosen commented in *USA Weekend*. "It's about time kids' musicians were taken seriously."

Selected discography

Rosenshontz Tickles You, RS Records, 1982.

Share It!, RS Records, 1983.
It's the Truth, RS Records, 1985, reissued, Lightyear, 1992.
Rock 'n' Roll Teddy Bear, RS Records, 1987, reissued, Lightyear, 1992.
Family Vacation, RS Records, 1988.
Big Bird and Oscar the Grouch: Camping in Canada (original songs for *Sesame Street*), Kids' Records.
(With Roberta Peters) *Raisins & Almonds*, Audiofidelity Records.
Vancouver Children's Festival, Festival Records.

Sources

Books

Parents' Choice Magazine Guide to Video Cassettes for Children, edited by Diane Huss Green, Consumer's Union, 1989.

Periodicals

Boston Sunday Globe, February 14, 1988.
Detroit Free Press, September 23, 1991.
Newsweek, November 11, 1985.
New York Daily News, September 25, 1988.
Parents, November 1989.
Parents' Choice, Vol. 12, No. 3, 1989.
USA Weekend, August 4, 1989.

Additional information for this profile was obtained from a Five Corners Music press packet, 1992.

—Jeanne M. Lesinski

Rick Rubin

Producer, record company executive

The *Village Voice* once dubbed Rick Rubin "Satan's Record Producer" and the highly successful and iconoclastic Rubin has been tagged with a bevy of similar epithets. His production and support of such controversial recording artists as horror-rappers the Geto Boys, satanic speed-metalists Slayer, and deliberately offensive comedian Andrew Dice Clay has placed him at odds with parents groups, political activists, and nervous record distributors; but Rubin has remained an unwavering proponent of absolute free speech. "You're either in or you're out" with respect to artistic freedom, he told *BAM* magazine. Nonetheless, Rubin's instincts about pop music talent and his approach to production have assured his status as a major player in the music business.

Founder of the groundbreaking record label Def Jam, which blazed new trails for rap and stunned the major labels, Rubin has since moved on to start Def American Records, signing only acts he himself enjoys. Unlike major label executives who scramble to sign acts that sound like current hits, Rubin told *BAM*'s Bill Holdship, "I just fall in love. It's just magic. I never think in terms of whether it can or can't sell. I never think in terms of how it fits into somebody else's market. It's just a personal thing. I always hope that somebody else will like it, but if they don't that's alright too. At least I'll be able to hold my head up and be proud of what I've done. I'm proud of all the records I've made." Regardless of Rubin's indifference to the market, he has signed and produced a number of highly successful acts. His production work aided the rise to fame of white punk-rappers the Beastie Boys and political hip-hoppers Public Enemy, and his innovative recording ideas and encouragement were an impetus for the Red Hot Chili Peppers' smash album *Blood Sugar Sex Magik.* As Rubin's Def Jam partner Russell Simmons told *Rolling Stone,* "Rick was one of the most talented producers I ever met. He could walk in and make a very different-sounding, special rap record that would set a trend. He wasn't just listening to other people's records and copying them."

From Hard Rock to Punk to Rap

According to *Music Express,* "Rubin is essentially a middle-class artist who is fascinated with street culture." Rubin's background is certainly a cultural universe away from the hardcore rap and metal scenes he has influenced so profoundly. He was born Frederick Jay Rubin in the early 1960s in the Lido Beach neighborhood of Long Island, New York. Raised by affluent parents, he discovered the liberating bombast of hard rock while in his teens. AC/DC's monster album *High-*

way to Hell would remain one of his all-time favorite records, as would early Aerosmith discs like *Rocks* and *Toys in the Attic.* And though Rubin's love for raunchy arena rock would not subside, he gravitated in his late teenage years to the even more intense and far angrier sound of punk rock. Soon he was playing guitar in a punk band called the Pricks. Even so, he noticed that the black students at his high school were listening to a new and vital music called rap.

"The high school I attended was about seventy percent white and thirty percent black," Rubin told Havelock Nelson of *Musician.* "The white scene was into Led Zeppelin, Yes, Pink Floyd—all groups that were completely *over*—whereas the black kids were always waiting for the latest rap or scratch record to come out." Rubin found it "exciting that people could be so progressive musically that they'd want the newest thing, love it and forget everything else. Rap was like the hardcore punk movement, the only difference being the white teenagers rejected the new music and the black teenagers accepted the new music. And I did too." Although he went on to play in another punk band, Hose, Rubin was becoming increasingly fascinated by rap.

Producing Rap Led to Birth of Def Jam

After high school Rubin attended New York University, where he studied philosophy. But his music hobby was about to blossom into a huge business. After hanging around the burgeoning New York hip-hop scene, Rubin paired rapper T. LaRock and D.J. Jazzy Jay, producing their single "It's Yours." The record was a club smash, and one of its admirers was influential rap producer Russell Simmons. When Simmons told Rubin

that "It's Yours" was his favorite rap record, the fledgling producer replied—as he later told *Musician*—that "the inspiration for it was all of the records you've ever made." The two teamed up to form Def Jam. Rubin found in Simmons a fellow believer in a hard, edgy sound far different from the disco-derived party grooves that characterized rap's first wave.

Def Jam began in Rubin's NYU dorm room in 1984. The label's first record was a single called "I Need a Beat" by a sixteen-year-old calling himself L. L. Cool J. "Freight trucks would roll up to my dorm from the pressing plant with 40,000 12-inch singles," Rubin told the *Los Angeles Herald Examiner.* "We then shipped [the records] to distributors across the country," he elaborated to Robert Hilburn of the *Los Angeles Times,* "I Need a Beat" cost $400 and sold 120,000 copies. Then 20 years old, Rubin would quickly attract the attention of the major labels with his fledgling enterprise. His innovative production and independent-minded talent were selling a lot of records, and in 1985 Def Jam made a lucrative distribution deal with Columbia Records. Realizing that he wouldn't be going to law school as he'd planned, Rubin broke the news to his parents by mailing them a xerox of his first advance: a check for $600,000.

Early Work With Beastie Boys and Public Enemy

In a 1987 interview with *Musician,* Rubin called Def Jam "unique in that we're in the music business; other record companies are in the banking business. They loan money, you make a record, you pay it back with your sales, and they take a piece from then on. It's really disgusting. We're not into fast money; we're into developing artists." Among the artists Def Jam developed were the Beastie Boys, a white punk-rap trio who enlisted Rubin as "DJ Double R." Rubin produced the group's smash 1986 debut, *Licensed to Ill.* Part of his pioneering contribution to the Beasties' sound was his use of hard-rock samples; this helped give the Beastie Boys crossover appeal. During his work with the Beasties Rubin was also pursuing rapper Chuck D. to assemble what would eventually become the hard-hitting political rap act Public Enemy.

In 1986 Rubin contributed to the first giant rap crossover hit, Run-D.M.C.'s reworking of the Aerosmith song "Walk This Way." Rubin selected the song, produced it, and recruited members of Aerosmith to guarantee the track's success. He proved to skeptics that rap was no passing fad and did so with a rock chestnut the lyrical cadences of which sounded perfectly apt coming from a rap group. Another of Rubin's feats at Def Jam was the coordination of the successful soundtrack album to the film *Less Than Zero,* for which he brought together artists from the rock and rap worlds. 1987 also saw Rubin direct the feature film *Tougher Than Leather,* which starred Run-D.M.C. The film flopped, hinting that the Def Jam Films enterprise Rubin and Simmons envisioned would not live up to their expectations.

Of his rap production technique, Rubin told *Musician's* Nelson that he bypassed the nonstop disco-groove approach, using different drum parts—with a rock backbeat rather than a disco-style pulse—to create tension and differentiate song parts. "I use beats to achieve the dynamics of melodies without melodies. Drum machines are the parts of the song; one beat happens during the verse, different pauses bring you into the chorus, then the chorus gets filled out—something is added or taken away. I create a song structure. This is the thing I might have brought to rap music."

Left Def Jam After Controversy

The glamour of Def Jam's Columbia distribution arrangement wore somewhat thin in 1986 when Rubin first encountered resistance to a controversial recording. Columbia declined to release *Reign in Blood,* brainchild of the heavy metal band Slayer, no doubt fearing negative publicity from parents groups concerning the band's preoccupation with satanism and suicide. "Who said rock 'n' roll was supposed to be nice?" Rubin asked rhetorically in a *Los Angeles Times* interview. "Rock 'n' roll is about going against the rules." He got the record distributed by Geffen and then decided to part ways with Simmons and start a new company. "In leaving Def Jam," he explained to *Music Express,* "my vision was always to start again. Part of that decision meant knowing I was giving up a really successful part of my past." He added that despite the temptation to stay with a successful outfit, he felt the attraction of "building a label from scratch." Rubin deemed it necessary to change locations, moving to Los Angeles to realize his new vision: Def American Records.

Rubin engineered a distribution deal between Geffen and Def American and began assembling a roster of talent. As usual, he followed his instincts entirely, signing Slayer, the metal group Danzig, outrageous comedian Andrew Dice Clay, hardcore rappers the Geto Boys, and bluesy rockers the Black Crowes. "This label represents my tastes 100 percent," he asserted in *Hits.* Except for the Geto Boys, Rubin had mostly lost interest in rap. "I got tired of the genre," he told *BAM.* "There was a time when I looked forward to every new rap

record that came out. That stopped happening a long time ago." Rubin added that he blamed indiscriminate signings by major labels eager to cash in for the homogenization of the form. In any case, Rubin took a fully hands-on approach to the records put out by his company, coaching bands at rehearsals and keeping his hand in as producer. Structurally, Rubin committed himself to gradual growth, hiring a small staff and few artists and letting the company take shape without indulging in the rapid expansion typical of some successful music ventures.

Blood Sugar Sex Magik

Soon Rubin was, in the words of *Los Angeles Times* music writer Hilburn, "one of the pop world's pivotal players for the '90s." The Black Crowes' debut album sold four million copies; most of Def American's other acts sold impressively as well. Rubin also maintained his career as a free-lance producer. He installed the hitherto cult-status band the Red Hot Chili Peppers in an old house reportedly haunted by rockers gone by to record their 1991 album *Blood Sugar Sex Magik* and convinced the group to record a ballad they hadn't planned to use. The song, "Under the Bridge," was the beginning of their mainstream success and sent the album shooting up the rock charts. "One of the great things about working with Rick is that he makes you feel comfortable," Chili Peppers lead singer Anthony Kiedis told Hilburn. "He is very up-front and makes you feel you can trust him, which is a key to getting someone to express your creative feelings." In 1990 Rubin's commitment to his artists earned him the Joel Webber Award for Excellence in Music and Business. "I put out quality records by quality acts," he told *NMS Today.* "They're not fictitious groups and I don't believe in hiring the newest guy to do the remix for the next pop single."

Controversy continued to follow Rubin's acts. The violent fantasies depicted by the Geto Boys and Andrew Dice Clay's objectionable remarks about women and gays angered many activists. Rubin, as usual, stood by the artists. The producer-executive was at one time also menaced by right-wing Jewish agitators who objected to sentiments expressed on some Public Enemy tracks. In *BAM,* Rubin answered all his critics the same way: "You have to put out records that you don't believe in politically just as much as records you do believe in, because that's freedom of speech." He responded in the *Los Angels Times* to those who objected to specific messages or images in rap or rock songs, saying "When you start being scared to let art reflect society, then something's wrong in the world, not in the music." Perhaps his strongest statement about free speech, however, came in *Hits:* "If you can't speak your mind in art, where can you? If you say no to the Nazis, you're saying no to opera. It's either everything or nothing."

Bounced Back From Geffen Goodbye

Eventually, however, even Geffen balked at the Geto Boys record, and Rubin had to put together an independent distribution package for the group. Soon thereafter Rubin found his company bounced by Geffen. In 1992 Def American made a distribution deal with Warner/Elektra/Atlantic Corp. "They paid me well for their involvement," Rubin admitted to *Hits.* "But the best thing about it is there's funding for me to build a really full-scale, free-standing company to rival any in the business."

1992 also saw another Def American artist sail to the top of the charts—rapper Sir Mix-a-Lot, whose single "Baby Got Back" became a summer radio staple. Mix-a-Lot was the first hip-hop act Rubin had shepherded since the Geto Boys and once again, his instincts had paid off. He then signed a number of untested acts, trusting what he saw as their potential. Rubin also continued producing for other labels, working with such artists as English rockers The Cult. In early 1993 *Spin* magazine reported that Rubin was embarking on yet another venture: to produce beat-heavy, synthesizer-laden "techno" and industrial dance music, signing acts from Belgium's Antler-Subway label, including Lords of Acid. To facilitate this pursuit, Rubin was reportedly establishing a spin-off of Def American called Whte Lbls. This off-shoot would in turn complement Def American's other new label, III Labels, which initially seemed a launching pad for new rap music.

Although Rubin's relatively brief music business career had already made him a sensation, he clearly appeared to be continuing his ascent. As Geffen president Ed Rosenblatt remarked to the *Los Angeles Times,* "He has created an incredibly [high-level] benchmark for himself with the success he has had in the past. It doesn't mean he is going to [match that level] on every record, but with someone who has this much talent and vision at such a young age, there is no reason he won't do even better." Rubin himself acknowledged in the *Times,* "My success has always been based on making records that I like. The bottom line has to be flipping in a cassette, turning it up and loving it . . . and counting on enough other people to think the same way I do."

Selected discography

As Producer

Singles

T. LaRock and D.J. Jazzy Jay, "It's Yours," 1982.
L. L. Cool J., "I Need a Beat," Def Jam, 1984.
Run-D.M.C., "Walk This Way," Def Jam, 1986.
The Cult, "The Witch" (from the *Cool World* soundtrack), Warner Bros., 1992.
Queen, "We Will Rock You/We Are the Champions" (rap version), 1992.

Albums

L. L. Cool J., *Radio,* Def Jam, 1985.
Run-D.M.C., *Raising Hell,* Def Jam, 1986.
Beastie Boys, *Licensed to Ill,* Def Jam, 1986.
Slayer, *Reign in Blood,* Def Jam, 1986.
Various artists, *Less Than Zero* (soundtrack), Def Jam, 1987.
Slayer, *South of Heaven,* Def Jam, 1987.
Slayer, *Seasons in the Abyss,* Def American, 1990.
Geto Boys, *Geto Boys,* Def American, 1990.
Geto Boys, *We Can't Be Stopped,* Def American, 1991.
Red Hot Chili Peppers, *Blood Sugar Sex Magik,* Warner Bros., 1991.
(Co-producer) Mick Jagger, *Wandering Spirit,* Atlantic, 1993.

Also producer of records by Danzig, Masters of Reality, Andrew Dice Clay, and other artists, and executive producer of Dan Baird's *Love Songs for the Hearing Impaired,* Def American, 1992.

Sources

BAM, September 7, 1990.
Billboard, July 27, 1991.
Hits, February 3, 1992.
Los Angeles Herald Examiner, March 24, 1989.
Los Angeles Times, April 16, 1989; May 10, 1992.
Melody Maker, January 3, 1987.
Music Express, March 1992.
Musician, May 1987.
NMS Today, July 16, 1990.
Rolling Stone, May 21, 1987; November 15, 1990; October 1, 1992.
Spin, November 1990; January 1993.
Village Voice, November 30, 1990.

—*Simon Glickman*

Dan Seals

Singer, songwriter

Singer and songwriter Dan Seals first came to fame as part of the pop duo England Dan and John Ford Coley. During the 1970s he and Coley released such pop and easy-listening hits as "I'd Really Love to See You Tonight," "Never Have to Say Goodbye Again," and "Love Is the Answer." After Seals broke with Coley, he went on to become one of the hottest country performers of the late 1980s and early 1990s with smashes like "Bop" and "Love on Arrival." As Bob Millard explained in *Country Music,* "Dan Seals has a lot of soul when he gets wound up around a really top notch song. He can sell a story and a feeling."

Despite his adoption of the stage name England Dan, Seals was actually born in McCarney, Texas. His was a musical family—older brother Jim is famed for his work in the folk duo Seals and Crofts, while another brother, Eddie, tours the Nashville nightclub circuit with his duo, Eddie & Joe. In addition, cousin Johnny Duncan is a country singer and another relative, Chuck Seals, wrote the tune "Crazy Arms." Dan Seals's first musical love was the country genre, and while he was still a young child he played in the family country band. Seals's father warned his children about the pitfalls of a performing career, though. "He'd sit down and say, 'Alcohol and dope and fast women killed every country singer there ever was,'" Seals remembered in the *Tennessean.* By the time he was a teenager, however, he had come to prefer rock and roll, and it was when they were members of a high school rock band that Seals first became acquainted with his future partner, John Ford Coley. Despite often practicing with one another, it took some time for the two of them to become good friends and begin writing songs together.

Meanwhile, the band was changing its focus from rock to soul, then acid rock. Not pleased with the group's direction, Seals and Coley left the band in 1969 to play milder music, especially folk. Unable to use Seals's last name because of his famous brother, they initially used his middle name, calling themselves Wayland and Coley. They finally settled on the England Dan tag, though, even before garnering some popularity in that country where they were the opening act for then-rising superstar Elton John. Encouraged by their success, Seals and Coley began looking for a recording contract, eventually signing with A&M Records in 1971.

England Dan and John Ford Coley made two albums for A&M—*Fables* and *I Hear the Music.* Not only did these efforts meet with less success than the duo had hoped, but the two men were dissatisfied with their lives in general. Accordingly, they decided to concentrate more on their religion, the Baha'i faith, which seeks to promote the belief that all people are part of a spiritual whole. After a year and a half without recording, and

For the Record. . .

Born Dan Wayland Seals, February 8, 1948, in McCamey, TX.

As England Dan, member of duo England Dan and John Ford Coley, 1969-80; signed with A&M Records, 1971; solo performer, c. 1983—.

Awards: Country Music Association duet of the year (with Marie Osmond), 1985, for "Meet Me in Montana," and single of the year, 1988, for "Bop."

Addresses: *Record company*—Warner Bros., 1815 Division St., Nashville, TN 37212.

performing only in small clubs or Baha'i Fireside shows, Seals and Coley were sufficiently refreshed to devote more attention to their professional careers. This time they signed with Atlantic Records, accepting songs written by other artists, and the hits began to come. Their first Atlantic album—released on the Atlantic subsidiary label Big Tree—was *Nights are Forever Without You.* It scored not only with the title track but with the duo's first gold single, "I'd Really Love to See You Tonight."

Seals's next effort with Coley, the 1977 *Dowdy Ferry Road,* garnered them a hit on the pop charts, in addition to the Number One spot on *Billboard*'s easy-listening chart with "It's Sad to Belong." Ironically, though England Dan and John Ford Coley became known and loved for the mellow sound of their chart-climbers, these songs were anomalies of a sort—much of the pair's other work was more rock-oriented, and their concert performances surprised their fans with vigorous, upbeat music. Seals and Coley made three more albums together—including a movie soundtrack called *Just Tell Me You Love Me*—scoring two more big hits with "Never Have to Say Goodbye Again" and the uplifting "Love Is the Answer," which was penned by singer and songwriter Todd Rundgren. In 1980, however, the duo decided to split up.

At that point Seals returned his attention to the country music he had loved so much as a child, hoping to establish a solo career. By 1985 he had hit the Top Ten on the country music charts three times, going as high as Number Two with "My Baby's Got Good Timin'." That year Seals released *Won't Be Blue Anymore* with which a *People* review stated he had "arrived at the . . . heart of country music," although he took "a far more circuitous route than a lot of Nashville mainstays." The album also included the immensely popular "Meet Me in Montana," a duet with country singer Marie Osmond.

The following year saw the release of *On the Front Line.* Alanna Nash of *Stereo Review* called the songs on this album "exceptionally well-crafted," further urging listeners to "give him a try." Apparently they took this advice to heart. "Bop," a song from Seals's next album, *The Best,* fared extremely well on the country charts—it was the Country Music Association Single of the Year—and received some crossover play as well.

As popular as his music is, Seals himself is thought of just as highly. Perhaps that's why his fans are so loyal. *Tennessean* correspondent Robert K. Oermann likened Seals's appeal to a "warm masculinity, quiet dignity or deep sensitivity. Whatever it is, it has kept country lovers coming back to him year after year, regardless of shifting fads and fashions." Much of Seals's character can be traced to his faith. Seeking to promote the international unity of all people, he participated in the 50th anniversary Voice of America show in Washington, D.C., in 1992. Later the same year Seals traveled to the remote town of Alma-Ata, located in what was once the Soviet republic of Kazakhstan, in order to attend the Voice of Asia Festival. Brotherhood was also the theme of the single "We Are One" on his *Walking the Wire* album, released in 1992. Seals was quoted as saying in the *Tennessean,* "We're all members of the human race. . . . If we were unified with each other we could knock out the problems in the world a lot quicker."

Selected discography

With John Ford Coley

Nights Are Forever Without You (includes "Nights Are Forever Without You" and "I'd Really Love to See You Tonight"), Big Tree, 1976.
Dowdy Ferry Road (includes "It's Sad to Belong"), Big Tree, 1977.
Dr. Heckle and Mr. Jive (includes "Love Is the Answer"), Big Tree, 1979.
Just Tell Me You Love Me (soundtrack), MCA, 1980.
Best of England Dan and John Ford Coley, Big Tree.
Fables, A&M.
I Hear the Music, A&M.

Solo releases

Won't Be Blue Anymore (includes "Meet Me in Montanna"), EMI, 1985.
On the Front Line, Capitol, 1986.
The Best (includes "Bop"), Liberty, 1988.
Rage On, Liberty, 1988.
On Arrival (includes "Love on Arrival" and "Good Times"), Liberty, 1990.
Classics Collection, Volume 1, Liberty, 1991.

Greatest Hits, Liberty, 1991.
Classics Collection, Volume 2, Liberty, 1992.
Early Dan Seals, Liberty, 1992.
The Songwriter, Liberty, 1992.
Walking the Wire, Warner Bros., 1992.

Sources

Books

Stambler, Irwin, and Grelun Landon, *The Encyclopedia of Folk, Country, and Western Music,* St. Martin's, 1984.

Periodicals

Atlanta Journal, May 13, 1989.
Atlanta Journal/Atlanta Constitution, July 26, 1986.
Billboard, October 31, 1992.
Boston Globe, October 14, 1986.
Chicago Tribune, February 23, 1986; October 14, 1986; February 19, 1989; August 5, 1990; May 14, 1992; July 12, 1992.
Country Music, March/April 1986; January/February 1987; May/June 1990.
Los Angeles Times, January 11, 1989.
People, September 30, 1985; November 3, 1986.
Stereo Review, October 1987.
Tennessean, August 1, 1992.
USA Today, July 9, 1992.

Additional information for this profile was obtained from Warner Bros. press material, 1992.

—Elizabeth Wenning

Ravi Shankar

Sitarist, conductor, composer

From his small, low platform covered with Indian rugs, Ravi Shankar has brought the music of India to audiences around the world. He has introduced the sitar—a long-necked Indian Lute—to such new domains as film, ballet, and orchestra. A complete musician, he is renowned equally as a concert soloist, composer, and conductor. He is also one of the few composers to have been greatly appreciated and embraced by such diverse audiences as the classical, jazz, pop, ethnic, and new age music circles. It seems inevitable that his greatest wish will come true: above all things to be remembered for his musical creations.

Shankar was born April 7, 1920, in Benares, which is considered the holiest of cities in India. He was the youngest son of a family of Bengali Brahmins, coming from an upper-class background. When he was ten years old Ravi was sent to Paris where his eldest brother, the great dancer Uday Shankar, had a troupe of gifted Indian dancers and musicians. Ravi became quite successful and was soon billed as a star dancer in their tours of Europe and the United States. He also attended school in Paris where he met many great musicians who exposed him to Western music.

In 1935 Uday invited sarod master Ustad Allauddin Khan to join the company and play as the principle soloist. Ravi was deeply impressed by his playing and spent most of the following year acting as Allauddin Khan's interpreter and guide in the hope of becoming his pupil. Before his departure Khan agreed to teach Ravi to play the sitar only if he gave up the fame and fortune of the artist's life in Paris and came to study with him in Maihar, a small village in India.

After a year of soul-searching Ravi decided to go to Maihar and submerge himself in intensive study and total dedication to his guru, Allauddin Khan. He shaved his head, wore clothes of course material, and slept only four or five hours a night with a one-hour nap in the afternoon. Ravi would then practice for 12 hours a day, sometimes until his fingers bled. The rest of the time was devoted to study, prayer, and meditation with the guru. "When music is not written down and you learn by an oral tradition," Shankar was quoted as saying in the *Washington Post,* "what is transmitted by the guru is not merely a technique but a feeling. My guru taught me that the best way to worship is by music."

After seven and a half years of study Ravi became a virtuoso and began playing concerts throughout India. He married his guru's daughter, Annapurna, once he had established himself as a success. He then founded the Vadya Vrinda, the Indian National Orchestra at All-India Radio. For the next seven years Shankar con-

For the Record. . .

B orn April 7, 1920, in Benares, India; married Annapurna Allauddin, 1945 (divorced, 1958); married Sukanya Rajan, 1989; children: (first marriage) Shubho.

Sitarist, conductor, and composer. International performer, beginning in 1956; performed with George Harrison at Hollywood Bowl, 1967; performed as classicist, 1979; engaged in instruction and development of the arts in India, late 1980s-early 1990s. Artistic director of ASIAD, the Olympic gathering of Asia, 1982. Composer of music for films, including *Pather Panchali*, *Kabuliwala*, and *Ghandi*, and for ballets. Author of autobiography *My Music, My Life*.

Awards: First prize in musical direction, Cannes Film Festival, 1955, for *Pather Panchali*; Silver Bear Prize for best film score at Berlin Film Festival, late 1950s, for *Kabuliwala*; President's Medal (India), 1961, for film score *Anuradha*, and 1962, for outstanding contribution to Indian music and culture; Grammy Award nomination for best folk recording, 1966, for *The Sound of the Sitar*, and for best chamber music performance, 1977, for *Improvisations*; classical record performance of the year, National Academy of Recording Arts and Sciences, 1967, for *West Meets East*; honorary member of American Academy of Arts and Letters; elected fellow of Sangeet Natak Academy; awarded Padma Visbushan, India's highest civilian honor.

Addresses: *Record company*—Private Music, 220 East 23rd Street, New York, NY 10010.

ducted most of the concerts and wrote some 200 compositions.

The Pioneer Period

In 1956 Shankar made his American debut in New York City and was received with critical and public acclaim. This began what he has referred to as the pioneer stage of his career, where he gradually became well known to the classical world and was simultaneously discovered in jazz circles. At first he played to modest audiences in town halls, college auditoriums, and the smaller stages on both of the American coasts. His manager had trouble booking engagements in the Midwest at all. Although he was one of the first performers of classical Indian music to tour the United States, interest in his work grew rapidly, and within a matter of a few years he played Carnegie Hall.

In Europe Shankar quickly established himself as a musical phenomenon through collaboration with other classical masters. In 1958 he appeared at the UNESCO Music Festival in Paris, performing with the great violinists Yehudi Menuhin and David Oistrakh. A couple of years later his first Concerto for Sitar and Orchestra was commissioned and recorded by the London Symphony Orchestra and conducted by Andre Previn. International recognition was decidedly achieved when Shankar wrote a composition for violin and sitar for Yehudi Menuhin and himself called "West Meets East." They appeared in concert at the United Nations to celebrate Human Rights Day. The recording of the piece was voted the classical record performance of the year by the American National Academy of Recording Arts and Sciences. Menuhin commented on the recording experience in *Life* magazine: "We sat incarcerated for three days in the aura of incense to which Ravi always plays. The whole object of the music lies in creating an aura which liberates men's thoughts and demands complete surrender."

Shankar's career suddenly shifted gears in the mid-1960s with the association of another gifted musician. In 1966 George Harrison heard one of Shankar's albums and quickly arranged to meet him at a dinner party. Ravi was impressed by Harrison's sincerity and reverence toward Indian music and invited him to come study in India. Harrison eventually spent seven weeks in India learning how to play the sitar but was required to return to England to rejoin the Beatles. To show his gratitude for the instruction Harrison flew in to join Shankar at his Hollywood Bowl concert in the summer of 1967 and the two of them held press conferences and fielded questions regarding their collaboration.

The Superstar Period

These events drew the attention of English and American youth cultures, which began attending Shankar's concerts in droves. Almost overnight he achieved superstar status. His record company put out ads stating: "We love Ravi, do you?" Record sales leapt up and his asking price per concert doubled from $2,000 to $4,000. Full-color posters of him posing next to his sitar were sold in record shops everywhere. Now that he was a part of the youth culture, he was invited to play with pop and rock groups at the Monterey Pop Festival later that year and again at Woodstock in 1969.

Shankar, however, was not entirely pleased with this burst of popularity and often scolded his audiences for their lack of respect toward the music. He repeatedly explained to journalists that he was not an advocate of the drug culture and that he was never on drugs when he played but rather in a deep spiritual state. "Though I understand it I feel a little bit sorry to be appreciated from a wrong angle," Shankar was quoted as saying in *Life* magazine. "It's a go-man-go attitude, not the proper one. . . . It's not [the audience's] fault that they are looking for instant Karma."

In 1971 Shankar joined Harrison for two sold-out charity concerts at Madison Square Garden to help the refugees of Bangladesh. At least $25,000 was raised from ticket sales and donated to the United Nations Children's Fund. A three-album recording of the concert called *The Concert for Bangladesh* was later released and generated an additional $15 million for the refugees. However, the strain of touring with Harrison and The Festival of India over the next few years finally got to Shankar and ultimately drove him to a nervous breakdown in 1975. He subsequently disappeared from the concert circuit for the next two years.

The Classicist Period

When he returned to the stage, Shankar chose to play only venues for classical or ethnic music and thereby avoided the popular music following. This new phase began with a U.S. premiere of the Concerto for Sitar and Orchestra at Carnegie Hall with the Baltimore Symphony Orchestra. Years later in an interview for *Musical America,* Shankar reflected on how his audience had changed from this point on in his career: "Yes, they have changed, changed for the better. It is no longer the esoteric, over-excited ethnic business it once

> "We sat incarcerated for three days in the aura of incense to which Ravi always plays. The whole object of the music lies in creating an aura which liberates men's thoughts and demands complete surrender."
> —Yehudi Menuhin

was." He retained only a small percentage of the mass youth culture but kept a large following of Indian immigrants and Indian music lovers.

The next few years saw a creative burst for Shankar in which he combined the sitar with the music of other cultures. In 1979 he embarked on his "East Greets East" tour, which blended the classical music of Japan and India. He wrote the piece for Hosan Yamamoto, a master of the Japanese bass flute, and for koto expert Musumi Miyashita. Afterwards he wrote new music for the French flute virtuoso Jean-Pierre Rampal. In the following year the New York Philharmonic, under the direction of Zubin Mehta, commissioned a second sitar concerto from Shankar. "The Garland of Ragas" or "Raga Mala" premiered at Lincoln Center's Avery Fisher Hall; this fusion of Indian music with Western classical orchestration was received with enthusiastic reviews.

In 1982 Shankar won great applause for his film score to the Academy Award-winning motion picture *Ghandi*. This was not unfamiliar territory for him, however. In the 1950s his film music to the *Pather Panchali* trilogy and to *Kabuliwala* had won him awards at the Cannes, Venice, and Berlin film festivals. These honors made him the first Indian musician to receive an award for best music direction from a foreign country. Shankar also composed film music for a number of American and European commercial movies, the most renowned being the incidental music to Jonathan Miller's controversial version of *Alice in Wonderland* on BBC.

In 1984 Shankar turned his attention to teaching. He felt it was important to continue the ancient guru/disciple tradition, and taught classes restricted to eight or ten of the most talented students in India. Teaching was nothing new to Shankar. As early as 1967 he founded the Kinnara school of Indian music in Bombay. A few years later he opened another branch in Los Angeles. He also chaired the department of Indian Music at the California Institute of Art. Afterwards he was to be the first musician invited as a Challigar Professor at City College in New York City. Even his autobiography, *My Music, My Life,* is still used as a textbook in ethnic music college courses.

In July of 1988 the Palace of Culture of the Soviet Union premiered Shankar's "Swar Milan," although the recording of the concert was called *Inside the Kremlin*. It was an epic piece with seven passages, using more than 140 musicians and singers from the Russian Folk Ensemble, the Chamber Orchestra of the Moscow Philharmonic, the Government Chorus from the Ministry of Culture, and Shankar's own Indian ensemble. The composition was successful in bringing together the various music of these greatly different cultures, and once again Shankar was able to create a completely new sound.

Ballet is yet another music medium to which he has contributed extensively over the years. Starting as far back as 1967, Shankar received great recognition for his American debut of *Samanya Ksnati*. He later wrote two other ballets, *India Immortal* and *Discovery of India*, which were inspired primarily by his native history and mythology. Both were well received critically and were considered landmarks in contemporary ballet music. 1990 saw the U.S. premiere of the ballet *Ghyanshyam: The Broken Branch*. It was about a dancer addicted to drugs; Shankar wrote it because he wanted to promote the need for a spiritual resurgence in modern society.

Since then Shankar has spent most of his time in India teaching and playing concerts. There has been a renaissance in the arts there, and he continues to contribute to it generously and innovatively. He has developed multimedia projects that involve music, dance, film, and performance art based on Indian themes. In 1990 he collaborated with minimalist composer Philip Glass and released an album of new age music called *Passages*. Perhaps this will herald a new period in his already rich and varied musical career.

Selected discography

The Sound of the Sitar, World-Pacific, 1966.
West Meets East (two volumes), Angel, 1967.
Improvisations, World-Pacific, 1977.
Inside the Kremlin (recorded in 1988), Private Music, 1989.
(With Philip Glass) *Passages*, Private Music, 1990.
(Contributor) *The Tiger and the Brahmin*, Kid Rhino, 1992.
The Concert for Bangladesh, Apple.
The Anthology of Indian Music, Volume 1, World-Pacific.
Classical Indian Music, Odeon.
Classical Music of India, Odeon.
East Greets East, Deutsche Grammophon.
Exotic Sitar and Sarod, Capitol.
The Genius of Ravi Shankar, Columbia.
Homage to Mahatma Ghandi and Baba Allauddin, Deutsche Grammophon.
In Concert, Ravi Shankar, World-Pacific.
India, Its Music and Its People, Desto.
India's Master Musician: Ravi Shankar, World-Pacific.
The Master Musicians of India, Prestige.
A Morning Raga, An Evening Raga, World-Pacific.
Music of India, Angel.
Pandit Ravi Shankar, Odeon.
(With Ali Akbar Kahn) *Raga Mishra Piloo*, Angel.
Raga Parameshwari, Capitol.
Ragas and Talas, World-Pacific.

Ragas Hameer and Gara, Deutsche Grammophon.
Ragas Jogeshwari, Deutsche Grammophon.
Ravi Shankar, Capitol.
Ravi Shankar and Ali Akbar Khan, Odeon.
Ravi Shankar and His Festival From India, World-Pacific.
Ravi Shankar at the Monterey International Festival, World-Pacific.
Ravi Shankar at the Woodstock Festival, World-Pacific.
Ravi Shankar, India's Master Musician in London, Odeon.
Ravi Shankar in New York, World-Pacific.
Ravi Shankar in San Francisco, World-Pacific.
Ravi Shankar, Portrait of Genius, World-Pacific.
Ravi Shankar, Sitar, Odeon.
Ravi Shankar's Festival From India, Dark Horse/A&M.
Shankar: Concerto #1 for Sitar and Orchestra, Angel.
Shankar: Concerto #2 for Sitar and Orchestra—Garland of Ragas, Angel.
Shankar Family and Friends, Dark Horse/A&M.
Six Ragas, Capitol.
The Song of God, Bhagavad Gita (narration by Shankar), World-Pacific.
Songs From the Hills and Dhun, World-Pacific.
The Sounds of India: Ravi Shankar, Columbia.
Chappaqua (soundtrack), Columbia.
"Charlie" (soundtrack), World-Pacific.
Raga (soundtrack), Apple.
Theme From "Pather Panchali" and Gat Kerwani, World-Pacific.
Three Ragas, World-Pacific.
Transmigration Macabre, Spark.
Two Raga Moods, Capitol.

Sources

Frets Magazine, November 1979.
Life, August 18, 1967.
Musical America, September 1982.
New York Times, December 27, 1968; January 5, 1972; December 14, 1974; November 12, 1979; March 16, 1980; September 13, 1985; April 24, 1987; December 24, 1990.
Pittsburgh Magazine, October 1984.
Time, June 14, 1968.
Twin Citian (Minneapolis-St. Paul, MN), December 1967.
Washington Post, June 19, 1985.

Additional information for this profile was obtained from press releases, World-Pacific Records, 1967, and Private Music Records, 1989.

—*Christian Whitaker*

Sonic Youth

Rock band

"Rock has never seen a band quite like Sonic Youth," *Rolling Stone* reviewer Robert Palmer commented in 1992. Noisy, arty, and unconventional, Sonic Youth has been unique in bringing its alienation-drenched melange of feedback, altered tunings, and tampered-with instruments to a larger audience.

Sonic Youth saw its genesis during the late 1970s avant-garde scene of New York City's Lower East Side, where experimental music was taken seriously yet was stoked by the intensity and freedom of punk. Guitarists Thurston Moore and Lee Ranaldo had played together in minimalist composer Glenn Branca's guitar choir and at a festival called Noisefest, which Moore organized. In 1981, Moore, Ranaldo, Ranaldo's friend—bassist Kim Gordon—and then-drummer Richard Edson formed Sonic Youth. "When we started," Moore told the *Boston Phoenix,* "we were being very reactionary, pulling against the norm at the time [and] trying to bring back and update the elements we liked that came out of bands like the Stooges and the MC5."

In 1982 the group released its first EP. Raw and primeval, the self-titled work's lyrics "started out a few steps past the taboo-busting of punk and heavy metal, calmly conflating sex and death and blasphemy amid barrages of noise," according to *New York Times* critic John Pareles. The next year, Bob Bert replaced Edson on drums for the album *Confusion Is Sex.* In a press release, Thurston Moore described the music on this second EP as "like having sex with the insane." Both *Sonic Youth* and *Confusion Is Sex*—which *Boston Phoenix* critic Ted Drozdowski described as capturing "the band as a hardcore-speed wad of warring sounds and screamed lyrics"—won Sonic Youth an underground following.

Musical Growth

On 1985's *Bad Moon Rising,* Sonic Youth began experimenting with dynamics, odd tunings, and song form while exploring the dangerous side of a 1960s revival. Gordon recited the chilling "Brave Men Run in My Family," and Moore and new wave artist Lydia Lunch recreated the frenzy of the famous 1960s Charles Manson murders on "Death Valley '69," a piece Drozdowski described as "more like a disfigured rock song than the result of primal-scream therapy."

The addition of Michigan-born, former Crucifucks drummer Steve Shelley upped the ante for 1986's *Evol*—"love" spelled backwards. Shelley, "whose rhythmic flexibility and subtle touch outclassed the group's previous stickmen" according to the *Boston Phoenix,* brought a firmer rhythmic backbone to the group's meditations on sex and death.

After releasing the tense, sensual, cathartic *Sister* in 1987, Sonic Youth made a big commercial breakthrough with 1988's double album *Daydream Nation.* Like *Evol* and *Sister* before it, *Daydream Nation* featured the band exploring a noisy, introspective world of alienation. It contained more conventional songwriting, and one of its songs, "Teen Age Riot," went to Number One on both the U.S. alternative charts and the British independent charts.

After releasing *Daydream Nation,* Sonic Youth toured extensively and became one of the first underground acts to visit the former Soviet Union. In 1988 the band recorded *The Whitey Album* under the name "Ciccone Youth"—which was inspired by pop icon Madonna's surname—and in 1989 they were the subject of a British television documentary called *Put Blood in the Music.*

Outgrew Small Labels

Underground success brought Sonic Youth to a crossroads. Would they continue in the alternative world where they could work on their own terms, or would they subject themselves to major label pressures and be accused of selling out? They managed to attain the best of both worlds when A&R Executive Gary Gersh, representing DGC Records promised Moore, Gordon, Ranaldo, and Shelley the creative control they desired, and in the fall of 1989 Sonic Youth committed to the label.

DGC, as it turned out, allowed the band as much freedom as it needed. Sonic Youth continued to work intuitively with tampered instruments and strange tunings. "Writing is a complicated process for us," Ranaldo explained in *Guitar World.* "Especially since we work in these weird tunings. It's not like someone comes in and says. 'Okay, the chords are G, C, and A.' The chords and finger positions are unknown to us. Most of the time we don't even have any idea whether they are major or minor, or what. If Thurston and I are in different tunings, as we seem to be more and more, it takes an even further leap to figure out how those tunings are going to complement each other."

With their 1990 major label debut, *Goo,* Sonic Youth stepped fully and boldly onto the national scene. Called a "meditation on stardom" by the *New York Times'* Pareles, *Goo* featured the single "Kool Thing," on which bassist/singer Kim Gordon collaborated with Public Enemy rapper Chuck D. "My theory is that women make natural anarchists," Gordon remarked in *Interview.* "They are outside of the system in so many ways—it's that unpredictable, wild female thing."

After the release of *Goo,* which eventually sold more than 220,000 copies, Sonic Youth toured big arenas with rocker Neil Young."It was three months of finding out about the politics of arena rock," Moore recalled in *Musician.* "We're interested in Neil Young's legacy, so the experience was cool. But he didn't learn much about us, and we just stayed in our room—put on black lights and played eight-tracks."

Sonic Youth took much of 1991 off to work on side projects; Gordon focused on his band Kitten, while Moore and Shelley, in collaboration with punk rocker Richard Hell, made music as Dim Stars. Gordon and Moore, who are married, also moved into a new apartment.

Released *Dirty*

For 1992's *Dirty* Sonic Youth brought in Butch Vig to produce and Andy Wallace to mix. Both had worked on Seattle-based grunge rock band Nirvana's *Nevermind.* It was the first time the band had worked with an outside producer. "The idea," Moore revealed in *Musician,* "was to make a record that sounded as solid as any other record on the marketplace without losing our ideas, which are somewhat off the beaten path or unorthodox commercially."

Dirty came out in a U.S. election year and had an overtly political stance. But while such political pieces as "Youth Against Fascism," the anti-sexual harassment "Swimsuit Issue," and "Chapel Hill"—a song condemning U.S. Senator Jesse Helms—showed the band had widened its lyrical scope, the album also contained personal pieces like Ranaldo's romantic "Wish Fulfillment," Gordon's "On the Strip"—a ballad about a prostitute's delusions—and Moore's "100 Percent," which rages against the senseless murder of a dead friend.

Some critics felt *Dirty* marked a turn toward conventionality; others saw it as providing a continuity for Sonic Youth's vision—one that has found a strong appeal among a growing alternative music audience. Pareles captured the essence of the band's distinct sound when he described the record as "[creating] maelstroms of dissonance, surrounding tunes with barbed noise and sending phantom overtones buzzing around listeners' ears."

In February of 1993 *Pulse!* reported that Sonic Youth had made an arrangement with Geffen/DGC Records that enables them to sign new bands to the label; as *unofficial* talent scouts, the band had recommended alternative acts Pavement, Mudhoney, and the colossal Nirvana to Geffen. Under the new agreement Sonic Youth has recruited the New York outfit Cell, which recorded its debut on Moore's Geffen-distributed Ecstatic Peace label, and a Connecticut band called St. Johnny. Meanwhile, what *Pulse!*'s Jon Wiederhorn called "the official Sonic Youth punkumentary," *1991: The Year Punk Broke,* in which Nirvana is featured as the warm-up act, was bringing concert footage and backstage antics to the Sonic faithful nationwide.

Selected discography

Sonic Youth (EP), SST, 1982.
Confusion Is Sex, SST, 1983.
Bad Moon Rising, Homestead, 1985.
Death Valley '69, Homestead, 1985.
Evol, SST, 1986.
Sister, SST, 1987.
Daydream Nation, Enigma/Blast First, 1988.
Goo, DGC, 1990.
Dirty, DGC, 1992.
(Contributors) "Ca Plane Pour Moi," *Freedom of Choice: Yesterday's New Wave Hits as Performed by Today's Stars,* Caroline, 1992.
Master-Dik, SST.
Sonic Death, SST.
Starpower, SST.

Sources

Atlanta Constitution, October 9, 1992.
Boston Globe, October 20, 1992.
Boston Phoenix, July 17, 1992.
Chicago Tribune, September 27, 1992.
Detroit Free Press, October 2, 1992.
Down Beat, February 1991.
Entertainment Weekly, June 26, 1992.
Guitar Player, September 1990; December 1992.
High Fidelity, March 1989.
Interview, March 1986; August 1990; August 1992.
Los Angeles Times, September 28, 1992.
Musician, September 1992.
Nation, January 9, 1989.
New Statesman, March 4, 1988.
New York, August 24, 1992.
New York Times, July 19, 1992; October 26, 1992.
People, July 7, 1986; August 17, 1992.
Pulse!, February 1993.

Rolling Stone, December 17, 1987; December 15, 1988; May 18, 1989; December 13, 1990; March 21, 1991; September 3, 1992.

Spin, November 1992.

Stereo Review, December 1992.

Variety, February 11, 1991.

—*Jordan Wankoff*

Rick
Springfield

Singer, songwriter, actor

In 1981 Rick Springfield gained a large audience in two mediums; he watched his smash hit single "Jessie's Girl" race up the charts from the vantage point of his newly landed spot as a regular on the popular television soap opera *General Hospital.* The pull of Springfield's musical success proved stronger than that of his soap career, however, and he left the show to follow up "Jessie's Girl" with spirited hits like "Don't Talk to Strangers" and "Affair of the Heart." As David Wild summed up in a *Rolling Stone* review, "Over the years [Springfield has] come up with some delectable ear candy."

Springfield was born August 23, 1949, in Sydney, Australia. His father was a career officer in the Australian Army, and the family moved around a great deal throughout Rick's childhood. Because of this, he had difficulty making friends and hated school, especially during the years his father was stationed in England. He told Edwin Miller of *Seventeen,* "In England, I was the Australian pig, the new kid with the funny accent. It was really traumatic. Because of the country schooling I had, I knew less than the English kids my age in the same class, and I got cut to pieces." Springfield's dislike of school, however, did not prevent him from becoming an avid reader; in fact, he would often stay home from school to read, favoring science fiction and humor. Eventually Springfield began writing stories like the ones he read.

Springfield also enjoyed listening to music and used it as a conscious form of rebellion against his parents. He tried to make his own guitars until his parents bought him one when he was 15 years old. While still in high school he formed a band called the Jordy Boys; the youngest member, he was also the least worldly. Springfield recollected in Irwin Stambler's *Encyclopedia of Pop, Rock, and Soul:* "The other members had been in jail for things like armed robbery. They were 25 and I was 16. One time we were parked near a milk bar and they ran into it and held it up. I stayed out in the car. Lucky we didn't get caught or it might have started me on the wrong foot."

Zoot Suited Him Fine

Eventually Springfield made his way into better bands, including Rock House, which even played for U.S. troops stationed in Vietnam, and Zoot, which became the most popular musical act in Australia during his

For the Record. . .

Born Richard Springthorpe, August 23, 1949, in Sydney, Australia; son of Norman James (a career officer in the Australian Army); immigrated to U.S., 1972; married; children: Liam.

Singer, songwriter, actor. Joined group Jordy Boys, c. 1964; performed with 1950s revival group Rock House; member of band Zoot, c. 1971; solo recording artist, 1971—, signed with Capitol Records, 1972. Actor in television programs, including *Battlestar Galactica, The Rockford Files, The Six-Million Dollar Man, Wonder Woman, Nick Knight, General Hospital,* and *The Human Touch;* actor in films, including *Hard to Hold,* 1984, and made-for-cable productions *Dead Reckoning,* USA, 1990, and *Silent Motive,* Lifetime, 1992.

Awards: Grammy Award for best male rock vocal performance, 1981.

Addresses: *Agent*—Triad Artists, Inc., 10100 Santa Monica Blvd., 16th Floor, Los Angeles, CA 90067. *Management*—Ron Weisner Entertainment, 9200 Sunset Blvd., Penthouse 15, Los Angeles, CA 90069.

tenure with the group. When Zoot split up, Springfield went solo, scoring an Australian hit in 1971 with "Speak to the Sky." As he had hoped, this recording received the attention of U.S. record companies; he was signed by Capitol Records in 1972, prompting his move to the United States.

Many of Springfield's other Australian efforts were included on his American debut album, *Beginnings.* "Speak to the Sky" became a minor hit in the United States, but much to Springfield's distress, he was pegged by fans and critics as a teen idol like singers David Cassidy and Donny Osmond. The following year, in hopes of circumventing Capitol's encouragement of his bubble gum rocker status, Springfield switched to Columbia Records and released *Comic Book Heroes.* The album failed miserably, and Columbia did not renew his contract.

Springfield's problems mounted as he became entangled in various legal disputes with his management and was forced to withdraw from the music business for a few years. When he returned, none of the major labels were interested in his demos, so he opted to record *Wait for the Night* on the smaller Chelsea label. Before the album could gain much exposure, however, Chelsea declared bankruptcy, dashing Springfield's plans. Still

able to live off his Australian royalties, he continued to write material and record demos, convinced that the right record deal would come along.

From "Working Class Dog" to Doctor

In the meantime, Springfield followed a friend to acting class and rapidly gained enthusiasm for dramatic performance. Soon he and a girlfriend decided to produce and direct themselves in a one-act play, and, as Springfield told *Seventeen's* Miller, "We invited every casting director and agent in Hollywood" to see it. Fortunately, the only one who accepted, a representative of Universal Studios, recognized the Australian's talent. Springfield was signed to a contract, which meant he got paid even when he didn't work, and soon began appearing in television programs such as *Battlestar Galactica, The Rockford Files, Wonder Woman, The Incredible Hulk,* and *The Six-Million Dollar Man.*

Though eventually dropped by Universal, Springfield was adequately consoled when RCA records, after listening to his demos, signed him to a contract in 1980. While he was recording what would become *Working Class Dog,* a casting director for *General Hospital* signed Springfield to play the role of Dr. Noah Drake, a young, eligible physician, and he began appearing on the show in 1981. The soap's audience found Springfield very appealing; he quickly became one of its most popular cast members. Then "Jessie's Girl," a song based on Springfield's experience of coveting a friend's love interest, was released as *Working Class Dog's* first single. The song won him a Grammy for best male rock vocal. Another cut from the album, "I've Done Everything for You," also became a smash. Suddenly, Springfield had to balance filming with concert appearances.

Springfield's follow-up album, *Success Hasn't Spoiled Me Yet,* featuring "Don't Talk to Strangers," also proved popular; his 1983 effort, *Living in Oz,* which included the hits "Human Touch" and "Affair of the Heart," was favorably received as well.

Not forgetting his acting career, though, Springfield made his 1984 big-screen debut in *Hard to Hold.* The film portrayed a rock star, played by Springfield, who survives an automobile accident and falls in love with a children's counselor. The woman, in turn, is torn between returning the musician's love and rejecting him because of his excessive lifestyle. Critics gave Springfield lukewarm acceptance at best; the romantic tale did relatively well at the box office, however, many female fans perhaps drawn by the promise of seeing Springfield's naked buttocks for a fleeting moment as his character loses his towel in one scene.

Traded Music for Movies

Despite his successes, which counted fans from many age groups, Springfield continued to be most popular with young girls—a curse that had always undermined his credibility with music critics. Perhaps to combat the teen idol image, he released a more ambitious album in 1985. But *Tao* was dismissed by *Rolling Stone's* Wild as "an overwrought, misguided bid for respectability." Voicing similar concerns, *Stereo Review* contributor Steve Simels explained what he viewed as "production overkill" by suggesting that Springfield may have had "lingering suspicions that he's a pretty face rather than a musician." Still, Simel did note that "when he's dealing with relationships, Springfield is capable of writing with a fair amount of verbal facility and genuine feeling." Springfield's 1988 album, *Rock of Life,* fared much better with critics; Wild praised the cut "Honeymoon in Beirut," and *People* reviewer Ralph Novak pointed out that "even [Springfield's] standard romantic tunes get away from romantic cliches."

Springfield continued to act, landing roles in various short-lived television series, including *Nick Knight* and in 1992, ABC's *The Human Target*. The latter was based on a DC comic book and starred Springfield as Christopher Chance, the "target"—a hero who aids crime victims by physically assuming the identity of whomever he's helping. Chance's sidekicks are a special-effects expert, a research assistant, and a chauffeur/bodyguard; all travel in Chance's rocket ship. Said *Entertainment Weekly's* Ken Tucker of the program, "If I were a kid, I guess I'd like all the nifty disguises, but to a grown-up, *The Human Target* seems campy in a dumb way, with stilted dialogue and stiff action scenes." Tucker gave the show a C-. *People* also coughed up a C-, complaining about the "truly dopey" dialogue, and exclaiming, "The summer wouldn't be complete without one really ludicrous, entirely implausible action series. Here it is!"

Objections to *The Human Target* seemed geared mostly toward the program itself, rather than Springfield's acting ability. In fact, Springfield has also found occasion to appear in made-for-television movies—a venue in which he has garnered a modicum of respect. For example, in 1990 he had a hefty part in the USA network's *Dead Reckoning,* which focused on a love triangle. David Hiltbrand commented in *People* that "all hands turn in good performances—particularly Springfield as the snake in the saw grass." Of particular interest has been Springfield's choice of characters; he's played good guys, bad guys, and even the in-

between, as in Lifetime's *Silent Motive,* which cast him, in the words of *New York's* John Leonard, as "a hairy nut."

As for Springfield's music career, he has never indicated that his recording hiatus is permanent. Given his versatile talent, Springfield is bound to please his fans wherever and whenever he pops up; for them, the adoration is truly an "Affair of the Heart."

Selected discography

Beginnings (includes "Speak to the Sky"), Capitol, 1972.
Comic Book Heroes, Columbia, 1973.
Wait for the Night, Chelsea, 1976.
Working Class Dog (includes "Jessie's Girl" and "I've Done Everything for You"), RCA, 1981.
Success Hasn't Spoiled Me Yet (includes "Don't Talk to Strangers"), RCA, 1982.
Living in Oz (includes "Human Touch" and "Affair of the Heart"), RCA, 1983.
Hard to Hold, RCA, 1984.
Tao, RCA, 1985.
Rock of Life (includes "Honeymoon in Beirut"), RCA, 1988.
Rick Springfield's Greatest Hits, RCA, 1989.

Sources

Books

Stambler, Irwin, *Encyclopedia of Pop, Rock, and Soul,* St. Martin's, 1989.

Periodicals

Chicago Tribune, July 26, 1985; March 20, 1988.
Dance Magazine, May 1986.
Entertainment Weekly, July 17, 1992.
High Fidelity, May 1988.
Los Angeles Times, May 19, 1985; November 25, 1985; July 20, 1992.
New York, October 21, 1991.
People, August 17, 1981; March 21, 1988; May 28, 1990; May 18, 1992; July 20, 1992.
Rolling Stone, May 5, 1988.
Seventeen, April 1982.
Stereo Review, September 1985; July 1988.
Variety, August 30, 1984; August 7, 1985; May 23, 1990; July 20, 1992.

—*Elizabeth Wenning and Lorna Mabunda*

Lisa Stansfield

Singer

Lisa Stansfield—the 23-year-old British pop and soul vocalist who won international fame in 1989 with the release of her first solo album, *Affection*—simultaneously achieved a strange kind of notoriety in the music world. Critics responding to her music have largely focused on her use of 1970s disco sounds, creating a controversy over the reemergence of a musical style that, since the "death" of disco in the early 1980s, many had come to assume was universally despised. *Rolling Stone* correspondent Rob Tannenbaum's description of Stansfield's impact on the music scene typifies the terms that many reviewers have used: "All right, so disco has never been scientifically proven to be harmful. But a dozen years ago, when Stansfield was necking to Sylvester records in England, [disco film] *Saturday Night Fever* backlash was turning 'Disco sucks' into an American motto. So when the musician describes her music as disco, without embarrassment or apology, a sociocultural moment has evolved."

Stansfield was born in 1966, the second of three daughters. Her family lived in the small suburb of Rochdale, in Northern England, not far from the industrial and economically depressed city of Manchester. The area has produced a number of England's most successful rock and pop music bands, particularly those with alternative or new wave sounds, but it was unlikely that Stansfield's musical influences would take her in that direction. She told Robert Hilburn of the *Los Angeles Times,* "Most of my influences were soul singers . . . Diana Ross, Chaka Khan, Gladys Knight, Dionne Warwick, among the women." It was their records that her mother had around the house; others included Barry White, George Benson, Sylvester, and Curtis Mayfield. However, a *People* correspondent wrote that her "dad . . . used to play his favorite records too. 'But I never sang Black Sabbath,' Stansfield [said]." The first record Stansfield ever bought herself was teen idol Donny Osmond's "Puppy Love" in 1972.

Despite the fact that, in the words of *Rolling Stone*'s Tannenbaum, there "was no evidence of musical talent in the family," Stansfield's performing career started quite early and rose steadily. At the age of 14, she left school to become the hostess for a variety show on a local television station. Stansfield described her role on the show in *People,* reporting, "I was 14 and being dressed like Joan Collins on a bad day." She eventually left this show for one called *Razzmatazz* that offered a larger audience and a larger paycheck, about which the singer added in *People,* "I was a minor celebrity getting £500 a week, just for saying a few words and smiling a lot. I thought, 'This is scandalous!'"

For the Record. . .

Born in 1966 in Rochdale, England; daughter of Keith (a draftsman) and Marian Stansfield; divorced.

Singer, 1980—. Performed in local clubs and on television variety shows, including *Razzmatazz,* early 1980s; collaborated with Andy Morris and Ian Devaney, c. 1984; with Morris and Devaney, formed group Blue Zone, 1986; produced dance singles with Coldcut (English production duo Matt Black and Jonathan More), 1988-89; released first solo album, *Affection,* 1989; contributed "Down in the Depths" to Cole Porter tribute anthology *Red, Hot and Blue* to raise money for AIDS research, 1990.

Selected awards: BRIT awards for best newcomer, 1989 and 1990, and best female artist, 1990 and 1991; Silver Clef Award for best new artist, 1990; Ivor Novello awards for best contemporary song, 1990, and best international song, 1991, both for "All Around the World."

Addresses: *Manager*—Jazz Summers, Big Life Management, 15 Little Portland St., London W1N 5DE, England. *Record company*—Arista Records, Arista Building, 6 West 57th St., New York, NY, 10019.

First Efforts "Total Embarrassment"

In the early 1980s, while she was smiling and singing on television, Stansfield also sang in some local social clubs and recorded a few singles that were never released. As she explained to Tannenbaum in *Rolling Stone,* Stansfield found those first efforts to be "a total embarrassment." It wasn't until 1984, at the age of 18, that Stansfield found the opportunity that allowed her to begin recording with greater success. She began working with two friends whom she had known in school, Andy Morris and Ian Devaney. The three had first worked together in a school production—a musical— in which Stansfield had a leading role and Devaney and Morris played in the band. The two young men began writing music with her—as well as playing guitar and horns on the recordings—and eventually became her producers.

In 1986 the trio chose a name for the group, calling themselves Blue Zone. Two years later they recorded the tracks for an album, tentatively titled *Big Thing,* but were ultimately dissatisfied with the work and chose not to release it. They did, however, release a single by the same title that became popular in British dance clubs. Consequently, an invitation arrived from Coldcut, the working name for producers Matt Black and Jonathan More. Black and More—an important duo in the British

music business—wanted a guest appearance from the group on their dance collection, *What's That Noise?* Blue Zone not only contributed "People Hold On," but also prepared another single with Coldcut, "This Is the Right Time." Both ventures became popular club tunes in England, inspiring the musicians to produce another album—this one presented as a solo vehicle for Stansfield—that was the beginning of *Affection,* released in 1989.

Helped Spur Disco Revival

While her career became increasingly successful, Stansfield's private life also underwent some dramatic changes. The singer made a point, however, of keeping the two worlds apart; consequently, according to Nick Coleman in *Vogue,* "Stansfield has a vanished past." Protected by this silence are details concerning a brief marriage that ended before Stansfield's rise to fame. After the break-up of that mysterious relationship, Stansfield became seriously involved with Devaney— the two started a home together sometime around 1988, before the production of *Affection.*

As soon as her first solo album hit the airwaves and record stores in 1989, Stansfield became the kind of celebrated "new face" in the music world that inspired euphoric commentary by reviewers. The excitement about her voice and her musical style blended fluidly into statements about her presence in general. David Fricke concluded in his *Rolling Stone* review of *Affection:* "Stansfield evokes the great black soul stylists of the mid-Seventies with a natural ease and practiced elegance that make the simple 'ay-ay-ay-ay' hook in 'All Around the World' sound like dancefloor Shakespeare. Stansfield could arguably have made it this year on her Ingrid Bergman-as-disco-urchin looks alone. That voice makes her a real Dreamgirl for the Nineties."

Affection Climbed Charts

Added to the generally positive tone of the reviews for *Affection* were the professional rewards that the album prompted. Soon after its release, the album jumped into the Top Ten on *Billboard's* Hot 100 chart. "All Around the World" quickly emerged as the hit single, reaching a Number One spot on rhythm and blues and dance charts in at least seven countries by June of

1990. Most notably, "All Around the World" and "You Can't Deny It" were consecutive Number One hits on the *Billboard* black music chart, making Stansfield the first British woman to achieve this distinction. The achievement was a particularly significant one—in 1990 Robert Hilburn reported in the *Los Angeles Times* that "'All Around the World' is one of the few singles in recent years by a white artist to reach No. 1 on the black music charts in the United States."

Something aside from music did eventually prompt derogatory remarks from a few quarters. After the release of *Affection,* journalists and fans commented a great deal on Stansfield's image, which tenaciously resisted sexual stereotypes with her closely cropped hair and menswear clothing. Upon the release of *Real Love* in 1991, however, Stansfield also unleashed a new image, including tight minidresses and chic curls.

This transformation in no way slowed the sales of *Real Love,* which garnered the same kind of attention for the quality of her voice and the "disco" sound in which she and her production duo continued to indulge. In 1992 Stephen Holden voiced the official *Rolling Stone* evaluation: "What makes the mix special is Stansfield's wantonly emotive singing, which is as luscious as melting chocolate. . . . Her voice is even richer and the arrangements more inventive and far-reaching than on *Affection.*"

Selected discography

Affection (includes "All Around the World" and "You Can't Deny It), Arista, 1989.
Real Love (includes "Change"), Arista, 1991.
(Contributor) *Red Hot and Blue,* Chrysalis, 1990.
(Contributor) *Red Hot and Dance,* Columbia, 1992.

Sources

Advocate, August 25, 1992.
Los Angeles Times, May 20, 1990.
Mademoiselle, June 1990.
People, July 30, 1990.
Rolling Stone, July 12, 1990; December 13, 1990; January 9, 1992.
Vogue, August 1990.

Additional information for this profile was obtained from an Arista Records press biography, 1991.

—*Ondine E. Le Blanc*

Marty Stuart

Singer, songwriter, guitarist, mandolinist

Marty Stuart is a man with a mission. The satin-and-rhinestone-clad country rocker aims to build on country's roots and bring an authentic hillbilly look and sound back to Nashville. An accomplished instrumentalist, Stuart has forged a path through the country ranks with a series of infectious hits such as "Hillbilly Rock" and "Little Things." He explained in the *Richmond Times-Dispatch* that his work is based on a fusion of bluegrass, vintage rock, and Western swing. "What I have a passion to do is to take what I've learned in the past with the masters and bridge it into the future," he said. "I'm crusading for hillbilly music."

Indeed he is; name a country or bluegrass master and chances are Stuart has played in that artist's band. At the age of 13, he was regularly performing with bluegrass pioneer Lester Flatt and he spent much of the late 1970s touring with Johnny Cash. Stuart has also done extensive studio work, backing up rockers Neil Young, Bob Dylan, and Billy Joel, in addition to a multitude of country artists. The multitalented Stuart even coproduced an album for the Sullivans, a gospel work that earned critical acclaim.

As a solo artist, Stuart has earned a measure of uniqueness with his passion for the flashiest stage attire he can borrow, buy, or collect from past country greats. The performer confessed in *Country America* that his fancy stage clothes are "uniforms." He contended, "[Clothes] transform you. In my case, they turn me into a hillbilly singer. When I get on my bus and put on these clothes, I can almost feel something coming together." *Entertainment Weekly* writer Kate Meyers raved, "Marty Stuart reeks of style. Country style." Stuart outlined his key to success: "The four things a hillbilly singer needs are a Cadillac, a Nudie [cowboy] suit, the right hairdo, and a pair of pointy-toed boots." And don't forget about the hair; curious about his massive pompadour, Meyers wondered, "What does it take to achieve such a resplendent coiffure?" The answer, according to Stuart: "About four minutes, a 60-mile-an-hour wind, a $1 hairbrush, and an 87-cent can of Aqua Net."

Marty Stuart grew up in Philadelphia, Mississippi, the grandson of a fiddler. A good deal of his youth was spent in front of the television, absorbing every country music show he saw. Porter Wagoner, Ernest Tubb, and the Wilburn Brothers ranked among Stuart's favorites, but one duo stood out in his mind. "My next-door neighbor got me a guitar when I was 4 or 5," he recounted in the *Richmond Times-Dispatch,* "and I used to stand in front of the TV pretending I was playing along with Flatt and Scruggs."

Landed Major Gig

Many children have indulged in such fantasies, but for Stuart, they became a reality. By the time he reached 12 years of age, Stuart had so progressed on both the guitar and the mandolin that he was hired to tour with the Sullivan Family, a gospel group. The stage experience and consequent exposure to other musicians helped young Stuart hone his skills. That summer, Stuart and his father journeyed to the famous Bean Blossom bluegrass festival in Indiana. There Stuart met his hero, Lester Flatt, and befriended a member of Flatt's band, the Nashville Grass. "It was hard going back to school after all that," he admitted in the Richmond Times-Dispatch. "I'd learned that summer that I could get paid for playing music, the girls liked it, I could let my hair grow, and sleep late in the morning."

Stuart took a quick trip to Nashville, where he jammed with Flatt's sidemen; Flatt overheard the youngster and invited him to join the band. Looking back Stuart remarked, "It was sort of a novelty—this old guy with this young kid—but the novelty was that I was so young and could really play." The 13-year-old dropped out of school and became a full-fledged professional musician, playing to crowds at the Grand Ole Opry and other venues. "My parents were very skeptical about letting me go," he held in the Richmond Times-Dis-

patch, "but they met with Lester and he assured them that he would assume all responsibility for me doing my schoolwork and sending most of my money home to go in the bank. Lester being who he was, they agreed. I don't think it would've happened if it had been the Rolling Stones."

Flatt proved to be an excellent role model, teaching Stuart a sure philosophy that has since served him well. "Lester used to preach to me about building a slow foundation so you have something to fall back on in a cold season," Stuart summed up in the Chicago Tribune. "I thought it best that I become a band member and do this right, and grow up and get the knowledge from the people that invented this music around here. So perhaps when I'm 28, 30 years old, I can give my solo career a chance. It won't be burned out. And that's kind of the way it worked."

Played With Greats

After playing with Flatt for several years, Stuart branched out. He did some bluegrass fusion work with fiddle great Vassar Clements; then he toured extensively with Johnny Cash, who was his father-in-law at the time. In 1982 Stuart released an album with bluegrass label Sugar Hill. Busy Bee Cafe featured Cash, Earl Scruggs, and Doc Watson in a bluegrass extravaganza. The work was a critical success, but sales were modest. Stuart kept busy in the studio, working for Emmylou Harris, Willie Nelson, and Waylon Jennings.

Stuart switched to CBS Records and released a self-titled album that indicated the direction he planned to take his solo work. He told the Wichita Eagle: "When I got a record deal in '85 with CBS, I saw that country music was becoming more video-oriented. There used to be a lot more color around here, with the fancy suits, but Willie [Nelson] and Waylon [Jennings] changed that. That's OK; it was a new time. But I like it. I went out and bought every Nudie suit I could get my hands on. I got the musicians' union directory and called and asked people to sell me their old suits. I bought some, and they gave me some. They're art pieces to me." Flamboyancy wasn't enough to help Marty Stuart crack the market, however.

Depression settled in as Stuart not only endured problems with his record company, but witnessed the breakup of his five-year marriage to Cindy Cash. Rather than let his troubles weigh him down for good, Stuart initiated his own cure; "I went to see my mother," he confessed in Country Music. "My motto is 'When in doubt, go see Momma,' 'cause I'm a card-carrying Momma's boy." His mother suggested he rediscover his roots. Such poignant advice led Stuart back to Mississippi, where he found the strength to continue.

Jumping labels again, Stuart joined MCA in 1989 and produced *Hillbilly Rock,* a rootsy, good-natured romp. That album languished too, until the title track caught on in the summer of 1990—thanks in no small part to a music video featuring Stuart in his vintage stage garb and oversized pompadour haircut. The title track, written by Stuart, pays tribute to the rural roots of rock in classic dance-hall style. "Hillbilly Rock" was the first song by Stuart to make the country Top 10. Even so, *Country Music's* Bob Allen acknowledged being puzzled: "It's still a mystery to me why *Hillbilly Rock . . .* didn't make more waves." As a bit of consolation, Allen noted, "For whatever it's worth, George Bush requested a copy of *Hillbilly Rock* to play on Air Force One [the presidential jet]."

Scored With *Tempted*

Not to be discouraged, Stuart released *Tempted* in 1991. The album featured a duet between Stuart and fellow "country boy" Travis Tritt. Stuart didn't have anyone in mind when he wrote "The Whisky Ain't Workin'" and he had never met Tritt before they got together for the song. The collaboration was kind of an accident, Stuart having chosen Tritt because, according to a *Tune In* interview, "I really like his voice." The twosome struck paydirt, however, when they chose to tour together under the auspices of the No Hats Tour. Stuart elaborated, saying in the same interview, "It's not that we have anything against singers with hats. We wish we could, but we can't find hats big enough for our hair!" In a more serious vein, Stuart commented, "I think that we have a little maverick in us, and there's a lot of renegade in both of us—those kinds of rules will make you work together. And hey, we are headed in the same direction."

They truly were; "The Whisky Ain't Workin'," co-written with Ronnie Scaife, went to Number One on the country singles chart and Stuart's album went Top 10. *Country Music* noted, "[*Tempted*] is the first contemporary country album to do a superb job of playing to the marketplace—it delivers five or six killer mainstream radio hits—while also seizing the neglected reins of country's historically strongest stalking horses and making that buggy run." Critics and fans alike were thrilled by Stuart's brand of country.

The follow-up, *This One's Gonna Hurt,* was described by *Entertainment Weekly's* Alanna Nash as "the record he was born to make." Nash went on to report, "Stuart achieves a nearly flawless integration of Southern rock,

pop, bluegrass, blues, honky-tonk, rockabilly, and boogie." She also applauded his "energy, wit, and soulful mandolin. . . ." Jack Hurst of the *Chicago Tribune* deemed the work "one of those albums knowledgeable critics look back at in 25 years or so and designate [as] one of the field's most important." For his part, press materials quoted Stuart as saying, "I've been aching to make a deep, deep mark that will sound off around the world for country music. I love every note of this album. I feel like I've done my job."

Since then Stuart has become a favorite on the country circuit, an honor for someone who is viewed as "the most ardent fan country music could hope for," according to *Country Music's* Patrick Carr. In fact Stuart has set about writing a script for an upcoming documentary. The film will capture life on the road and will feature artists he has worked with in the past.

For the present, the singer-songwriter continues defending hillbilly music as a viable modern form. He asserted in the *Chicago Tribune:* "The only thing I've ever wanted to do my whole life is play country music, and that's all I've ever done. Sometimes the energy that is in my music gets confused with rock 'n' roll. To me, I hear more bluegrass than anything. Bluegrass is just a revved-up form of picking." Hillbilly, he told *Country America,* doesn't necessarily mean hick. "I was watching reruns of old country music shows from the Sixties the other day," he said. "The set in the TV studio had a front porch, fake flowers, hay bales, wagon wheels and a singer. That's what a lot of people *still* think Nashville is." Stuart concluded, "I got news for you. We're as hip down here as you can get."

Selected discography

Marty, With a Little Help From My Friends, Ridge Runner, 1977.
Busy Bee Cafe, Sugar Hill, 1982.
Marty Stuart, CBS, 1986, reissued, 1992.
Hillbilly Rock (includes "Hillbilly Rock"), MCA, 1989.
Tempted (includes "Little Things" and "The Whiskey Ain't Workin'"), MCA, 1991.
This One's Gonna Hurt You, MCA, 1992.
Let There Be Country (recorded in 1987), Columbia, 1992.

Sources

Books

Vaughan, Andrew, *Who's Who in New Country Music,* St. Martin's, 1989.

Periodicals

Atlanta Journal, July 20, 1991.

Chicago Tribune, August 10, 1990; October 27, 1991.

Country America, October 1990.

Country Music, July/August 1985; September/October 1985; September/October 1986; January/February 1990; March/April 1991; May/June 1991; July/August 1992; November/December 1992.

Entertainment Weekly, July 24, 1992; September 18, 1992.

Guitar Player, September 1986; December 1986.

Los Angeles Times, January 15, 1992.

Nashville Banner, May 1, 1992.

New York Times, July 12, 1992.

People, November 16, 1992.

Richmond Times-Dispatch, March 10, 1991, April 12, 1991.

Stereo Review, April 1990; October 1992.

Tune In, February 1992.

Washington Post, March 13, 1991.

Wichita Eagle, November 30, 1990.

Additional information for this profile was obtained from MCA Records press materials, Gurley and Co. publicity materials, and the Marty Stuart Fan Club, 1992.

—Anne Janette Johnson and Lorna Mabunda

Matthew Sweet

Singer, songwriter, guitarist

Matthew Sweet released two widely acclaimed albums before getting the listening public's attention. Despite critical approval of his first two solo efforts, 1986's *Inside* and 1989's *Earth,* Sweet had anything but a smooth path to success. Beset by personal crises—a divorce from his wife of six years and a flood in his Princeton, New Jersey, home that destroyed his guitars and records—he was also forced to maneuver through record-company politics; although *Inside* received such accolades as three-and-a-half stars from *Rolling Stone* and *Earth* was singled out as a "Platter dJour" by *Spin,* Columbia Records chose not to distribute the latter, and when Sweet's A&R representative left A&M Records, which had picked up *Earth,* that label dropped him. "The year before [*Girlfriend*] came out was really hard," Sweet told *Musician,* though this hardship apparently offered considerable inspiration to the struggling artist. "I thought I might have to find another career or get a job at the 7-Eleven," he admitted. But when Zoo Entertainment offered Sweet a deal to produce and distribute *Girlfriend,* in 1990, Sony, which had acquired Columbia, was smart enough to re-release *Inside,* and Sweet's popularity took off.

Matthew Sweet was born and raised in Lincoln, Nebraska, where he worked in a music store and played in various new-wave cover bands during high school. He graduated in 1983 and moved to Athens, Georgia, for summer school. Briefly attending the University of Georgia, he quickly became part of the Athens music scene, joining the band Oh-OK and then forming Buzz of Delight; both bands released EPs on Atlanta's DB Records in the mid-1980s. Sweet then moved to New York, encouraged by Columbia Records' Steve Ralbovsky, who pushed for the release of Sweet's first solo disc, *Inside.* In 1987 Sweet shouldered bass duties for the Golden Palominos, touring with the loose assemblage of artists and helping to record their 1987 album *Blast of Silence,* for which he co-wrote and sang "Something Becomes Nothing." Two years later, Sweet recorded his second album, *Earth,* which again provoked a response from critics though not from the general listener. *Girlfriend* was his breakthrough.

Broke Through With Harder-Edged *Girlfriend*

The appeal of this third record was widespread; though *Girlfriend* fit most comfortably under the rubric of pop, critics could hear a considerable rock and roll influence. Gene Santoro of *The Nation* felt that the work recalled Bob Dylan, the Jefferson Airplane, the Doors, and even the Beatles. *Rolling Stone's* Paul Evans added Neil Young and Crazy Horse to the list, and Michael

For the Record. . .

Born October 6, 1964, in Lincoln, NE; married c. 1984 (divorced c. 1990). *Education:* Attended the University of Georgia.

Worked in music store and played with various bands during high school; played guitar with band Oh-OK, Athens, GA, which released *Furthermore What,* DB Records, 1984; formed band Buzz of Delight, Athens, which released *Soundcastles,* DB Records, 1984; signed with Columbia Records and released *Inside,* 1986; toured with the Golden Palominos, 1987, Lloyd Cole, c. 1990, and the Indigo Girls, 1992. Co-produced Velvet Crush's *In the Presence of Greatness,* Ringers Lactate/Caroline, 1992.

Addresses: *Home*—Princeton, NJ. *Record Company*— Zoo Entertainment, 6363 Sunset Blvd., Hollywood, CA 90028.

Azerrad, also of *Rolling Stone,* heard echoes of the legendary 1970s guitar band Television.

Indeed, on *Girlfriend* Sweet was accompanied by the guitars of Richard Lloyd, originally of Television, and Robert Quine, who has played with Lou Reed and Richard Hell and the Voidoids. Ric Menck, of Velvet Crush, whose album was co-produced by Sweet and recorded in his living room, played drums, singer-songwriter Lloyd Cole contributed acoustic guitar, and Greg Leisz of k. d. lang's country-rockin' Reclines lent his talents on pedal steel. Sweet had worked with Lloyd and Quine on *Earth,* during which, he reported in *Pulse!,* "I got just a taste of what they were capable of and I sort of regretted that there wasn't more room that wasn't plotted out in advance." *Girlfriend's* live studio approach provided that room.

Critics who detected the influence of rock and roll appreciated what *Musician's* Jon Young called the "tougher edge" of *Girlfriend,* due in part to the emphasis on guitars. *Nation* contributor Santoro testified, "The lunatic guitars . . . thrash and burn with deliciously vicious postpunk edges," and *Rolling Stone's* Azerrad remarked that "the heavily autobiographic *Girlfriend* plays Sweet's impeccable pop sense off noisy, passionate guitar work." *Pulse!* contributor Marc Weidenbaum concluded that *Girlfriend* actually "would have been a rock'n'roll record were it not for the marvelous, sugary haze of [Sweet's] vocals." But Sweet himself perhaps best summed up the album's "unproduced" sound. Of his first two releases, he told *Rolling Stone,* "There was something missing for me." He explained to Weidenbaum that *Earth* "was just the culmination of this plan we'd

had for a long time: to try and make a record that had really good drum programming that seemed real." When he discovered the loose and largely undiluted noise of Neil Young and Jimi Hendrix, Sweet decided to forgo his drum machine altogether in favor of the genuine article to make "a really raw, totally blatant, in-your-face kind of record."

"Luscious Pure Pop"

Still, the strains of rock that weave themselves through *Girlfriend* do not preclude the presence of pop. *Musician's* Young, for one, referred appreciatively to the "luscious pure pop" found throughout. In fact, some critics have discerned a unique balance in Sweet's music between pop and rock. Attested *Rolling Stone's* Evans, "This is popcraft raised to the level of artistry—a rock and roll valentine that delivers subtle wisdom with an exhilarating kick."

While exploring Sweet's distinctive pop-rock stylings, critics have also focused on the upheavals in Sweet's life that they see translated into both the lyrics and music of *Girlfriend.* Some have viewed the album as an emotional musical autobiography. Comparing Sweet to his pop forbears, Evans wrote, "While quivering at times like a teenager gripped by a fearsome crush, he's actually a knowing lover—the spirit of his songs suggest a grown-up Everly Brothers, straining still to be starry-eyed but savvy enough to have survived love's disenchantments." In *Spin,* Thom Jurek declared, "Matthew Sweet is giving American music something that it has been known to lack: honesty. Not since [pop cult favorite] Big Star have we heard songs so lyrically fragile (to the point of embarrassment) that are also so sharp, lean, and powerful musically." Like Big Star's Alex Chilton, who inspired a generation of songwriters, Sweet is a romantic. "Anyone who has ever been in love to the point of obsession," added Jurek, "will feel that songs like 'Looking at the Sun' and 'Your Sweet Voice' were written just for them." Perhaps Evans pegged Sweet best, though, stating, "[With] virtually all of [*Girlfriend's*] fifteen tunes offering joyous or yearning or bittersweet statements about romance, [the album] is the breathless testimony of a fool for love."

Emotional Honesty

Sweet, too, acknowledges the impact of his emotional life on his musical life. Of his separation and divorce, he said in *Rolling Stone,* "It was the most terrible experience of my life." Of the timing of his next bout with love, he explained he was "needless to say, really on edge when I went in to make this record." Cutting *Girlfriend,*

Sweet insisted, was a key aspect of his emotional recovery. "It's funny," he remarked in *Rolling Stone,* "how the album ended up showing everything I needed to feel. Everything I needed as an antidote is there." But Sweet expressed his desire that the release act as a tonic to others as well, telling *Spin's* Jurek, "I wanted to make a record that people could listen to in personal terms. It comes out of my life to a point, but it offers the listeners a chance to interject themselves, because these are experiences we all share."

Of his chosen profession, Sweet averred modestly in *Spin,* "I don't call it craft. That would be lying. I just write the songs and hopefully they're honest enough from the outset not to even need crafting." And with an edgy bit of good humor, Sweet noted to Elysa Gardner in *Entertainment Weekly,* "People say, 'This is your big breakup record—will you still be able to write good songs?' I'm sure I'll be just as depressed at some other point in my life."

It is this disarming candor—both musical and personal—that has seduced so many critics and, with *Girlfriend,* fans. Azerrad concluded admiringly of Sweet's method on that record, "[He] and his friend and producer Fred Maher traded perfectionism for spontaneity. . . . Sweet found his fullest expression in [the album's] bluesy base and loose, jam-session feel. Alternating blistering rockers with lyrical acoustic numbers, the album documents both the torment of a disintegrating relationship and the giddy rush of a new one." Sweet believes that honesty will, in fact, be the key to his continued success. He has even expressed thankfulness for the ebb and flow of his moods. "Some days I'm happy," he admitted in *Musician,* "others I'm weighed down and crushed. I've always regarded it as a valuable asset that I don't feel good about myself. I'll keep striving to do better."

Selected discography

(With Oh-OK) *Furthermore What,* DB Records, 1984.
(With Buzz of Delight) *Soundcastles,* DB Records, 1984.
Inside, Columbia, 1986, reissued, Sony, 1990.
(With the Golden Palominos), *Blast of Silence* (includes "Something Becomes Nothing"), Celluloid Records, 1987.
Earth, A&M, 1989.
(Contributor) Lloyd Cole, *Lloyd Cole,* Capitol, 1990.
Girlfriend (includes "Looking at the Sun" and "Your Sweet Voice"), Zoo Entertainment, 1991.
(Contributor) Lloyd Cole, *Don't Get Weird on Me, Babe,* Capitol, 1991.
(Contributor) *Buffy the Vampire Slayer* (soundtrack; "Silent City"), Columbia, 1992.
(Contributor) Ultra Vivid Scene, *Rev,* 4AD/Columbia.
(Contributor) *Yuletunes,* Black Vinyl Records.

Sources

Entertainment Weekly, April 17, 1992.
Musician, February 1992.
Nation, February 3, 1992.
Pulse!, December 1991; August 1992.
Rolling Stone, November 28, 1991; June 23, 1992.
Spin, March 1992.

Additional information for this profile was obtained from a Zoo Entertainment press biography, 1991.

—*Diane Moroff*

Cecil Taylor

Pianist, composer

"**I** was washing dishes in a restaurant at the same time I was being written about in places like *Down Beat,*" the iconoclastic jazz pianist and composer Cecil Taylor told *Down Beat* correspondent Gene Santoro, "and it was very good for me, because I had to decide what I really wanted to do. Did I want to pursue my ideals badly enough? It was the only way to learn that I did." Ranked with jazz innovators Louie Armstrong, Lester Young, Charlie Parker, Miles Davis, and John Coltrane, Taylor, along with Ornette Coleman, pioneered the 1960s free jazz movement with unorthodox play. Pounding out notes with fingers, fists, palms, elbows, and forearms, Cecil Taylor does not tickle the ivories so much as attack them. He forged a new concept of jazz with his improvisational compositions that disseminated conventional meter and melody. A paradigm of the misunderstood artist, Taylor was more influential than popular in his early years.

"In a more embracing cultural climate," Stephanie Stein related in *Down Beat,* "Taylor, one of our most significant contemporary musicians, would stand a pivotal link in a musical time-line: Bach, Mozart, Beethoven, Bartok, Tatum, Taylor; or for his absolute command of the piano, would share the esteem regarded his world-class peers." Awarded a Guggenheim Fellowship in 1973 and entry into *Down Beat* magazine's Critics Poll Hall of Fame in 1975, Taylor has been named *Down Beat's* number one pianist in numerous issues since his career began.

Taylor was born on March 25, 1929, in Long Island City, New York, and grew up in a two-family brick home in the borough of Queens. His father, Percy Clinton Taylor, was head chef at the Rivercrest Sanitarium in Astoria. When he came home from his 17-hour work day during the week, Taylor's father sang hymns and listened to popular performers, including Louie Armstrong and Judy Garland. Almeida Ragland Taylor, Cecil's mother, was his father's second wife. A woman of many talents who spoke French and German, played piano, and danced, she was an actress in black silent films.

Early Musical Influences

Taylor began piano lessons at age five under the tutelage of his mother, who preferred a professional career in medicine or law for Taylor. She died of cancer when he reached adolescence. Taylor's Uncle Bill, a pianist, violinist, and drummer, subsequently moved in with Taylor and his father. Hoping Cecil would become a pianist, Uncle Bill took the youngster to hear jazz

For the Record. . .

Born Cecil Percival Taylor, March 25, 1929 (some sources say March 15, 1929; March 15, 1930; or March 15, 1933), in New York, NY; son of Percy Clinton (a chef) and Almeida (Maitie) Ragland (an actress) Taylor. *Education:* Attended New York College of Music; graduated from New England School of Music, 1953 (some sources say 1952 or 1955).

Pianist, composer, and educator. Leader of jazz group, 1953—; released debut LP, *Jazz Advance,* 1956; performed at Five Spot Cafe, New York City, 1956; led onstage band in play *The Connection,* 1960; toured Europe, 1962; organized Jazz Composers Guild, 1964; recorded with Jazz Composers orchestra, 1968; played for Maeght Foundation, France, 1969, and Metropolitan Museum of Art, New York City, 1972; performed in ensembles and as a solo artist at various jazz festivals, including Newport, 1957 and 1972, Great South Bay, 1958, Montreux, 1974, and Kool Jazz, 1984; two-piano performance with Mary Lou Williams, Carnegie Hall, 1977; performed with ballet dancer Mikhail Baryshnikov; composed short ballet *Tetra Stomp: Eatin' Rain in Space,* 1979; performed for President Jimmy Carter at the White House, 1979 (one source says 1978). Instructor in music, University of Wisconsin, 1970-71; Antioch College, Yellow Springs, OH, 1972-74; and Glassboro State College, NJ.

Selected awards: Guggenheim fellow, 1973.

joined Taylor on some old classics and original numbers when the record debuted in late 1956.

Originally engaged for six weeks at the Five Spot Cafe that same year, Taylor experienced his first success at the neighborhood bar when his contract was extended. With his seminal quartet, he transformed the cafe into the foremost jazz club in New York City. Though he mesmerized the crowd, the club's owners were unhappy when patrons, who were immersed in Taylor's performance, neglected to order drinks. As the 1950s ended, Taylor won accolades for defying established jazz forms with his percussive, irregular rhythmic style in his performances at prestigious jazz festivals, including Newport. Yet, the musician was unable to find steady work.

Heralded New Jazz Movement

In 1961 Taylor's father, who had never remarried, died at the time Taylor inaugurated the free jazz movement. Alto saxophonist Jimmy Lyons and drummer Sunny Murray joined Taylor to produce his key album entry in improvisational autonomy, 1962's *Nefertiti, the Beautiful One Has Come.* That same year the musician was unemployed when he was honored with *Down Beat* magazine's New Star Pianist Award but followed with a fairly successful Scandinavian tour.

In 1964 Taylor, who had already begun to perform original numbers solely on his albums, became one of the founders of the Jazz Composers Guild. Drummer Andrew Cyrille joined Taylor and ally Jimmie Lyons the following year in an association that continued for decades. Although his devotees were not numerous in 1966, Taylor's release of *Unit Structures* solidified his reputation as the foremost pianist/composer of the era. Critics objected to the strain placed on listeners by his totally unconventional rhythmic and lyric patterns, but Taylor remained uncompromising in his pursuit of a black methodology in jazz composition. His interpretation of the piano as a percussive, rather than string, instrument rather than string, mingled European avant-garde influences with the blues.

As the decade of the 1970s began, Taylor was a frustrated educator, teaching music at the University of Wisconsin. He felt his students lacked seriousness and gave failing grades to two-thirds of his class. After Wisconsin University officials overturned the grades, Taylor accepted a position at Antioch College in Ohio. He then moved to Glassboro State College in New

performances in New York City. In addition, Taylor received classical training in public school and at the New York School of Music.

After reading that jazz great Duke Ellington believed future jazz musicians would need conservatory training, Taylor left for Massachusetts to attend the New England Conservatory of Music. Although he studied four years at the conservatory, he felt his real education began when he listened to Charlie Parker, Sarah Vaughan, and other musicians in the jazz clubs around Boston.

Taylor lived at home with his father after graduating from the conservatory in 1953. Rarely employed more than twice a year, he played an eclectic mix of stints, in Harlem and Greenwich Village, at West Indian dances, and for the Art Students League. He gigged with alto saxophonist Johnny Hodges before making the album that portended his idiosyncratic approach, *Jazz Advance,* in 1955. Bassist Buell Neidlinger, drummer Dennis Charles, and tenor saxophonist Steve Lacy

Jersey, where he stayed until 1974, the same year he began recording without accompaniment. Audiences found his solo albums accessible, heightening a new era of acceptance for Taylor; his public performances, however, were controversial.

Down Beat's Lee Jeske was baffled by Taylor's April 17, 1997, Carnegie Hall appearance with Mary Lou Williams, commenting that the two-piano exhibition struck him "like two heavyweight prizefighters ferociously maintaining their individual styles for 15 rounds." When ballet superstar Mikhail Baryshnikov teamed with Taylor, who claimed dance as an impetus for his work, their jazz-dance acts opened to mixed reactions in Philadelphia, Chicago, and Los Angeles.

The effect of lackluster press on Taylor was minimal, however. He maintained a dogged hold on his inimitable style. "At the start of the Sixties," noted Bob Blumenthal in *Rolling Stone,* "Taylor's music broke the binds imposed by straight-ahead swing and, along with the more rhythmically regular work of Ornette Coleman and John Coltrane, ushered in an era of bold jazz discovery. Two decades later, it is still called 'new music.'" An inspired Taylor concluded the decade by composing the ballet *Tetra Stomp: Eatin' Rain in Space* and holding a concert at the White House upon the invitation of President Jimmy Carter.

Secured His Audience

Taylor was named number one pianist for the ninth consecutive year in *Down Beat* magazine's Critics Poll in 1986, the same year Jimmie Lyons, his master alto sax player of more than 25 years, died. Recovering from his grief, Taylor led Leroy Jenkins, Thurman Barker, and Freddie Waits in a quintet in 1987. The following year, the release of two of Taylor's albums on compact disc (CD), *Conquistador!* of 1966 and *Cecil Taylor* of 1978, received a rave review from *Down Beat's* Art Lange, "If Taylor's career can be seen as an ocean which approaches and recedes, this music is the first indications of an oncoming tidal wave."

Responding to the barrage of Taylor re-releases that had appeared by 1990, Lange commented, "A recent avalanche of *Cecil Taylor* recordings serves to remind us of certain things that shouldn't require prompting: of the longevity of his rich, variegated recording career . . . of the depth and breadth of his creative abilities and attitudes; of the appreciation for his art outside of the United States." The momentary lapses of "insecure or uninspired playing" by a few of Taylor's accompanists, surmised Lange, exposed Taylor's demands on jazz musicians who "had to invent their roles" when accompanying a musical nonconformist like Taylor. The effort accompanists had to exert to follow Taylor was fulfilling to sidemen like the late Jimmie Lyons. Lyons once noted, reported Kevin Lynch in *Down Beat,* "Playing with Cecil made me think differently about what the music's about. It's not about any cycle of fifths—it's about sound."

An influential presence on the jazz music scene for more than three decades, Cecil Taylor confided to *Down Beat's* Santoro the ideals by which he fulminated music's formal limits, "You have to try to understand that pursuing music is a choice that you make. . . . So you then begin the process of really getting down to it: the distance between whatever excellence it is you're striving for in whatever it is you're trying to convey and the person you would like to be. . . . After all, it's a life's work."

Selected discography

Jazz Advance, Transition, 1956, reissued, Blue Note, 1991.
Nefertiti, the Beautiful One Has Come, Arista/Freedom, 1962.
Unit Structures, Blue Note, 1966.
Conquistador!, Blue Note, 1966.
Silent Tongues, Arista/Freedom, 1974.
Air Above Mountains (Buildings Within), Enja, 1976.
Cecil Taylor, New World, 1978.
3 Phasis, New World, 1978.
One Too Many Salty Swift and Not Goodbye (recorded in 1978), hat Art, 1986.
For Olim, Soul Note, 1986.
Garden (recorded in 1981), hat Art, 1986.
The Eight (recorded in 1981), hat Art, 1987.
Cecil Taylor in Berlin '88, FMP, 1988.
Looking (Berlin Version), FMP, 1989.
In Florescence, A&M, 1990.
Dark to Themselves (recorded in 1976), Enja, 1990.
Looking Ahead (recorded in 1958), Fantasy/OJC, 1990.
The Great Concert of Cecil Taylor, Prestige.
Solo, Trio.
Cecil Taylor Jumpin' Punkins, Candid.
Cell Walk for Celeste, Candid.
Indent, Freedom.
The World of Cecil Taylor, Candid.
(With Art Ensemle of Chicago) *Thelonious Sphere Monk,* DIW.
(With Buell Neidlinger) *New York City R&B,* Candid.
(With Max Roach) *Historic Concerts,* Soul Note.
(With John Coltrane) *Coltrane Time,* United Artists.
(With Segments II) *Winged Serpent,* Soul Note.

Sources

Billboard, January 13, 1990.
Down Beat, April 1980; June 1982; May 1986; November 1986;
   May 1987; January 1988; May 1989; June 1990; May 1992.
New Yorker, May 5, 1986.
High Fidelity, March 1986; April 1989.
Rolling Stone, June 28, 1979; December 13, 1990.

—Marjorie Burgess

Henry Threadgill

Saxophonist, composer

"**A**s a kid, I wanted to learn how to play all this great music, the way these great people had been doing it," jazz composer, bandleader, and performer Henry Threadgill told *Down Beat's* Howard Mandel. "It wasn't in my head to have a Mercedes. . . . To grapple with the music was enough." Winner of numerous awards in *Down Beat's* International Critics and Readers Polls, including top composer, he has led his own groups—Air, the Henry Threadgill Sextett, and Very Very Circus, among others—to probe all possibilities of sound.

Threadgill, an alto saxophonist and multi-reed player who finds that even hubcaps can be rhythmic, is a first generation member of the 1960s Association for the Advancement of Creative Musicians (AACM). Although the renowned artist has graced mass media magazines in Dewar's Profile Scotch advertisements and the stage of the Metropolitan Opera as a musician in *Porgy and Bess*, since his days with the AACM, Threadgill has admirably maintained the organization's original quest—to create "great black music."

"Threadgill's way to the forefront of contemporary creative music has always been oblique and circuitous; he's a collector of musical styles," appraised Kevin Lynch in *Down Beat*, "and an explorer who constantly stops to observe the surrounding world." Mandel conjectured, "Threadgill's originality of sound seems to render him 'too contemporary' for regular employment in taverns that showcase jazz, though his music is based in gospel, the blues, and parade marches, as well as his serious research into what's beyond." The unconventional composer, who includes funeral dirges in his repertoire, envisions a workplace in any of life's settings. He told Gene Santoro in *The Nation*, "I'd like to put a band in a funeral parlor and work there."

Developed Eclectic Musical Tastes

Born on February 15, 1944, in Chicago, Illinois, Threadgill was raised in the bleak atmosphere of the ghetto, but music brightened his household and surroundings. Exposed to country music on the radio and to classical music by an aunt who studied to become an opera singer, Threadgill developed eclectic tastes at an early age. "My grandmother took me to churches where there was music, record shops had speakers outside so you walked down the street hearing music, bands played, and still play, at the Maxwell Street flea market," he related to Mandel. "Even at grammar school, teachers played records during rest periods, good music we would cool out and sleep to."

For the Record. . .

Born February 14, 1944, in Chicago, IL; married; children: one daughter. *Education:* Received B.M. from American Conservatory of Music; attended Governors State University.

Jazz saxophonist and composer. Member of sextet that included Roscoe Mitchell, early 1960s; performed with Experimental Band and Heritage Ensemble, early 1960s; member of Association for the Advancement of Creative Musicians (AACM), early 1960s; toured with gospel singer Jo Jo Morris, 1965-67; formed trio Reflection, 1971, re-formed as Air, 1975; led Henry Threadgill Sextett, Windstring Ensemble, and Society Situation Orchestra, mid-1970s; composed score for *Diggers,* National Public Radio, mid-1980s; performed at Carnegie Hall, New York City, mid-1980s; appeared in Metropolitan Opera production of *Porgy and Bess,* New York City, mid-1980s; appeared in print advertisements for Dewars, 1988; formed ensemble Very Very Circus, early 1990s—.

Addresses: *Record company*—Axiom Records, 825 8th Ave., New York, NY 10019.

While in grade school, Threadgill studied piano and marched in street bands as a percussionist. Jazz great Charlie Parker's recordings inspired him to learn to play the saxophone. In high school, he played tenor and baritone sax in the marching band. Threadgill mastered alto saxophone, clarinet, and flute while he performed with local rhythm and blues groups in his spare time. After a stint in the Army, he spent 11 years taking university courses, including flute, piano, and composition at the American Conservatory of Music and at Governors State University. "I was never interested in a degree," Threadgill confessed to Mandel, "I was interested in the catalog."

Playing gospel music while traveling the gospel circuit with church musicians and evangelists, Threadgill procured his first professional experience. He alternated his education with blues sessions on Sundays and jazz sessions on Mondays and performed in any mix of gigs—V.F.W. bands, marching bands, polka bands, and light classical orchestras—to earn his daily bread. Disenchanted with bebop, the prevalent jazz form of the early 1960s, Threadgill commented to Santoro, "Bebop couldn't service me: it didn't have anything to do with people standing up for their rights, it didn't have anything to do with the Vietnam War, didn't have anything to do with the Gray Panthers, the Black Panthers." The musician thus joined the free jazz movement, performing in a sextet with Roscoe Mitchell and Joseph

Jarman as well as Phil Cohran's Heritage Ensemble and Muhal Richard Abrams's Experimental Band.

Boosted "Great Black Music"

"Notes per se became less important than the effects that could be conjured up through instrumental sounds—any sounds, from bleeps and blatts and burps to childlike whimpering and sobbing sighs and whinnying overblown shrieks," wrote Santoro, characterizing the radical bent of the AACM in Chicago during the sixties. Threadgill joined the nonprofit organization, an outgrowth of Abrams's Experimental Band—which sponsored performances and recording sessions—late in the decade.

Fashioning a double-tiered string of auto hubcaps into a percussion instrument, Threadgill sired his own version of composition that coincided with the AACM's "new movement" in Great Black Music. "In the AACM what was happening was an expression of what I was about, and the moment," he recounted to Mandel. "I knew that it expressed the times . . . the revolution in America, God is dead, America shooting down its kids, the [Vietnam] War, the questioning of traditional philosophies. . . . I was tied into that moment."

Threadgill formed the trio Reflection with percussionist Steve McCall and bassist Fred Hopkins in 1971 and kept McCall and Hopkins when he reformed the group under the name Air in 1975. "It is a different kind of fusion music," Charles Mitchell observed in *Down Beat* about the "beauty" of the threesome in concert. Though the group made several albums, including *Air Song, Air Raid, New Air,* and *Air Show No. 1,* Threadgill garnered more popularity after his move to New York City in the mid-1970s.

In New York he led the Windstring Ensemble and the Society Situation Orchestra and formed the Henry Threadgill Sextett, which had seven members; the two drummers functioned as one component of Threadgill's outfit. Threadgill released several albums, including *When Was That?, Just the Facts and Pass the Bucket,* and *Subject to Change,* that merited approval, but they were recorded on minor labels and received little publicity during the mid-1980s.

Acclaim at Last

In 1987 Threadgill's sextet saw its first release on a major record label. *You Know the Number,* on RCA Novus, was followed the same year by *Easily Slip Into*

Another World. Placing in 11 of *Down Beat*'s International Critics and Readers Polls in 1988, Threadgill won top composer honors as well as passage out of the relative obscurity of the previous decades with the widely acclaimed *Easily Slip Into Another World.* "The album is a brash, swaggering vindication of the tradition that regenerates itself in a dialectic of individual imagination and democratic dynamism," cheered Lynch. "It's music of the moment that echoes familiar images of the past with the elemental eloquence of myth."

Further accolades came from Eric Levin in *People:* "The emotions that Threadgill's music expresses are not only diverse, they color, comment upon and compound each other as his compositions strut, shimmy, and tumble along." Bill Milkowski concluded in *Down Beat,* "The guy's prolific and important. . . . Maybe with this wider exposure, more people will be able to appreciate Henry Threadgill's genius."

Viewing his music as "a reflection of social reality," Threadgill disclosed to Santoro that he is mystified by any revival of traditional jazz: "It's funny to see a lot of musicians involved with music that's older than they are . . . where they're playing stuff that isn't relevant today." The progressive jazz musician closed the decade of the 1980s championing invention with the release *Rag, Bush, and All,* a romp that John Ephland described in *Down Beat* as "everybody running. . . . All that running lands them in the sky."

Threadgill then opened the 1990s with a new album, *Spirit of Nuff . . . Nuff,* by his new group Very Very Circus. Planning a book and film documentary to highlight his 1991 U.S. tour, a performance of which was captured on the LP *Live at Koncepts,* Threadgill offered his mix of jazz, blues, gospel, Southern brass, and European classical music to more offbeat locales, including churches, hospitals, town squares, and zoos. "I want to give music to people in parts of this country I can't ordinarily get to," the innovative musician divulged to Suzanne McElfresh in *Down Beat.* "When you bring music to them, you make our country smaller in a good way. You break down isolation; everyone gains."

Due to release an album entitled *Too Much Sugar for a Dime* in 1993, the well-respected Threadgill, having entered his fourth decade in the business, has played an integral role in the world of jazz music. Reviewing Very Very Circus's live album in 1993, *Musician* correspondent Tom Moon praised Threadgill's ensemble: "Very Very Circus, one of the most flexible and interactive small groups currently working, is heard melding brusque funk horn lines, jittery Latin rhythms and com-

plex orchestral counterpoint into an invigorating compositional assault on the knotty *Live at Koncepts* . . . an album that defines this year's true zeitgeist."

Selected discography

X-75 Volume 1, Arista-Novus, 1979.
When Was That?, About Time, 1982.
Subject to Change, About Time, 1986.
You Know the Number, RCA Novus, 1987.
Easily Slip Into Another World, RCA Novus, 1987.
(Contributor) *Weird Nightmare: Meditations on Mingus,* Columbia, 1992.
Just the Facts and Pass the Bucket, About Time.
Rag, Bush, and All, RCA Novus.

With Air

Air Song, Why Not, 1975.
Air Time, Nessa, 1977.
Air Lore, Arista-Novus, 1979.
Air Mail, Black Saint, 1980.
80 Degrees Below '82, Antilles, 1982.
Air Show No. 1, Black Saint, 1986.
Air Raid, India Navigation.
New Air, Black Saint.

With Muhal Richard Abrams

Young at Heart, Wise in Time, Delmark, 1969.
Nonaah, Nessa, 1977.
1-OQA+19, Black Saint, 1977.
L-R-G, The Maze, S II Examples, Nessa, 1978.

With Very Very Circus

Spirit of Nuff. . . Nuff, Black Saint, 1991.
Live at Koncepts, Taylor Made, 1992.
Too Much Sugar for a Dime, Axiom, 1993.

Sources

Down Beat, August 1983; July 1985; March 1986; June 1987; July 1988; August 1988; February 1989; July 1989; April 1991; February 1993.
Musician, January 1993.
Nation, July 18, 1987.
People, May 30, 1988.
Pulse!, December 1992; February 1993.
Spin, February 1993.

—*Marjorie Burgess*

Tanita Tikaram

Singer, songwriter

Around 1982 Tikaram's family moved to Basingstoke, a
suburb south of London. At the same time, her brother
gave her a guitar. While she was learning to play,
Tikaram immersed herself in the folk-rock sound of the
1960s and 1970s; Leonard Cohen, Van Morrison, Joni
Mitchell, and Tom Waits all contributed to the development of her vocal and musical style. Tikaram staunchly
resisted the most popular musical trends around her; in
1989 she told *Melody Maker:* "Going into the Eighties I
remember Visage and all the new romantic stuff—my
brother was a member of the Duran fan club and I
remember being appalled by that."

At the time at which Tikaram began writing her own
songs, she was preparing to enter university (the equivalent of the American undergraduate system) and expecting that she would eventually study law. Writing
music began as a break from the study. This approach
to producing songs stuck with Tikaram even when she
became a professional; she explained to Jon Wilde in a
Melody Maker interview: "I associate song-writing with
everything anti-intellectual. It was a great freedom for
me when I started writing songs because I'd been
studying at school and college for so long. . . . I knew it
had to be a quick, spontaneous process." Apparently,
the shift from writing songs in her bedroom and playing
guitar for her family to international success happened
with similar ease. While singing at a South London

For the Record. . .

Born in 1970 in West Germany; father (with the British military) is from Fiji and mother from Borneo.

Singer and songwriter. Began playing guitar and writing songs while preparing for university, c. 1982-87; discovered while playing at London tavern, c. 1987; recorded material for first album with producers Rod Argent and Peter Van Hooke, 1988; signed with Reprise/Warner Bros. and released debut album, *Ancient Heart*, 1988.

Addresses: *Record company*—Reprise Records, 3300 Warner Blvd., Burbank, CA, 91505-4694.

Tavern, Tikaram caught the attention of a music agent. From there, as Wilde later described it, Tikaram's career took off with story-book speed: "She's immediately rushed into a recording-studio where she knocks her own songs into shape. With a place being held for her at university, she puts an academic career on hold and signs to the biggest record label in the world. Her debut single storms the hit parade. Her debut album sells millions and makes her an international success."

Real-Life Overnight Success Story

Tikaram's first effort, *Ancient Heart,* appeared in late 1988 and was handled by two important English producers: Rod Argent and Peter Van Hooke; the latter had worked with one of Tikaram's idols, Irish folk-rock musician Van Morrison. The recording process that Argent and Van Hooke chose, described in *Musician,* set up the sound that would ensure Tikaram's recognition: "The pair took the inexperienced singer into the studio to record . . ., first laying down her voice and guitar to a click track, then creating the record's lush soundscape with layers of synthesizer, bass and drum machine."

Fans bought the album in droves, pushing its sales up to 3.5 million within a year. *Ancient Heart* remained in the top ten—and often the top five—on U.K. charts for more than six months. By the spring of 1989, *Ancient Heart* had gone double platinum in Britain and had become the number one album on charts across Europe. Her most striking successes were in Norway, where *Ancient Heart* remained at number one for over 15 weeks, and Turkey, where Tikaram became the most popular international musician. British and American critics couldn't say enough about her voice and the enigmatic lyrics that showcased it so well. A reviewer for *Glamour* epitomized the kind of excitement that

listeners expressed: "Haunting. Primal. Passionate. The most impressive album so far this year is *Ancient Heart.* . . . Her deep rich voice is unusually mature." She was frequently compared to other female musicians who have earned respect as folk musicians, including Tracy Chapman, Michelle Shocked, Lucinda Williams, and Suzanne Vega.

In the early spring of 1989 Tikaram went on a six-week tour of Europe; during the tour, she collected a gold record from virtually every country in which she stopped. Mat Smith in *Melody Maker* described the effect that she had on an audience in Switzerland: "In Zurich, loyalty means an unprecedented three encores and a wild Swiss crowd who just won't go home even when the house lights are turned up. During the gig there were moments so pure they could only be described in tears, moments when Tanita's soul hovered above our heads glinting like a lighthouse in a storm." By April of the same year, she had started on her tour of the United States, consolidating her popularity with American fans.

Received Mixed Reviews

While on tour, Tikaram was already writing the songs for her second release, *The Sweet Keeper,* which she cut with the same producers and musicians who worked on her first album. She told Wilde that the "title for the album came from this book I have by the Indian writer, RK Narayan, called *The Vendor of Sweets.* I remember thinking that the title had a great childlike quality to it." The unrestrained praise for the first album, however, was not repeated with the second; although sales were still strong, many critics, including *Melody Maker*'s Bob Stanley, were more skeptical: "While Tanita is a huge fan of Leonard Cohen and Joni Mitchell, her lyrics barely compare. On *The Sweet Keeper* . . . they have progressed to the point where they sound simple but are often impenetrable." Stanley was even ambivalent about that mainstay of Tikaram's success, her voice: "It's her voice which remains the centerpiece of *The Sweet Keeper.* Tan sounds even older than she did on *Ancient Heart,* 20 going on 46, but her voice now wavers and changes from song to song. On the single, 'We Almost Got It Together,' while it's still identifiably Tanita, it sounds as if she had a couple of gins before the tapes started rolling."

With 1991's *Everybody's Angel,* her third release in as many years, Tikaram tried changing her production style, albeit still working with Van Hooke, Argent, and most of the same musicians. She shifted the style of the music some, moving towards a rhythm and blues sound: "I'd been listening to a lot of these collections with people like Otis Redding and Sam Cooke, and I realized that most of these '60s soul singers weren't particularly loud, they just knew how to control their voices." Moreover, making the most of her first attempt at co-production, she insisted on *live* recording sessions—during which the musicians are taped playing together, rather than the more common pasting together of a song that has been recorded piecemeal.

The production created a sound that *Musician*'s Cronin found particularly successful: "Throughout her new record Tikaram puts that lesson to good use, coaxing wide-ranging dynamics out of her extraordinary voice." He declared that "Tikaram found the warmth she was looking for." Other reviewers, however, as well as fans, received this album with less enthusiasm than they had the first two. As with *The Sweet Keeper, Everybody's Angel,* according to critics, suffered from too much musical production; Jenny Jedeikin in *Rolling Stone* explained: "*Everybody's Angel* adds horns, backing harmonies and strings to the Celtic arrangements that Tikaram fans have come to expect. However, because her voice is her strongest asset, Tikaram would be better served by less cluttered accompaniment."

Image Attacked in Press

The drop in Tikaram's critical success with the release of *Everybody's Angel,* which several reviewers characterized as simply too much too soon, was accompanied by an occasionally vicious attack on her public image. She had started out as the darling both of the teen pop scene—gracing the pages of *Seventeen* and *Glamour*—and of serious music critics precisely because she would not conform to the self-advertisement expected of music celebrities; eventually, however, a number of critics rejected her for taking herself *too* seriously. For the critics who did not care for Tikaram's music, this quickly became the focus, as they lambasted the singer for her choice not to market herself as a sex symbol.

At the lenient end of the spectrum are Wilde's comments about *The Sweet Keeper:* "Like its predecessor, *Ancient Heart,* it's a strangely self-contained work. These songs, like the ones which launched Tikaram's career, are emotionally detached to the verge of frigidity. . . . Lyrically too, they never quite emote, always hanging back, preferring to keep themselves ambigu-

ous and unresolved." Paul Lester, writing for *Melody Maker,* picked up on that charge: "That voice is something. It really is starved of emotional expression"; he went on to administer deeper criticism by stating, "Horny she ain't. *Horn-rimmed,* maybe. Welcome to Librarian rock." Stanley closed a review with a similar sentiment, commenting that "now if only she'd swap that black outfit for something a little more cheery—a gold lamé suit, perhaps?," and another *Melody Maker* reviewer began a piece with the observation that "she's not exactly sexy is she?"

Although these reviewers clearly saw Tikaram's understated persona as a fault in a female performer, the majority of her listeners—according to sales—still find something valuable in her music and image. And the extent to which she controls the production of her music and her image has increased. Continuing at her previous pace, Tikaram prepared a fourth album, *Eleven Kinds of Loneliness,* for release in the spring of 1992; for this work, she again augmented her own role as producer.

Selected discography

Ancient Heart (includes "Twist in My Sobriety" and "For All These Years"), Reprise, 1988.
The Sweet Keeper, Reprise, 1990.
Everybody's Angel, Reprise, 1991.
(Contributor) *Mark Isham,* Virgin, 1991.
Eleven Kinds of Loneliness, Reprise, 1992.

Sources

Entertainment Weekly, May 22, 1992.
Glamour, September 1989.
Life, May 1989.
Melody Maker, March 11, 1989; June 10, 1989; December 23-30, 1989; January 27, 1990; February 24, 1990.
Musician, April 1991.
People, March 12, 1990.
Rolling Stone, March 7, 1991.
Seventeen, April 1989.
Stereo Review, May 1990; January 1991.
Vanity Fair, April 1991.

—*Ondine E. Le Blanc*

Randy Travis

Singer, songwriter

Randy Travis was among the first performers of his generation to find a mainstream audience for traditional country music. By 1986, Travis, who grew up listening to his father's recordings of past country greats, had parlayed his down-home good looks, distinctive voice, and intelligent choice of material into country stardom. He was inducted into the Grand Ole Opry at the age of 28 and was the first country artist ever to have a debut album sell over one million copies. As Jay Cocks put it in *Time* magazine, Travis had "not redefined country so much as reminded everyone of its truest instincts."

Travis was "discovered" in Nashville just as public taste began to reacquaint itself with conventional country music. His songs of love, heartache, and the realities of blue-collar life endeared him—and thus, country music itself—to a generation of listeners raised on rock and roll. In 1991 *Pulse!* contributor Robert Gordon equated Travis with country music's return to basics, explaining how the singer "rode the crest of the New Traditionalist movement which began halfway through the last decade, establishing an expansive audience that Nashville never knew existed."

Whether writing his own songs or choosing others to record, Travis steered clear of material even slightly pop- or rock-oriented. He has sung duos with such country music standard-bearers as George Jones, Roy Rogers, and Tammy Wynette. Travis's heartfelt dedication to pure country forms indeed proved the catalyst to his success; as *Pulse!* contributor Gordon suggested, he was in the right place at the right time, with a powerful strain of conviction in his performance. "You will know the voice right away, even if you have never heard it," Cocks reported. "A backcountry baritone canters along a line of swaying melody, taking it easy, taking everything easy. The prides, the miseries, the dalliances and departures that are the mother lode of country music, all are delved into and delivered up with the sidling grace of an unordained preacher taking the back door to honky-tonk heaven."

Learned From Williams, Haggard, and Jones

"I do try to sing with as much feeling as I can," Travis told the *New York Times Magazine*. "I lived a lot. I *did* a lot. I got started early, doin' a lot of things. That's some of what I learned from Hank [Williams Sr.] and [Merle Haggard] and [George] Jones—because when you listen to them sing a song, they can just make you believe everything about it. They just sing to you like it really happened to them. And to me, that's what singin's all about."

Travis was born Randy Traywick in Marshville, North Carolina, on May 4, 1959, one of five children. Both of his parents worked full-time—his father owned a construction company and his mother worked in a textile mill. The Traywicks owned a farm, too, and Randy helped raise turkeys and cattle. Harold Traywick, however, had other ambitions for his son. The elder Traywick was a fan of old-time country music, especially the works of Hank Williams, Lefty Frizzell, Ernest Tubb, Gene Autry, and Roy Rogers. Young Randy grew up listening to recordings from another era and despite the pull of rock and roll, fell in love with the country sound. "My brothers and sisters, people I went to school with—I mean, all of them—were definitely into rock 'n' roll," Travis told *Time.* "Sure, I heard it. I mean, if I was riding in a car with them, I didn't have a lot of choice. But it never really appealed to me that much."

Father Encouraged Performing Career

What did appeal to Travis was country music, especially the George Jones and Merle Haggard songs of the late 1960s and early 1970s. When Travis was only ten, his father bought him a Gibson guitar for Christmas. A brother, Ricky, received a set of drums. With their parents' enthusiastic approval, the two began performing as "The Traywick Brothers" at local functions. Randy was still in grade school. "My folks pushed me to do it," Travis told *People* magazine. "It has always been in Daddy's mind especially." Travis absolutely hated school, dropping out before finishing the ninth grade. For a while he worked on his father's turkey farm and in the construction business, but he seemed more bent on getting into trouble than making a living.

He continued to perform—now as a solo singer—in tough venues where acts would be protected from the audience by chain link fence. Soon Travis was drinking excessively and using drugs. He has been brutally candid about his troubled teen years, telling *Newsweek* that he began drinking at 12 and using drugs at 14. "Sometimes a lot harder drugs, but at least marijuana every day," he admitted. "I think all that was part of why I got into so much trouble. Because I drank *so* much and did *so* many drugs that it was like it wasn't me. It was like another person was in control. Nobody can handle that kind of abuse. You go crazy, you're not mentally in control. I'm just thankful that cocaine wasn't around when I was going through my bad time. I'd have probably died. I'd have probably killed myself with it."

As it was, Travis nearly ruined his health and almost landed in prison before his eighteenth birthday. "I can't count the times I've been in jail," he told *Time.* Once he was arrested for leading police on a high-speed chase. Another time the charge was breaking and entering. Travis was saved, literally, by his voice. During one of his stable periods he had won a talent contest at Country City U.S.A., a nightclub in Charlotte, North Carolina. The club's owner, Lib Hatcher, was bowled over by his sincere delivery and shy presence on stage. Hatcher gave Travis the second chance he needed to stay out of jail and reconstruct his life. She told him he could be a big star and that she could help him get to the top. He believed her. "The main reason I eventually got straightened out was that I met my manager, Lib Hatcher," Travis told *Stereo Review* in 1989. "She gives great advice, and finally I found someone I could talk to. I never had that before. It was really a combination of her and my music. For the first time I took the music business seriously. It gave me something actually to do."

Rescued by Lib Hatcher

At 17, facing five years in prison for the breaking and entering charge, Travis was spared prison when Hatcher appeared in court on his behalf; she told the judge she would employ Travis full-time and take responsibility for him. She was granted custody, and Travis was warned that the next time he appeared in court, he had better bring his toothbrush. Thus, in 1976, a partnership began that would bring stardom to Travis and a millionaire lifestyle to the woman who believed in him. Travis moved in with Hatcher and her husband and began to sing regularly at Country City U.S.A. Hatcher's marriage ended shortly thereafter, and she devoted more and more of her energy to advancing Travis's career. She moved her club into a new building with more seats and scraped together $10,000 to record two singles on a tiny Louisiana record label.

Faith alone propelled the pair through some lean years. Travis told *Country America* magazine: "Lib and I have seen numerous Christmases together, and sometimes we didn't feel like we had very much to celebrate. Before we moved to Nashville, there were some pretty hard times in North Carolina. . . . For several years there, neither of us could really afford to buy much of anything for anybody. I was working at the nightclub in Charlotte that Lib owned, and it wasn't doing too well. There was hardly any money changing hands."

In 1980 Hatcher sold her Charlotte club and moved with Travis to Nashville. There they rented a bungalow on 16th Avenue, in the famed Music Row area, and sought work in which Travis would be most visible. Hatcher found a position managing the Nashville Palace, one of the many restaurants featuring live music located within a stone's throw of the Opryland complex. Travis went to work at the Palace as a short-order cook and singer. Billed as "Randy Ray," he would cook, wash dishes, sing, and then wash more dishes. He often worked from dawn until two a.m. "I don't know why I didn't get discouraged," he told *People*. "Lack of sense or something." Almost every record company in Nashville turned down "Randy Ray" at least once; Warner Bros. passed him over twice. Still Hatcher persisted, inviting Grand Ole Opry stars in to sing at the Palace and to hear her young protege.

Signed With Warner Bros.

Then Travis's style caught up with the times. The early 1980s saw the emergence of George Strait, Ricky Skaggs, and Reba McEntire, all performers with pure country—rather than pop, or "countrypolitan," as the 1970s trend toward watered-down country was called—orientation. Though Nashville executives still preferred artists with crossover potential, pointing to the success of the Charlie Daniels Band and Alabama among teens, Warner Bros. senior vice president Martha Sharp nevertheless went to the Palace to hear "Randy Ray" perform in 1985 and offered him a contract on the spot. "I loved his voice," she told the *Los Angeles Times*. "But I knew I was going to get a lot of guff. The prevailing opinion ·at that time was that he was too country, nothing that country would work. Still, my gut told me to go ahead."

The first thing Sharp did was change Randy Traywick's stage name to Randy Travis. Then she encouraged him to focus on his strengths—especially his robust but edgy voice and the vein of irony that helped temper his

---

> *"I don't know why I didn't get discouraged—lack of sense or something."*

---

more sentimental songs. Travis's first album, *Storms of Life,* was released by Warner Bros. in June of 1986 with anticipated sales of 20,000 units. By the end of the year it had sold more than a million copies and yielded four hit singles: "1982," "On the Other Hand," "Diggin' Up Bones," and "Reasons I Cheat." *Storms* catapulted Travis from anonymity to becoming the winner of the Country Music Association's coveted Horizon Award— the equivalent of a "rookie of the year" honor.

During his years of struggle Travis and his band had journeyed to concerts in a converted bread truck; equipment was hauled in a van and horse trailer. By the beginning of 1987, the Travis entourage—still ably managed by Hatcher—traveled in the comfort of a $500,000 bus. Hatcher also found Travis a publicist, who signed the engaging young singer to some unlikely television appearances, including one on the rock-oriented *Saturday Night Live*. Through shrewd management and sheer hard work, Travis soon eclipsed many of the other New Traditionalists. His second album, *Always and Forever,* sold well over three million copies and remained at the Number One position on the country charts for a record 43 weeks. The release's most popular hit single, "Forever and Ever, Amen" was named favorite country single of 1987 by both the

Country Music Association and the Academy of Country Music.

Developed Talents

In 1988 the former cook at the Nashville Palace found himself performing at London's Royal Albert Hall, with Rolling Stone Mick Jagger in the audience. By that time Travis had massed three platinum albums and scores of fans, many of whom had never before given country music a second glance. As Bob Millard put it in *Country Music* magazine, Travis's popularity had grown to the point that he "can sell a million copies of anything with his voice on it." Still, Travis is not the type to rest on his laurels. As a member of the Grand Ole Opry, he could have settled in and comfortably churned out his trademark hits year after year as other singers came and went. Instead, the singer stretched his musical skills by writing more of his own material and tinkering with his style—without abandoning the pure country sound that made him famous. His 1991 album, *High Lonesome,* yielded two hits he co-wrote with country up-and-comer Alan Jackson, "Better Class of Losers" and "Forever Together." The latter, a heartfelt ballad of devotion to a loved one, crested the charts just as Travis married Lib Hatcher, in May of 1991.

Through it all Travis has remained modest about his success and grateful that he has made his mark without compromising to fit markets beyond country. "I have a voice that sounds like a country singer, and there's no way around that," he told *Stereo Review.* "Plus, I don't *want* to do anything else. I love country music." *Country Music* contributor Michael Bane called Travis "your basic lightning rod," adding, "With his successes, the floodgates opened, and, as it always has, country music changed, evolved. Within a few years, the business belonged to the 'men with hats,' traditional male vocalists." Some of these "hat acts," in fact—most notably country phenomenon and pop music fan Garth Brooks—outshined Travis in the early 1990s. As Alanna Nash concluded in *Entertainment Weekly,* "Travis's success opened the door to all those guys . . . and they owe him more than a wave as they pass him by on the charts."

What they also owe Travis is respect for his tenacity and his integrity as a country musician first and a crossover artist second. The singer who lists his own personal favorites as George Jones and Merle Haggard told *Pulse!,* "Country music has changed some, but it still addresses the things that everyday people go through

in everyday life. To me that's what country music is about."

Selected discography

On Warner Bros. Records, except where noted

Storms of Life (includes "1982," "On the Other Hand," "Diggin' Up Bones," and "Reasons I Cheat"), 1986.
Always and Forever, 1987.
Old 8 x 10, 1988.
An Old Time Christmas, 1989.
No Holdin' Back, 1989.
Heroes and Friends, 1990.
High Lonesome (includes "Better Class of Losers" and "Forever Together"), 1991.
Greatest Hits (2 volumes), 1992.
(Contributor) *Barcelona Gold,* 1992.
(Contributor) *A Very Special Christmas II,* A&M, 1992.
Soundtrack, 1993.

Sources

Books

Newsmakers 1988, Gale, 1989.
Vaughan, Andrew, *Who's Who in New Country Music,* St. Martin's, 1989.

Periodicals

Chicago Tribune, November 13, 1986; February 22, 1987.
Country America, January 1992.
Country Music, January/February 1991; March/April 1991; November/December 1991; January/February 1992; July/August 1992.
Entertainment Weekly, March 20, 1992.
Los Angeles Times, March 6, 1988.
Newsweek, October 27, 1986; October 16, 1989; October 22, 1990.
New York Times Magazine, June 25, 1989.
People, November 10, 1986; June 24, 1991.
Pulse!, November 1991.
Stereo Review, September 1987; June 1989.
Time, June 22, 1987; July 25, 1988.
Washington Post, February 15, 1987.

Additional information for this profile was obtained from Warner Bros. media information, 1992.

—Anne Janette Johnson

Turtle Island String Quartet

Acoustic quartet

Winnipeg Symphony cellist Mark Summer had a jarring revelation halfway through a performance of a progressive classical piece: "I remember being in the middle of playing Berlioz's 'Symphonie Fantastique,'" he told *Newsweek*. "This amazing piece, way ahead of its time, and I'm going, 'I'm really *bored*.'" Shortly thereafter, Summer teamed up with violinists Darol Anger and David Balakrishnan to form the iconoclastic Turtle Island String Quartet. Summer no longer complains of boredom; neither do his audiences.

Dedicated to eradicating the distinction between highbrow and low, Turtle Island String Quartet has been credited in the *Detroit News* with having "erected a wondrous musical bridge that spans the chasm between the twangy mountain sounds of bluegrass and the rarefied elegance of classical chamber music." Balakrishnan explained, "We're a string quartet, we're jazz musicians, we're composers and we grew up listening to [British rock group] the Beatles." Combining the classical quartet format with a varied American repertoire, Turtle Island has created a unique formula

For the Record. . .

Members include **Darol Anger** (violin; born c. 1953), **David Balakrishnan** (violin; born c. 1954; received master's degree in composition from Antioch University), **Jeremy Cohen** (violin, viola; studied with Itzhak Perlman; replaced **Katrina Wreede**, 1992), and **Mark Summer** (cello; born c. 1958; attended Cleveland Institute of Music).

Quartet formed in San Francisco, CA, c. 1986; signed with Windham Hill Jazz Records; released debut album, *Turtle Island String Quartet*, 1988.

Selected awards: Grammy Award nomination, 1988, for "Night in Tunisia," from *Turtle Island String Quartet.*

Addresses: *Agent*—Jeff Laramie, SRO Artists, Inc., P.O. Box 9532, Madison, WI 53715.

that has drawn a broad-based following. Chamber music aficionados are attracted to the group's technical prowess, while a wider audience finds its "swinging strings" irresistible. Whatever its appeal, Turtle Island has won a spot at the forefront of a new movement among young classical musicians.

Accomplished Musical Backgrounds

The name Turtle Island, derived from the Native American word for North America, reflects the group's preference for a homegrown repertoire. Committed to what they call "American vernacular," the group's members draw on such diverse musical traditions as jazz, world beat, bluegrass, folk, and rock. In the course of a typical performance, the ensemble moves effortlessly from works by the likes of Chick Corea, Benny Goodman, and George Gershwin to such irreverent pieces as Balakrishnan's suite "Waterfall With Blenders," a spoof of New Age music. During one New York City recital, jazz great Dizzy Gillespie's classic "A Night in Tunisia" was masterfully interwoven with Harburg-Arlen's "If I Only Had a Brain" and the theme song to the 1950s television sitcom *Leave It to Beaver.*

The Turtle Island String Quartet is able to pull off its blending of eclectic musical styles because of the members' impeccable technique—the result of accomplished musical backgrounds. Darol Anger, an international performing and recording artist, is the product of northern California's jazz and bluegrass movements. A central figure in the development of the "new acoustic" style, which combines folk and jazz, he is widely respected for his ingenious technical innovations.

David Balakrishnan, Turtle Island's principal composer and arranger, holds a masters degree in composition from Antioch University. Balakrishnan's work has received both critical acclaim and honors; he was the recipient of the National Endowment for the Arts' Meet the Composer Grant in 1988 and was nominated for a Grammy Award for his arrangement of "A Night in Tunisia" on the album *Turtle Island String Quartet.*

Known for his improvisational skills, Mark Summer is regarded by critics as one of the premier jazz cellists on the contemporary scene. Classically trained, he played for the Winnipeg Symphony after attending the Cleveland Institute of Music.

Jeremy Cohen, who plays both violin and viola, has extensive classical experience. He performed with the New Jersey Philharmonic, the New York Pro Arte Chamber Orchestra, and the National Orchestral Association after studying under Itzhak Perlman. Well versed in jazz, he has recorded with Ray Charles and Horace Silver.

Distinctive Debut Album

Collectively, Turtle Island utilizes its members' skills by combining the techniques each brings to the ensemble. Through their classical training, Balakrishnan told *Newsweek,* the Turtle Islanders learned standard techniques for precision playing such as bowing in unison. Under the guidance of its jazz players, the group mastered the art of improvisation and the "subtle shades and inflections" basic to jazz, Summer added. What's more, the musicians' skills are complementary: "Balakrishnan's conservatism keeps Anger's adventurousness from getting out of hand. And the others keep Balakrishnan . . . from getting too academic," remarked a *Newsweek* correspondent.

Based in the San Francisco Bay Area, Turtle Island was formed in the mid-1980s by Balakrishnan and Anger, fellow members of the David Grisman String Quartet, a new acoustic ensemble. Summer met Anger at the 1985 Winnipeg Folk Festival, where he heard his band Montreaux perform. Following a concert by Anger, Balakrishnan, and Matt Glaser as part of the Bay Area's Jazz Violin Celebration, Summer became the group's third member. In 1992 Jeremy Cohen took the quartet's fourth seat, a position previously held by Katrina Wreede.

Turtle Island made its Windham Hills recording debut in 1988 with *Turtle Island String Quartet,* an album that *Down Beat* commented "swings with distinction." Featuring such jazz standards as Miles Davis's "Milestones," Dizzy Gillespie's "Night in Tunisia," Oliver Stone's "Stolen Moments," and Bud Powell's "Tempus Fugit," it also includes original compositions that are a hybrid of bluegrass, Indian, and European music. The album is made distinctive by its unusual rhythmic techniques. With no traditional piano or bass drum accompaniment, the Turtle Islanders create a strong backbeat by stretching their strings to the limit. "The violin can produce acoustically all the sounds rock guitar players buy those pedals to create electronically," Balakrishnan told *Newsweek*. To do so, the musicians pluck strings, run their bows over miked instruments or the side of a violin to create a brush effect, and use the "chop." "The chop is something we use . . . to get the sound of the drums or the rhythm guitar sound," Balakrishnan explained in the *Detroit News*. "That gives the really important backbeat groove that we need to create the Swing feel."

Expanded Scope of String Quartet Format

Turtle Island String Quartet introduced the eclectic approach to repertoire that would become the group's trademark. On *Metropolis,* released in 1989, the quartet explored that repertoire further, presenting arrangements of pop-jazz works by Pat Methany, Horace Silver, Lee Morgan, and John Coltrane alongside its own, original compositions. The album also gave the Turtle Islanders the opportunity to demonstrate their well-honed improvisational skills. Indeed, *Metropolis*'s rise to the Top 20 on the jazz charts is a tribute to the group's musical prowess.

Turtle Island's next two albums reflect an interest in a more focussed repertoire. *Skylife,* released in 1990, features original compositions, while the 1991 album *On the Town* concentrates on conventional jazz material from the swing era. "Instead of making albums that have something of everything on them," Anger noted, "we're going to concentrate album by album, so we can really immerse ourselves in the style and see how far we can take it, and put the Turtle Island stamp on it."

If the quartet's performance since its inception is any indication, the Turtle Island stamp is bound to make a lasting impression. The group has distinguished itself with its adventurous repertoire, technical innovations, and able improvisations. Having achieved an acceptance in both classical and jazz circles that has helped to significantly expand the scope of the string quartet format, the Turtle Island String Quartet is not about to quit. "There is so much to explore," Balakrishnan told the *Detroit News*. "We see a life's work here, no problem at all."

Selected discography

On Windham Hill Jazz Records

Turtle Island String Quartet, 1988.
Metropolis, 1989.
Skylife, 1990.
A Shock to the System (soundtrack), 1990.
On the Town, 1991.
Spider Dreams, 1992.

Sources

Billboard, November 30, 1991; September 19, 1992.
Chamber Music, summer 1989.
Detroit Free Press, March 6, 1992.
Detroit News, April 11, 1991.
Down Beat, April 1988; December 1991.
Los Angeles Times, April 8, 1991.
Newsweek, September 24, 1990.
People, August 21, 1989.
Pittsburgh Press, June 22, 1992.
Reading Times (PA), March 25, 1991.
Stereo Review, November 1990.
Topeka Capital-Journal (KS), October 8, 1991.

Additional information for this profile was obtained from a Windham Hill Records press release, 1992.

—*Nina Goldstein*

Dawn Upshaw

Opera singer

Even though Dawn Upshaw is one of the most sought-after contemporary performers on the operatic and concert stage, she is in some ways an unlikely star. Raised by parents who, as amateur performers, specialized in songs by folk greats Peter, Paul and Mary and Bob Dylan, her early musical heroes were Linda Ronstadt and Barbra Streisand, and she even briefly considered a career singing commercial jingles. She was not at all impressed by her first exposure to opera—a production of Rossini's *Barber of Seville*—while she was in high school and did not become serious about singing operatic roles until her audition in 1984 for the Metropolitan Opera's (Met) Young Concert Artists program.

Even after achieving international fame, Upshaw is something of an atypical celebrity—an "anti-diva," as David Patrick Stearns of *Stereo Review* has called her. In a profession where monumental egos have become legendary, Upshaw remains modest and self-critical, once telling *Gramophone*'s Edward Seckerson, "I don't have an incredible voice; I don't think that I have a particularly individual sound." And although the rigorous demands of a performing career have been known to wreak havoc on the families of many artists, Upshaw has carefully guarded her private life, often bringing her husband and daughter with her on tour and insisting on at least one full month off a year to spend with them. As she confided to Stearns, "I've always found my sense of identity from my family, not through performing. And that will always be most important."

An Inventive Performer

As remarkable as Upshaw's path to stardom has been, her choice of repertoire and the manner in which she has presented it in recital and on recording. Although she has been widely acclaimed in mainstream operatic roles, such as those in Mozart's operas, she made a commitment early in her career to champion contemporary music, especially works by American composers. She has followed through on her decision by premiering roles—such as the lead in William Mayer's controversial *Death in the Family*—programming contemporary vocal literature on her recitals, and recording works by such American composers as John Harbison, Gian Carlo Menotti, Samuel Barber, and Charles Ives.

Upshaw has also tried to bring a new freshness to the time-honored traditions of the vocal recital; she enjoys chatting with the audience during her performances and occasionally builds recitals around a single theme. In one performance she chose "Childhood," beginning with the Mussorgsky song cycle *The Nursery* and end-

Born July 17, 1960, in Nashville, TN; daughter of a psychotherapist and a teacher; married Michael Nott (a musicologist), 1986; children: Sarah Elizabeth. *Education:* Illinois Wesleyan University, B.A., 1982; Manhattan School of Music, M.A., 1984; studied with Jan DeGaetani at summer workshops in Aspen, CO.

Opera singer and concert performer. Attended apprenticeship program and debuted as Countess Ceprano in Verdi's *Rigoletto,* Metropolitan Opera, New York City, 1984-85; sang soprano lead in premiere of William Mayer's *Death in the Family,* St. Louis, MO, 1986; replaced Kathleen Battle as Adina in Donizetti's *L'elisir d'amore,* Metropolitan Opera, 1988; sang in four Mozart productions, Metropolitan Opera, 1991-92; appeared in concert with Los Angeles Philharmonic, Atlanta Symphony, Cleveland Orchestra, and other ensembles; toured with Chamber Music Society of Lincoln Center; performed in festivals in Edinburgh, Scotland, and Aix-en-Provence, France, 1992.

Selected awards: Winner of Young Concert Artists International Auditions, 1984; first prize, Walter Naumberg Vocal Competition, 1985; Grammy awards, 1989, for *Knoxville: Summer of 1915,* and 1991, for *The Girl With Orange Lips.*

Addresses: *Agent*—Agnes Bruneau and Associates, 155 West 68th Street, No. 1010, New York, NY 10023. *Record company*—Elektra/Nonesuch, 75 Rockefeller Plaza, New York, NY 10019.

Susan Elliott of the *New York Times,* "I was always aware of Jan's particular devotion to 20th-century music; but also, just from watching and listening to her, I learned how important it is to have a lot of respect for myself. To do things I think are important."

Began Road to International Career

The first important stepping-stone in Upshaw's career was her success in 1984 at international auditions sponsored by Young Concert Artists, which led to an apprenticeship at the Metropolitan Opera. Upshaw made her operatic debut there during the 1984-85 season, singing the small role of Countess Ceprano in Verdi's *Rigoletto.* She also developed a friendship and important working relationship with the Met's artistic director, James Levine, with whom she has since appeared on several recordings.

In 1985 Upshaw shared first prize in the Naumberg competition, subsequently giving a recital at the Lincoln Center and recording her first solo disc for Musicmasters. Another major break came at the Met in 1988, when she filled in for an ailing Kathleen Battle in the role of Adina in Donizetti's *L'elisir d'amore.* Upshaw's career has skyrocketed ever since; she has received requests to perform at opera houses and festivals throughout the United States and Europe, has traveled on lengthy recital tours, and has appeared on several highly acclaimed recordings, two of which have won Grammy Awards.

Natural Talent Combined With Scholarship

Throughout her career Upshaw has been praised for the warmth and freshness of her tone and the effortlessness of her vocal technique. Reviewing Upshaw's performance as Pamina in Mozart's *Magic Flute,* Bernard Holland of the *New York Times* called her "the radiant pure center of the evening." In addition, David Stearns has written of her "spring-water-fresh vocal quality, rare directness, and simplicity of manner."

Yet, part of what has made Upshaw a truly outstanding artist has been her striving for more than just sheer beauty of tone. As she told *Connoisseur's* Elizabeth Riely, "I don't think about sound alone in singing. That comes before. Ultimately, in performance I forget about the technique. I try to get the message across through the music the composer has written." To do this, Upshaw studies the texts of the pieces she sings in tremendous depth, exploring the details and nuances of the words in order to communicate them to her audience. "I try to have a solid understanding of the text—not just what it's

ing with Brahms's lullaby. Her inventiveness is even visible in the packaging of her second solo recording, *The Girl With Orange Lips,* which features a provocative photo of her taken at the Bronx Botanical Gardens. "People have an idea of what classical records should look like," she expressed to Stearns, "and I think that's a little ridiculous."

Although she sang informally with her parents and was a choir member in high school, Upshaw began her formal music training at Illinois Wesleyan, where she studied with David Nott. Nott's son Michael, a musicologist, became Upshaw's husband in 1986. After graduating, the singer moved to New York, where she studied voice with Ellen Faull at the Manhattan School of Music. During summer workshops in Aspen at this time, she became acquainted with Jan DeGaetani, considered one of the country's outstanding vocal interpreters of contemporary music. DeGaetani had a profound impact on Upshaw's career; as Upshaw told saying, but what it means and why the composer has set it in a particular way," she commented to Elliot. "And I go for a certain naturalness and simplicity, because through that, the message gets across much more easily than fussing about how I'm standing or even singing."

It is the unlikely collection of elements she embodies—the informal, "girl-next-door" image combined with a brash sense of musical adventure and a profound dedication to the art of singing—that has no doubt endeared Upshaw to audiences, critics, and fellow musicians. Although the singer herself may at times seem surprised at the turns her life has taken, there are those who find her talent a natural gift that could not go unexpressed. As the great conductor Robert Shaw declared, according to Elliott, "It's [Upshaw's] nature to sing, just like it's a bird's nature. That's why she's here on earth."

Selected discography

Naumberg Foundation Presents: Works by Wolf, Strauss, Rachmaninoff, Ives and Weill, Musicmasters, 1986.
Strauss, *Ariadne auf Naxos,* Deutsche Grammophon, 1986.
Knoxville, *Summer of 1915,* Elektra/Nonesuch, 1989.
Vivaldi, *Gloria in D; J. S. Bach, Magnificat in D,* Telarc, 1989.

Donizetti, *L'elisir d'amore,* Deutsche Grammophon, 1990.
Schubert, *Mass No. 2,* Telarc, 1990.
American Elegies, Elektra/Nonesuch, 1991.
Charpentier, *Te Deum, Magnificat,* EMI, 1991.
The Girl With Orange Lips, Elektra/Nonesuch, 1991.
Mozart, *Lucio Silla,* Teldec, 1991.
Mozart, *The Magic Flute,* EMI, 1991.
Mozart, *The Marriage of Figaro,* Deutsche Grammophon, 1991.
Gorecki, *Symphony No. 3,* Elektra/Nonesuch, 1992.
Mozart, *La Finta Giardiniera,* Teldec, 1992.

Sources

Connoisseur, February 1988.
Gramophone, November 1991.
New York Times, February 4, 1990; February 10, 1990; September 28, 1991; November 10, 1991; December 17, 1991; February 15, 1992.
Opera News, February 2, 1991.
Stereo Review, June 1992; July 1992; September 1992.
Wall Street Journal, April 27, 1990.

Additional information for this profile was obtained from Agnes Bruneau and Associates, 1992.

—*Jeffrey Taylor*

Jody Watley

Singer, songwriter

"I know what I like and don't like," vocalist and performer Jody Watley told Rory O'Connor in *Vogue.* "I fight for what I want—and I get it." A dancer on the television show *Soul Train,* Watley sang with the popular rhythm and blues trio Shalamar before making her way to solo stardom in the late 1980s. An award-winning recording artist, Watley designed a successful marketing strategy that has netted multiplatinum-selling albums and numerous Top Ten singles. "Some performers are great singers, some can dance, some have a great look, and others project a lot of energy," Watley, who wanted to be a fashion designer once, disclosed to O'Connor. "But I'm all those things rolled into one."

Born in Chicago, Illinois, Watley is the daughter of a radio talk show evangelist. As a child, she met several prominent black entertainers, including Sam Cooke and Joe Tex, through her father's program. When Jody was eight years old, her godfather, "Mr. Entertainment" Jackie Wilson, invited her to perform live with him onstage. She recalled to Anthony DeCurtis in *Rolling Stone,* "It was really funny—I didn't freak out or anything. Once I was out there, I became Little Miss Excitement."

The Watley family moved frequently throughout Jody's childhood because of her father's schedule. She revealed to DeCurtis that although her mother sang in church choirs, "it never interested me. It always seemed like too many people to be in the midst of." Instead, Watley remained in her room "dancing up a storm" in front of her mirror to the secular strains of James Brown and Motown. Her parents made no objection to her musical taste. "I started finding myself through short stories and little poems I wrote as a kid," Watley recounted to David Ritz in *Essence.* "I always loved writing. And dressing up. My mother has wonderful taste in clothes. She'd dress me for school so immaculately that I'd get run home."

Became *Soul Train* Dancer

After her family moved from Kansas City, Missouri, to Los Angeles, Watley landed a spot on *Soul Train,* beginning her dancing career at the age of 14. When Jeffrey Daniel became her television dance partner, the pair devised eye-catching routines. "We started doing things that would make us stand out," Jody divulged to DeCurtis. "We'd do stuff that none of the other dancers would have the nerve to do." The couple enhanced their act using such things as roller skates and oriental fans. When Watley was 17, she was encouraged by *Soul Train* producer Don Cornelius to start a singing career. The high school graduate, who had received her diploma with honors, confided to Ritz, "It wasn't

For the Record. . .

B orn January 30, c. 1960, in Chicago, IL; daughter of a radio evangelist; children: Lauren.

Singer and songwriter. Dancer on television show *Soul Train* at age 14; member of trio Shalamar for eight years; released self-titled solo album on MCA Records, 1987; producer of exercise video *Jody Watley: Dance to Fitness*, 1990.

Selected awards: Grammy Award for best new artist, 1988; two multiplatinum albums.

Addresses: *Home*—Los Angeles, CA. *Record company*—MCA Records, 70 Universal Plaza, 3rd floor, Universal City, CA 91608.

easy deciding not to go to college, since learning's important to me. But deep down, I knew this was my destiny."

Cornelius persuaded Watley and Daniel to form a trio with Howard Hewett called Shalamar, marketing the single "Uptown Festival," which Cornelius had previously made with studio musicians. Although Shalamar produced numerous successful albums, songwriter Watley was disillusioned during her eight years with the group since Shalamar recorded only two of her songs. "Spiritually, creatively, artists must grow," Watley told Ritz. "After a few years, it was clear that my artistic growth was stunted. I was stuck. . . . I couldn't stand being treated like a brainless doll. It wasn't a matter of money, it was a matter of happiness. Success isn't being rich; it's being happy." Watley left Shalamar to launch her own career in 1984.

Launched Solo Recording Career

After a brief sojourn in England making pivotal professional contacts, Watley returned to Los Angeles where she paired up with ex-Prince bassist Andre Cymone. Cymone, producer Bernard Edwards—who had worked with Diana Ross—and Watley developed songs, while Watley put together "the design, the details, the videos, the concept as a whole," she told *Vogue's* O'Connor. Her 1987 multiplatinum, self-titled debut album was carefully calculated to present Jody as a savvy *femme fatale* in the same league with her late eighties competitors Janet Jackson and Whitney Houston. Although *High Fidelity* posted "warning signs" about Watley being an "all watered-down Janet Jackson," *Rolling Stone* asserted the artist was a worthy rival whose "vocals establish her as a serious pro." The magazine

continued, "She gets to the song's emotional point." Watley's profile appeared in several magazines, including *Vogue, Essence, Rolling Stone,* and *Harper's Bazaar.* Winning a Grammy Award in 1988 for best new artist, she devoted the next years to making herself a headliner.

Watley's second release, 1989's *Larger Than Life,* went platinum, convincing critics the singer was durable. *People's* David Hiltbrand declared that the young star is "likely to be with us for a while if she continues to put out strong, sassy, records like [*Larger Than Life*]." The reviewer commented that her "voice, though limited, has a sultry edge," but her "music throughout is rich, crisp and clear."

In 1991 Watley's third album, *Affairs of the Heart,* received accolades from Arion Berger in *Entertainment Weekly:* "*Affairs* may be unserious dance fluff, but Watley's commitment to the music is real. She sings love songs as if they matter, and the record turns out to be another solid collection of heavy-breathing dance workouts." Diane Cardwell in *Rolling Stone* and David Hiltbrand in *People* noted Watley lacked the vocal strength to carry off the numerous ballads on the album, but Hiltbrand stated, "Watley still furnishes abundant reasons to move" on her "dance grooves."

Renowned for Style

A single mother, Watley balances a career and raising her daughter, Lauren, in Los Angeles. Renowned for her fashion sense, she favors Japanese designers but donned a $40 thrift shop bargain when she attended the 1988 Grammy Awards. Watley told Lynn Hirschberg in *Vanity Fair,* "I style myself. . . . It drives the record company crazy. . . . But I know my goals better than anyone—I want to be megafamous *and* I want to do my own grocery shopping."

Watley's early 1990s plans included worldwide tours and acting roles. An advocate of charities for AIDS victims, she sang composer Cole Porter's "After You, Who?" on the AIDS benefit album *Red Hot + Blue.* The multitalented performer told Larry Flick in *Billboard,* "We all have an obligation to lend a helping hand to people in pain. It's all about compassion and humanity. What good is there in success if you can't use it to help people who need it?"

Selected discography

On MCA Records

Jody Watley, 1987.

Larger Than Life, 1989.

(Contributor), "After You, Who?," *Red Hot + Blue,* Chrysalis, 1990.

Affairs of the Heart, 1991.

You Wanna Dance With Me?

Sources

Billboard, November 30, 1991.

Ebony, February 1988; April 1992.

Entertainment Weekly, December 13, 1991.

Essence, July 1982; May 1988.

Glamour, June 1988.

Harper's Bazaar, September 1989.

High Fidelity, September 1987.

Interview, December 1991.

Jet, June 22, 1987.

Musician, July 1987.

People, May 22, 1989; July 1, 1991; January 13, 1992.

Performing Arts, 1983/1984.

Playboy, October 1989.

Rolling Stone, May 21, 1987; June 18, 1987; August 24, 1989; January 23, 1992.

Vanity Fair, October 1991.

Vogue, September 1987.

—Marjorie Burgess

John Williams

Composer, conductor

"In recent decades the American whose music is heard by the most people at home and abroad is probably not George Gershwin, Cole Porter, Michael Jackson, or Bruce Springsteen," William Livingstone claimed in *Stereo Review,* "but the film composer John Williams." Indeed, having written the musical scores for ten of the Top 12 money-making motion pictures of all time—*Star Wars, Close Encounters of the Third Kind, Jaws,* and *E.T. The Extraterrestrial* among them—Williams has been assured of a vast audience. But his music has been not merely an accompaniment to the action on the screen; it stands alone. His soundtracks have sold into the millions. And Williams's dozen-year tenure as director of the Boston Pops, one of the world's most widely recognized orchestras, has further ensconced his name and music in the minds of contemporary listeners.

Williams's commitment to quality was evidenced early on. Born in 1932, in Flushing, New York, Williams first studied piano at the age of six. By the time he was in grade school, this son of a CBS radio orchestra percussionist had learned to play bassoon, cello, clarinet, trombone, and trumpet. He also organized a small band, but found that since the clarinet and piano are in different keys, they could not be played from the same music. Not to be thwarted, he learned to transpose the music. "I used to sit in the basement of our house . . . and pour over orchestration books," he recalled to Richard Dyer in *Ovation.* "I applied the principles of Rimsky-Korsakov to the pop tunes of 1940 and 1941, and by the time our band was in high school, we were already quite sophisticated." In effect, his writing and orchestration career had begun.

Started Career as Studio Pianist

Around 1950, Williams attended UCLA and Los Angeles City College, concentrating on the study of orchestration. He also studied composition privately with Italian composer Mario Castelnuovo-Tedesco. Serving in the U.S. Air Force during the Korean War, Williams played, conducted, and arranged music for military bands. In 1954, after having completed two years of military duty, Williams enrolled at the Juilliard School of Music in New York, studying piano with Madame Rosina Lhevinne. When his apprenticeship at the conservatory ended, he played jazz piano in nightclubs. Williams returned to Los Angeles in 1956, securing his first job with the film industry as a studio pianist. Among Williams's first projects was *South Pacific.*

But his talent lay in composition and orchestration, and established film composers such as Bernard Herrmann,

For the Record. . .

Born John Towner Williams, February 8, 1932, in Flushing, NY; son of John (a percussionist) and Esther Williams; married Barbara Ruick, c. 1956 (died, 1974); married Samantha Winslow (a photographer), 1980; children: (first marriage) Jennifer, Mark, Joe. *Education:* Attended University of California, Los Angeles; studied orchestration with Robert van Epps at Los Angeles City College; studied composition with Mario Castelnuovo-Tedesco, c. 1950-1952; studied piano with Rosina Lhevinne at Juilliard School of Music, 1954-55.

Composer and conductor. Worked as jazz pianist in New York City nightclubs, c. 1954-55; pianist for Columbia Pictures and Twentieth Century Fox staff orchestras, beginning in 1956; album arranger, late 1950s and early 1960s; composer of film scores and television theme music, 1960—; conductor and music director of the Boston Pops Orchestra, 1980-93; artist-in-residence at Tanglewood Music Center, 1993—. Frequent guest conductor.

Selected awards: Seventh Annual Career Achievement Award, Society for the Preservation of Film Music, 1991; numerous Academy Award nominations; Academy awards for best original film score or song for *Fiddler on the Roof, Jaws, Star Wars,* and *E.T. The Extraterrestrial;* 16 Grammy awards; two Emmy awards; three Golden Globe awards; honorary degrees from numerous institutions including Boston University, New England Conservatory of Music, Tufts University, and the University of Southern California; numerous gold and platinum records.

Addresses: *Home*—Los Angeles, CA. *Agent*—Michael Gorfaine, The Gorfaine/Schwartz Agency, Inc., 3301 Barham Blvd., No. 201, Los Angeles, CA 90068.

Alfred Newman, and Franz Waxman took note, encouraging him to orchestrate their material and pursue his own creations. Working for Columbia Pictures, Williams also arranged albums for such diverse Columbia Records artists as singer Vic Damone and gospel star Mahalia Jackson. At this same time, he was also under contract to write music for television series, often for as many as 39 programs a season. The workshop intensity forced Williams to compose and adapt music to almost any setting—an invaluable ability for his upcoming career.

In 1960 Williams scored his first film, *Because They're Young,* starring Dick Clark. Neither the film nor the score made a lasting impression, but his work for television was soon recognized with Emmy and Grammy nominations and awards, and his musical screen credits began to mount. Albeit with notable exceptions, Williams's subsequent film scoring career can be divided chronologically into four genres: comedies, musicals, disasters, blockbusters.

Light comedic fare like *Bachelor Flat* and *Gidget Goes to Rome* marked his first phase, which Williams described to *Ovation's* Dyer as having "lots of brass chords on cuts to brassieres." Hollywood began recognizing his work during the 1960s with Academy Award nominations, but it wasn't until his second phase that an award was finally bestowed—he was given an Oscar for his work on the 1971 film adaptation of *Fiddler on the Roof.* Popular recognition for Williams finally came in the mid-1970s when the film market was flooded with several disaster movies he had scored, including *The Poseidon Adventure, Earthquake, The Towering Inferno,* and culminating in the unforgettable 1975 release *Jaws.* The menacing two-note phrase signaling the approach of the shark has become one of the most famous leitmotifs in contemporary film. *Jaws* earned Williams two Academy awards and marked the beginning of his long and fruitful collaboration with director Steven Spielberg, out of which would come two more award-winning productions—1977's *Close Encounters of the Third Kind* and 1982's *E.T. The Extraterrestrial.*

Star Wars Created New Dimension

Another directorial wunderkind, George Lucas, selected Williams to score his mythic fantasy *Star Wars* in 1977. The resultant composition placed Williams in his final phase and at the forefront of modern film composers. "I have no pretensions about that score, which I wrote for what I thought was a children's movie," he told Livingstone in *Stereo Review.* "All of us who worked on it thought it would be a great Saturday-morning show. None of us had any idea that it was going to become a great world success." The music Williams created, expansive and symphonic in character, has almost become standard concert material, taking on its own life apart from the movie. Some critics, like Dyer, believed the music not only transcended the movie but helped define it: "There is a sense in which the music really created the characters of *Star Wars*—when anyone thinks of Princess Leia, does he [or she] remember Carrie Fisher, or the sinuous flute theme that transmutes her into a gorgeous creature of myth?"

With such thorough successes, it was surprising when Williams, at the top of his field, accepted the position as conductor of the Boston Pops Orchestra in 1980. The then 95-year-old orchestra had previously been led by the venerable Arthur Fiedler, who died after a 50-year reign that made The Pops and Fiedler nearly synonymous. But famed conductor André Previn, who encouraged Williams to pursue and accept the position, believed Williams had something to offer the Boston Pops. "He knows the orchestra from the point of view of the man with the pencil, and that means intimately," Previn was quoted as saying by Daniel B. Wood in the *Christian Science Monitor.* "He can make superlative arrangements of pop materials, and he can edit, fix, handle anything that comes up in someone else's arrangement, make it better, and all in a matter of minutes."

With his classical compositional training and his experience in jazz, Williams gave the Pops a broader musical sensibility while continuing, and even expanding, its popular appeal. He took the Pops on tour to Japan and the Far East, exposing audiences to a repertoire previously unheard in those regions. He also continued to create lauded scores for the biggest movies of the 1980s and early 1990s, including the *Indiana Jones* series, *Home Alone,* and *JFK.*

Resigned From Pops

Williams announced his resignation from the Boston Pops effective at the end of the 1993 season. His tenure had been productive and satisfying, and, as he explained to Dyer, this time in the *Boston Globe,* "With every birthday ending in a zero, you want to reconsider and reprioritize your life." Scaling back his conducting and film scoring responsibilities to move beyond his past accomplishments in pursuit of a deeper challenge, Williams was serving as an artist-in-residence at the classically oriented Tanglewood Music Center. "All through the last 30 years I've done so much composing," he explained to Andrew L. Pincus in the *Berkshire Eagle,* "but most of it's been to order—film music and background music of a kind of utilitarian nature. I've always wished that somewhere along the line in life there could be time and the opportunity for a little more thoughtful composition."

Time is definitely on the side of this prolific artist. Showered with accolades and celebrity, Williams remains resolutely devoted to a stalwart ideal behind the production of his work: "Will it be good enough?" he explained to Livingstone. "That keeps me going, and that challenge is the key to my obsession with what I am doing in my work."

Selected compositions

Film scores

Because They're Young, Columbia, 1958.
Gidget Goes to Rome, Columbia, 1963.
Valley of the Dolls, Twentieth Century Fox, 1967.
Goodbye Mr. Chips, MGM, 1969.
Jane Eyre, British Lion, 1971.
Fiddler on the Roof, United Artists, 1971.
The Poseidon Adventure, Twentieth Century Fox, 1972.
Cinderella Liberty, Twentieth Century Fox, 1973.
Earthquake, Universal, 1974.
The Towering Inferno, Twentieth Century Fox/Warner Bros., 1974.
Jaws, Universal, 1975.
Star Wars, Twentieth Century Fox, 1977.
Close Encounters of the Third Kind, Columbia, 1977.
Superman, Warner Bros., 1978.
Dracula, Twentieth Century Fox, 1979.
The Empire Strikes Back, Twentieth Century Fox, 1980, reissued, Varese Sarabande, 1992.
Raiders of the Lost Ark, Paramount, 1981.
E.T. The Extraterrestrial, Universal, 1982.
Return of the Jedi, Twentieth Century Fox, 1983.
Indiana Jones and the Temple of Doom, Paramount, 1984.
Empire of the Sun, Warner Bros., 1987.
The Witches of Eastwick, Warner Bros., 1987.
The Accidental Tourist, Warner Bros., 1988.
Born on the Fourth of July, Universal, 1989.
Indiana Jones and the Last Crusade, Paramount, 1989.
Presumed Innocent, Warner Bros., 1990.
Home Alone, Twentieth Century Fox, 1990.
JFK, Warner Bros., 1991.
Hook, Tri-Star, 1991.
Far and Away, Imagine Entertainment, 1992.
Home Alone 2, Arista, 1992.

Compositions broadcast on television include the "Mission Theme" for NBC News; "Olympic Fanfare and Theme" for the 1984 Summer Olympics; "The Olympic Spirit" for the 1988 Summer Olympics; and music for the 1988 Winter Olympics.

Other compositions include two symphonies; bassoon, clarinet, flute, and violin concertos; an *Essay for Strings;* and chamber music pieces.

Selected discography

With the Boston Pops

Pops in Space, Philips, 1981.
Pops on the March, Philips, 1981.
We Wish You a Merry Christmas, Philips, 1981.
Pops Around the World, Philips, 1982.
On Stage, Philips, 1984.

(With James Ingram) *America, the Dream Goes On,* Philips, 1985.

(With Dudley Moore) *Prokofiev—Peter and the Wolf,* Philips, 1985.

Swing, Swing, Swing, Philips, 1986.

Pops in Love, Philips, 1987.

Holst—The Planets, Philips, 1988.

Pops Brittania, Philips, 1989.

Music of the Night: Pops on Broadway, Sony Classical, 1990.

I Love a Parade, Sony Classical, 1991.

The Spielberg/Williams Collaboration, Sony Classical, 1991.

The Green Album, Sony Classical, 1992.

Iberia, Sony Classical, 1992.

Kid Stuff, PolyGram, 1992.

Joy to the World, Sony.

Night Before Christmas.

Sources

Berkshire Eagle (Pittsfield, MA), July 19, 1992.

Boston Globe, July 24, 1992.

Christian Science Monitor, April 30, 1985.

High Fidelity/Musical America, May 1981; September 1981.

Los Angeles Times, April 15, 1991; December 21, 1991.

Ovation, June 1983.

Stereo Review, July 1988; September 1988.

Additional information for this profile was obtained from the Gorfaine/Schwartz Agency, Inc., 1992.

—Rob Nagel

Sonny Boy Williamson

Singer, harmonica player

Rice Miller, better known as Sonny Boy Williamson, was one of the founding fathers of electric blues and rock and roll. Sporting a goatee, pin-striped suit, and bowler hat, the aging Williamson appeared an elder statesman of the blues. During his lifetime, his brilliant harmonica and vocal style attracted numerous understudies. In the early 1940s and 1950s, bluesmen like B. B. King, Junior Parker, and James Cotton traveled hundreds of miles from their homes to watch him perform. At the height of the sixties blues revival, rock groups from the Yardbirds to the Band played with the harmonica legend. Through live radio broadcasts, recordings, and stage performances, Williamson brought his music to audiences throughout America and Europe. To those who knew him, he was fiercely independent and often confrontational—a streetwise genius whose music helped shape nearly every bluesman of the post-World War II era.

Williamson was born Aleck Ford, the son of Millie Ford, on December 5, 1899, in Glendora, Mississippi. One of many children, Williamson began teaching himself harmonica at the age of five. Adopting the surname of his stepfather, Jim Miller—Millie Ford never married her son's natural father—the young boy later became known to local Mississippians as Rice Miller. In the 1920s, Williamson performed throughout the South as a spiritual musician called "Little Boy Blue." During the next decade, he billed himself as "The One Man Band," entertaining crowds with his skills on harmonica, drums, and zoothorn.

After leaving home around the age of thirty, Williamson earned his livelihood working for tips at jukejoints, picnics, carnivals, and lumbercamps. A drifter and incessant gambler, he took to wearing cut-off rubber boots and a self-fashioned leather belt that held his large collection of harmonicas. By the mid-1930s, Williamson crossed the Delta with the likes of Robert Johnson, Elmore James, Robert Nighthawk, and Johnson's stepson, Robert Junior Lockwood. In the years that followed, Williamson played plantations throughout Mississippi with his brother-in-law, Howlin' Wolf.

From Rambler to Radio Personality

None of his years on the road, however, brought Williamson as much notoriety as did his radio show on KFFM in Helena, Arkansas. In 1941, Williamson, along with guitarist Lockwood, began broadcasting his show from the second floor of the Floyd Truck Lines building. The broadcast could be heard within a range of fifty to sixty miles and was one of the first in the country to feature electric blues. With the sudden commercial

Born Aleck Ford, December 5, 1899, in Glendora, MS; died March 25, 1965, in Helena, AR; buried in White-field Baptist Church Cemetery, Tutwiler, MS, gravestone erected, 1977; took name Sonny Boy Williamson from bluesman John Lee Williamson; also known as Rice Miller; son of Millie Ford; stepson of Jim Miller; married, 1930s; married Mattie Lee Gordon, 1949.

Began playing harmonica c. 1904; performed as religious musician "Little Boy Blue," 1920s; appeared as one-man band, 1930s; traveled the South with various bluesmen, mid-1930s; hosted King Biscuit Time radio program, KFFM, Helena, AR, 1941-45; performed in clubs in Detroit, MI, 1945-49; radio show host, KWEM, West Memphis, TN, 1949; recorded for Trumpet record label, 1951-54; recorded for Chess Records, 1955; toured Europe with American Blues Festival, 1963-64. Annual King Biscuit Blues Festival inaugurated, Helena, 1986; Sonny Boy Blues Society founded, Helena, 1988.

success of the program, the sponsor decided to market Sonny Boy Corn Meal, displaying a caricature of Williamson on every sack. Eventually, other musicians became members of Sonny Boy's King Biscuit Boys, including drummer James "Peck" Curtis, guitarist Willie Wilkins, and pianist Robert Dunlow. Upon leaving the show in 1945, Williamson journeyed to Detroit where he performed in clubs with pianist Boogie Woogie Red. Four years later, Williamson moved to West Memphis where he hosted a fifteen minute broadcast on KWEM radio, sponsored by Hadacol Tonic. Among the show's listeners was a singer-guitarist named B. B. King who appeared as an occasional guest artist.

Williamson's radio show also attracted the notice of Lillian McMurray, who in 1951 invited him to record for her newly formed Trumpet label in Jackson, Mississippi. He was joined in the studio by longtime veterans Wilkins, Elmore James, James's drummer Frock O'Dell, and Willie Love. These sessions captured Williamson's maturing musical style and unusual vocal ability. His first single, "Eyesight to the Blind," became an immediate regional hit. Many of his recordings for Trumpet exhibited a lively jump dance sound.

Williamson's vocals were, as music writer Robert Palmer described in his book Deep Blues, "autobiographical" in nature, revealing "sharp private images." This quality imbued recordings like "Nine-Below Zero" and "West Memphis Blues," a song describing how fire ravaged his home in West Memphis in 1949. But Williamson's career at Trumpet ended in 1955 when the

company sold its rights to the Chicago-based Chess label.

Chicago-Bound

Upon joining the ranks at Chess that same year, Williamson began turning out sides for the company's new subsidiary, the Checker label. Along with Muddy Waters, Howlin' Wolf, and Little Walter, Williamson became one of the major forces responsible for transforming a small unknown label into a legendary institution.

Williamson's first session featured the Muddy Waters Band—Waters and Jimmy Rogers on guitars, Otis Spann on piano, and Freddy Below on drums. Together, they recorded Williamson's first single, "Don't Start Me to Talking," which later that year became a Top Ten R&B hit. For the next eight years, Williamson produced numerous classic numbers for Chess, like "Cross My Heart," "Checking Up on My Baby," "My Younger Days," "Help Me," "Bring It On Home," and the eerie "Your Funeral and My Trial."

With the exception of a few sessions in 1956-1957, most of Williamson's Chess recordings showcased the standard Chicago line-up: piano, two guitars, bass, drums, and harmonica. Longtime friend Lockwood remained Williamson's preferred guitarist, as his sophisticated chordal work and fills created a rich contrapuntal sound with Williamson's voice-like harmonica. Another major sessionman, bassist and producer Willie Dixon, recalled in his autobiography I Am the Blues, that if Williamson "didn't have the right song [he] would make up something just as good and keep right on playing." And it was this gift for improvisation that gave Williamson's lyrics a flowing poetic quality unmatched by many of his contemporaries.

Blues Ambassador

During his career at Chess, Williamson continued to tour and play club dates. In 1960 he convinced Lockwood to move to Cleveland where they worked for thirteen months. Restless, Williamson moved on to play in the Chicago and Milwaukee areas. But 1963 was a major turning point, when he joined the American Folk Blues Festival, a tour that stopped in France, Holland, Germany, Denmark, Sweden, and England. Williamson received a warm reception from thousands of European fans—some of whom followed him around on the streets for days. While in England, he played in Chris Barber's band; and on his second tour in 1964, he performed and recorded with rock groups like the Yardbirds and the Animals. "It's likeable in England," related Williamson to Max Jones in *Melody Maker* magazine. "They seem to appreciate the blues."

Despite Williamson's appreciation for his British admirers, he returned home that same year to Helena where he hosted the "King Biscuit Hour" and played local clubs. While on a visit to Helena, a young white rock group named Levin and the Hawks (later known as the Band) invited Williamson to an impromptu jam session in their motel room. "When we played, something happened," commented Hawk's guitarist Robbie Robertson in *Rolling Stone*. "It was quite magical." The musical combination proved so impressive, the Hawks made plans to tour with Williamson. But such aspirations came to an end when, on March 25, 1965, the blues legend passed away in his Elm Street apartment in Helena.

Upon his death, Williamson left behind thousands of musical admirers and devoted listeners. Over the years, he was known to have taught harmonica—to such later blues greats as Junior Parker, James Cotton, Howlin' Wolf, and Billy Boy Arnold. Across the Atlantic, Williamson's songs became standards in the repertoire of English rock and blues bands. More recently, his music has survived in the harmonica stylings of James Harmon and the Fabulous Thunderbirds' Kim Wilson. "There's not a night that I don't play one or two Sonny Boy songs," related Wilson in the *Arkansas Gazette*. "He was one of the key people in the blues." Other forms of tribute include the founding of the Sonny Boy Blues Society and the King Biscuit Blues Festival, both based in Williamson's former home of Helena.

"Sonny Boy had a wonderful life. He was one of the greatest deliverers of the soul blues," declared Willie Dixon in the liner notes to Chess's *Sonny Boy Williamson: The Real Folk Blues*. A master storyteller, gifted musician, and originator of over 80 songs, Williamson remains one of the most influential and respected musicians of electric blues.

Selected discography

Sonny Boy Williamson: The Real Folk Blues, Chess, 1965.
Sonny Boy Williamson: More Real Folk Blues, Chess, 1967.
Sonny Boy Williamson: One Way Out, Chess, 1984.

The Unissued 1963 Blues Festival, Red Lightning, 1985.
Keep It to Ourselves (recorded in 1963), Alligator, 1992.
King Biscuit Time, Arhoolie.
Down and Out Blues, Checker.
Sonny Boy Williamson, Chess.
Sonny Boy Williamson: Bummer Road, Chess.
Sonny Boy Williamson and Memphis Slim, Crescendo.
Sonny Boy Williamson: A Portrait in Blues, Storyville.
Sonny Boy Williamson: Final Sessions 1963-6, Blue Night.

Sources

Books

Barlow, William, *Looking Up at Down: The Emergence of Blues Culture*, Temple University Press, 1989.
The Blackwell Guide to the Blues Records, edited by Paul Oliver, Basil Blackwell, 1989.
Dixon, Willie, and Don Snowden, *I Am the Blues: The Willie Dixon Story*, Da Capo, 1989.
George, Nelson, *The Death of Rhythm & Blues*, Dutton, 1989.
Guralnick, Peter, *Feel Like Going Home: Portraits in Blues & Rock n' Roll*, Harper, 1988.
Harris, Sheldon, *Blues Who's Who: Biographical Dictionary of Blues Singers*, Da Capo, 1979.
Palmer, Robert, *Deep Blues*, Viking Press, 1989.
Rowe, Mike, *Chicago Blues: The Music and the City*, Da Capo, 1975.
Scott, Frank, *The Down Home Guide to the Blues*, Cappola Books, 1977.
Shaw, Arnold, *The World of Soul: Black Americans' Contribution to the Pop Music Scene*, Cowler, 1970.

Periodicals

Arkansas Gazette (Helena), August 13, 1991.
Daily World (Helena, AR), October 10, 1991.
Living Blues, March/April 1990.
Melody Maker, January 11, 1964.
Rolling Stone, November 14, 1991.

Additional information for this profile was obtained from liner notes by Willie Dixon to *Sonny Boy Williamson: The Real Folk Blues*, Chess, 1965.

—John Cohassey

George Winston

Composer, pianist, guitarist

George Winston is known as one of the great popularizers of minimalist, acoustic solo piano music. His best-selling albums *Autumn, December, Winter Into Spring,* and *Summer* feature pleasant, uncluttered melodies that invite the listener to relax. On the concert stage, however, Winston likes to get the audience tapping their toes to the boogie-woogie and stride piano pieces of such celebrated jazz pianists as Fats Waller and Doctor Longhair.

Although born in Michigan in 1949, Winston grew up elsewhere: Florida, Mississippi, Montana. With each move his family made, the young boy was exposed to different musical styles. George enjoyed many kinds of music, including 1960s-brand Top 40 and rock and roll. At the age of eight he took piano lessons but quit playing when he decided that he preferred partaking in baseball with the other boys in his neighborhood. After a hiatus of several years Winston came back to the piano, inspired by Jimmy Wisner's playing on "Asia Minor," a song recorded with the group Kokomo, and Floyd Cramer's tunes "On the Rebound" and "The Last Date." Winston was also influenced by Vince Guaraldi's music for the Peanuts animated television specials in 1965, Artie Butler's piano on Joe Cocker's hit song "Feelin' Alright," and Nicky Hoplins's melodic piano work on guitarist Jeff Beck's album *Beck-Ola.*

As a teenager Winston played rock and roll organ and electric piano with a Miami band until 1971, when he discovered the music of Fats Waller. Waller's stride, or acoustic, piano playing was a style of jazz developed in the 1920s as an offshoot of ragtime. In an interview with *Down Beat* writer Bill Milkowski, Winston described his discovery of stride: "I was playing electric piano at the time . . . when I heard Fats do 'Got a Brand New Suit' off one of the old RCA Vintage albums. I remember saying, 'This is how I wanted to play all my life.' I had seen a couple of stride players . . . but I wasn't really interested in stride until I heard Fats. I literally left the electric stuff behind." Winston immersed himself in playing stride piano and began to compose and arrange his own works, which included rhythm and blues, blues, rock, standards, and highly melodic solo piano pieces. In 1972 he recorded *Ballads and Blues,* his first solo piano album.

Career Suffered Ups and Downs

Discouraged by the music business and frustrated at not being able to reach his goal of playing stride piano like Fats Waller, Winston quit playing piano altogether in 1977. "For a while it just broke my heart," he told Milkowski. "I knew I could never play like Fats, with that power and delicacy." A few years later Winston's interest was piqued by a tune called "Hey Now Baby," by Roy Byrd, known as Professor Longhair. He again immersed himself in piano, this time playing Professor Longhair songs.

Winston also learned to play the guitar and became interested in the works of several Hawaiian slack key guitarists. Slack key refers to the Hawaiian style of solo guitar finger picking using open tunings on a classical or steel-stringed guitar. It was Winston's interest in guitar that led to the piano music for which he is best known. After hearing a Christmas album for solo guitar by John Fahey entitled *The New Possibility,* Winston started trying to work out some of Fahey's tunes on his guitar. Then he began experimenting with the songs on the piano and developing his own highly melodic pieces.

Meeting Brought Unexpected Success

Winston's musical career had already sputtered and taken odd turns. When he approached William Ackerman, guitarist and founder of Windham Hill, an independent record label, about re-releasing an out-of-print album by a Brazilian guitarist, he had no inkling of what was to happen. Ackerman and Winston met after a year of corresponding. "I originally intended to sign George as a guitarist. I was sleeping at his house in L.A., and he played me this slide-guitar stuff," Ackerman told *Rolling Stone*'s Kurt Loder. "I said, 'George, this is fabulous, we're gonna do an album.' He said, 'Great.' Then he said, 'Hey do you mind if I play the piano a bit while you're going to sleep?'" Ackerman was so impressed by Winston's introspective, melodic piano compositions, that he changed his mind about the guitar album deal. Winston instead recorded the solo piano albums *Autumn, Winter Into Spring, December,* and *Summer.* He subsequently became the most popular artist on the

Windham Hill label's roster, with cassettes selling in the hundreds of thousands of copies.

Winston's uncluttered solo piano music is never frenetic or aggressive and has become for many a prime acoustic example of what is popularly called new age space music. According to *The New Age Music Guide,* "Space music carries visions in its notes; it is transcendent inner and outer space music that opens, allows, and creates space. Though born of electronics, it is harmonic, beautiful, and emotionally compelling." Winston remarked to *Down Beat*'s Milkowski, "With the *Autumn, Winter Into Spring,* and *December* records, I try to communicate season changes and the thoughts of what people are doing in those changes. I've come up with something personal so that it doesn't really matter how good or bad it is pianistically. It just reflects what I'm trying to say personally."

Thrilling Concerts

In 1983 Winston founded Dancing Cat Productions, a Santa Cruz, California-based independent record label that enjoys distribution rights under an agreement with record giant BMG. Winston's company has brought out several albums of stride piano tunes, including *Rock 'n' Roll Gumbo* and *The London Concert,* performed by Professor Longhair, and soundtracks to the children's classics *The Velveteen Rabbit* and *Sadako and the Thousand Paper Cranes,* which employ Winston's evocative solo piano. Winston tentatively plans to record solo piano albums on the themes of the forest and the plains as well as collections of Vince Guaraldi compositions, rhythm and blues pieces, and stride tunes. According to Winston, works by Hawaiian slack key guitarists will figure prominently on Dancing Cat lists in the 1990s.

Winston has garnered a loyal following in the United States and Europe. Although best known for his melodic, evocative piano music, Winston surprises live audiences when he pulls out his harmonica or guitar, or when he breaks into stride and boogie-woogie piano tunes, inviting listeners to take the stage and dance. Audiences may also be startled by the balding, grizzly bearded Winston's casual appearance. He once took the stage at New York City's Avery Fischer Hall wearing jeans, a plaid work shirt, and no shoes. In 1992 Winston was studying the style of rhythm and blues/jazz pianists Henry Butler and James Booker, as well as working on solo guitar, particularly pieces by the masters of the Hawaiian slack key style. With such a varied career, it is difficult not to wonder what Winston will be involved with next.

Selected discography

Ballads and Blues, Windham Hill, 1972.

Autumn, Windham Hill, 1980.

December, Windham Hill, 1982.

Winter Into Spring, Windham Hill, 1982.

Evening With Windham Hill Live, Windham Hill, 1983.

(With Meryl Streep) *The Velveteen Rabbit,* Rabbit Ears Presents, 1985.

Summer, Windham Hill, 1991.

(With Streep) *The Night Before Christmas,* Rabbit Ears Presents, 1992.

(With Liv Ullman) *Sadako and the Thousand Paper Cranes,* Dancing Cat, 1992.

(Contributor) *Windham Hill: The First Ten Years,* Windham Hill, 1992.

December, Windham Hill, 1993.

Variations on the Kanon by Pachelbel, Windham Hill.

Sources

Books

The New Age Music Guide, compiled by Patti Jean Birosik, Collier Books, 1989.

Periodicals

Audio, August 1983.

Christian Science Monitor, May 2, 1984.

Down Beat, December 1982; March 1983; March 1986.

Guitar Player, November 1981; November 1989; December 1990.

High Fidelity, December 1981.

New York Times, December 9, 1983; December 14, 1983.

People, August 9, 1982.

Rolling Stone, March 17, 1983.

Stereo Review, March 1984.

Variety, February 20, 1985; July 22, 1987; December 20, 1989; January 31, 1990.

Washington Post, December 12, 1982; April 22, 1983; July 9, 1983; February 20, 1984.

Additional information for this profile was obtained from a Dancing Cat Productions, Inc., press biography, 1992.

—Jeanne M. Lesinski

Yo Yo

Rap singer

"Hip hop may have taken sexual politics out of the halls of black academia and into the 'hood," reflected Joan Morgan in a 1991 *Village Voice* review, "but *feminist* remains a word so loaded even a super-woman like [rapper] Queen Latifah steps from it. So as hip hop's first self-proclaimed feminist activist, 19-year-old Yo Yo should be given her props on bravery alone." Indeed the young rapper did arrive on the scene riding a wave of fierce and successful female rhymesters, but she claimed the mantle of feminism more openly than most of her peers. With the help of producer-mentor Ice Cube, Yo Yo established herself as a potent force in rap; then she launched the Intelligent Black Woman's Coalition (IBWC) to "help sisters of all races make positive changes in their lives," as she explained in *Essence*. Although the social agenda underlying many of her songs helped secure her place in the forefront of the hip-hop community, Yo Yo achieved fame primarily via her skills on the microphone. "She rhymes with charm and mischievous attitude," commented Michael Small of *People* magazine, declaring also that Yo Yo "makes an unwavering call for self-respect that reaches her young urban audience as no polite pre-election speech could."

Born Yolanda Whitaker in 1971, Yo Yo grew up in south central Los Angeles with her mother and seven siblings. A school security guard, Mrs. Whitaker's energy and determination provided an early example for her daughter. "My mother is my inspiration," Yo Yo told *The Source,* noting that with her own children grown, Mrs. Whitaker "works with young girls with babies, group home kids, you know, kids like us." Following her mother's lead, Yo Yo began swinging at sexism from an early age. By age 16 she had earned quite a reputation at George Washington Preparatory High School. "I came out rapping from a woman's point of view 'cause I saw that no one was speaking up for the ladies," she told *Essence*. "And I don't give a damn if men label me a feminist. It's about time someone gave men feedback and said, 'I'm not your ho or your bitch, I'm a strong, intelligent black woman!'"

"Profemale Agenda" on Debut

Soon the rapper Ice Cube—known for his work with the group N.W.A.—wanted to meet her. He finally approached her at a flea market, "liked the way she sassed him," in the words of Dimitri Ehrlich in *Pulse!,* and eventually signed her to his production company, Street Knowledge. Despite having made part of his reputation on the basis of lyrics widely condemned by critics as misogynist, Ice Cube asked Yo Yo to lend her feminist perspective to a track on his album *AmeriKKKa's Most Wanted.* The two went head to head on "It's a Man's World," and though critics were divided about who came out ahead, most admitted that Yo Yo held her own.

Ice Cube aided Yo Yo in brokering a deal with East West Records and then, he and his Lench Mob cohorts produced her 1991 debut album, *Make Way for the Motherlode.* Kim France of *Rolling Stone* instantly dubbed Yo Yo "the strongest female rapper to come out of the Los Angeles scene," admiring the rapper's toughness and her "profemale agenda." Though she had reservations about the preachiness of some of Yo Yo's raps, a note about the record in the magazine's year-end issue added that "the arrangements are slammin', as steely as anything on Ice Cube's own records, but with a surprising, fluid sensuality in spots." *Make Way* yielded "You Can't Play With My Yo Yo" and "Stompin' to the 90's" as well as the "Intelligent Black Woman's Anthem"; on "What Can I Do?" Ice Cube stepped in to spar with the star. "Blessed with a range of rhyme styles and an uncanny ability for role play, Yo Yo speaks to the strengths, insecurities, f----ups, and epiphanies particular to our gender," opined Morgan in her *Village Voice* review.

Bit Part in *Boyz*

1991 also saw Yo Yo join Ice Cube on the big screen, though her role in John Singleton's film *Boyz N the Hood* was far smaller than his. She contributed the song "Mama Don't Take No Mess" to the movie's soundtrack; *Rolling Stone* noted that she "raises a good ruckus" with her rapping. In the wake of her album, Yo Yo was also able to publicize the IBWC, and

chapters around the country hosted discussions of current issues. Describing her outlook to *Spin,* Yo Yo remarked, "I'm not Sister Yo Yo, one of those Afrocentric, X-cap wearing niggas that won't bust a gut for the cause." Of her organizational goals she said, "I don't want to be one of these sisters on a black thing mission. I'm on a sister-to-sister mission and that's worldwide."

Yo Yo's sophomore record, *Black Pearl,* utilized a variety of producers with Ice Cube serving as executive producer. The album's title song sampled the 1969 soul tune of the same name by Sonny Charles and The Checkmates. As Yo Yo remarked in her East West biography, "Back in the '60s, that song meant a lot to my parents. . . . Young people don't know. Being black or too dark was supposed to be ugly. Back then the song was so powerful. It meant so much to black people who had been scared to express themselves." Morgan, writing for *Spin,* commented that "*Black Pearl* certainly rocks harder. Its production mixes gospel R&B moments, sinewy bass lines, and Afro-club classics—a refreshing deviation from the South Central standard of '70s funk and manic urban hysteria. Yo Yo's skills have also improved. Her rapid-fire delivery and syncopation allows her to coast past hardcore beasts as she drops science with her new school feminism."

Black Pearl a Mixed Bag

Another review in *Spin,* however, complained that the record was "subdued." Arion Berger of *Entertainment Weekly* remarked that Yo Yo's "high, husky voice is sometimes hard to hear, and the record meanders at first, but *Black Pearl* is a much-needed reassertion of feminine dignity from the all-too-misogynistic West Coast rap scene." The album includes "Homegirl Don't Play Dat," an attack on philandering men called "Hoes," and the seductive finale "Will You Be Mine," a song *Rolling Stone's* Diane Cardwell nonetheless called the album's "only true low point" and "about as sexy as Monopoly."

That comment notwithstanding, Yo Yo evidently needs no coaching in matters of romance. Dream Hampton of *The Source* described a night on the town with the star, during which Yo Yo was approached by scores of smitten young men. As Hampton observed, "Yo Yo's 'around the way girl' position in the politics of hip-hop has created a space for sistas who refuse to support anyone unconditionally (brotha or no) and want, in addition to respect, the freedom to shake their thangs— if the beat so moves them." After all, the IBWC never said anything about not having a good time.

Selected discography

(Contributor) Ice Cube, "It's a Man's World," *AmeriKKKa's Most Wanted,* Priority, 1990.
Make Way for the Motherlode (includes "You Can't Play With My Yo Yo," "Stompin' to the 90's," "Intelligent Black Woman's Anthem," and "What Can I Do?"), East West, 1991.
(Contributor) *Boyz N the Hood* (soundtrack; "Mama Don't Take No Mess"), Qwest/Warner Bros., 1991.
Black Pearl (includes "Black Pearl," "Homegirl Don't Play Dat," "Hoes," and "Will You Be Mine"), East West, 1992.
(Contributor) "Get the Fist" (single), 1992.

Sources

Entertainment Weekly, August 7, 1992.

Essence, August 1991.
People, September 14, 1992.
Pulse!, August 1992.
Rolling Stone, May 2, 1991; December 12, 1991; August 6, 1992.
Source, October 1992.
Spin, July 1992.
Village Voice, June 11, 1991.
YSB, November 1991.

Additional information for this profile was obtained from an East West Records publicity biography, 1992.

—*Simon Glickman*

Warren Zevon

Singer, songwriter

Warren Zevon's career has taken almost as many strange twists and turns as the stories of the bizarre characters in his songs. Before beginning his solo career, Zevon worked extensively as a backing musician on stage and in the studio; he even wrote jingles. His first commercial success as a solo artist came in 1978 with the Top Ten single "Werewolves of London," from the gold album *Excitable Boy.* Zevon's next few recordings did not attain the same popularity, however, and Zevon did not release any new material for five years. Since then, though, he has returned to the studio for three solo albums and a collaboration with members of the pop group R.E.M. Ironic and darkly humorous lyrics remain his trademark, but he also has a serious side that *Rolling Stone* critic Elysa Gardner called "an almost folk-like earnestness." The range of his lyrics, combined with his talents as a musician and composer, have made Zevon a long-standing favorite of critics, fellow musicians, and his devoted fans.

Zevon spent his youth studying classical piano, but at 16, he left his family's California home, guitar in tow, for the New York folk scene of the early 1960s. From there he moved to San Francisco, then to Los Angeles, where he met and worked with Jackson Browne, Linda Ronstadt, members of the Eagles, and other performers immersed in the popular southern California rock sound of the 1970s. Even then Zevon was busy writing his own songs, and one of his compositions, "She Got Me Man," appeared in the movie *Midnight Cowboy.* Finally in 1970 he got the opportunity to record his first album, *Wanted Dead or Alive,* which flopped.

Success at Last

Lack of success put Zevon's solo career on hold for a while. He worked as a musical director and band member for the Everly Brothers, and then in 1974, went to Spain, where he played piano in a club for tourists. Meanwhile, Zevon's friends in California were working on his behalf. Linda Ronstadt recorded some of Zevon's songs, making his "Hasten Down the Wind" the title track of a 1976 album, but the most help came from Jackson Browne, who persuaded Asylum to release a solo album by Zevon. The resulting album, *Warren Zevon,* while not a big commercial success, did well enough with the public and with critics to give Zevon the opportunity to record another one.

Browne and Ronstadt both clocked in on the new album as did Waddy Wachtel, Ronstadt's guitarist, who became a regular collaborator with Zevon. The result was 1978's *Excitable Boy,* which went gold and contained such hits as "Excitable Boy," "Lawyers, Guns, and Money," and "Roland the Headless Thompson

For the Record. . .

Born January 24, 1947, in Chicago, IL. *Education:* Studied music with Robert Craft.

Singer and songwriter. Released *Wanted Dead or Alive,* Imperial, 1970; musical director for the Everly Brothers, 1971-73; played lounge piano in Spain, 1974; scored first Top Ten single, "Werewolves of London," 1978.

Awards: Gold record for *Excitable Boy,* 1978.

Addresses: *Office*—1880 Century Park E., #900, Los Angeles, CA 90067.

Gunner," as well as the hit "Werewolves of London." The popularity of "Werewolves of London" surprised Zevon, who told Stephen Fried of *GQ* that it was "a song that was really just a joke between friends." But that joke gave Zevon the clout to become a concert headliner.

Unfortunately Zevon has never matched the commercial success of *Excitable Boy.* His next album, *Bad Luck Streak in Dancing School,* made it into the Top 20 in 1980; that same year he released a live album, *Stand in the Fire,* which, according to Irwin Stambler in *The Encyclopedia of Pop, Rock and Soul,* "caught much of the fervor and excellent musicianship that made Zevon shows among rock's best in the early 1980s." *The Envoy,* recorded in 1982, flopped commercially and was to be Zevon's last until 1987.

Five Years of Silence

The move from obscurity to sudden stardom and then back off the charts mirrored the turmoil of Zevon's life in the late 1970s. Leaning on the same friends who had supported him musically, Zevon sought treatment for alcoholism. *The Envoy* was his first sober studio effort, but its lack of success cost him his recording deal with Asylum. Instead of writing new songs and seeking a new deal, Zevon took to the road, playing solo acoustic sets in small clubs. Reflecting on that time to Fried in *GQ,* Zevon said that the notion that he was down and out during this time made a good story but not a true one: "I wasn't starving or anything. I was making a living as a musician. In fact, on a purely economic level, you can make more money touring that way than with a band."

Zevon also told Fried, "I thought that when I had ten or twelve songs I'd get a deal." He did, this time with Virgin Records, and in 1987 Zevon released *Sentimental*

Hygiene. As in the past Zevon received musical help from his friends, who now included Peter Buck, Mike Mills, and Bill Berry of R.E.M. The trio performed on most of the album's tracks while Bob Dylan and Neil Young played on one song each. Speaking of how it felt to return to the studio and tour with a band again, Zevon told Anthony DeCurtis of *Rolling Stone,* "I sort of like starting my career over every seven years or so, or I sort of *have* to, whether I like to or not."

"You Know, Dear, This Album Isn't Funny"

Zevon returned to his pace of releasing a new album every two years or so. 1989's *Transverse City* so turned away from his characteristic humor that even his mother noticed. In an interview with Gary Graff of the *Detroit Free Press,* Zevon confessed that his mother told him, "You know, dear, this album isn't funny."

The tone of Zevon's 1990 release was not humorous either. *Hindu Love Gods,* officially issued by a band of the same name, resulted from one day of recording with members of R.E.M. during the *Sentimental Hygiene* sessions. It consisted entirely of covers from a diverse group of performers, including Muddy Waters, Woody Guthrie, the Georgia Satellites, and Prince. Paul Evans reviewed the album in *Rolling Stone,* saying, "It's real roots rocking—done by smart, delighted fans."

In 1991 Zevon returned to more characteristic territory with *Mr. Bad Example,* which featured "Model Citizen" and "Things to Do in Denver When You're Dead"— shining examples of his trademark sense of ironic humor. Craig Tomashoff's review of the album in *People* also summed up Zevon's career: "Few people in rock have Zevon's knack for spinning strange tales over memorable melodies. This will surely be the album that breaks him into the big time. If not, guaranteed the next one will." Though Tomashoff's assessment could point to any part of Zevon's history, be assured that Zevon's high marks have been true pinnacles indeed.

Selected discography

Wanted Dead or Alive, Imperial, 1970.
Warren Zevon, Asylum, 1976, reissued, Elektra, 1992.
Excitable Boy (includes "Werewolves of London"), Asylum, 1978.
Bad Luck Streak in Dancing School, Asylum, 1980, reissued, Elektra, 1992.
Stand in the Fire, Asylum, 1980.
The Envoy, Asylum, 1982.
Sentimental Hygiene, Virgin, 1987.
Transverse City, Virgin, 1989.

(With Hindu Love Gods) *Hindu Love Gods*, Giant, 1990.
Mr. Bad Example, Giant, 1991.
Learning to Flinch, Giant, 1993.
A Quiet Normal Life (The Best of Warren Zevon), Asylum.

Sources

Books

The Rolling Stone Encyclopedia of Rock & Roll, edited by Jon Pareles and Patricia Romanowski, Rolling Stone Press/Summit Books, 1983.

Stambler, Irwin, *The Encyclopedia of Pop, Rock and Soul*, St. Martin's, 1989.

Periodicals

Detroit Free Press, January 3, 1992.
GQ, January 1988.
People, January 20, 1992.
Rolling Stone, June 18, 1987; November 15, 1990; November 29, 1990; November 28, 1991.

—*Lloyd Hemingway*

Cumulative Indexes

Cumulative Subject Index

Volume numbers appear in **bold**.

A cappella
The Nylons **6**
Take 6 **6**

Accordion
Buckwheat Zydeco **6**
Chenier, Clifton **6**
Queen Ida **9**
Richard, Zachary **9**
Yankovic, "Weird Al" **7**

Banjo
Clark, Roy **1**
Crowe, J.D. **5**
Eldridge, Ben
See the Seldom Scene
Fleck, Bela **8**
Also see the New Grass Revival
Hartford, John **1**
Johnson, Courtney
See the New Grass Revival
Scruggs, Earl **3**
Seeger, Pete **4**
Also see the Weavers
Skaggs, Ricky **5**
Stanley, Ralph **5**
Watson, Doc **2**

Bass
Bruce, Jack
See Cream
Clarke, Stanley **3**
Collins, Bootsy **8**
Entwistle, John
See The Who
Hill, Dusty
See ZZ Top
Hillman, Chris
See the Desert Rose Band
Also see the Byrds
Johnston, Bruce
See the Beach Boys
Jones, John Paul
See Led Zeppelin
Lake, Greg
See Emerson, Lake & Palmer/Powell
McCartney, Paul **4**
Also see the Beatles
McVie, John
See Fleetwood Mac
Meisner, Randy
See the Eagles
Mingus, Charles **9**
Porter, Tiran
See the Doobie Brothers
Rutherford, Mike
See Genesis
Schmit, Timothy B.
See the Eagles
Simmons, Gene
See Kiss
Sting **2**
Sweet, Matthew **9**
Vicious, Sid
See the Sex Pistols
Also see Siouxsie and the Banshees
Waters, Roger
See Pink Floyd
Weymouth, Tina
See Talking Heads

Wyman, Bill
See the Rolling Stones

Big Band/Swing
The Andrews Sisters **9**
Arnaz, Desi **8**
Bailey, Pearl **5**
Basie, Count **2**
Bennett, Tony **2**
Berrigan, Bunny **2**
Calloway, Cab **6**
Carter, Benny **3**
Clooney, Rosemary **9**
The Dorsey Brothers **8**
Dorsey, Jimmy
See the Dorsey Brothers
Dorsey, Tommy
See the Dorsey Brothers
Eckstine, Billy **1**
Eldridge, Roy **9**
Ellington, Duke **2**
Ferguson, Maynard **7**
Fitzgerald, Ella **1**
Fountain, Pete **7**
Gillespie, Dizzy **6**
Goodman, Benny **4**
Jones, Spike **5**
Lee, Peggy **8**
Miller, Glenn **6**
Parker, Charlie **5**
Roomful of Blues **7**
Severinsen, Doc **1**
Shaw, Artie **8**
Sinatra, Frank **1**
Torme, Mel **4**
Vaughan, Sarah **2**

Bluegrass
Auldridge, Mike **4**
The Country Gentlemen **7**
Crowe, J.D. **5**
Flatt, Lester **3**
Fleck, Bela **8**
Also see the New Grass Revival
Gill, Vince **7**
Hartford, John **1**
Martin, Jimmy **5**
Also see the Osborne Brothers
Monroe, Bill **1**
The New Grass Revival **4**
O'Connor, Mark **1**
The Osborne Brothers **8**
Parsons, Gram **7**
Also see the Byrds
Scruggs, Earl **3**
The Seldom Scene **4**
Skaggs, Ricky **5**
Stanley, Ralph **5**
Stuart, Marty **9**
Watson, Doc **2**

Blues
Bailey, Pearl **5**
Berry, Chuck **1**
Blood, Sweat and Tears **7**
The Blues Brothers **3**
Charles, Ray **1**
Clapton, Eric **1**
Collins, Albert **4**
Cray, Robert **8**

Diddley, Bo **3**
Dr. John **7**
Earl, Ronnie **5**
Also see Roomful of Blues
The Fabulous Thunderbirds **1**
Guy, Buddy **4**
Handy, W. C. **7**
Hawkins, Screamin' Jay **8**
Healey, Jeff **4**
Holiday, Billie **6**
Hooker, John Lee **1**
Howlin' Wolf **6**
James, Elmore **8**
James, Etta **6**
Johnson, Robert **6**
King, Albert **2**
King, B.B. **1**
Leadbelly **6**
Led Zeppelin **1**
Little Feat **4**
Mayall, John **7**
Plant, Robert **2**
Also see Led Zeppelin
Professor Longhair **6**
Raitt, Bonnie **3**
Redding, Otis **5**
Rich, Charlie **3**
Robertson, Robbie **2**
Robillard, Duke **2**
Roomful of Blues **7**
Smith, Bessie **3**
Snow, Phoebe **4**
Taj Mahal **6**
Vaughan, Stevie Ray **1**
Waits, Tom **1**
Walker, T-Bone **5**
Wallace, Sippie **6**
Washington, Dinah **5**
Waters, Muddy **4**
Williamson, Sonny Boy **9**
Winter, Johnny **5**
ZZ Top **2**

Cajun/Zydeco
Buckwheat Zydeco **6**
Chenier, Clifton **6**
Doucet, Michael **8**
Queen Ida **9**
Richard, Zachary **9**

Cello
Casals, Pablo **9**
Gray, Walter
See Kronos Quartet
Harrell, Lynn **3**
Jeanrenaud, Joan Dutcher
See Kronos Quartet
Ma, Yo-Yo **2**

Children's Music
Harley, Bill **7**
Lehrer, Tom **7**
Nagler, Eric **8**
Raffi **8**
Rosenshontz **9**
Sharon, Lois & Bram **6**

Christian Music
Grant, Amy **7**

King's X **7**
Patti, Sandi **7**
Petra **3**
Stryper **2**

Clarinet
Adams, John **8**
Dorsey, Jimmy
  See the Dorsey Brothers
Fountain, Pete **7**
Goodman, Benny **4**
Shaw, Artie **8**

Classical
Anderson, Marian **8**
Arrau, Claudio **1**
Bernstein, Leonard **2**
Boyd, Liona **7**
Bream, Julian **9**
Bronfman, Yefim **6**
The Canadian Brass **4**
Casals, Pablo **9**
Chang, Sarah **7**
Clayderman, Richard **1**
Copland, Aaron **2**
Davis, Chip **4**
Fiedler, Arthur **6**
Galway, James **3**
Gingold, Josef **6**
Gould, Glenn **9**
Harrell, Lynn **3**
Horne, Marilyn **9**
Horowitz, Vladimir **1**
Jarrett, Keith **1**
Kennedy, Nigel **8**
Kissin, Evgeny **6**
Kronos Quartet **5**
Levine, James **8**
Liberace **9**
Ma, Yo-Yo **2**
Marsalis, Wynton **6**
Midori **7**
Ott, David **2**
Parkening, Christopher **7**
Perlman, Itzhak **2**
Phillips, Harvey **3**
Rampal, Jean-Pierre **6**
Salerno-Sonnenberg, Nadja **3**
Schickele, Peter **5**
Segovia, Andres **6**
Shankar, Ravi **9**
Stern, Isaac **7**
Takemitsu, Toru **6**
Upshaw, Dawn **9**
von Karajan, Herbert **1**
Wilson, Ransom **5**
Yamashita, Kazuhito **4**
Zukerman, Pinchas **4**

Composers
Adams, John **8**
Anka, Paul **2**
Atkins, Chet **5**
Bacharach, Burt **1**
Benson, George **9**
Berlin, Irving **8**
Bernstein, Leonard **2**
Bley, Carla **8**
Brubeck, Dave **8**
Byrne, David **8**
  Also see Talking Heads
Cage, John **8**
Cale, John **9**
Casals, Pablo **9**
Clarke, Stanley **3**
Coleman, Ornette **5**
Cooder, Ry **2**
Cooney, Rory **6**

Copland, Aaron **2**
Crouch, Andraé **9**
Davis, Chip **4**
Davis, Miles **1**
de Grassi, Alex **6**
Elfman, Danny **9**
Ellington, Duke **2**
Eno, Brian **8**
Enya **6**
Gillespie, Dizzy **6**
Glass, Philip **1**
Gould, Glenn **9**
Grusin, Dave **7**
Guaraldi, Vince **3**
Hamlisch, Marvin **1**
Hancock, Herbie **8**
Handy, W. C. **7**
Hartke, Stephen **5**
Hunter, Alberta **7**
Jarre, Jean-Michel **2**
Jarrett, Keith **1**
Jones, Quincy **2**
Jordan, Stanley **1**
Kitaro **1**
Lee, Peggy **8**
Lincoln, Abbey **9**
Lloyd Webber, Andrew **6**
Mancini, Henry **1**
Masekela, Hugh **7**
Metheny, Pat **2**
Mingus, Charles **9**
Monk, Meredith **1**
Monk, Thelonious **6**
Morton, Jelly Roll **7**
Nascimento, Milton **6**
Newman, Randy **4**
Ott, David **2**
Parker, Charlie **5**
Ponty, Jean-Luc **8**
Reich, Steve **8**
Reinhardt, Django **7**
Ritenour, Lee **7**
Rollins, Sonny **7**
Satriani, Joe **4**
Schickele, Peter **5**
Shankar, Ravi **9**
Shaw, Artie **8**
Shorter, Wayne **5**
Solal, Martial **4**
Sondheim, Stephen **8**
Story, Liz **2**
Summers, Andy **3**
Sun Ra **5**
Takemitsu, Toru **6**
Talbot, John Michael **6**
Taylor, Cecil **9**
Threadgill, Henry **9**
Tyner, McCoy **7**
Washington, Grover Jr. **5**
Williams, John **9**
Winston, George
Zimmerman, Udo **5**

Conductors
Bacharach, Burt **1**
Bernstein, Leonard **2**
Casals, Pablo **9**
Copland, Aaron **2**
Domingo, Placido **1**
Fiedler, Arthur **6**
Jarrett, Keith **1**
Levine, James **8**
Mancini, Henry **1**
Marriner, Neville **7**
Rampal, Jean-Pierre **6**
Schickele, Peter **5**
von Karajan, Herbert **1**
Williams, John **9**

Zukerman, Pinchas **4**

Contemporary Dance Music
Abdul, Paula **3**
The B-52's **4**
The Bee Gees **3**
Brown, Bobby **4**
Brown, James **2**
Cherry, Neneh **4**
Clinton, George **7**
Deee-Lite **9**
De La Soul **7**
Depeche Mode **5**
The English Beat **9**
Eurythmics **6**
Exposé **4**
Fox, Samantha **3**
Gang of Four **8**
Hammer, M.C. **5**
Harry, Deborah **4**
Ice-T **7**
Idol, Billy **3**
Jackson, Janet **3**
Jackson, Michael **1**
James, Rick **2**
Jones, Grace **9**
Madonna **4**
Pet Shop Boys **5**
Prince **1**
Queen Latifah **6**
Rodgers, Nile **8**
Salt-N-Pepa **6**
Simmons, Russell **7**
Technotronic **5**
The Village People **7**
Was (Not Was) **6**
Young M.C. **4**

Contemporary Instrumental/New Age
Ackerman, Will **3**
Clinton, George **7**
Collins, Bootsy **8**
Davis, Chip **4**
de Grassi, Alex **6**
Enya **6**
Hedges, Michael **3**
Jarre, Jean-Michel **2**
Kitaro **1**
Kronos Quartet **5**
Story, Liz **2**
Summers, Andy **3**
Winston, George **9**

Cornet
Handy, W. C. **7**

Country
Acuff, Roy **2**
Alabama **1**
Anderson, John **5**
Asleep at the Wheel **5**
Atkins, Chet **5**
Auldridge, Mike **4**
Black, Clint **5**
Brooks, Garth **8**
Buffett, Jimmy **4**
The Byrds **8**
Campbell, Glen **2**
Carpenter, Mary-Chapin **6**
Carter, Carlene **8**
The Carter Family **3**
Cash, Johnny **1**
Cash, June Carter **6**
Cash, Rosanne **2**
Clark, Roy **1**
Cline, Patsy **5**
Coe, David Allan **4**

Cooder, Ry **2**
The Cowboy Junkies **4**
Crowe, J. D. **5**
Crowell, Rodney **8**
Daniels, Charlie **6**
Denver, John **1**
The Desert Rose Band **4**
Dickens, Little Jimmy **7**
Dylan, Bob **3**
Flatt, Lester **3**
Ford, Tennessee Ernie **3**
Gayle, Crystal **1**
Gill, Vince **7**
Gilley, Mickey **7**
Griffith, Nanci **3**
Haggard, Merle **2**
Hall, Tom T. **4**
Harris, Emmylou **4**
Hartford, John **1**
Hay, George D. **3**
Hiatt, John **8**
Highway 101 **4**
Jackson, Alan **7**
Jennings, Waylon **4**
Jones, George **4**
The Judds **2**
The Kentucky Headhunters **5**
Kristofferson, Kris **4**
Lang, K. D. **4**
Lee, Brenda **5**
Little Feat **4**
Loveless, Patty **5**
Lovett, Lyle **5**
Lynn, Loretta **2**
Lynne, Shelby **5**
Mandrell, Barbara **4**
Mattea, Kathy **5**
Miller, Roger **4**
Milsap, Ronnie **2**
Monroe, Bill **1**
Murphey, Michael Martin **9**
Murray, Anne **4**
Nelson, Willie **1**
Newton-John, Olivia **8**
The Nitty Gritty Dirt Band **6**
The Oak Ridge Boys **7**
O'Connor, Mark **1**
Oslin, K. T. **3**
Owens, Buck **2**
Parsons, Gram **7**
        Also see the Byrds
Parton, Dolly **2**
Pearl, Minnie **3**
Pride, Charley **4**
Rabbitt, Eddie **5**
Raitt, Bonnie **3**
Rich, Charlie **3**
Robbins, Marty **9**
Rodgers, Jimmie **3**
Rogers, Kenny **1**
Rogers, Roy **9**
Scruggs, Earl **3**
Seals, Dan **9**
Skaggs, Ricky **5**
The Statler Brothers **8**
Stevens, Ray **7**
Strait, George **5**
Stuart, Marty **9**
The Texas Tornados **8**
Tillis, Mel **7**
Tillis, Pam **8**
Travis, Randy **9**
Tritt, Travis **7**
Tubb, Ernest **4**
Tucker, Tanya **3**
Twitty, Conway **6**
Van Shelton, Ricky **5**
Watson, Doc **2**

Wells, Kitty **6**
West, Dottie **8**
Whitley, Keith **7**
Williams, Don **4**
Williams, Hank, Jr. **1**
Williams, Hank, Sr. **4**
Wills, Bob **6**
Wynette, Tammy **2**
Yoakam, Dwight **1**
Young, Faron **7**

Dobro
    Auldridge, Mike **4**
        Also see the Country Gentlemen
        Also see the Seldom Scene
    Burch, Curtis
        See the New Grass Revival
    Knopfler, Mark **3**

Drums
    See **Percussion**

Dulcimer
    Ritchie, Jean **4**

Fiddle
    See **Violin**

Film Scores
    Anka, Paul **2**
    Bacharach, Burt **1**
    Berlin, Irving **8**
    Bernstein, Leonard **2**
    Byrne, David **8**
        Also see Talking Heads
    Cafferty, John
        See the Beaver Brown Band
    Cliff, Jimmy **8**
    Copland, Aaron **2**
    Crouch, Andraé **9**
    Donovan **9**
    Eddy, Duane **9**
    Elfman, Danny **9**
    Ellington, Duke **2**
    Ferguson, Maynard **7**
    Gould, Glenn **9**
    Grusin, Dave **7**
    Guaraldi, Vince **3**
    Hamlisch, Marvin **1**
    Hancock, Herbie **8**
    Harrison, George **2**
    Hedges, Michael **3**
    Jones, Quincy **2**
    Knopfler, Mark **3**
    Lennon, John **9**
        Also see the Beatles
    Mancini, Henry **1**
    Mayfield, Curtis **8**
    McCartney, Paul **4**
        Also see the Beatles
    Metheny, Pat **2**
    Nascimento, Milton **6**
    Richie, Lionel **8**
    Robertson, Robbie **2**
    Rollins, Sonny **7**
    Sager, Carole Bayer **5**
    Schickele, Peter **5**
    Shankar, Ravi **9**
    Taj Mahal **6**
    Waits, Tom **1**
    Williams, Paul **5**
    Young, Neil **2**

Flute
    Anderson, Ian
        See Jethro Tull

Galway, James **3**
Rampal, Jean-Pierre **6**
Wilson, Ransom **5**

Folk/Traditional
    Arnaz, Desi **8**
    Baez, Joan **1**
    Belafonte, Harry **8**
    Blades, Ruben **2**
    Brady, Paul **8**
    Bragg, Billy **7**
    The Byrds **8**
    The Carter Family **3**
    Chapin, Harry **6**
    Chapman, Tracy **4**
    The Chieftains **7**
    Childs, Toni **2**
    Clegg, Johnny **8**
    Cockburn, Bruce **8**
    Cohen, Leonard **3**
    Collins, Judy **4**
    Crosby, David **3**
        Also see the Byrds
    de Lucia, Paco **1**
    Donovan **9**
    Dr. John **7**
    Dylan, Bob **3**
    Elliot, Cass **5**
    Enya **6**
    Estefan, Gloria **2**
    Galway, James **3**
    The Gipsy Kings **8**
    Griffith, Nanci **3**
    Guthrie, Arlo **6**
    Guthrie, Woodie **2**
    Harding, John Wesley **6**
    Hartford, John **1**
    Iglesias, Julio **2**
    Indigo Girls **3**
    The Kingston Trio **9**
    Kuti, Fela **7**
    Ladysmith Black Mambazo **1**
    Larkin, Patty **9**
    Lavin, Christine **6**
    Leadbelly **6**
    Lightfoot, Gordon **3**
    Los Lobos **2**
    Makeba, Miriam **8**
    Masekela, Hugh **7**
    McLean, Don **7**
    Mitchell, Joni **2**
    Morrison, Van **3**
    Nascimento, Milton **6**
    N'Dour, Youssou **6**
    Near, Holly **1**
    Ochs, Phil **7**
    O'Connor, Sinead **3**
    Odetta **7**
    Parsons, Gram **7**
        Also see the Byrds
    Paxton, Tom **5**
    Peter, Paul & Mary **4**
    The Pogues **6**
    Prine, John **7**
    Redpath, Jean **1**
    Ritchie, Jean, **4**
    Rodgers, Jimmie **3**
    Santana, Carlos **1**
    Seeger, Pete **4**
        Also see the Weavers
    Shankar, Ravi **9**
    Simon, Paul **1**
    Snow, Pheobe **4**
    Sweet Honey in the Rock **1**
    Taj Mahal **6**
    Thompson, Richard **7**
    Tikaram, Tanita **9**
    Vega, Suzanne **3**

Joplin, Janis **3**
Kennedy, Nigel **8**
Kiss **5**
Knopfler, Mark **3**
Kravitz, Lenny **5**
Led Zeppelin **1**
Lennon, John **9**
    Also see the Beatles
Lennon, Julian **2**
Lindley, Dave **2**
Little Feat **4**
Living Colour **7**
Loggins, Kenny **3**
Los Lobos **2**
Lydon, John **9**
    Also see the Sex Pistols
Lynne, Jeff **5**
Lynyrd Skynyrd **9**
Martin, George **6**
Marx, Richard **3**
McCartney, Paul **4**
    Also see the Beatles
The MC5 **9**
Megadeth **9**
Mellencamp, John "Cougar" **2**
Metallica **7**
Miller, Steve **2**
Morrison, Jim **3**
    Also see the Doors
Morrison, Van **3**
Mötley Crüe **1**
Myles, Alannah **4**
Nelson, Rick **2**
Newman, Randy **4**
Nicks, Stevie **2**
Nirvana **8**
Nugent, Ted **2**
Ocasek, Ric **5**
O'Connor, Sinead **3**
Orbison, Roy **2**
Osbourne, Ozzy **3**
Page, Jimmy **4**
    Also see Led Zeppelin
Palmer, Robert **2**
Parker, Maceo **7**
Parsons, Gram **7**
    Also see the Byrds
Petty, Tom **9**
Perkins, Carl **9**
Phillips, Sam **5**
Pink Floyd **2**
Plant, Robert **2**
    Also see Led Zeppelin
The Pogues **6**
Pop, Iggy **1**
Presley, Elvis **1**
The Pretenders **8**
Prince **1**
Prine, John **7**
Queen **6**
Queensrÿche **8**
Raitt, Bonnie **3**
The Ramones **9**
The Red Hot Chili Peppers **7**
Reed, Lou **1**
    Also see the Velvet Underground
Reid, Vernon **2**
    Also see Living Colour
R.E.M. **5**
The Replacements **7**
Robertson, Robbie **2**
The Rolling Stones **3**
Roth, David Lee **1**
    Also see Van Halen
Rubin, Rick **9**
Rush **8**
Satriani, Joe **4**
The Sex Pistols **5**

Shocked, Michelle **4**
Simon, Carly **4**
Simon, Paul **1**
Siouxsie and the Banshees **8**
Smith, Patti **1**
The Smiths **3**
Sonic Youth **9**
Soundgarden **6**
Spector, Phil **4**
Spinal Tap **8**
Springsteen, Bruce **6**
Squeeze **5**
Steely Dan **5**
Stevens, Cat **3**
Stewart, Rod **2**
Stills, Stephen **5**
Sting **2**
Stone, Sly **8**
Stryper **2**
Summers, Andy **3**
Tears for Fears **6**
10,000 Maniacs **3**
The Texas Tornados **8**
They Might Be Giants **7**
Thompson, Richard **7**
Three Dog Night **5**
Timbuk 3 **3**
Townshend, Pete **1**
    Also see The Who
Turner, Tina **1**
U2 **2**
Vai, Steve **5**
Van Halen **8**
Vaughan, Stevie Ray **1**
The Velvet Underground **7**
Walsh, Joe **5**
    Also see the Eagles
Whitesnake **5**
The Who **3**
Winter, Johnny **5**
Winwood, Steve **2**
Yes **8**
Young, Neil **2**
Zappa, Frank **1**
Zevon, Warren **9**
ZZ Top **2**

Rock and Roll Pioneers
Berry, Chuck **1**
Clark, Dick **2**
Darin, Bobby **4**
Didley, Bo **3**
Dion **4**
Domino, Fats **2**
Eddy, Duane **9**
The Everly Brothers **2**
Haley, Bill **6**
Hawkins, Screamin' Jay **8**
Holly, Buddy **1**
James, Etta **6**
Lewis, Jerry Lee **2**
Little Richard **1**
Nelson, Rick **2**
Orbison, Roy **2**
Paul, Les **2**
Perkins, Carl **9**
Phillips, Sam **5**
Presley, Elvis **1**
Professor Longhair **6**
Sedaka, Neil **4**
Spector, Phil **4**
Twitty, Conway **6**
Wilson, Jackie **3**

Saxophone
Carter, Benny **3**
Clemons, Clarence **7**
Coleman, Ornette **5**

Coltrane, John **4**
Dorsey, Jimmy
    See the Dorsey Brothers
Kirk, Rahsaan Roland **6**
Morgan, Frank **9**
Parker, Charlie **5**
Parker, Maceo **7**
Rollins, Sonny **7**
Sanborn, David **1**
Shorter, Wayne **5**
Threadgill, Henry **9**
Washington, Grover, Jr. **5**

Songwriters
Acuff, Roy **2**
Adams, Bryan **2**
Anderson, Ian
    See Jethro Tull
Anderson, John **5**
Anka, Paul **2**
Armatrading, Joan **4**
Atkins, Chet **5**
Bacharach, Burt **1**
Baez, Joan **1**
Baker, Anita **9**
Balin, Marty
    See Jefferson Airplane
Barrett, (Roger) Syd
    See Pink Floyd
Basie, Count **2**
Becker, Walter
    See Steely Dan
Belew, Adrian **5**
Benton, Brook **7**
Berlin, Irving **8**
Berry, Chuck **1**
Black, Clint **5**
Blades, Ruben **2**
Bono
    See U2
Brady, Paul **8**
Bragg, Billy **7**
Brickell, Edie **3**
Brooks, Garth **8**
Brown, Bobby **4**
Brown, James **2**
Browne, Jackson **3**
Buck, Peter **5**
    See R.E.M.
Buck, Robert
    See 10,000 Maniacs
Buckingham, Lindsey **8**
    Also see Fleetwood Mac
Buffett, Jimmy **4**
Bush, Kate **4**
Byrne, David **8**
    Also see Talking Heads
Cale, John **9**
Calloway, Cab **6**
Carpenter, Mary-Chapin **6**
Carter, Carlene **8**
Cash, Johnny **1**
Cash, Rosanne **2**
Cetera, Peter
    See Chicago
Chapin, Harry **6**
Chapman, Tracy **4**
Charles, Ray **1**
Childs, Toni **2**
Clapton, Eric **1**
Cleveland, James **1**
Clinton, George **7**
Cockburn, Bruce **4**
Cohen, Leonard **3**
Cole, Lloyd **9**
Cole, Nat King **3**
Collins, Albert **4**
Collins, Judy **4**

Cumulative Musicians Index

Volume numbers appear in **bold.**

Gorman, Steve
    See the Black Crowes
Gould, Billy
    See Faith No More
Gould, Glenn **9**
Gradney, Ken
    See Little Feat
Gramolini, Gary
    See the Beaver Brown Band
Grant, Amy **7**
Grant, Lloyd
    See Metallica
The Grateful Dead **5**
Gray, Ella
    See Kronos Quartet
Gray, Tom
    See the Country Gentlemen
    See the Seldom Scene
Gray, Walter
    See Kronos Quartet
Grebenshikov, Boris **3**
Green, Al **9**
Green, Karl Anthony
    See Herman's Hermits
Green, Peter
    See Fleetwood Mac
Green, Susaye
    See the Supremes
Green, Willie
    See the Neville Brothers
Greenspoon, Jimmy
    See Three Dog Night
Griffin, Bob
    See the BoDeans
Griffith, Nanci **3**
Grohl, Dave
    See Nirvana
Groucutt, Kelly
    See Electric Light Orchestra
Grove, George
    See the Kingston Trio
Grusin, Dave **7**
Guaraldi, Vince **3**
Guard, Dave
    See the Kingston Trio
Guerin, John
    See the Byrds
Guest, Christopher
    See Tufnel, Nigel
Guns n' Roses **2**
Gunther, Cornell
    See the Coasters
Gustafson, Steve
    See 10,000 Maniacs
Guthrie, Arlo **6**
Guthrie, Woodie **2**
Guy, Billy
    See the Coasters
Guy, Buddy **4**
Hackett, Steve
    See Genesis
Hagar, Sammy
    See Van Halen
Haggard, Merle **2**
Haley, Bill **6**
Hall & Oates **6**
Hall, Daryl
    See Hall & Oates
Hall, Randall
    See Lynyrd Skynyrd
Hall, Tom T. **4**
Hall, Tony
    See the Neville Brothers
Hamilton, Frank
    See the Weavers
Hamilton, Tom
    See Aerosmith
Hamlisch, Marvin **1**

Hammer, M.C. **5**
Hammerstein, Oscar
    See Rodgers, Richard
Hammett, Kirk
    See Metallica
Hammond, John **6**
Hammond-Hammond, Jeffrey
    See Jethro Tull
Hampson, Sharon
    See Sharon, Lois & Bram
Hampton, Lionel **6**
Hancock, Herbie **8**
Handy, W. C. **7**
Hanna, Jeff
    See the Nitty Gritty Dirt Band
Harding, John Wesley **6**
Harley, Bill **7**
Harrell, Lynn **3**
Harrington, David
    See Kronos Quartet
Harris, Damon Otis
    See the Temptations
Harris, Emmylou **4**
Harris, Evelyn
    See Sweet Honey in the Rock
Harrison, George **2**
    Also see the Beatles
Harrison, Jerry
    See Talking Heads
Harry, Deborah **4**
Hart, Lorenz
    See Rodgers, Richard
Hart, Mickey
    See the Grateful Dead
Hartford, John **1**
Hartke, Stephen **5**
Hartman, Bob
    See Petra
Hartman, John
    See the Doobie Brothers
Hassan, Norman
    See UB40
Hauser, Tim
    See The Manhattan Transfer
Hawkins, Screamin' Jay **8**
Hay, George D. **3**
Haynes, Warren
    See the Allman Brothers
Hays, Lee
    See the Weavers
Hayward, Richard
    See Little Feat
Headon, Topper
    See The Clash
Healey, Jeff **4**
Heart **1**
Hedges, Michael **3**
Hellerman, Fred
    See the Weavers
Helm, Levon
    See the Band
    Also see the Nitty Gritty Dirt Band
Hendrix, Jimi **2**
Henley, Don **3**
    Also see the Eagles
Herman's Hermits **5**
Herndon, Mark
    See Alabama
Hetfield, James
    See Metallica
Hewson, Paul
    See U2
Hiatt, John **8**
Hidalgo, David
    See Los Lobos
Highway 101 **4**
Hijbert, Fritz
    See Kraftwerk

Hill, Dusty
    See ZZ Top
Hillman, Chris
    See the Byrds
    Also see the Desert Rose Band
Hirt, Al **5**
Hitchcock, Robyn **9**
Hodo, David
    See the Village People
Hoffman, Guy
    See the BoDeans
Holiday, Billie **6**
Holland, Brian
    See Holland-Dozier-Holland
Holland-Dozier-Holland **5**
Holland, Eddie
    See Holland-Dozier-Holland
Holland, Julian "Jools"
    See Squeeze
Holly, Buddy **1**
Honeyman-Scott, James
    See the Pretenders
Hooker, John Lee **1**
Hopwood, Keith
    See Herman's Hermits
Horn, Shirley **7**
Horn, Trevor
    See Yes
Horne, Marilyn **9**
Hornsby, Bruce **3**
Horovitz, Adam
    See the Beastie Boys
Horowitz, Vladimir **1**
Hossack, Michael
    See the Doobie Brothers
Houston, Cissy **6**
Houston, Whitney **8**
Howe, Steve
    See Yes
Howlin' Wolf **6**
Hubbard, Preston
    See the Fabulous Thunderbirds
    Also see Roomful of Blues
Hudson, Garth
    See the Band
Hughes, Glenn
    See Black Sabbath
Hughes, Glenn
    See the Village People
Hughes, Leon
    See the Coasters
Hunt, Darryl
    See the Pogues
Hunter, Alberta **7**
Hunter, Shepherd "Ben"
    See Soundgarden
Hutchence, Michael
    See INXS
Hütter, Ralf
    See Kraftwerk
Hutton, Danny
    See Three Dog Night
Hyman, Jerry
    See Blood, Sweat and Tears
Hynde, Chrissie
    See the Pretenders
Ian, Janis **5**
Ibbotson, Jimmy
    See the Nitty Gritty Dirt Band
Ice Cube
    See N.W.A.
Ice-T **7**
Idol, Billy **3**
Iglesias, Julio **2**
Indigo Girls **3**
INXS **2**
Iommi, Tony
    See Black Sabbath

Lamm, Robert
  See Chicago
Lang, K. D. **4**
Lanois, Daniel **8**
Larkin, Patty **9**
Lataille, Rich
  See Roomful of Blues
Laurence, Lynda
  See the Supremes
Lavin, Christine **6**
Lavis, Gilson
  See Squeeze
Lawry, John
  See Petra
Lawson, Doyle
  See the Country Gentlemen
Leadbelly **6**
Leadon, Bernie
  See the Eagles
  See the Nitty Gritty Dirt Band
Leavell, Chuck
  See the Allman Brothers
LeBon, Simon
  See Duran Duran
Leckenby, Derek "Lek"
  See Herman's Hermits
Ledbetter, Huddie
  See Leadbelly
Led Zeppelin **1**
Lee, Brenda **5**
Lee, Geddy
  See Rush
Lee, Peggy **8**
Lee, Sara
  See Gang of Four
Lee, Tommy
  See Mötley Crüe
Leese, Howard
  See Heart
Lehrer, Tom **7**
Lennon, John **9**
  Also see the Beatles
Lennon, Julian **2**
Lennox, Annie
  See Eurythmics
Leonard, Glenn
  See the Temptations
Lesh, Phil
  See the Grateful Dead
Levene, Keith
  See The Clash
Levine, James **8**
Levy, Ron
  See Roomful of Blues
Lewis, Huey **9**
Lewis, Jerry Lee **2**
Lewis, Otis
  See the Fabulous Thunderbirds
Lewis, Roy
  See Kronos Quartet
Liberace **9**
Lifeson, Alex
  See Rush
Lightfoot, Gordon **3**
Lilienstein, Lois
  See Sharon, Lois & Bram
Lincoln, Abbey **9**
Lindley, David **2**
Linnell, John
  See They Might Be Giants
Lipsius, Fred
  See Blood, Sweat and Tears
Little Feat **4**
Little, Keith
  See the Country Gentlemen
Little Richard **1**
Living Colour **7**

Llanas, Sammy
  See the BoDeans
L.L. Cool J. **5**
Lloyd Webber, Andrew **6**
Loggins, Kenny **3**
Los Lobos **2**
Los Reyes
  See the Gipsy Kings
Loughnane, Lee
  See Chicago
Love, Mike
  See the Beach Boys
Loveless, Patty **5**
Lovett, Lyle **5**
Lowe, Chris
  See Pet Shop Boys
Lowe, Nick **6**
Lozano, Conrad
  See Los Lobos
Lucia, Paco de
  See de Lucia, Paco
Lupo, Pat
  See the Beaver Brown Band
LuPone, Patti **8**
Lydon, John **9**
  Also see the Sex Pistols
Lynn, Loretta **2**
Lynne, Jeff **5**
  Also see Electric Light Orchestra
Lynne, Shelby **5**
Lynyrd Skynyrd **9**
Ma, Yo-Yo **2**
MacGowan, Shane
  See the Pogues
Madonna **4**
Magoogan, Wesley
  See the English Beat
Maher, John
  See the Buzzcocks
Makeba, Miriam **8**
Malone, Tom
  See Blood, Sweat and Tears
Mancini, Henry **1**
Mandrell, Barbara **4**
Maness, J. D.
  See the Desert Rose Band
The Manhattan Transfer **8**
Manilow, Barry **2**
Manuel, Richard
  See the Band
Manzarek, Ray
  See the Doors
Marini, Lou, Jr.
  See Blood, Sweat and Tears
Marley, Bob **3**
Marley, Ziggy **3**
Marr, Johnny
  See the Smiths
Marriner, Neville
Mars, Chris
  See the Replacements
Mars, Mick
  See Mötley Crüe
Marsalis, Wynton **6**
Martin, Barbara
  See the Supremes
Martin, Christopher
  See Kid 'n Play
Martin, Dean **1**
Martin, George **6**
Martin, Greg
  See the Kentucky Headhunters
Martin, Jim
  See Faith No More
Martin, Jimmy **5**
  Also See the Osborne Brothers
Martin, Tony
  See Black Sabbath

Marx, Richard **3**
Masekela, Hugh **7**
Maseo, Baby Huey
  See De La Soul
Mason, Nick
  See Pink Floyd
Masse, Laurel
  See The Manhattan Transfer
Mathis, Johnny **2**
Matlock, Glen
  See the Sex Pistols
Mattea, Kathy **5**
May, Brian
  See Queen
Mayall, John **7**
Mayfield, Curtis **8**
Mazibuko, Abednigo
  See Ladysmith Black Mambazo
Mazibuko, Albert
  See Ladysmith Black Mambazo
MCA
  See Yaunch, Adam
McCarrick, Martin
  See Siouxsie and the Banshees
McCartney, Paul **4**
  Also see the Beatles
MC Clever
  See Digital Underground
McCracken, Chet
  See the Doobie Brothers
McDaniels, Darryl "D"
  See Run-D.M.C.
McDonald, Barbara Kooyman
  See Timbuk 3
McDonald, Michael
  See the Doobie Brothers
McDonald, Pat
  See Timbuk 3
McDorman, Joe
  See the Statler Brothers
McDowell, Hugh
  See Electric Light Orchestra
MC Eric
  See Technotronic
McEuen, John
  See the Nitty Gritty Dirt Band
McFee, John
  See the Doobie Brothers
McFerrin, Bobby **3**
The MC5 **9**
McGeoch, John
  See Siouxsie and the Banshees
McGuinn, Jim
  See McGuinn, Roger
McGuinn, Roger
  See the Byrds
McIntosh, Robbie
  See the Pretenders
McIntyre, Joe
  See New Kids on the Block
McKagan, Duff
  See Guns n' Roses
McKay, John
  See Siouxsie and the Banshees
McKean, Michael
  See St. Hubbins, David
McKernarn, Ron "Pigpen"
  See the Grateful Dead
McKnight, Claude V. III
  See Take 6
McLean, Don **7**
McLeod, Rory
  See Roomful of Blues
MC Lyte **8**
McMeel, Mickey
  See Three Dog Night
McRae, Carmen **9**

Paxton, Tom **5**
Payne, Bill
 See Little Feat
Payne, Scherrie
 See the Supremes
Pearl, Minnie **3**
Peart, Neil
 See Rush
Pedersen, Herb
 See the Desert Rose Band
Peduzzi, Larry
 See Roomful of Blues
Pegg, Dave
 See Jethro Tull
Pendergrass, Teddy **3**
Pengilly, Kirk
 See INXS
Penn, Michael **4**
Perez, Louie
 See Los Lobos
Perkins, Carl **9**
Perkins, Steve
 See Jane's Addiction
Perlman, Itzhak **2**
Perry, Doane
 See Jethro Tull
Perry, Joe
 See Aerosmith
Pet Shop Boys **5**
Peter, Paul & Mary **4**
Peters, Bernadette **7**
Petra **3**
Petty, Tom **9**
Phelps, Doug
 See the Kentucky Headhunters
Phelps, Ricky Lee
 See the Kentucky Headhunters
Phife
 See A Tribe Called Quest
Philips, Anthony
 See Genesis
Phillips, Chynna
 See Wilson Phillips
Phillips, Harvey **3**
Phillips, Sam **5**
Phungula, Inos
 See Ladysmith Black Mambazo
Piaf, Edith **8**
Piccolo, Greg
 See Roomful of Blues
Pierson, Kate
 See the B-52's
Pilatus, Rob
 See Milli Vanilli
Pink Floyd **2**
Pinnick, Doug
 See King's X
Pirroni, Marco
 See Siouxsie and the Banshees
Plant, Robert **2**
 Also see Led Zeppelin
The Pogues **6**
Poindexter, Buster
 See Johansen, David
Pointer, Anita
 See the Pointer Sisters
Pointer, Bonnie
 See the Pointer Sisters
Pointer, June
 See the Pointer Sisters
Pointer, Ruth
 See the Pointer Sisters
The Pointer Sisters **9**
Poland, Chris
 See Megadeth
Ponty, Jean-Luc **8**
Pop, Iggy **1**

Porter, Tiran
 See the Doobie Brothers
Posdnuos
 See De La Soul
Potts, Sean
 See the Chieftains
Powell, Billy
 See Lynyrd Skynyrd
Powell, Cozy
 See Emerson, Lake & Palmer/Powell
Prater, Dave
 See Sam and Dave
Presley, Elvis **1**
The Pretenders **8**
Price, Leontyne **6**
Price, Louis
 See the Temptations
Price, Rick
 See Electric Light Orchestra
Pride, Charley **4**
The Primettes
 See the Supremes
Prine, John **7**
Prince **1**
Professor Longhair **6**
Public Enemy **4**
Pyle, Artemis
 See Lynyrd Skynyrd
Q-Tip
 See A Tribe Called Quest
Queen **6**
Queen Ida **9**
Queen Latifah **6**
Queensrÿche **8**
Querfurth, Carl
 See Roomful of Blues
Rabbitt, Eddie **5**
Rabin, Trevor
 See Yes
Raffi **8**
Raitt, Bonnie **3**
Rakim
 See Eric B. and Rakim
Ramone, C.J.
 See the Ramones
Ramone, Dee Dee
 See the Ramones
Ramone, Joey
 See the Ramones
Ramone, Johnny
 See the Ramones
Ramone, Marky
 See the Ramones
Ramone, Ritchie
 See the Ramones
Ramone, Tommy
 See the Ramones
The Ramones **9**
Rampal, Jean-Pierre **6**
Ranaldo, Lee
 See Sonic Youth
Ranken, Andrew
 See the Pogues
Ranking Roger
 See the English Beat
Ray, Amy
 See Indigo Girls
Reagon, Bernice Johnson
 See Sweet Honey in the Rock
Redding, Otis **5**
Reddy, Helen **9**
The Red Hot Chili Peppers **7**
Redpath, Jean **1**
Reed, Lou **1**
 Also see the Velvet Underground
Reeves, Martha **4**
Reich, Steve **8**

Reid, Christopher
 See Kid 'n Play
Reid, Don
 See the Statler Brothers
Reid, Harold
 See the Statler Brothers
Reid, Vernon **2**
 Also see Living Colour
Reinhardt, Django **7**
R.E.M. **5**
Ren, M.C.
 See N.W.A.
Reno, Ronnie
 See the Osborne Brothers
The Replacements **7**
Reyes, Andre
 See the Gipsy Kings
Reyes, Canut
 See the Gipsy Kings
Reyes, Nicolas
 See the Gipsy Kings
Reynolds, Nick
 See the Kingston Trio
Rhodes, Nick
 See Duran Duran
Rich, Charlie **3**
Richard, Keith
 See Richards, Keith
Richard, Zachary **9**
Richards, Keith
 See the Rolling Stones
Richie, Lionel **2**
Ritchie, Jean **4**
Ritenour, Lee **7**
Robbins, Marty **9**
Roberts, Marcus **6**
Robertson, Robbie **2**
 Also see the Band
Robeson, Paul **8**
Robillard, Duke **2**
 Also see Roomful of Blues
Robinson, Chris
 See the Black Crowes
Robinson, Rich
 See the Black Crowes
Robinson, Smokey **1**
Rockenfield, Scott
 See Queensrÿche
Rodgers, Jimmie **3**
Rodgers, Nile **8**
Rodgers, Richard **9**
Roeder, Klaus
 See Kraftwerk
Rogers, Kenny **1**
Rogers, Roy **9**
The Rolling Stones **3**
Rollins, Sonny **7**
Romm, Ronald
 See the Canadian Brass
Ronstadt, Linda **2**
Roomful of Blues **7**
Roper, De De
 See Salt-N-Pepa
Rosas, Cesar
 See Los Lobos
Rose, Axl
 See Guns n' Roses
Rosen, Gary
 See Rosenshontz
Rosenshontz **9**
Rosenthal, Phil
 See the Seldom Scene
Ross, Diana **1**
 Also see the Supremes
Rossi, John
 See Roomful of Blues
Rossington, Gary
 See Lynyrd Skynyrd

Roth, David Lee **1**
   Also see Van Halen
Rotten, Johnny
   See Lydon, John
   Also see the Sex Pistols
Rourke, Andy
   See the Smiths
Rubin, Rick **9**
Rudd, Phillip
   See AC/DC
Ruffin, David **6**
   Also see the Temptations
Run-D.M.C. **4**
Rush **8**
Russell, Mark **6**
Rutherford, Mike
   See Genesis
Rutsey, John
   See Rush
Ryland, Jack
   See Three Dog Night
Sade **2**
Sager, Carole Bayer
Sahm, Doug
   See the Texas Tornados
St. John, Mark
   See Kiss
St. Hubbins, David
   See Spinal Tap
Salerno-Sonnenberg, Nadja **3**
Saliers, Emily
   See Indigo Girls
Salt-N-Pepa **6**
Sam and Dave **8**
Samuelson, Gar
   See Megadeth
Sanborn, David **1**
Sanders, Steve
   See the Oak Ridge Boys
Sanger, David
   See Asleep at the Wheel
Santana, Carlos **1**
Satriani, Joe **4**
Savage, Rick
   See Def Leppard
Saxa
   See the English Beat
Schermie, Joe
   See Three Dog Night
Schickele, Peter **5**
Schlitt, John
   See Petra
Schmit, Timothy B.
   See the Eagles
Schmoovy Schmoove
   See Digital Underground
Schneider, Florian
   See Kraftwerk
Schneider, Fred III
   See the B-52's
Schuur, Diane **6**
Scofield, John **7**
Scott, Bon (Ronald Belford)
   See AC/DC
Scruggs, Earl **3**
Seals & Crofts **3**
Seals, Dan **9**
Seals, Jim
   See Seals & Crofts
Sears, Pete
   See Jefferson Starship
Sedaka, Neil **4**
Seeger, Pete **4**
   Also see the Weavers
Segovia, Andres **6**
The Seldom Scene **4**
Seraphine, Daniel
   See Chicago

Severin, Steven
   See Siouxsie and the Banshees
Severinsen, Doc **1**
The Sex Pistols **5**
Shabalala, Ben
   See Ladysmith Black Mambazo
Shabalala, Headman
   See Ladysmith Black Mambazo
Shabalala, Jockey
   See Ladysmith Black Mambazo
Shabalala, Joseph
   See Ladysmith Black Mambazo
Shallenberger, James
   See Kronos Quartet
Shane, Bob
   See the Kingston Trio
Shankar, Ravi **9**
Sharon, Lois & Bram **6**
Shaw, Artie **8**
Shearer, Harry
   See Smalls, Derek
Sheila E. **3**
Shelley, Peter
   See the Buzzcocks
Shelley, Steve
   See Sonic Youth
Sherba, John
See Kronos Quartet
Sherman, Jack
   See the Red Hot Chili Peppers
Shock G
   See Digital Underground
Shocked, Michelle **4**
Shogren, Dave
   See the Doobie Brothers
Shontz, Bill
   See Rosenshontz
Shorter, Wayne **5**
Siberry, Jane **6**
Siegal, Janis
   See the Manhattan Transfer
Sills, Beverly **5**
Silva, Kenny Jo
   See the Beaver Brown Band
Simmons, Gene
   See Kiss
Simmons, Joe "Run"
   See Run-D.M.C.
Simmons, Patrick
   See the Doobie Brothers
Simmons, Russell **7**
Simon, Carly **4**
Simon, Paul **1**
Simonon, Paul
   See The Clash
Simpson, Ray
   See the Village People
Sinatra, Frank **1**
Singer, Eric
   See Black Sabbath
Sioux, Siouxsie
   See Siouxsie and the Banshees
Siouxsie and the Banshees **8**
Sixx, Nikki
   See Mötley Crüe
Skaggs, Ricky **5**
   Also see the Country Gentlemen
Skillings, Muzz
   See Living Colour
Slash
   See Guns n' Roses
Sledd, Dale
   See the Osborne Brothers
Slick, Grace
   See Jefferson Airplane
Slovak, Hillel
   See the Red Hot Chili Peppers

Smalls, Derek
   See Spinal Tap
Smith, Bessie **3**
Smith, Chad
   See the Red Hot Chili Peppers
Smith, Curt
   See Tears for Fears
Smith, Fred
   See the MC5
Smith, Garth
   See the Buzzcocks
Smith, Patti **1**
Smith, Robert
   See The Cure
   Also see Siouxsie and the Banshees
Smith, Smitty
   See Three Dog Night
Smith, Willard
   See DJ Jazzy Jeff and the Fresh Prince
The Smiths **3**
Sneed, Floyd Chester
   See Three Dog Night
Snow, Don
   See Squeeze
Snow, Phoebe **4**
Solal, Martial **4**
Soloff, Lew
   See Blood, Sweat and Tears
Sondheim, Stephen **8**
Sonic Youth **9**
Sonnenberg, Nadja Salerno
   See Salerno-Sonnenberg, Nadja
Sosa, Mercedes **3**
Soundgarden **6**
Spector, Phil **4**
Spence, Skip
   See Jefferson Airplane
Spencer, Jeremy
   See Fleetwood Mac
Spinal Tap **8**
Spitz, Dave
   See Black Sabbath
Springfield, Rick **9**
Springsteen, Bruce **6**
Squeeze **5**
Squire, Chris
   See Yes
Stacey, Peter "Spider"
   See the Pogues
Stanley, Ian
   See Tears for Fears
Stanley, Paul
   See Kiss
Stanley, Ralph **5**
Stansfield, Lisa **9**
Starling, John
   See the Seldom Scene
Starr, Ringo
   See the Beatles
Starship
   See Jefferson Airplane
The Statler Brothers **8**
Steele, David
   See the English Beat
Steely Dan **5**
Sterban, Richard
   See the Oak Ridge Boys
Stern, Isaac **7**
Stevens, Cat **3**
Stevens, Ray **7**
Stewart, Dave
   See Eurythmics
Stewart, Ian
   See the Rolling Stones
Stewart, John
   See the Kingston Trio
Stewart, Rod **2**
Stills, Stephen **5**

Sting **2**
Stinson, Bob
　See the Replacements
Stinson, Tommy
　See the Replacements
Stipe, Michael
　See R.E.M.
Stoltz, Brian
　See the Neville Brothers
Stone, Curtis
　See Highway 101
Stone, Sly **8**
Stookey, Paul
　See Peter, Paul & Mary
Story, Liz **2**
Stradlin, Izzy
　See Guns n' Roses
Strait, George **5**
Street, Richard
　See the Temptations
Streisand, Barbra **2**
Strickland, Keith
　See the B-52's
Strummer, Joe
　See The Clash
Stryper **2**
Stuart, Marty **9**
Summer, Mark
　See Turtle Island String Quartet
Summers, Andy **3**
Sun Ra **5**
Super DJ Dmitry
　See Deee-Lite
The Supremes **6**
Sutcliffe, Stu
　See the Beatles
Sweet Honey in the Rock **1**
Sweet, Matthew **9**
Sweet, Michael
　See Stryper
Sweet, Robert
　See Stryper
Sykes, John
　See Whitesnake
Tabor, Ty
　See King's X
Taj Mahal **6**
Take 6 **6**
Takemitsu, Toru **6**
Talbot, John Michael **6**
Talking Heads **1**
Tandy, Richard
　See Electric Light Orchestra
Tate, Geoff
　See Queensrÿche
Taylor, Andy
　See Duran Duran
Taylor, Cecil **9**
Taylor, Dick
　See the Rolling Stones
Taylor, Earl
　See the Country Gentlemen
Taylor, James **2**
Taylor, John
　See Duran Duran
Taylor, Mick
　See the Rolling Stones
Taylor, Roger
　See Duran Duran
Taylor, Roger Meadows
　See Queen
Tears for Fears **6**
Technotronic **5**
Te Kanawa, Kiri **2**
The Temptations **3**
Tennant, Neil
　See Pet Shop Boys
10,000 Maniacs **3**

Terminator X
　See Public Enemy
Terrell, Jean
　See the Supremes
The Texas Tornados **8**
Thayil, Kim
　See Soundgarden
They Might Be Giants **7**
Thomas, David
　See Take 6
Thomas, David Clayton
　See Clayton-Thomas, David
Thomas, Mickey
　See Jefferson Starship
Thompson, Dennis
　See the MC5
Thompson, Les
　See the Nitty Gritty Dirt Band
Thompson, Porl
　See The Cure
Thompson, Richard **7**
Threadgill, Henry **9**
Three Dog Night **5**
Tiffany **4**
Tikaram, Tanita **9**
Tilbrook, Glenn
　See Squeeze
Tillis, Mel **7**
Tillis, Pam **8**
Timbuk 3 **3**
Timmins, Margo
　See the Cowboy Junkies
Timmins, Michael
　See the Cowboy Junkies
Timmins, Peter
　See the Cowboy Junkies
Tolhurst, Laurence
　See The Cure
Toller, Dan
　See the Allman Brothers
Tone-Lōc **3**
Tony K
　See Roomful of Blues
Tork, Peter
　See the Monkees
Torme, Mel **4**
Tosh, Peter **3**
Townes, Jeffery
　See DJ Jazzy Jeff and the Fresh Prince
Townshend, Pete **1**
　Also see The Who
Travers, Brian
　See UB40
Travers, Mary
　See Peter, Paul & Mary
Travis, Randy **9**
A Tribe Called Quest **8**
Tritt, Travis **7**
Trucks, Butch
　See the Allman Brothers
Trugoy the Dove
　See De La Soul
Tubb, Ernest **4**
Tubridy, Michael
　See the Chieftans
Tucker, Moe
　See the Velvet Underground
Tucker, Tanya **3**
Tufnel, Nigel
　See Spinal Tap
Turner, Tina **1**
Turtle Island String Quartet **9**
Twitty, Conway **6**
2Pac
　See Digital Underground
Tyler, Steve
　See Aerosmith
Tyner, McCoy **7**

Tyner, Rob
　See the MC5
Tyson, Ron
　See the Temptations
U2 **2**
UB40 **4**
Ulrich, Lars
　See Metallica
Upshaw, Dawn **9**
Vachon, Chris
　See Roomful of Blues
Vai, Steve **5**
　Also see Whitesnake
Vandenburg, Adrian
　See Whitesnake
Vandross, Luther **2**
Van Halen **8**
Van Halen, Alex
　See Van Halen
Van Halen, Edward
　See Van Halen
Vanilla Ice **6**
Van Shelton, Ricky **5**
Van Zant, Johnny
　See Lynyrd Skynyrd
Van Zant, Ronnie
　See Lynyrd Skynyrd
Vaughan, Jimmie
　See the Fabulous Thunderbirds
Vaughan, Sarah **2**
Vaughan, Stevie Ray **1**
Vega, Suzanne **3**
The Velvet Underground **7**
Vettese, Peter-John
　See Jethro Tull
Vicious, Sid
　See the Sex Pistols
　　Also see Siouxsie and the Banshees
The Village People **7**
Vincent, Vinnie
　See Kiss
Virtue, Michael
　See UB40
Vito, Rick
　See Fleetwood Mac
Volz, Greg
　See Petra
Von, Eerie
　See Danzig
von Karajan, Herbert **1**
Vox, Bono
　See U2
Wadenius, George
　See Blood, Sweat and Tears
Wahlberg, Donnie
　See New Kids on the Block
Waits, Tom **1**
Wakeling, David
　See the English Beat
Wakeman, Rick
　See Yes
Walker, Colin
　See Electric Light Orchestra
Walker, Ebo
　See the New Grass Revival
Walker, T-Bone **5**
Wallace, Sippie **6**
Waller, Charlie
　See the Country Gentlemen
Waller, Fats **7**
Walsh, Joe **5**
　Also see the Eagles
Ward, Bill
　See Black Sabbath
Warnes, Jennifer **3**
Warren, Mervyn
　See Take 6
Warwick, Dionne **2**